THE 20TH CENTURY LEGAL PHILOSOPHY SERIES

VI

MAX WEBER ON LAW IN ECONOMY AND SOCIETY

20TH CENTURY LEGAL PHILOSOPHY SERIES: VOL. VI

MAX WEBER

on

Law in Economy and Society

EDITED WITH INTRODUCTION AND ANNOTATIONS BY

MAX RHEINSTEIN

Max Pam Professor of Comparative Law
University of Chicago Law School

TRANSLATION FROM

Max Weber, *Wirtschaft und Gesellschaft*, Second Edition (1925)

BY

EDWARD SHILS

Professor of Sociology
Committee on Social Thought, University of Chicago

AND

MAX RHEINSTEIN

CAMBRIDGE · MASSACHUSETTS
HARVARD UNIVERSITY PRESS
1966

Second Printing

Distributed in Great Britain by

OXFORD UNIVERSITY PRESS

LONDON

The publication of this volume is financed by the publication funds of the Harvard Law School.

LIBRARY OF CONGRESS CATALOG CARD NUMBER 54–5023

PRINTED IN THE UNITED STATES OF AMERICA

GENERAL INTRODUCTION TO THE SERIES

By the Editorial Committee

This book is one of the 20th Century Legal Philosophy Series, published under the auspices of the Association of American Law Schools. At its annual meeting in December, 1939, the Association authorized the creation of a special committee "for the purpose of preparing and securing the publication of translations on the same general lines as the Modern Legal Philosophy Series, sponsored by this association at the annual meeting thirty years ago . . . the materials to represent as nearly as possible the progress of Continental Legal thought in all aspects of Philosophy and Jurisprudence in the last fifty years."

Whereas the earlier Series was a very daring venture, coming, as it did, at the beginning of the century when only a few legal scholars were much interested in legal philosophy, the present Series could be undertaken with considerable assurance. In 1909 only a few of the leading law schools in this country included Jurisprudence in their curricula, and it was usually restricted to the Analytical School. By 1939 Jurisprudence was being taught in many law schools, and the courses had been broadened to include not only Analytical Jurisprudence, but also the Philosophy and the Sociology of Law. The progress in logical theory, in ethics, and in social science between 1909 and 1939 was without doubt an important factor in the expansion of Jurisprudence. In 1939 there was not only the successful precedent of the earlier Series, now completely out of print, but also the known rise of a very substantial body of interested readers, including students and practicing lawyers as well as professional scholars. This thoroughly admirable change, especially in the English-speaking countries, has been widely recognized as productive of a great enrichment of Anglo-American law. The Modern Legal Philosophy Series has been justly credited with a major part of that influence by making readily available the Continental jurisprudence of the last century.

The primary task of the legal philosopher is to reveal and to maintain the dominant long-run influence of ideas over events, of the general over the particular. In discharging this task he may help his generation to understand the basic trends of the law from one generation to the next, and the common cultural ties of seemingly disparate national legal systems. He may, again, create from these common ideal goods of the world's culture general theories, beliefs, and insights that will be accepted and used as guides by coming generations. The works of great legal philosophers serve not only the needs of the practitioner and other utilitarian ends; they also contribute abundantly to our theoretical knowledge. Indeed, in a deeper sense, we have come to understand the superficiality of setting utility against theory. The day is past when jurisprudence can defensibly be regarded as a curious hobby or as "merely cultural" in the sense that the fine arts contribute to the rounded education of a gentleman at the Bar. The issues are now correctly formulated in terms of whether one wishes to be a highly competent lawyer or a technician. Since the question, thus put, is obviously rhetorical, it is but another mode of asserting the considered judgment of those best qualified to pass on such matters, that the science and philosophy of law deal with the chief ideas that are common to the rules and methods of all positive law, and that a full understanding of any legal order therefore eludes those whose confining specialties keep them from these important disciplines.

The recent revival of interest in American history also reminds us emphatically that the great Fathers of the Republic, many of them lawyers, were men of universal intellectual outlook. They were as thoroughly grounded in French thought as in English. Grotius and Pufendorf were almost as widely read as the treatises on common law. Indeed, Jefferson and Wilson, to select two of the many great lawyers who come to mind, were able philosophers and social scientists. They apparently regarded it as essential to the best conduct of their professional careers to study philosophy and, especially, jurisprudence, Jefferson remarking that they are "as necessary as law to form an accomplished lawyer." The current movements in politics and economics have raised innumerable problems which, just as in the formative era of the Republic, require for their solution the sort of knowledge and skills that transcend specialization and technical proficiency. They call for a competence that is grounded in a wide perspective, one that represents an integration of the practitioner's technical skills with a knowledge of the various disciplines that bear directly on the wise solution of the present-day problems; and these are by no means confined to public affairs — they equally concern the daily practice of the private practitioner. With many such legal problems, with methods relevant to sound solutions, with the basic ideas and values involved, the eminent legal philosophers whose principal works appear in this Series have been particularly concerned. If it seems to some that the literature of jurisprudence is rather remote from the immediate practical problems that occupy the attention of most lawyers, it is necessary to reassert our primary dependence for the solution of all such problems upon theory — a truth that has been demonstrated many times in the physical sciences but which holds, also, in the realm of social problems. The publication of such a Series as this rests on the premise that it is possible to discover better answers than are now given many problems, that a closer approximation to truth and a greater measure of justice are attainable by lawyers, and that in part, at least, this can be brought about through their greater sensitivity to the relevant ideals of justice and through a broader vision of the jurisprudential fundamentals.

In the General Introduction to the first Series, it was noted that "The value of the study of comparative law has only in recent years come to be recognized by us. Our juristic methods are still primitive, in that we seek to know only by our own experience, and pay no heed to the experience of others." As the nations are drawn closer together by forces not wholly in human control, it is inevitable that they should come to understand each other more fully. The legal institutions of any country are no less significant than its language, political ideals, and social organization. The two great legal systems of the world, the civilian and the common law, have for some years been moving toward what may become, in various fields of law, a common ground. The civilian system has come more and more to recognize actually, if not avowedly, the importance of case-law, whereas the common law system has been exhibiting an increasing reliance on legislation and even on codes. In a number of fields, e.g., commercial law, wills, and criminal law, there is such an agreement of substantive principles as to make uniformity a very practical objective. While economic interests will undoubtedly provide the chief stimulus to that end, in the long-range view the possibility of focusing the energies of leading scholars and lawyers, the whole world over, on the same problems is the most inviting ideal of all. The problems of terminology, legal methods, the role of precedent, statutory interpretation, underlying rationale, the use of different types of authority, the efficacy of various controls and their operation in diverse factual conditions, the basic issues concerning the values that are implemented — these and innumerable other fundamental problems of legal science and philosophy may and should receive collaboration on a scale never before attainable. The road to the attainment of these objectives is not an easy one, but if any such avenue exists it is surely that indicated by the best literature in jurisprudence.

These fundamentals are also invaluable aids to better understanding of one's own law. On the side of insight into legal methods and substantive doctrines alone, the gain is immeasurably great. The common lawyer, at least until very recent times, was wont to accept a rigorous adherence to the rule of precedent as axiomatic in any modern system. He was apt to regard the common law through Blackstonian eyes; and he can hardly be said to have been even initiated into the criticism of statutes from other perspectives than those required by an unquestioning acceptance of the primacy of case-law. The gains should be no less great as regards organization of the substantive law. A century and a quarter ago John Austin remarked that the common law was a "mess." Although much progress in systematization has been made since that time, we still have a great deal to learn from our civilian friends — particularly from those who have attained wide recognition for their jurisprudential analyses of the common problems of modern legal systems. In addition, there is that vast illumination to be had from the discovery that other advanced legal systems, representing cultures of high achievement, sometimes apply to the solution of many problems different rules of law and even different basic doctrines than does our own. What better avenue to sound criticism of our legal system, what easier road to its early enrichment than by way of intimate knowledge of the innumerable ideas, some identical with our own but otherwise enunciated, some slightly divergent, others directly opposite, that are supplied so generously in the works of legal philosophers!

With the above objectives in view, the Editorial Committee, appointed early in 1940, immediately took up its task. For almost an entire year it engaged in active correspondence with practically all the legal philosophers in the United States, with many European, including English, legal philosophers; and, later on, when the Committee decided to include in the Series a volume devoted to Latin-American jurisprudence, there was much correspondence with legal philosophers of the various countries of Latin America. In addition, like activities centered on the engagement of translators qualified to translate correctly great works of jurisprudence into readable English. Anyone who has undertaken such translation will realize the difficulties involved, and the very high competence that is required. The Committee was able to set very rigorous standards in this regard because of the presence in the United States of an exceptionally able group of European legal scholars, some of whom had for many years been well versed in the English language.

In making its selection of works for inclusion in this Series, the Editorial Committee has been guided in part by the originality and intrinsic merit of the works chosen and in part by their being representative of leading schools of thought. The first Series, the Modern Legal Philosophy Series, had made available some of the work of nineteenth-century European legal philosophers — including Jhering, Stammler, del Vecchio, Korkunov, Kohler, and Gény. That Series and other publications had brought Duguit to the English-reading public. In 1936 the Harvard University Press published a translation of Ehrlich's *Fundamental Principles of the Sociology of Law.* The present century has also seen the rise of a number of brilliant legal philosophers who have attained very wide recognition. Among those whose inclusion in this Series was clearly called for were Max Weber, Kelsen, Petrazycki, Radbruch, the French Institutionalists, chiefly Hauriou and Renard, the Interests-Jurisprudence School centering around Heck, and some others. The opinion of the Committee as to these men was abundantly confirmed by the numerous communications received from legal philosophers of many countries, and the chief problem was to decide which of their works should be translated. But distinction in jurisprudence is not confined to a few writers, and any choice solely on the basis of scholarly merit would be enormously difficult, if not impossible. The Committee, like its predecessors, sought "to present to Anglo-American readers, the views of the best modern representative writers in jurisprudence . . . but the selection has not centered on the notion of giving equal recognition to all countries. Primarily, the design has been to represent the various schools of thought." (General Introduction to the Modern Legal Philosophy Series.) Some schools of thought have been much more productive than others; especially has this been true of those of Legal Positivism and Sociology of Law, which number many very able representatives. Without further presentation of the numerous phases of this problem, it may be stated that the Committee, whose members represent various legal philosophies, has endeavored to make the best selection possible under the conditions of its appointment, the objectives set before it, and the rigorous restriction resulting from the size of the Series.

The success of such a project as this required considerable assistance of many kinds, and the Committee is pleased to acknowledge the abundant aid extended to it. Our greatest debt is to the late John H. Wigmore, whose broad experience as Chairman of the Editorial Committee of the Modern Legal Philosophy Series was placed at our disposal, and who advised us frequently on many problems that arose in the initial stages of the work. As Honorary Chairman of this Committee until his death on April 20, 1943, he participated in many of its conferences and took an active and highly important part in launching the project and assuring its success. It was Mr. Wigmore who, in the early uncertain days of the enterprise, interested his former student, a Trustee of Northwestern University, Mr. Bertram J. Cahn, and Mrs. Cahn to contribute a substantial sum to defray the expenses of translation. The publication of the Series involved the expenditure of a considerable sum of money, and would have been impossible had not the Committee received a very substantial subsidy from Harvard Law School. No less a debt does the Committee acknowledge to the authors who contributed their work and, in some instances, their close personal collaboration. The translators have earned the Committee's admiration for their splendid achievements in the face of serious obstacles and with very little financial assistance to ease their task. We of the Committee wish, also, to give our very hearty thanks to the many legal philosophers, American, Continental, English, and Latin-American, who made many valuable suggestions and encouraged us greatly by their interest in the project. They are far too numerous to be named, as are those many persons in various positions, some of them rather humble ones, who lightened our tasks by their kindly aid. Finally the Committee acknowledges the special help given by Harvard Law School, the University of San Francisco Law School, Columbia University Law School, and Indiana University Law School. Each of the first two schools provided at its own cost a member of its faculty to serve as a translator, as well as stenographic assistance, and the other schools provided considerable stenographic, clerical, and other help. To each of the above persons and institutions the Committee gives its grateful thanks for assistance, without which the publication of this Series would not have been possible.

ERRATA

Page	*Note*	
125	62, l. 1	*For* n. 43 *read* n. 45
150	130	*For* 70 *read* n. 70
172	200	*For* n. 165 *read* n. 166
206	30	*For* 236 *read* 336
211	44, l. 3	*For* Schubart-Kikentscher *read* Schubart-Fikentscher
224	5	*For* 56 *read* 89
236	35, l. 2	*For* n. 28 *read* n. 31
257	9	*For* 233 *read* 322
276	59, l. 2	*For* Ch. VII, n. 186 *read* Ch. VI, n. 191
316	39, l. 10	*For* 22 *read* 221

CONTENTS

General Introduction to the Series vii

Preface xv

List of Books Cited in Abbreviated Form xix

Introduction by Max Rheinstein xxv

Max Weber on Law in Economy and Society

I. BASIC CONCEPTS OF SOCIOLOGY 1

II. THE ECONOMIC SYSTEM AND THE NORMATIVE ORDERS 11

Sec. 1. Legal Order and Economic Order 11

Sec. 2. Law, Convention, and Usage 20

Sec. 3. Significance and Limits of Legal Coercion in Economic Life 33

III. FIELDS OF SUBSTANTIVE LAW 41

IV. CATEGORIES OF LEGAL THOUGHT 61

V. EMERGENCE AND CREATION OF LEGAL NORMS 65

VI. FORMS OF CREATION OF RIGHTS 98

Sec. 1. Logical Categories of "Legal Propositions" — Liberties and Powers — Freedom of Contract . . 98

Sec. 2. Development of Freedom of Contract — "Status Contracts" and "Purposive Contracts" — The historical origin of the Purposive Contracts . . . 100

Sec. 3. Institutions Auxiliary to Actionable Contract: Agency; Assignment; Negotiable Instruments . . 122

Sec. 4. Limits of Freedom of Contract 125
Sec. 5. Extension of the Effect of a Contract beyond Its Parties — "Special Law" 140
Sec. 6. Associational Contracts — Juristic Personality . 154
Sec. 7. Freedom and Coercion 188
Supplement to Chapter VI. The Market 191

VII. THE LEGAL HONORATIORES AND THE TYPES OF LEGAL THOUGHT 198

VIII. FORMAL AND SUBSTANTIVE RATIONALIZATION IN THE LAW (SACRED LAWS) 224

IX. IMPERIUM AND PATRIMONIAL MONARCHICAL POWER AS INFLUENCES ON THE FORMAL QUALITIES OF LAW: THE CODIFICATIONS . 256

X. THE FORMAL QUALITIES OF REVOLUTIONARY LAW — NATURAL LAW 284

XI. THE FORMAL QUALITIES OF MODERN LAW . 301

XII. DOMINATION 322
Sec. 1. Power and Domination. Transitional Forms . . 322
Sec. 2. Domination and Administration — Nature and Limits of Democratic Administration 330
Sec. 3. Domination through Organization — Bases of Legitimate Authority 334

XIII. POLITICAL COMMUNITIES 338
Sec. 1. Nature and "Legitimacy" of Political Communities 338
Sec. 2. Stages in the Formation of Political Communities 342

XIV. RATIONAL AND IRRATIONAL ADMINISTRATION OF JUSTICE 349

INDEX 357

PREFACE

THE Max Weber volume was the first scheduled for publication in the 20th Century Legal Philosophy Series. Its completion turned out to present formidable difficulties and to require many years of work.

As a speaker, Weber was easy to understand and to listen to. In his lectures the right word would come to him naturally. The glow of his passionate zeal to discover the truth and awaken the active coöperation of his hearers gave vividness and color to his presentation, which was underscored at appropriate places by the easily found and perfectly formulated *bon môt* or by some witty sarcasm. Little of this oratorical brilliancy can be found in Weber's writing, and least of all in his *Economy and Society,* where his style is heavy, involved and cumbersome. One of the reasons for this unpleasantness of his written style lies in his passion for accuracy. Every sentence had to be just right; quite particularly, he would not tolerate overgeneralization. So every statement is narrowed by a qualifying statement, which in turn is qualified again and again, and the main proposition is combined with its qualifiers and sub-qualifiers in just one sentence, which often enough is of such monstrous length and involvement that even a German reader does not find it easy to unwind the thread and hunt for the predicate. The uncommon aspect of Weber's style is aggravated by his use of words newly and artificially coined by him. Most of these terms of art are precise and poignant; but they cannot be understood without constantly keeping in mind the definitions by which he explains his linguistic creations or his highly technical use of words which also occur in the common language; and many of these definitions are involved enough and based upon terms which in turn cannot be understood, or are likely to be misunderstood, without Weber's elaborate explanations. None of Weber's newly coined terms can, of course, be found in any German-English dictionary and many of those terms which can be found are not used in their common meaning. To make things worse, Weber died before he could apply any finishing touch to his manuscript, of which considerable parts were left in the stage of a draft, jotted down to give expression to a course of thought, but without regard to beauty of style or even readability, and meant to be worked over and rephrased before publication.

The translators' work was thus beset with extraordinary difficulties.

Many a sentence of Weber's had to be studied over and over again to unravel its structure and to discover its meaning. Completely literal translation is, of course, never possible in the case of any text. In Weber's case even that measure of literalness which is possible in most instances of prose, could not be considered. His sentences had to be divided into new ones of reasonable length and structure, and English equivalents had to be found for his terms of art. As, contrary to German, new English words cannot ordinarily be formed by simply joining together existing ones into new composites, circumscribing explanations had to be formed and formulated. Finally, the English text had to be readable with at least some measure of ease, although it could never be hoped to make it read like a piece of literature.

The translation was made by Professor Edward A. Shils, then of the University of London, and now of the Committee on Social Thought of the University of Chicago. It was then worked over by the editor, whose mother tongue happens to be German, and who had had the privilege of attending classes of Max Weber's at the University of Munich. He was assisted by Mrs. Elizabeth Mann Borgese and by Mr. Samuel Stoljar, the latter being a member of the Comparative Law Research Staff of the University of Chicago Law School. It is hoped that this combined effort has produced an English text which is not only accurate but also more readable than the German original.

However, Weber's text had not only to be translated. In order to make it fully intelligible and useful to American readers it had also to be commented upon. As the reader will observe, the range of Weber's knowledge was phenomenal. The materials for inquiry are taken from all civilizations and from all ages. Weber draws upon Hindu, Chinese, Islamic or primitive Polynesian law just as well as on the legal systems of Rome, England, medieval Europe, or modern Germany, America, or France. In many, if not in most cases, he hints at the phenomena referred to rather than explain them. Innumerable terms of Roman, Germanic, Hindu, Arabic, or what not origin are used without explanation. But what reader can be expected to be familiar with such terms as *chrenechruda, hadith, tannaim, diadikasia,* or *actio quod iussu*? Such terms had to be explained.

Also, how can the reader know whether Weber is correct in all those statements about the most diverse legal and social systems which he uses as the basis of his generalizations and conclusions? They had to be checked and their sources had to be found, at least as far as possible. In most cases this task could be performed; there are, indeed, few propositions for which it was not possible to locate Weber's source or to find at least some other confirmation. Not even Max Weber could be expected to be infallible, but the number of serious mistakes turned out to be unbelievably small. In some cases, however, Weber's sources have been corrected by more recent specialists' research, particularly in the field of Roman law, where research in papyri, the discovery of "interpolations" in the Digest of Justinian, and the discovery of new manuscripts, especially newly found fragments of Gaius' Institutes, have in many respects altered the views of that generation of scholars whose works were used by Weber. Such new discoveries or changes of view had to be presented to the reader of our edition. Lastly, it was held to be desirable to indicate to the reader the literature in which he can find further information on those topics which are treated but briefly by Weber. As Weber's sources mostly consisted of works of German scholars, pains were taken to include in the bibliographical lists books which are available in English.

The search for Weber's sources and for supplementary literature, the task of explaining the numerous, often exotic, terms of his text and, quite particularly, that of checking the accuracy of Weber's statements and of providing the reader with supplementary information, all these efforts took much time and pains. The editor was assisted by Doctor Alise Vagelis, Mr. Samuel Stoljar, and Dr. Stoyan Bayitch, of the Comparative Law Research Staff of the University of Chicago Law School. Without their help the work could never have been done. Where not even Weber could be infallible, the editor cannot harbor the hope of having avoided errors and omissions. He can only count on the indulgence of the reader and in advance express his gratitude for any criticism and suggestion that may be offered to him.

Max Rheinstein

University of Chicago Law School

List of Books Cited in Abbreviated Form

Books which are marked by an asterisk appear to have been extensively used by Max Weber. No book published after 1921 could, of course, have been used by Weber. Such books are cited to give the reader references for further reading.

Alabaster	Alabaster, E., Notes and Commentaries on Chinese Criminal Law. 1899.
Allen	Allen, C. K., Law in the Making, 3rd ed. 1939.
*Amira	Grundriss des germanischen Rechts, 3rd ed. 1913.
*Blackstone	Blackstone, W., Commentaries on the Laws of England, 1765–69.
Bonner and Smith	Bonner, R. and Smith, G., The Administration of Justice from Homer to Aristotle, 2 vols. 1930–38.
*Brunner, Abh.	Brunner H., Abhandlungen zur Rechtsgeschichte, 2 vols. 1931. (Contains reprints of articles published at earlier times in other places.)
*Brunner, Rechtsgeschichte	Brunner, H., Deutsche Rechtsgeschichte. Vol. 1, 1st ed. 1892, 2nd ed. 1906. Vol. 2, 1st ed. 1892, 2nd ed. 1928 by C. Freiherr von Schwerin.
*Bryce	Bryce, J., Studies in History and Jurisprudence. 1901.
Buckland	Buckland, W. W., Textbook of Roman Law, 2nd ed. 1932.
Diamond	Diamond, A. S., Primitive Law. 1935.
*Ehrlich	Ehrlich, E., Fundamental Principles of the Sociology of Law, Transl. by Moll, 1936. Weber used the German original s.t. Grundlegung der Soziologie des Rechts. 1913.

Encyc. Soc. Sci. — Encyclopedia of the Social Sciences, ed. by Seligman, E. R. A., and Johnson, A., 13 vols. 1933.

Engelmann — Engelmann, W., Die Wiedergeburt der Rechtskultur in Italien. 1938.

Engelmann and Millar — Engelmann, A. and Millar, R. W., History of Continental Civil Procedure. 1927.

*Enneccerus — Enneccerus, L., Lehrbuch des bürgerlichen Rechts, 1928 ed.

*Gierke — von Gierke, O., Development of Political Theory, Transl. by Freyd. 1939.

*Gierke, Genossenschaftsrecht — von Gierke, O., Das deutsche Genossenschaftsrecht, 4 vols. 1868–1913.

*Gierke, Privatrecht — von Gierke, Deutsches Privatrecht, 3 vols. 1895, 1905, 1917.

*Goldschmidt — Goldschmidt, L., Universalgeschichte des Handelsrechts. 1891.

*Hatschek — Hatschek, O., Englisches Staatsrecht, 2 vols. 1905.

Hedemann — Hedemann, J. W., Die Fortschritte des Zivilrechts im 19. Jahrhundert, 3 vols. 1910, 1920, 1930.

Holdsworth — Holdsworth, Sir W., History of English Law, 13 vols.; vols. 1–3, 3rd ed. 1922–23; vols. 4–12, 1924–38; Tables and Index by E. Potton, 1932; vol. 13, ed. by Goodhart, 1952.

*Huebner — Huebner, R., History of Germanic Private Law, Transl. by Philbrick, 1918. Weber used the German original s.t. Grundzüge des Deutschen Privatrechts. 1913.

*Jellinek — Jellinek, G., Allgemeine Staatslehre, 3rd ed. 1914.

*Jellinek, System — Jellinek, G., System der subjektiven öffentlichen Rechte. 1892.

*Jhering — von Jhering, R., Der Geist des römischen Rechts auf den verschiedenen Stufen seiner Entwicklung, 3 vols., 5th–6th eds. 1906–07.

Jörs and Kunkel	Jörs, P., Römisches Privatrecht, 2nd ed. by Kunkel, W., 3rd ed. 1949.
Jolowicz	Jolowicz, H. F., Historical Introduction to Roman Law. 1932.
*Karlowa	Karlowa, O., Römische Rechtsgeschichte. 1901.
Kaser	Kaser, M., Das altrömische Jus. 1949.
Kelsen	Kelsen, H., General Theory of Law and State. 1945.
*Kohler and Wenger	Kohler, J., and Wenger, L., Allgemeine Rechtsgeschichte. 1914.
*Leist	Leist, B. W., Gräco-Italische Rechtsgeschichte. 1884.
*Maine	Maine, Sir H. S., Ancient Law. 1906.
*Maine, Institutions	Maine, Sir H. S., Lectures on the Early History of Institutions, 7th ed. 1897.
*Maine, Early Law	Maine, Sir H. S., Dissertations on Early Law and Custom. 1907.
*Maitland, Forms	Maitland, F. W., The Forms of Action at Common Law. 1936 ed.
*Maitland, Papers	Maitland, F. W., Collected Papers, 3 vols. 1911.
*Mitteis	Mitteis, L., Römisches Privatrecht. 1908.
*Mitteis, Reichsrecht	Mitteis, L., Reichsrecht und Volksrecht in den östlichen Provinzen des römischen Kaïserreichs. 1891.
*Mommsen	Mommsen, T., Abriss des römischen Staatsrechts. 1893, 2 ed. 1907.
Noyes	Noyes, R., The Institution of Property. 1936.
*Pauly and Wissowa	Pauly, A. F., and Wissowa, G., Realenzyklopädie der klassischen Altertumswissenschaft. 1894 et s.
Planitz	Planitz, H., Deutsche Rechtsgeschichte. 1950.
Plucknett	Plucknett, T. F. T., Concise History of the Common Law. 1948.
*Pollock and Maitland	Pollock, Sir F. and Maitland, F. W., The History of English Law before

	THE TIME OF EDWARD I, 2 vols., 1st ed. 1899, 2nd ed. 1923.
RADIN	RADIN, M., ANGLO-AMERICAN LEGAL HISTORY. 1936.
RHEINSTEIN, DECEDENTS' ESTATES	RHEINSTEIN, M., CASES AND OTHER MATERIALS ON THE LAW OF DECEDENTS' ESTATES. 1947.
RHEINSTEIN, STRUKTUR	RHEINSTEIN, M., DIE STRUKTUR DES VERTRAGLICHEN SCHULDVERHÄLTNISSES IM ANGLO-AMERIKANISCHEN RECHT. 1932.
ROSTOVTZEV	ROSTOVTZEV, M. J., SOCIAL AND ECONOMIC HISTORY OF THE ROMAN EMPIRE. 1926.
SAV. Z. GERM.	ZEITSCHRIFT DER SAVIGNY STIFTUNG FÜR RECHTSGESCHICHTE, GERMANISTISCHE ABTEILUNG.
SAV. Z. ROM.	ZEITSCHRIFT DER SAVIGNY STIFTUNG FÜR RECHTSGESCHICHTE, ROMANISTISCHE ABTEILUNG.
*SCHRÖDER	LEHRBUCH DER DEUTSCHEN RECHTSGESCHICHTE, 16th ed. 1922.
SCHULZ, HISTORY	SCHULZ, F., HISTORY OF ROMAN LEGAL SCIENCE. 1946.
SCHULZ, PRINCIPLES	SCHULZ, F., PRINCIPLES OF ROMAN LAW. 1936.
SEAGLE	SEAGLE, W., THE QUEST FOR LAW. 1941.
SMITH	SMITH, M., DEVELOPMENT OF EUROPEAN LAW. 1922.
*SOHM	SOHM, R., INSTITUTES OF ROMAN LAW, Transl. by Ledlie, 3rd ed. 1907. Weber used the German original s.t. INSTITUTIONEN DES RÖMISCHEN RECHTS, 15th ed. 1917.
*STOBBE	STOBBE, O., GESCHICHTE DER DEUTSCHEN RECHTSQUELLEN. 1864.
STONE	STONE, J., THE PROVINCE AND FUNCTION OF LAW, 1946.
THURNWALD	THURNWALD, R., WERDEN, WANDEL UND GESTALTUNG DES RECHTS, 1934.
VINOGRADOFF	VINOGRADOFF, P., OUTLINES OF HISTORICAL JURISPRUDENCE, 2 vols. 1922.

WEBER, AGRARGESCHICHTE	WEBER, M., RÖMISCHE AGRARGESCHICHTE. 1891.
WEBER, ESSAYS	From MAX WEBER, ESSAYS IN SOCIOLOGY, Transl. by H. Gerth and C. Mills. 1946.
WEBER, HISTORY	WEBER, M., GENERAL ECONOMIC HISTORY, Transl. by F. Knight. 1927.
WEBER, THEORY	WEBER, M., THEORY OF SOCIAL AND ECONOMIC ORGANIZATION, Transl. by A. M. Henderson and T. Parsons. 1947.
WEBER, WIRTSCHAFTSGESCHICHTE	WEBER, M., WIRTSCHAFTSGESCHICHTE. 1922.
WENGER	WENGER, L., INSTITUTES OF THE ROMAN LAW OF CIVIL PROCEDURE, Transl. by O. H. Fisk. 1940.
Z. F. HANDELSR.	ZEITSCHRIFT FÜR DAS GESAMTE HANDELSRECHT.
Z. F. VGL. RW.	ZEITSCHRIFT FÜR VERGLEICHENDE RECHTSWISSENSCHAFT.

INTRODUCTION

By Max Rheinstein

I. The Context of Weber's Sociology of Law

The main part of this book is constituted by the seventh chapter, entitled "Sociology of Law" (*Rechtssoziologie*), of Max Weber's *Economy and Society*.[1] It is accompanied by a few other sections of that book, which are closely connected with the Sociology of Law.

Economy and Society forms part of a major whole, an encyclopedic work which was planned on vast proportions, but modestly entitled *Outline of Social Economics*.[2] That term "social economics" was a new

[1] The first edition of Wirtschaft und Gesellschaft was published by Verlag von J. C. B. Mohr (Paul Siebeck) in Tübingen, Germany, 1922; an "enlarged" second edition was published in 1925. In that latter edition, the work, without the index, contains 869 pages. Of these, 160 pages have been translated and published in the present volume; to these have been added this Introduction and the Notes.

[2] Grundriss der Sozialökonomik. The work consists of 9 Parts in 13 volumes and contains the following Parts:

I. Abteilung, I. Teil, *Wirtschaft und Wirtschaftswissenschaft* (*The Economy and the Science of Economics*) by K. Bücher, J. Schumpeter, and E. v. Philippovich, 2nd ed., 1924.

I. Abt., II. Teil, *Theorie der gesellschaftlichen Wirtschaft* (*Economic Theory*) by F. v. Wieser, 2nd ed., 1924.

II. Abt., I. Teil, *Wirtschaft und Natur* (*Economy and Nature*), by A. Hettner, P. Mombert, R. Michels, K. Oldenberg, and H. Herkner, 2nd ed., 1923.

II. Abt., II. Teil, *Wirtschaft und Technik* (*Economy and Technology*), by F. v. Gottl-Ottilienfeld, 2nd ed., 1923.

III. Abt., *Wirtschaft und Gesellschaft* (*Economy and Society*), by M. Weber, 2nd ed., 1925.

IV. Abt., I. Teil, *Spezifische Elemente der modernen kapitalistischen Wirtschaft* (*Specific Elements of The Modern Capitalistic Economy*), by W. Sombart, A. Leist, H. Nipperdey, C. Brinkmann, E. Steinitzer, F. Leitner, A. Salz, F. Eulenburg, E. Lederer, O. v. Zwiedineck-Südenhorst, 1925.

V. Abt., I. Teil, *Entwicklung, Wesen und Bedeutung des Handels* (*Development, Nature, and Significance of Trade*), by H. Sieveking, 2nd ed., 1925.

V. Abt., II. Teil, *Der moderne Handel* (*Modern Trade*), by J. Hirsch, 2nd ed., 1925.

V. Abt., III. Teil, *Transportwesen* (*Transportation*), by K. Wiedenfeld, 1930.

VI. Abt., *Industrie, Bauwesen, Bergwesen* (*Industry, Building Trade, Mining*), by H. Sieveking, E. Schwiedland, A. Weber, F. Leitner, M. R. Weyermann,

creation. "Institutional economics" is perhaps its closest American equivalent. But its meaning is broader. The ambitious plan was to investigate, upon the broadest possible scale, the interrelationships between economic institutions and relationships, and all other phenomena and relationships of society, of the present and the past. In other words, the plan was to assemble all leading scholars of German tongue in the fields of economics and sociology and collectively to produce a comprehensive treatise on sociology and its interrelationships with all other phenomena of society. In this connection it ought to be remembered that in Europe the word sociology does not have exactly the same meaning as in America. In this country sociology is usually meant to refer to that branch of learning which concerns itself with those social groupments and relationships of our own modern Western society which are neither politically formalized, nor, primarily, concerned with economic activities. Description, analysis, and critique of the state and other political communities is thought to constitute the domain of the political scientist. The study of economic phenomena, relationships, and institutions constitutes the domain of the economist. The phenomena of so-called primitive peoples are studied by the cultural anthropologist. The regulation through the state of social relationships in our own society of present-day America and the adjustment of social trouble situations through the courts is the field of legal science and practice. The study of significant events of the past in their causal relationships constitutes the concern of the historian.

O. v. Zwiedineck-Südenhorst, Ad. Weber, E. Gothein, and T. Vogelstein, 2nd ed., 1923.

VII. Abt., *Land- und forstwirtschaftliche Produktion. Versicherungswesen* (*Agriculture, Forestry, Insurance*), by T. Brinkmann, J. B. Esslen, and others, 1922.

VIII. Abt., *Aussenhandel und Aussenhandelspolitik* (*Foreign Trade and Foreign Trade Policy*), by F. Eulenburg, 1929.

IX. Abt., I. Teil, *Die gesellschaftliche Schichtung im Kapitalismus* (*Social Stratification under Capitalism*), by C. Brinkmann, L. Pesl, G. Albrecht, E. Lederer, G. Briefs, R. Michels, G. Neuhaus, and J. Marschak, 1926.

IX. Abt., II. Teil, *Die autonome und staatliche soziale Binnenpolitik im Kapitalismus* (*Social Policy under Capitalism*), by K. Schmidt, O. Swart, W. Wygodzinski, V. Totomianz, E. Lederer, J. Marschak, T. Brauer, R. Wilbrandt, and Ad. Weber, 1927.

The idea of the work was conceived by Max Weber, who also elaborated its general plan, advised by many of the contributors and, especially, by K. Bücher and E. v. Philippovich. Bücher has become known principally by his work in the field of typology of economic development (DIE ENTSTEHUNG DER VOLKSWIRTSCHAFT, 1922). Philippovich was the author of a widely used treatise of economic theory and policy (GRUNDRISS DER POLITISCHEN OEKONOMIE, 3 vols., 1913, 1914, 1915).

What remains for the sociologist is the study of those social groupments and relationships which have not been preëmpted by the other branches of the social sciences, that is, principally the informal groups such as the family, the gang or the professions, or the problems of race relations, urbanization, or rural society life.

In Europe, sociology, while it has paid attention to the study of these informal social groupments and relationships, is rather regarded, however, as the science of social relationships in general or, even more ambitiously, of society in general. Its ultimate question is: What makes society tick? More concretely, the European sociologists try to find out what are the basic phenomena and relationships of society in all its aspects: political, legal, literary, artistic, economic, etc.; what are the relationships between these various aspects of social life, and in what ways do they interact upon each other. It would not be correct to say that sociology, in that sense, is simply the sum total of all the social sciences. The European sociologist does not try to duplicate the work of the economist, the political scientist, the jurist, the musicologist, the philologist, etc. He rather starts where they leave off. He tries to find out what there is in common in all those social activities which constitute the subject-matter of the specialized sciences, and how they influence and interact upon each other, in our society as well as in societies of other cultures, past and present, developed or primitive. Understood in this sense, sociology is basic for all social and natural sciences, its aim being the discovery of those ultimate units of society which might, in a sense, be called the atoms of the social structure, the type-patterns according to which the boundless manifold of social phenomena may be taxonomically classified, and, lastly, to find out what regularities, if any, one might find in the coincidence or sequence of social phenomena. It thus resembles the natural sciences, whose methods of exact observation it tries to emulate in so far as they can be applied to the complex social phenomena, and which it also parallels in its endeavor to describe the phenomena and their interrelationships with the impartiality of the scientist. It therefore differs from the tasks of the social philosopher, who tries to discover the nature or essence of society by speculation rather than exact observation, and the political philosopher who professes, by the use of reason, to be able to evaluate different ways of social life against each other and thus to prove which kind of society constitutes that "good society" which ought to be the aim of all good men.

While sociology thus aims at being as exact as possible and refraining from ethical evaluation (to be *wertfrei*), it stands in conscious contrast to the natural sciences through the awareness of the fact that social phenomena cannot be understood through the mere observation of external behavior. In so far as it is apprehended by the senses human behavior has no social meaning. The observation that one man hands to another a piece of greenish paper is as such irrelevant in the study of human relationships. The observed phenomenon does not assume social significance until we know that a large group of human beings, of which our two actors are members, regard the greenish paper as a piece of paper money or, in other words, that they ascribe to it the function of serving as a generally recognized means of exchange and payment; that one of our two actors handed the paper to the other for the purpose of paying a debt, or making a loan, or buying some goods or services, or making a gift, or giving a tip or alms, or what not; and that, finally, the paper was taken by the other with the same or, perhaps, with some different understanding. In other words, the sociologist has to pay attention to the meaning which human beings ascribe to their behavior and without which behavior belongs to the field of physiology rather than that of social conduct to be studied by the sociologist. The study of the mere behavior of atoms as observable by the senses, either directly or through the medium of instruments, constitutes the task of the physicist; that of molecules, of the chemist; that of cells and their consociation in the organisms of plant and animals is the task of the physiologist. None of these scientists has to concern himself with the meaning which an atom, a molecule, a star, or a cell might ascribe to its movements and other changes. A science of social life would be senseless, however, if it would limit itself to external activities. For the physiologist, who measures muscle energy and use of calories, it makes no difference with what meaning a wooden staff is thrown by a man. To the sociologist this fact is relevant only in so far as he can know that the thrower ascribes to the staff the meaning of being a spear and to his act that of warfare, murder, revenge, hunting, athletic competition, or play.

It is this necessity of considering the meaning of human behavior which has constantly been emphasized as the sociologist's special task by the author of our book, Max Weber. But before discussing the special features of his work, we must obtain some impression of that major framework within which his principal book was to be published. The *Outline of Social Economics*, of which it forms a part, was intended to do no less than tie together the results of all the sociological work that had been done by scholars of German tongue by the late 1920's and early 1930's, in so far as it was related to the economic phenomena of society. This emphasis upon the economic aspects of society can, probably, be traced to two, in a sense, accidental causes.

The first is that, in German-speaking countries, the new science of sociology had largely been created by scholars coming from economics, such as, above all, Max Weber, his brother Alfred Weber, Ernst Lederer, Werner Sombart, Othmar Spann, Max Oppenheimer, and Karl Bücher.

The second reason for the placement of the emphasis upon the economic sphere can be found in the fact that to a considerable extent the work of the German sociologists constituted the response to the challenge of one of their earliest representatives, Karl Marx. Deeply moved by the misery of the working classes as he observed it in mid-nineteenth-century capitalism, Marx set out to investigate the economic system which, he believed, had produced such misery along with the immense growth of wealth, science and technology. His analysis of capitalism broadened out into a general theory of society when he discovered, as he at least believed, that all of the world's history could be comprehended as a series of class struggles which were caused, and in their forms determined, by the relations of production of the particular period. Here, so he was convinced, was the prime mover of all the world's activities: the economic fact of the relations of production by which mankind satisfied its physical needs. These material economic circumstances were the base which determined for every civilization the ideological superstructure of its religion, philosophy, law, political apparatus, art, literature, and all other activities of the mind. This superstructure was created by every ruling class to underpin its position of power in the class struggle. None of these ideological phenomena has any existence or truth value of its own. With every change of positions in the class struggle for economic power, the superstructure of rationalizations and ideological props changes accordingly. The economy, i.e., matter, is the historical *prius* which determines all the creations of the so-called mind. Any belief in the independent existence of a sphere of the mind and spirit which might proceed along its own ways independent of, or even causative for, the events in the material sphere, was either a lie or self-deception.

Here was a general theory of society of impressive unity, brilliantly propounded and used with explosive effectiveness as a weapon in the economic and political struggle of those political workers' parties which had been founded or inspired by Marx. Was it true, this theory of historical materialism with its primacy of the economic sphere?

Here was a challenge which had to find its response in an intensive study of the structure and workings of society aiming in particular at determining within the social whole the role of the economic sector and its relation to all others. Manifold answers were given. The theory of the primacy of the economic facts was confronted with a whole set of theories finding the basic factor of society in race, climate and topography, philosophical ideas, political power, or some other single factor to be proclaimed as the base and all other factors as the superstructure, just as Marx had proclaimed the prius of the relationships of production.

In contrast to such attempts to substitute for the monolithic Marxian theory some other theory of equal one-sidedness but usually less impressiveness, other scholars resorted to exact historical investigation of economic development. The results of the painstaking research of this historical school of Roscher, Schmoller, Brentano, and their pupils have been invaluable, but the concern about the often minuscule detail threatened to become the very end itself. But there were those, too, who endeavored to utilize the rich results of the historical, statistical, and other factual research for the major end of obtaining insight into the workings of society. Notable among them were Wilhelm Dilthey, philosopher-historian, Ernst Troeltsch, historian and theologian, Werner Sombart, economic historian, and Max Weber.

Dilthey, least preoccupied with economic problems, devoted his life work to the study of the role played in history by ideas.[3] Sombart, beginning as a socialist and as historian of socialist movements,[4] came to interest himself in the origins, growth, and development of that phase of history which had produced socialism, viz., modern capitalism, the rise of which he described in rich detail and on the basis of painstaking historical research in his monumental *History of Modern Capitalism*.[5] By these facts he found himself driven to the conclusion that modern capitalism could not have arisen without a fundamental change in spirit that took place in Western Europe at the end of the Middle Ages. Modern capitalism, he found, would not have been possible without that break with the set ways of tradition which occurred in the age of the discoveries, the Renaissance, and the Reformation, and quite particularly would it not have been possible without that new attitude toward economic activities which made working for profit respectable, "usury" permissible, and strict rational calculation and competition for market chances necessary and proper. It was this latter change of attitude toward economic activity that Sombart found the most effective among

[3] Cf. Arnold Bergsträsser, *Wilhelm Dilthey and Max Weber: an Empirical Approach to Historical Synthesis* (1947) 57 ETHICS 92.

[4] SOZIALISMUS UND SOZIALE BEWEGUNG IM 19. JAHRHUNDERT, 1896; 10th ed., as DER PROLETARISCHE SOZIALISMUS, 2 vols. (1924); tr. from 6th ed., by M. Epstein as SOCIALISM AND THE SOCIAL MOVEMENT (1909).

[5] DER MODERNE KAPITALISMUS, 3 vols., in 6 (1928).

the many factors which had contributed in making possible and bringing about modern capitalism. What had been the cause of this change of spirit? Sombart was inclined to ascribe a major role in this development to the infiltration of the Jewish spirit into the economy of Western Europe, which he thought he could discover to have followed the expulsion of the Jews from Spain.[6] The rich tapestry which Sombart himself had woven in his *History*, was too complex, however, seriously to suggest this or any other single *causa causans*, but Sombart's suggestions were eagerly taken up by popularizers who simplified and then presented them to those craftsmen, peasants, and tradesmen whose traditionalist ways were increasingly endangered by the wave of capitalism which they were easily induced to identify with the successful Jewish competitor. Sombart, the scholar and historian, thus found himself among the prophets of National-Socialism,[7] from which he turned away in disgust, however, when he saw what it meant in action.

Immediately concerned with the problem of the ethical teachings of Christianity, Ernst Troeltsch was driven to the investigation of the influence of these teachings, clearly a phenomenon of the mental or spiritual sphere, upon human action including, of course, economic activity,[8] and this approach indicated that it was just as defensible to regard in the social fabric the mental and spiritual element as the cause of certain economic effects as vice versa.

The scholar who was to tie together all these various threads and to show, what should have been obvious all along, that all search for a primal cause or base of the complex social phenomena had to be futile, was Max Weber,[9] for many years Troeltsch's friend and colleague in Heidelberg. Possibly stimulated by the range of Troeltsch's research, Weber concluded that in order to find out the peculiar cause or causes of modern capitalism it might be best to compare the developments of the Western world where alone capitalism in its typical sense had arisen, with other civilizations, especially those of the Orient, where nothing comparable to modern Western capitalism had ever originated. What

[6] Die Juden und das Wirtschaftsleben, 1911, tr. by M. Epstein as The Jews and Modern Capitalism (1913).

[7] See especially his Deutscher-Sozialismus (1934), tr. by Karl F. Geiser as A New Social Philosophy (1937).

[8] Die Soziallehren der christlichen Kirchen (1912), tr. by O. Wyon as The Social Teaching of the Christian Churches, 2 vols. (1931).

[9] 1864–1920. On his life see the biography written by his widow, Marianne Weber, s.t. Max Weber, Ein Lebensbild (1926); 2nd ed. (1950); for a short description of Weber's life see Talcott Parsons' Introduction to Weber, Theory.

were the peculiar features by which the modern Western world is distinguished from all other civilizations? As far as Weber was able to find an answer, it is laid down in his last, unfinished work, *Economy and Society,* which, constituting the center piece of the plan for the great, collective *Outline of Social Economics,* also represents a mighty attempt to give a full typology and classification of significant social phenomena and to investigate their interrelations.

The chapter devoted to the analysis of the relationships between the social phenomenon "Law" and the social phenomena of the economic sphere constitutes the main part of our present book. In that chapter, as in all others of *Economy and Society,* Weber takes seriously the postulate that sociology has to be the science of society in general. He thus gathered his material from all the world's great civilizations as well as from primitive society. It is this universality of knowledge together with the author's gift of penetrating analysis, his objectivity, his passion for accurate formulation, and his genius for recognizing the essentials and the relations between seemingly remote phenomena which gives Weber's work its unique character.

The extraordinary qualities of Weber's mind became apparent in his very earliest writings. Stemming from a long line of ancestors distinguished in the professions, especially that of the Lutheran clergy, Max Weber, who was born in 1864, devoted himself to the study of law. His doctoral dissertation, however, hardly resembled the typical juristic dissertation of which hundreds are annually produced by German law candidates. The topic "A Contribution to the History of Medieval Business Organizations" [10] was suggested to Weber by Levin Goldschmidt, the historian of the Law Merchant, for whom Weber was soon called upon to substitute in his courses. The theme, concerned with the forerunners and earliest beginnings of modern capitalism, was to be a fitting start of Weber's life work.

While engaged in the regular in-service training of a candidate for the bench or the bar, Weber wrote the book by which he formally qualified as an instructor in law at the University of Berlin, his *Roman Agrarian History and Its Significance in Public and Private Law.*[11] Based upon original research in a field generally neglected until then, the book comprehensively presented the history of the legal institutions of Roman agriculture in constant interrelation with political, economic,

[10] Zur Geschichte der Handelsgesellschaften im Mittelalter (1889).

[11] Die römische Agrargeschichte in ihrer Bedeutung für das Staats- und Privatrecht (1891).

and social developments. Weber's teacher and sponsor in this extraordinary enterprise was the great Mommsen himself.

Weber, successfully engaged in the teaching of commercial law and legal history at the University of Berlin, made a fateful decision when, in 1894, he accepted the call to a newly created chair of economics at the University of Freiburg. Apparently, the nascent science of economics appeared more challenging to him than legal history. But the facts that Weber had been trained to be a lawyer and had taught law to regular law students were to leave their mark on all his future work. When he found it necessary in his investigations of the workings of society to consider the law and its functions, he did so with the sure touch of the trained expert.

In addition to working out and teaching highly original courses on economic theory and history, Weber's early years of academic life were filled with much practical activity, including an investigation of the status of farm workers [12] and the evaluation of a parliamentary inquiry into the functioning of the stock exchange,[13] whose report was to become the basis of the German "Securities and Exchange Act, 1908." [14]

After the influence of Mommsen, the jurist-historian-philologist, and Goldschmidt, the investigator of the medieval ways of commerce, a new dimension was added to Weber's mind through his friendship with Troeltsch, the explorer into the relationships between the religious and the other spheres of social life. What had been the role of religion in the development of Western capitalism? There was one religion which was completely peculiar to the West: Protestantism; also the period of its rise coincided with that of the early beginning of Western capitalism. Could there, perhaps, be some connection? Weber began to study the historical materials, and with Troeltsch undertook a trip to America,[15] the country of the most unbridled capitalism.

[12] Die Verhältnisse der Landarbeiter im Ostelbischen Deutschland (1892), Schriften des Vereins für Sozialpolitik, vol. 55; Privatenqueten über die Lage der Landarbeiter, 1892 Mitteilungen des evangelisch-sozialen Kongresses; Die ländliche Arbeitsverfassung (1893) Schriften des Vereins für Sozialpolitik, vol. 58; Entwicklungstendenzen in der Lage der ostelbischen Landarbeiter (1894) Archiv für soziale Gesetzgebung, vol. 7.

[13] Ergebnisse der deutschen Börsenenquete (1894–96) Zeitschrift für das gesamte Handelsrecht, vols. 43, 44, 45.

[14] Börsengesetz, of 27 May 1908, R.G. Bl. 1908. 215.

[15] The trip was officially undertaken to participate in the World Congress of Art and Science which was held in St. Louis in 1904 on the occasion of the St. Louis World's Fair. Weber's paper on *The Rural Community* is published in vol. 7 of the Reports of The Congress, ed. by H. J. Rogers (1906).

In an essay entitled *Protestant Ethics and the Spirit of Capitalism*,[16] Weber maintained that the latter was indeed, linked to the former. Protestantism in general had removed certain obstacles from the course of other factors which had given help to the rise of what was to become the capitalistic spirit. Protestantism's most peculiar form, Calvinism, especially as Puritanism, had also by itself helped to engender new ideas: devotion to the duties inherent in the strictly rational conduct of commerce or industry, when carried on as a "calling" and combined with a virtuous mode of life, could, as intra-wordly *askesis*, be as religiously meritorious as the monk's strictly disciplined devotional life had been in the old Church; and success in such devotion could be regarded as a sign of belonging to the community of the elect, in contrast to the profligacy and irresponsibility of the damned.

Human striving for the accumulation of wealth has been almost universal in the world, especially when sought to be satisfied in the "irrational" (i.e., unsystematic) ways of war, piracy, or treasure hunt. Both inside and outside the Western world, wealth has also been pursued in the "rational" ways of "political capitalism" through the utilization, by way of purchase, pledge acquisition or rent, of power positions, especially the renting by publicans of the right to levy taxes. In various forms wealth has been pursued rationally in trade or, through the use of slaves or other unfree labor, in plantation agriculture. However, none of these types of "capitalism" shows those features which are characteristic of modern Western capitalism, viz., the consistent use of capital accounting (*Kapitalrechnung*), rational orientation of economic activity toward exchange possibilities in a free market, and investment of economic values in means of technological production. Weber contrasted these features of formally rational economic conduct with economic conduct oriented toward some particular ethical ideal or political goal, and regarded them as being closely connected with the specifically Calvinist-Puritan way of life.

This is not the place for a critical evaluation of this thesis, for which Weber adduced a wealth of evidentiary material which has found acceptance and support by competent scholars, but which has also met with criticism, of which some at least has been founded on respectable historical evidence. Notable among those who have found Weber's thesis suggestive has been Richard Henry Tawney, whose analysis of the

[16] *Die protestanische Ethik und der Geist des Kapitalismus* (1904/5) ARCHIV FÜR SOZIALWISSENSCHAFT, vols. 20 and 21; repr. in 1 GESAMMELTE AUFSÄTZE ZUR RELIGIONSSOZIOLOGIE (2nd ed., 1922), tr. by Talcott Parsons as THE PROTESTANT ETHIC AND THE SPIRIT OF CAPITALISM (1930).

"acquisitive society" has been based upon the work of Weber and who was the first to introduce Weber to the English-speaking world.[17] In evaluating Weber's ideas on the role of Protestantism in the development of modern capitalism it must not be overlooked that Weber never postulated a simple cause and effect relationship. It is essential that we understand that, like Sombart, Weber recognized modern capitalism as a phenomenon of the mind, a specific human attitude, the rise of which from medieval traditionalism required a specific combination of circumstances, political, economic and, among others, religious.

In his article on Protestantism this religious element was treated so to speak in isolation from others. The rise of Calvinist Protestantism was taken as the starting point, from which its influence was traced upon the economic sphere. This method turned out to be so fascinating and fruitful that Weber applied it in a series of further studies of the influence played upon economic conduct by several of the world's great religions, viz., Judaism of the prophetic age, Hinduism, Buddhism, and Confucianism.[18] In these Weber presented a wealth of historical data and utilized them for new sociological insights. He also demonstrated that in the presentation and analysis of the interconnection of social phenomena it was possible to start out from those of the religious just as well as from those of the economic sphere. However, the more Weber concentrated upon this study of the interrelations between religious and economic conduct, the clearer it became to him that concentration upon religion as a single, isolated phenomenon was apt to result in a distortion of the complex social fabric. What was needed even for the limited goal of understanding the rise of Western capitalism was an analysis of society as a whole.

As a preliminary to that task Weber recognized the necessity of a clear definition, classification, and systematization of those social phenomena whose interrelationships were to be traced. After all, modern science could not achieve its spectacular results until the phenomena to be observed had been described, classified, and systematically arranged for ready reference. Linnaeus, Laplace, and their companions in the creation of taxonomic systems in zoology, botany, mineralogy, anatomy, etc., had to precede the physiologists. The task of these taxonomic scien-

[17] THE ACQUISITIVE SOCIETY (1920); RELIGION AND THE RISE OF CAPITALISM (1926).

[18] GESAMMELTE AUFSÄTZE ZUR RELIGIONSSOZIOLOGIE (1922/23). Weber's essay on Judaism has been translated by Hans H. Gerth, s.t. ANCIENT JUDAISM (1952); his essay on religion in China by Hans H. Gerth, s.t. THE RELIGION OF CHINA, CONFUCIANISM AND TAOISM (1951); that on Hinduism by Hans H. Gerth and Don Martindale, s.t. HINDU SOCIAL SYSTEM (1950).

tists had been comparatively easy, however. The units of observation existed as such in nature in the form of its separate species. Nature presented the wolf, the squid, the rose, or the blue spruce, and others as so many different species. These species had to be described, occasionally also first to be discovered, and then to be arranged in some system so as to promote economy of thought and facilitate ready reference.

In social science it also seems at a first glance that we know those phenomena whose interrelations we are trying to unravel. We think that we know the species of, let us say, political organization, such as monarchy and republic, or aristocracy, democracy, and dictatorship; or the species of economic systems such as capitalism, the manorial system, or the types of economy of primitive food gatherers, hunters, or cattle-raising nomads. But let us try to define the exact borderline between monarchy or republic, between aristocracy and democracy, or between capitalism and pre-capitalist economy. Or let us try to classify a particular historical situation. The Roman state of Caesar's days, was it a republic or a monarchy? The Florentine Republic of the days of Savonarola, was it a democracy, or an aristocracy, or if neither, what else? England in 1760, was its economy of the capitalist or the pre-capitalist type?

None of these questions can be answered for the simple reason that clearly defined species do not exist in the realm of social phenomena. We are fairly certain that the present-day United States is a republic and a democracy, and Libya a monarchy; is the latter also a democracy? If not, what is it? And what of the U.S.S.R. and the People's Democracies? Or Canada; or Viet-Nam? Of both democracy and dictatorship we have certain more or less vaguely defined ideas. But do those ideas coincide with any concrete reality? What we find are mixtures. Even the dictatorship of Hitler in National-Socialist Germany had democratic features, and in the democracy of the United States we find certain dictatorial elements. The question is always one of more or less, or one of defining the position of a concrete phenomenon upon a scale of infinite transitions between the two extremes of clear-cut polarity. Every political, or more generally, every social, scientist has always had to apply the method which Polybius used when he described the constitution of Rome by indicating that the consuls constituted the monarchical element, the senate the aristocratic, the *comitia* the democratic, etc., and that the peculiar characteristics of the Roman constitution lay in the way in which these various elements were blended.

However, unless we content ourselves with vague approximations, we encounter a new difficulty. How can we characterize a concrete historical phenomenon as such and such a combination of such and such elements, until we know what the elements are. Let it be emphasized again that nature, while it presents us with species of plants or animals, does not present us with species of social phenomena. Whatever species' terms we use in our social science discourse, we have created ourselves. Capitalism, manorial system, monarchy, feudalism, marriage, monotheism, etc., all these concepts are creations of the human mind, but when we look at these concepts more closely we find that many, if not most of them, are but vaguely defined, that they are used with different meanings by different people, that they overlap, and that their sum total does not cover the totality of social phenomena.

In view of this situation Weber apprehended the need of creating a comprehensive system of concepts and of establishing a clear-cut terminology as a preliminary for all further analysis of interrelations of social phenomena.[19] He thus undertook to formulate, as the vocabulary of further work, a set of concepts, i.e., of rigorously defined situations of what may be called a "pure" type. What would be the characteristics of an economy in which all conduct was carried on strictly along the lines of tradition, or of this or that system of ethical or religious values, or of rigorous pursuit of the chances of the market, and in complete disregard of all tradition and all consideration of religious or ethical commands? Or what would be the characteristics of a society in which all precepts for social conduct are obeyed because they have always been obeyed and have thus become accepted as inveterate; or because the ruler is regarded as "charismatically" qualified to be the man of destiny; or because its governmental system is carried on in accordance with a set of rules which have been worked out rationally and are regarded as the "right" ones? Situations of such "pure" type have never existed in history. They are artificial constructs similar to the pure constructs of geometry. No pure triangle, cube, or sphere has ever existed. But never could reality have been penetrated scientifically without the use of the artificial concepts of geometry. For the "pure" concepts created by him, Weber used the term "ideal type" (*Idealtyp*). The term is not very fortunate. If we encounter it without knowing how Weber meant it to be understood, we may be misled to assume that the ideal types are models for the actualization of which men ought to strive.

[19] Weber's various essays on methodology have been collected in the volume entitled GESAMMELTE AUFSÄTZE ZUR WISSENSCHAFTSLEHRE (1922; 2nd ed. 1951); the most important of these essays have been translated and edited by EDWARD A. SHILS AND HENRY A. FINCH, as MAX WEBER ON THE METHODOLOGY OF THE SCIENCES (1949).

Such an interpretation would be erroneous. In his scholarly work, in contrast to his political activities, Weber did not intend to advocate any particular line of social conduct as against another. Such an approach would imply evaluation, and evaluation is not the task of the social scientist, who has to limit himself to observation, description, and explanation. The "ideal types" of Weber's sociology are simply mental constructs meant to serve as categories of thought the use of which will help us to catch the infinite manifoldness of reality by comparing its phenomena with those "pure" types which are used, so to speak, to serve as guides in a filing system. The use of such "pure-type concepts" in the social sciences is in no way a new invention of Weber's. They have been applied in political science ever since Aristotle formulated his concepts of monarchy, oligarchy, democracy, etc., as the filing system for the apprehension of the phenomena of the political life of the city-states and kingdoms of antiquity. The entire science of economics has to a large extent been based upon the use of the ideal type of the *homo economicus*, the human being who is motivated exclusively by the desire for economic goods and who follows in this pursuit exclusively the commands of reason to the exclusion of all emotional irritants or traditionalistic, ethical, or other inhibitions. No human being of this kind has ever existed or is likely ever to exist. Yet, this mental construct has been useful, or even indispensable, in our endeavor to understand the working and functioning of the economic system.

What has been new in the case of Weber has thus not been the use of ideal concepts as such but the consistent way in which they are used and the manner in which an entire system of them has been elaborated as that set of categories within which the social phenomena, or at least a large part of them, can be filed, and thus observed, described, analyzed, and understood in their continuous changes as well as in those interrelations by which these changes are produced.

Weber's system of ideal concepts is presented in the First Part of *Economy and Society*. These first one hundred and eighty pages are the basic part of the entire work.[20] In four chapters he presents "The Basic Concepts of Sociology; Sociological Categories of Economic Conduct"; "The Type Situations of Domination"; and the basic concepts for the understanding of "Estates and Classes."

All these concepts, among them the concept of law, are presented as definitions, which are, of course, nominal rather than real definitions. From all we have said it ought to be clear that Weber does not pretend

[20] This part has been translated by A. M. Henderson and Talcott Parsons as THEORY OF SOCIAL AND ECONOMIC ORGANIZATION (1947).

to define what democracy, capitalism, law, society, feudalism, bureaucracy, patrimonialism, sultanism, etc., "really" are. All he intends to do is to let us know what *he* means when *he* uses these terms so that we know clearly what he is talking about. Thus he never says "law (or convention, or ethics, etc.) *is* such and such" but rather "when I speak of law (or convention, etc.) I mean a phenomenon having such and such characteristics." The terms thus defined are used with consistency throughout the book. Clearly, the meaning of the terms, referring to ideal types of social situations, is not always the same as that in which the same words are used in common parlance. One might grossly misunderstand Weber if one read later parts of his work without knowledge of his terminology and thus with the inclination to interpret his language in the sense of common parlance. The main difference between the meaning of words in Weber's terminology and in common parlance is the greater precision of the former. What do we mean, for instance, when we speak of bureaucracy? It would be difficult to ascribe any clear meaning to this term of common language. Compare with it the precision of Weber's definition, which is developed as follows:[21]

1. (a) *Domination* shall mean the probability that all, or certain, commands are obeyed by a definable group of human beings. . .

(b) Experience shows that no domination has ever been content with the probability of its continued existence being dependent exclusively upon considerations of self-interest of the ruled, or upon their emotions, or upon their belief that obedience as such is an ethical duty. Every domination will rather be anxious to raise and cultivate the belief in its *legitimacy.* According to the type of legitimacy claimed, the type of obedience on the part of the administrative staff required to guarantee this obedience will vary just as the ways in which the domination is exercised as well as its effects. It will thus be helpful to establish the various type categories of domination in accordance with the kind of legitimacy typically claimed by it. It will be helpful, too, in this task to start with the contemporary scene which is, of course, the most familiar to us. . .

2. There are three pure types of *legitimate domination.* (a) A domination can be legitimately valid because of its rational character: such *legal domination* rests upon the belief in the legality of a consciously created order and of the right to give commands vested in the person or persons designated by that order. Or

(b) A domination can be legitimately valid because of its traditional character: such *traditional domination* rests upon the general and continuous belief in the sacredness of settled traditions and the legitimacy of the person or persons called to authority by such tradition; or

[21] Wirtschaft und Gesellschaft (2nd ed.) 122 *et seq.*

(c) A domination can be legitimately valid because of its charismatic character: such *charismatic domination* rests upon the uncommon and extraordinary devotion to the sacredness or the heroic force or the exemplariness of an individual and the order revealed or created by him.

In the case of domination by virtue of consciously made rules obedience is given to the legally created *impersonal* order and the *superior* designated by it, by virtue of the formal legality of his commands, and within the scope of authority assigned to him by the order. In the case of traditional domination obedience is given by virtue of piety and within the scope of usage to the *person* of the *lord* who is designated as well as bound by tradition. In the case of charismatic domination obedience is given to the charismatically qualified *leader* as such by virtue of personal faith in his revelation, heroism, or exemplariness within the confines of the validity of such faith in this charisma of his. . .

3. *Legal domination* rests upon the existence of the following notions, which are independent of each other:

(a) that any kind of law can be rationally made. . . ;

(b) that every legal system is essentially a cosmos of abstract, and in the normal case, consciously made rules; that in the administration of justice these rules are applied to individual cases, and that in the administration those interests which are designated by the order of the organization are consciously promoted within the confines of the rules of law; . . .

(c) that the typically legal master, i.e. the *superior*, who gives commands, in turn obeys the impersonal order toward which his commands are oriented;

(d) that *those who obey* do so solely as members of the organization and solely "to the law"; and

(e) that in accordance with the notion stated *sub* (c) the members, when obeying the superior, do so not out of respect for his person but out of *respect for the impersonal order*, and that, consequently, obedience is owed to the superior exclusively within that limited scope of jurisdiction which is rationally assigned to him by the order.

4. We thus find that *rational domination* is characterized by the following basic features:

(a) acts of *official business* are continuously carried on in the manner of being bound to definite rules;

(b) This conduct of official business is carried on within the scope of definite jurisdictions. This fact means (1) that the official business is carried on within the spheres of duties objectively determined in accordance with the principle of division of labor; (2) that to every such branch of jurisdiction there are assigned its proper powers of command; and (3) that those means of coercion which are admissible as well as the conditions of their application are clearly determined.

A line of conduct showing these characteristics shall be called *agency* (*Behörde*).

(c) In addition to the characteristics of rational domination just stated *sub* (a) and (b) we find, furthermore, the principle of *official hierarchy* which means that the order provides for every agency another one by which it is controlled or supervised so that the latter can be invoked in appeal or remonstrance against the measures of the former. . . .

(d) The rules according to which the agencies act may be either (1) technical rules; or (2) norms.

In both cases professional training is necessary if full rationality is to be achieved in the application. Hence nobody is allowed to be a member of the administrative staff unless he can prove that he has successfully undergone the professional training and no one but a person thus qualified can be employed as an *official*. "Officials" thus constitute the typical administrative staff of rational organization, irrespective of whether it is political, hierocratic, economic (especially capitalistic), or of any other kind.

(e) Where rationality obtains the *administrative staff* is completely *separated from* the supplies and other *means of administration*. The officials, employees or workers in the administrative staff do not own the supplies or other means of administration; they are rather supplied to them in kind or in money, and they are accountable for them. The official funds are completely separated from the official's private funds and his place of work, the office, is separated from his private home.

(f) In the case of full rationality *no office is appropriated to its incumbent*. For judges, certain other officials and even workers it is to an increasing extent recognized that they have a "right" to their official positions, but the recognition of such a right is not meant to constitute the official as the owner of his job but rather to safeguard the purely objective ("independent") fulfillment of his duties as being determined exclusively by the appropriate norms.

(g) All administrative activities are *recorded*, even where oral discussion takes place or is prescribed. At least the preliminary discussion, the grounds, and the final decision, decrees and orders are recorded in writing. The files and the continuous conduct of the business by officials constitute the *bureau* as the focal point of all modern organizational activity.

(h) *Legal domination can assume several different forms* (viz. especially those of bureaucracy, of administration by honoratiores, or of direct democracy).

5. The purest type of legal domination is that which is carried on by means of a *bureaucratic administrative staff*. Only the chief of the organization possesses his position as master by virtue of appropriation, or election, or designation by his predecessor. But his powers, too, are legally defined jurisdictions. The administrative staff is, in the pure type case, composed exclusively of officials every one of whom is acting by himself rather than as the member of a board, bench or committee. Every one of these officials presents the following further characteristics:

(a) He is personally free and only obeys objectively defined official duties.

(b) He stands with all others in a fixed pyramid of hierarchy of office.

(c) His office is endowed with a definitely fixed jurisdiction.

(d) He is not elected but hired by contract.

(e) He is selected upon the basis of his objective qualification for his job, which, in the case of full rationality, is ascertained by an examination and proven by an official diploma.

(f) He is paid a fixed money salary and in most cases he is entitled to a pension. The employment can always be terminated by the official and, in private organizations, as a general rule also by the master. The amount of the salary is determined by the official's position in the hierarchical pyramid, frequently also by the amount of responsibility involved in his position, and also by the consideration to enable the official to live in accordance with his proper social status.

(g) The office constitutes the official's sole and full-time job.

(h) The official enters a career in which he will be promoted in accordance with seniority, or with achievement, or both, depending upon the judgment of his superiors.

(i) The official does not own the supplies or other means of administration nor does he own his job.

(j) He is subject to a strictly unitary official discipline and control.

The system just defined can and does occur not only in political or hierocratic, but also in economic, charitable, or other private organizations, irrespective of whether they are meant to serve ideal or material purposes.

In the following section Weber then explains why the bureaucratic type of administration thus defined is the one through which "formal rationality," i.e., efficiency of administration, can be achieved in the highest degree and why its increasing use has become inevitable in all kinds of modern mass organization.

"1. The only choice is between 'bureaucratization' and 'dilettantization' of the administration, and the great superiority of bureaucracy consists in technical knowledge and competency" which have become indispensable especially in the economic sphere, irrespective of whether it is organized capitalistically or whether it were to be organized along socialist lines. If the bureaucratic machinery of the modern state were to cease to function, sheer physical existence would become impossible for all except the immediate owners of the food supplies.

Hence the bureaucratic machinery continues to function for the successful revolutionaries or the occupying enemy just as it had been functioning for the legal government. The essential question is always: Who dominates the bureaucratic machinery? But on the other hand, it can never be completely dominated by the non-professional. . . . Bureaucratic administration means domination by virtue of knowledge. Upon this fact rests its specifically rational character. . . .

Only one type of person is superior to the bureaucratic officials in knowledge and experience, viz., the capitalistic entrepreneur, although even his superiority is limited to his own field of interests. But within this field he is the only one who is immune against the otherwise ineluctable domination of bureaucratic knowledge.

2. In a general way, bureaucracy results in the following social consequences.

(a) In consequence of its interest in universal recruitment from among those best qualified objectively, bureaucracy produces a trend toward social *equalization.*

(b) In consequence of the interest in the longest possible professional training, which often lasts almost until the end of the third decade of life, bureaucracy produces a trend toward *plutocracy.*

(c) Bureaucracy tends toward the rule of *formalistic impersonality.* The ideal official administers his office *sine ira et studio*, without hatred or passion, hence also without "love" or "enthusiasm"; under the pressure of a plain sense of duty, "without regard of the person" he treats equally all persons who find themselves in factually equal situations.

Better than any attempted description this lengthy quotation will give an impression of the peculiar way in which Weber formed the concepts of his ideal types of social situations, of the meticulous care with which he articulated their definitions, and the systematic manner in which these concepts are related to each other. Beginning with the most general concepts of social conduct and social relations, Weber formulates new, ever more specialized and thus ever more concrete concepts by emphasizing ever more detailed and concrete traits. Our specimen also demonstrates the way in which Weber presents the effects which a particular social phenomenon would produce upon others if it occurred in its pure form, or which are actually produced by these phenomena of real life in which the ideal type is approximated. What the illustration does not show is the vast range of historical material from which Weber's concepts are derived. Many illustrations of this impressive characteristic will be found, however, in this present book.

II. "Economy and Society"

The systematic presentation of the basic ideal types of social phenomena in general and in the fields of economic conduct and dominational organization in particular was published in early 1921 as the first part of *Economy and Society.* At that time its author was dead. For a long time his health had been impaired. At various times illness had compelled him to interrupt his activities. On 14th October 1920 it put an end to his indefatigable activities in the sphere of learning and in the political life of the German Republic, which he had helped to prepare and establish in the turmoil of World War I and the Revolution of 1918–19.

In the last years of his life the sallowness of Weber's complexion indicated the frailty of his state of health, but it hardly ever penetrated to the consciousness of the students who were enthralled by Weber's volcanic personality when they listened to his lectures, to which he attracted in his few years in Munich crowds of a thousand or more students from all departments of the university. Discussion was carried on only in his seminars to which none would be admitted but a dozen or so of the most highly qualified graduate students. The course which Weber taught in Munich during these last years was called General Economic History. From students' notes its text was reconstructed after Weber's death and, through Frank Knight, made accessible in English.[22] This was no routine course but a presentation of the quintessence of Weber's research and thought. On a world-wide scale, the rise of modern capitalism was presented against the background of ancient and later pre-capitalist society, in continuous confrontation with the different phenomena of the Orient and in consistent search for the interrelations between the economic phenomena on the one hand and those in other social spheres, especially the political, on the other. Weber's lecturing was no reading, however, from a prepared text. All he brought with him into the classroom were little slips of paper upon which he had apparently noted a few key terms of an outline. The students could thus watch the fascinating process of scholarly and artistic creation. The words and thoughts were produced with eruptive force. Weber spoke fast, indeed rapidly. It was not always easy to follow this torrent. But everything was presented in the most strictly elaborated systematic order and in the most precise verbal formulation. There were no "ahs" or "hms," no repetitions, except where indicated by didactic considerations. Everything was said in the right words and at the proper place. The presentation was cool and objective, but behind this remoteness of the scholar we students could feel the fire of the passion which was burning in that extraordinary man and the iron will which kept it under control and which prevented the entry into his work as a scholar and teacher of those deep emotions and convictions for which he would plead so eloquently when he allowed himself to take a stand on the political problems of the day, always carefully announcing in such cases that he would now speak as a politician and not as a scientist.

[22] HISTORY (1922; 2nd ed. 1950).

Yes, Weber was an impressive personality, a man unforgettable to one who had the good fortune of having had him as a teacher. His death, occurring in the midst of the academic year, was a blow to the world of learning, and a loss deeply felt by his students.

On the date of Weber's sudden death nothing was completed of *Economy and Society* except those Sections of Part I which he had personally seen into the press. In addition there were manuscripts in various stages of completion, ranging from chapters almost finished, but for the last revision, to mere notes.[23] The parts which were nearest to completion were meant to form the bulk of Parts II and III of *Economy and Society*, as the book had been planned by Weber, to be entitled respectively "Types of Consociation and Association" and "Types of Domination." These chapters were posthumously published by Weber's widow, as he had left them, but in a chapter sequence which had to be determined by her. In the second edition, which became soon necessary, she added Weber's essay on "The Rational and Sociological Bases of Music," which had previously been published as a separate pamphlet and which had been written by Weber as a first approach to a comprehensively planned sociology of the arts. The essay fits in well with the other chapters which are now assembled in *Economy and Society*. Why is it, Weber asks, that Western music is different from that of all other civilizations? In the course of his investigations he found a startling answer. Although flowing from sentiment more directly than any other art, music, in order to develop as an art, required the discipline of rationality. The type of musical system, such as those of Greece, China, India, or the Western Middle Ages, is determined by its peculiar type of rationality, and the type of rationality which has given its imprint to the music of the West appears to be akin to that type of rationality which has determined other phenomena of Western civilization, especially in the religious sphere and with, and perhaps through, it in the economic.

For further parts of the book, nothing was ready at Weber's death but notes and outlines, too sketchy to permit publication. They were meant to grow into a comprehensive sociology of the arts and sciences.

In those chapters which now form Part II of *Economy and Society*, Weber presents his analysis of social groupments with a view to determining the relationships between different kinds of consociation and ways of economic organization. Starting with the basic groupments of kinship, sex relationships, and neighborhood, Weber proceeds to a brief discussion of ethnic association and a more extensive one of re-

[23] On the making of ECONOMY AND SOCIETY and its posthumous publications, see MARIANNE WEBER, MAX WEBER (1926).

ligious association, the latter presenting the quintessence of his long research in the field of sociology of religion. After a fragmentary, uncompleted sketch on that type of social relationship which forms the characteristic core of the capitalistic economy, the market, there follow the two chapters which constitute the bulk of our present book. Starting from a general discussion of the significance of the legal order in economic life, Weber proceeds to that sociology of legal thought in which the breadth of his knowledge and depth of thought have found their most fascinating expression.

The sociology of law would seem to connect naturally with those chapters which now form the Third Part of *Economy and Society* and which are concerned with those types of domination through which law is created and made effective. The editor, Weber's widow, has interposed, however, as a last chapter of Part II of *Economy and Society*, Weber's essay on "The City," in which he contrasts the autonomous, organized, and structured city of the West with the mere agglomeration of people in the cities of the Orient, again investigating the role of the former in the evolution of modern capitalism.

Of the Third Part of *Economy and Society* we have included in the present book the first chapter, which is closely connected with the sociology of law. The basic forms in which the phenomenon of domination and authority occurs are here in more readable form than that of the rigorous definitions in which they are established in the First Part of *Economy and Society*. In the remaining ten chapters the details are filled in. Indeed, they constitute the material from which Weber has derived his general categories. As a specimen we have included in the present book those parts of the chapter on the bureaucratic form of domination which constitute a close sequence to or, better, a basis, of those parts of the sociology of law in which Weber investigates the influence which bureaucracy has exercised on legal thought. Other parts, especially those concerned with the Chinese forms of bureaucracy and patrimonialism, have recently been made available in English by Gerth and Mills.

Gradually, Weber's thought and work are thus being opened up to the English-speaking parts of the world, but even now, more than thirty years after his death, considerable parts not only of his work in general but even of *Economy and Society*, are waiting for a translator. All of them, and quite particularly those which have been assembled in the present book, can stand by themselves. The reader should not forget, however, that they all are but parts of a major whole, that they were not intended by the author to be read separately, but that he meant them to constitute necessary constituents of his vast-scale investigation into the social bases of economic organization in general and of modern capitalism in particular. This aim of Weber's should especially be kept in mind by the reader of the present book.

III. Weber's Sociology of Law

If understood in its full purport, sociology of law would have to comprise an investigation into the relationship between *all* legal and all other social phenomena. It should thus concern itself first of all with the question of why law, in the sense of politically organized enforcement of a social order, has arisen at all; how the enforcement machinery can be organized and how it operates; to what extent it is effective, and by what factors the varying degrees of its effectiveness are determined; what factors influence the content of those rules of social conduct which are legally enforced; why, how, and in which ways the content of these rules is changed with changing social conditions; which factors determine which fields of human conduct are under given circumstances to be subject to legal control, which are to be subject to ethical, religious, conventional, or other forms of social control, and which are to be left free of all social control altogether. These are just some of the problems which would have to constitute the subject matter of a systematic sociology of law aiming at comprehensiveness. Weber has not attempted to write such a systematic sociology of law. His interest in law came to be centered around that problem which in this country is usually referred to as that of legal thought or of the judicial process. That latter term would be too narrow, however, for Weber's planetary thought. In the Common Law the judge is commonly regarded as the central figure in the legal universe. His activity decisively affects our lives and towards him are the activities of all other members of the legal profession oriented. In a Common Law country the analysis of the judicial process is thus all but coterminous with an analysis of legal thought in general.

It has not been the least of Weber's merits that he has shown that this judge-centeredness of the Common Law is not a general feature of all legal systems. He has shown not only that legal systems may be dominated by figures other than judges, such as priests, consultants of predominantly temporal or sacred learning, conveyancers, or professors, but that it is decisive for the entire character of a legal system by what kind of such "honoratiores" it is thus dominated. Weber is thus concerned with the process of legal thought in general rather than with special phenomena of judicial thought. But that problem of legal thought does indeed constitute the central problem of his sociology of law and it is this very fact which renders Weber's ideas significant for present American jurisprudence in which, too, the process of legal thought has come to occupy the center of the stage.

Weber's starting point is his observation that, as in so many other respects, in the field of legal thought, too, the West has developed a method which cannot be found in any other civilization. It is the method which Weber calls that of logical formalism. Its characteristics are stated concisely or even cryptically and at a place where the central significance of the matter is in no way made apparent. If Weber would ever have had the opportunity of completing his work, the present first Section of the chapter on Sociology of Law would most likely have been rewritten and rearranged. A brief explanation would thus seem to be called for so as to indicate more clearly the particular problem which Weber tried to clarify.

In the field of law the two basic activities are those of creating law and of finding the law once created. With respect to both, Weber establishes two methodological categories: they can be irrational or rational. Also, law making and law finding can proceed rationally or irrationally either with respect to formal or to substantive criteria.

Law makers and law finders proceed in a formally irrational manner in so far as they are guided by means which are beyond the control of reason, such as an oracle, a prophetic revelation, or an ordeal.

Irrationality of the substantive kind exists in so far as law makers or law finders fail to be guided by general norms and proceed either in pure arbitrariness or jump to their conclusions in a completely casuistic manner upon the basis of emotional evaluations of every single case. This ideal type which has no counterpart in reality is approximated by the tyrant as well as the khadi, i.e., the Moslem judge who sits in the market place and, at least seemingly, renders his decisions without any reference to rules or norms but in what appears to be a completely free evaluation of the particular merits of every single case. The type would also be approximated by that kind of wise man who, ably applying the Solomonic hunch, would seem to represent the ideal of the German school of free law or of the American realists.

Rational on the other hand are the activities of law makers and law finders in so far as they are guided by rational considerations, which, in turn, can again be of the substantive or the formal kind.

Substantively rational are law makers or finders in so far as they consciously follow (more or less) clearly conceived and articulated general principles of some kind. These principles may be those of a religion, or a system of ethical thought, or of a notion of *raison d'état*, or power policy planfully formulated and conceived. Substantively rational, for instance, is Mohammedan law in so far as its "makers" and finders have been trying to implement the religious thought and commands of the Prophet; substantively rational is Soviet law in so far as it is conceived as a means to bring about, to preserve, and to elaborate the social system of the Communist ideology; substantively rational, too, is any law which a conqueror imposes upon a subject population as a means of maintaining and strengthening his rule, or the law by means of which a ruling nation tries to "elevate" the population of a backward territory to its own, "higher" level of civilization.

Finally, the methods of law making and law finding may be rational not in a substantive but in a formal way. Formally rational is a law in so far as significance in both substantive law and procedure is ascribed exclusively to operative facts which are determined not from case to case but in a generically determined manner. Again, such formal rationality may be of two different kinds. Those facts which are to be significant in the determination of legal relationships, especially of rights and duties, may be of a purely extrinsic character: a contract is binding or not depending on whether or not it has been reduced to writing, or whether a seal has been employed, or whether certain formulary words have been used; whether or not a defendant has been validly summoned depends on whether or not certain visible or audible acts have been performed under exact observance of clearly prescribed formalities such as oral communication of the summons before a certain number of witnesses, or personal delivery of a formulary writing by a certain public official, and so on. Whether or not an interest in a piece of land has been effectively conveyed depends upon whether or not a clod of earth or some other symbol of the land or a formalized instrument in writing has been delivered in a particular manner, for instance on the very land itself, or before a judge, or in the presence of witnesses, and so on.

Lastly, law making and law finding can be logically rational in so far as they proceed upon the basis of generic rules which neither are determined by any religious, ethical, political, or other system of ideology, nor regard as relevant the observance of formalized acts observable by the senses, but are formulated by the use of generic concepts of an abstract character. In Weber's own words, law making and law finding are formally rational in the logical manner in so far as "the legally relevant facts are determined in a process of logical interpretation of meaning and as fixed legal concepts are thus created and applied in the form of strictly abstract rules." The way in which the term "logically formal rationality" is applied later on makes it clear that by it Weber means exactly that method of legal thought which in modern jurisprudence has become known as "jurisprudence of concepts" or "conceptual jurisprudence (*Begriffsjurisprudenz*)," and which has been so ardently attacked by the New Jurisprudence of Free Law and Jurisprudence of Interests in Germany, by Gény and Lambert in France, and by Sociological Jurists and Realists in America.

To Weber this kind of legal thought appears as a peculiar product of Western civilization and one which cannot be found in other legal systems, especially those of the Orient. Hence he raises the problem of determining the relationship between this peculiar type of legal thought and that type of economy which is peculiar to the West, modern capitalism. Has, perhaps, the rise of formal rationality in legal thought contributed to the rise of capitalism; or has, possibly, capitalism contributed to the rise of logical rationality in legal thought? This is the main problem to which Weber addresses himself in his Sociology of Law. Nowhere is it expressly stated, however, in these words and quite possibly Weber might regard our formulation as an oversimplification of his more subtle inquiry. We nevertheless believe that Weber's text can be more easily understood and followed if we keep in mind that the problem just formulated at least constitutes a starting point or perhaps, the very center, of his endeavor.

The point is so basic, indeed, that before proceeding to explain the way in which Weber has attacked his problem, it may be appropriate to recapitulate the scheme of ideal type categories within which Weber has tried to apprehend the vast variety of kinds of legal thought as they can be found in the actuality of the world's legal systems. According to this scheme legal thought as appearing in law making and law finding can approximate, or constitute combinations of, any one of the following types:

1. *irrational*, i.e., not guided by general rules
   a. *formal*: guided by means which are beyond the control of reason (ordeal, oracle, etc.);
   b. *substantive*: guided by reaction to the individual case;
2. *rational*, i.e., guided by general rules
   a. *substantive*: guided by the principles of an ideological system other than that of the law itself (ethics, religion, power politics, etc.);
   b. *formal*:
      (1) *extrinsically*, i.e., ascribing significance to external acts observable by the senses;
      (2) *logically*, i.e., expressing its rules by the use of abstract concepts created by legal thought itself and conceived of as constituting a complete system.

In that concrete system of law in which logically formal rationality of the law has found its most perfect expression, i.e., that which was elaborated by the German legal scholars of the nineteenth century, it has, according to Weber, resulted in the formulation of the following postulates:

(1) that every decision of a concrete case consists in the "application" of an abstract rule of law to a concrete fact situation;

(2) that by means of legal logic the abstract rules of the positive law can be made to yield the decision for every concrete fact situation;

(3) that, consequently, the positive law constitutes a "gapless" system of rules, which are at least latently contained in it, or that the law is at least to be treated for purposes of legal practice as if it were such a gapless system;

(4) that every instance of social conduct can and must be conceived as constituting either obedience to, or violation, or application, of rules of law.

As we have observed already, the type of legal thought thus characterized was developed to its highest degree of perfection by the German Pandectists of the nineteenth century. In a more general sense it constitutes the method of the Civil Law as it was developed from the twelfth century on in the universities first of Italy, then of France, Holland, and Germany. The main difference between the Civil Law and the Common Law consists in the fact that the latter has developed a different method of thought, which, in Weber's terminology, approximates the substantively irrational type. However, the method of logically formal rationality, that is, conceptual jurisprudence, can also be found in the Common Law, especially in those of its parts in which Civil Law influence has been strong. In order to understand Weber's presentation it is necessary to know exactly what he understands by that key term of logically formal rationality of legal thought. To American readers the meaning can probably be explained best through some illustrations drawn from the Common Law.

Assume *D* and *S* own neighboring pieces of land respectively called Blackacre and Whiteacre. *D*, the owner of Blackacre, finds it advantageous for the utilization of his land to use a way leading across Whiteacre. He thus agrees with *S* that he and all his successors in the ownership of Blackacre shall in perpetuity and as against all later owners of Whiteacre have the right to walk and drive over the latter. A right of this kind is commonly known as servitude or easement. Now let us assume that at some subsequent time *X*, a later owner of Whiteacre, called the servient tenement, also acquires Blackacre, the dominant tenement, but shortly thereafter, resells and conveys it to *Y*. In spite of the terms of its creation, the easement no longer exists and *Y* has no right of way against *X*. This rule is based upon an entirely formal chain of reasoning, which was developed by the Roman jurists and simply taken over from them into English and American law: a servitude is defined as a *ius in re aliena*, a right in a thing belonging to another. If both the dominant and the servient tenement happen to come into the hands of one and the same owner the easement *can* no longer exist, as the very basis of its definition, viz., that of being the right of one person in the thing of another, has been destroyed.

This purely formal line of argumentation foregoes all considerations of economical, social, or other policy. If we shift from the method of logically formal rationality to that of substantive rationality we would consider such questions as these: Is it desirable in the interest of more efficient utilization of land that incumbrances by which such utilization might be adversely affected come at some time to an end even contrary to their terms of original creation? If so, by what events should such termination be brought about: by the expiration of a maximum period of time once and for all fixed by the law in the manner of a statute of limitation or of the rule against perpetuities; or by an important change of circumstances concerning the mode of utilization of the lands in question such as, for instance, a change from rural to urban or industrial use; or by the accidental circumstance of title to both becoming united in the hands of the same owner? If we answer the first question affirmatively, we might conceivably choose the last mentioned mode of termination, although it is more likely that our consideration of economic and social policy would cause us to prefer a mode of termination which is less dependent upon accidental circumstances and which may, perhaps, never occur. Whatever our answer may be, it will be reached in a manner different from that of logically formal rationality, but the latter happens to be the one in which the problem is solved in both the Civil and the Common Law. The other method, which we have sketched as a possible one and which would, indeed, seem to be more appealing to the general modes of thought of our times, is that advocated by the German jurisprudence of interests or the sociological jurisprudence of Roscoe Pound, or the "social interpretation" of François Gény or Edouard Lambert.

For a considerable period of time jurists in both Civil Law and Common Law countries were puzzled by the problem of how to handle the situation of a corporation of which all shares of stock have become united in the hands of a single stockholder. Has the corporation come to an end or does it continue to exist as a separate legal entity? Again there are two possible methods of approach. We may say that by definition a corporation is an association of a plurality of persons; hence, if there is left only one, by very definition the corporation must have ceased to exist. We might also argue, however, as follows: corporation is a legal device which has been invented to achieve certain practical effects, viz., to make it possible for a number of persons to unite capital contributions for the purpose of establishing a business enterprise and to carry it on separate and apart from their other property and estate so as, quite particularly, not to expose their other assets to liability for the debts incurred in the business. Shall this device also be made available to a single person who wishes to carry on a business without engaging in it all his property, but is willing to comply with the formalities which have been established to prevent abuses of the corporate device? In answering this question we will then pay attention to a number of considerations of economic policy and expediency, perhaps also of fiscal policy or of business ethics, i.e., considerations of substantive rather than logically formal rationality. How we finally come out is immaterial for our present purposes, which are concerned with methods of thought rather than with concrete legal problems.

In conflict of laws a lively dispute has been carried on for some time with respect to the proper method by which its problems ought to be approached. In this country the "conceptual" method has become identified with the name of the late Joseph Henry Beale, while a "modern" approach has been advocated by such writers as the late Walter Wheeler Cook, Ernest Lorenzen, Wilfred Stumberg, and the author of the present essay. The conceptualists' reasoning starts with a definition and an axiom. Conflict of laws is defined as that branch of the law which is concerned with the enforcement of foreign created rights. The axiom, which in turn is derived from the concept of sovereignty defined as exclusive power over a territory, states that no state other than that in which an event occurs *can* determine what rights if any shall arise out of that event. From these premises it is then concluded that a contract *must*, by logical necessity, be "governed" by the law of the state in which it was made, and that a tort *must* be "governed" by the law of the place where it was committed, etc.

The "modern" approach proceeds in a different way: For practical reasons each court normally decides its cases under the law of its own state. This normal application of the *lex fori* may bring about, however, that we may take by surprise individual parties who have been carrying on business or other activities with a view toward some other law, as they would normally have done where they had been acting abroad. If we wish to avoid such surprise and the consequential upsetting of credit, business, and other expectations, we ought to find out as far as possible which law, if any, the party or parties had in mind when they were acting, and then judge the legal consequences of their conduct by that law in so far at least as we do not thereby endanger important social interests of the political community of our own state.

Here, again, we have the difference between the jurisprudence of concepts or, in Weber's terminology, the method of logically formal rationality, and, on the other side, the method of substantive rationality or, as Roscoe Pound would call it, sociological jurisprudence.

We could continue with illustrations but those given will, we hope, suffice to illustrate the difference between the two kinds of legal thought which Weber calls those of logically formal and of substantive rationality. Both, incidentally, are methods of *rational* thought, i.e., of thought which tries to proceed upon the basis of general principles and to maintain consistency in the sense of avoiding contradictions within itself. In other words, both methods of thought proceed "logically." This observation would seem to be called for by the continuous attacks which have been made by at least some of the American modernists upon the use of logic in legal thinking. All these attacks can be traced back to Holmes's *bon mot* that the life of the law has not been logic but experience.[24] Not only the context in which this famous passage appears but Holmes's entire life and work should have made it clear that he would have been the last to disparage logical thinking, that is, thinking which tries to avoid intrinsic contradiction and to maintain consistency within a given line of argumentation. Clearly, Holmes was also far from disparaging the use of concepts. Thinking without concepts is as unthinkable as painting without paints or making music without sounds. The only problem is what sort of concepts we use or, from what premises we start when we begin to think. This is what Holmes means: that we derive our premises from the experience of life rather than formulating them as artificial and purely formal concepts. It is not the least of the merits of the work of Weber that he helps us to understand what Holmes really meant and what constitutes the real issue in our present methodological polemics. Both sides, the Bealites and the realists, are standing for rationality in legal thought. The only question is whether this rationality shall be of the logically formal or of the substantive kind.

The legal technique which does indeed dispense with logic is that of irrationality. That kind which Weber calls formally irrational, and which

[24] THE COMMON LAW (1881) 1.

is typical of primitive and archaic stages of civilization, no longer plays an important role in modern law, although it has not entirely disappeared. While we no longer resort to the ordeal as a mode of trial or to prophecy as the method of creating new law, we have maintained the oath, that is, the conditional self-curse; our law of evidence, while it does no longer resort to irrational means of finding the truth, still excludes several thoroughly rational methods of truth finding, and charismatic law creators like Hitler or Lenin are not qualitatively different from Mohammed, Moses, or other (real or legendary) law prophets of the past.

Neither has the substantively irrational mode of legal thought entirely disappeared. In trying to gauge its present significance we must be particularly careful, however, that Weber's categories represent ideal types, that is, that they do not as pure forms occur in real life. The jury, which we may be inclined to regard as the very embodiment of substantively irrational decision, is in no way entirely swayed by blind emotion. Jurymen, too, try to be rational and consistent. They differ from professional lawyers in that they may start from different premises and that the logic of their mental processes may, and indeed is expected to, be tempered with occasional interferences by the emotions.

Even less should we apply the unqualified label of substantive irrationality to case law, as some of Weber's passages, especially in Chapter VII, may induce us to do. Case law may tend toward irrationality, but even in that most extreme form in which it appears, that is, the practice of the khadi, it does not lack all rationality. Neither the Mohammedan khadi nor his counterpart, the English (or American) justice of the peace, is expected to administer justice according to his own arbitrary whim or momentary fancy. The "good" khadi is the one whose decision is in accordance with popular conviction, that is, with the religious or ethical value system prevailing at the time and place. In primitive or archaic circumstances this value system may be more felt than consciously known, but it exists wherever there exists a society and it is the very art of the khadi to articulate it as it applies to a concrete case. He is the one who is able to express in words, although of concrete application, what the common man but vaguely feels but cannot so easily apply and even less put into words. Only where he has succeeded in articulating in his decision the "sound feeling of the people," will the khadi's decision meet with that approval without which he cannot permanently maintain his authority. This practice will often contain a good measure of irrationality, but basically his thought is of the pattern of the substantively rational, although largely inarticulate, kind.

Even less irrational is judicial case law in the sense of judge-made law, as occurring particularly, but by no means solely, in the Common Law. Consistency, which indeed is the essence of rationality, is required by the very principle of *stare decisis*. As no case is ever completely identical with any other, we can never follow precedent in any way other than by trying to follow its *ratio decidendi*, i.e., the principle, broad or narrow, upon which we find, or believe, it to be based. Often enough this *ratio decidendi* may be expressed not at all or so vaguely that we cannot discover it easily. Often enough too the judge in the more recent case may, unconsciously, misread the *ratio decidendi* of the precedent. With much justification the judicial process of the Common Law has been characterized as reasoning by example in the Aristotelian sense.[25] But reasoning by example is still reasoning although in it the major premise of the syllogism is less distinctly articulated than in that kind of reasoning in which every part of every syllogism appearing in the chain of reasoning is articulated. In reasoning by example, results may be reached in the way of a short circuit, that is, by jumping over intermediate steps and by refraining from articulating in neat terms the various major and minor propositions, especially the former. But granting all these factors of possible disturbance and possible interference of emotional elements, basically the process remains a rational one. What has endeared it to Common Law lawyers is its special aptness to hide behind a screen of verbal formulae of apparent logically formal rationality, those considerations of substantive rationality, that is, of social policy, by which the decision has been actually motivated but which judges are reluctant to reveal to the public and, often enough, to themselves. In the major part of that chapter to which Weber himself has given the title of Sociology of Law he shows how different kinds of legal thought are characteristic of different kinds of legal honoratiores such as judges, theologians, consultants, conveyancers, professors, bureaucrats, and so forth. He thereby offers profound insights into the varieties of legal thought and legal systems and into their connections with political, administrative, economic, and other social phenomena. In this connection Weber proves the usefulness of his scheme of classification of types of legal thought, but he also demonstrates the necessity of constant awareness on the part of the reader that his categories are ideal types of which reality never presents anything but approximations and ever varying combinations.

If we keep this fact in mind we may also suppress criticism to which

[25] Edward Levi, Introduction to Legal Reasoning (1949) 1.

we might incline with respect to one of Weber's categories, viz., his very basic category of logically formal rationality. A legal system in which all concepts are of a purely formal character has never existed in the world and can hardly be even conceived as a theoretical possibility. Even the most highly abstract legal concepts have been derived from typical constellations of actual life and in connection with considerations of some social policy, that is, of substantive rationality. Such a highly abstract concept as *dominium* (title) describes in a shorthand manner the complex situation which exists when the community ascribes to one of its members (or to an aggregate of them; or to the member of another community, or an aggregate of them, which our community for reasons of ethical, religious, or expediential policy has decided in that respect to treat like its own members) the legitimate power to enjoy the use of a tangible good in all such ways as are not prohibited or ascribed to another by the community, and to dispose of this power for the benefit of others in those ways which are provided by the community. This concept will be useful in any community which to some extent ascribes the use and enjoyment of at least some of its economic goods to individuals or to any aggregate subdivisions of the regulating community. It loses its sense only in a community in which no such assignment whatsoever exists and in such a community the concept will hardly be maintained. But where it is maintained it expresses a social reality which is, in turn, the effect of a social policy, for economical, ethical, religious, power, or other purposes to put, at least to some extent, the existing economic goods to individual rather than to communal use or, in other words, at least for some purpose to prefer individual to community ownership.

This fact that the concept of title expresses a social reality and actual social policy, that is, substantive rationality, does not exclude that it be put to occasional uses for which it is not designed and that conclusions are drawn from it which are not justified by its reality content. There is no policy reason, for instance, why, in a contract to sell, the passing of the risk should be coupled with the passing of the title; or why an easement or a mortgage should be extinguished where the title to the two tenements concerned, or to the mortgage and the land encumbered by it, happen to be united in the same person. These conclusions have been drawn by law specialists who have lost sight of the actualities of life which lie behind the concepts. Whenever this process sets in we can speak of jurisprudence of concepts or formal rationality. We must not overlook, however, that even where such processes occur, the bulk of legal concepts and the normal use to which they are put is of the substantive rather than the formal kind of rationality. If we keep this fact in mind or, in other words, if we remain aware of the fact that the contrast between substantive and formal rationality is but relative, the two concepts are indeed helpful categories for the classification of the actual phenomena of methods of legal thought.

If we consider the principal interest of Weber and the general direction of his thought it is easy to see why he established his categories of legal thought along the lines just stated. Modern capitalism was for him characterized by a particular state of mind. His categories of social conduct in general, and of economic conduct in particular, are formulated as different kinds of mental attitudes. They are four: traditionalistic, emotional, value rational, and purpose rational. Social conduct is of the traditionalistic pattern if it is carried on in the way it is simply because it has always been carried on in that way. It is of the emotional kind if it is determined by passions and feelings. It is value rational (*wertrational*) where it is oriented toward a value system which, as one of religion, ethics, or aesthetics, is regarded as the expression of the proper one as such and without regard to its immediate practical consequences. Social conduct is, finally, purposively rational (*zweckrational*) where it is oriented toward some practical purpose and determined by rational choice. Modern capitalism constitutes the very prototype of purposively rational conduct, viz., of conduct oriented toward profit and rational choice of the means conducive to that purpose. The categories of legal thought are obviously conceived along lines parallel to the categories of economic conduct. The logically formal rationality of legal thought is the counterpart to the purposive rationality of economic conduct. Indeed, there are many indications that Weber at some stage of his work regarded it as possible that a peculiar relationship existed between the logically formal rationality of legal thought and the purposively rational kind of economic conduct and thus with modern capitalism. But Weber's own work shows that this connection is not one of absolute correlation. In England where capitalism developed earliest, logically formal rationality never came to dominate legal thought to the same degree to which it was developed in Germany, where capitalism had a much later start. Only in so far is a relationship shown to exist as modern capitalism requires a legal system which guarantees predictability and, in particular, freedom from arbitrary, unpredictable government interference. This guarantee is to a high degree given where legal thought is of the kind of logically formal rationality, but, as the example of England proves, it can also exist where that type of legal thought has not become dominant. It has also been shown by Weber that legal thought was directed toward the pattern of logically formal rationality not so much by the economic needs of capitalism as by the fact that in those parts where it achieved its highest degree of perfection, legal thought happened to be dominated by scholars who are driven by the requirements of oral and written teaching to conceptual articulation and systematic arrangement of the legal phenomena. An economic cause might be found, however, if we go a step beyond Weber's scope of inquiry and ask ourselves why it was that scholars came to occupy the role of the legal honoratiores in the countries of the Civil Law and especially in nineteenth-century Germany. Have they not been pushed into their position of prominence by the lack of national legislatures and supreme courts in late medieval Italy, the seventeenth-century Netherlands, eighteenth-century France, and nineteenth-century Germany? Where a country is a political, social, and, quite particularly, an economic unit, it requires a certain minimum of legal uniformity. The modern economy cannot be carried on where legal certainty is jeopardized by too many differences between local laws, which, where their territories are small, are often enough ill defined and difficult to ascertain. Where legal uniformity is achieved neither by a national legislature nor by a national supreme court the task of achieving at least some measure of legal uniformity must be undertaken by some other agency, and that very role was undertaken on the European continent by the scholars of the university law schools. That Western European law developed upon the uniform pattern of the rediscovered and rejuvenated Roman law was the work of the Glossators and Commentators of Bologna and their schools; that legal diversity within their countries was kept within the bounds tolerable for trade and nascent capitalism was the merit of the scholars of Leyden, Paris, and Orléans; that politically disunited Germany could maintain that measure of legal uniformity and certainty without which its economic growth in the nineteenth century would hardly have been possible has been the achievement of the Pandectist professors. We may also add: the need for maintaining in the United States that minimum uniformity without which business and industry could not operate on a nation-wide basis has created tasks for the legal scholars which did not exist in the motherland of the Common Law, where the nation-wide, or indeed, empire-wide uniformity of the law was maintined for centuries by a central supreme court and a centralized legal profession. The results of this rise of a new type of legal honoratiores is already observable in American law which is no longer simply a judge-made law as the English Common Law was for so many centuries, but which has assumed, through the influence of the national law schools, the national law reviews, and the great treatises of the Grays, the Willistons, the Wigmores, the Bogerts, and the other nationally influential scholars, a good many of those traces which are characteristic of scholarly, professional influence.

The problem of legal thought, its various kinds and their relationships with other social phenomena, while occupying the major part of the chapter on Sociology of Law, is not the only one which is treated therein. Its discussion is preceded by that of two others, viz., the problem of the conditions under which law can be expected to be made and changed rationally, and that of the development of that legal institution which has been the most indispensable condition for the rise of modern capitalism, viz., freedom of contract. All these topics are, in turn, preceded by a brief sketch of the significance which law plays for economic conduct in general, and by a definitional statement of what Weber means when he speaks of law and how certain important concepts of the lawyer's terminology appear when they are observed from the point of view of the sociologist.

Arrangement and presentation of Chapter V, dealing with the conditions under which rational law making, i.e., legislation, has arisen, are so clear that no explanatory comment would seem to be called for. Legislation which, at least for the Continental lawyer, appears as the normal, if not the only possible, form of law making, is shown to be anything but original, and its antecedents are traced through those various ways in which legal innovations could arise in more primitive or archaic stages, either as legal prophecy, or as slow growth of new practices of private transactions and conveyancing, or in the disguised forms in which an unchangeable law of a sacred book or immutable precedent is changed by way of "interpretation" or "distinguishing."

More complicated is the line of thought in Chapter VII in which Weber traces the growth, in the Western world, of the institution of freedom of contract. In contrast to the preceding chapter, which is concerned with the forms in which *law* is created, the heading of Chapter VI indicates as its subject matter the "forms in which *rights* are created." Accordingly, the chapter opens with a sociological definition of the concept of right. In consequence of his general position in society a person can find himself as factually occupying a position in which he is likely to be able to exercise a power of disposition over other persons or over economic goods. This factual position can be fortified by the likelihood that the members of a special staff of the community will go into action to guarantee him his position. The situation in which he thus finds himself is that of having a *right*. The circumstances under which the community's staff will go into action on his behalf are indicated by the rules of *law*. Through the guaranty of legal protection, he who is factually in the possession of the power of disposition over a thing or person obtains a specific security for the permanency of this position; especially one to whom a promise has been made obtains through the legal guarantee a superadded security for the performance of the promise. Such is, indeed, the most elementary relationship between law and economy.

Freedom of contract is thus a misnomer. The essential feature is not that persons are left free to make agreements, as they please, but that their agreements are enforced in the specific way of the law, that is, by the action, in favor of the promisee, of the special enforcement staff of the society.

How did this state of affairs develop out of an earlier stage in which either no social enforcement staff existed at all or only in some rudimentary form, or in which it would go into action only upon special and extraordinary occasions and where, consequently, one who regarded himself as injured in his "rights," had to resort to self-help, normally with the support of the fellow members of his kinship group? This process is traced in the first 24 pages of Chapter VI (pp. 98 to 121).

The possibility of obtaining "legal" enforcement for all, or at least most, kinds of agreements freely made, does not suffice, however, for the needs of developed and rationally conducted business, which requires that contractual rights as well as obligations can be created for a person by an agent acting for him, that contractual rights once created can be transferred to others and that in the case of such transfer the transferee obtains a position in which he cannot be disturbed by unknown defenses. Without these institutions of agency, assignment, and negotiable instruments it would not be possible to carry on business in the way necessary for modern capitalism, which particularly requires reliable means for speedy mass transfers of credit claims, especially of investments created as such claims. The mere fact that most of these institutions were barely developed in Roman law goes far to indicate how different from modern capitalism Roman capitalism was as far as it can be found to have existed at all. The problems arising in this respect are discussed in the second part of the chapter, on pages 122–125.

Wherever freedom of contract has existed, including the broad measure to which it exists today, it has never been without limits. What are the factors which determine to what extent and in what respects freedom of contract, in the sense of legal enforcement of private agreements, can be found in different kinds of society? This is the problem to which

Weber has addressed himself in the third part of Chapter VI, on pages 125–140. There emerges the significant fact that in certain periods of history freedom of contract was limited in the economic field, in which it has become all important for us, while it was much broader than it is with us in other spheres, especially in that of sexual relations.

In the extensive fourth part of the chapter (pp. 140–188) Weber discusses a phenomenon whose connection with freedom of contract is not obvious at a first glance. While normally concluded between two parties and thus primarily affecting their positions, every contract also has some necessary repercussions upon outsiders. By incurring new obligations a debtor affects his general credit status, a transfer of land imposes upon other landowners a new neighbor, etc. There are certain transactions, however, by which the positions of third parties are affected even more strongly, especially the creation of a corporation or some other juristic person. By establishing a corporation its members create for themselves and for their relations with outsiders a "special law" (*Sonderrecht*), which is different from the general law of the land. This modern type of special law is contrasted with other, older types, especially with that state of affairs where a general law of the land hardly existed and the kind of law under which a person lived depended on the personal group to which he belonged, such as the tribe in the Frankish Empire, or the religious community, even at this day, in the Near and Middle East. In what ways in the West did the old system of personal special laws give way to a general law of the land, and to what extent and in what ways have new forms of special law developed within the general law? In this connection Weber traces the history of associations from antiquity to the modern corporation. This mainstay of capitalism emerges as being principally an organization of ecclesiastical origin which was adopted in England, the homeland of capitalism, more reluctantly than on the European continent. Again, as in many other cases, Weber points out that this fact is due mainly to differences in the political structure of the countries concerned.

The chapter closes with a brief, but trenchant, inquiry into the relationship between the extent to which freedom of economic contract exists in a given society and the extent to which it affords real freedom of the individual from domination by others. The correlation is shown to be in no way a necessary one.

That part of the book which is entitled Sociology of Law is limited to the discussion of the problems just stated, that is, the types of legal thought and their relationship to other social phenomena; the methods of making and changing law in general and the development of rational law making through legislation in particular; and freedom of contract, i.e., legal enforcement of private transactions and the creation of special law by private arrangement as the indispensable condition of modern capitalism.

These problems, especially those of legal thought, are closely related, however, with some of the problems dealt with by Weber in the Third Part of his book and concerned with certain relations between law and political and administrative organization. A presentation of Weber's thought on law would have been incomplete without these sections. They have thus been included in the present book.

Whether Weber would have maintained the sequence of his text in which it appears in the German original, we do not know. To us it seems that his thought might be more easily understood if it is pursued in the order in which we have tried to present it in this Introduction. In the following text, the sequence of the German original has been maintained, however. We have changed only the numbering of the subdivisions so as to render it appropriate for a book which is to constitute a unit in itself. The original numbers of the subdivisions are, of course, indicated in the footnotes.

IV. Weber's Concept of Law

From what we have said so far about Weber's sociology of law, it might already be clear in what sense he is using the term "law." As in the case of all other terms used by him, he gives a careful definition, which, of course, is not meant as the statement of any "true" nature or essence of the law or the idea of law, but simply as an explanation of what he, Weber, means when he chooses to use the word law. His definition is thus a working definition, which, however, is not made up arbitrarily but with regard to both common usage and the ends of the inquiry within which Weber wishes to explore the phenomenon to which common usage applies the term law, although in a more vague sense than that which is required in a scientific context. Clearly, Weber's working definition must be expressed in purely factual terms and must thus be free of all elements implying value judgments of an ethical or political character.

Weber's definition of law is given in the first two Sections of Chapter VI of *Economy and Society,* Part II, which will be found in this volume on pages 11 to 33. It is more fully developed, however, in Part I of *Economy and Society,* of which we have also included the relevant sections in this volume.

The starting point is the concept of *social conduct* (*soziales Handeln*), which is defined in the very first Section of *Economy and Society* as that kind of human conduct which is related to the conduct of others and in its course oriented to it. Social conduct can be oriented to the idea that there exists some *legitimate order*. Such an order does, in turn, effectively exist or, which means the same, possess validity in exactly that measure in which social conduct is actually oriented to it. An order is called (by Weber) *convention* when its validity is guaranteed by the likelihood (*die Chance*) that conduct which does not conform to the order will meet with the (relatively) general and actually observable disapproval of some given group of people. An order shall be called *law* where it is guaranteed by the likelihood that (physical or psychological) coercion, aiming at bringing about conduct in conformity with the order, or at avenging its violation, will be exercised by a staff of people especially holding themselves ready for this purpose.

Every single part of this definition is carefully explained by Weber, and the reader is hereby referred to those passages of the text. It may not be inappropriate, however, to indicate here some of those implications of Weber's definition of law which have not been expressly stated by him.

We have already observed that the definition uses none but factual terms, and that it carefully refrains from implying judgments of ethical or other evaluation. Sociology, if it wishes at all to be a science, has to refrain from passing moral or political value judgments, it has to be *wertfrei*. In legal philosophy we find time and again definitions of law which imply some ethical or political value as a necessary element of the very concept of law and which thus excludes from the concept of law every phenomenon which does not live up to the particular value postulated. Law, it is said, must by intrinsic necessity be conducive toward freedom (Kant, Hegel) or justice, or equality, or democracy, or the welfare of the people, or law is said not to exist unless it constitutes not only an imperative means of social coördination but one which is ethically approved; or law is defined as necessarily implying its conformity with reason (St. Thomas Aquinas). None of these definitions can be used by the sociologist, who has to concern himself with any kind of organizationally coercive order, regardless of whether or not he is pleased by its contents or by the ends for which it is used by those who have the power to manipulate it. The sociologist has to deal equally with the social order of primitive cannibals, the ancient Babylonians, Greeks or Romans, Angevin England, or the contemporary United States, the Soviet Union, or National-Socialist Germany of the recent past. Nothing in the nature of things prevents him from reserving the term "law" to those orders which happen to please him because of their more or less close conformity with his own ethical and political ideals, and to apply some term other than law, for instance, arbitrary rule, tyranny, or bum-bum to those orders which he happens to dislike. The only question is whether or not such a variation of terms is helpful within the framework of a scientific inquiry. Physicists do not reserve the term atomic energy to those cases in which the underlying phenomenon is used by human beings for "peaceful" or other "constructive" purposes, while using another term for those cases in which the phenomenon is used in war, nor do they in the latter case distinguish between such use by our side and that of the enemy. So in his field Weber would see no practical use in making a terminological distinction between those orders which happen to please and those which would displease his ethical, political, or aesthetic sensitivities.

To the sociologist such value-loaded definitions of law as are used in philosophy are not without interest, however. It is indeed a sociological problem to find out why philosophers do make use of such definitions and why in a given social situation the philosophers prefer to include in their definitions of law one value rather than another. This problem is touched upon by Weber in his discussion of the phenomenon of natural law thought and theories, but it has not been followed up by him in all its ramifications. Here we can only hint at the possibility of an explanation. Every expert in advertising or propaganda knows that it is good, that is, effective, psychology to pass off as already existing or as certain to occur that state of affairs which he, the propagandist, wishes to bring about: "Everybody smokes *Non plus ultra* cigarettes"; "The victory of our cause (country, party, doctrine, etc.) is certain" is proclaimed with special vigor when it is uncertain. Perhaps the most grandiose illustration of the effectiveness of this psychological trick is afforded by Marxism: the proletariat and its friends are urged to the utmost exertion by the assertion that its victory over the capitalist-imperialist class will inevitably come by the intrinsic necessity of the dialectical process. It belongs to the same order of ideas if the philosopher, to whom a particular type of social order appears as the only desirable one, proves, not only to others but also to himself, that this order either exists already although in a not yet fully realized shape, or that it will be achieved by inevitable necessity or, quite particularly, that it is the only one which is compatible with the definition of a term which, by itself, signifies a phenomenon with which positive value feelings are commonly combined. Law, so often appearing in the euphonious combination of law and order, is a conspicuous example of such a term. Besides, all, not only those to whose benefit the legal order may specifically operate in one or the other case, but indeed all who are interested in the maintenance of a peaceful order, are interested in the law being obeyed, unless it should happen to infringe outrageously upon our interests or sensitivities. The likelihood of law observance is increased when we prove, to others and to ourselves, that, by its very definition, the law is just, conducive of freedom, reasonable, or simply "good"; and vice versa, our fight against an order which is disliked by us, or by those who want us to fight against it, increases in vigor, when we can prove to ourselves that the rules established and enforced by the tyrant, the conqueror, or the occupant are not law but just brute force and violence. Perhaps it is the very social function of the philosopher to provide us with such psychological ammunition as we need to fight the good fight. The sociologist's task, however, is just to observe and carefully to refrain from evaluation in general and quite particularly from that disguised evaluation which is given to us, as a social necessity, by the philosopher. Clearly this method of the social scientist may have the dangerous effect of diminishing the effectiveness of those myths which society seems to require for its integration and continued cohesion. Yet its development can as little be stopped as that of psychoanalysis or nuclear physics. Besides, social ideals can, must, and will be maintained and, if needs, fought for also even though their necessity might not be proved by means of the philosopher's reason. Ethical ideals and convictions are effective just because they spring from strata which are deeper than that of consciously working reason. By what they are determined we do not know, by environment, by inner secretion, or by divine grace. But once we have taken a stand for or against a life in social harmony and order, we need reason to help us find the way this ideal may be approximated, even though we know that it cannot be achieved as long as men are men rather than angels. There is a task and function for the philosopher in society, but there is also one for the social scientist. Tensions may exist between their callings, but tension is of the essence of life and both the philosopher and the social scientist are needed to help us live in this world, which is so full of mystery and tension that only religion, perhaps, can help us to accept it.

In its positivity Weber's concept of law is reminiscent of Austin's definition of law as the command of the sovereign. But it is in better correspondence with common parlance and the actuality of facts in at least two respects. Weber speaks neither of the sovereign nor of a command. Law, it is true, is for him, too, an order system, i.e., a set of normative ideas which are held in the minds of the members of a given community, which thus influence their conduct, and the effectiveness of which is increased by the existence of a staff of specialists, whom we may call the enforcement officers of the community, and who are likely to go into action for the purpose of bringing about coercive compliance with the rules of law. But this staff must not necessarily be an agency of the sovereign. By introducing the concept of sovereign Austin has limited his concept of law to that of the modern state, which was, indeed, quite satisfactory for his purposes. Such a concept of law would be too narrow, however, for the sociologist, who must consider such phenomena as ecclesiastical law, gang law, the law merchant of the Middle Ages, or tribal, international, or other forms of primitive law. All these phenomena are covered by Weber's definition, with the only exception, perhaps, of international law, the state of which, at least in the days before the League of Nations and the United Nations, was too undeveloped even to have a staff of enforcement specialists who would go into action on behalf of the international community. Now, even international law can be fitted in with Weber's definition, as can be visibly observed when the international guards are changed monthly at the gate of the "war criminals" prison in Spandau.

Weber also avoids speaking of law as the command of the sovereign or anyone else. Law is an order, i.e., a set of ought ideas which are held in the minds of certain people. How and whence these ideas originate is a problem of interest to the sociologist. Weber in particular has taken great pains to classify the reasons why the ideas of order are regarded as legitimate, that is, as entitled to obedience. The source of its legitimacy is not decisive, however, for the classification of an order as law. What stamps it as law, in contradistinction to ethics, religion, or convention, is the mode of its enforcement or, more correctly, the way in which the likelihood of its being obeyed is increased. If that guarantee of obedience is due to the existence of an enforcement staff of a social group, the order is one of law; if the enforcement staff is an agency of the state, the order constitutes the law of the state, without regard as to how and by whom the rules thus enforced have been created. This approach of Weber's makes it possible to understand phenomena which remain unexplained and unexplainable if we use Austin's definition of law, which, indeed, has resulted in confusion not only in jurisprudential theory but in actual legal practice.

Unexplained under the Austinian approach remains quite particularly the phenomenon of the Common Law. In the view held by every Common Law lawyer whose observation and perception has not been biased by

Austinian jurisprudence, the Common Law is that body of rules, principles, techniques, and attitudes which is common to all those countries, states, and territories in which there have come to prevail those professional traditions and ideals which were originally developed by the royal courts of England. Daily observation demonstrates that there indeed exists an Anglo-American Common Law and even more tangibly a general American Common Law. We teach it in our law schools, we write or read about it in our law books and law reviews, and the attempt to "restate" it has been made by the American Law Institute. Yet, we have been told by the Supreme Court of the United States, in *Erie Railroad Company v. Tompkins*,[26] that it does not, nay, that it cannot, exist. All law in the United States, we are told there, is the law of either a state or of the federal government. The law-making power of the latter is limited by the federal Constitution to the regulation of the topics enumerated therein. The regulation of ordinary matters of private and commercial life is not stated in the catalogue. Hence it *must* be state law and a general common law *cannot* exist. This argumentation, which was preceded by that of Mr. Justice Holmes in *Black and White Taxicab Co. v. Brown and Yellow Taxicab Co.*,[27] is based upon the Austinian notion that law must be the command of, i.e., created by, a sovereign. In this country, law must be created either by a state or by the federal government, hence, common law is possible only as state law, but never as a law independently to be explained and applied by federal courts. The contradiction between that notion and everyday observation and parlance evaporates when we free ourselves of the idea that law must necessarily be the command of the sovereign. Law is that set of normative ideas which are (sought to be) enforced by the enforcement staff of some social group. Nothing thus stands in the way of courts of the United States enforcing rules which have not been created by the United States law-making organs, i.e., the Congress or the federal courts, but which have originated in some other way but are held to constitute part of that treasure of ideas which is common to all American or, indeed, all Anglo-American jurisdictions. That those ideas are not held uniformly in every one of these jurisdictions and that, in practical application, they may be "interpreted" differently by different sets of courts is a regrettable fact but does not necessarily deprive those rules of their character as Common Law.

It may not be superfluous to state that we do not mean to say that

[26] (1938) 304 U.S. 64, 58 S. Ct. 817, 87 L. ed. 1188, 114 A.L.R. 1487.

[27] (1928) 276 U.S. 518, 532, 48 S. Ct. 404, 409, 57 A.L.R. 426, 432.

the decision reached by the Supreme Court of the United States in *Erie Railroad v. Tompkins* is "wrong." In order to make such a statement we would first have to establish a standard by which we could measure the rightness or wrongness of a decision of a court of ultimate appeal. There may have been excellent reasons of policy for substituting legal uniformity within every state for legal uniformity among the states (or, more correctly, among the federal courts sitting in the several states). All we wish to say is that the method of jurisprudence of concepts or, to use Weber's term, of logically formal rationality, which appears in the published opinion of Mr. Justice Brandeis, is not convincing. It is derived from a definition of law which one scholar, Austin, happened to use for the purposes of his inquiry, which is not capable, however, of covering the, after all, existing, phenomenon of the Common Law, and which was thus inappropriate to be made the conceptual cornerstone of a decision in which the very application of the Common Law was at stake.

The narrowness of the definition of law as the command of the sovereign has also made it difficult to understand the phenomenon dealt with in the law of conflict of laws, i.e., the phenomenon that the courts of state *F* every now and then decide a case in conformity with the law of states *A*, *B*, or *X*. Tortured attempts have been made to explain this phenomenon, and a score of particular difficulties have arisen as a result. The theoretical difficulties are, indeed, considerable, if we regard law as necessarily constituting the command of the sovereign. The courts of *F* have to obey the command of the sovereign of *F*, whoever or whatever that term may mean. Why should they ever obey, or apply, the command of the sovereign of *X*? The difficulty disappears, however, if we regard as law every norm which is enforced by the enforcement staff, and thus as the law of *F* every rule which is applied and enforced by the courts of *F*, irrespective of whence and how it originated. This, indeed, has been the answer of the so-called local law theory. Its acceptance is hardly possible to an Austinian; it presents no "logical" difficulty, however, if we define law in the way in which it is done by Weber.

All through his work Weber proves himself to be a realist in the sense of a scholar who is interested in the reality of social life, its correct description, and the discovery of the relationships existing between its various factors and aspects. This very realism caused him to define law as an order, that is, a set of norms rather than as "that which the judges or other law people do." Not that he would have been disinterested in the activities of these, or any other, people. His description of the activities of the legal honoratiores and the analysis of their functions in society constitute one of the main parts of his work. But he still defines law as a set of rules, i.e., as the set of those rules which some people are holding in their minds and which in some way influence their behavior. What these ways are does again constitute one of the topics of Weber's inquiry. In order to make this inquiry in a clear manner he has to separate the socially significant facts, that the ideas are held by some people, that they somehow arise in those minds, and that their existence in the minds somehow influences human conduct, from the content of these ideas.

Nothing in the nature of things prevents us from saying that music consists in the activities of musicians, and a drama in those of the actors. Such a concept would be of little help, however, if we should wish to look at Beethoven's *Ninth Symphony* or Shakespeare's *Hamlet* in a library. We might, of course, say that the symphony or the play consists in the book or the notations or letters which we find in it. But that definition again does not cover the case of the conductor or actor or art lover who knows the piece by heart, or of the composer or poet who had it, or part of it, in his mind, at least for some moment, before he could write it down. Thus for some or perhaps most purposes, for example, that of determining the scope of a copyright and its violation, the "best" definition, the one most helpful for our purposes, is that which defines the symphony or play or the poem as a content of some human mind or minds. In the same way, the ideas that a person who has bought a thing ought to pay the price, that one who has earned an income of $10,000 ought to pay a certain income tax, or that one who has committed murder ought to be prosecuted, tried, sentenced, and executed, can actually be found to be held by human beings and in some ways to influence their conduct.

These facts that the ideas are held in actual human minds and that they actually influence social conduct belong to the world of the "is"; the ideas themselves, however, form the realm of the "ought." Each of them constitutes a legitimate field of investigation, the former of the social scientist, the latter of the lawyer and the analytical jurist. Their investigation requires different methods, however. Nothing but confusion can result when they are mixed together. This purity of the method is being insisted upon by both Weber, the sociologist, and Kelsen, the jurist. Their work is complementary. Kelsen, in his pure theory of law,[28] concerns himself with the norms and their structure. What is the dis-

[28] The principal statement in English is given in KELSEN, GENERAL THEORY OF LAW AND STATE (1945).

tinctive mark of those ideas which are rules of law as against other ideas? In what way are these ideas related to the ideas of the state? In what order are the law ideas related to each other? These are the questions asked by Kelsen. Why do people have law ideas? How is their content formed? How and why does it change? In what ways does it influence social conduct? These are the questions asked by Weber.

The difference between the two sets of problems and the methods in which they are approached is strikingly illustrated by the difference between social concepts and legal concepts. The latter are absolute, the former gradual. For the judge a statute is either valid or invalid; the sociologist may find that one statute, for instance, the Illinois Sales Act, is more valid than another, for instance, the gambling acts. In that discussion of principal legal categories which now appears, somewhat out of context, in Chapter III, Weber gives some additional illustrations. The judge of a French civil court must answer with a clear-cut yes or no the question of whether a certain problem is one of private law and thus within his own jurisdiction, or one of public law and thus reserved for decision to the administrative tribunals. From the point of view of the sociologist it is impossible to draw such a clear-cut line between private and public law, and the same difference occurs as to such distinctions as those between crime and tort, substance and procedure, etc. The lawyer has to decide, the sociologist to observe. Their problems and methods are different, but this does not mean that they would not have something to tell each other. What the sociologist can have to tell and to teach the lawyer, that question may be answered by the reader of Max Weber's work.

THE WORKS OF MAX WEBER

Zur Geschichte der Handelsgesellschaften im Mittelalter, 1889.

Die römische Agrargeschichte in ihrer Bedeutung für das Staats- und Privatrecht, 1891.

Wirtschaft und Gesellschaft, 1922, 2nd ed. 1925.

Wirtschaftsgeschichte, ed. by S. Hellmann and M. Palyi, 1923.

Weber's major articles have been collected in the following volumes:

Gesammelte Politische Schriften, 1921.

Gesammelte Aufsätze zur Religionssoziologie, 3 vols., 1920–21, 2nd ed. 1922–23.

Gesammelte Aufsätze zur Wissenschaftslehre, 1922, 2nd ed. 1951.

Gesammelte Aufsätze zur Sozial- und Wirtschaftsgeschichte, 1924.

Gesammelte Aufsätze zur Soziologie und Sozialpolitik, 1924.

The most important of Weber's articles have been republished in the following two volumes of the Series entitled *Civitas Gentium*, ed. by Max Graf zu Solms:

Schriften zur Theoretischen Soziologie der Politik und Verfassung, 1947 (contains a bibliography of all of Max Weber's works and of the extensive literature about Max Weber).

Aus den Schriften zur Religionssoziologie, 1948.

The following editions of Max Weber's works are available in English:

From Max Weber. Essays in Sociology, transl., edited and with an introduction by H. H. Gerth and C. W. Mills, 1946.

General Economic History, tr. by Frank Knight, 1927, 2nd ed. 1950.

Max Weber on the Methodology of the Social Sciences, tr. and ed. by E. A. Shils and H. A. Frisch.

The Protestant Ethic and the Spirit of Capitalism, tr. by T. Parsons, with a Foreword by R. H. Tawney, 1930. 2nd ed., also containing *The Evolution of the Capitalist Spirit*, tr. by Frank Knight, 1945.

The Theory of Social and Economic Organization, tr. by A. M. Henderson and T. Parsons, with an introd. by T. Parsons, 1947.

The Hindu Social System, tr. by H. H. Gerth and D. Martindale, 1950.

The Religion of China: Confucianism and Taoism, tr. by H. H. Gerth, 1951.

Ancient Judaism, tr. by H. H. Gerth, 1952.

For bibliographies of the vast literature on Weber, see:

Weinreich, Marcel, *Max Weber, l'homme et le savant; étude sur ses idees directrices*. Paris, Librairie Scientifique et Philosophique. J. Vrin, 1939, pp. 189–205.

Mayer, Jacob Peter, *Max Weber and German Politics; a Study in Political Sociology*. London, Faber, 1944, pp. 107–119.

Gerth, H. H. and Gerth, H. J., *Bibliography on Max Weber* (1949) 16 Social Research 70–89.

Weber, Marianne, *Max Weber, Ein Lebensbild*. 2nd ed. Heidelberg, 1950, pp. 755–760.

MAX WEBER

LAW IN ECONOMY AND SOCIETY [1]

[1] W.u.G., Part I, ch. I (*passim*); Part II, ch. V, VI, VII; Part III, chs. I, II, VI (*passim*).

CHAPTER I

BASIC CONCEPTS OF SOCIOLOGY[2]

Section 1. The word "sociology" is used in many different senses. In our context it shall mean that science which aims at the interpretative understanding of social conduct and thus at the explanation of its causes, its course, and its effects. Human behavior shall be called "conduct" (*Handeln*) when, and in so far as, the person or persons acting combine with their behavior some subjective meaning. The behavior may be mental or external; it may consist in action or in omission to act. Conduct will be called "social conduct" where its intention is related by the actor or actors to the conduct of others and oriented accordingly in its course.[3]

. . . . .

Section 2. Like any other conduct, social conduct may be determined in any one of the following four ways:

It may, first, be determined rationally and oriented toward an end. In that case it is determined by the expectation that objects in the world outside or other human beings will behave in a certain way, and by the use of such expectations as conditions of, or as means toward, the achievement of the actor's own, rationally desired and considered, aims. This case will be called *purpose-rational conduct.*

Or, social conduct may be determined, second, by the conscious faith in the absolute worth of the conduct as such, independent of any aim, and measured by some such standard as ethics, aesthetics, or religion. This case will be called *value-rational conduct.*

[2] The following text constitutes a part of the first chapter of Part I of *Economy and Society*. This entire Part I is available in English in the translation by A. M. Henderson and T. Parsons, edited by Parsons s.t. MAX WEBER: THE THEORY OF SOCIAL AND ECONOMIC ORGANIZATION (1947). Certain passages of this Part are essential within the framework of Weber's thought on sociology of law. They are therefore published in this present book. Our translation, it will be observed, is different from that of Henderson and Parsons. The latter is undoubtedly correct, and so, it is hoped, is this one. The divergence of the two translations may serve, however, as an illustration of the impossibility of a literal rendering of Weber's German text.

[3] W.u.G. 1.

Or, third, social conduct may be determined *affectually,* especially *emotionally,* by actual constellations of feelings and emotions.

Or, it may, fourth, be determined *traditionalistically*.[4]

. . . . .

Section 3. The term "social relationship" will be used to mean the case where two or more persons are engaged in conduct the meaning of which is directed and thus oriented from one person to the other. Hence a social relationship simply consists in the probability that human beings will act in some (sensibly) determinable way; it is completely irrelevant why such a probability exists. Where it exists there is a social relationship, and absolutely no more is required for its existence.[5]

. . . . .

Section 4. Within the realm of social conduct one finds factual regularities, that is, courses of action which, with a typically identical meaning, are repeated by the actors or simultaneously occur among numerous actors. It is with such *types* of conduct that sociology is concerned, in contrast to history, which is interested in the causal connections of important, i.e., fateful, *single* events.

An actually existing probability of a *regularity* of an orientation of social conduct will be called "usage" (*Brauch*) where, and in so far as, the probability of its existence within a group of people is based on *nothing but actual habit* (*Übung*). A usage will be called a "custom" if the actual habit is based upon long standing. Where, on the other hand, a usage is determined *exclusively* by the fact that all the actors' conduct is *aim-rationally* oriented toward identical expectations, it will be called a "usage determined by the interest situation."

Fashion constitutes a special case of usage. In contrast to custom we shall speak of fashion where the conduct in question is motivated by its *novelty* rather than long standing as in the case of custom.

. . . . .

In contrast to "convention" and "law" we shall speak of "custom" where the rule is not externally guaranteed but where the actor conforms to it "without thinking" or for such reasons as simple convenience, and where others belonging to the same group of people can be expected to act in the same way for the same reasons. In this meaning custom thus

[4] W.u.G. 12.

[5] W.u.G. 13.

does not claim any "validity"; nobody is in any way required to abide by it. However, the transition from this case to those of convention or law is indefinite. Factual custom everywhere has begotten a feeling of oughtness. At present it is a custom that in the morning we eat a breakfast of some definable content. However, nobody (except a hotel guest) "ought" to do so. Besides, the custom has not prevailed at all times. On the other hand, the ways in which we dress are, today at least, no longer mere custom. They have become convention.[6]

. . . . .

Section 5. Conduct, especially social conduct, and quite particularly a social relationship, can be oriented on the part of the actors toward their *idea* (*Vorstellung*) of the existence of a *legitimate order*. The probability of such an orientation shall be called the *validity* of the order in question.

1. "Validity" of an order is thus to mean more than the mere regularity of the course of social conduct as determined by custom or interest situations. The fact that movers regularly advertise near the dates people are moving from one apartment to another is caused exclusively by their interest situation. The fact that a salesman regularly visits a certain customer on a certain day of the week or month is either habit of long standing or also caused by his interests (he may follow a regular turn). But the fact that a public officer shows up at his office every day at the same hour is determined not only by routine (custom) or his interest situation but regularly also by the validity of an order (viz., the civil service rules) as a command the violation of which will not only involve detriments but will also, at least normally, be abhorrent to his sense of duty in the value-rational manner.

2. Only then will the content of a social relationship be called a social order if the conduct is, approximately and on the average, oriented toward determinable "maxims." Only then will an order be called "valid" if the orientation toward those maxims occurs, among other reasons, also because it is in some appreciable way regarded by the actor as in some way obligatory or exemplary for him. In actual life, conduct may

[6] W.u.G. 14.

The chapters on usage and custom in the second volume of JHERING'S LAW AS A MEANS TO AN END are still worth while reading. See also P. OERTMANN, RECHTSREGELUNG UND VERKEHRSSITTE (1914) and, more recently, E. WEIGELIN, SITTE, RECHT UND MORAL (1919), whose opinions agree with mine and disagree with those of Stammler [WIRTSCHAFT UND RECHT (1896)] [Weber's note.]

be oriented toward an order for a great variety of motives. But the fact that, among other motives, the order appears to at least some of the actors as exemplary or obligatory and thus as binding, increases, often considerably, the probability that conduct will really be oriented toward the order. An order which is obeyed for the sole reason of aim-rationality is generally less stable than conduct which, because of its long standing, is oriented toward a custom. Indeed, that latter attitude is the much more frequent. But even more stable is the conduct oriented toward a custom which is endowed with the prestige of exemplariness or obligatoriness or, in other words, of "legitimacy." But, of course, the transitions from the orientation of conduct toward an order by virtue of mere tradition or mere aim-rationality to the belief in legitimacy are indeterminate in actual life.

3. There can be orientation toward an order even where its meaning (as generally understood) is not necessarily obeyed. The probability that the order be to some extent valid (as an obligatory norm) can also occur where its meaning is "evaded" or "violated." Such orientation may be of a merely aim-rational kind: The thief orients his conduct toward the validity of the criminal law, viz., by trying to conceal it. The very fact that the order is valid within a group of people makes it necessary for him to conceal its violation. This case is, of course, marginal. Very frequently the order is violated only in one or another partial respect, or its violation is sought to be passed off as legitimate, with a varying measure of good faith. Or several different interpretations of the meaning of the order coexist alongside each other. In that case the sociologist will regard each one as valid in exactly so far as it is actually determinative of conduct. It is, indeed, in no way difficult for the sociologist to recognize that several, possibly mutually contradictory, orders are valid within the same group. Even one and the same individual may orient his conduct toward mutually contradictory orders. He can do so successively; such cases can, indeed, be observed all the time; but orientation of conduct toward mutually contradictory orders can occur with respect to one and the same conduct. One who engages in a duel orients his conduct toward the honor code; but he also orients it toward the criminal law [by which duelling is prohibited] by keeping the duel secret or, in the opposite manner, by voluntarily appearing in court. Where, however, evasion or violation of the order (i.e., of the meaning generally ascribed to it) has become the rule, the order has come to be valid in but a limited sense or has ceased to be valid altogether. For the lawyer an order is either valid or not; but no such alternative exists for the sociologist. Fluid transitions exist between validity

and nonvalidity, and mutually contradictory orders can be valid alongside each other. Each one is valid simply in proportion to the probability that conduct will actually be oriented toward it.[7]

. . . . .

Section 6. The legitimacy of an order can be *guaranteed* in several ways:

I. It may be guaranteed purely *subjectively* and such subjective guaranty may be either

1. merely affectual, i.e., through emotional surrender; or

2. value-rational, i.e., determined by the faith in the absolute validity of the order as the expression of ultimate, binding values of an ethical, aesthetical, or other kind; or

3. religious, i.e., determined by the belief that salvation depends upon obedience to the order.

II. The legitimacy of an order may, however, be guaranteed also by the expectation of certain external effects, i.e., by interest situations.

An order will be called *convention* where its validity is externally guaranteed by the probability that a violation will meet with the (relatively) general and practically significant *disapproval* of a determinable group of people.[8]

An order will be called *law* if it is externally guaranteed by the probability that coercion (physical or psychological), to bring about conformity or avenge violation, will be applied by a *staff* of people holding themselves specially ready for that purpose.

1. Under *convention* we shall thus understand that *custom* which, within a given group, is approved as "valid" and guaranteed against deviation by disapproval. It differs from "law," as defined here, by the absence of a *staff* holding itself ready to use coercion. Stammler's distinction of convention from law according to whether or not submission is "voluntary,"[9] neither corresponds to common linguistic usage nor does it fit his own illustrations. Everybody is seriously expected and regarded as obliged to conform to such conventions as those of the usual modes of salutation, of decent dress, or of the general modes of social intercourse. Conformance to such conventions is in no way so voluntary as, for example, the choice of the manner of cooking. A violation of con-

[7] W.u.G. 16/17.

[8] On convention see JHERING, *op. cit.*, WEIGELIN, *op. cit.*, and TÖNNIES, DIE SITTE (1909). [Weber's note.]

[9] *Op. cit. supra* n. 6. [Weber's note.]

vention, especially in the frame of so-called professional ethics, often meets with most effective and serious retribution in the form of social boycott by the members of the profession, a retribution which may be more effective than any legal coercion. Nothing is lacking but the staff which could hold itself specifically ready for action meant to guarantee obedience, such as judges, prosecutors, policemen, or sheriffs. Again, however, there is no clear-cut dividing line. There is a marginal case, consisting in the formally threatened and *organized* boycott. In our terminology this already constitutes a means of legal coercion. It is irrelevant in the present context that in certain cases a convention may, in addition to general disapproval, be protected by other means. An illustration of this situation is presented by the case of the visitor who refuses to leave another's house when asked to do so. He violates a convention; but the master of the house may also expel him bodily. In such a case coercion is applied not by a special staff, but by some particular individual who is able to do so just in consequence of the general disapproval of the violation of the convention.[10]

2. In our context the concept of law will be defined as an order which depends upon an enforcement *staff*. In other connections different definitions may well be appropriate. The enforcement staff does, of course, not necessarily have to be of the kind we know today. It is unnecessary, in particular, that there be any *judicial* organ. In the case of blood vengeance and feud the enforcement staff consists in the clan, provided that its reaction is actually determined by some kind of regulatory order. We must recognize, however, that this case represents the very limit of what can still be regarded as "legal coercion." Time and again international law has been said not to be "law," because it lacks a supra-national enforcement agency. Indeed, our definition of law, too, would not apply to an order which is guaranteed merely by the expectation of disapproval and reprisals on the part of those who are harmed by its violation, i.e., merely by convention and self-interest rather than by a staff of persons whose conduct is *specially* oriented toward the observation of the regulatory order. Yet, legal terminology may be quite different.

Irrelevant, too, are the means of coercion. The friendly "admonition," as it could be found in some sects as the first degree of mild coercion of the sinner, constitutes coercion in our sense, provided it is regulated by some order and applied by a staff. The same is to be said about the censorial "reprimand" as a means to guarantee the observance of "ethical" duties and, even more so, about psychological coercion through

[10] W.u.G. 17–19.

ecclesiastical discipline. Hence "law" may be guaranteed by hierocratic authority just as it may be guaranteed politically, or through the statute of an association, or domestic authority, or through a sodality or some other association. The [peculiar] rules of [German students' fraternities, known as] the *comment* [and regulating such matters as convivial drinking or singing] are also "law" in our sense, just as the case of those [legally regulated but unenforceable] duties which are mentioned in Section 888, par. 2 of the [German] Code of Civil Procedure [for instance, the duty arising from an engagement to marry].

Not every valid order is necessarily of an abstract, general character. Nowadays we strictly distinguish between the general "norm of law" and the concrete "judicial decision." Such a distinction was not made at all times. An "order" may thus consist in the ordering of one single concrete situation.

. . . . .

An "externally" guaranteed order may also be guaranteed "internally." The relationship between law, convention, and ethics does not present any problem to the sociologist. To him an "ethical" standard is one which applies to human conduct that specific kind of evaluating *faith* which claims to determine what is "ethically good," just as any conduct which claims to be "beautiful," by so doing, subjects itself to the standard of aesthetics. Normative ideas of this kind can have a powerful influence upon conduct even though they may lack any external guaranty. External guaranties will be usually lacking where the violation of the standard does not appreciably affect the interests of others. On the other hand, they are frequently guaranteed religiously. Possibly, they may also be guaranteed by convention (in our sense of the term), i.e., through disapproval or boycott; in addition, there may be the legal guaranty through the police or the means of criminal or private law. "Ethics," which is valid in the sociological sense, usually is guaranteed by convention, i.e., by the probability of its violation meeting with disapproval. Not every conventionally or legally guaranteed norm, however, claims also to be one of ethics. Legal norms are frequently motivated by mere expediency and thus claim ethical character even less than the norms of convention. Whether or not a normative idea which is actually held by human beings belongs to the realm of ethics or, in other words, whether or not a given norm is one of "mere" law or convention must be decided *by the sociologist* exclusively in accordance with that notion of the "ethical" which is actually held by the people in question. It is not possible, however, to state any general propositions in this respect.[11]

. . . . .

Section 7. The actors can ascribe legitimate validity to an order in a variety of ways.

The order can be recognized as legitimate, *first*, by virtue of tradition: valid is that which has always been.

Second, the order may be treated as legitimate by virtue of affectual, especially emotional, faith; this situation occurs especially in the case of the newly revealed or the exemplary.

Third, the order may be treated as legitimate by virtue of value-rational faith: valid is that which has been deduced as absolutely demanded.

Fourth, legitimacy can be ascribed to an order by virtue of positive enactment of recognized *legality*.

Such legality can be regarded as legitimate either (a) because the enactment has been agreed upon by all those who are concerned; or (b) by virtue of imposition by a domination of human beings over human beings which is treated as legitimate and meets with acquiescence.

The details will be discussed in the chapters dealing with the sociology of domination and of law. At present the following brief remarks will suffice.

(1) The oldest and most universally found type of validity of orders is that which is based upon the sacredness of tradition. The psychological blocks to any change of an inveterate usage are strengthened by the apprehension of magical detriments. An order which has once become valid is furthermore perpetuated by those manifold interests which arise with respect to the continuation of acquiescence in its existence.

(2) In early society, down to the statutes of the Hellenic *aisymnetes,* conscious creation of new orders appeared almost exclusively as prophetic oracle or at least as revelation enjoying prophetical sanction and thus held sacred. Acquiescence thus depended upon the faith in the legitimacy of the prophet. In periods of strict traditionalism no new order could thus arise without new revelation unless the new order was not looked upon as such but was regarded as a truth that had already been valid although it had been temporarily obscured and had thus been in need of rediscovery.

(3) The purest type of value-rational validity is represented by nat-

[11] W.u.G. 18/19.

ural law. The influence of its logically deduced propositions upon actual conduct may lag far behind their theoretical claims; that they have had some influence cannot be denied, however. Its propositions must be distinguished from those of revealed, of enacted, and of traditional law.

(4) Today the most common form of legitimacy is the belief in legality, i.e., the acquiescence in enactments which are formally correct and which have been made in the accustomed manner. The contrast between agreed and imposed enactments is not an absolute one. In the past it was often necessary for an order to be agreed upon unanimously if it was to be treated as legitimate. Today, however, it frequently happens that an order is agreed upon only by a majority of the members of the group in question, with the acquiescence, however, of those who hold different opinions. In such cases the order is actually imposed by the majority upon the minority. Very frequent also is the case that a violent, or ruthless, or simply energetic minority imposes an order which is also regarded as legitimate by those who were originally opposed. Where voting is the legal method of creating or changing an order, it happens very often that a minority achieves formal majority, but with the acquiescence of the actual majority, so that majority rule is a mere appearance.

The faith in the legality of an agreed order can be traced to fairly early periods and can also be found among so-called primitive peoples; almost always is it supplemented, however, in such cases, by the authority of oracles.

(5) Acquiescence in an imposed order, in so far as it does not depend upon mere fear or upon considerations of purpose-rationality, presupposes the belief that the power of domination of him or those by whom the order is imposed is in some sense legitimate. This phenomenon will be discussed *infra*.

(6) Unless the order is an entirely new one, acquiescence in it is generally based upon a combination of considerations of self-interest, of tradition, and of belief in legality. Very often those who thus acquiesce are in no way aware of whether the case is one of custom, convention, or law. It is then the sociologist's task to find out which kind of validity is the typical one.[12]

. . . . .

Section 8. A social relationship will be called *struggle* in so far as the conduct of a party is oriented toward the intention of making his own will prevail against the resistance of the other party or parties. Such

[12] W.u.G. 19.

means of struggle as do not consist in actual physical violence shall be called *peaceful means of struggle.* The peaceful struggle will be called *competition* if it is carried on as formally peaceful endeavor to obtain the power of disposition over opportunities which are coveted also by others.[13]

[13] W.u.G. 20.

CHAPTER II

THE ECONOMIC SYSTEM AND THE NORMATIVE ORDERS[1]

Section 1. Legal Order and Economic Order

1. *The Sociological Concept of Law.* When we speak of "law," "legal order," or "legal proposition" (*Rechtssatz*), close attention must be paid to the distinction between the legal and the sociological points of view. Taking the former, we ask: What is intrinsically valid as law? That is to say: What significance or, in other words, what *normative* meaning ought to be attributed in correct logic to a verbal pattern having the form of a legal proposition. But if we take the latter point of view, we ask: What *actually* happens in a community owing to the *probability* that persons participating in the communal activity (*Gemeinschaftshandeln*), especially those wielding a socially relevant amount of power over the communal activity, subjectively consider certain norms as valid and practically act according to them, in other words, orient their own conduct towards these norms? This distinction also determines, in principle, the relationship between *law* and *economy*.

The juridical point of view, or, more precisely, that of legal dogmatics[2] aims at the correct meaning of propositions the content of which constitutes an order supposedly determinative for the conduct of a defined group of persons: in other words, it tries to define the facts to which this order applies and the way in which it bears upon them. Toward this end, the jurist, taking for granted the empirical validity of the legal propositions, examines each of them and tries to determine its logically correct meaning in such a way that all of them can be combined in a system which is logically coherent, i.e., free from internal contradictions.

Sociological economics,[3] on the other hand, contemplates the inter-

[1] W.u.G. 368–385.

[2] Legal dogmatics (*dogmatische Rechtswissenschaft*) — the term frequently used in German to mean the legal science of the law itself as distinguished from such ways of looking upon law from the outside as philosophy, history, or sociology of law.

[3] *Sozialökonomie* — the term used in the title of the encyclopedic series of which WEBER'S ECONOMY AND SOCIETY forms part, and meant to indicate the author's

connections of human activities as they actually take place and as they are conditioned by their necessary orientation toward the "economic situation of facts." We shall thus use the term "economic order" for the situation which arises from the combination of the following two factors, viz., first, the mode of distribution of factual power over goods and economic services as it emerges consensually from the process of balancing conflicting interests; and, second, the mode in which both goods and services are actually used by virtue of that power and the underlying intentions.

It is obvious that these two approaches deal with entirely different problems and that their "objectives" cannot come directly into contact with one another. The ideal "legal order" of legal theory has nothing directly to do with the world of real economic conduct, since both exist on different levels. One exists in the ideal realm of the "ought," while the other deals with the real world of the "is." If it is nevertheless said that the economic and the legal order are intimately related to one another, the latter is understood, not in the legal, but in the sociological sense, i.e., as being *empirically* valid. In this context "legal order" thus assumes a totally different meaning. It refers, not to a set of norms of logically demonstrable correctness, but rather to a complex of actual determinants (*Bestimmungsgründe*) of actual human conduct. This point requires further elaboration.

The fact that some persons act in a certain way because they regard it as prescribed by legal propositions (*Rechtssaetze*) is, of course, an essential element in the actual emergence and continued operation of a "legal order." But, as we have seen already in discussing the significance of the "existence" of social norms,[4] it is by no means necessary that all, or even a majority, of those who engage in such conduct, do so from this motivation. As a matter of fact, such a situation has never occurred. The broad mass of the participants act in a way corresponding to legal norms, not out of obedience regarded as a legal obligation, but either because the environment approves of the conduct and disapproves of its opposite, or merely as a result of unreflective habituation to a regularity of life that has engraved itself as a custom. If the latter attitude were universal, the law would no longer "subjectively" be regarded as such, but would be observed as custom. However slight, objectively, may be the chance of the coercive apparatus [in the sense defined elsewhere] [5]

---

endeavor to present the economic order as a constituent part of the phenomena of social life. *Cf. supra* Introduction, p. IX.

[4] *Supra* p. 3 *et seq.*

[5] *Infra* p. 16 *et seq.*

enforcing, in a given situation, compliance with those norms, we nevertheless have to consider them as "law." Neither is it necessary — according to what was said above — that all those who share a belief in certain norms of behavior, actually live in accordance with that belief at all times. Such a situation, likewise, has never obtained, nor need it obtain, since, according to our general definition, it is the "orientation" of an action toward a norm, rather than the "success" of that norm that is decisive for its validity. "Law," as understood by us, is simply an "order system" endowed with certain specific guarantees of the probability of its empirical validity.

The term "guaranteed law" shall be understood to mean that there exists a "coercive apparatus," i.e., that there are one or more persons whose special task it is to hold themselves ready to apply specially provided means of coercion (legal coercion) for the purpose of norm enforcement. The means of coercion may be physical or psychological, they may be direct or indirect in their operation, and they may be directed, as the case may require, against the participants in the consensual community (*Einverstaendnisgemeinschaft*), the consociation, the corporate body or the institution within which the order system is (empirically) valid; or they may be aimed at those outside. They are the "legal norms" of the community in question.

By no means all norms which are consensually valid in a community — as we shall see later — are "legal norms." Nor are all official functions of the persons constituting the coercive apparatus of a community concerned with legal coercion; we shall rather consider as legal coercion only those actions whose intention is the enforcement of conformity to a norm as such, i.e., because of its being formally accepted as binding. The term will not be applied, however, where conformity of conduct to a norm is sought to be produced because of considerations of expediency or other material circumstances. It is obvious that the effectuation of the validity of a norm may in fact be pursued for the most diverse motives. However, we shall designate it as "guaranteed law" only in those cases where there exists the probability that coercion, that is, legal coercion, will be applied "for its own sake." As we shall have opportunity to see, not all law is guaranteed law. We shall speak of law — albeit in the sense of "indirectly guaranteed" or "unguaranteed" law — also in all those cases where the validity of a norm consists in the fact that the mode of orientation of an action toward it has some "legal consequences"; i.e., that there are other norms which associate with the "observance" or "infringement" of the primary norm certain probabilities of consensual action guaranteed, in their turn, by legal coercion.

We shall have occasion to illustrate this case, which occurs in a large area of legal life. However, in order to avoid further complication, whenever we shall use the term "law" without qualification, we shall mean norms which are directly guaranteed by legal coercion. Such "guaranteed law" is by no means in all cases guaranteed by "violence" in the sense of the prospect of physical coercion. In our terminology, law, including "guaranteed law" is not characterized sociologically by violence or, even less, by that modern technique of effectuating claims of private law through bringing "suit" in a "court," followed by coercive execution of the judgment obtained. The sphere of "public" law, i.e., the norms governing the conduct of the organs of the state and the activities carried on within the framework of public administration and in relation to itself [6] recognizes numerous rights and legal norms, upon the infringement of which a coercive apparatus can be set in motion only through the "remonstrance" by members of a limited group of persons, and often without any means of physical coercion. Sociologically, the question of whether or not guaranteed law exists in such a situation depends on the availability of an organized coercive apparatus for the nonviolent exercise of legal coercion. This apparatus must also possess such power that there is in fact a significant probability that the norm will be respected because of the possibility of recourse to such legal coercion.

Today legal coercion by violence is the monopoly of the state. All other consociations applying legal coercion by violence are today considered as heteronomous and mostly also as heterocephalous.[7] This view is characteristic, however, only of certain stages of development. We shall speak of "state" law, i.e., of law guaranteed by the state, only when, and to the extent that, the guaranty for it, that is, legal coercion, is exercised through the specific, i.e., normally direct and *physical,* means of coercion of the political community. Thus, the existence of a "legal norm" in the sense of "state law" means that the following situation obtains: In the case of certain events occurring there is general agreement that certain organs of the community can be expected to go into official action, and the very expectation of such action is apt to induce conformity with the commands derived from the generally accepted interpretation of that legal norm; or, where such conformity has become unattainable, at least to effect reparation or "indemnification." The

[6] *Infra* p. 41.

[7] Heteronomous — receiving its order from the outside; opposite — autonomous; heterocephalous — headed by one who is not chosen by the members of the group in question, as, for instance, the Governor of the Territory of Hawaii, who is appointed by the President of the United States.

event inducing this consequence, the legal coercion by the state, may consist in certain human acts, for instance, the conclusion or the breach of a contract, or the commission of a tort. But this type of occurrence constitutes only a special instance, since, upon the basis of some empirically valid legal proposition, the coercive instruments of the political powers against persons and things may also be applied where, for example, a river has risen above a certain level. It is in no way inherent, however, in the validity of a legal norm as normally conceived, that those who obey do so, predominantly or in any way, because of the availability of such a coercive apparatus as defined above. The motives for obedience may rather be of many different kinds. In the majority of cases, they are predominantly utilitarian or ethical or subjectively conventional, i.e., consisting of the fear of disapproval by the environment. The nature of these motives is highly relevant in determining the kind and the degree of validity of the law itself. But in so far as the formal sociological concept of guaranteed law, as we intend to use it, is concerned, these psychological facts are irrelevant. In this connection nothing matters except that there be a sufficiently high probability of intervention on the part of a specially designated group of persons, even in those cases where nothing has occurred but the sheer fact of a norm infringement, i.e., on purely formal grounds.

The empirical validity of a norm as a legal norm affects the interests of an individual in many respects. In particular, it may convey to an individual certain calculable chances of having economic goods available or of acquiring them under certain conditions in the future. Obviously, the creation or protection of such chances is normally one of the aims of law enactment by those who agree upon a norm or impose it upon others. There are two ways in which such a "chance" may be attributed. The attribution may be a mere by-product of the empirical validity of the norm; in that case the norm is not *meant* to guarantee to an individual the chance which happens to fall to him. It may also be, however, that the norm is specifically meant to provide to the individual such a guaranty, in other words, to grant him a "right." Sociologically, the statement that someone has a right by virtue of the legal order of the state thus normally means the following: He has a chance, factually guaranteed to him by the consensually accepted interpretation of a legal norm, of invoking in favor of his ideal or material interests the aid of a "coercive apparatus" which is in special readiness for this purpose. This aid consists, at least normally, in the readiness of certain persons to come to his support in the event that they are approached in the proper way, and that it is shown that the recourse to such aid is actually guaranteed to him by a "legal norm." Such guaranty is based simply upon the "validity" of the legal proposition, and does not depend upon questions of expediency, discretion, grace, or arbitrary pleasure.

A law, thus, is valid wherever legal help in this sense can be obtained in a relevant measure, even though without recourse to physical or other drastic coercive means. A law can also be said to be valid, viz., in the case of unguaranteed law, if its violation, as, for instance, that of an electoral law, induces, on the ground of some empirically valid norm, legal consequences, for instance, the invalidation of the election, for the execution of which an agency with coercive powers has been established.

For purposes of simplification we shall pass by those "chances" which are produced as mere "by-products." A "right," in the context of the "state," is guaranteed by the coercive power of the political authorities. Wherever the means of coercion which constitute the guaranty of a "right" belong to some authority other than the political, for instance, a hierocracy, we shall speak of "extra-state law."

A discussion of the various categories of such extra-state law would be out of place in the present context. All we need to recall is that there exist nonviolent means of coercion which may have the same or, under certain conditions, even greater effectiveness than the violent ones. Frequently, and in fairly large areas even regularly, the threat of such measures as the exclusion from an organization or a boycott, or the prospect of magically conditioned advantages or disadvantages in this world or of reward and punishment in the next, are under certain cultural conditions more effective in producing certain behavior than a political apparatus whose coercive functioning is not always predictable with certainty. Legal forcible coercion exercised by the coercive apparatus of the political community has often come off badly as compared with the coercive power of other, e.g., religious, authorities. In general, the actual scope of its efficiency depends on the circumstances of each concrete case. Within the realm of sociological reality, legal coercion continues to exist, however, as long as some socially *relevant* effects are produced by its power machinery.

2. *State Law and Extra-State Law.* The assumption that a state "exists" only if and when the coercive means of the political community are superior to *all* others, is anti-sociological. "Ecclesiastical law" is still law even where it comes into conflict with "state" law, as it has happened many times and as it is bound to happen again in the case of the relations

between the modern state and certain churches, for instance, the Roman-Catholic. In imperial Austria, the Slavic *Zadruga* not only lacked any kind of legal guaranty by the state, but some of its norms were outright contradictory to the official law.[8] Since the consensual action constituting a *Zadruga* has at its disposal its own coercive apparatus for the enforcement of its norms, these norms are to be considered as "law." Only the state, if invoked, would refuse recognition and proceed, through its coercive power, to break it up.

Outside the sphere of the European-Continental legal system, it is no rare occurrence at all that modern state law explicitly treats as "valid" the norms of other corporate groups and reviews their concrete decisions. American law thus protects labor union labels or regulates the conditions under which a candidate is to be regarded as "validly" nominated by a party. English judges intervene, on appeal, in the judicial proceedings of a club. Even on the continent German judges investigate, in defamation cases, the propriety of the rejection of a challenge to a duel, even though duelling is forbidden by law.[9] We shall not enter into a casuistic inquiry into the extent to which such norms thus become "state law." For all the reasons given above and, in particular, for the sake of terminological consistency, we categorically deny that "law" exists only where legal coercion is guaranteed by the political authority. There is no practical reason for such a terminology. A "legal order" shall rather be said to exist wherever coercive means, of a physical or psychological kind, are available; i.e., wherever they are at the disposal of one or more persons who hold themselves ready to use them for this purpose in the case of certain events; in other words, wherever we find a consociation specifically dedicated to the purpose of "legal coercion." The possession of such an apparatus for the exercise of physical coercion has not always been the monopoly of the political community. As far as psychological coercion is concerned, there is no such monopoly even today, as demonstrated by the importance of law guaranteed only by the church.

We have also indicated already that direct guaranty of law and of rights by a coercive apparatus constitutes only one instance of the existence of "law" and of "rights." Even within this limited sphere the coercive apparatus can take on a great variety of forms. In marginal cases,

[8] But see *infra* p. 69.

[9] Weber was himself involved in a suit of this kind when, in 1911, he brought action against a faculty colleague at the University of Heidelberg who had spread the — false — rumor that Weber, when insulted, had rejected a challenge to a duel; see MARIANNE WEBER, MAX WEBER, EIN LEBENSBILD (2nd ed. 1951) 472.

it may consist in the consensually valid chance of coercive intervention by *all* the members of the community in the event of an infringement of a valid norm. However, in that case one cannot properly speak of a "coercive apparatus" unless the conditions under which participation in such coercive intervention is to be obligatory, are firmly fixed. In those cases where the protection of rights is guaranteed by the organs of the political authority, the coercive apparatus may be reinforced by pressure groups: the strict regulations of associations of creditors and landlords, especially their blacklists of unreliable debtors or tenants, often operate more effectively than the prospect of a lawsuit. It goes without saying that this kind of coercion may be extended to claims which the state does not guarantee at all; such claims are nevertheless based on *rights* even though they are guaranteed by authorities other than the state. The law of the state often tries to obstruct the coercive means of other consociations; the English Libel Act thus tries to preclude blacklisting by excluding the defense of truth. But the state is not always successful. There are groups stronger than the state in this respect, for instance, those groups and associations, usually based on social class, which rely on the "honor code" of the duel as the means of resolving conflicts. With courts of honor and boycott as the coercive means at their disposal, they usually succeed in compelling, with particular emphasis, the fulfillment of obligations as "debts of honor," for instance, gambling debts or the duty to engage in a duel; such debts are intrinsically connected with the specific purposes of the group in question, but, as far as the state is concerned, they are not recognized, or are even proscribed. But the state has been forced, at least partially, to trim its sails.

It would indeed be bad legal reasoning to demand that such a specific delict as duelling be punished as "attempted murder" or assault and battery. Those crimes are of a quite different character. But it remains a fact that in Germany the readiness to participate in a duel is still a *legal* obligation imposed by the state upon its army officers even though the duel is expressly forbidden by the Criminal Code.[10] The State itself has connected legal consequences with an officer's failure to comply with the honor code. Outside of the class of army officers the situation is different, however. The typical means of statutory coercion applied by "private" organizations against refractory members is exclusion from the corporate body and its tangible or intangible advantages. In the professional organizations of physicians and lawyers as well as in social or political clubs, it is the *ultima ratio*. The modern political organization

[10] Written before the Revolution of 1918.

has to a large extent usurped the application of these measures of coercion. Thus, recourse to them has been denied to the physicians and lawyers in Germany; in England the state courts have been given jurisdiction to review, on appeal, exclusions from clubs; and in America the courts have power over political parties as well as the right of reviewing, on appeal, the legality of the use of a union label.

This conflict between the means of coercion of the various corporate groups is as old as the law itself. In the past it has not always ended with the triumph of the coercive means of the political body, and even today this has not always been the outcome. A party, for instance, who has violated the code of the group, has no remedy against a systematic attempt to drive him out of business by underselling. Similarly, there is no protection against being blacklisted for having availed oneself of the plea of illegality of a contract in futures. In the Middle Ages the prohibitions of resorting to the ecclesiastical court contained in the statutes of certain merchants' guilds were clearly invalid from the point of view of canon law, but they persisted nonetheless.[11]

To a considerable extent the state must tolerate the coercive power of organizations even in cases where it is directed not only against members, but also against outsiders on whom the organization tries to impose its own norms. Illustrations are afforded by the efforts of cartels to force outsiders into membership, or by the measures taken by creditors' associations against debtors and tenants.

An important marginal case of coercively guaranteed law, in the sociological sense, is presented by that situation which may be regarded as the very opposite of that which is presented by the modern political communities as well as by those religious communities which apply their own "laws." In the modern communities the law is guaranteed by a "judge" or some other "organ" who is an impartial and disinterested umpire rather than a person who would be characterized by a special relationship with one or the other of the parties. In the situation which we have in mind the means of coercion are provided by those very persons who are linked to the party by close personal relationship, for example, as members of his kinship group. Just as war under modern international law, so under these conditions "vengeance" and "feud" are the only, or at least, the normal, forms of law enforcement. In this case, the "right" of the individual consists, sociologically seen, in the mere probability that the members of his kinship group will respond to their obligation of supporting his feud and blood vengeance (an obligation

[11] See *infra* p. 253.

primarily guaranteed by fear of the wrath of supernatural authorities) and that they will possess strength sufficient to support the right claimed by him even though not necessarily to achieve its final triumph.

The term "legal relationship" will be applied to designate that situation in which the content of a right is constituted by a relationship, i.e., the actual or potential actions of concrete persons or of persons to be identified by concrete criteria. The rights contained in a legal relationship may vary in accordance with the actually occurring actions. In this sense a state can be designated as a legal relationship, even in the hypothetical marginal case in which the ruler alone is regarded as endowed with rights (the right to give orders) and where, accordingly, the opportunities of all the other individuals are reduced to reflexes of his regulations.

Section 2. Law, Convention, and Usage

Significance of Usage in the Formation of Law — Change through Intuition and Empathy — Borderline Zones between Convention, Usage, and Law

Law, convention, and usage belong to the same continuum with imperceptible transitions leading from one to the other. We shall define *usage* to mean a typically uniform activity which is kept on the beaten track simply because men are "accustomed" to it and persist in it by unreflective imitation. It is a collective way of acting, the perpetuation of which by the individual is not "required" in any sense by anyone.

Convention, on the other hand, shall be said to exist wherever a certain conduct is sought to be induced without, however, any coercion, physical or psychological, and, at least under normal circumstances, without any direct reaction other than the expression of approval or disapproval on the part of those persons who constitute the environment of the actor.

"Convention" must be distinguished from *customary law.* We shall abstain here from criticizing this not very useful concept.[12] According to the usual terminology, the validity of a norm as customary law consists in the very likelihood that a coercive apparatus will go into action for its enforcement although it derives its validity from mere consensus rather than from enactment. Convention, on the contrary, is characterized by the very absence of any coercive apparatus, i.e., of any, at least relatively clearly delimited, group of persons who would continuously hold themselves ready for the special task of legal coercion through physical or psychological means.

[12] Cf. *infra* p. 66.

The existence of a mere usage, even unaccompanied by convention, can be of far-reaching economic significance. The level of economic need, which constitutes the basis of all "economic activity," is comprehensively conditioned by mere "usage." The individual might free himself of it without arousing the slightest disapproval. In fact, however, he cannot escape from it except with the greatest difficulty, and it does not change except where it comes gradually to give way to the imitation of the different usage of some other social group.

We have already seen [13] that the uniformity of mere usages can be of importance in the formation of groups of social intercourse and of intermarriage. It may also give a certain, though rather intangible, impetus toward the formation of feelings of "ethnic" identification and, in that way, contribute to the creation of community.[14] At any rate, adherence to what has as such become customary is such a strong component of all conduct and, consequently, of all collective conduct, that legal coercion, where it transforms a usage into a legal obligation (by invocation of the "usual") often adds practically nothing to its effectiveness, and, where it opposes "usage," frequently fails in the attempt to influence actual conduct. Convention is equally effective, if not even more. In countless situations the individual depends on his environment for a spontaneous response, not guaranteed by any earthly or transcendental authority. The existence of a "convention" may thus be far more determinative of his conduct than the existence of legal enforcement machinery.

Obviously, the borderline between usage and convention is fluid. The further we go back in history, the more we find that conduct, and particularly collective conduct, is determined, in an ever more comprehensive sphere, exclusively by orientation to what is customary. The more this is so, the more disquieting are the effects of any deviation from the customary. In this situation, any such deviation seems to act on the psyche of the average individual like the disturbance of an organic function, from which it appears indeed to derive.

Present ethnological literature does not allow us to determine very clearly the point of transition from the stage of mere usage to the, at first vaguely and dimly experienced, "consensual" character of communal action, or, in other words, to the conception of the "oughtness" of certain accustomed modes of conduct. Even less can we trace the changes of the scope of activities with respect to which this transition

[13] W.U.G. 13; Parsons' tr. 118.

[14] See W.U.G. 216.

took place. We shall thus by-pass this problem. It is entirely a question of terminology and convenience at which point of this continuum one shall assume the existence of the subjective conception of a "legal obligation." Objectively the chance of the factual occurrence of a violent reaction against certain types of conduct has always been present among human beings as well as among animals. It would be far-fetched, however, to assume in every such case the existence of a communally valid norm, or that the action in question would be directed by a clearly conceived conscious purpose. Perhaps, a rudimentary conception of "duty" may be determinative in the behavior of some domestic animals to a greater extent than may be found in aboriginal man if we may use this highly ambiguous concept in what is in this context a clearly intelligible sense. We have no access, however, to the "subjective" experiences of the first *homo sapiens* and such concepts as the allegedly primordial, or even *a priori,* character of law or convention are of no use whatsoever to empirical sociology. It is not due to the assumed binding force of some rule or norm that the conduct of primitive man manifests certain external factual regularities, especially in his relation to his fellows. On the contrary, those organically conditioned regularities which we have to accept as psychophysical reality, are primary. It is from them that the concept of "natural norms" arises.

The inner psychological orientation towards such regularities contains in itself very tangible inhibitions against "innovations," a fact which can be observed even today by everyone in his daily experiences, and it constitutes a strong support for the belief in "oughtness." In view of such observation we must ask how anything new can ever arise in this world, oriented as it is toward the regular and the empirically valid. No doubt innovations have been induced from the outside, i.e., by changes in the external conditions of life. But the response evoked by external change may be the extinction of life as well as its reorientation; there is no way of foretelling. Furthermore, external change is by no means a necessary precondition for innovation: in some of the most significant cases, it has not even been a contributing factor in the establishment of a new order. The evidence of ethnology seems rather to show that the most important source of innovation has been the influence of individuals who have experienced certain types of "abnormal" states (which are frequently, but not always, regarded by present-day psychiatry as pathological) and who, as a result of these experiences, have been capable of exercising a special influence on others. We are not discussing here the origin of these experiences which appear to be "new" as a consequence of their "abnormality," but rather their effects. These influences which overcome the inertia of the customary may originate from a variety of psychological occurrences. To Hellpach [14a] we owe the distinction between two categories which, despite the possibility of intermediate forms, nonetheless appear as polar types. The first, inspiration, consists in the sudden awakening, through drastic means, of the awareness that a certain action "ought" to be done by him who has this experience. In the other form, that of empathy or identification, the influencing person's attitude is empathically experienced by one or more others. The types of action which are produced in these ways may vary greatly. Very often, however, a collective action is induced which is oriented toward the influencing person and his experience and from which, in turn, certain types of consensus with corresponding contents may be developed. If they are "adapted" to the external environment, they will survive. The effects of "empathy" and, even more so, of "inspiration" (usually lumped together under the ambiguous term "suggestion") constitute the major sources for the realization of actual innovations whose "establishment" as a regularity will, in turn, reinforce the sense of "oughtness," by which it may possibly be accompanied. The feeling of oughtness, it is true, may undoubtedly appear as something primary and original even in the case of innovation, as soon as there are but the rudiments of a conscious and purposive concept of innovation. Particularly in the case of "inspiration" it may constitute a psychological component. It is confusing, however, when imitation of a new type of conduct is regarded as the basic and primary element in its diffusion. Undoubtedly, imitation is of extraordinary importance, but as a general rule it is secondary and constitutes only a special case. If the conduct of a dog, man's oldest companion, is "inspired" by man, such conduct, obviously, cannot be described as "imitation of man by dog." In a very large number of cases, the relation between the persons influencing and those influenced is exactly of this kind. In some cases, it may approximate "empathy," in others, "imitation," conditioned either by rational purpose or in the ways of "mass psychology."

In any case, however, the emerging innovation is most likely to produce consensus and ultimately law, when it derives from a strong inspiration or an intensive "identification." In such cases a convention will result or, under certain circumstances, even consensual coercive action against deviants. As long as religious faith is strong, convention, that is, the approval or disapproval by the environment, engenders, as

[14a] Willy Hellpach (born 1877), professor of medicine, known by his highly original investigations on the influence of meteorological and geographic phenomena upon the mind.

historical experience shows, the hope and faith that the supernatural powers too will reward or punish those actions which are approved or disapproved in this world. Convention, under appropriate conditions, may also produce the further belief that not only the actor himself but also those around him may have to suffer from the wrath of those supernatural powers, and that, therefore, reaction is incumbent upon all, acting either individually or through the coercive apparatus of some organization. In consequence of the constant recurrence of a certain pattern of conduct, the idea may arise in the minds of the guarantors of a particular norm, that they are confronted no longer with mere usage or convention, but with a legal obligation requiring enforcement. A norm which has attained such practical validity is called customary law. Eventually, the interests involved may engender a rationally considered desire to secure the convention, or the obligation of customary law, against subversion, and to place it explicitly under the guarantee of an enforcement machinery, i.e., to transform it into enacted law.

Particularly in the field of the internal distribution of power among the organs of an institutional order experience reveals a continuous scale of transitions from norms of conduct guaranteed by mere convention to those which are regarded as binding and guaranteed by law A striking example is presented by the development of the British Constitution.

Finally, any rebellion against convention may lead the environment to make use of its coercively guaranteed rights in a manner detrimental to the rebel; for instance, the host uses his right as master of the house against the guest who has infringed upon the conventional rules of social amenity; or a war lord uses his legal power of dismissal against the officer who has infringed upon the code of honor. In such cases the conventional rule is, in fact, indirectly supported by coercive means. The situation differs from that of "unguaranteed" law in so far as the initiation of the coercive measures is a factual, but not a legal, consequence of the infringement of the convention. The legal right to exclude anyone from his house belongs to the master as such. But a directly unguaranteed legal proposition draws its validity from the fact that its violation engenders consequences somehow *via* a guaranteed legal norm. Where, on the other hand, a legal norm refers to "good morals" (*die guten Sitten*),[15] i.e., conventions worthy of approval, the fulfillment of the conventional obligations has also become a legal obligation and we have a case of indirectly guaranteed law. There are also numerous in-

[15] Cf. German Civil Code, Sec. 138: "A transaction which is contrary to good morals is void"; Sec. 826: "One who causes harm to another intentionally and in a manner which is against good morals, has to compensate the other for such harm."

stances of intermediate types, as, for example, the courts of love of the Troubadours of Provence which had "jurisdiction" in matters of love;[16] or the "judge" in his original role as arbitrator seeking to procure a settlement between feuding antagonists, perhaps also rendering a verdict, but lacking coercive powers of his own; or, finally, modern international courts of arbitration. In such cases, the amorphous approval or disapproval of the environment has crystallized into a set of commands, prohibitions, and permissions authoritatively promulgated, i.e., a concretely organized pattern of coercion. Excepting situations of mere play, as, for instance, the courts of love, such cases may be classified as "law" provided the judgment is normally backed not only by the personal, and therefore irrelevant, opinion of the judge, but by, at least, some boycott as self-help of the kinship group, the state, or some other group of persons whose right has been violated, as in the last two of the illustrations above. According to our definition, the fact that some type of conduct is "approved" or "disapproved" by ever so many persons is insufficient to constitute it as a "convention"; it is essential that such attitudes are likely to find expression in a specific environment. This latter term is, of course, not meant in any geographical sense. But there must be some test for defining that group of persons which constitutes the environment of the person in question. It does not matter in this context whether the test is constituted by profession, kinship, neighborhood, economic estate, race, religion, political allegiance, or anything else. Nor does it matter that the membership is changeable or unstable. For the existence of a convention in our sense it is not required that the environment be constituted by a corporate organized group as we understand that term. The very opposite is frequently the case. But the validity of law, presupposing, as we have seen, the existence of an enforcement machinery, is necessarily a corollary of organized collective action. Of course, we do not imply that the collective would regulate only its own corporate or collective action. It is rather that the organized collectivity must be said to be the "sustainer" of the law.

[16] The "courts of love" (cours d'amour) belonged to the amusements of polite society at the high period of chivalry and the troubadours (twelfth to thirteenth century). They are reported to have consisted of circles of ladies who were organized in the way of courts and rendered judgments and opinions in matters of courtly love and manners. They flourished in southern France, especially Provence, where they came to an end with the collapse of Provençal society in the "crusade" against the Albigensian heretics. In the late Middle Ages, a brilliant court of love is reported to have flourished for some years at the Burgundian court; cf. HUIZINGA, WANING OF THE MIDDLE AGES (1924), c. 8, p. 103. On the courts of love in general, see CAPEFIGUE, LES COURS D'AMOUR (1863); RAJNA, LE CORTI D'AMORE (1890); and the article by F. Bonnardot in 2 LA GRANDE ENCYCLOPÉDIE 805, with further literature.

On the other hand, we are far from asserting that legal rules, in the sense here used, would offer the only standard of subjective orientation for consensual, communal, corporate, or institutional action, which, we must remember, is nothing but a segment of sociologically relevant conduct in general. If "collective order" is understood to be constituted by all those determinable regularities of conduct which are characteristic of, or indispensable to, the actual course of the communal (community creating or community influenced) action, then this order is only to a small extent the result of an orientation toward legal rules. To the extent that it is consciously oriented towards rules at all and does not merely spring from unreflective habituation, the rules are of the nature of "usage" and "convention," or, in part, and often predominantly, they are rational maxims of purposeful self-interested action of the individual participants, on the effective operation of which each participant is counting for his own conduct as well as for that of all others. This expectation is, indeed, justified objectively, especially since the maxim, though lacking legal guaranties, often constitutes the subject matter of some special consociation or consensus. The chance of legal coercion which, as already mentioned, motivates even "legal" conduct only to a slight extent, is also objectively an ultimate guaranty for no more than a fraction of the actual course of consensually oriented conduct.

It should thus be clear that, from the point of view of sociology, the transitions from mere usage to convention and from it to law are fluid.

Even from a non-sociological point of view it is wrong to distinguish between law and ethics by asserting that legal norms regulate mere external conduct, while moral norms regulate only matters of conscience. The law, it is true, does not by any means always regard the intention of an action as relevant, and there have been legal propositions and legal systems in which legal consequences, including even punishment, are causally connected exclusively with external events. But this situation is not the normal one. Legal consequences attach to *bona* or *mala fides*, or "intention," or moral turpitude, and a good many other purely subjective factors. Moral commandments, on the other hand, are aiming at overcoming in practical, and thus external, conduct those anti-normative impulses which form part of the "mental attitude."

From the normative point of view we should thus distinguish between the two phenomena not as external and subjective, but as representing different degrees of normativeness.

From the sociological point of view, however, ethical validity is normally identical with validity "on religious grounds" or "by virtue of convention." Only an abstract standard of conduct subjectively conceived as derived from ultimate axioms could be regarded as an "exclusively" ethical norm, and this only in so far as this conception would acquire practical significance in conduct. Such conceptions have in fact often had real significance. But wherever this has been the case, they have been a relatively late product of philosophical reflection. In the past, as well as in the present, "moral commandments" in contrast to legal commands are, from a sociological point of view, normally either religiously or conventionally conditioned maxims of conduct. They are not distinguished from law by hard and fast criteria. There is no socially important moral commandment which would not have been a legal command at one time or another.

Stammler's distinction between convention and legal norm according to whether or not the fulfillment of the norm is dependent upon the free will of the individual[17] is of no use whatsoever. It is incorrect to say that the fulfillment of conventional "obligations," for instance of a rule of social etiquette, is not "imposed" on the individual, and that its nonfulfillment would simply result in, or coincide with, the free and voluntary separation from a voluntary consociation. It may be admitted that there are norms of this kind, but they exist not only in the sphere of convention, but equally in that of law. The *clausula rebus sic stantibus* in fact often lends itself to such use. At any rate, the distinction between conventional rule and legal norm in Stammler's own sociology is not centered on this test. Not only the theoretically constructed anarchical society, the "theory" and "critique" of which Stammler has elaborated with the aid of his scholastic concepts, but also a good number of consociations existing in the real world have dispensed with the legal character of their conventional norms. They have done so on the assumption that the mere fact of the social disapproval of norm infringement with its, often very real, indirect consequences will suffice as a sanction. From the sociological point of view, legal order and conventional order do thus not constitute any basic contrast, since, quite apart from obvious cases of transition, convention, too, is sustained by psychological as well as (at least indirectly) physical coercion. It is only with regard to the sociological *structure* of coercion that they differ: The conventional order lacks specialized personnel for the implementation of coercive power (enforcement machinery: priests, judges, police, the military, etc.).

Above all, Stammler confuses the ideal validity of a norm with the assumed validity of a norm in its actual influence on empirical action. The former can be deduced systematically by legal theorists and moral philosophers; the latter, instead, ought to be the subject of empirical

[17] Wirtschaft und Recht (1896) 125.

observation. Furthermore, Stammler confuses the normative regulation of conduct by rules whose "oughtness" is factually accepted by a sizable number of persons, with the factual regularities of human conduct. These two concepts are to be strictly separated, however.

It is by way of conventional rules that merely factual regularities of action, i.e., usages, are frequently transformed into binding norms, guaranteed primarily by psychological coercion. Tradition thus makes convention. The mere fact of the regular recurrence of certain events somehow confers on them the dignity of oughtness. This is true with regard to natural events as well as to action conditioned organically or by unreflective imitation of, or adaptation to, external conditions of life. It applies to the accustomed course of the stars as ordained by the divine powers, as well as to the seasonal floods of the Nile or the accustomed way of remunerating slave laborers, who by the law are unconditionally surrendered to the power of their masters.

Whenever the regularities of action have become conventionalized, i.e., whenever a statistically frequent action has become a consensually oriented action (this is, in our terminology, the real meaning of this development), we shall speak of "tradition."

It cannot be overstressed that the mere habituation to a mode of action, the instinct to preserve this habituation, and, much more so, tradition, have a formidable influence in favor of a habituated legal order, even where such an order originally derives from legal enactment. This influence is more powerful than any reflection on impending means of coercion or other consequences, considering also the fact that at least some of those who act according to the "norms" are totally unaware of them.

The transition from the merely unreflective formation of a habit to the conscious acceptance of the maxim that action should be in accordance with a norm is always fluid. The mere statistical regularity of an action leads to the emergence of moral and legal convictions with corresponding contents. The threat of physical and psychological coercion, on the other hand, imposes a certain mode of action and thus produces habituation and thereby regularity of action.

Law and convention are intertwined as cause and effect in the actions of men, with, against, and beside, one another. It is grossly misleading to consider law and convention as the "forms" of conduct in contrast with its "substance" as Stammler does. The belief in the legal or conventional oughtness of a certain action is, from a sociological point of view, merely a superadditum increasing the degree of probability with which an acting person can calculate certain *consequences* of his action. Economic theory therefore properly disregards the character of the norms altogether. For the economist the fact that someone "possesses" something simply means that he can count on other persons not to interfere with his disposition over the object. This mutual respect of the right of disposition may be based on a variety of considerations. It may derive from deference to conventional or legal norms, or from considerations of self-interest on the part of each participant. Whatever the reason, it is of no primary concern to economic theory. The fact that a person "owes" something to another can be translated, sociologically, into the following terms: a certain commitment (through promise, tort, or other cause) of one person to another; the expectation, based thereon, that in due course the former will yield to the latter his right of disposition over the goods concerned; the existence of a chance that this expectation will be fulfilled. The psychological motives involved are of no primary interest to the economist.

An exchange of goods means: the transfer of an object, according to an agreement, from the factual control of one person to that of another, this transfer being based on the assumption that another object is to be transferred from the factual control of the second to that of the first. Of those who take part in a debtor-creditor relationship or in a barter, each one expects that the other will conform to his own intentions. It is not necessary, however, to assume conceptually any "order" outside or above the two parties to guarantee, command, or enforce compliance by means of coercive machinery or social disapproval. Nor is it necessary to assume the subjective belief of either or both parties in any "binding" norm. For the partner to an exchange can depend on the other partner's *egoistic interest* in the future continuation of exchange relationships or other similar motives to offset his inclination to break his promise — a fact which results most tangibly from the so-called "silent trade" among primitive peoples as well as from modern business, especially on the stock exchange.

Assuming the availability of purely expediential rationality, each participant can and does, in fact, depend on the probability that under normal circumstances the other party will act "as if" he accepted as "binding" the norm that one has to fulfill his promises. Conceptually this is quite sufficient. But it goes without saying that it makes a difference whether the partner's expectation in this respect is supported by one or both of the following guaranties: 1. the factually wide currency, in the environment, of the subjective belief in the objective validity of such a norm (consensus); 2. even more so, the creation of a conventional guaranty through regard for social approval or disapproval, or of a legal guaranty through the existence of enforcement machinery.

Can it be said that a stable private economic system of the modern type would be "unthinkable" without legal guaranties? As a matter of fact we see that in most business transactions it never occurs to anyone even to think of taking legal action. Agreements on the stock exchange, for example, take place between professional traders in such forms as in the vast majority of cases exclude "proof" in cases of bad faith: the contracts are oral, or are recorded by marks and notations in the trader's own notebook. Nevertheless, a dispute practically never occurs. Likewise, there are corporate groups pursuing purely economic ends the rules of which nonetheless dispense entirely, or almost entirely, with legal protection from the state. Certain types of "cartels" were illustrative of this class of organization. It often happened also that agreements which had been concluded and were valid according to private law were rendered inoperative through the dissolution of the organization, as there was no longer a formally legitimated plaintiff. In these instances, the corporate group with its own coercive apparatus had a system of "law" which was totally lacking in the power of forcible legal coercion. Such coercion, at any rate, was available only so long as the organized group was in existence. As a result of the peculiar subjective attitude of the participants, cartel contracts often had not even any effective conventional guarantee. Those consociations often functioned nonetheless for a long time and quite efficiently in consequence of the convergent interests of all the participants.

Despite all such facts, it is obvious that forcible legal guarantee, especially where exercised by the state, is not a matter of indifference to such organizations. Today economic exchange is quite overwhelmingly guaranteed by the threat of legal coercion. The normal intention in an act of exchange is to acquire certain subjective "rights," i.e., in sociological terms, the probability of support of one's power of disposition by the coercive apparatus of the state. Economic goods today are normally at the same time *legitimately acquired rights*; they are the very building material for the universe of the economic order. Nonetheless, even today they do not constitute the total range of objects of exchange.

Economic opportunities which are not guaranteed by the legal order, or the guaranty of which is even refused on grounds of policy by the legal order, can and do constitute objects of exchange transactions which are not only not illegitimate but perfectly legitimate. They include, for instance, the transfer, against compensation, of the goodwill of a business. The sale of a goodwill today normally engenders certain private law claims of the purchaser against the seller, namely, that he will refrain from certain actions and will perform certain others, for instance, "introduce" the purchaser to the customers. But the legal order does not enforce the claims against third parties. Yet, there have been and still are cases in which the coercive apparatus of the political authority is available for the exercise of direct coercion in favor of the owner or purchaser of a "market," as for instance in the case of a guild monopoly or some other legally protected monopoly. It is well known that Fichte [18] considered it as the essential characteristic of modern legal development that, in contrast to such cases, the modern state guarantees only claims on concrete usable goods or labor services. Besides, so-called "free competition" finds its legal expression in this very fact. Yet, although such "opportunities" have remained objects of economic exchange even without legal protection against third parties, the absence of legal guaranties has nevertheless far-reaching economic consequences. But from the point of view of economics and sociology it remains a fact that, on general principle, at least, the interference of legal guaranties merely increases the degree of certainty with which an economically relevant action can be calculated in advance.

The legal regulation of a subject matter has never been carried out in all its implications anywhere. This would require the availability of some human agency which in every case of the kind in question would be regarded as being capable of determining, in accordance with some conceived norm, what ought to be done "by law." We shall by-pass here the interaction between consociation and legal order: as we have seen elsewhere, any rational consociation, and therefore, any order of communal and consensual action is posterior in this respect. Nor shall we discuss here the proposition that the development of communal and consensual action continually creates entirely new situations and raises problems which can be solved by the accepted norms or by the usual logic of jurisprudence only in appearance or by spurious reasoning (cf. in this respect the thesis of the "free-law" movement).[19]

We are concerned here with a more basic problem: It is a fact that the most "fundamental" questions often are left unregulated by law even in legal orders which are otherwise thoroughly rationalized. Let us illustrate two specific types of this phenomenon:

(1) A "constitutional" monarch dismisses his responsible minister and fails to replace him by any new appointee so that there is no one to countersign his acts. What is to be done "by law" in such a situation? This question is not regulated in any constitution anywhere in the world. What is clear is no more than that certain acts of the government cannot be "validly" taken.

[18] Der geschlossene Handelsstaat (1800), Bk. I, c. 7.

[19] See *infra* p. 309.

(2) Most constitutions equally omit consideration of the following question: What is to be done when those parties whose agreement is necessary for the adoption of the budget are unable to reach an agreement?

The first problem is described by Jellinek as "moot" for all practical purposes.[20] He is right. What is of interest to us is just to know why it is "moot." The second type of "constitutional gap," on the other hand, has become very practical, as is well known.[21] If we understand "constitution," in the sociological sense, as the modus of distribution of power which determines the possibility of regulating communal action, we may, indeed, venture the proposition that any community's constitution *in the sociological sense* is determined by the fact of where and how its constitution *in the juridical sense* contains such "gaps," especially with regard to basic questions. At times such gaps of the second type have been left intentionally where a constitution was rationally enacted by consensus or imposition. This was done simply because the interested party or parties who exercised the decisive influence on the drafting of the constitution in question expected that hè or they would ultimately have sufficient power to control, in accordance with their own desires, that portion of communal action which, while lacking a basis in any enacted norm, yet had to be carried on somehow. Returning to our illustration: they expected to govern without a budget.

Gaps of the first type mentioned above, on the other hand, usually remain open for another reason: Experience seems to teach convincingly that the self-interest of the party or parties concerned (in our example, of the monarch) will at all times suffice so to condition his or their way of acting that the "absurd" though legally possible situation (in our example, the lack of a responsible minister) will never occur. Despite the "gap," general consensus considers it as the unquestionable "duty" of the monarch to appoint a minister. As there are legal consequences attached to this duty, it is to be considered as an "indirectly guaranteed legal obligation." Such ensuing legal consequences are: the impossibility of executing certain acts in a valid manner, i.e., of attaining the possibility of having them guaranteed through the coercive apparatus.

[20] Gesetz und Verordnung (1887) 295; Verfassungsänderung und Verfassungswandel (1906) 43.

[21] The situation arose in Prussia when the predominantly liberal Diet early in 1860 refused to pass Bismarck's budget because of its disapproval of his policy of armaments (so-called Era of Conflict or *Konfliktsperiode*). In Austria, too, Parliament (*Reichsrat*) repeatedly was unable to reach agreement on a budget during that period of conflict between the several ethnic groups of the Monarchy which preceded the outbreak of World War I.

But for the rest, it is not established, either by law or convention, what is to be done to carry on the administration of the state in case the ruler should not fulfill this duty; and since this case has never occurred thus far, there is no "usage" either which could become the source for a decision. This situation constitutes a striking illustration of the fact that law, convention, and usage are by no means the only forces to be counted on as guarantee for such conduct of another person as is expected of, promised by, or otherwise regarded as due from, him. Beside and above these, there is another force to be reckoned with: the other person's self-interest in the continuation of a certain agreed action as such. The certainty with which the monarch's compliance with an assumedly binding duty can be anticipated is no doubt greater, but only by a matter of degree, than the certainty — if we may return now to our previous example — with which a partner to an exchange counts, and in the case of continued intercourse, may continue to count, upon the other party's conduct to conform with his own expectations. This certainty exists even though the transaction in question may lack any normative regulation or coercive guaranty.

What is relevant here is merely the observation that the legal as well as the conventional regulation of consensual or societal action may be, as a matter of principle, incomplete and, under certain circumstances, will be so quite consciously. While the orientation of communal action to a norm is constitutive of consociation in any and every case, the coercive apparatus does not have this function with regard to the totality of all stable and institutionally organized corporate action. If the absurd case of illustration No. 1 were to occur, it would certainly set legal speculation to work immediately and then perhaps, a conventional, or even legal, regulation would come into existence. But in the meantime the problem would already have been actually solved by some communal or consensual or societal action the details of which would depend upon the nature of the concrete situation. Normative regulation is one important causal component of consensual action, but it is not, as claimed by Stammler,[22] its universal "form."

Section 3. Significance and Limits of Legal Coercion in Economic Life

Sociology is a discipline searching for empirical regularities and types. In so far as it is concerned with legal guaranties and those normative conceptions on which they depend as the motives underlying their crea-

[22] *Op. cit. supra* n. 17.

tion, interpretation, and application, its interest is thus of a special kind. They are to be considered as consequences as well as, and more so, as causes or concomitant causes of certain regularities. These may be regularities of human action which are as such directly relevant to sociology, or regularities of natural occurrences, engendered by human action, and as such indirectly relevant to sociology.

Factual regularities *of* conduct ("usages") can, as we have seen, become the source of rules *for* conduct ("conventions," "law"). The reverse, however, may be equally true. Regularities may be produced by legal norms, acting by themselves or in combination with other factors. This applies not only to those regularities which directly realize the content of the legal norm in question, but equally to regularities of a different kind. The fact that an official, for example, goes to his office regularly every day is a direct consequence of the order contained in a legal norm which is accepted as "valid" in practice. On the other hand, the fact that a traveling salesman of a factory visits the retailers regularly each year for the solicitation of orders is only an indirect effect of legal norms, viz., of those which permit free competition for customers and thus necessitate that they be wooed. The fact that fewer children die when nursing mothers abstain from work as a result of a legal or conventional "norm" is certainly a consequence of the validity of that norm. Where it is an enacted legal norm, this result has certainly been one of the rationally conceived ends of the creators of that norm; but it is obvious that they can decree only the abstention from work and not the lower death rate. Even with regard to directly commanded or prohibited conduct, the practical effectiveness of the validity of a coercive norm is obviously problematic. Observance follows to an "adequate" measure, but never without exceptions. Powerful interests may indeed induce a situation in which a legal norm is violated, without ensuing punishment, not only in isolated instances, but prevalently and permanently, in spite of the coercive apparatus on which the "validity" of the norm is founded. When such a situation has become stabilized and when, accordingly, prevailing practice rather than the pretense of the written law has become normative of conduct in the conviction of the participants, the guaranteeing coercive power will ultimately cease to compel conduct to conform to the latter. In such case, the legal theorist speaks of "derogation through customary law."

"Valid" legal norms, which are guaranteed by the coercive apparatus of the political authority, and conventional rules may also coexist, however, in a state of chronic conflict. We have observed such a situation in the case of the duel, where private law has been transformed by convention. And while it is not at all unusual that legal norms are rationally enacted with the purpose of changing existing "usages" and conventions, the normal development is more usually as follows: a legal order is empirically "valid" owing not so much to the availability of coercive guaranties as to its habituation as "usage" and its "routinization." To this should be added the pressure of convention which, in most cases, disapproves any flagrant deviation from conduct corresponding to that order.

For the legal theorist the (ideological) validity of a legal norm is conceptually the *prius*. Conduct which is not directly regulated by law is regarded by him as legally "permitted" and thus equally affected by the legal order, at least ideologically. For the sociologist, on the other hand, the legal, and particularly the rationally enacted, regulation of conduct is empirically only one of the factors motivating communal action; moreover, it is a factor which usually appears late in history and whose effectiveness varies greatly. The beginnings of actual regularity and "usage," shrouded in darkness everywhere, are attributed by the sociologist, as we have seen, to the impulsive and instinctive habituation of a pattern of conduct which was "adapted" to given necessities. At least at first, this pattern of conduct was neither conditioned nor changed by an enacted norm. The increasing intervention of enacted norms is, from our point of view, only one of the components, however characteristic, of that process of rationalization and consociation whose growing penetration into all spheres of communal action we shall have to trace as a most essential dynamic factor in development.[23]

This discussion has been restricted to a consideration of the broad relations between law and economic activity. Summing up, we may now make the following statements:

(1) Law (in the sociological sense) guarantees by no means only economic interests but rather the most diverse interests ranging from the most elementary one of protection of personal security to such purely ideal goods as personal honor or the honor of the divine powers. Above all, it guarantees political, ecclesiastical, familial, and other positions of authority as well as positions of social preëminence of any kind which may indeed be economically conditioned or economically relevant in the most diverse ways, but which are neither economic in themselves nor sought for preponderantly economic ends.

(2) Under certain conditions a "legal order" can remain unchanged

[23] This programmatic statement has been carried out by Weber in Parts II and III of W.u.G. The present book contains those sections of these Parts which are concerned with the relations between social structure and law.

while economic relations are undergoing a radical transformation. In theory, a socialist system of production could be brought about without the change of even a single paragraph of our laws, simply by the gradual, free contractual acquisition of all the means of production by the political authority. This example is extreme; but, for the purpose of theoretical speculation, extreme examples are most useful. Should such a situation ever come about — which is most unlikely, though theoretically not unthinkable — the legal order would still be bound to apply its coercive machinery in case its aid were invoked for the enforcement of those obligations which are characteristic of a productive system based on private property. Only, this case would never occur in fact.[24]

(3) The legal status of a matter may be basically different according to the point of view of the legal system from which it is considered. But such differences [of legal classification] need not have any relevant economic consequences provided only that on those points which generally are relevant economically, the *practical* effects are the same for the interested parties. This not only is possible, but it actually happens widely, although it must be conceded that any variation of legal classification may engender some economic consequences somewhere. Thus totally different forms of action would have been applicable in Rome depending on whether the "lease" of a mine were to be regarded legally as a lease in the strict sense of the term, or as a purchase. But the practical effects of the difference for economic life would certainly have been very slight.[25]

[24] The norms of the legal order, existing before the total socialization took place could also be applied after its occurrence, if legal title to the various means of production were to be ascribed not to one single, central public authority but to formally autonomous public institutions or corporations which are to regulate their relationships to each other by contractual transactions, subject to the directions of, and control by, the central planning authority. Such a situation does indeed exist in the Soviet Union. Cf. H. J. BERMAN, JUSTICE IN RUSSIA (1950), and review by Rheinstein (1951) 64 HARV. L. REV. 1387.

[25] Cf. in American law the controversy as to the correct legal classification of a mining or oil and gas lease: does the transaction create a profit a prendre, or does it give to the "lessee" the title to the minerals, or does it result in the creation of a leasehold interest in the strict sense of the term? As in Rome, the "proper" classification may be relevant in some practical respect as, for instance, with regard to the question of whether, in the case of the death of the lessee — if he should ever be an individual! — his interest descends as real, or is to be distributed as personal, property. In the former case it would, ordinarily, not be touched for the payment of debts of the deceased until all the personal property has been exhausted; in the latter, the "lease" would be immediately available for the creditors along with the other "personal" assets of the decedent. But, by and large, the economic situation is one and the same whichever of the various legal classifications is applied.

(4) Obviously, any legal guaranty is directly at the service of economic interests to a very large extent. Even where this does not seem to be, or actually is not, the case, economic interests are among the strongest factors influencing the creation of law. For, any authority guaranteeing a legal order depends, in some way, upon the consensual action of the constitutive social groups, and the formation of social groups depends, to a large extent, upon constellations of material interests.

(5) Only a limited measure of success can be attained through the threat of coercion supporting the legal order. Owing to a number of external circumstances as well as to its own peculiar nature, this applies especially to the economic sphere. It would be quibbling, however, to assert that law cannot "enforce" any particular economic conduct, on the ground that we would have to say, with regard to all its means of coercion, that *coactus tamen voluit.*[26] For this is true, without exception, of all coercion which does not treat the person to be coerced simply as an inanimate object. Even the most drastic means of coercion and punishment are bound to fail where the subjects remain recalcitrant. In a broad mass such a situation would always mean that its members have not been educated to acquiescence. Such education to acquiescence in the law of the time and place has, as a general rule, increased with growing pacification. Thus it should seem that the chances of enforcing economic conduct would have increased, too. Yet, the power of law over economic conduct has in many respects grown weaker rather than stronger as compared with earlier conditions. The effectiveness of maximum price regulations, for example, has always been precarious, but under present-day conditions they have an even smaller chance of success than ever before.

Thus the measure of possible influence on economic activity is not simply a function of the general level of acquiescence towards legal coercion. The limits of the actual success of legal coercion in the economic sphere rather arise from two main sources. One is constituted by the limitations of the economic capacity of the persons affected. There are limits not only to the stock itself of available goods, but also to the way in which that stock can possibly be used. For the patterns of use and of relationship among the various economic units are determined by habit and can be adjusted to heteronomous norms, if at all, only by difficult reorientations of all economic dispositions, and hardly without losses, which means, never without frictions. These frictions increase with the degree of development and universality of a particular form of

[26] "Although coerced, it was still his will."

consensual action, or, in other words, with the interdependence of the individual economic units in the market, and, consequently, the dependence of every one upon the conduct of others. The second source of the limitation of successful legal coercion in the economic sphere lies in the relative proportion of strength of private economic interests on the one hand and interests promoting conformance to the rules of law on the other. The inclination to forego economic opportunity simply in order to act legally is obviously slight, unless circumvention of the formal law is strongly disapproved by a powerful convention, and such a situation is not likely to arise where the interests affected by a legal innovation are widespread. Besides, it is often not difficult to disguise the circumvention of a law in the economic sphere. Quite particularly insensitive to legal influence are, as experience has shown, those effects which derive directly from the ultimate sources of economic action, such as the estimates of economic value and the formation of prices. This applies particularly to those situations where the determinants in production and consumption do not lie within a completely perspicuous and directly manageable complex of consensual conduct. It is obvious, besides, that those who continuously participate in the market intercourse with their own economic interests have a far greater rational knowledge of the market and interest situation than the legislators and enforcement officers whose interest is only ideal. In an economy based on all-embracing interdependence on the market the possible and unintended repercussions of a legal measure must to a large extent escape the foresight of the legislator simply because they depend upon private interested parties. It is those private interested parties who are in a position to distort the intended meaning of a legal norm to the point of turning it into its very opposite, as has often happened in the past. In view of these difficulties, the extent of factual impact of the law on economic conduct cannot be determined generally, but must be calculated for each particular case. It belongs thus to the field of case studies in social economics. In general no more can be asserted than that, from a purely theoretical point of view, the complete monopolization of a market, which entails a far greater perspicuity of the situation, technically facilitates the control by law of that particular sector of the economy. If it, nevertheless, does not always in fact increase the opportunities for such control, this result is usually due either to legal particularism arising from the existence of competing political associations,[27] or to the power of the private interests amenable to the monopolistic control and thus resisting the enforcement of the law.

[27] See *infra* pp. 188 *et seq.*

From the purely theoretical point of view, legal guaranty *by the state* is not indispensable to any basic economic phenomenon. The protection of property, for example, can be provided by the mutual aid system of kinship groups. Creditors' rights have sometimes been protected more efficiently by a religious community's threat of excommunication than by political bodies. "Money," too, has existed in almost all of its forms, without the state's guaranty of its acceptability as a means of payment.[28] Even "chartal" money, i.e., money which derives its character as means of payment from the marking of pieces rather than from their substantive content, is conceivable without the guaranty by the state. Occasionally chartal money of non-statal origin appeared even in spite of the existence of an apparatus of legal coercion by the state: the ancient Babylonians, for instance, did not have "coins" in the sense of a means of payment constituting legal tender by proclamation of the political authority, but contracts were apparently in use under which payment was to be made in pieces of a fifth of a shekel designated as such by the stamp of a certain "firm" (as we would say).[29] There was thus lacking any guaranty "proclaimed" by the state; the chosen unit of value was derived, not from the state, but from private contract. Yet the means of payment was "chartal" in character, and the state guaranteed coercively the concrete deal.

"Conceptually" the "state" thus is not indispensable to any economic activity. But an economic system, especially of the modern type, could certainly not exist without a legal order with very special features which could not develop except in the frame of a "statal" legal order. Present-day economic life rests on opportunities acquired through contracts. It is true, the private interests in the obligation of contract, and the common interest of all property holders in the mutual protection of property are still considerable, and individuals are still markedly influenced by convention and usage even today. Yet, the influence of these factors has declined due to the disintegration of tradition, i.e., of the tradition-determined relationships as well as of the belief in their sacredness. Furthermore, class interests have come to diverge more sharply from one another

[28] Cf. W.u.G. 38, 97; Parsons' tr. 173, 280.

[29] No reference to a practice of the kind mentioned could be located except the following passage in B. Maissner, Babylonien und Assyrien (1920) 356: "As one could not generally rely upon the weight and fineness of the silver and thus had to check (*xâtu*), one preferred to receive silver bearing a stamp (*kanku*) by which the weight and fineness would be guaranteed. In contracts from the period of the first Babylonian dynasty we find shekels mentioned 'with a stamp'(?) of Babylon (Vorderasiatische Bibliothek VI, No. 217, 15) or shekels 'from the city of Zahan' or 'from Grossippar' (Brit. Mus. Cuneiform Tablets IV, 47, 19a)."

than ever before.[30] The tempo of modern business communication requires a promptly and predictably functioning legal system, i.e., one which is guaranteed by the strongest coercive power. Finally, modern economic life by its very nature has destroyed those other associations which used to be the bearers of law and thus of legal guaranties. This has been the result of the development of the market. The universal predominance of the market consociation requires on the one hand a legal system the functioning of which is *calculable* in accordance with rational rules. On the other hand, the constant expansion of the market consociation has favored the monopolization and regulation of all "legitimate" coercive power by *one* universal coercive institution through the disintegration of all particular status-determined and other coercive structures, which have been resting mainly on economic monopolies.

[30] On "classes," see W.u.G. 177, Parsons' tr. 424.

CHAPTER III

FIELDS OF SUBSTANTIVE LAW [1]

1. *Public Law and Private Law.* One of the most important distinctions in modern legal theory and practice is that between "public" and "private" law.[2] But the exact criteria of this distinction are surrounded by controversy.

(a) In accordance with the sociological test, one might define public law as the total body of those norms which regulate the activities of the state as such, that is, those activities which the state in a given legal sysem is legally empowered to pursue. In this sense we mean by "activities of the state as such" [3] those activities which are instrumental for the maintenance, development, and the direct fulfillment of the objectives of the state, objectives however which must themselves be valid by virtue of enactment, or by virtue of the consensus of those concerned. Correspondingly, private law would be defined as the totality, not of those norms which relate to the state as such, but of those norms which, while issuing from the state, regulate conduct other than state activity. This kind of definition is rather non-technical and, therefore, difficult to apply. But it seems nevertheless to constitute the basis of almost all other attempted distinctions of the two great branches of the law.

(b) The distinction just stated is often intertwined with another one.

[1] W.u.G. Part II, Chap. VII (Sociology of Law) 387–395.

[2] Weber refers here to Continental, and especially German, legal theory, where the distinction between public law and private law is given particular emphasis. The distinction was familiar to the Roman jurists and well known especially is Ulpian's definition (DIGEST 1.1.4.) of public law as that which "is concerned with the Roman state" (*quod ad statum rei Romanae spectat*) and of private law as that which "is concerned with the interest of individuals" (*quod ad singulorum utilitatem pertinet*). The distinction has been of practical significance where a government, although being prepared to guarantee a firm legal order with regard to the private relations among the citizens themselves, yet remained unwilling to fix those relations between them in hard and fast rules. This situation was typical of the late Roman Empire as well as of the absolute monarchies of the modern age. To the degree to which the organs of the state became subject to rules of law, the distinction between public and private law lost importance, ultimately to become no more than a convenient classification of certain legal rules, especially for the purposes of legal writing and education.

[3] *Staatsanstaltsbezogenes Handeln.*

Public law might be regarded as identical with the total body of the "reglementations," i.e., those norms which only embody instructions to state officials as regards their duties, but, in contradistinction to what may be called "claim norms," do not establish any "rights" of individuals. This distinction, however, must be correctly understood. For the norms of public law can establish rights of individuals, for instance, the right to vote as established in a law on presidential elections. Such a law nonetheless falls within the domain of public law.

But today such a "public right" belonging to an individual is not regarded as a vested right in the same sense as a property right, which the legislator himself views as in principle inviolable. From a legal point of view, the public rights of individuals are but those spheres of activity in which he acts as an agent of the state for specifically delimited purposes. Thus, in spite of the fact that they formally appear as rights, they may still be regarded as but another aspect, a "reflex," of a "reglementation" rather than as the result of a "claim-norm." Furthermore, by no means all claims which exist in a legal system and which belong to private law, as previously defined, are vested rights.[4]

Indeed, even those incidents of ownership which are fully recognized at any given time, may be looked upon as being but reflexes of the legal order. As a matter of fact, the question as to whether a given right is "vested" means frequently no more than whether or not it is liable to expropriation without compensation. Thus one might assert that all public law is in the legal sense no more than a body of reglementations, without asserting that reglementations belong exclusively to the sphere of public law. But not even such a definition would be correct. For in some legal systems the governmental power itself may be regarded as a vested property right belonging to the monarch, and in some others certain constitutional rights belonging to the citizen may be regarded as inalienable and, therefore, as vested rights.[5]

(c) Finally, private law might be contrasted with public law as the law of coördination as distinguished from that of subordination. Private law would then be concerned with those legal affairs in which several parties are confronting each other so that the law treats them as being coördinated and that their legal spheres are to be "properly" defined against each other by the legislature, the judiciary or, by means of legal transactions, by the parties themselves. In the domain of public law, however, a holder of preëminent power, having authoritative power of command, is confronting those persons who are his subjects by virtue

[4] Cf. *infra* pp. 98 *et seq.*

[5] The reference is to the patrimonial state, as to which see *infra* n. 6.

of the legal meaning of the norms. Yet not every functionary of the state has authority to command and not all those activities of the organs of the state which are regulated by public law are commands. Furthermore, the regulation of the relations among the various public organs, i.e., among power holders of equal status, belongs to the proper sphere of "public law." Besides, one must include within the field of public law not only the relations between the organs of the state and those subject to them but also those activities of the subjects by which they create and control those organs. Once this is admitted, the definition here discussed leads us back to the one previously presented, i.e., the definition that does not regard as falling within the field of public law every regulation of the power to exercise authority or of the relations between those who exercise authority and those who are subject to it. For example, an employer's exercise of power would obviously be excluded because it originates in a contract between parties of equal legal status. Again, the authority of the head of a family will be regarded as falling within the sphere of private law — for no other reason than the fact that public law is only concerned with those activities within a given legal system which are directed toward the maintenance of the state as well as toward the realization of those objectives of the state which are its prime concern. Of course, the question as to what these particular objectives should be is answered in varying ways even today. Lastly, certain public activities may be intentionally regulated in such a way that, with respect to the same subject matter, rights vested in individuals and powers conferred upon state agencies coexist and compete with each other.

As we have seen, the delimitation of the spheres of public and private law is even today not entirely free from difficulty. It was even less clear in the past, and there was once a situation in which such a distinction was not made at all. Such was the case when all law, all jurisdictions, and particularly all powers of exercising authority were personal privileges, such as, especially, the "prerogatives" of the head of the state. In that case the authority to judge, or to call a person into military service, or to require obedience in some other respect was a vested right in exactly the same way as the authority to use a piece of land; and just like the latter, it could constitute the subject matter of a conveyance or of inheritance. Under this system of "patrimonialism,"[6] political authority was not organized in an institutionalized pattern, but was represented by the concrete consociation of individual power-holders, or per-

[6] On patrimonialism, see W.u.G. 679; Parsons' tr. 62, 346.

sons claiming powers, and by the concrete arrangements made between them. It was a kind of political authority which was not essentially different from that of the head of a household, or a landlord, or a master of serfs. Such a state of affairs has never existed as a complete system, but, in so far as it did exist, everything which we legally characterize as falling within the sphere of "public law" constituted the subject matter of the private rights of individual power-holders and was in this respect in no way different from a "right" in private law.

2. *Right-granting Law and Reglementation.* A legal system may also assume a character exactly opposite to the one just described, that is to say, "private law," of the kind defined above, may be completely absent in wide areas of social life which would today fall within its sphere. This occurs where there exist no norms having the character of right-granting laws. In such a situation, the entire body of norms consists exclusively of "regulations." In other words, all private interests enjoy protection, not as guaranteed rights, but only as the obverse aspect of the effectiveness of these regulations. This situation, too, has never prevailed anywhere in its pure form, but in so far as it obtains, all forms of law become absorbed within "administration" and become part and parcel of "government." [7]

3. *"Government"* [8] *and "Administration."* "Administration" is not a concept of public law exclusively. For we must recognize the existence of private administration, as in the case of a household or a business enterprise, alongside the kind of administration carried on either by the state or by other public institutions (i.e., either institutional organs of the state itself, or heteronomous institutions deriving their powers from the state, or recognized coercive agencies established by the state for particular purposes. These latter agencies are heteronomous public coercive organizations).[9]

[7] This description of the "ideal type" of the totalitarian state was written before it emerged in its modern form.

[8] Weber's term "government" has been retained here, although the term "executive" might better correspond to American parlance.

[9] Weber calls the state as well as public bodies within the state *Zwangsorganisationen*, here rendered by the expression "coercive agency or organization." The point about these coercive organizations is that they have not only certain delegated powers of legislation but also that membership in the bodies or organizations is not a matter of choice but of compulsion. The most common examples are: municipal corporations, school and sanitary districts, "established" churches, and certain professional guilds or associations, such as an "integrated" bar association.

In its widest sense, the expression "public administration" includes not only legislation and adjudication but also those other residuary activities which we usually call "government." "Government" can be bound by legal norms and limited by vested rights. In these respects it resembles legislation and adjudication. But there are two aspects to be distinguished. First, and in a positive sense, government must have a legitimate basis for its own jurisdiction; a modern government exercises its functions as a "legitimate" jurisdiction, which means legally that it is regarded as resting on authorization by the constitutional norms of the state. Secondly, and in a negative sense, the limitations on the power of the state by law and vested rights create those restraints upon its freedom of action to which it must adjust itself. One specific characteristic of government, however, resides in the fact that it aims not only at acknowledging and enforcing the law simply because the law exists and constitutes the basis of vested rights, but also in that it pursues other concrete objectives of a political, ethical, utilitarian, or some other kind. To the government, the individual and his interests are in the legal sense objects rather than bearers of rights.

In the modern state, it is true, there exists a trend formally to assimilate adjudication to "administration" (in the sense of "government"). A judge is frequently instructed, either by the positive law or by legal theory, to render his decision on the basis of ethics, equity, or expediency. In the administrative field, on the other hand, the modern state has provided for the citizen, to whom, on principle, its activities are directed, a possibility of protecting his interests by granting remedies which are formally identical with those existing in the field of the administration of justice, namely, the right to resort to administrative tribunals.[10] But none of these guaranties can eliminate the basic contradiction between adjudication and "government." Law creation, too, is approximated by government wherever government promulgates general rules dealing with typical situations rather than merely intervening in specific cases — and, to a certain extent, even when it does not feel bound by them. After all, observance by the government of the rules is regarded

[10] An Anglo-American lawyer would regard this right as an ordinary instance of the "right" of access to the courts. But as a continental lawyer, Weber thinks of the protection of this right as that entrusted to the specially established administrative tribunals of either the French or the German type. This kind of protection of the citizen against abuses of governmental powers is organized on lines different from those known in the countries of the Common Law, but it should not be regarded as less effective. *Cf.* E. Freund, *Administrative Law*, 1 Encyc. Soc. Sci. (1930) 452, and Garner, *Anglo-American and Continental European Administrative Law* (1929), 7 N.Y.U.L.Q. Rev. 387.

as the normal thing and a total disregard of them would ordinarily be disapproved as "arbitrary" conduct.

The primeval form of "administration" is represented by patriarchal power, i.e., the rule of the household. In its primitive form, the authority of the master of the household is unlimited. Those subordinated to his power have no rights as against him, and norms regulating his behavior toward them exist only as indirect effects of heteronomous religious checks on his conduct. Originally, we are confronted with the coexistence of the theoretically unrestrained administrative power of the master of the household within the domestic group, on the one side and, on the other, arbitration proceedings, originating in arrangements made between kinship groups and relating to the proof and composition of alleged injury. Only in the latter are "claims," i.e., rights, at issue and are verdicts rendered; and only in relations between kinship groups do we find established formalities, limitations as to time, rules of evidence, etc., that is, the beginnings of "judicial" procedure. None of these exist within the sphere of patriarchal power, which represents the primitive form of "government," in the same way as the inter-group arrangements represent the primitive form of adjudication. The two are distinct from one another also with regard to the spheres in which they operate. Even such a relatively late phenomenon as the ancient Roman administration of justice stopped at the threshold of the household.[11] We shall later see how domestic authority came to be diffused beyond its original sphere and was carried over into certain forms of political power, viz., patrimonial monarchy, thereby also entering into the administration of justice.

Whenever this happened, the distinctions between legislation, adjudication, and government were broken down. The consequences have been one or the other of the following:

In the first place, adjudication assumed the character of "administration," both formally and materially, and was operated simply through decrees or commands issued by the lord to his subjects according to considerations of mere expediency or equity, and without fixed forms and at arbitrary times. This situation, however, never obtained with full force except in borderline cases; but approximations to it have occurred in "inquisitorial" procedures as well as in all those systems of procedure in which the conduct of trial and proof is dominated by the judge.[12]

[11] M. Kaser, *Zur altrömischen Hausgewalt* (1950), 67 SAV. Z. RÖM. 474.

[12] German, and generally continental, theory of procedure distinguishes between two types of trial: (1) the trial according to the *Offizialmaxime*, and (2) the trial

The other, rather different, possible consequence of the diffusion of the pattern of domestic authority into extra-household spheres consists in "administration" assuming the form of judicial procedure, as happened to a large extent, and in some sense still happens today, to be the case in England. Parliament deals with "private bills," i.e., with such purely administrative acts as licensing, etc., in exactly the same way that it treats public bills. The failure to distinguish between the two types of legislation has been a general feature of older parliamentary procedure; for the English Parliament it was, indeed, a decisive factor in the establishment of its position.[13] Parliament arose originally as a judicial body, and, in France, it became such to the exclusion of all other activities. This confusion between legislative and judicial functions was conditioned by political circumstances. The budget, which is a purely administrative matter,[14] is also treated as a legislative act, in adherence to a pattern established in England as well as for political reasons.

---

according to the *Verhandlungsmaxime*. Under (1), the trial is dominated by the presiding judge whose function it is to ascertain what has really happened and who is, therefore, alone or primarily entitled to call and examine the witnesses and to require such proof as he thinks necessary. Under (2), the judge only assumes the role of umpire in a trial mainly conducted by the parties; each party decides upon the witnesses he wishes to call, the questions he wishes to ask in examination and cross-examination, and the kind of evidence he wishes to submit. Actually, neither type of trial has in practice ever existed in a pure form. Continental procedure, both civil and criminal, follows today mainly the *Verhandlungsmaxime*, although the latter is modified, especially in criminal procedure, by certain concessions to the *Offizialmaxime*. Cf. ENGELMANN AND MILLAR, 11; Millar, *Formative Principles of Civil Procedure* (1923) 18 ILL. L. REV. 1, 94, 150; and his article on Procedure in 12 ENCYC. SOC. SCI. 439 (with list of further literature). Concerning modern continental procedure see also SCHLESINGER, COMPARATIVE LAW (1950) 197, 510, 523; and Hamson, *Civil Procedure in France and England* (1950), 10 CAMB. L.J. 411.

[13] Cf. JELLINEK, SYSTEM 3; R. GNEIST, HISTORY OF THE ENGLISH CONSTITUTION (Ashworth's tr. 1891) 338; HATSCHEK, 503; J. E. A. JOLIFFE, CONSTITUTIONAL HISTORY OF MEDIAEVAL ENGLAND (1937) 337; also ANSON, LAW AND CUSTOM AND THE CONSTITUTION (1892) 262; on the present practice, see WADE AND PHILLIPS, CONSTITUTIONAL LAW (1950) 111.

[14] Weber's classification of private bills and the budget as "purely administrative matters" derives from German legal and constitutional theory, which distinguishes between laws in the *formal* and the *substantive* sense. A law in the substantive sense means an enactment authorizing interference by the state with the life, liberty, or property of the citizens. A law in the formal sense is simply an act issuing from the legislature, irrespective of its contents. One of the postulates of the "rule of law" as understood on the Continent is that the state is not allowed to interfere with life, liberty, or property without the consent of the people or their duly elected representatives. Hence, any law in the substantive sense must be, or at least have its basis in, an act of the legislature, i.e., a law in the formal sense. It is this political

The distinction between "administration" and "private law" becomes fluid where the official actions of the organs of official bodies assume the same form as agreements between individuals. This is the case when officials in the course of their official duties make contractual arrangements for exchange of goods or services either with members of the organization or with other individuals. Frequently such relationships are withdrawn from the norms of private law, are arranged in some way different from the general legal norms as to substance or as to the mode of enforcement, and are thus declared to belong to the sphere of "administration." [15] As long as claims treated in this way are guaranteed by some

---

theory of the rule of law which constitutes the basis of the principle so firmly held in the continental countries, which requires that all law be expressed in a code or statute, and which thus excludes the recognition as legitimate of any "common law" which would not be based on statute but solely on judicial precedent. The notion that law could be made or applied by courts without approval of the legislature expressly given in a statute, so that there could be a government by the judiciary rather than by the people's duly elected representatives, appears repugnant to the traditional continental notions of the rule of law and democracy.

On the other hand, measures which do not constitute public interference with the life, liberty, or property of the subjects are classified as "administrative acts" which generally do not require for their validity a law in the formal sense. But modern constitutional law often requires that even an "administrative act" be embodied in a formal law, that is, be properly passed by the legislature. As regards the budget, it is, in theoretical analysis, only a program of public revenue and expenditure, and thus an administrative act. This analysis does not, of course, apply to the tax and customs provisions which constitute interferences with property. But even for the budget as such, positive constitutional law requires that it be embodied in an act of the legislature. The budget, therefore, albeit an administrative act, constitutes also a law in the formal sense. Cf. JELLINEK, SYSTEM 226; also KELSEN 123, 131; JELLINEK, VERWALTUNGSRECHT (1949) 8, 385; FLEINER, INSTITUTIONEN DES DEUTSCHEN VERWALTUNGSRECHTS (1922) 17; LABAND, DEUTSCHES REICHSSTAATSRECHT (1912) 130.

[15] Cf. the special rules applying in this country to government contracts and the enforcement of contractual claims against the government. The special status of government contracts is even more pronounced in France, where they are subject to a body of special rules to a large extent judicially elaborated, not by the ordinary courts, but by the Council of State and the administrative tribunals subordinate to it. Cf. GOODNOW, COMPARATIVE ADMINISTRATIVE LAW (1893) I, 86, 107; II, 217; WALINE, LA NOTION JUDICIAIRE DE L'EXCÈS DU POUVOIR (1926) 7–10, 76 *et seq.*; F. A. OGG, EUROPEAN GOVERNMENTS AND POLITICS (2nd ed. 1943) 572, 768. On the other hand, under the fisc theory, which prevails in Germany and the other countries following the German system, government contracts are treated like contracts concluded between private parties and are subject to the jurisdiction of the ordinary courts. The same treatment applies to torts committed by public officials in the course of their official duties. Cf. E. Borchard, *State Liability*, 14 ENCYC. SOC. SCI. 338, with bibliography; also 2 GOODNOW, *op. cit.* 240, 258–261; as to

possibility of enforcement, they do not cease to be "rights," and the distinction is no more than a technical one. However, even as such, the distinction may be of considerable practical significance. Nonetheless, the total structure of ancient Roman private law is completely misunderstood if one regards as belonging to its sphere only those claims which were enforced in a regular jury trial and on the basis of a *lex*, and excludes from it all those rights which were enforced solely through the magistrate's "cognitio" and which, at times, were of preponderant economic significance.[16]

4. *Criminal Law and Private Law.* The authority of magi and prophets [17] and, under certain conditions, the powers of the priesthood, can, to the extent that they have their source in concrete revelation, be as unrestrained by rights and norms as the primitive power of the master of a household. Belief in magic is also one of the original sources of criminal law, as distinguished from "private law." [18] The modern view

---

government contracts in England, see Wade and Phillips, *op. cit. supra* n. 13 at p. 309.

[16] Following Gaius IV. 103, 105, it has become customary to distinguish between *iudicium legitimum* and the *iudicia quae imperio continentur.* The former is the regular civil procedure in which the issue is defined before the praetor, formally stated in the *formula*, and then tried before and decided by the lay judge (*iudex*). The latter term covers a variety of special proceedings in which, as a common feature, the issue is not only formulated by the magistrate but also tried before and decided by him or, under his authority, by a substitute (*subrogatus*, surrogate). One of these procedures was the so-called bureaucratic *cognitio*, which applied to the litigation concerning the lands owned by the state as *ager publicus*. This procedure differed from the ordinary civil procedure not only through the absence of a *iudex*, but also through the fact that judgment could be rendered not only for money damages but also for specific performance. As Weber indicates, its significance has been commonly neglected in the literature on Roman law. For further information on the legal aspects of the bureaucratic *cognitio*, see Wenger, 28, 62 *et seq.*, 239, 250, 255 *et seq.*; as to its significance in connection with the *ager publicus*, see Weber, 167 *et seq.*; *cf.* also Mommsen, 290.

[17] For further discussion of the role of law prophets see *infra* p. 86.

[18] On the role of magic in legal development, see G. Gurvitch, *Magic and Law* (1942), 9 Social Research 104, and same, Essais de sociologie (1939) 204. For a general account of the role of magic in primitive societies as regards the criminal law and the peculiar nature of private or civil law, see Malinowski, Crime and Custom in Savage Society (1926) 50–59, 67–68, 98–99, 119–121. See also Hogbin, Law and Order in Polynesia (1934) and Malinowski's introduction thereto, especially pp. xvii–lxxii; Lowie, Primitive Religion (1925); Tylor, Primitive Culture (6th ed. 1920); Radcliffe-Brown, The Andaman Islanders (1922); Westermarck, Ritual and Belief in Morocco (1926). Usually regarded as the basic

of criminal justice, broadly, is that public concern with morality or expediency decrees expiation for the violation of a norm; this concern finds expression in the infliction of punishment upon the evil doer by agents of the state, the evil doer, however, enjoying the protection of a regular procedure. The redress of the violation of private rights, on the other hand, is left to the injured party, and action by the latter leads not to punishment, but to the restoration of a situation which the law has guaranteed. But even today this distinction is not always applied in clear-cut fashion. It was certainly unknown in primitive administration of justice. Even in the late stages of otherwise complex legal developments, every action was simply looked upon as sounding in tort and the notions of "contract" and *obligatio* were completely unknown.[19] Indeed, Chinese law still manifests some traces of this situation,[20] which in the history of civilization has been of such great importance in legal development. Every infringement by an outsider upon a member of a kinship group or his property calls for either revenge [21] or composition, the pursuit of which is left to the injured party, supported by his kin.

---

work is SIR JAMES FRAZER, THE GOLDEN BOUGH, vols. I and II; THE MAGIC ART (3rd ed. 1911, abridged ed. 1925). For a short introduction to the problem, see ROBSON, CIVILISATION AND THE GROWTH OF LAW (1935) 74 *et seq.*

[19] See on all this in general: ENGELMANN AND MILLAR, 118, 129, 211, 652; R. DE LA GRASSERIE, THE EVOLUTION OF CIVIL LAW (1918) 609; DIAMOND 301, 307; LOWIE, PRIMITIVE SOCIETY (1920) 397, 425. See also as regards:

(a) Roman law: NOYES 201–207; A. HÄGERSTRÖM, DER RÖMISCHE OBLIGATIONSBEGRIFF (1927) 600; KASER 308–316, 322–336.
(b) Greek law: P. Vinogradoff, *Greek Law*, in COLLECTED PAPERS vol. 2 (JURISPRUDENCE, 1928) 43, 44.
(c) Oriental law: Articles "law" in 9 ENCYC. SOC. SCI. (1933) and literature there cited, especially the articles by Seidl on Egyptian Law, p. 209; Koschaker on Cuneiform Law, p. 211; and Gulak on Jewish Law, p. 219.
(d) Slavic law: L. J. STRACHOVSKY, A HANDBOOK OF SLAVIC STUDIES (1949); R. DARESTE, ETUDES D'HISTOIRE DU DROIT (1889) 158–222 (L'ANCIEN DROIT SLAVE).
(e) Germanic law: AMIRA 280–282; 2 BRUNNER, RECHTSGESCHICHTE 328.

In English law the distinction between tort and contract developed at a rather late stage. Cf. MAITLAND, FORMS 8, 48, 53 *et seq.*; HOLDSWORTH, II, 43 *et seq.*, III, 375 *et seq.*, 412 *et seq.*; PLUCKNETT.

[20] The reference is to Chinese law as it existed before the reforms following the revolution of 1912; see J. H. WIGMORE, WORLD'S LEGAL SYSTEMS (1928) 141; W. S. H. HUNG, OUTLINES OF MODERN CHINESE LAW (1934) 5, 249; ALABASTER.

[21] The German text contains an obvious typographical error; instead of *Recht* it should read *Rache* ("revenge").

The procedure for obtaining composition either shows no trace at all or at most the mere beginnings of the distinction between felony that calls for vengeance, and tort that merely requires restitution. Furthermore, the absence of a distinction between actions for what we call "civil" redress and criminal prosecution aiming at punishment, and the designation of both these phenomena by the single expression of satisfaction for wrong suffered, is connected with two peculiarities of primitive law and procedure. There is a complete unconcern with a notion of guilt, and, consequently, with any degrees of guilt, reflecting the inner motivations and psychological attitudes. He who thirsts for vengeance is not interested in motives; he is concerned only with the objective happening of the event by which his desire for vengeance has been aroused. His anger expresses itself equally against inanimate objects, by which he has been unexpectedly hurt, against animals by which he has been unexpectedly injured, and against human beings who have harmed him unknowingly, negligently, or intentionally. This, for example, was the original sense of the Roman *actio de pauperie*, i.e., that an animal had behaved in a way other than it should have, as well as of the *noxae datio*, i.e., the surrender of the animal for vengeance.[22] Every wrong is, therefore, a "tort" that requires expiation, and no tort is more than a wrong that requires expiation.

The primitive indistinctiveness of crime and tort also found expression in the ways in which "judgments" were "enforced." Procedure did not vary, whether the suit was about a piece of land or about homicide. But even when that stage was reached when fairly well-established compositions began to be imposed, there was still a lack of "official" machinery for the enforcement of these judgments. It was rather believed that a judgment which had been arrived at by the interpretation of oracles or other magical devices, or the invocation of magical or divine powers, carried with it sufficient magical authority to enforce itself, so that disobedience constituted a kind of serious blasphemy. Where, as a result of certain developments connected with military organization (to be dealt with shortly),[23] the trial took place before an assembly of the whole community, with all members participating in the making of the judgment (as was the case, for instance, in early Germanic recorded history), it might be expected that as a consequence of such

[22] On the *actio de pauperie* and *noxae datio* see SOHM 280, 331 (*actio de pauperie*); and 191, 194, 280, 331 (*noxae datio*); WENGER 153, where further literature is cited.

[23] See *infra* pp. 91 *et. seq.*

coöperation in the rendering of a judgment, none of its members would obstruct its enforcement, provided it had not been publicly challenged in the assembly. Nevertheless, the victorious litigant could not depend on anything more than mere passivity on the part of those outside of his own kinship group. It was entirely incumbent upon him, by way of self-help, to enforce the judgment with the assistance of his kinfolk unless, of course, the unsuccessful party obeyed the judgment. Both in Rome and among the Germanic tribes, this self-help usually consisted in the capture of the condemned to remain as hostage for the payment of the composition, the amount of which was either fixed by the judgment itself or was to be agreed on by the litigants themselves. Nor did this self-help vary for different types of litigation: self-help was resorted to whether the suit had been about a piece of land or whether it had been about homicide. An official machinery for the enforcement of judgments did not become available until princes or magistrates saw the necessity, for political reasons and in the interest of public order, to use their *imperium* against persons interfering with the enforcement of a judgment and to threaten such persons with legal sanctions, especially outlawry.[24] All this, however, took place without any distinction between civil and criminal proceedings. In those legal systems in which under the influence of certain legal *honoratiores*[25] there remained some continuity with the

[24] As to Rome, see WENGER 8 *et seq.*; as to Germanic law, see HUEBNER, 427, 477, 478. Cf. also the source materials collected in STONE AND SIMPSON, LAW AND SOCIETY (1948) 132 *et seq.*, 284 *et seq.*

[25] *Honoratiores* (Lat. "those of higher honor"). In German the word *Honoratioren* is used, often with a slight implication of friendly ridicule, to mean the more respectable citizens of a town. Weber uses the word as a term of art, which he defines as applying to persons having the following characteristics: "(1) By virtue of their economic situation they are able on a continuous basis to occupy positions of leadership or authority in a corporate group without remuneration or with a remuneration which is merely nominal; and (2) they occupy a position of social prestige, which may rest on any one of many different grounds and which is such that in a formally democratic process they are likely to enjoy the confidence of their fellow members, so that they will hold office first upon the basis of free choice, and then by tradition." (W.u.G., 170) This definition is closely connected with the characterization of the peculiar situation which exists when authority is exercised by such *honoratiores* as compared with other types of authority (THEORY, Parsons' tr. 413; see also W.u.G. 609, 674, 681, 719). As defined in this way, Parsons is justified in translating *honoratiores* by "amateurs." However, Weber does not consistently adhere to his own definition. In the present context Weber means by "legal *honoratiores*" (*Rechtshonoratioren*), those classes of persons who have (1) in some way made the occupation with legal problems a kind of specialized expert knowledge, and (2) enjoy among their group such a prestige that they are able to impress some peculiar characteristics upon the legal system of their respective

ancient forms of expiatory justice, and in which there was a lesser degree of "bureaucratization," i.e., those of Rome and England, this original state of complete nondifferentiation continued to show itself in the rejection of specific performance for the restoration of concrete objects. Even in an action concerning title to land, the judgment was ordinarily rendered in terms of money.[26] This was not due at all to a highly developed market economy which would evaluate everything in terms of money. Rather was it a consequence of the primitive principle that every wrong, including the wrongful possession of property, demanded satisfaction and nothing but satisfaction, and that this liability attached to the culprit's own person. On the Continent, specific performance emerged relatively early in the early Middle Ages, owing to the rapidly growing power of the *imperium* of the princes.[27] English procedure, on the other hand, even down to recent times, had to resort to peculiar fictions in order to introduce the possibility of specific performance in actions concerning real property.[28] In Rome the persistence of condemnation to money damages instead of specific performance was the result of the general tendency to keep official activities to a minimum, which, in turn, was due to the system of rule by *honoratiores*.

5. *Tort and Crime*. Substantive law too was deeply influenced by the notion that litigation implied a wrong committed by the accused and not just the existence of a state of affairs objectively regarded as unlawful. Originally, all "obligations" were, without exception, obligations *ex delicto*; hence, contractual obligations were, as we shall see,[29] at first conceived as arising out of tort. In England, as late as the Middle Ages, a contractual action was formally connected with a fictitious tort.[30]

---

societies. The context makes it clear, however, that persons of this kind can be *honoratiores* even though they receive a more than nominal remuneration for their activities. As to the role of legal *honoratiores* in general, see *infra* p. 198 *et seq.*

[26] As to the Roman rule that *omnis condemnatio est pecuniaria*, see WENGER 143 *et seq.*

[27] Cf. ENGELMANN AND MILLAR 166–168; also, M. Esmein, *L'origine et la logique de la jurisprudence en matière d'astreintes* (1903), 2 REVUE TRIMESTRIELLE DE DROIT CIVIL 5.

[28] Here Weber seems to be mistaken. What he may have had in mind are the fictions resorted to in the action of ejectment; cf. MAITLAND, FORMS. For the doctrine of specific performance in English law, see MAITLAND, EQUITY (1936) 301–317; H. HAZELTINE, *Early History of Specific Performance of Contract in English Law* (FESTGABE FÜR KOHLER, 1913) 68–69.

[29] *Infra*, p. 110.

[30] This statement is too broad. It applies to the action of assumpsit, but not to the actions of covenant, debt, and detinue.

The abatement of the debts upon the death of the debtor was as much because of this concept as of the absence of any notion of a "law of succession."[31] The heirs' liability for contractual debts was, as we shall see,[32] developed with varying results by means of the joint liability for wrongful acts, first of the kindred and later of the fellow members of the household or of the participants in a power relation as either subordinates or superiors. Even the principle of protection of bona fide purchasers, a principle allegedly indispensable for modern commerce,[33] has its origin in the ancient idea that no lawsuit could be anything but one *ex delicto* against a thief or his accessory. Only later, in consequence of the development of actions *ex contractu* and the distinction between "real" and "personal" actions, did the old rule undergo divergent developments in different legal systems. Thus its place came to be occupied by the owner's action against every possessor (*rei vindicatio*) [34] in ancient Roman [35] and in English law [36] as well as in Hindu law,[37] which, in contrast to Chinese law, was relatively highly rationalized. Still later the protection of the bona fide purchaser was revived again in the case of purchasers in market overt in English [38] and Hindu law [39] on the rational

[31] See Goudy, *Two Ancient Brocards*, in P. VINOGRADOFF, ESSAYS OF LEGAL HISTORY (1913) 216–227; HOLDSWORTH, III, 576 *et seq.*

[32] Cf. *infra*, p. 154.

[33] Weber cites here the ancient German maxim of *Hand muss Hand wahren* ("hand must warrant hand"). It means that where a bailee has transferred the chattel to a third party, the bailor has an action only against the bailee. See HUEBNER, 407, 421, 448; 2 BRUNNER, RECHTSGESCHICHTE 512; (1928), 668; HOLMES, COMMON LAW (1951), 164; 2 POLLOCK AND MAITLAND (1899) 155. As to the alleged indispensability for modern business of the protection of bona fide purchasers far beyond the modest scope of protection existing in American law, see 3 MOTIVE ZU DEM ENTWURFE EINES BUERGERLICHEN GESETZBUCHES FUER DAS DEUTSCHE REICH (1888) 344.

[34] The action which Weber means here is, as indicated by his reference to the *rei vindicatio*, that action which has been developed in all more elaborate systems and which is now constituted in American law by the action of replevin. It is the remedy by which the owner as such, and without reference to any contract or tort, can obtain restitution of a chattel to which he has the title, but which he finds in the hands of another person to whom he has not given a special permission or right to hold or to use it.

[35] As to the Roman *rei vindicatio*, see WENGER 127; SOHM 189, 248, 269; BUCKLAND, MANUAL 139–142; JOLOWICZ 142–144; cf. *infra* p. 111.

[36] Cf. MAITLAND, FORMS, 22 *et seq.*; POLLOCK AND MAITLAND, 107, 137, 146–148, 166; HOLDSWORTH, III, 318 *et seq.*

[37] Cf. Jolly, *Recht und Sitte*, in BÜHLERS, GRUNDRISS DER INDO-ARISCHEN PHILOLOGIE (1896) 8.

[38] On the history of market overt in English law see HOLDSWORTH V, 98, 105, 110–111.

[39] See 1 MILL AND WILSON, HISTORY OF BRITISH INDIA (1858) 160.

grounds of providing security for business dealings. The absence of general protection of bona fide purchasers in English and Roman law, as contrasted with German law, is yet another instance of the adaptability of commercial interest to the most diverse systems of substantive law. It illustrates, moreover, the high degree of independence which characterizes the development of law. Perhaps another example of this delictual conception of legal obligation can be found in the expression *malo ordine tenes*[40] that occurs in the Frankish action for the restitution of land, although the correct interpretation of these words is a debatable matter.

It is quite possible, however, that entirely different ideas may have been at work in such legal institutions as the bilateral Roman *vindicatio*,[41] the Hellenic *diadikasia*,[42] or the Germanic actions for land.[43] In all these cases one may conclude that they were originally regarded as *actiones de recursu*, i.e., actions tending to ascertain a person's full membership in a certain community as based upon his title to a certain piece of land.[44] After all, *fenites*[45] means "comrades," and *Kleros*[46] means "comrade's share." Again, originally, the regular *ex officio* prosecution for a delict was as nonexistent as the official enforcement of a judgment. Within the household, chastisement derived from the patriarch's authority over his household. Disputes among members of a kinship group were settled by the elders. However, in all these situations, the decision whether punishment was to be meted out or not, and, if it was, in what form and to what degree, was an entirely discretionary matter, for

[40] Lat. — literally: "You are holding by bad order," i.e., "unlawfully."

[41] See *supra* n. 34.

[42] *Diadikasia* is a dispute between two claimants aiming at a judicial declaration as to who is "really" the holder of the title. It is thus not an action for damages brought by an alleged title holder against an alleged wrongdoer. Cf. MEIER UND SCHOEMANN, DER ATTISCHE PROCESS (1824) 367; 2 BONNER AND SMITH 79, 101.

[43] These, as Weber adds, "are of a totally different structure." As to these actions, see AMIRA 192–199, 266; GIERKE, GENOSSENSCHAFTSRECHT II, 268–325; R. Sohm, *Fränkisches Recht und römisches Recht* (1880), 1 SAV. Z. GERM. 27.

[44] See also WEBER'S GENERAL ECONOMIC HISTORY (1950), c. I. [WIRTSCHAFTSGESCHICHTE (1923) 17, 19] and literature there cited.

[45] The reference could not be ascertained; possibly it is to Celtic, especially Irish, law. The word *Fenites* may derive from the old Irish name *Feni* which means the landowning class, but by etymology means the military caste; see MacNeill, *Celtic Law*, 9 ENCYC. SOC. SCI. 246; and by the same author, *Early Irish Laws and Institutions* (1930), 7 N.Y.U.L.Q. REV. 849–853; cf. also the present Gaelic word *Fein* as in "Fennian Brotherhood" or "Sinn Fein Party."

[46] *Kleros* (Greek) is that which is assigned by lot, i.e., an allotment of land; cf. LIDDEL AND SCOTT, GREEK-ENGLISH LEXICON (1925); 2 VINOGRADOFF 6, 52, 61, 202, 210, 253.

"criminal law" was nonexistent. A primitive form of criminal law did develop outside the boundaries of the household, particularly in situations in which the conduct of an individual endangered *all* the members of his neighborhood, kinship, or political association. Such situations could be brought about by two types of misconduct: religious blasphemy or military disobedience. The whole group was endangered when a magical norm, e.g., a taboo, was infringed and, in consequence, the wrath of magical forces, spirits or deities, threatened to descend with evil consequences not merely upon the blasphemer (or criminal) himself but upon the whole community which suffered him to exist within their midst. Stimulated by magi or priests, the members of the community would outlaw the culprit or lynch him, as for instance through stoning among the Jews. Or else they might conduct an expiatory religious trial. Blasphemous acts were thus the main source of what may be called "intra-group punishment" as distinguished from "inter-group vengeance." The second source for such punishment was political or, originally, military. Anyone endangering by treachery or cowardice the security of the collective fighting forces or, after some code of military discipline became established, by disobedience, had to reckon with the punitive reactions of the war lord or the army.[47] And although, of course, a person's military misbehavior had first to be established as a fact, the procedure for the finding of this fact was very summary indeed.

6. *Imperium.* From the predominance of vengeance to the formation of a firmly fixed and formalized criminal procedure a direct line of development can be traced. As we have seen, the punitive reactions of the master of a domestic group, or of the religious or military authorities, were in general free from procedural formality or rule. It is true that the punitive powers of the master of a household became to some extent restricted by the intervention of the elders of his own group or the religious or military authorities in charge of certain intra-group relations, but by and large the master remained a law unto himself within his sphere and he was bound by legal rules only in very special cases.

A slow, and in its result varying, subjection to rules occurred, however, as to the primitive nondomestic powers, i.e. the householdlike power exercised by patrimonial monarchy in relations quite different from those of a household, or, in other words, as to those powers which are contained in the concept of *imperium*. We shall not discuss here the

[47] For the military punishment imposed by the Roman *comitia centuriata* see MAINE 374–382; LOWIE, ORIGIN OF THE STATE (1927) 102–108; and the same author's PRIMITIVE SOCIETY (1920) 385, 394–396.

origins of the process by which definite rules became established. Nor shall we discuss, at any rate at present, whether the holder of *imperium* imposed them on himself in his own interest, or whether he had to do so in view of the factual limits within which he would find obedience, or whether they were imposed upon him by other powers. All these questions will be dealt with in our analysis of domination.[48] *Imperium* has always included, however — and in the past to an even greater extent than today — the power to punish and, in particular, the power to crush disobedience not merely through the direct application of force but through the threat of detriment as well. The power to punish could be directed against certain subordinate "officials" who exercised *imperium* or against those who were subjected to its power. In the former case, we speak of *disciplinary power*, and in the latter, of the *power to inflict punishment*. In this context, "public law" is directly connected with criminal law; and we can state, at any rate, that both criminal law and criminal procedure do not begin to be systematically treated unless there are at least some rules which are recognized as factually binding.

7. *Limitation of Power and Separation of Powers.* Such norms as those just mentioned always act as restraints upon the imperium within the sphere in which they obtain. On the other hand, not every restraint possesses "normative" character. Now there are two kinds of restraints, viz., (1) limitations of power, and (2) separation of powers. Limitation of power exists where, due to sacred tradition or enactment, a particular *imperium* is restrained by the rights of its subjects. The power-holder may issue only commands of a certain type, or he may issue all sorts of commands except in certain cases or subject to certain conditions. Whether these limitations possess "legal," "conventional," or merely "customary" status, is to be answered in each case by ascertaining whether the maintenance of the limitations is guaranteed by a coercive organization (whose coercive means may be more or less effective) or whether they are maintained only by conventional disapproval or whether in the last analysis there is no *agreed* limitation at all. The other kind of restraint ("separation of powers") exists where one *imperium* conflicts with another *imperium*, either equal or in certain respects superior to it, but the legitimate validity of which is fully recognized as limiting the extent of its authority. Both limitation of power and separation of powers may exist together, and it is this coexistence which so distinctively characterizes the modern state with its distribution of competence among its various organs. Indeed, this modern state is essentially characterized by

[48] *Infra* c. XII.

the following criteria: It is a consociation of bearers of certain defined *imperia*; these bearers are selected according to established rules; their *imperia* are delimitated from each other by general rules of separation of powers; and internally each of them finds the legitimacy of its power of command defined by set rules of limitation of power.

Both separation of powers and limitation of power may assume structural forms quite different from those in which they appear in the modern state. Especially is this true of the separation of powers. Its structure was different in the ancient Roman law of intercession of *par majorve potestas*[49] as well as in the patrimonial, the corporate, and the feudal types of state organization.[50] Nonetheless, there is truth in Montesquieu's assertion that it was only through the separation of powers that the very concept of public law was made possible.[51] But this proposition must be understood correctly in the sense that the separation of powers need not necessarily be of the sort that he thought he had found in England. On the other hand, not every kind of separation of powers leads to the idea of a public law, but only that type which is peculiar to the idea of the state as a rationally organized institution. The reason why a systematic theory of public law was developed only in Western countries is simply that only in these countries had the political organization assumed the form of an institution with rationally dovetailed jurisdictions and a separation of powers. As far as antiquity is concerned, it had a systematic theory of the state precisely to the extent that there existed a rational separation of powers: the doctrine of the *imperia* of the several Roman magistrates was elaborated in a systematic manner.[52] Everything else was essentially political philosophy rather than constitutional law. In the Middle Ages, separation of powers appeared only in the competition among privileges, feudal claims, and other rights; consequently, there was no separate treatment of constitutional law. Whatever there was of it was contained in feudal and manorial law. The decisive legal conceptions of modern public law owe their origin to a peculiar combination of several factors. As a matter of historical fact, they owe it to the rational formal consociation of privileged persons in public corporations of the

[49] An official of equal or higher power (*par maiorve potestas*) could, through his "stepping in" (*intercessio*), stop the activities of other officials; cf. MOMMSEN 22; L. HOMO, ROMAN POLITICAL INSTITUTIONS (1929) 29, 45, 221–223; JOLOWICZ 11, 43, 45, 47, 337; cf. also W.u.G. 567; Weber, *Die Stadt* (47 ARCHIV FÜR SOZIALWISS. UND SOZIALPOLITIK, 1920/21) 712.

[50] W.u.G. Part III, cc. VI and VII.

[51] MONTESQUIEU, SPIRIT OF THE LAWS (Nugent transl. 1949) 151.

[52] Cf. HOMO, *op. cit.*, *sub tit.* "imperium" (index), esp. pp. 206–235; 1 MOMMSEN 76–191; W. HEITLAND, ROMAN REPUBLIC (1909) vol. I, *sub tit.* "imperium."

corporative state which increasingly combined both separation and limitation of powers with institutional structure. As a matter of legal theory, they owe it to the Roman concept of the corporation, the ideas of natural law, and, finally, French legal theory. We shall deal with this development of modern public law in our chapter on authority.[53] In the following sections we shall deal mainly with lawmaking and lawfinding, but only in connection with those economically relevant spheres which today are left to private law and civil procedure.

8. *Substantive Law and Procedure.* According to our contemporary modes of legal thought, the activities of political organizations fall, as regards "law," into two categories, viz., lawmaking and lawfinding, the latter involving "execution" as a technical matter. Today we understand by lawmaking the establishment of general norms which in the lawyers' thought assume the character of rational rules of law. Lawfinding, as we understand it, is the "application" of such established norms and the legal propositions deduced therefrom by legal thinking, to concrete "facts" which are "subsumed" under these norms. However, this mode of thought has by no means been common to all periods of history. The distinction between lawmaking as creation of general norms and lawfinding as application of these norms to particular cases does not exist where adjudication is "administration" in the sense of free decision from case to case. In such a situation, it is not only the legal norm that is lacking, but also the idea of a party's right to have it applied to his case. The same is true where law appears as "privilege"[54] and where, accordingly, the idea of an "application" of legal norms as the foundation of a legal claim could not have arisen. Again, the distinction between lawmaking and lawfinding is absent wherever, but only to the extent that, lawfinding is not conceived as an application of general norms to concrete cases. In other words, the distinction is absent in all cases of irrational adjudication, which has been not only the primitive form of adjudication but which, as we shall see,[55] has also prevailed, either in its pure or in some modified form, throughout all history in all parts of the world except those in which Roman law came to obtain. Similarly, the distinction between rules of law to be applied in the process of lawfinding, and rules regarding that process itself, has not always been drawn as clearly as that which is drawn today between substantive and procedural law. Where legal procedure rested upon the *imperium*'s influence upon the pleadings, as,

[53] W.u.G., Part III, c. VI.
[54] See *infra*, p. 267.
[55] *Infra*, c. V.

for instance, in early Roman law, or, in a technically quite different way, in English law, it is easy to hold the notion that substantive legal claims are identical with the right to make use of procedural forms of action such as the Roman *actio*[56] or the English writ.[57] In older Roman legal doctrine the line of demarcation between procedural and private law was thus not drawn in the way it is drawn by us. For quite different reasons, a similar mixture of problems which we would respectively call procedural and substantive was apt to arise where adjudication was based on irrational modes of proof, such as the oath or wager of law in their original magical significance, or upon ordeals. The right or duty to resort, or submit, to such significant acts of magic was then a component of a substantive legal claim or even identical with it. Nevertheless, the distinction between rules of procedural and of substantive law was inherent in the distinction made in the Middle Ages between *Richtsteige*, on the one hand, and "mirrors of law,"[58] on the other. This distinction was no less clear than that which was made in the Romans' early efforts at systematization,[59] although it was made in a somewhat different way.

[56] KASER 174; NOYES 146.

[57] See MAITLAND, FORMS 78.

[58] RICHTSTEIG — a book containing advice as to how to initiate and prosecute a lawsuit.

RECHTSBUCH (*Spiegel*, "Mirror of Law") — a handbook of law, especially of substantive law. As to both, see STOBBE I, 286 *et seq.*, 390 *et seq.*, II, 143 *et seq.*

[59] GAIUS' INSTITUTES (*ca.* 161 A.D.) is the oldest work accessible to us in which we find that arrangement of the materials in the three parts of Persons, Things, and Actions, which was traditionally followed until the eighteenth century.

Chapter IV

CATEGORIES OF LEGAL THOUGHT[1]

As we have already pointed out, the mode in which the current basic conceptions of the various fields of law have been differentiated from each other has depended largely upon factors of legal technique and of political organization. Economic factors can therefore be said to have had an indirect influence only. To be sure, economic influences have played their part, but only to this extent: that certain rationalizations of economic behavior, based upon such phenomena as a market economy or freedom of contract, and the resulting awareness of underlying, and increasingly complex conflicts of interests to be resolved by legal machinery, have influenced the systematization of the law or have intensified the institutionalization of political society. We shall have occasion to observe this time and again. All other purely economic influences merely occur as concrete instances and cannot be formulated in general rules. On the other hand, we shall frequently see that those aspects of law which are conditioned by political factors and by the internal structure of legal thought have exercised a strong influence on economic organization. In the following paragraphs, we shall deal briefly with the most important conditions by which the formal characteristics of law, i.e., lawmaking and lawfinding, have been influenced. We shall be especially interested in observing the extent and the nature of the rationality of the law and, quite particularly, of that branch of it which is relevant to economic life, viz., private law.

A body of law can be "rational" in several different senses, depending on which of several possible courses legal thinking takes toward rationalization. Let us begin with the apparently most elementary thought process, viz., generalization, i.e., in our case, the reduction of the reasons relevant in the decision of concrete individual cases to one or more "principles," i.e., legal propositions. This process of reduction is normally conditional upon a prior or concurrent analysis of the facts of the case as to those ultimate components which are regarded as relevant in the juristic valuation. Conversely, the elaboration of ever more comprehensive "legal propositions" reacts upon the specification and delimitation of the potentially relevant characteristics of the facts. The process both

[1] W.u.G. 395–397.

depends upon, and promotes, casuistry. However, not every well-developed method of casuistry has resulted in, or run parallel to, the development of "legal propositions of high logical sublimation." Highly comprehensive schemes of legal casuistry have grown up upon the basis of a merely paratactic association analogy of extrinsic elements. In our legal system the analytical derivation of "legal propositions" and the decision of specific cases go hand in hand with the synthetic work of "construction" of "legal relations" and "legal institutions," i.e., the determination of which aspects of a typical kind of communal or consensual action are to be regarded as *legally* relevant, and in which logically consistent way these relevant components are to be regarded as *legally* coördinated, i.e., as being in "legal relationships." Although this latter process is closely related to the one previously described, it is nonetheless possible for a very high degree of sublimation in analysis to be correlated with a very low degree of constructional conceptualization of the legally relevant social relations. Conversely, the synthesis of a "legal relationship" may be achieved in a relatively satisfactory way despite a low degree of analysis, or occasionally just because of its limited cultivation. This contradiction is a result of the fact that analysis gives rise to a further logical task which, while it is compatible with synthetic construction, often turns out to be incompatible with it in fact. We refer to "systematization," which has never appeared but in late stages of legal modes of thought. To a youthful law, it is unknown. According to present modes of thought it represents an integration of all analytically derived legal propositions in such a way that they constitute a logically clear, internally consistent, and, at least in theory, gapless system of rules, under which, it is implied, all conceivable fact situations must be capable of being logically subsumed lest their order lack an effective guaranty. Even today not every body of law (e.g., English law) claims that it possesses the features of a system as defined above and, of course, the claim was even less frequently made by the legal systems of the past; where it was put forward at all, the degree of logical abstraction was often extremely low. In the main, the "system" has predominantly been an external scheme for the ordering of legal data and has been of only minor significance in the analytical derivation of legal propositions and in the construction of legal relationships. The specifically modern form of systematization, which developed out of Roman law, has its point of departure in the logical analysis of the meaning of the legal propositions as well as of the social actions.[2] The "legal relationships" and casuistry,

[2] The elaboration of this modern form of "systematization" was particularly the work of the eighteenth-century scholars of Natural Law and the German Pandectists

on the other hand, often resist this kind of manipulation, as they have grown out of concrete factual characteristics.

In addition to the diversities discussed so far, we must also consider the differences existing as to the technical apparatus of legal practice; these differences to some extent associate with, but to some extent also overlap, those discussed so far. The following are the possible type situations:

Both lawmaking and lawfinding may be either rational or irrational They are "formally irrational" when one applies in lawmaking or lawfinding means which cannot be controlled by the intellect, for instance when recourse is had to oracles or substitutes therefor. Lawmaking and lawfinding are "substantively irrational" on the other hand to the extent that decision is influenced by concrete factors of the particular case as evaluated upon an ethical, emotional, or political basis rather than by general norms. "Rational" lawmaking and lawfinding may be of either a formal or a substantive kind. All formal law is, formally at least, relatively rational. Law, however, is "formal" to the extent that, in both substantive and procedural matters, only unambiguous general characteristics of the facts of the case are taken into account. This formalism can, again, be of two different kinds. It is possible that the legally relevant characteristics are of a tangible nature, i.e., that they are perceptible as sense data. This adherence to external characteristics of the facts, for instance, the utterance of certain words, the execution of a signature, or the performance of a certain symbolic act with a fixed meaning, represents the most rigorous type of legal formalism. The other type of formalistic law is found where the legally relevant characteristics of the facts are disclosed through the logical analysis of meaning and where, accordingly, definitely fixed legal concepts in the form of highly abstract rules are formulated and applied. This process of "logical rationality" diminishes the significance of extrinsic elements and thus softens the rigidity of concrete formalism. But the contrast to "substantive rationality" is sharpened, because the latter means that the decision of legal problems is influenced by norms different from those obtained through logical generalization of abstract interpretations of meaning. The norms to which substantive rationality accords predominance include ethical imperatives, utilitarian and other expediential rules, and

---

of the nineteenth century; as to their work, see EHRLICH, c. 14; v. HIPPEL, GUSTAV HUGOS JURISTISCHER ARBEITSPLAN (1931); same author, ZUR GESETZMÄSSIGKEIT JURISTISCHER SYSTEMBILDUNG (1930); WIEACKER, VOM RÖMISCHEN RECHT (1944) 256; for further bibliographical references see 20th Century Legal Philosophy Series, THE JURISPRUDENCE OF INTERESTS (1948) 200; cf. *infra* c. IX.

political maxims, all of which diverge from the formalism of the "external characteristics" variety as well as from that which uses logical abstraction. However, the peculiarly professional, legalistic, and abstract approach to law in the modern sense is possible only in the measure that the law is formal in character. In so far as the absolute formalism of classification according to "sense-data characteristics" prevails, it exhausts itself in casuistry. Only that abstract method which employs the logical interpretation of meaning allows the execution of the specifically systematic task, i.e., the collection and rationalization by logical means of all the several rules recognized as legally valid into an internally consistent complex of abstract legal propositions.

Our task is now to find out how the various influences which have participated in the formation of the law have influenced the development of its formal qualities. Present-day legal science, at least in those forms which have achieved the highest measure of methodological and logical rationality, i.e., those which have been produced through the legal science of the Pandectists' Civil Law, proceeds from the following five postulates: viz., first, that every concrete legal decision be the "application" of an abstract legal proposition to a concrete "fact situation"; second, that it must be possible in every concrete case to derive the decision from abstract legal propositions by means of legal logic; third, that the law must actually or virtually constitute a "gapless" system of legal propositions, or must, at least, be treated as if it were such a gapless system; [3] fourth, that whatever cannot be "construed" legally in rational terms is also legally irrelevant; and fifth, that every social action of human beings must always be visualized as either an "application" or "execution" of legal propositions, or as an "infringement" thereof. However, for the moment we shall not concern ourselves with these theoretical postulates, but shall rather investigate certain general formal qualities of the law which are important for its functioning.[4]

[3] This conclusion has been drawn particularly by Stammler, although not explicitly. He holds that the "gaplessness" of the legal system must result in a gapless "legal ordering" of all social conduct [see his WIRTSCHAFT UND RECHT (1924) 541]. [Weber's note.]

[4] Chapter XIV, *infra* p. 349, might profitably be read in connection with the chapter just ended.

Chapter V

EMERGENCE AND CREATION OF LEGAL NORMS[1]

1. *The Emergence of New Legal Norms — Theories of Customary Law Insufficient as Explanations.* How do new legal rules arise? At the present time, they usually arise by way of legislation, i.e., conscious human lawmaking in conformity with the formal constitutional requirements, be they customary or "made," of a given political society. Obviously, this kind of lawmaking is not aboriginal; it is not the normal one even in economically or socially complex and advanced societies. In England, the "common law" is regarded as the very opposite of "made" law. In Germany, non-enacted law is usually called "customary law." But the concept of "customary law" is relatively modern; in Rome it did not emerge before the very late period; in Germany it resulted from Civilian doctrine. Of such academic origin was especially that theory which was developed in Germany and according to which a custom, in order to be law, must be actually observed, must be commonly believed to be binding, and must be rational.[2] Also the other definitions which are current today are but theoretical constructs. For purposes of legal dogmatics, the concept of customary law is still indispensable, however, provided it is used in such refined ways as those formulated by Zitelmann or Gierke.[3] Otherwise we would have to confine our concept of law to statute law on the one side and judge-made law on the other. The violent struggle against the concept of customary law which the legal sociologists have carried on, especially Lambert and Ehrlich, is not only devoid of any foundation but also represents a confusion between the legal and sociological methods of analysis.[4]

[1] W.u.G. 397–412.

[2] The classical formulation of the German Pandectist doctrine of customary law is that by PUCHTA, DAS GEWOHNHEITSRECHT, 2 vols. (1828/37); for a concise modern treatment, see 1 ENNECCERUS, ALLGEMEINER TEIL (1928) 31, 64, 79; see also MAINE (1861), c. i; J. C. GRAY, NATURE AND SOURCES OF LAW (2nd ed. 1927), c. XII; Vinogradoff, *The Problem of Custom*, COLLECTED PAPERS, II, 410; furthermore, ALLEN (5th ed. 1951), cc. i and ii, where the rather different tests of the legal validity of customs in the common law are fully discussed.

[3] E. Zitelmann, *Gewohnheitsrecht und Irrtum* (1883), 66 ARCHIV FÜR DIE CIVILISTISCHE PRAXIS, 323 O. GIERKE, PRIVATRECHT, I, 159.

[4] E. LAMBERT, LA FONCTION DU DROIT CIVIL COMPARÉ (1903), 172, 216; EHRLICH, 436; see also GRAY, *op. cit. supra* n. 2, at 297. Both Lambert and Ehrlich argued

But we are concerned with a different problem, viz., that of discovering the empirical processes in which nonstatutory norms arise as valid customary law. On that problem the traditional doctrines tell us little if anything. As a matter of fact, they are even incorrect where they purport to explain the actual development of law in the past, particularly in periods in which there was little or no enacted law. It is, of course, true that these doctrines find some support in late Roman as well as medieval conceptions, both continental and English, about the meaning and the presuppositions of *consuetudo* as a source of law.[5] There, however, the problem was that of finding an adjustment between a body of rational law claiming universal validity and a multitude of actually prevailing systems of laws of locally or personally limited application. In the late Roman Empire the conflict was between the imperial law and the laws of the peoples of the provinces;[6] in England, between the law of the land (*lex terrae*), i.e., the Common Law, and the local laws;[7] on the Continent it was between the "received" Roman law and the indigenous bodies of law.[8] Only the various particularistic bodies of law were classified by the jurists as "customary law," and in order to give legal recognition to customary law the jurists devised certain tests of validity which customary law had to fulfill. This was a necessary step in view of

---

that the origin of custom was not to be found in VOLKSRECHT but predominantly in JURISTENRECHT. More particularly, their argument (especially Lambert's) was that custom becomes only then established when those who use the custom have become clearly convinced that the courts will not depart from the line of conduct which the judges have laid down and that it is better to adapt oneself to these rules in the same way as one has to adapt himself to the rules laid down by the legislature. This view of custom was meant to drive another nail into the coffin of the Historical School, whose arguments were that custom derived first and foremost from the *consensus utentium* before receiving judicial and legal recognition. Ehrlich was less radical than Lambert, although he too insisted strongly on the creative agency of judge-made law. He distinguished between *Rechtssätze*, i.e., rules for decision, and *Rechtsverhaeltnisse*, i.e., the legal arrangements actually existing in society, such as property, family, etc. In dealing with *Rechtsverhältnisse* the judge's function might be less original and more restricted, for the judge must always give due attention to the private arrangements or conventions existing in society; but according to Ehrlich, the process of judicial lawmaking was still clearly discernible.

[5] On the medieval doctrines about *consuetudo* as a source of law, see BRIE, LEHRE VOM GEWOHNHEITSRECHT (1899), §§ 12 *et seq.*; ENGELMANN (1938) 81; for England, see POLLOCK AND MAITLAND 183; ALLEN; HOLDSWORTH, III, 167–170.

[6] For a discussion of this conflict, see MITTEIS, REICHSRECHT (1891); JOLOWICZ, 66–71.

[7] Cf. 1 POLLOCK AND MAITLAND 107, 184, 186, 220, 222; HOLDSWORTH I, 1–20; II, 3–21; 206–207; ALLEN, 86–88.

[8] Cf. *supra* n. 5, see also SAVIGNY, GESCHICHTE DES RÖMISCHEN RECHT IM MITTELALTER (2nd ed. 1850) esp. I, 115, 178.

the fact that the universal law claimed an exclusive applicability. But it would not have occurred to anyone to classify as customary law the English Common Law, which certainly was not statute law. Similarly, the definition of the Islamic *Idjmâ* as the *tacitus consensus omnium* [9] is completely unconnected with "customary law," simply because it purported to be "sacred" law.

2. *The Role of Party Practices in the Emergence and Development of Legal Norms.* Theoretically, the origin of legal norms might, as we have already seen, be thought of most simply in the following way: The psychological "set" which arises with the habituation of an action causes conduct which in the beginning constitutes plain habit later to be experienced as binding; then, with the awareness of the diffusion of such conduct among a plurality of individuals, it comes to be incorporated as "consensus" into people's semi- or wholly conscious "expectations" as to the meaningfully corresponding conduct of others. Finally these "consensual understandings" acquire the guaranty of coercive enforcement by which they are distinguished from mere "conventions." Even on this purely hypothetical construction there arises the question of how anything could ever change in this inert mass of canonized custom which, just because it is considered as binding, seems as though it could never give birth to anything new. The Historical School of Jurisprudence tended to accept the hypothesis that evolutionary impulses of a "folk spirit" are produced by a hypostatized supra-individual organic entity.[10] Karl Knies also inclined toward this view.[11] Scientifically, however, this conception leads nowhere. Of course, empirically valid rules of conduct, including legal rules, have at all times emerged, and still emerge today, unconsciously, i.e., without being regarded by the participants as newly created. Such unconscious emergence has occurred primarily in the form of unperceived changes in meaning; it also takes place through the belief that a factually new situation actually presents no new elements of any relevance for legal evaluation. Another form of "unconscious" emergence is represented by the application of what actually is new law to old or somewhat different new situations with the conviction that the law so applied has always obtained and has always been applied in that manner. Nonetheless, there also exists a large class of cases in

[9] *Idjmâ* — in Mohammedan law that consent of the scholars which has been held necessary to establish law supplementary to the word of the Prophet as expressed in the Koran and his other alleged sayings (*hadith*).

[10] On the Historical School, see now the full treatment by Stone, 421.

[11] K. Knies, Die politische Oekonomie vom geschichtlichen Standpunkte (1883).

which both the situation as well as the rule applied are felt to be "new," although in different degrees and senses.

What is the source of such innovation? One may answer that it is caused by changes in the external conditions of social life which carry in their wake modifications of the empirically prevailing "consensual understandings." But the mere *change of external conditions* is neither sufficient nor necessary to explain the changes in the "consensual understandings." The really decisive element has always been *a new line of conduct* which then results either in a change of the meaning of the existing rules of law or in the creation of new rules of law. Several kinds of persons participate in these transformations. First we should mention those individuals who are interested in some concrete communal action. Such an individual may change his behavior, especially his communal actions, either to protect his interests under new external conditions or simply to promote them more effectively under existing conditions. As a result, there arise "new" consensual understandings and sometimes new forms of rational association with substantively new meanings; these, in turn, generate the rise of new types of customary behavior.

It may also be, however, that, without any such reorientation of behavior by individuals, the total structure of communal action changes in response to changes in external conditions. Of several types of action, all may have been well suited to existing conditions; but, when the conditions change one may turn out to be better suited to serve the economic or social interests of the parties involved; in the process of selection it alone survives and ultimately becomes the one used by all so that one cannot well point out any single individual who would have "changed" his conduct. In its pure form, such a situation may be a theoretical construct, but something of the kind does actually occur in the selective process which operates between ethnic or religious groups which cling tenaciously to their own respective usages. More frequent, however, is the injection of a new content into communal actions and rational associations as a result of individual invention and its subsequent spread through imitation and selection. Not merely in modern times has this latter situation been of significance as a source of economic reorientation, but in all systems in which the mode of life has reached at least a measure of rationalization. The parties to the new arrangements are frequently unconcerned about the fact that their respective positions are insecure in the sense of being legally unenforceable. They regard legal enforceability by the state as either unnecessary or as self-evident; even more frequently do they simply rely upon the self-interest or the loyalty of their partners combined with the weight of convention.

Prior to the existence of any coercive machinery, and prior even to the regulated enforcement of norms through the sib members' duty to participate in vengeance, the function later fulfilled by the "legal" guaranty of a norm was undoubtedly performed by the general convention that the person who was admittedly "in the right" could find others who would help him against an offender; and, where some special guaranty appeared desirable, magical self-malediction, i.e., the oath, superseded under very diversified circumstances and to a very large extent, as far as the interested parties themselves were concerned, all other forms of guaranty, including an existing guaranty of legal coercion. In most periods, the preponderant part of the consensual order, including that of economic matters, has operated in this way and without concern for the availability of the legal coercive power of the state or of any coercive enforcement at all. Such an institution, however, as the Yugoslav Zadruga [12] (household community),

[12] *Zadruga* (accent on the first syllable) is the south-Slavic kind of the frequently occurring phenomenon of the house community (cf. Peake, *Village Community*, 15 ENCYC. SOC. SCI. 253, 256). According to TROYANOVITCH, MANNERS AND CUSTOMS IN SERBIA, ed. Stead, London, 1909, c. xii, it was a large family or clan, organized on a patrilineal basis, dwelling in one large house and holding all its land, livestock, and money in common. These *zadrugas* continued for several generations without division, often including as many as 100 individuals. They were ruled by an elder (*stareshina*), usually the oldest member of the household capable of exerting authority, who apportioned the work among the different members. When a *zadruga* broke up, the stores were divided equally among all the members, but the land among the males only.

The *zadruga* has been regarded as evidence for the Marxist theory of "aboriginal" communal property or as a model for the communist society of the future (S. Marcovic, 10 ENCYC. SOC. SCI. 144). Quite particularly has the *zadruga* been used as the prime illustration for the superfluousness or ineffectiveness of state law as a means of social regulation. This notion seems to derive from the use which Ehrlich made of the investigation of South Slavic law by Bogišič (see Demelic, *De droit coutumier des Slaves méridionaux d'après les recherches de v. Bogišič*, 6 REV. LÉGISL. ANCIENNE ET MODERNE (1876) 253). The famous passage in Ehrlich (at 371) is as follows:

"Bogišič's investigation revealed that among all the Southern Slavs within the territory within which the Austrian Civil Code is in effect the well-known South Slavic family community, the Sadruga, is in existence; this is altogether unknown to the Civil Code and absolutely irreconcilable with its principles."

This proposition, which has been taken over by Weber, is not tenable, however.

In the former Austro-Hungarian Monarchy the kingdom of Croatia-Slavonia, a semi-autonomous part of Hungary, constituted the area of principal occurrence of the *zadruga*. The Austrian Civil Code of 1811 was introduced there in 1852 (Law of November 29, 1852, Austrian REICHS-GESETZ-BLATT 1852, No. 246). In the course of the implementation of the Code as the law of Croatia-Slavonia, the Decree of the Austrian Minister of Justice of April 18, 1853 (R.G. Bl. 1853, No. 65) provided for

which is so often cited as evidence of the dispensability of legal coercion, actually dispensed only with the coercive legal power of the state, while during the period of its universal diffusion it undoubtedly enjoyed effective protection through the coercive power of the village authorities. Such forms of consensual action, once they have become firmly embedded in usage, may continue to exist for centuries without

---

the introduction of the Austrian system of registration of land titles. Section 29 of this decree provided expressly that in the case of lands owned by a "house communion" the family as such was to be entered as the owner rather than any single individual. This decree constituted a clear recognition of the *zadruga* by the official law. It continued a tradition which had been established by official Austrian legislation from the beginning of the Austrian rule over the regions of the so-called *Militär-Grenze* ("Military Border Region," i.e., the region adjacent to the Turkish border). The *zadruga* is expressly mentioned in the very statute of 1754 by which the *Militär-Grenze* was established (*Militär-Gräntz-Rechte für das Carlstädter und Varasdiner Generalat*, Part IV, § 37; see also *Grenz-Grundgesetz* of 1807; cf. M. Stopfer, Erläuterungen der Grundgesetze für die Carlstädter 1, Varasdiner, Banat, slavonische und croatische Militärgrenze [Vienna, 1830]; see also Vanicek, Geschichte der Militärgrenze, 4 vols., [1875]; Hostinek, Die K.K. Militärgrenze, 2 vols. [1861]).

The Basic Law of 1850 (*Kaiserl. Patent v. 7. Mai, 1850, R.G. Bl. 1850, No. 243*) stated expressly that "The patriarchal life of the border population is placed under the protection of the law" (§ 31); in accordance with this maxim an extensive set of provisions was established to clarify the internal structure of the "family houses" and their relation to outsiders (§§ 16, 22, 27, 33–45). By a later Croatian Statute of 1870, the disciplinary powers of the family head and the village authorities over *zadruga* members were again expressly recognized and regulated (cf. Bidermann, *Législation autonome de la Croatie* [1876], 8 Rev. dr. intl. et législ. comp. 215, 266). In Austria proper the *zadruga* existed only in the small district of White Carniola. There, too, judicial practice regarded *zadruga* lands as owned, not by individuals, but by the family. Official Austrian, including Croatian-Slavonian, law was thus far from hostile to the *zadruga*. It would also be difficult to see in what respects the *zadruga* would have been incompatible with any of the provisions of the Austrian Civil Code. Like all modern codifications, the Austrian code leaves wide room for private parties to regulate their affairs according to their own wishes. The majority of its rules on contracts are stopgap law (*ius dispositivum*) to be applied only in so far as the parties have failed to make their own arrangements. Its rules on real property and decedents' estates are so formulated that they can easily be adapted to various forms of joint tenancy. It is thus difficult to see how the *zadruga* can be used as an illustration for the ineffectiveness of legal regulation.

For further information on the *zadruga* see Maine, Early Law 232–282; Weber, History (1950) 12, 47; Y. Peritch, *Opposition between communism and bourgeois democracy as typified in the Serbian Zadruga Family* (1922) 16 Ill. L. Rev. 423; S. H. Cross, *Primitive Civilization of the Eastern Slavs* (1946) 5 American Slavic and East-European Rev. 50; P. E. Moreley, *Adaptation for Survival: The Varzic Zadruga* (1942/43) 2 Slavonic and East-European Rev. 147–170; for recent developments concerning the *zadruga* see M. Isic, Les problèmes agraires en Yougoslavie (1926) 32, 48, 319.

any recourse to the coercive power of the state. Although the Zadruga was not recognized by, and was even contrary to many of the rules of, official Austrian law, it still dominated the life of the peasantry. But such instances should not be regarded as normal and should not be used as a basis for general conclusions.

Where several religiously legitimated legal systems coexist side by side on a completely equal footing, with equal religious legitimacy, and with freedom of choice between them for the individuals, the fact that one of them is supported not only by the religious sanction but also by the coercive power of the state may well decide the rivalry between them, even though state and economic life are dominated by traditionalism. Thus, in Islam the same status is officially enjoyed by all the four orthodox schools of law.[13] Their application to the individuals is determined by the principle of personality in much the same way in which the application of the several tribal laws was determined in the Frankish empire.[14] At the University of Cairo [15] all four schools are represented. Nevertheless, the fact that the Hanefite system was adopted by the Osmanic sultans and that, in consequence, its rules were enjoying the sanction of coercive enforcement by the secular officialdom and the courts,[16] condemned to a slow death the Malekite system by which that support was once enjoyed in the past, as well as of the other two systems; and this development has taken its course despite the complete absence of any other negative factors. In business affairs proper, that is, in the contracts of the market, the interested parties' concern for the availability of the coerçive power of the state is considerable. In this field, the development of new forms of association has taken place, and still does so through exact estimates of the probability of enforcement by the courts as organs of the political authority. The contracts to be concluded are being adapted to this estimate and the invention of new contractual forms proceeds by taking these estimates into account.

[13] The four orthodox schools of Islamic jurisprudence are the Hanefite, Shafiite, Malekite, and Hanbalite; see Schacht 8 ENCYC. SOC. SCI. 344, and literature there cited.

[14] For the system of "personal laws" in the Frankish empire, see Maitland, *Prologue to a History of English Law* (1907) SELECTED ESSAYS IN ANGLO-AMERICAN LEGAL HISTORY 20; see also 1 BRUNNER, 259; SMITH, 115 *et seq.*; K. SCHRÖDER, DIE FRANKEN UND IHR RECHT (1881) 36.

[15] The reference is to the school of El-Azhar, Islam's most celebrated center of learning, founded in Cairo in A.D. 988.

[16] Weber's reference is to the old Turkey of the time before the Kemalist reforms of the 1920's; cf. VESEY-FITZGERALD, MUHAMMEDAN LAW (1931) 36–49.

While changes in the meaning of the prevailing law are thus initiated by the parties or their professional counselors, they are consciously and rationally adapted to the expected reaction of the judiciary. As a matter of fact, this kind of activity, the *cavere* of the Romans,[17] constitutes the very oldest type of activity performed by "professional," rationally working lawyers. Among the conditions for the development of a market economy, the calculability of the functioning of the coercive machinery constitutes the technical prerequisite as well as one of the incentives for the inventive genius of the cautelary jurists (*Kautelarjuristen*), whom we find as an autonomous element in legal innovation resulting from private initiative everywhere, but most highly developed and most clearly perceptible in Roman and English law.[18]

On the other hand, the spread of consensual and rational agreements of a certain type naturally exercises a marked influence upon the probability of their coercive enforcement by the law. While under normal circumstances only the unique case lacks the guaranty of enforcement, established custom and type agreement, once they enjoy universal diffusion, cannot be persistently ignored except under the compelling necessity of certain formal considerations or because of the intervention of authoritarian powers, or where the agencies of legal coercion have no contact with the life of business as is the case where they are imposed by an ethnically or politically alien authority, or where, in consequence of extreme vocational specialization, the organs of legal coercion have become far removed from private business as occasionally happens under conditions of sharp social differentiation. The intended meaning of an agreement may be in dispute or its use may be

[17] Traditionally one enumerates three main types of lawyers' activity in ancient Rome: *respondere*, *agere*, and *cavere*. *Respondere* was the exposition of a point of law, especially in the answer to a question addressed to the jurist (*responsa prudentium*); *agere* was the activity on behalf of a client in a court of law; *cavere* meant the drafting of contracts, wills, and other transactions. A distinction was made between the "jurisconsult" and the "advocate" (orator, rhetor). The latter would act in those courts, especially criminal, in which oratory would be counted on to be helpful. Legal training was neither necessary nor usual for an orator. Cicero's knowledge of the law, for instance, does not seem to have surpassed that of the well-educated citizen and statesman in general. Cf. Schulz, History; see also the popular account of "how the Roman law factory worked" by Wormser, The Law (New York, 1949), c. ix; for further discussion by Weber, see *infra*, pp. 212 *et seq.*

[18] *Kautelarjuristen* — those lawyers who, like the English conveyancer or the modern American corporation lawyer, are using their skill in drafting instruments and especially in inventing new clauses for the purpose of safeguarding their clients' interests and of preventing future litigation. The term has been used with special reference to the German seventeenth- and eighteenth-century specialists in that art.

an as yet unstabilized innovation. In such situations the judge, as we shall call the agency of legal coercion *a potiori*, is a second autonomous authority. But even in more normal cases the judge is doing more than merely placing his seal upon norms which would already have been binding by consensual understanding or agreement. His decision of individual cases always produces consequences which, acting beyond the scope of the case, influence the selection of those rules which are to survive as law. We shall see that the sources of "judicial" decision are not at first constituted by general "norms of decision" that would simply be "applied" to concrete cases, except where the decision relates to certain formal questions preliminary to the decision of the case itself. The situation is the very opposite: in so far as the judge allows the coercive guaranty to enter in a particular case for ever so concrete reasons, he creates, at least under certain circumstances, the empirical validity of a general norm as "law," simply because his maxim acquires significance beyond the particular case.

3. *The Emergence of Judge-Made Law.* The phenomenon just described is in no way aboriginal or universal. It certainly does not exist at all in a primitive decision arrived at through the magical means of legal revelation. Indeed in all other adjudication which is not yet formally rationalized in a juristic way, even where it has passed beyond the stage of the ordeal, the irrationality of the individual case is still significant. No general "legal norm" is applied, nor does the maxim of the concrete decision, provided it exists and is perceived at all, obtain as a norm of decision, including even ecclesiastical dooms. In the "suras" of the Koran, Mohammed repeatedly rejects earlier directives of his own, irrespective of their divine origin, and even Jehovah "regrets" some of his decisions, including some of a legal character. Through an oracle, Jehovah ordained the daughters' right of inheritance (Num. 27), but upon remonstration by the interested parties, the oracular pronouncement was corrected (Num. 36). Thus even a "weistum"[19] of a general character is unstable, and where the

[19] *Weistum* (pl. *Weistümer*), similar to the costumals or customaries of England, is a collection of legal customs of a particular locality, especially a manor. "As far back as into the Carlovingian period we can trace the practice of an *inquisitio* into existing customs to be made annually by an officer of the manor. The materials so collected were recited every year or, later, reduced to writing and annually read in public. From the manorial communities this custom spread to communities of free peasants and to free villages." (VON SCHWERIN, DEUTSCHE RECHTSGESCHICHTE [2nd ed. 1915], with bibliography).

individual case is decided by drawing lots,[20] by combat, by some other ordeal, or by concrete oracular pronouncement, we cannot, of course, find any "rule-orientation" in a decision either in the sense of rule application or of rule creation. The decisions of lay judges, too, require a long development and much travail to reach the idea that they represent "norms" going beyond the individual case.[21] As a matter of fact, the greater the degree to which the decision is a concern of "laymen," the less it proceeds upon purely objective lines and the more it takes into account the persons involved and the concrete situation. A certain measure of stabilization and stereotyping in the direction of the formation of norms emerges inevitably, however, as soon as the decision becomes the subject matter of discussion, or whenever rational grounds for the decision are being sought or presupposed. In other words, norm-formation occurs wherever there is a weakening of the originally purely oracular character of the decision. But, within certain limits, it was just the magical character of the primitive law of evidence which tended to more rational norm-formation, because it required that the question to be asked had to be precisely formulated.

There also exists another intrinsic element. Obviously, it is difficult, and often impossible, for a judge who wishes to avoid the charge of bias to disregard in a later case a norm which he has consciously used as his maxim in an earlier similar decision, and to deny his power of enforcement when he has once granted it before. The same considerations hold true for the judges who succeed him. The more stable the tradition, the more the judges will depend on these maxims which guided their predecessors, because it is just then that every decision, regardless of how it came into existence, appears as being derived from the exclusively and persistently correct tradition, as part of it or as its manifestation. It thus becomes a pattern which has, or at least lays claim to, permanent validity. In that sense, the subjective conviction that one is applying only norms already valid is in fact characteristic of every type of adjudication born in a prophetic age, and it is in no way peculiarly modern.

New legal norms thus have two primary sources, viz., first, the standardization of certain consensual understandings, especially purposive

[20] As among the Jews by Urim and Thummim (see *infra* p. 89). [Weber's note.]

[21] As it is shown, for instance, by the investigations of Vladimirski-Budanov [Vladimirski-Budanov, Mikhail Flegontovich, 1838–1916, Russian legal historian; cf. the biographical article on him in 15 ENCYC. SOC. SCI. 271]; see his Russian Legal History (OBZOR ISTORII RUSSKAGO PRAVA, 1907) 59, 88. [Weber's note.]

agreements, which are made with increasing deliberateness by individuals who, aided by professional "counsel," thereby demarcate their respective spheres of interest; and, second, judicial precedent. In this way, for example, the English common law developed.[22] The extensive participation in the process of juridically experienced and trained experts, who to an ever increasing degree devoted themselves "professionally" to the tasks of "counsel" or judge, has placed the stamp of "lawyers' law" upon the type of law thus created.

There is not excluded, of course, the role played in the development of the law by purely "emotional" factors, such as the so-called "sense of justice." Experience shows, however, that the "sense of justice" is very unstable unless it is firmly guided by the "pragma" of objective or subjective interests. It is, as one can still easily see today, capable of sudden fluctuations and it cannot be expressed except in a few very general and purely formal maxims.[23] No national legal peculiarities, in particular, can be derived from any differences in the operation of the "sense of justice," at least not as far as present knowledge goes.[24] Being mainly emotional, that "sense" is hardly adequate for the maintenance of a body of stable norms; it rather constitutes one of the diverse sources of irrational adjudication. Only upon this basis can one ask to what extent "popular" attitudes, i.e., attitudes widely diffused among those actually concerned in these interests, can prevail against the "lawyers' law" of the professionals (attorneys and judges) who are continuously engaged in the invention of new contracts and in adjudication. The answer to this question depends, as we shall see, upon the type of adjudicative procedure prevailing in a given situation.

4. *Development of New Law through Imposition from Above.* But aside from the influence and, mostly, the confluence of these factors,

[22] For the latest and most comprehensive presentation of the development of the principle of *stare decisis* in English law, see ALLEN 43, 150 *et seq.*, 525 *et seq.*

[23] For recent discussions of the "sense of justice," see E. N. CAHN, THE SENSE OF INJUSTICE (1949); E. RIEZLER, DAS RECHTSGEFÜHL (2nd ed. 1946); HOCHE, DAS RECHTSGEFÜHL IN JUSTIZ UND POLITIK (1932); H. COING, GRUNDZÜGE DER RECHTSPHILOSOPHIE (1950) 48.

[24] Weber's remark is directed against those scholars of the historical school of jurisprudence who regarded all law as the emanation of every nation's peculiar "national spirit" (*Volksgeist*); see especially SAVIGNY, VOM BERUF UNSERER ZEIT FÜR GESETZGEBUNG UND RECHTSWISSENSCHAFT (1814), translated by HAYWARD (ON THE VOCATION OF OUR AGE FOR LEGISLATION AND JURISPRUDENCE, 1831); cf. STONE 421. The theory of the national peculiarity of the sense of justice was taken up by the National-Socialists and used by them as one of the foundations of their legal theory.

innovation in the body of legal rules may also occur through their deliberate imposition *from above*.[25] Of course, this took place at first in ways very different from those we know in our present society. Originally there was a complete absence of the notion that rules of conduct possessing the character of "law," i.e., rules which are guaranteed by "legal coercion," could be intentionally created as "norms." As we have seen, legal decisions did not originally have any normative element at all. Today, we take it for granted that legal decisions constitute the "application" of fixed and stable rules; [26] but in earlier times they were not looked upon in that way at all. Even where there had emerged the conception that norms were "valid" for behavior and binding in the resolution of disputes, they were not conceived as the products, or as even the possible subject matter, of human enactment. Their "legitimacy" rather rested upon the absolute sacredness of certain usages as such, deviation from which would produce either evil magical effects, such as the restlessness of the spirits, or the wrath of the gods. As "tradition" they were, in theory at least, immutable. They had to be correctly known and interpreted in accordance with established usage, but they could not be created. Their interpretation was the task of those who had known them longest, i.e., the physically oldest persons or the elders of the kinship group, quite frequently the magicians and priests, who, as a result of their specialized knowledge of the magical forces, knew and had to know the techniques of intercourse with the supernatural powers.

Nevertheless, new norms have also emerged through explicit imposition. But this could happen in one way only, viz., through a new charismatic revelation which could assume two forms. In the older it would indicate what was right in an individual case; in the other, the revelation might also point to a general norm for all future similar cases. Such revelation of law constitutes the primeval revolutionary element which undermines the stability of tradition and is the parent of all types of legal "enactment." The revelation could, and indeed often was, revelation in the literal sense; the new norms found their source in the inspiration or impulses, either actual or apparent, of the charismatically qualified

[25] On the slow development of conscious creation of new law by legislation in England, see ALLEN 354, 365 *et seq.*; S. THORNE, INTRODUCTION TO A DISCOURSE UPON THE EXPOSITION AND UNDERSTANDING OF STATUTES, WITH SIR THOMAS EGERTON'S ADDITIONS (1942).

[26] The view expressed here by Weber is typically that of continental legal thinking; for the radically different view of the American realists, see especially JEROME FRANK, LAW AND THE MODERN MIND (1930); for a more realistic description of the American approach, see EDWARD LEVI, INTRODUCTION TO LEGAL REASONING (1949); cf. also STONE 192; and see *infra* p. 315.

person and without being in any way required by new external conditions. But, usually, revelation was an artificial process. Various magical devices were used to obtain new rules when a change in economic or social conditions had created novel and unsolved problems. The men who normally used these primitive methods of adapting old rules to new situations were the magicians, the prophets, or the priests of an oracular deity. Of course, the line where interpretation of old tradition slides into the revelation of new norms is unprecise. But the transition must take place once the interpretative wisdom of the priests or elders proves inadequate. A similar need may also arise for the determination of disputed facts.

What is now of interest are the ways in which these modes of inventing, finding, or creating law affect its formal characteristics. The presence of the magic element in the settlement of disputes and in the creation of new norms results in the rigorous formalism so peculiar to all primitive legal procedure. For, unless the relevant question has been stated in the formally correct manner, the magical technique cannot provide the right answer. Furthermore, questions of right or wrong cannot be settled by any magical method indiscriminately or arbitrarily selected; each legal problem has its own technique appropriate to it. We can now understand the fundamental principle characteristic of all primitive procedure once it has become regulated by fixed rules, viz., that even the slightest error by one of the parties in his statement of the ceremonial formula will result in the loss of the remedy or even the entire case, as, for instance, in the Roman procedure by *legis actio* or in early medieval law.[27] The lawsuit, however, was, as we have seen, the oldest type of "legal transaction," because it was based upon a contract, i.e., the contract of composition.[28] Accordingly, we find the corresponding principle in the solemn private transactions of the early Middle Ages as well as in the Roman *negotia stricti juris*.[29] Even the

[27] For the formalistic features of the *legis actio*, see JOLOWICZ 87, 181; WENGER 123; ENGELMANN AND MILLAR 269, 281; 2 JHERING, 496–695. As to formalism in medieval procedure, see Brunner, *Wort und Form im altfranzösischen Prozess* in SITZUNGSBER. DER AKAD. DER WISS. ZU WIEN, PHIL-HIST. CLASSE LVII (1867), 655; ENGELMANN AND MILLAR 174, 386, 649; O. v. ZALLINGER, WESEN UND URSPRUNG DES FORMALISMUS IM ALTDEUTSCHEN PRIVATRECHT (1898); SCHROEDER, §§ 13, 25, 37, 63. See also *infra* p. 199 (*fautes volent exploits*).

[28] See *supra* p. 54.

[29] In classical Roman law a distinction was made between *negotia stricti iuris* and *negotia bonae fidei*. In the former the debtor has to perform exactly as he has promised, no more and no less. The principal example is the formalized promise of the solemn *stipulatio*. In the latter, which are a product of later development, the debtor has to do whatever is required by good faith and fair dealing, especially in

slightest deviation from the magically effective formula renders the whole transaction void. More particularly we find in this early formalism of procedure a formalistic "law of evidence," which was not at all to regulate procedural proof in the modern sense. No proof was offered to show the allegation of a particular fact to be either "true" or "false." The issue was rather which party should be allowed or required to address to the magical powers the question of whether he was right and in which of the several ways this might or ought to be done.[30] The formal character of procedure thus stands in sharp contrast to the thoroughly irrational character of the technique of decision. Hence, the "law" that found expression in these decisions was entirely fluid and flexible, unless rigorously traditional norms had come to be generally acknowledged. Logical or rational grounds for a concrete decision were entirely lacking not only where the decision was given by a divine power or found through magical means of proof, but also where it consisted in the verdict of a charismatically qualified sage or, later, by an elder steeped in tradition, or an elder of the kinship group, or an arbitrator selected *ad hoc*, or a permanently elected expounder of the law (*lag saga*),[31] or a judge appointed by a political ruler. The verdict had to state that the particular problem had always been dealt with in the particular way; or it had to state that a divine power had decreed that the problem should be dealt with in that way in the specific case in hand or in all future cases, too. Such also was the nature of that great innovation of King Henry II, which was to become the origin of all civil trial by jury. The *assisa novae disseisinae*,[32] which was granted to the petitioning party by royal

view of local or mercantile custom. Cf. SOHM, 367; JÖRS AND KUNKEL 165 (with bibliography); see also SCHULZ, PRINCIPLES 223 *et seq.*

[30] Among the historians of the Germanic laws it has become customary to speak of the "right" to offer proof and to contrast it with the modern "burden" of proof. Cf. 2 BRUNNER, RECHTSGESCHICHTE § 105; SCHROEDER 84; AMIRA, 130, 161; MAURER, GESCHICHTE DES ALTGERMANISCHEN GERICHTSVERFAHRENS (1824); see also 1 POLLOCK AND MAITLAND 39; 2 HOLDSWORTH 107, 112. In England the right of the defendant in the more archaic forms of action to prove his case by wager of law survived, at least formally, until its official abolition by the statute 3 and 4 William 4 c. 42, Sec. 13 (1833). On proof in archaic procedure in general, see *Declareuil, Preuves judiciaires dans le droit franc* (1898) 22 NOUVELLE REVUE HISTORIQUE DE DROIT 220.

[31] "Lag saga" was the recitation of the laws, occasionally in poetic form, at the periodically held popular assemblies of Scandinavia and Iceland. The same word applies to the person by whom the law is thus recited. See BRYCE, 327; see *infra* n. 65.

[32] For the Assize of Novel Disseisin (the German text says: *assisa novae disciplinae*, an obvious error of transcription), established at the Assize of Clarendon in 1166, see POLLOCK AND MAITLAND 145–147; PLUCKNETT 339–342; cf. also JOÜON

writ, replaced in real actions [33] the older magical-rational modes of proof, i.e., wager of law and combat, by the interrogation of twelve neighbors sworn to tell whatever they knew about the seisin in question. The "jury" emerged when the parties voluntarily or, shortly afterwards, under the pressure of compulsion,[34] agreed in all types of litigation [35] to accept the verdict of twelve jurors rather than to derive the finding of guilt from the old irrational modes of trial.[36] The jury, as it were, thus took the place of the oracle, and indeed it resembles it inasmuch as it does not indicate rational grounds for its decision. There was to be a distribution of functions between presiding "judge" and jury. The popular view which assumes that questions of fact are decided by the jury and questions of law by the judge is clearly wrong. Lawyers esteem the jury system, and particularly the civil jury, precisely because it decides certain concrete issues of "law" without creating "precedents" which might be binding in the future, in other words, because of the very "irrationality" in which a jury decides questions of law. Indeed, it is this aspect of the civil jury's function which explains the very slow development in English law of certain rules of long-time practical validity to the status of fully recognized rules of law. As the verdicts intermingled issues of law with questions of fact, it was only to the extent that the judges freed the properly legal from the factual portions of a verdict and articulated the former as legal principles, that these verdicts could become part of the growing body of law. It was in this manner that a major part of English commercial law was formulated by Lord Mansfield in the course of his judicial career. He endowed with the dignity of legal

---

DES LONGRAIS, LA SAISINE (1925), and by the same author, *La portée politique des réformes d'Henri II* (1936) REVUE HISTORIQUE DE DROIT 540.

[33] The "real actions" were those common law actions which were brought for the recovery of land. They were cumbersome and subject to numerous delays (*essoins*) and became obsolete in the sixteenth century, when the action of ejectment largely took their place. Cf. MAITLAND, FORMS 7; PLUCKNETT 336–337, 354.

[34] The form of compulsion referred to is the *peine forte et dure*. This was first imposed by the Statute of Westminster (1275) upon felons who refused to submit to trial by jury. In the sixteenth century, the *peine* became a form of torture: the accused was placed between two boards and weights were piled upon him until he accepted trial by jury or finally succumbed.

[35] Compulsion was only used in the case of felonies. Jury trial soon became the normal mode of trial in civil cases. See especially PLUCKNETT 125; BRUNNER, SCHWURGERICHTE (1876); HOLTZENDORFF'S RECHTSLEXICON 559, repr. 1 ABHANDLUNGEN ZUR RECHTSGESCHICHTE (1931) 82.

[36] The classical work on the origins of the jury is BRUNNER, ENTSTEHUNG DER SCHWURGERICHTE (1872); for a comprehensive presentation see 1 POLLOCK AND MAITLAND 138; 1 HOLDSWORTH 298; THAYER, THE JURY AND ITS DEVELOPMENT (1892) 5 HARV. L. REV. 249; see also RADIN, 204.

propositions what had hitherto been but the "feeling for law and justice" of the juries when they settled legal problems without distinguishing between law and fact.[37] Incidentally, the jury performed this task quite well, at least when it included experienced businessmen. Similarly, in Roman law the creative function of the "responding jurists" emerged from their giving advice to civil jurors; but in this case the legal problems were analyzed outside the court by an independent and legally competent agency.[38] This in due course produced a tendency to shift the work of the jurors onto the responding jurists and promoted in Rome the extraction of rational propositions of law from vaguely felt ethical maxims, just as in England the temptation to shift the work from the judge to the jury could, and probably often did, produce the opposite effect. Because of the jury, some primitive irrationality of the technique of decision and, therefore, of the law itself, has thus continued to survive in English procedure even up to present time.[39]

Again, in so far as settled ways of judging typical fact situations have developed from the interaction of private business practices and judicial precedents, they do not possess the rational character of "legal propositions" as evolved by modern legal science. The legally relevant fact situations were distinguished from each other in a thoroughly empirical way in accordance with their objective characteristics rather than in accordance with their meanings as disclosed by formal legal logic. Certain distinctions were made, but only in the context of determining in a particular case which question should be addressed to the god or the charismatic authority, how this question should be put, and upon which of the parties it should be incumbent to apply the appropriate means of proof. As primitive legal coercion had for this purpose become rigorously formal and consistent, it always led to the "conditional judgment." [40] One

[37] On Lord Mansfield, see 12 Holdsworth 464–560; also C. H. S. Fifoot, Lord Mansfield (1936), esp. 82–117.

[38] *Infra* p. 212.

[39] Cf. in this respect the opinion of Jerome Frank as expressed in Law and the Modern Mind, c. xvi and App. 5; also in Courts on Trial (1949), c. viii.

[40] The conditional or proof-judgment of early German procedure (i.e., before the reception of Roman law) merely decided which allegations were decisive of the cause, which allegations had therefore to be proved, and which of the parties was to make the proof. Failing proof, judgment went automatically to the other party. In other words, "the legal consequences of such success or failure in the proof needed no express statement: the nature of the proof-judgment was such as to leave not the slightest doubt on this score" (Engelmann and Millar 143–144). This type of judgment differed from Roman procedure, where the plaintiff sought to establish conclusively his claim and thus to secure authority to have his claim enforced in case judgment was given in his favor. In the Germanic system, the claim and its

of the parties was declared to have the right or the duty to furnish proof in a certain way, and success or failure in the case was, explicitly or by implication, declared to depend upon the result of his proof. Although different in many technical respects, the procedural dichotomy of both the praetorian formulary procedure [41] of Rome and the English procedure by writ and jury trial were connected with this basic phenomenon.

The problem of just what question was to be addressed to the magical powers constituted the first stage in the development of technical-legal concepts. But there is as yet no distinction between questions of fact and questions of law; or between objective norms and subjective "claims" of individuals which they guarantee; or between the claim for performance of an obligation and the demand for vengeance for a wrong; [42] or between public and private rights; or between the making and the application of the law. Nor is there a distinction between "law" meaning the normative claims of certain individuals, and "administration" meaning the purely technical decrees which indirectly result in certain persons obtaining certain opportunities. Of course, all such distinctions exist in a latent and primitively inarticulate form. For, when seen from our point of view, the different kinds of coercion or of coercive authorities

---

enforcement were, as it were, left open, and the defendant, in case he was unsuccessful as against the plaintiff's proof, was bound to give satisfaction not by virtue of the judgment itself but by virtue of his undertaking to accept the results of the proofs which were directed by the court. ENGELMANN AND MILLAR, *ibid.*

In his text, Weber continues as follows: "in close correspondence to our present practice in those cases where one party is charged with swearing a decisory oath." The reference is to Sections 445–463 of the German Code of Civil Procedure in its original version of 1877. Under these provisions the party who has the burden of proof and would otherwise be unable to prove a material fact within the knowledge of the other, could challenge the latter to swear that the former's factual allegation is not true. In such cases the court would render a conditional final judgment to the effect that decision would go to the party challenged if he would swear the oath, but to the challenger if the oath were not sworn. One or the other alternative would take effect immediately depending on whether or not the oath would be sworn. This kind of procedure was abolished by the Law of October 27, 1933 (R.G. Bl. 1933 I 779, 781).

[41] The parallel drawn by Weber is first that between the Roman *litis contestatio* on the one hand and the Germanic *Urteilserfüllungsgelöbnis* on the other. The similarity between them is that both constituted, as it were, agreements between the parties to submit to the decision that would be rendered. The second parallel seems to be that between the Roman *litis contestatio* and the Germanic conditional or proof judgment (see n. 40 *supra*), which also existed in England until trial by jury replaced the other modes of proof such as the ordeal and trial by battle.

[42] Originally, everything which could constitute the basis of a suit was a wrong. [Weber's note.]

to some extent correspond to these distinctions. Thus the distinction between the religious lynch justice (employed by a community which feels threatened by magical dangers because of the conduct of one of its members) and the composition proceedings between kinship groups corresponds in a certain sense to the present-day distinction between criminal prosecution *ex officio* and civil proceedings initiated by private parties. Likewise we have come to see the original seed bed of "administration" in the arbitration of disputes by the master of the household, unbound by formal restraints or principles; and we distinguished this type of "administration" from the first steps toward an organized "administration of justice" which evolved in disputes between kinship groups by way of the rigorously formal composition procedure and its strict tendency to apply only existing rules. Furthermore, wherever there arose an *imperium* (i.e., an authority whose functions are specifically particularized as distinguished from the unlimited domestic authority), we find the beginnings of the distinction between "legitimate" command and the norms by which it is "legitimated." Both sacred tradition and charisma bestowed upon an individual command either an impersonal or a personal legitimacy, as the case may be, and thus also indicated the limits of their "lawfulness." [43] But since *imperium* conferred upon its holder a specific "legal quality" rather than impersonal jurisdiction, there was for a long time no clear-cut distinction between the legitimate command, the legitimate claim, and the norm by which both are legitimated. Again, what separated immutable tradition from *imperium* was also rather vague. The reason is that the *imperium*-holder made no important decision, however great the power he might claim, without resorting as nearly as possible to the method of obtaining a revelation of the law.

5. *Approaches to Legislation.* (a) Even within the framework of tradition, the law that is actually applied does not remain stable. As long, at least, as the tradition has not yet fallen into the domain of a group of specially trained "preservers," who are at first usually the magicians and priests developing empirically fixed rules of operation, it will be relatively unstable in wide areas of social life. Valid "law" is what is "applied" as such. The decisions of the African "palavers" have been transmitted over generations and been treated as "valid law." [44]

[43] Cf. *infra* pp. 334 *et seq.*, 349 *et seq.*

[44] *Palaver* — "A talk, parley, conference, discussion; chiefly applied to conferences, with much talk, between African or other uncivilized natives, and traders or travellers," 7 OXFORD ENGLISH DICTIONARY (1933) 390; cf. LETOURNEAU, L'ÉVOLUTION JURIDIQUE (1891) 78, 89.

Munzinger reports the same phenomenon as to the East African dooms (*buthas*).[45] "Case law" is the oldest form of changing "customary law." As far as subject matter is concerned, we have seen that, at first, this kind of legal development is limited to the tested devices of the art of magical inquiry. Only as the importance of the magicians declined did tradition acquire that character which it possessed, for example, in the Middle Ages and under which the existence of a legally valid usage could, just like a fact, become the subject matter of proof by the interested party.[46]

(b) The most direct path of development led from the charismatic revelation of new commandments over the *imperium* to the conscious creation of law by compact or imposed enactment. The heads of kinship groups or local chieftains are the earliest parties to such compacts. Where in addition to villages and kinship groups, territorially more inclusive political or other associations come into existence for some political or economic reason, their affairs were managed through the regular or *ad hoc* meetings of the authorities just referred to. The compacts at which they arrived were of a purely technical or economic nature, that is, they concerned themselves, according to our notions, with mere "administration" or strictly private settlements. These compacts expanded, however, into the most diverse spheres. The assembled authorities might, in particular, incline toward imputing to their common declarations a particularly high authority for the interpretation of the sacred tradition. Under certain circumstances they might even dare to interfere, through their interpretation, with magically sanctioned institutions, for instance, those ordering kinship exogamy. At first this process would be initiated mostly by the charismatically qualified magician or sage presenting the assembly with the revelation of the new principle with which he has been inspired in a state of ecstasy or in a dream; then the members, acknowledging the charismatic qualification, would accept this revelation and would communicate it to their own groups as a new principle to be observed. However, the boundaries between technical decree, interpretation of tradition by individual decision, and revelation of new rules were vague and the magicians' prestige was unstable. Hence, the creation of law could, as for instance in Australia, be increasingly secularized [47] and revelation could be either completely excluded or applied only as an *ex post facto* legalization of the compacts. As a result, wide

[45] W. Munzinger, Ostafrikanische Studien (1864) 478.

[46] Cf. *supra*, p. 65.

[47] See A. Elkin, The Australian Aborigines (1938) 28–31, 36–37, 102; and literature there cited; Spencer, The Arunta (1927) I, 11–13.

areas in which lawmaking was once possible only through revelation become subject to regulation by the simple consensus of the assembled authorities. This notion of "enactment" of law is thus frequently found to be fully developed even among African tribes, although the elders and other *honoratiores* may not always be able to impose upon their fellow tribesmen the new laws upon which they have agreed. Menrad[48] has found, for instance, that on the Guinea Coast the agreements of the *honoratiores* are imposed by fines upon the economically weak, that the new norms are disregarded, however, by the wealthy and the eminent unless they had been assented to by them in exact analogy to the behavior of the "great of the realm" in the Middle Ages. On the other hand, the Ahentas and the Dahomey Negroes would, either periodically or incidentally, revise their enacted statutes and decide upon new ones.[49] Such a situation, however, can no longer be called primitive.

(c) As a general rule, enactment of statutes was either entirely nonexistent, or, where it existed, the absence of any distinction between finding and making law usually prevented the emergence of any idea of the legislative act as a general rule to be "applied" by the judge. The doom simply carried the authority of precedent. This type of intermediate stage between the interpretation of an already prevailing law and the creation of new law is still to be found in the German "customals" (*Weistümer*), which are pronouncements regarding either concrete or abstract legal problems, issued by an authority legitimated by either personal charisma or age, knowledge, honorific family status, or official position.[50] It is also exemplified by the pronouncements of the Nordic *lag saga*.[51] These Germanic sources did not distinguish between laws and rights,[52] or between statutory enactment and judicial decision, or between private and public law, or even between administrative decree and normative rule. Depending on the case at hand, they fluctuated from one to the other. Even English parliamentary resolutions retained such an ambiguous character almost up to the threshold of modern times. As indicated by the term *assisa*, not only in the Plantagenet era but, at least basically, even well into the seventeenth century, a parliamentary

[48] The reference could not be located.

[49] M. J. Herskovits, Dahomey, An Ancient West African Kingdom (1938) II, 5–16; R. Rattray, Ashanti Law and Constitution (Oxford, 1929); D. Westermann, The African To-day and To-morrow (3rd ed. 1949) 72; E. C. Meck, Law and Authority in a Nigerian Tribe (1937) 247 *et seq.*

[50] *Supra* n. 19.

[51] *Supra* n. 31.

[52] In the German language this distinction is obscured by the fact that the same word "Recht" means both "law" and "right."

resolution had the same character as any other doom.[53] Even the king did not regard himself as unconditionally bound by his own *assisae.* By various means Parliament sought to counteract that tendency. The keeping of records and "rolls" of various kinds was meant to serve the purpose of conferring the status of precedent upon those Parliamentary resolutions which had met with royal assent. Consequently, the resolutions of Parliament have always retained, even until today, the character of mere amendments to the existing law, in contrast to the codifying character of the modern continental legislative enactment, which, unless otherwise indicated, always purports to constitute a complete regulation of the subject matter in question. Hence, the principle that old law is completely repealed by new law has not yet been fully accepted in England even today.[54]

(d) That concept of statute which in England was favored by the rationalism of the Puritans and later of the Whigs derives from Roman law, where it had its source in the *ius honorarium,* i.e., in the originally *military* imperium *of the magistrate. Lex rogata* was that decree of the magistrate which had been rendered binding for the citizens by the consent of the citizens in arms and which was thus binding also for the magistrate's successor in office.[55] The original source of the modern concept of statute was, accordingly, Roman military discipline and the peculiar nature of Roman military communality. In medieval continental Europe, Frederick I of Hohenstaufen was the first to utilize the Roman conception of statute,[56] apart from the Carlovingians, to whom

[53] On the slow development of the English "statute" from a specific royal grant or command into an act of legislation in the modern sense, see ALLEN 357; PLUCKNETT, STATUTES AND THEIR INTERPRETATION IN THE FIRST HALF OF THE 14TH CENTURY (1922); THORNE, *op. cit. supra* n. 25; Richardson and Sayles, *The Early Statutes* (1934) 50 L.Q. REV. 201, 540; see also the concise survey in RADIN 327 *et seq.*

[54] "Statutes in derogation of the common law are to be interpreted narrowly!"

[55] The decree of a Roman magistrate was not binding upon his successor; the *praetor*'s edict had thus to be repromulgated whenever a new *praetor* took office. The situation was different, however, where the magistrate had asked for (*rogare*) and obtained the assent of the popular assembly (*comitia*). In that case his act was formally elevated to the rank of a *lex* or, more specifically, a *lex rogata.* It was distinguished from the *lex data,* which was a decree issued by the magistrate alone and without the assent of the popular assembly. It was used mostly for purposes of provincial and local government and of emergency legislation. It was characteristic of the Roman legislative process that the popular assemblies could neither initiate legislation nor discuss it. The draft law was placed before the assembly by the moving magistrate (*rogatio*) and the assembly would only express its assent (*uti rogas*) or its refusal. Cf. 3 MOMMSEN, 310 *et seq.*

[56] Frederick I (Barbarossa), Emperor 1152–1190. Whether it can really be said

it had been of a merely incipient significance.[57] But even the early medieval, particularly English, conception of the statute as an enacted amendment to the law was by no means reached quickly.

(e) Characteristics of the charismatic epoch of lawmaking and lawfinding have persisted to a considerable extent in many of the institutions of the period of rational enactment and application of the law. Remnants still survive even at the present day. As late a writer as Blackstone called the English judge a sort of living oracle; [58] and as a matter of fact, the role played by decision as the indispensable and specific form in which the common law is embodied corresponds to the role of the oracle in ancient law: What was hitherto uncertain, viz., the existence of the particular legal principle, has now, through the decision, become a permanent rule. The decision cannot be disregarded with impunity unless it is obviously "absurd" or "contrary to reason" [59] and therefore lacking charismatic quality. The only distinction between the genuine oracle and the English precedent is that the oracle does not state rational grounds, but it shares this very feature with the verdict of the jury. Historically, of course, the jurors are not the successors of the charismatic legal prophets; they rather represent the displacement of the irrational means of proof in the administration of justice through popular assemblies, by the testimony in the King's courts of neighbors, especially in matters concerning property and possession. The jury is thus a product of monarchical rationalism. On the other hand, however, charismatic declaration of law has been the source of the relations between the Germanic aldermen (*scabini, schepen, schoeffen*) [60] and the "judge" as well as of the Nordic institution of the *lag saga*.

6. *The Role of the Law Prophets and of the Folk Justice of the*

---

that he was "the first" to utilize the Roman conception of statute is open to doubt. The idea that the Germanic emperors were the successors of the Roman caesars can be found ever since the renewal of the Empire by Charlemagne in A.D. 800; cf. C. DAWSON, THE MAKING OF EUROPE (1935) 214 *et seq.*; P. KOSCHAKER, EUROPA UND DAS RÖMISCHE RECHT (1947) 6–54, and the vast literature cited there.

Frederick I was particularly outspoken in this idea and in his insistence upon Roman law constituting the continuing law of the Empire, in which his own *constitutiones* were to occupy the same position as those of his predecessors of antiquity. Cf. 1 STOBBE 617.

[57] For a concise account of the "written law" in the Frankish Empire see SMITH 124 *et seq.*

[58] BLACKSTONE I, 172, 173.

[59] BLACKSTONE I, 173.

[60] As to the *Schöffen* see BRUNNER I, 209; II, 296–303; ENGELMANN AND MILLAR 98 *et seq.*, 144 *et seq.*; SMITH 135, 247, *et seq.*

Germanic Assembly. Of striking importance is a fundamental principle which has had an extraordinary influence upon the development of corporative and estate autonomy in the medieval West.

(a) This principle, which was adhered to with great consistency for political and other reasons already mentioned, required that the lord of the court or his deputy would not participate in the decision of the case but would only occupy the chair and keep order in the court; the decision was to be arrived at by charismatic "declarers" of the law or, later, by aldermen appointed from the community within which the decision was to stand as law.[61] In certain respects, this principle partakes of the nature of charismatic adjudication. The judge, by whom the court is convoked and held in his official capacity, cannot participate in the lawfinding simply because in the charismatic view his office as such does not confer upon him the charismatic quality of legal wisdom. His task is done when he has brought the parties to the point where they choose composition in preference to vengeance and the peace of the court in preference to self-help, and where they are ready to perform those formalities which both force them to adhere to the trial agreement and, at the same time, constitute the correct and effective way of putting the question to the deity or to the charismatically qualified sages. Originally, these legal sages were men of some general magical qualifications who were called upon in individual cases because of their very charisma; or they were priests, as the Brehons in Ireland [62] or the Druids among the Gauls,[63] or special juridical *honoratiores* acknowledged as such by election as *lag sagas* among the North Germans or as *rachimburgi* among the Franks.[64] The charismatic *lag saga* later became a functionary whose position was legitimated as such by periodic election and eventually by appointment; the *rachimburgi* gave way to the aldermen legitimated as juridical *honoratiores* by royal patent. Yet, the principle still survived that the law could not be disclosed by the lord himself but only by persons qualified by the possession of charisma. Thanks to his charismatic status, many a Nordic *lag saga* or German alderman was a politically influential spokesman for his district with the sovereign, especially in

[61] Cf. *infra*, p. 90.

[62] As to the ancient laws of Ireland and the so-called Brehon laws, see MAINE, INSTITUTIONS 9, 24, 279 *et seq.*; J. H. WIGMORE, PANORAMA OF THE WORLD'S LEGAL SYSTEMS (1936) 669–713, and literature cited at 730; E. MacNeill, *Law — Celtic* 9 ENCYC. SOC. SCI. 246, 266 (bibliography).

[63] MAINE 662–669; MACNEILL, *loc cit.*

[64] BRUNNER, RECHTSGESCHICHTE I, 204, 209; II, 295–300, 302, 472; SMITH, 134; see also Haff, *Der germanische Rechtsprecher* (1948) 66 SAV. Z. GERM. 364.

Sweden.[65] Always, these men were descended from eminent families and quite naturally the office was often hereditary in a family regarded to be charismatically qualified. It can be shown that since the tenth century no *lag saga* has ever been a "judge." He had nothing to do with the enforcement of any judgment; originally he had no coercive powers at all and only later did he acquire a limited coercive power in Norway. Coercive power, to the extent that it existed in legal matters at all, lay rather in the hands of political officials. From one called upon from case to case to find the law, the lag saga developed into a permanent official; and with the growing need for a rational calculability and regularity of the law, he became responsible for stating annually before the assembled community all those rules in accordance with which he would declare or "find" the law from case to case. The purpose was to make these rules known to the whole community but also to keep them alive in the memory of the *lag saga* himself. In spite of certain differences, the similarity with the annual publication of the praetorian edict is considerable. The succeeding *lag saga* was not bound by the saga of his predecessor, since, by virtue of his charisma, every *lag saga* could "create" new law. He could, of course, take into account suggestions and resolutions of the popular assembly, but he was not required to do so, and such resolutions were not law until they were received into the *lag saga*. Law could only be revealed; this fundamental principle as well as its implications in regard to the creation and declaration of law must now have become quite obvious. Traces of such institutions can be found in all Germanic legal systems, especially in Frisia, where we find the so-called *asega*.[66] Thuringia seems to constitute the only exception.[67] The "editors" mentioned in the Preamble to the *Lex Salica* [68] probably were also such

[65] The "law speaker" in Sweden was the *laghmather*; see E. Künssberg, *Germanic Law* 9 ENCYC. SOC. SCI. 237; v. AMIRA, NORDGERMANISCHES OBLIGATIONENRECHT (1882) 5, 15, 20, 143; see also WIGMORE, *op. cit. supra* n. 62, at 818; BRYCE 328, 329, 332; MAURER, VORLESUNGEN ÜBER ALTNORDISCHE RECHTSGESCHICHTE (1907/10) IV, 263 *et seq.*, 280; v. AMIRA, *op. cit.*; R. Schröder, *Gesetzsprecheramt und Priestertum bei den Germanen* (1883) 4 SAV. Z. GERM. 215, and literature there cited; K. Haff, *Der germanische Rechtsprecher als Träger der Kontinuität* (1948) 66 SAV. Z. GERM. 364.

[66] The elected *iudex* — *âsega* — had to find the appropriate law and to submit it to the community for approval. BRUNNER I, 205; SMITH 37; see also SCHRÖDER 221.

[67] Authority for this proposition could not be located.

[68] Weber speaks of the Introduction to the "Lex Salica." The older version of the Salic Laws, which alone is prefaced by the Introduction mentioned in the text, is more correctly referred to as the "Pactus legis Salicae." Its text is as follows:

"Between the Franks and their great ones it was agreed and resolved that one should cut down all causes of quarrels in order to preserve the zeal for peace among

prophets of the law, and we may therefore rightly assume that the peculiar origin of the Frankish *Capitula legibus addenda* [69] is in some way connected with the incorporation of this legal prophecy into the organization of the state.

(b) Similar developments, or traces of them, can be found everywhere. The primitive method of deciding legal disputes by resorting to an oracle was frequent in civilizations of otherwise highly rationalized political and economic structure as, for instance, Egypt (the oracle of Ammon) or Babylonia.[70] Certainly the practice also contributed to the power of the Hellenic oracles.[71] Similar functions were performed by the legal institutions of the Israelites.[72] Indeed, legal prophecy seems to have been universal. Everywhere the power of the priests rested largely upon their activities as dispensers of oracles or as the "directors" of the procedure in ordeals. Their powers thus increased considerably with the growing pacification of society due to the increased replacement of vengeance, at first by composition and eventually by complaint and trial. In Africa, the significance of irrational means of proof has been greatly reduced by the "chieftain's trial"; nevertheless, the terrifying power of the fetish-priest still rests upon the partial survival of the older practice of the sacred magical trial and ordeal, which was not only held under his supervision but which also allowed him to bring charges of sorcery and thus to deprive of life and property anyone who had incurred his displeasure or that of one who knew how to win him to his side. Even purely secular forms of the administration of justice have

---

them. As they surpass all neighboring tribes by the strength of their arms, so they should also surpass them by the authority of their laws. Claims for amends should thus be terminated according to the kinds of dispute. Hence there were chosen from among several men those called Visogast, Salegast, Arogast, and Vidogast, from places on the other side of the Rhine, to wit, Bodoheim, Saleheim, and Vidoheim. They assembled at three gemots, carefully discussed all causes of disputes, and decreed the decisions for every one of them." (Prologue to the "Lex Salica," translated from the Latin text in K. A. ECKHARDT, DIE GESETZE DES MEROWINGERREICHES (1935) 481.

[69] *Capitula legibus addenda* — royal acts (*capitula*) amending those popular laws which had been officially compiled, such as the *lex Salica* or the *lex Ribuaria*; cf. BRUNNER I, 543–550; on the Frankish capitularies in general, see POLLOCK AND MAITLAND I, 16.

[70] P. CARUS, ORACLE OF YAHVEH (1911) 22–26, 32; S. A. STRONG, ON SOME ORACLES TO ESARHADDON AND ASURBANIPAL (1893).

[71] F. W. H. Myers, *Greek Oracles* (in E. ABBOTT, HELLENICA, 1880) 425, 453–465; W. HALLIDAY, GREEK DIVINATION (1913), cc. iv, x; BOUCHÉ-LECLERQ, HISTOIRE DE LA DIVINATION DANS L'ANTIQUITÉ (1879), 4 vols.; see esp. III, 147, 149–152, 156–161.

[72] See CARUS, *op. cit.* 1–21, 33, 35. For a comparison of Israel and Egypt, *ibid.*, pp. 11–12.

under certain conditions retained important traces of the old charismatic methods of adjudication. It is probably correct to regard the Athenian *thesmothetes* [73] as a body of persons who, through a process of formalization, changed from a group of charismatic legal prophets into an elective council of officials. But we cannot say with any certainty to what extent the participation of the Roman *pontifices* in legal matters was originally organized in a way similar to that of other forms of legal prophecy. The principle of separating the formal direction of the lawsuit from the finding of law applied in Rome as well, although the technical details were different from those of Germanic law. As regards the edict of the *praetor* and the *aediles*, their similarity with the *lag saga* is also evident from the fact that its binding effect upon the individual official himself was preceded by a stage in which the official enjoyed wide discretionary powers. The principle that the *praetor* should be bound by his own edict did not evolve into a rule of law until the imperial period; and we must assume that both the pontifical disclosure of the law as resting upon an esoteric body of technical rules and the *praetor's* instruction to the *iudex* were at first rather irrational. In traditional historiography the demand of the plebs for the codification and publication of the law is presented as resulting from their opposition to both an esoteric law and the power of the magistrate.

(c) The separation of lawfinding from law enforcement has often been claimed to be a peculiar trait of German law as well as the source of the special power of the German sodalities (*Genossenschaften*).[74] Actually, however, it is anything but a German peculiarity. The German council of aldermen simply took the place of the old charismatic prophets. The unique feature of German legal development can rather be found in the maintenance of that separation, the way in which it was technically worked out, and its connection with certain other important peculiarities of German law. Of these, one must mention particularly the continuous importance of the so-called *Umstand*.[75] This was the participation in the process of adjudication by members of the legal community who were not juridical *honoratiores*, whose concurrence or rather, acclamation expressive of concurrence, was indispensable for

[73] The college of *thesmothetai* seems to have been a judicial body in Athens, created the administration of justice and appear to have been called legislators, to relieve the executive magistrates (*archontes*) of some of the burden of their judicial duties. See 1 BONNER AND SMITH, 85.

[74] See *infra* p. 154.

[75] The *Umstand* are the members of the popular assembly (*thing*, *gemot*) who surround the judgment place and give or refuse their assent to the judgment proposed.

ratification of the verdict as found by the "lawfinders," and every one of whom could, by way of *Urteilsschelte*, challenge the verdicts proposed.[76] The phenomenon of participating in adjudication by way of concurring acclamation can be found outside the area of Germanic procedure. One is justified in assuming, for instance, that elements of this practice are contained in Homer's description of a trial as depicted upon the shield of Achilles; [77] or in the trial of Jeremiah,[78] and elsewhere. The right of every freeman to challenge the decision of the lawfinders, i.e., the so-called *Urteilsschelte,* is a peculiar feature of German law, however. Yet it is by no means necessary to regard it as rooted in immemorial, aboriginal Germanic tradition. It seems rather to be a product of special developments, largely military in nature.

(1) Among the most important factors which secularized the thinking about what should be valid as a norm and especially its emancipation from magically guaranteed traditions, were war and its uprooting effects. Although the *imperium* of the conquering warrior chief was inevitably very wide, he could not exercise it in important cases without the free consent of the army. It was in the very nature of the situation that this imperium was in the vast majority of cases oriented towards the regulation of conditions which in times of peace could have been regulated only by revealed norms, but which in times of war required that new norms be created by agreed or imposed enactment. The war lord and the army disposed of prisoners, booty, and particularly of conquered land. They thus created new individual rights and, under certain circumstances, new law. On the other hand, the war lord, both in the interest of common security and to prevent breaches of discipline and the instigation of domestic disorder, had to have more comprehensive powers than a "judge" possessed in times of peace. These circumstances would alone have been sufficient to increase the imperium at the expense of tradition. But war also disrupts the existing economic and social order, so that it becomes clear to everyone that the things one has been accustomed to are not absolutely sacred. It follows that war and warlike expansion have at all stages of historical development often been connected with a systematic fixation of the law both old and new. Again, the pressing need for security against internal and foreign enemies

[76] On *Urteilsschelte* see *infra* at n. 86; also BRUNNER II, 471.

[77] This is Homer's famous description in the *Iliad* (Σ497–508); cf. MAINE, 385, and note "S" (by F. POLLOCK) at 405–407; and especially, H. J. Wolff, *The Origin of Judicial Litigation among the Greeks* 4 TRADITIO (1946) 34–49, with bibliography on p. 82.

[78] Jer. 26:7–24.

induces a growing rationalization of lawmaking and lawfinding. Above all, those various social elements by whom legal procedure is guided and presided over, enter into new relationships with each other. In the same way as the political association assumes a permanently military character because of war and preparation for war, the military as such increases its decisive influence over the settlement of disputes between its members and, consequently, upon the development of the law. The prestige of age and, to a certain extent, the prestige of magic tend to decrease. But many different solutions would be found for the problem of how to adjust the various claims for a share in the making of new law among the war lord, the secular and spiritual guardians of sacred tradition, and the army, which is likely to be comparatively free from the restraints of tradition.

From this point of view, the type of military organization is a highly important factor. The Germanic *thing* of the district and also the *gemot* (*Landsgemeinde*) of the total political community were assemblies of the men who were able to bear arms and, consequently, were owners of land. Similarly, the Roman *populus* consisted of the property-holders assembled in their tactical units.[79] During the great upheavals of the migration of the Germanic tribes, the assemblies of the Germanic political communities seem to have assumed, as against the war lord, the right to participate in the creation of new law. Sohm's contention that all enacted law was the King's law is quite improbable.[80] In fact, the bearer of the *imperium* does not seem to have played a predominant role in this kind of lawmaking. Among more sedentary peoples, the power of the charismatic legal sage continued unbroken; among those who were faced with new situations in the course of their warlike wanderings, especially the Franks and the Langobards, the sense of power of the warrior class increased. They claimed and exercised the right of active and decisive participation in the enactment of laws and the formation of judgments.

In early medieval Europe, on the other hand, the Christian Church, by its example of episcopal power, everywhere strongly encouraged the interference of the princes in the administration and enactment of the law. Indeed, the church often instigated this intervention for its own interests as well as in the interests of the ethics it taught. The capitularies of the Frankish kings developed in the same way as the subtheocratic courts of the itinerant justices.[81] In Russia, very shortly after

[79] Cf. *infra*, p. 333.

[80] Sohm, *Fränkisches Recht und römisches Recht* (1880) 1 Sav. Z. Germ. 1, 9.

[81] Annual visitation of the diocese by the bishop seems to have been an ancient

the introduction of Christianity, the second version of the *Russkaya Pravda* is evidence of the prince's intervention in adjudication and enactment which had been lacking in the first version; the result was the development of a considerable body of new substantive law having its source in the prince.[82] In the Occident, this tendency of the *imperium* conflicted with the firm structure of charismatic and corporative justice within the military community. On the other hand, the Roman *populus* could, in accordance with the development of discipline in the hoplite army,[83] only accept or reject what was proposed by the holder of the *imperium,* i.e., apart from legal enactments, nothing but decisions in capital cases brought before it by *provocatio*.[84] In the German *thing* a valid judgment necessarily required the acclamation of the audience (*Umstand*).[85] The Roman *populus,* on the other hand, was not concerned with any judgment save its power to rescind, by way of grace, a death sentence rendered by a magistrate. The right of every

---

custom in the church. In the Frankish empire this custom seems to have been neglected during the later Merovingian period. It was revived under the Carlovingians in the seventh century, and there was separated from the general visitation a special institution for the discovery and punishment of ecclesiastical crimes, the so-called itinerant court (*Sendgericht*). It was held as an inquest at which in each parish a group of "mature, honest, and truthful men" (*iuratores*) were required under oath to inform the bishop's itinerant judge of all crimes of which they had knowledge. Cf. 5 HINSCHIUS, SYSTEM DES KATHOLISCHEN KIRCHENRECHTS (1895) 425. On the role of the ecclesiastical *Sendgericht* as a model for the royal inquest and thus for the development of the jury system, see BRUNNER, SCHWURGERICHTE (1876).

[82] Weber's assumption of the existence of successive versions of the RUSSKAYA PRAVDA seems to be based upon the writings of Goetz (*Das russische Recht* [1910] 24 Z.F. VGL. RW. 241; [1914] 31 Z.F. VGL. RW. 1) and Kohler (*Die Russkaja Prawda und das altslawische Recht* [1916] 33 Z.F. VGL. RW. 289). Upon these studies doubt has been thrown by the latest investigation (Academy of the U.S.S.R., PRAVDA RUSSKAYA, 1940, I, 29, 55), where it is pointed out that the oldest existing manuscript dates from 1282 and that all earlier dates ascribed to later editions have been purely conjectural. Controversy also exists with reference to the nature of the RUSSKAYA PRAVDA. According to KLUCHEVSKY (HISTORY OF RUSSIA, trans. Hogarth [1911], cc. ix and x) the book is neither a princely enactment nor a private law book but a collection of secular customs which was made by the Church to be applied in its courts when they had to exercise general jurisdiction over its nonclerical subjects. For an English translation of the RUSSKAYA PRAVDA see VERNADSKY, MEDIEVAL RUSSIAN LAWS (1947).

[83] Hoplite army (Greek): an army composed of heavily-armed soldiers. The term is used by Weber as a term of art. Cf. W.U.G. 568, 592, 644; ESSAYS 57, 227, 256, 345.

[84] *Provocatio* — the right of a Roman citizen convicted of a capital crime to appeal to the people assembled in the *comitia centuriata*. See JOLOWICZ 320 *et seq.*

[85] See BRUNNER I, 204; SMITH 38; ENGELMANN AND MILLAR 96.

member of the German *thing* assembly to challenge the decision proposed (*Urteilsschelte*) [86] was due to its lesser degree of military discipline. The charismatic quality of adjudication was not the exclusive possession of a special occupational group, but every member of the *thing* community could at all times express his superior knowledge and attempt to have it prevail over the judgment proposed. Originally, a decision between them could only be arrived at by an ordeal, frequently with penal sanctions for the one whose "false" judgment constituted blasphemy against the divine guardians of the law. In fact, of course, the murmur of approval or disapproval by the community, whose voice was, in this sense, the "voice of God," would always carry considerable weight. The strict discipline of the Romans found expression in the magistrate's exclusive right of guiding the course of the lawsuit as well as in the exclusive right of initiative (*agere cum populo*) of the several magistrates who were competing with each other.[87]

The Germanic dichotomy between lawfinding and law enforcement constitutes one type of separation of powers in the administration of justice; another is represented by the Roman system of concurrent powers of several magistrates entitled to "intercede" against each other and of dividing the functions of a law suit between magistrate and *judex*. Separation of powers in the administration of justice was also guaranteed by the necessity of collaboration in various forms among magistrates, juridical *honoratiores*, and the military or political assembly of the community. It was on this basis that the formalistic character of the law and its administration were preserved.

(2) Where, however, "official" authorities, that is, the imperium of the prince and his officials or the power of the priests as the official guardians of the law succeeded in eliminating the independent bearers of charismatic legal knowledge on the one side, and the participation of the popular assembly or its representatives on the other, the development of law acquired quite early that theocratic-patrimonialistic character which, as we shall see, produced peculiar consequences for the formal aspects of the law. Although a different course developed where, as for instance in the Hellenic democracies, a politically omnipotent popular assembly completely displaced all magisterial and charismatic agents of adjudication and set itself up as the sole and supreme authority in the creation and the finding of the law, the effects upon the formal qualities of the law were similar. We shall speak of "lawfinding by the folk assembly" (*dinggenossenschaftliche Rechtsfindung*) whenever the folk

[86] *Supra* n. 76.
[87] *Supra* p. 85.

assembly, while it participates in adjudication, does not have supreme authority over it but can accept or reject the decision recommended by the charismatic or official possessor of legal knowledge and can influence the decision in some particular way, for instance, through the challenge of the judgment proposed. Illustrations of this situation are the Germanic military community as well as, although in a highly rationally modified way, the military community of Rome. The type is not characterized, however, by the mere fact of the popular assembly participating in adjudication, examples of which occur frequently, e.g., among the Negroes of Togoland [88] or among the Russians of the period of the first pre-Christian version of the *Russkaya Pravda*.[89] In both these situations we can find a small body of "judgment finders" — twelve among the Russians — corresponding to the Germanic council of aldermen. Among the Negroes of Togoland the members of this body are taken from among the elders of the kinship or neighborhood groups, and we may assume a similar basis more generally for the origin of the council of judgment finders. In the *Russkaya Pravda*, the prince did not participate at all; among the Togoland Negroes, however, he presides over the deliberations, and the judgment is arrived at by the joint and secret consultation between him and the elders. In neither case, however, does the participation of the people impart any charismatic character to the process of decision finding. Cases where popular participation does have that character seem to be rare in Africa and elsewhere.

(3) Where the folk community exists, the formal character of the law and of lawfinding is largely preserved because the lawfinding is the product of revelation of the legal sage rather than the whimsical or emotional enunciation of those for whom the law is effective, i.e., those whom it purports to dominate rather than to serve. On the other hand, the sage's charisma, like every other genuine charisma, must "prove" itself by its own persuasive and convincing power. Indirectly, the sense of fairness and the everyday experience of the members of the legal community can thus make themselves felt strongly. But formally, the law is a "lawyers' law," for without specific expert knowledge and skill, it cannot assume the form of a rational rule. However, as far as its content is concerned, it is at the same time also "popular law." It is probable that the origin of "legal proverbs" may be ascribed to the

[88] Cf. L. Asmis, DIE *Stammesrechte der Bezirke Misahöhe, Anecho und Lomeland* (*Schutzgebiet Togo*) (1911) 26 Z.F. VGL. RW. 1.

[89] See *supra* n. 82; cf. J. Kohler, *Die Russkaja Prawda und das altslawische Recht* (1916) 33 ZEITSCHRIFT FÜR ÖFFENTLICHES RECHT 289; but see *infra* p. 258.

epoch of administration of justice by the folk assembly. It should be realized, however, that the folk assembly was not a universal phenomenon, if we use the term in the precise sense of a peculiar variety of several possible ways of dividing power between the authority of legal charisma and ratification by the popular and military community. The specific feature of such legal proverbs is usually a combination of the formal legal norms with a concrete and popular reason, as, for example, in such sayings as these: "Where you have left your faith, there you must seek it again,"[90] or "Hand must warrant hand."[91] They originate, on the one hand, in the popular character of the law which arises both from the participation of the community and the relatively considerable knowledge which it has of the law. On the other hand, legal proverbs also originated in certain maxims formulated by individuals, who, either as experts or as interested observers, gave thought to the common features of frequently recurring decisions. It is certain that legal prophets must have coined many a maxim in this fashion. In short, legal proverbs are fragmentary legal propositions expressed as slogans.

7. *The Role of the Law Specialists.* Yet formally elaborated law constituting a complex of maxims consciously applied in decisions has never come into existence without the decisive coöperation of trained specialists. We have already become acquainted with their different categories. The stratum of "practitioners of the law" concerned with adjudication comprises, in addition to the official administrators of justice, the legal *honoratiores,* i.e., the *lag sagas, rachimburgi,* aldermen, and, occasionally, priests. As the administration of justice requires more and more experience and, ultimately, specialized knowledge, we find as a further category private counselors and attorneys, whose influence in the formation of the law through "legal invention" has often been considerable. The conditions under which this group has developed will later be discussed in detail.[92] The increased need for specialized legal knowledge created the professional lawyer. This growing demand for experience and specialized knowledge and the consequent stimulus for increasing rationalization of the law have almost always come from increasing significance of commerce and those participating in it. For the solution of the new problems thus created, specialized, i.e., rational, training is an ineluctable requirement. Our interest is centered upon the ways and consequences of the "rationalization" of the law, that is the develop-

[90] "Wo du deinen Glauben gelassen hast, da musst du ihn suchen"; see *supra* 00.

[91] "Hand wahre Hand." See *supra* p. 54.

[92] *Infra* c. VII.

ment of those "juristic" qualities which are characteristic of it today. We shall see that a body of law can be "rationalized" in various ways and by no means necessarily in the direction of the development of its "juristic" qualities. The direction in which these formal qualities develop is, however, conditioned directly by "intrajuristic" conditions: the particular character of the individuals who are in a position to influence "professionally" the ways in which the law is shaped. Only indirectly is this development influenced, however, by general economic and social conditions. The prevailing type of legal education, i.e., the mode of training of the practitioners of the law, has been more important than any other factor.

CHAPTER VI

FORMS OF CREATION OF RIGHTS[1]

Section 1. Logical Categories of "Legal Propositions" — Liberties and Powers — Freedom of Contract

The fusion of all those organizations which had respectively engendered their own bodies of law into the one comprehensive organization of the state, now claiming to be the sole source of all "legitimate" law, is characteristically reflected in the formal mode in which the law serves the interests, especially the economic interests, of the parties concerned. We have previously defined the existence of a right as being no more than an increase of the probability that a certain expectation of the one to whom the law grants the right will not be disappointed. We shall continue to consider the creation of a right as the normal method of increasing such probability, but we must recognize that, in a sociological analysis, there is but a gradual transition from this normal case to the situation where the legally secured interest of a party is but the "reflex" of a "regulation" and where the party does not possess a "right" in the strict sense.[2]

To the person who finds himself actually in possession of the power to control an object or a person the legal guaranty gives a specific certainty of the durability of such power. To the person to whom something has been promised the legal guaranty gives a higher degree of certainty that the promise will be kept. These are indeed the most elementary relationships between law and economic life. But they are not the only possible ones. Law can also function in such a manner that, in sociological terms, the prevailing norms controlling the operation of the coercive

[1] W.u.G. 413–456.

[2] See *supra* p. 42. As to the distinction between claim norms and reglementations, cf. JELLINEK, SYSTEM, esp. 63–76 (*Reflexrecht und subjectives Recht*); W. JELLINEK, VERWALTUNGSRECHT (1948) 200, 305. The validity of the distinction is denied by LABAND, STAATSRECHT (1911) I, 331; III, 207. A synthesis is tried by H. KELSEN, REINE RECHTSLEHRE (1934) 39; THEORY 77, 78, 84. The influence on Weber of Georg Jellinek, his Heidelberg colleague and personal friend, was considerable, not only in matters of detail but in giving support to Weber's sociological approach to law in general. It was applied by Jellinek especially in his ALLGEMEINE STAATSLEHRE, 3rd ed. 1914.

apparatus have such a structure as to induce, in their turn, the emergence of certain economic relations which may be either a certain order of economic control or a certain agreement based on economic expectations. This occurs when law is expressly created for a particular purpose. Such a situation presupposes, of course, a specific stage of legal development about which it will be appropriate to make some observations.

From the juridical point of view, modern law consists of "legal propositions," i.e., abstract norms the content of which asserts that a certain factual situation is to have certain legal consequences. The most usual classification of legal propositions distinguishes, as in the case of all norms, between prescriptive, prohibitory, and permissive ones; they respectively give rise to the rights of individuals to prescribe, or prohibit, or allow, an action vis-à-vis another person.[3] Sociologically, such legally guaranteed and limited power over the action of others corresponds to the expectation that other persons will either engage in, or refrain from, certain conduct or that one may himself engage, or fail to engage, in certain conduct without interference from a third party. The first two expectations constitute claims, the latter constitutes a privilege.[4] Every right is thus a source of power of which even a hitherto entirely powerless person may become possessed. In this way he becomes the source of completely novel situations within the community. Nevertheless, we are not at present concerned with this phenomenon, but rather wish to deal with the qualitative effect of legal propositions of a *certain* type inasmuch as they affect an individual right-holder's power of control. This type with which we shall deal is constituted by the third kind of legally guaranteed expectations previously mentioned, i.e., the *privileges*. In the development of the present economic order they are of particularly great importance. Privileges are of two main kinds: The *first* is constituted by the so-called freedoms, i.e., situations of simple protection against certain types of interference by third parties, especially by state officials acting within the sphere of otherwise legally

[3] For a typical presentation of this trichotomy see ENNECCERUS 56; 1 AUSTIN, LECTURES ON JURISPRUDENCE (1885) 39, 92, 684, 710 *et seq.* As to the third kind of right the text is not entirely clear. What is meant is not the situation in which *A* can allow *B* to engage in certain conduct but, as the following sentences show, the situation in which *A* can engage in certain conduct without being subject to legally justified interference by one, or more, or all, others.

[4] Weber is using the term *Freiheitsrecht* ("privilege") in the sense in which it had been developed by G. JELLINEK in SYSTEM 89. It might be noted that Jellinek's and Weber's use of the terms "claim" and "privilege" resembles Hohfeld's terminology; cf. HOHFELD, FUNDAMENTAL LEGAL CONCEPTIONS (1923).

permitted conduct; instances are freedom of movement, freedom of conscience, or freedom of disposition over property. The *second* type of privilege is that which grants to an individual *autonomy* to *regulate* his *relations with others* by his own transactions. Freedom of contract, for example, exists exactly to the extent to which such autonomy is recognized by the legal order. There exists, of course, an intimate connection between the expansion of the market and the expanding measure of contractual freedom or, in other words, the scope of arrangements which are guaranteed as valid by the legal order or, in again different terms, the relative significance within the total legal order of those rules which authorize such transactional dispositions. In an economy where self-sufficiency prevails and exchange is lacking, the function of the law will naturally be otherwise: it will mainly define and delimit a person's non-economic relations and privileges with regard to other persons in accordance, not with economic considerations, but with the person's origin, education, or social status.

Section 2. Development of Freedom of Contract — "Status Contracts" and "Purposive Contracts" — The Historical Origin of the Purposive Contracts

1. "Freedom" in the legal sense means the possession of rights, actual and potential, which, however, in a marketless community naturally do not rest predominantly upon legal transactions but rather directly upon the prescriptive and prohibitory propositions of the law itself. Exchange, on the other hand, is, within the framework of a legal order, a "legal transaction," viz., the acquisition, the transfer, the relinquishment, or the fulfillment of a legal claim. With every extension of the market, these legal transactions become more numerous and more complex. However, in no legal order is freedom of contract unlimited in the sense that the law would place its guaranty of coercion at the disposal of all and every agreement regardless of its terms. A legal order can indeed be characterized by the agreements which it does or does not enforce. In this respect a decisive influence is exercised by diverse interest groups, which varies in accordance with differences in the economic structure. In an increasingly expanding market, those who have market interests constitute the most important group. Their influence predominates in determining which legal transactions the law should regulate by means of power granting norms.

That extensive contractual freedom which generally obtains today has, of course, *not always existed*; and even where freedom of contract did exist, it did not always prevail in the spheres in which it prevails today. Freedom of contract once existed indeed in spheres in which it is no longer prevalent or in which it is far less prevalent than it used to be. We shall survey the main stages of development in the following brief sketch.

In contrast to the older law, the most essential feature of modern substantive law, especially private law, is the greatly increased significance of legal *transactions*, particularly *contracts*, as a source of claims guaranteed by legal coercion. So very characteristic is this feature of private law that one can *a potiori* designate the contemporary type of society, to the extent that private law obtains, as a "contractual" one.

a. From the legal point of view, the juridico-economic position of the individual, i.e., the totality of his legitimately acquired rights and valid obligations, is determined on the one hand by *inheritance* based upon a legally recognized family relationship, and, on the other hand, directly or indirectly, by contracts concluded by him or for him in his name. The law of inheritance constitutes in contemporary society the most important survival of that mode of acquisition of legitimate rights which was once, especially in the economic sphere, the exclusive or almost exclusive one. In the case of inheritance the operative facts generally occur independently of the interested individual's own conduct. These facts constitute the starting-point for his further legally relevant activities. But a person's membership in such a group as a given family is based upon natural relationship, which is socially and economically regarded as a special and intrinsic quality and is attributed to him by the law independently of his own acts of consociation.

Obviously the contrast is only relative, for claims of inheritance may also be based on contract; [5] and in testate succession the legal basis of acquisition is not the membership in the kinship circle but rather the unilateral disposition of the testator. However, contracts to devise or bequeath are infrequent nowadays. The normal and, in many systems of law, for example, the Austrian, the only possible case is that of the marriage settlement.[6] Mostly such a settlement is made before marriage in order simultaneously to regulate succession upon death and marital property rights *inter vivos*. In other words, the contract regulates the

[5] Weber is thinking here of the contract to devise or bequeath. In American law such a contract binds the promisor to make a certain will which, in turn, creates the right of the devisee or legatee. In German law the "contract of inheritance," if properly concluded, is as such the basis for the beneficiary's right upon the death of the promisor; it does not thus need to be implemented by a will. See German Civil Code, Secs. 2278–2302.

[6] See Austrian Civil Code, Sec. 1249.

property incidents of a family relationship about to be created. As regards wills, the great majority of them nowadays aim, in addition to munificence regarded as an obligation of decency, at the balancing of interests among family members in view of special economic needs created either by the peculiar nature of the assets of the estate or by peculiar circumstances of the persons concerned. Besides, at least outside of the area of Anglo-American law, freedom of testation is narrowly limited by the rights of certain near relatives to indefeasible portions.[7] The significance of the wider freedom of testation in certain ancient and modern systems of law and the correspondingly greater significance in the past, as well as the causes of their decline, are discussed in another place.[8] At the present time, legal transactions with freely chosen content and freely concluded according to the free choice of the parties are of but limited importance in the sphere of family and inheritance law.[9]

b. In *public law* the role of contractual transactions is, quantitatively at any rate, by no means slight. Every appointment of an official is made by contract and many important phenomena of constitutional government, especially certain determinations with regard to the budget, presuppose in substance, if not formally, a free agreement among a number of independent organs of the state, none of which can legally coerce the other. Yet, in the legal sense, the public official's legally fixed obligations are not regarded as flowing from a contract of appointment, as would happen in the case of a freely made contract of private law, but from his act of submission to the authority of the state as a public servant.[10] Similarly a freely arrived at agreement preceding the budget is not treated as a "contract"; nor is the agreement as such treated as a legally essential event. The reason is that, for good juristic reasons, "sovereignty" is accepted as the essential attribute of the modern state, conceived as a "unity," while the acts of its organs are looked upon as instances of the exercise of public duties. Thus, in the sphere of public

[7] Cf. McMurray, *Succession, Laws of*, 14 ENCYC. SOC. SCI. 435, 440; Nussbaum, *Liberty of Testation* (1937) 23 A.B.A.J. 183; RHEINSTEIN, DECEDENTS' ESTATES 403, 406.

[8] Cf. *infra* p. 137.

[9] For a discussion of the relations between inheritance and marital property rights on the one hand, and military and economic organization on the other, see also W.u.G., Part II, c. ii, § 5 (p. 204).

[10] All this is current German theory of administrative law. Cf. especially W. JELLINEK, 352 *et seq.* and further literature there cited; A. LOTZ, GESCHICHTE DES DEUTSCHEN BEAMTENTUMS (1914); W. SOMBART, BEAMTENSCHAFT UND WIRTSCHAFT (1927); F. WINTERS, ABRISS DER GESCHICHTE DES BEAMTENTUMS (1929); LABAND, DAS STAATSRECHT DES DEUTSCHEN REICHES (1911) 433 *et seq.*; see also Weber's discussion of Bureaucracy in W.u.G., Part III, c. vi (p. 650).

law the domain of free contract is essentially found in international law. This conception, however, has historically not always been the prevailing one and it would not accurately express the actual relationships of political organization in the past. Formerly the position of a public official was less based upon a free contract than it is today; indeed it rested rather upon his entire submission to the personal, quasi-familial, authority of a lord.[11] But other political acts, for instance those intended to provide means for public purposes as well as many other administrative acts, were, under the conditions of the corporately organized political structure, nothing but contracts between the prince and the estates, who, as the owners of their powers and prerogatives in their totality, constituted the political community. Legally, their joint acts were looked upon in precisely this manner.[12] The feudal bond, too, was in its innermost essence based upon contract, and the expression "pactus" was applied with all seriousness to such a collection of existing laws as the *leges barbarorum*, which at the present time we would call statutory codifications.[13] As a matter of fact, even real innovations in the law could only be brought about by a freely made agreement between the official authorities and the whole community assembled in the "thing."

The last example we may give of the use of the contract concept is the primitive political associations which, at any rate as far as their legal form was concerned, were based on freely concluded agreements between autonomous groups, such as, e.g., the "houses" of the Iroquois.[14] The so-called "men's houses," too, were in the first place voluntary associations which were intended, however, to be of permanent duration, and which were in this respect distinguished from those earlier voluntary associations which were established for the purpose of adventure and which were entirely based upon free agreement.[15] The phenomenon of

[11] The matter is discussed in LOTZ, *op. cit.* 28 (*Beamte als Hofbeamte*); LABAND, *op. cit.* 433.

[12] O. GIERKE, 91; same author, GENOSSENSCHAFTSRECHT I, 535; CARLYLE, HISTORY OF MEDIEVAL POLITICAL THEORY (1903), vol. iii, part 1; SPANGENBERG, VOM LEHENSSTAAT ZUM STÄNDESTAAT (1912); Luschin v. Ebengreuth, *Die Anfänge der Landstände* (1897) 78 HIST. Z. 427.

[13] The *leges barbarorum* were those "codifications" of the customary laws which were undertaken by the Germanic peoples after their conquest of the western parts of the Roman Empire, as, for example, the *Lex Salica* of the Salic Franks or the *Lex Visigothorum* of the Visigothic conquerors of Spain; cf. AMIRA 15, 16; Jenks, *Development of Teutonic Law* (1907) 1 SELECTED ESSAYS IN ANGLO-AMERICAN LEGAL HISTORY 35; HUEBNER 2.

[14] Cf. LEWIS H. MORGAN, LEAGUE OF THE IROQUOIS (1922); same author, ANCIENT SOCIETY (1878) 399, 446.

[15] On men's houses, see LOWIE, PRIMITIVE SOCIETY (1925) 197, 299, 306, 315, 368;

free agreement also appears at quite primitive levels in the field of *adjudication.* Indeed, it marks its very beginnings. The arbitration agreement which developed out of the agreement for composition between kinship groups, i.e., the voluntary submission to a verdict or an ordeal, is not only the source of all procedural law but also the point of departure to which even the oldest contracts of private law can, very broadly speaking, be traced.[16] Furthermore, most of the important technical advances of procedure have, at least formally, been products of voluntary agreement among the parties. Thus the intervention of the sovereign authorities, e.g., the lord mayor or praetor, took the very characteristic form of compelling the parties to make certain agreements designed to facilitate the progress of the cause.[17] They therefore are

---

H. Schurtz, Altersklassen und Männerbünde (1902); W. Schmidt und W. Koppers, Gesellschaft und Wirtschaft der Völker (1924) 244. Cf. also *infra* p. 343.

[16] This view of the origin of procedural law was also maintained by Maine, at 385. The opposite view that the law of procedure originated in the power of rulers to command their subjects to submit to arbitration has been advanced especially by F. Oppenheimer, The State (1914) 78–81, and L. Gumplowicz, Outlines of Sociology (1899), 179; cf. Seagle 62. It is an oversimplification to say that all procedural law had its origin either in voluntary or in commanded submission, for many other factors must have been involved. Where the disputes between primitive kinship groups were mediated or arbitrated, some additional circumstances must have occurred to change voluntary submission into compulsory submission to adjudication. It is, therefore, perhaps more correct to say that different rules of procedure had different origins; that this was so in Roman law has been argued by so careful a scholar as Wenger (at 11); but see, for another differentiating view, Ehrlich 137 *et seq.* As to the controversy in general, see Thurnwald 145 *et seq.*; Diamond, cc. xxx, xxxi.

[17] As to the Lord Mayor, Weber seems to be referring to the Mayor's Court in London; on its history, see A. Thomas, Illustrations of the Medieval Municipal History of London from the Guildhall Records (1921) in Transactions of the Royal Historical Society, 4th Ser., IV, 81 *et seq.* One of the peculiar usages of the Mayor's Court was the custom of *foreign attachment*: "By this custom, when a plaintiff brought an action for debt, and the debtor had no goods in his own hands, whereby he might be attached, but goods or money owed, in the hands of a third person, who was called the garnishee, the court would sequestrate such goods, and in case the garnishee made no denial, attach them. If the debtor pleaded to the suit and found bail, the attachment would be discharged. But on failure to do so, the Court would order the goods to be valued and delivered to the plaintiff in satisfaction of his claim, unless the debtor within a year and a day put in his appearance" (p. 98). See also A. Thomas, Calendar of Early Mayor's Court Roles (1924) and literature cited there; 20 Halsbury, The Laws of England (1911) 283. With respect to the Roman *praetor* Weber seems to be thinking primarily of the *litis contestatio* of the formulary procedure. Through the threat of property sequestration (*missio in bona*) the *praetor* could compel the parties to

but instances of the "compulsory contract" (*Rechtszwang zum Kontrahieren*); the compulsory feoffment, too, played a considerable role in the sphere of feudal, i.e., political, law.[18]

2. The "contract," in the sense of a voluntary agreement constituting the legal foundation of claims and obligations, has thus been widely diffused even in the earliest periods and stages of legal history. What is more, it can also be found in spheres of law in which the significance of voluntary agreement has either disappeared altogether or has greatly diminished, i.e., in public law, procedural law, family law, and the law of decedents' estates. On the other hand, however, the farther we go back in legal history, the less significant becomes contract as a device of economic acquisition in fields other than the law of the family and inheritance. The situation is vastly different today. The present-day significance of contract is primarily the result of the high degree to which our economic system is market-oriented and of the role played by money. The increased importance of the private law contract in general is thus the legal reflex of the market orientation of our economy. But contracts characteristic of a market economy are completely different from those contracts which in the spheres of public and family law once played a greater role than they do today. In accordance with this fundamental transformation of the general character of the voluntary agreement we shall call the more primitive type "status contract" and that which is peculiar to the exchange or market economy "purposive contract."

The distinction is based on the fact that all those primitive contracts by which political or other personal associations, permanent or temporary, or family relations are created involve, substantially, a change in

---

agree upon the formula proposed by him or worked out, with his coöperation, before him. Once the formula has been settled "the praetor gives the document to the plaintiff. . . And now follows the formal contract between the parties: the one who has now come out . . . as actor hands the document to the defendant, who accepts it." WENGER 139. As to the numerous controversies concerning the *litis contestatio* and its character as a compulsory contract, see WENGER 17, 139. Other compulsory contracts may be found in those various cases in which the *praetor* could compel one party to promise to give security to the other (*cautiones*; *stipulationes in iure*); cf. WENGER 102.

[18] In the pure form of feudalism, the relation between lord and vassal was created by a contract which either party was free to make. In European feudalism the fiefs tended to become hereditary in the sense that, at the death of the vassal, the lord was bound to enter upon a new contract with his heir, i.e., to accept his act of homage and fealty. Similarly the vassal was bound to render homage to the heir of the lord; cf. 5 ENCYC. SOC. SCI. 205, 219; POLLOCK AND MAITLAND I, 296, 310.

what may be called the total legal situation (the universal position) and the social status of the persons involved. To have this effect these contracts were originally either straightforward magical acts or at least acts having a magical significance. For a long time their symbolism retained traces of that character, and the majority of these contracts are "fraternization contracts." By means of such a contract a person was to become somebody's child, father, wife, brother, master, slave, kin, comrade-in-arms, protector, client, follower, vassal, subject, friend, or, quite generally, comrade. To "fraternize" with another person did not, however, mean that a certain performance of the contract, contributing to the attainment of some specific object, was reciprocally guaranteed or expected. Nor did it mean that the making of a promise to another would, as we might put it, have ushered in a new orientation in the relationship between the parties. The contract rather meant that the person would "become" something different in quality (or status) from the quality he possessed before. For unless a person voluntarily assumed that new quality, his future conduct in his new role could hardly be believed to be possible at all. Each party must thus make a new "soul" enter his body. At a rather late stage the symbolism required the mixing and imbibing of blood or spittle or the creation of a new soul by some animistic process or by some other magical rite.[19]

One whose thinking is embedded in magic cannot imagine any other than a magical guaranty for the parties to conform, in their total behavior, to the intention of the "fraternization" they contracted. But as the notion of the divinity gradually replaces animism, it is found necessary to place each party under the dominion of a supernatural power, which power constitutes not only their collective protection but also jointly and severally threatens them in case of antifraternal conduct. The *oath*, which originally appears as a person's conditional self-surrender to evil magical forces, subsequently assumes the character of a conditional self-curse, calling for the divine wrath to strike.[20] Thus the oath remains even in later times one of the most universal forms of all fraternization pacts. But its use is not so limited.

3. In contrast to the true magical forms of fraternization, the oath is also technically suited to serve as a guaranty for purposive contracts, i.e., contracts neither affecting the status of the parties nor giving rise to new qualities of comradeship but aiming solely, as, for instance, bar-

[19] See THURNWALD 51. R. SCHRÖDER 66; BRUNNER I, 132. SCHMIDT UND KOPPERS, *op. cit.* (in *Völker und Kulturen*) III, 167, 234; MAINE, EARLY LAW 69 *et seq.*

[20] On the oath, see THURNWALD 176; WENGER 125, 336; POLLOCK AND MAITLAND I, 39; II, 600; DIAMOND 52, 111, 336–339, 350–390.

ter, at some specific (especially economic) performance or result. This type of contract, however, does not appear in the most primitive society. In earliest times, *barter*, the archetype of all merely instrumental contracts, would seem to have been a general phenomenon among the comrades of an economic or political community only in the noneconomic sphere, particularly as barter of women between exogamous sibs whose members seem to confront each other in the strange dual role of being partly comrades and partly strangers. In the state of exogamy barter appears also as an act of fraternization; however much the woman may be regarded as a mere object, there will rarely be missing the concurrent idea of a change of status to be brought about by magical means.[21] The peculiar duality in the relations between the exogamously cartelized sibs, created by the rise of regulated exogamy, may perhaps help to explain a much discussed phenomenon, namely, the phenomenon that certain formalities were sometimes required for the marriage with a concubine while the marriage with the legitimate wife might be entered into without any formalities.[22] It may be that the latter remained formless because it was the original and pre-exogamous type of marriage, while barter in pre-exogamous times did not yet have anything to do with fraternization. It is more plausible, however, that fixed contractual formalities were necessitated by the need for special arrangements regarding the economic security of the concubine who lacked the generally fixed economic status of the legitimate wife.

Economic barter was always confined to transactions with persons who were not members of one's own "house," especially with outsiders in the sense of non-kinsmen, non-"brothers"; in short, non-comrades. For precisely this reason barter also lacked in the form of "silent" trade any trace of magical formalism. Only gradually did it acquire religious protection through the law of the market. Such protection, however, would not arise as a set of settled forms until a belief in gods had taken its place alongside those magical conceptions which had provided appropriate means of direct guaranty only for status contracts.[23] Occasionally it would also happen that a barter transaction might be placed under the guaranty of the status-contract through some special act of fraternization or some equivalent. This would not generally happen, however, unless land were involved. Normally, barter enjoyed practically no guar-

[21] Schmidt und Koppers, *op. cit.* I, 497; 1 Westermarck, History of Human Marriage (1925) 233.

[22] The place of the discussions referred to by Weber could not be ascertained.

[23] See M. Ebert, Real-Lexikon der Vorgeschichte (1926) VI, sub tit. "Kauf," 246–248; VIII, sub tit. "Markt," 34.

anty, and the conception was nonexistent that barter could mean the assumption of an "obligation" which would not be the product of a natural or artificial all-inclusive fraternal relationship. As a result, barter at first took effect exclusively as a set of two simultaneous and reciprocal acts of immediate delivery of possession. Possession, however, is protected by the claim for vengeance on, and expiation by, the thief. Thus, the kind of "legal protection" accorded to barter was not the protection of an obligation, but of possession. Where, at a later time, the obligation of warranty of title came to develop at all, it was protected only indirectly in the form of an action for theft against the seller who lacked title.[24]

Formal legal construction of barter does not begin until certain goods, especially metals, have acquired a monetary function, i.e., where sale has arisen. This development does not depend upon the existence of chartal or even state money,[25] but, as shown especially in Roman law, on mere pensatory means of payment. The transactions *per aes et libram* constitute one of the two original forms of legal transaction in ancient Roman *ius civile*. In the domain of Roman urban developments this form of cash purchase acquired an almost universal function for the most diverse classes of private legal transactions, regardless of whether they involved questions of family or inheritance law or of exchange proper.[26] The agreements of fraternization as well as other forms of

[24] In Roman law, at least with respect to the sale of *res mancipi* by way of *mancipatio* (see *infra*, n. 26) the original source of the seller's obligation arising in the case of a defect of title or quality is predominantly said to have consisted in a wrong committed by him (see E. RABEL, DIE HAFTUNG DES VERKÄUFERS WEGEN MANGELS IN RECHT [1902] 8/9). Jhering, whose opinion seems to have influenced Weber, believed that the wrong consisted in a *furtum* ("theft") which would be committed by the seller when he accepted the buyer's money as the price for goods which did not belong to him (GEIST DES RÖMISCHEN RECHTS, I, 157; III, Part i, 138). It is more probable, however, that the seller's wrong consisted in his failure to come to the buyer's defense when the latter's right to quiet possession and enjoyment was questioned by a third party's claim of superior title. A duty of the seller to defend the buyer against such attacks has been found to have existed in the archaic stages of Greek, Germanic, Slavic, and numerous other laws; cf. RABEL, *loc. cit.* 6; DARESTE, *op. cit.* 166, 184, 202, 232, 263; but compare now H. Coing, *Die* clausula doli *im klassischen Recht* (1951) FESTSCHRIFT FRITZ SCHULZ 97.

[25] Chartal money: all types of money which is either stamped or coined, in contrast with the natural means of exchange or payment; see WEBER, THEORY 174, 178, 280, 291; also WEBER, HISTORY 50, 236.

[26] In transactions *per aes et libram* ("by copper and scales") the money was weighed for the recipient in the presence of five witnesses and a weigher (*libripens*); certain ritual words had to be spoken. This institution was principally used in the *mancipatio*, by which title to goods was transferred, i.e., goods which were the

status contract were oriented toward the total social status of the individual and his integration into an association comprehending his total personality. This form of contract with its all-inclusive rights and duties and the special attitudinal qualities based thereon thus appears in contrast to the money contract, which, as a specific, quantitatively delimited, qualityless, abstract, and usually economically conditioned agreement, represents the archetype of "coercing contract" (*Zwangskontrakt*). The money contract, as such a coercing contract of ethical indifference, was the appropriate means for the elimination of the magical and sacramental elements from legal transactions and for the secularization of the law. In Roman law, for example, the civil marriage form of *coemptio* thus came to confront the sacred marriage form of *confarreatio*.[27] The money contract was, it is true, not the only suitable means, but it was the most suitable. Indeed, as a specific cash transaction it was of a rather conservative nature since, originally at least, it was completely devoid of any promissory elements oriented towards the

---

mainstay of a Roman farm household (land, slaves, and cattle), the so-called *res mancipi* (*supra* n. 24). Title to other goods could be transferred, at least in classical times, in the less formal way of simple *traditio*. Transaction *per aes et libram* was also used in connection with the *nexum*, the archaic way of creating a debt for a loan, and also for purposes of adoption, making wills, and marriage. See *infra* n. 27. Cf. BUCKLAND 236; JOLOWICZ, 151; As Weber states, the transactions *per aes et libram* were, or better seem to have been, one of the two principal methods by which legally binding transactions could be made in the archaic stage of Roman law. The other method was the *in iure cessio*, which, similar to the common law fine, seems essentially to have been a mock trial before the magistrate intended to result in an authoritative authentication of the fact that a grantor had yielded his title to his grantee.

[27] *Coemptio* and *confarreatio* are usually stated as the two forms of marriage of early Roman law. The latter was an elaborate religious ceremony, which seems to have been impractical for anyone but the members of the patrician aristocracy. *Coemptio* was a transaction *per aes et libram* which seems to have been essential not so much for the creation of the marriage relation as such as for the acquisition by the husband of the old-style marital power (*manus*) over his wife. In later republican times both kinds of formality became obsolete. The marriage was regarded as validly concluded by the informal consent of the parties, usually evidenced by the celebration of the bride's entry into the groom's house (*in domum deductio*). In the old-style *coemptio* the head of the household to which the bride belonged seems to have transferred for a nominal price his power over her to the groom. In so far as *coemptio* was at all used in classical times, the *mancipatio* with the groom seems to have been performed by the bride herself. Cf. 1 BONFANTE, CORSO DI DIRITTO ROMANO (1925) 39 *et seq.*; Kunkel, 14 PAULY-WISSOWA, REALENZYKLOPÄDIE DER KLASSISCHEN ALTERTUMSWISSENSCHAFT 2259; F. SCHULZ, CLASSICAL ROMAN LAW (1951) 103; CORBETT, ROMAN LAW OF MARRIAGE (1930); for further literature, see JÖRS AND KUNKEL 271 *et seq.* 416.

future. For the effect of this transaction, too, was solely to provide secure possession as well as a guaranty that the goods were properly acquired; however, at any rate originally, the transaction did not constitute a guaranty that the promises involved in it would be fulfilled.

4. The concept of obligation [28] through contract was entirely alien to primitive law; it knew but one form of obligation and claim, viz., that arising *ex delicto*. The amount of the claim of an injured party was rigorously fixed by the practice of composition and its attendant conventions. The *wergilt* debt as set by the judge was the most ancient true debt and all other forms of obligation have derived from it.[29] Conversely it can be said that only such actions were cognizable by the courts as arose from an obligation. As regards disputes between members of different kinship groups, no formal procedure existed for the restitution of chattels or the surrender of immovables. Every complaint was necessarily based upon the argument that the defendant had personally done the plaintiff a wrong which would have to be expiated. Hence there was no place for an action *ex contractu* or for the recovery of a chattel or a piece of land or for actions to determine personal status.

a. The problem of whether a person was properly a member of a household, a kinship group, or a political association could, as an internal affair, be decided solely by the group itself. But things underwent a change in this very respect. It was the basic norm of every type of brotherhood or loyalty-bound relationship that a brother should neither summon into court, nor bear witness against, his brother, nor kinsman against kinsman, nor guild brother against guild brother, nor patron against client, and vice versa, in the same way as there was no possibility of blood vengeance in any of these relationships. Vengeance for felony amongst them was a matter for the spirits or gods, the priestly power of excommunication, the master of the household, or the lynching procedures of the group. But when political association had come to constitute the military community, and when military duty and political

[28] The term obligation is more commonly used in the civil law than in the common law jurisdictions. In civil law terminology obligation (Lat. *obligatio*) means personal duty of any kind, such as duty to pay money, to deliver goods, to convey a piece of land, to render services, to refrain from engaging in certain conduct, etc. The obligation can arise out of a contract (*ex contractu*), out of a tort (*ex delicto*), or directly out of a command of the legal order (*ex lege*); subdivisions of the latter category are the obligations *quasi ex contractu* and *quasi ex delicto*.

[29] *Wergilt* (*wergeld*) — expiatory payment for wrong, especially as fixed by tradition. The word is Germanic, but the institution seems to have been almost universal. Weber follows here the theory primarily expressed by Amira, Nordgermanisches Obligationenrecht (1882).

rights had become intertwined with birth in legitimate wedlock so that unfree persons or those born in inferior station had no military rights and thus no rights to share in booty, there had to be a legal procedure for the determination of a person's disputed status.

The emergence of actions concerning land was closely connected with this situation. Power over certain areas of usable land became, as scarcity increased, an increasingly important element in the life of every corporate body, both political associations and house communities. The right of full membership in the group provided a claim to a share in the land and, conversely, only the landholder was a full member of the group. Disputes between the groups about land thus always meant that the victorious group would receive the disputed land. As the individual appropriation of the land developed, the role of plaintiff devolved from the group to the individual member who would sue another, both plaintiff and defendant claiming the land by virtue of their right of membership. In any such dispute concerning membership right in land the subject matter had of necessity to be found to belong to one party or the other, as it constituted the very basis of his entire political and social existence. Only one of the two could as a group member be legitimately entitled thereto, just as a person could only be a member or a non-member, a freeman or unfree. Especially in military associations, like the ancient *polis*, the litigation about the *fundus* or *kleros* had to assume the form of a bilateral dispute. Instead of one party's being charged by an allegedly injured person as a wrongdoer, who would then have to seek to establish his innocence, each of the parties had to claim to be in the right at the risk of being in default. Thus, where the dispute turned about a membership right as such, the pattern of the tort action was inapplicable. Nobody could steal a *fundus*, not just because of naural obstacles, but because one could not steal from a person his status as a member of the group. Hence, there developed for disputes about status or land, alongside the unilateral tort action, the bilateral action, such as the Hellenic *diadikasia*, or the Roman *vindicatio* with necessary cross-action of the defendant against the claim of the plaintiff.[30] In

[30] The *rei vindicatio* was the action for the specific recovery of a chattel or a piece of land. It was brought against the possessor by the person who claimed to be the legal owner. It has been described by Gaius (iv, 16, 17) as follows: [transl. by L. Mears (1882), 518]:

"§ 16: If it was a real action in respect of movables or moving things, which could be brought or led into court, they were claimed before the praetor thus: The claimant, holding a staff, took hold of the thing, for example, a slave, and spoke as follows: 'I say this slave is mine, according to the law of the quirites, by the title

this litigation involving status, which included the conflict over a group member's right to his share in the land, we have to find the root of the distinction between rights *in rem* and rights *in personam.* This distinction was the product of a development and appeared only with the disintegration of the old personal groups, especially the decline of the strict dominion of the kinship group over property. One might locate it approximately at the stage of the emergence of the market association and the individual allotment of hides, i.e., at the stage of an initial system of individual property. Primitive legal thought was characterized not by the distinction between rights *in rem* and rights *in personam* but by two

---

which I have shown. Thus, upon him I place my lance,' at the same time placing the staff on the slave. His adversary then said and did the same, and when both had thus laid claim to the slave, the praetor said: 'Both claimants quit hold of the slave.' Upon this, they both let go. The first claimant then said: 'I demand of you the ground of your claim.' The other replied: 'I declared my right when I placed my lance upon him.' Then the first claimant said: 'Since you claim him in defiance of right, I challenge you to stake five hundred pounds of copper upon the issue of a trial.' His adversary replied by a similar challenge, but if the subject matter of the suit was of less value than one thousand pounds of copper, then they named fifty pounds of copper as the sum reciprocally staked. Then the same proceedings were gone through as in a personal action, after which the praetor temporarily assigned to one of the parties the subject matter of the suit, that is, appointed one of them to be interim possessor and ordered him to give security to his opponent for the subject matter of the suit and the interim possession, that is, for the thing in dispute, and the produce, whilst the praetor himself took security from both parties in respect of the penal sum for costs as that would be forfeited to the public treasury. A staff was used, as it were, in the place of the spear, which was the symbol of lawful ownership; since that was especially looked upon as a man's own property which had been taken from the enemy, and for this reason a spear is placed before the centumviral tribunal.

"§ 17: If the thing was of such a nature that it could not be conveniently brought or led into court, as for example, if it were a column, or a ship, or a herd of cattle of any sort, some part of it only was taken, and the claim was made in respect of that part as if the whole were before the court. . . Similarly, when the dispute was about a piece of land, or a building, or an inheritance, some part was taken and brought into court, and the claim was made in respect of this portion, as if in the presence of the whole. . ."

WENGER, p. 127, adds the following observation: "That is a symbolic reminder of the manual struggle for the thing, of self-help, before the state established the order of peace. This last is represented by the Praetor: *cum uterque vindicasset, praetor dicebat: Mittite ambo hominem* ('since both of you claimed [him], leave both the man'). That is still clearer in the symbolic fight for a *fundus* (tract of land) from which the parties bring a clod, in order to enact with it the aforementioned reciprocal *vindicatio*-proceeding before the Praetor." As to the Greek *diadikasia* (διαδικασία), see 2 BONNER AND SMITH 79, 101, 163, 260, 265; LEIST 490. See also *supra* c. III, notes 34, 35, and 41.

types of fundamental facts. The first was that an individual would say: By virtue of having been born or brought up in the house of *X*, by marriage, adoption, fraternization, military consociation, or initiation I am a member of the *Y* group and am entitled thereby to claim the use of the piece of property called *Z*. Or, secondly, one would say *X*, a member of Group *Y*, has committed against me, *A*, or my fellow group member, *B*, a wrong of the type of *C*, and for this reason he and his comrades owe expiation to us, the fellow members of *A*.[31] With the increasing individual appropriation of property the former configuration developed into the claim of a right *in rem* against everyone, especially actions of the type of the *hereditatis petitio*[32] and the *rei vindicatio*. The latter fact-situation developed into the right *in personam* against a particular person, viz., that one is held to be bound to perform a certain duty toward the obligee; and the duty exists only toward the obligee. The clarity of the original situation and the directness of the line of development are blurred by the dualism of legal relations within the kinship group and between different kinship groups. Among kinship members, we have seen there could be neither vengeance nor litigation but only arbitration by the group elders; against those who resisted, only the sanction of boycott or ostracism could be applied. All the magical formalities of procedure were lacking; arbitration of disputes within the kinship group was an administrative matter. Legal procedure and law in the sense of claims guaranteed by judicial decision and the coercive power attached thereto existed only between those different kinship groups and their members who belonged to the same political community.

When the kinship group disintegrated and gave place to a combination of house communities, neighborhood bodies, and the political association, the question arose as to how far the legal procedure of the political association would intrude into the relations among members of the same kinship group or even the same community. To the extent that this was the case, individual claims to land also became the object of litigation before the judge even between group members, at first, in the above-mentioned form of the bilateral vindication. On the other hand, the political power could assume patriarchal form and the method of dispute settlement would then more or less generally assume that

[31] In Arabic legal parlance one does not say: "the blood of *A* has been shed," but "our blood has been shed." [Weber's note.]

[32] *Hereditatis petitio*: action for the recovery of the total estate of a decedent, brought by the person claiming heirship against one who is alleged to have no right to the estate.

form of administrative settlement which was formerly applicable to internal disputes. Then this type could also influence the characteristics of the legal procedure of the political association. As a result, the clear-cut classification of the old as well as the newer conception of the distinction between the two categories of claims was blurred. The technical form of the distinction shall not concern us here, however. We shall rather return to the question of how the personal responsibility for delicts produced the contractual obligation, and how the delictual fault as a cause of action gave rise to the obligation *ex contractu*. The connecting link consisted in the liability for composition as determined by, or acknowledged in, the legal procedure.

b. One of the earliest type situations in which the acknowledgment of an enforceable *contractual obligation* had to become an economic need is the debt arising out of a *loan*. It is in this very situation, moreover, that we can perceive the gradualness of the process of emancipation from the original stage of exclusive liability of the debtor's person. The loan originally was a typical, interest-free form of emergency aid among brothers. Hence it could not be actionable, as no action at all would be admissible among brothers, i.e., between members of a kinship group or a guild, or as between patron and client, or within any other type of relationship of personal loyalty. A loan made to someone outside the fraternal group, if it occurred at all, was in itself not legally subject to the prohibition of taking interest. But within the scheme of personal liability it was not actionable. As means of enforcement the disappointed creditor had only available to him magical procedures, sometimes of a rather grotesque character, remnants of which have survived for long periods. In China the creditor would threaten suicide and eventually even commit it in the expectation of pursuing his debtor after death.[33] In India the creditor would seat himself in front of the debtor's house and there either starve or hang himself; in this way he could compel his sib to revenge him against the debtor; and where the creditor was a Brahmin, the debtor as the murderer of a Brahmin, would even become subject to the intervention of the judge.[34] In Rome *improbitas* as provided by the Law of the XII Tables and *infamia* as later provided

[33] Sternberg, *Der Geist des chinesischen Vermögensrechts* (1911) 26 Z.F. VGL. RW. 142/3, cf. ALABASTER 317.

[34] On this institution of "sitting dharma" see MAINE, INSTITUTIONS 38 *et seq.*; 297–305; E. S. HARTLAND, PRIMITIVE LAW (1924) 186. A similar custom is reported for ancient Irish law by MAINE, *op. cit.* 280, 296, 303: If the debtor was of chieftain grade, the creditor had "to fast upon him," i.e., to go to his residence and wait a certain time without food.

in cases of severe breaches of *fides* were probably survivals of the social boycott as it occurred in the case of disrespect for the requirements of good faith and fair dealing as a substitute for the actionability that was lacking.

c. The development of a unified law of obligations was certainly derived from the action for tort. The delictual liability of the entire kinship group was, for instance, the source of the widespread joint liability of all kin or house community members for the performance of the contract made by one of them.[35] However, the development of the various actionable contracts largely proceeded along its own ways. The entry of money into economic life often played the decisive role. Both primitive forms of contract in Roman *ius civile*, viz., *nexum*, the debt contracted *per aes et libram*, and *stipulatio*, the debt contracted by symbolic pledge,[36] were money contracts. This fact, which is clear for the *nexum*, seems also to be certain for the *stipulatio*. As to both, the connections with the precontractual stage are clear. They were rigorously formal oral transactions and they required that the necessary acts be performed by the parties themselves. Both have the same origin. As to the *stipulatio* we may agree with Mitteis [37] who, on the basis of analogies in Germanic

[35] A. Kocourek and J. Wigmore, *Sources of Ancient and Primitive Law* (1915) in 1 EVOLUTION OF LAW 328, on Fanti Customary Law; MAINE, INSTITUTIONS 187, on Irish law. See *supra* p. 69 on the Slavonic *zadruga*.

[36] The *nexum* seems to have been the money loan contract which was formally created *per aes et libram*, i.e., by weighing the copper amount in the presence of five witnesses and a weigher (*libripens*); see *supra*, n. 26. It had disappeared in historical times, and the references in the sources are so fragmentary that its origin and nature are still obscure. The theory accepted by Weber is that of Mitteis (25 SAV. Z. ROM. 282), who believed that the *nexum* was a transaction by which the debtor symbolically sold himself to the creditor. This theory has, however, been attacked from various quarters. The extensive literature is listed at JÖRS AND KUNKEL 219; to this should be added Koschaker, *Eheschliessung und Kauf nach alten Rechten* [1951], ARCHIV ORIENTÁLNY 210, 288; and v. Lübtow, *Zum Nexumproblem* (1950) 67 SAV. Z. ROM. 112. *Stipulatio* was the contract which was bindingly concluded by the exchange of certain ritualistic words. Upon the creditor's question: *Sestertios mille dare spondesne* ("do you promise to pay 1,000 sestertii"?) the debtor would answer, "spondeo" ("I promise"). Later it became permissible to use other terms instead of the words "spondesne? spondeo," especially, "promittisne– promitto," or "dabisne– dabo." Whether, as Weber believes, such a promise or stipulation could only relate to the payment of money, is controversial. The literature is listed at JÖRS AND KUNKEL 97. See also *ibid.* 218.

[37] "Aus römischem und bürgerlichem Recht" (FESTSCHR. F. BECKER) 109 *et seq.* Mitteis' theory of the origin of the *stipulatio* has been doubted by Segré, 108 ARCHIVIO GIURIDICO 179; Luzzatto, *Per una ipotesi sulle origini e la natura delle obbligazioni romane*, 8 FOND. CASTELLI 253; and Weiss, PAULY-WISSOWA,

law, regards it as having originated in procedure, outside of which it originally played only a very modest role, essentially in connection with agreements on such collateral terms as interest and similar matters. In addition to barter, the composition agreement, which formed the basis of the trial, also constituted a step on the way to the coercing contract in the sense that, being a contract among enemies rather than one of fraternization, it required a precise formulation of the issue and, quite particularly, of the point or points to be proved. As its attendant formalities became more and more fixed, increasingly numerous occasions occurred for incidental transactions creating contractual obligations. The giving of security by one party to the other is one of the most important of these transactions. In many legal systems the very procedure which was intended to eliminate self-help had to be initiated by some act of self-help. The plaintiff would drag the defendant into court and would not release him unless he received security that the defendant, if found guilty, would not evade the payment of the composition. Such self-help was always directed against the body of the adversary, as the action was based upon the allegation that a felony had been committed by the defendant against the plaintiff, for which the defendant had to answer with his person, rather than on a complaint that the defendant's conduct constituted an objective wrong. The security which the defendant had to give in order to remain unmolested until the time of judgment was provided through sureties or by way of pledge.[38]

Realenzyklopädie der klass. Altertumswissenschaft, 2. Reihe, III, 2540; Jörs and Kunkel 96. These authors declare that the origin of the *stipulatio* has as yet not been cleared up.

[38] Weber is thinking here of the *in ius vocatio*, by which an action was initiated in archaic Roman law and which is described by Wenger 96, as follows: "*In ius vocatio*. In the Twelve Tables it is placed at the head of the whole statute, and it is handed down to us in its crude archaic primitiveness: I, (1) *Si in ius vocat, ito. Ni it, antestamino: igitur em capito.* (2) *Si calvitur pedemve struit, manum endo iacito.* (3) *Si morbus aevitasve vitium escit, iumentum dato. Si nolet, arceram ne sternito* [translation by J. Wigmore, Sources of Ancient and Primitive Law (1915), vol. I. of Evolution of Law, by Kocourek and Wigmore, p. 465]. "*If* [a man] *call* [another] *to law, he shall go. If he go not, they shall witness it; then he shall be seized. If he flee or evade, lay hands on him as he goes. If illness or age hinder, an ox-team shall be given him, but not a covered carriage, if he does not wish.*"

"In these provisions, probably handed down with later additions, appear already fundamental legal principles, special regulations which we today would leave to an enforcing ordinance. Further, such enforcing ordinances were indeed issued by the Praetor in great numbers. — The defendant may not personally offer resistance to the *in ius vocatio*, but it is possible for him to find an appropriate *vindex*, who frees him from the hands of the plaintiff who is applying force, and guarantees —

It is thus in the course of procedure that these two legal institutions appear for the first time as compulsorily enforceable transactions. Later on, in the place of a third party surety, the defendant himself was allowed to warrant the fulfillment of the judgment. The legal view was that the defendant was his own surety, just as the oldest juridical form of the free labor contract was everywhere the sale of oneself into temporary slavery taking the place of the formerly normal sale by father or master. The most ancient contractual obligations consisted in the transposition of certain procedural arrangements into the common legal life. In Germanic law the giving of a pledge or a hostage was the most ancient means of contracting debts, not only economically but also as far as legal formalities are concerned. Suretyship, from which the pledging of oneself was derived in both Roman and German law, was in the latter undoubtedly connected in legal thought with the solidary personal liability of the members of the kinship group and the house community. The second form of security for future obligation, i.e., the pledge, was both in Roman and in Germanic law [39] at first either taken as a distress or given to avoid the personal liability of being sued and taken in execution; hence it was not, as it is today, a security for a claim existing separately. The giving of the pledge rather constituted a transfer of possession of goods which, as long as the debt remained unpaid, were to be in the creditor's possession lawfully, while upon timely payment of the debt his possession was to become unlawful and thus to constitute a wrong towards the former debtor. It thus easily fitted in with the usual pattern of the most ancient causes of action, viz., actual injury to the person or to his possessions. The very widespread legal transaction of the conditional self-sale into slavery for debt also attached itself in part directly to the possible modes of execution and partly to the giving of a hostage, which, as we have seen, was also connected with procedure.[40] The body of the debtor was to constitute the creditor's pledge

---

in some manner no longer surely recognizable — the appearance of the defendant in court. If no appropriate *vindex* is found, then the defendant is, according to the Twelve Tables, dragged by force before the judicial magistrate. The calling of witnesses by the plaintiff means for the defendant at least a certain guaranty against the unlawful use of force."

[39] As to Roman law, Weber obviously has in mind the archaic *legis actio per pignoris capionem*, which seems not to have been generally available, however, but only for certain claims of sacred law and public law, especially taxes; cf. WENGER 228. In the Germanic law distress seems to have been more generally available. As to both Roman and Germanic law, Weber seems to follow the exposition of MAINE, INSTITUTIONS 257 *et seq.*

[40] See *supra*, n. 38.

and was to be forfeited into his lawful posession if the debt was not properly paid. Originally the liability for contracted debt, like liability for vengeance and composition, from which it derived, was not a personal liability with one's assets but a liability of the debtor's physical body and of it alone. Originally there was no execution upon the debtor's assets at all. In the event of nonpayment, the creditor's only resort was execution upon the person, whom he could kill or imprison as a hostage or hold as a bond-servant or sell as a slave; where there were several creditors, they could, as the Twelve Tables show, cut him into pieces.[41] The creditor could also establish himself in the home of the debtor, and the latter would have to serve and provide for him (Einleger); [42] but this already

[41] The famous passage is related by Gellius XX, 48 (Bruns, Fontes juris romani antiqui; Tab. II. 6) to have read as follows: "Tertiis nundinis partis secanto. Si plus minusve secuerint, se fraude esto." ("After sixty days [60 days after the seizure of the defaulting debtor by one of his several creditors] let them cut parts. If thy cut more or less, it shall be without prejudice.") The translation of the archaic Latin is not too certain and the meaning of the passage has been controversial. Weber follows the opinion which regards the passage as permitting the creditors bodily to cut the debtor in pieces. Joseph Kohler has used the same interpretation in his famous essay on Shylock's claim to his debtor's "pound of flesh," in which he sees a survival of a once general idea into a time when it came to clash with changed moral ideas. (SHAKESPEARE VOR DEM FORUM DER JURISPRUDENZ [2nd ed. 1919] 50.) An entirely different view has been expressed by Max Radin ("*Secare partis*: The Early Roman Law of Execution against a Debtor" [1922] 43 AMER. J. OF PHILOSOPHY 32), who applies the *secare* to the piecemeal alienation of the debtor's property. For further references to the extensive literature, see WENGER, § 21, n. 8.

[42] The German text is as follows: "oder der Gläubiger setzte sich in das Haus des Schuldners, und dieser musste ihn bewirten (*Einleger*)." — There exists a German word "Einleger," but none of its meanings fits the passage of the text (see 2 PREUSSISCHE AKADEMIE DER WISSENSCHAFTEN. DEUTSCHES RECHTSWÖRTERBUCH [1934] 1422). Probably there has occurred an error of transcription or typography, and the word meant is *Einlager*. However, this term refers to the exactly opposite method of debt collection, viz., the exertion of pressure upon the debtor by exacting that he or his surety live away from home at some agreed place until the debt is paid (see the references in 2 DEUTSCHES RECHTSWÖRTERBUCH 1414). Ordinarily the duty to submit to such "quartering" had, in German law, to be assumed by special agreement (HUEBNER 482). Von Schwerin (*op. cit.*) describes the institution as follows: "Hostageship has survived terminologically in the institution of *Einlager* (*giselschaft*, *obstagium*) which was taken over (sc. in Germany) from France in the 12th century. It was common, especially among knights; usually it was undertaken by contract, but there were also cases where it was provided by statute. It was a kind of captivity into which the surety surrendered himself by riding up to an inn and remaining there together with a fixed number of retainers until the debt was paid. The institution was abolished by imperial legislation in the 16th century, but in certain regions, for instance, of Switzerland, it survived into the modern age."

The only instance of a situation in which, in the territory of German law, the creditor would have submitted to "quartering" is referred to in the following state-

marks the transition to liability of the debtor's assets. Yet, the transition proceeded but slowly, and liability of the person for nonpayment of debt disappeared in Rome only in the course of the class conflict,[43] while in Germany it did not disappear until the nineteenth century.[44] The most ancient purely obligatory contracts, i.e., *nexum* and *stipulatio*, and, among the Germans, *vadiatio*,[45] obviously signified the voluntary sub-

---

ment of R. His (*Gelobter und gebotener Friede im deutschen Mittelalter* [1912] 33 SAV. Z. GERM. 169): "To prevent an abuse of force, of the two parties, the Dutch and West-Frisian cities of the 15th century ordered *both* litigants — the creditor and the debtor — to submit themselves to 'quartering.'" For further references see M. Rintelen, *Schuldhaft und Einlager im Vollstreckungsverfahren des alt-niederländischen und sächsischen Rechtes* (1908); 1 AMIRA, *op. cit.* (1882) 362, 392 *et seq.*

While no reference could thus be found which would indicate a connection of the German *Einlager* with the mode of exacting a debt by the creditor's installing himself in the house of a debtor, the latter custom has, indeed, occurred as indicated by a remark of Kohler's about China (KOHLER AND WENGER 143).

[43] Traditionally, a *lex Poetelia*, dated at 326 B.C., is cited as an important milepost of this development. It is reported to have prohibited the chaining and killing of the debtor and to have compelled the creditor to accept the debtor's willingness to work off the debt. The reports, which are all by historians who wrote centuries later (Livy, Dionysius, Cicero, etc.), are suspect as to the details of the development but probably accurate in so far as they represent the transition from liability of the person to liability of the property as an aspect of the struggle between patricians and plebeians. As to literature on the problem, see WENGER, § 21, n. 10.

[44] In the United States imprisonment for debt was generally abolished in the nineteenth century, when its prohibition was expressly stated in numerous state constitutions. It has nevertheless survived in the form of punishment for contempt of court for nonobedience of equity decrees, as well as, in certain states, judgments for damages rendered at law upon a verdict which finds the debtor guilty of malice or of reckless or wanton negligence. For obligations to pay family support the threat of imprisonment in alimony row still constitutes one of the principal guaranties of enforcement.

In Germany, by Bundesgesetz of 29 May 1868, as in probably all countries of Western and Central Europe (e.g., Bundesverfassung der Schweizerischen Eidgenossenschaft of 29 May 1874, Art. 59), imprisonment for debt has been radically and completely abolished by nineteenth-century legislation. Public opinion would not tolerate it even as a means of enforcement of duties of family support. Theoretically, but hardly ever used, imprisonment is still possible as a means to induce a person to comply with certain judgments ordering him to do, or to refrain from doing, an act other than that of the payment of money. See German Code of Civil Procedure, §§ 888, 890; cf. A. SCHÖNKE, ZWANGSVOLLSTRECKUNGSRECHT (1948) 168–189. On the abolition of imprisonment for money debt, see HEDEMANN, I; L. ROSENBERG, LEHRBUCH DES DEUTSCHEN ZIVILPROZESSRECHTS (1949) 806–807.

[45] *Vadiatio* (Wadiation) — Germanic transaction establishing suretyship: a staff is handed by the debtor to the creditor, who hands it on to the surety, asking him to assume the suretyship for the debtor's debt. There exists a voluminous literature which is particularly concerned with the symbolism of the transaction. According to AMIRA (*Die Wadiation*, SITZUNGSBERICHTE DER BAYERISCHEN AKADEMIE DER

mission to a *conditional liability of the person as security for* the delivery of goods promised for the future.[46] Immediate liability of the person was thus avoided. But if the promise remained unfulfilled, the only recourse possible was again that of resorting to the debtor's person.

Originally all contracts were contracts relating to a change in the possession of goods. Hence, all those legal transactions which really represented old forms of contractual liability, especially those particularly rigid and formal ones which were universally required for the creation of a money debt, were symbolically connected with the legal forms of transfer of possession.[47] Many of these symbolic forms undoubtedly rested upon magical conceptions. Of permanent influence, however, was the fact that legal thought did not at first recognize as relevant any such intangible phenomena as simple promises but was interested only in wrong, i.e., a misdeed against the goods or a violation of life or limb or visible possession. A contract, to be legally relevant, had thus to contain a disposition over tangible goods, or had at least to be susceptible of such an interpretation.[48] If this was the case, it could, in the course of development, come to incorporate the most diverse contents. A transaction, on the other hand, which could not be formulated in this way could not become legally effective except as a transaction against cash or, at least, against the deposit of a part payment which would preclude a change of mind on the part of the promisor. Thus arose the principle which is basic in many legal systems, namely, that no contractual promise can be binding unless it is not gratuitous. This attitude was so effective that even at the end of the Middle Ages the English doctrine of "consideration" was derived from it: where a consideration, even though it be only a nominal one, was actually paid the contract could assume any content which was not legally frowned upon; it would be valid even where, without that fact, there would be no legal pigeonhole into which it would fit. The provision in the Twelve Tables on *mancipatio*, the

WISSENSCHAFTEN, PHILOS.-PHILOL. KLASSE [1911]), the staff constitutes an instance of the magically spelled messenger's staff, which is found to play a considerable role in the symbolism of the Germanic laws; see AMIRA, DER STAB IN DER GERMANISCHEN RECHTSSYMBOLIC (1909). For a different view about the *vadiatio* see O. GIERKE, SCHULD UND HAFTUNG (1910); see also HUEBNER 497.

[46] The counterpart to the words printed in italics are missing in the German text. As it stands it does not make sense, and it is clear that certain words must have dropped out by typographical error. The interpolation seems to be the one called for by the context.

[47] Cf. *supra* p. 54.

[48] As to the effects of this feature in the common law, where it remained influential into the very present, see STREET, THE FOUNDATIONS OF LEGAL LIABILITY (1916) II, 75; III, 129; RHEINSTEIN, STRUKTUR 55 *et seq.* 61.

meaning of which has been much disputed,[49] probably constituted a more primitive method of sanctioning a kind of freedom of disposition; while its possibilities of development were more limited, the underlying formal concept was essentially similar.

In addition to the patterns developed from the formalistic monetary transactions on the one hand, and procedural suretyship on the other, the law has evolved a third type of contract, namely, the "coercing contract." The capacity of the law to create guaranties through the use of force was utilized for the artificial creation of new contractual actions out of actions *ex delicto*. This method was resorted to even in a legal system so highly developed technically as the English of the late Middle Ages. The economic rationalization of the law favored the rise of the conception that the liability for composition was not so much, as it had been conceived originally, a buying off of vengeance but rather a compensation for the harm suffered. Thus nonperformance of a contract could now be characterized as a harm requiring compensation. Since the thirteenth century the lawyers and judges of the royal courts of England declared in an ever increasing number of contractual situations that nonperformance constituted a "trespass" and thus provided legal protection, especially by means of the *writ of assumpsit*,[50] just as in a technically quite different situation the praetorian practice of the Romans extended the sphere of legal protection first through the extensive application of delictual actions and then through the concept of *dolus*.[51]

[49] Tab. VI.1: "Cum nexum facit mancipiumque, uti lingua nuncupassit, ita ius esto." — "When he makes a *nexum* and a *mancipium*, as the tongue has spoken, so it shall be the law." For attempts to explain this passage and the numerous controversies around it, see Jörs and Kunkel 90 *et seq.*; Buckland 426; Jolowicz 139, 145–150, 164; for a new and apparently well-founded theory, see Koschaker, *op. cit. supra* n. 36, at 210, 288.

[50] Of the extensive literature, see especially Maitland, Forms, 2 Pollock and Maitland 196, 214, 220, 348; Holdsworth, I, 456; II, 379, 440, 442; III, 281, 323, 455, 457, 422, 430 *et seq.*

[51] The German text says: "durch Erklärung der Dilatioklagen." This passage must contain an error of the editors of Weber's posthumous manuscript, or of the printer. There is no such word as "Dilatioklagen." What is meant is obviously "Deliktsklagen." As the following reference to the use of the concept of *dolus* indicates, Weber is apparently following here the famous description given of the development by Mitteis, 1, 315 *et seq.*, who finds one of the principal sources of what later came to be regarded as liability for breach of contract in the idea that a man who fails to live up to certain duties which he has assumed is not acting "like a gentleman," that he is guilty of *dolus*, and if so found officially, has incurred forfeiture of civil rights (*infamia*). For discussions of this theory, see Sohm 423; R. Sohm and L. Mitteis, Institutionen (1949) 190, 460 ("infamia"); Jörs and Kunkel 170, 222.

Section 3. Institutions Auxiliary to Actionable Contract: Agency; Assignment; Negotiable Instruments.

Even after the creation of actionable contractual claims capable of assuming any content we are still far from that legal state of affairs which is required by advanced and completely commercial social intercourse.

1. Every rational business organization needs the possibility, for particular cases as well as for general purposes, of acquiring contractual rights and of assuming obligations through agents. Advanced trade, moreover, needs not only the possibility of transferring legal claims but also, and quite particularly, a method by which transfers can be made legally secure and which eliminates the need of constantly testing the title of the transferor. The development of those legal institutions, indispensable for a modern capitalistic society, will be discussed in another part of this work.[52] In the present connection we shall do no more than briefly touch upon the developments of early times. In contrast to Greek law, where direct representation was well known in the creation of obligations, "agency" was almost impossible in Roman law.[53] Obviously this legal situation, which was connected with the formalism of the civil actions, made possible the use of slaves in those really capitalistic enterprises for which representation was widely acknowledged in practice. Again, as a result of the highly political character of the debt-relationship, assign-

[52] Viz., by G. Leist [in GRUNDRISS DER SOZIALÖKONOMIK. IV Abt. "Spezifische Elemente der modernen kapitalistischen Wirtschaft." 1. Teil (1925), p. 27, s.t. *Die moderne Privatrechtsordnung und der Kapitalismus* (ed. by Hans Nipperdey)].

[53] In a general sense continental legal theory distinguishes between two types of representation or (broadly) agency, i.e., between (i) direct representation where the agent makes a contract or creates an obligation expressly in the name and on behalf of his principal, and (ii) indirect representation, in which the principal is neither mentioned nor disclosed. In the technical sense only the former is called agency. Roman law had, apart from *mandatum*, no term of art for "agency" in the technical sense. Indeed, according to Paulus, DIG. 45, 1, 126, 2, "per liberam personam obligationem nullam adquirere possumus" — the making of contracts through free persons (or agents) is impossible. Gaius is to the same effect: 1.2, 95. But in practice Roman law diverged from this negative position by creating exceptions which the Roman lawyers handled in their customary subtle manner. See WENGER, DIE STELLVERTRETUNG IM RECHTE DER PAPYRI (1906), esp. pp. 157–166 and p. 219 for the selling of a slave through an agent; cf. also SOHM, § 45 "Representation"; BUCKLAND 276 *et seq.*, 529. In Greek law, on the other hand, direct representation was well known not only because of the role which the slaves played in commerce but also because the concept of agency was used in the *tutela* and in other institutions; see WENGER 166–172; BEAUCHET, HISTOIRE DU DROIT PRIVÉ DE LA RÉPUBLIQUE ATHÉNIENNE (1897).

ment of choses in action was unknown in both ancient Roman and Germanic law.[54] At a rather late time Roman law created a substitute by means of indirect representation and also ultimately arrived at a law of assignment, the utility of which for business transactions was impaired, however, by the substantive ethical tendencies of the later Imperial legislation.[55] As a matter of fact, up to the beginning of modern times, no strong practical demand existed for the assignability of choses in action, except for those which were the subject matter of regular trade or which directly served the purpose of transferring claims to third parties.[56] To meet these needs commercialization was achieved through instruments payable to the order of the payee or to the bearer, which served for the transfer both of claims, especially monetary claims, and of powers of disposition over commercial goods and membership rights in commercial enterprises. They had been utterly unknown in Roman law, and it is still uncertain whether, as Goldschmidt believed, the Hellenistic, or, as Kohler thinks, the Babylonian instruments which go back as far as Hammurabi and were payable to the bearer, were really genuine negotiable instruments.[57] At any rate, however, they facilitated payment to and through third parties in a way which was possible only indirectly under official Roman law. True right-creative instruments are completely unknown to Roman law, unless one considers as such the *contractus literalis*, i.e., the

[54] As to Roman law, see SOHM, § 87; BUCKLAND 518, 550; JÖRS AND KUNKEL 205. In practice the effect of substituting a new creditor for an old one could be achieved by means of novation: by agreement with the debtor the old obligation toward the original creditor was extinguished, and a new one with a new creditor was substituted for it.

As to Germanic Law, see HUEBNER, §§ 78, 79.

As to the slow development of assignment in the Common Law, see 2 WILLISTON ON CONTRACTS 1164 *et seq.* and literature cited there.

[55] By the Lex Anastasiana of A.D. 506 an assignee who had purchased the assignor's claim could recover from the debtor no more than the purchase price which he, the assignee, had paid the assignor; as to the surplus, the debt was discharged. Under a law of A.D. 422, which was restated in Codex 2, 13, 2, a creditor was prohibited to assign his claim to a socially more powerful (*potentior*) person. Cf. Mitteis, *Über den Ausdruck "potentiores" in den Digesten*, 2 MÉLANGES GIRARD (1911). On the role which the fear of maintenance and champerty played in the reluctance of the Common Law to recognize the assignability of choses in action, see WILLISTON, *op. cit.* n. 51 *supra.*

[56] *Sic*: ". . . oder direkt dem Zweck der Übermittlung von Ansprüchen an Dritte dienten."

[57] L. GOLDSCHMIDT 80, 82, 387, 390; see also his VERMISCHTE SCHRIFTEN (1901) II, 172; KOHLER AND PEISER, HAMMURABI'S GESETZ (1904) III, 237; compare this with the doubts in GOLDSCHMIDT, *loc. cit.* 167, as well as those of Koschaker, 9 ENCYC. SOC. SCI. 211, 217/8.

book entry by a banker.[58] In Hellenistic and late Roman law the use of instruments in writing, which had been so highly developed in the Orient even in the most ancient times, was developed into the compulsory documentation of certain transactions and the use of certain quasi-negotiable instruments, perhaps through the state's insistence upon recordation, which at first had been meant essentially to serve fiscal purposes.[59] In the Hellenic and Hellenistic cities the technique of documentation was carried on, for the sake of publicity, by two officials who had been unknown to the Romans, viz., the courts' remembrancer and the notary.[60] The institution of the notary was taken over from the Eastern part of the Empire by the West. But in the Occident the late Roman practice of using instruments in writing was not really promoted before the seventh century and in connection with post-Roman practices, possibly through the strong influx of Oriental, especially Syrian, traders. Then, however, the instrument in writing, both as the instrument payable to the order of the payee and to the bearer, developed very rapidly,[61] a fact which is surprising in a period whose intensity of commerce we have to visualize as extremely limited in comparison to classical Antiquity. As has been the case so often, the particular legal techniques adopted seem also in this connection to have followed their own paths. The decisive factor was that now, after the disappearance of legal unity, developments were determined by the centers of commerce and their merely technically trained notaries and that the notariat constituted the only remaining bearer of the commercial traditions of Antiquity and thus was the only creative force. However, with respect to the very use of instruments, the development was favored also by the irrational modes of thought of Germanic law. In popular ideas the instrument

[58] The *contractus literalis* (Roman law) was the contractual obligation created or, more probably, re-created, by the ledger entry by a banker or some such person; cf. BUCKLAND 459; see also Goldschmidt, *Inhaber-, Order- und executorische Urkunden im Classischen Altertum* (1889) 10 SAV. Z. ROM. 373, at 393. Many problems are as yet unsolved; cf. the literature listed by JÖRS AND KUNKEL 188, 410.

[59] For the insistence of the state upon registration of title to land see Zachariae v. Lingenthal, *Zur Geschichte des römischen Grundeigenthums* (1888), 9 SAV. Z. ROM. 263 *et seq.*, 270 *et seq.*; H. LEWALD, BEITRÄGE ZUR KENNTNIS DES RÖMISCH-ÄGYPTISCHEN GRUNDBUCHWESEN IN RÖMISCHER ZEIT (1909). See the review of these last two books by Mitteis (1909), 30 SAV. Z. ROM. 457; see also MITTEIS, REICHSRECHT 465, 480, 493, 514–517, 532.

[60] On the origin of the notary and his role in later antiquity, see MITTEIS, REICHSRECHT 52, 95, 171; DRUFFEL, PAPYROLOGISCHE STUDIEN ZUM BYZANTINISCHEN URKUNDENWESEN (1915); STEINWENTER, BEITRÄGE ZUM ÖFFENTLICHEN URKUNDENWESEN DER RÖMER (1915).

[61] GOLDSCHMIDT 390.

appeared as a sort of fetish, by the formal delivery of which, at first made before witnesses, specific legal effects were produced, just as by other, originally quasi-magical symbols such as the throwing of the spear or the *festuca* of Germanic, or the corresponding *barkonu* of Babylonian law.[62] Originally one did not deliver, as the symbol, the instrument with the writing upon it but the parchment without writing, and only afterwards was the record entered upon it.[63] But while in Italian law, owing to the concomitance of German legal symbolism and the practices of the notaries, the development of documentary evidence was greatly favored even in the Early Middle Ages,[64] it remained unknown for a long time in English law, where the decisive legally constitutive role was played by the seal.[65] The development of the types of commercial paper characteristic of modern commerce took place in the Middle Ages to a large extent, however, under Arabic influence, as a result of partly administrative and partly commercial needs.[66] Ancient Roman commerce apparently could and had to get along without these technical devices, which today seem to us to be so indispensable.

Section 4. Limits of Freedom of Contract

1. *In general.* Today it is fundamentally established that any content whatsoever of a contract, in so far as it is not excluded by limitations on the freedom of contract, creates law among the parties and that particular forms are necessary only to the extent that they are prescribed for reasons of expediency, especially for the sake of the unambiguous demonstrability of rights, and thus of legal security. This stage was reached only quite late: in Rome, by means of the gradual internationalization of the law and in modern times under the influence of the Civil Law doctrine and the needs of trade. Yet, despite this generally existing freedom of contract, modern legislation does not content itself with the general rule that parties to a contract may agree to whatever they please, provided they do not violate certain specially established restrictions. Instead, it rather regulates various types of agreements by certain spe-

[62] *Festuca* (Frankish) — "staff." See *supra* n. 43. On the Babylonian *barkonu* see KOHIER AND WENGER 60.

[63] See Brunner, *Carta und Notitia, Commentationes philologae in honorem Theodori Mommseni* (1877) 570, 577, repr. 1 *Abh.* 458, 469.

[64] GOLDSCHMIDT 151; BRUNNER, *loc. cit.* 458, 466 *et seq.*

[65] POLLOCK AND MAITLAND II, 223 *et seq.*; on the seal see the articles by Hazeltine, Pollock, and Crane in ASS. OF AMER. LAW SCHOOLS, SEL. READINGS ON THE LAW OF CONTRACTS (1931) 1, 10, 598.

[66] GOLDSCHMIDT 97, 99; n. 14a, 390.

cial rules of *ius dispositivum,* i.e., rules which are to be operative only where the parties have not provided otherwise.[67] However, this phenomenon is, in general, due to considerations of mere expediency. As a rule, the parties do not think of really taking care of all the possibly relevant points, and it is also convenient to be able to stick to tried and well-known types. Without these, modern commercial intercourse would scarcely be possible. But the significance of the enabling norms and of freedom of contract are by no means exhausted in this respect. They can have an even more fundamental significance.

In certain situations the normative control through enabling rules necessarily extends beyond the task of the mere delimitation of the range of the parties' individual spheres of freedom. As a general rule, the permitted legal transactions include a power of the parties to the transaction to affect even third parties. In some sense and to some degree almost every legal transaction between two persons, inasmuch as it modifies the mode of the distribution of disposition over legally guaranteed powers of control, affects relations with an indeterminately large body of outsiders. This effect takes place in many different ways. To the extent that, from a purely formalistic point of view, the agreement creates claims and obligations only between the immediate parties, no external effects at all seem to result, as in that case nothing appears legally guaranteed except the prospect that the promise will be fulfilled.

[67] The distinction between *ius dispositivum* — "permissive rules" — and *ius cogens* — "mandatory rules," i.e., rules which cannot be contracted out by the parties, is common in civilian legal theory. *Ius dispositivum* (stopgap law) will be applied when the parties have failed to provide for a contingency which has arisen and for which they should have provided and probably would have provided had they ever thought of it. It is thus constituted by those rules of law which apply only where they have not been "contracted out" by the parties. A large number of the rules of the law of contracts and of the law of wills are of such character. The provisions, for instance, of the law of sales concerning the seller's "implied" warranty for defects of quality apply only where the parties have not made their own provisions for the case; in the law of wills the rules on lapse or abatement of legacies apply only where the testator has failed to provide for the contingency by dispositions of his own.

Since the time of the Roman jurists it has been characteristic for the Civil Law that elaborate rules of stopgap have been established for the various types of contract of daily life, such as sale, donation, lease, contract for services, suretyship, partnership, mandate, etc. All the modern Codes thus contain chapters respectively dealing with these various types of contract, giving for each those rules of stopgap law which apply in default of different arrangement by the parties. As the statutory rules correspond to the intentions of typical parties, few terms of a contract need to be spelled out expressly. Contractual instruments can thus be shorter and simpler than in this country where contractual terms are not so easily assumed to be "implied."

Again, to the extent that the transaction only concerns legal transfer of possession from one hand to another, as is usually the case, the interest of third parties seems to be hardly affected. The goods remain as inaccessible to them as they were before and all they have to do is to recognize a new person as the proprietor. In truth, however, this lack of effect on third parties' interests is never more than relative. The interests of every creditor of a person contracting a debt are affected by the latter's increased liabilities, and the interests of the neighbors are affected by every sale of land, for instance, through the changes in its use which the new owner may, or may not, be economically able to introduce. These are empirically possible repercussions which the law generally admits and guarantees. Their existence is by no means always ignored by a legal system; for an illustration we may refer to the prohibition of the assignment of claims to "a more powerful creditor" as existed in late Roman law.[68]

There are, moreover, cases in which the interests of third parties can be affected in still another way through the utilization of freedom of contract. When, for example, someone sells himself into slavery, or a woman, through contracting marriage, submits to the marital power of her husband, or when a parcel of land is subjected to a family settlement, or when a corporation is formed by a number of individuals, interests of third persons are thereby affected in a way which is qualitatively different from that in which they are affected in the cases stated earlier, although the actual degree of affectedness may be quantitatively lesser and its actual manner may greatly vary from case to case. In the second group of cases there is created for the benefit of the contracting parties an entirely new *special law* which binds every third person's claims and expectations to the extent to which legal validity and coercive guaranty are ascribed to the arrangement of the contracting parties. This situation is thus different from the former since the rules of the new special law take the place of the hitherto prevailing general rules concerning such matters as the validity of agreements or a creditor's power to seize assets of property. The entirely new rules of a special law now apply not only to all new but often also to the already existing contracts of the person who has become a slave, a married woman, or a life tenant under a strict family settlement, and, in the case of the persons who have become stockholders of a corporation, a new special law applies to at least some of their contracts. The peculiar technique of juridical expression may frequently obscure the meaning of the situation

[68] *Supra* n. 55.

and the way in which the interests of third parties are affected by it. A corporation, for example, must legally possess a certain declared "capital," which may be reduced, under certain precautions, by a decision of a stockholders' meeting. In practice this means that the persons who have combined to form a corporation are compelled by the law to declare a certain surplus of the common property in goods and claims over and above the "debts" to be permanently available for creditors and members acquiring stock at a later date. When they compute the profits annually to be distributed, the managers and members of the corporation are bound to this declaration by the threat of criminal prosecution for the infringement of the rule which provides that no profits may be distributed unless the fund, which has been declared as "capital," remains covered by tangible goods or choses in action as computed under the rules of proper evaluation and accounting. Provided that certain precautions are observed, the members of the corporation are allowed, however, to withdraw their declaration and thus to reduce the corresponding guaranty for the creditors and later stockholders. In other words, they may henceforth distribute profits despite the fact that the originally declared amount is not covered. It is obvious that the possibility of creating a corporation as it is provided by such and similar enabling special rules of law affects in qualitatively specific ways the interests of third parties who are not at the moment members of the corporation, viz., creditors and later purchasers of stock. The same is true of the significance for third parties of the limitations of contractual freedom which arise from a person's voluntary entry upon slavery, or of the creation of the mortgage in favor of the wife on all the assets of the husband as it arises under several legal systems where, upon marriage, the wife becomes a mortgagee even with priority over older mortgages.[69] It is clear that this mode of influencing the legal situation of third parties, which deviates from the otherwise valid legal rules, goes beyond those "repercussions" which can arise outside the circle of the immediate participants from almost any legal transaction. We shall not discuss here the various tran-

[69] Following the model of the Code of Justinian (C. 8. 18. 12) a legal mortgage is given to the wife in the assets of the husband by the French Civil Code (art. 2121) and numerous other codes patterned upon it, e.g., those of Belgium, Italy, Spain, Mexico, Brazil, and Quebec. It is meant to protect those claims for damages which may arise for the wife against the husband, especially out of the management by him of the community fund and certain assets of the wife. The mortgage arises automatically upon the marriage, without need of recordation, and with priority over certain others of the husband's creditors. Cf. 2 PLANIOL, TRAITÉ ÉLÉMENTAIRE DE DROIT CIVIL (3rd ed. 1949) 1237 *et seq.*; T. Rohlfing, *Hypothek*, 4 RECHTSVERGLEICHENDES HANDWÖRTERBUCH (1933) 274.

sitional stages by which these two classes of phenomena are connected with one another. In the sense in which we discuss it now, "freedom of contract" means the power to participate effectively in such legal transactions as extend beyond the immediate circle of the participants not only by indirect repercussions but by the creation of special law. Even where this power is subject to some restrictions protecting interests of third parties, it means more than the mere concession of a "right of freedom" in the sense of a simple empowerment to perform, or to abstain from the performance of, certain concrete acts.

On the other hand, the law can refuse legal validity to agreements which do not appear at all directly to affect the interests of outsiders, or which at least do not involve any sort of special law apart from the generally valid law, and which even seem to confer upon third parties advantages rather than harm. The reasons for such *limitations of contractual freedom* may be very diverse. Thus classical Roman law did not admit the creation of a corporation or resort to any other device which would amount to affecting the interests of third parties through the establishment of special law; it refused to admit that in the establishment of a partnership the general law could be modified through the creation of a special partnership fund or the assumption of joint and several liability by the partners. It also refused validity to the creation of permanent rent charges through rent purchase or emphyteusis even though they would affect third parties only indirectly. The use of the last named institution was denied, at least to private persons, as the institution of the *ager vectigalis* was originally available only to the municipalities and only later became available to the owners of landed estates.[70] Classical Roman law also did not know negotiable instruments and originally did not even allow the assignment of choses in action. Modern law not only prevents the creation of special law through a contract by which an individual would subject himself to a relationship of slavery but, like Roman law, also for a long time excluded the encumbering of landed property with perpetual rent charges; only quite recently and under

[70] The ordinary lease (*locatio conductio rei*) of Roman law was a personal contract. Hence, if the lessor sold the land, the lessee had no right of continued use as against the purchaser but only a claim for damages against his lessor. In contrast, emphytheusis was the special kind of inheritable lease of land which gave the lessee a property interest in the land which he could enforce against everybody. It originated in Greece and, in the fourth century, became fused in a practical and modern manner, with the *ager vectigalis*, i.e., the Roman long-term lease (*ius perpetuum*) in public lands. Cf. KOHLER AND WENGER 228; BUCKLAND 275; WEBER, AGRARGESCHICHTE 170 *et seq.*; MITTEIS, ZUR GESCHICHTE DER ERBPACHT IM ALTERTUM (1901).

strictly limited conditions did the latter become permissible in Germany.[71] Modern law, furthermore, regards many agreements which were regarded as quite normal in antiquity as violating good morals and thus invalid, even though they affect third parties neither through the creation of special law nor by indirect repercussion. There are particularly excluded individual agreements as to sexual relations for which full freedom of contract existed in ancient Egypt,[72] while legitimate marriage is the only form today. The same observation obtains for other family arrangements, such as the major part of those agreements on paternal and domestic authority which were common in antiquity.[73]

The reasons for these differences in the ways of limiting freedom of contract are of many different kinds. Certain empowerments may be lacking simply because the legal recognition of the particular institution or commercial technique was not felt at the time as a real need. This would probably explain the absence of negotiable instruments in ancient law, or, more exactly, in the official law of the Roman empire; instruments of an at least externally similar sort were not altogether unknown in antiquity; they occur, for instance, as early as in Old Babylonian

[71] Perpetual rents were a common institution of medieval law. While canon law prohibited the lending of money upon interest, it did not prevent a person having capital to invest from "purchasing" a perpetual rent, secured by the possibility of levying execution upon a piece of, mostly urban, land in the case of nonpayment, and subject to termination upon repayment of the capital to the purchaser. Other perpetual rent charges came into being when ancient feudal and manorial claims to services or deliveries in kind were transformed into money rents. In France all these ancient charges were swept away by the Revolution of 1789. In Germany and the other countries of central and western Europe they were made subject to speedy amortization in the course of the so-called "liberation of the soil" ("Bodenbefreiung," see *infra* n. 101), which had been one of the principal postulates of Liberalism as it had become dominant in the nineteenth century. (Cf. HEDEMANN II, part ii, 9, 27.) The law of real property was reorganized in a way which excluded the creation of new perpetual rents. To a strictly circumscribed and narrowly limited extent their creation was permitted again for certain special purposes by the German Civil Code of 1896 (§§ 1105–1112, 1199–1203) and a few special statutes of later date (see M. WOLFF, SACHENRECHT, 8th ed. 1929, 307).

[72] On the freedom of sexual contract in Ptolemaic-Roman Egypt, see J. NITZOLD, DIE EHE IN ÄGYPTEN ZUR PTOLEMÄISCH-RÖMISCHEN ZEIT (1903).

[73] Roman institutions of this kind were *arrogatio* (transaction to establish paternal power over an adult man not previously subject to the paternal power of any other *paterfamilias*), *adoptio* (transaction to transfer parental power over a *filiusfamilias* by one *paterfamilias* to another), and *emancipatio* (remission of a person from parental power). Similar institutions were common in antiquity; cf. Robert H. Lowie, *Adoption*, in 1 ENCYC. SOC. SCI. 459, 463 (literature). On Germanic laws, see HUEBNER 660; L. Talheim, *Adoption* in 1 PAULY-WISSOWA 396.

times.[74] The same explanation may hold true of the absence of modern capitalistic forms of association, for which antiquity had no parallels other than the various forms of state capitalist associations, as ancient capitalism was essentially living off the state. But the absence of an economic need is by no means the only explanation of the lack of certain legal institutions in the past. Like the technological methods of industry, the rational patterns of legal technique to which the law is to give its guaranty must first be "invented" before they can serve an existing economic interest. Hence the peculiar kinds of technique used in a legal system or, in other words, its modes of thought, are of far greater significance for the likelihood that a certain legal institution will be invented in its context than is ordinarily believed. Economic situations do not automatically give birth to new legal forms; they merely provide the opportunity for the actual spread of a legal technique if it is invented. Many of our specifically capitalistic legal institutions are of medieval rather than Roman origin, although Roman law was much more rationalized in a logical sense than medieval law. While this fact has certain economic reasons, it is also due to a variety of reasons deriving entirely from differences of legal technique. The modes of thought of western medieval law were in many respects "backward." Thus it was not logic but a sort of legal animism or magic when the instrument in writing was conceived as a tangible embodiment of "rights" rather than as a rational mode of proof. Not logical either was the customary practice, derived from legal particularism, of imposing upon all sorts of communal groups solidary responsibility towards outsiders for all their members; [75] or the readiness to recognize separate funds in the most diverse spheres,[76] a phenomenon which, like the one mentioned just before, is explicable only in the light of purely political conditions. These very elements of "backwardness" in the logical and governmental aspects of legal development enabled business to produce a far greater wealth of practically useful legal devices than had been available under the more logical and technically more highly rationalized Roman law.[77] Quite generally one may observe that those special institutions which, like those of medieval commercial law, were particularly well suited for the emerging modern capitalism, could arise more easily in the context of a society which, for political reasons, produced a variety of bodies

[74] Cf. *supra* n. 57.

[75] Cf. *infra* p. 154.

[76] As to these "special funds" see HUEBNER 181.

[77] The German text reads "technisch-politisch rationalisiert," i.e., "rationalized technically-politically."

of law corresponding to the needs of different concrete interest groups.[78] Moreover, this lack of logical rationalization as well as of "scientific" treatment of the law was a factor of some importance; its consequence was that there could not then exist the subsequently established doctrine that for a principle to have legal validity it had to be "construed" out of a system of given concepts, and that nothing outside such logical construction could juristically even be "conceived." [79] Under certain circumstances, legal rationalism may indeed imply an impairment of creative ability, although this point should not be so exaggerated as it has occasionally been done in recent times.[80] Predominantly ethical or political interests and considerations are responsible for such other limitations on the freedom of contract as its exclusion or restriction in family matters, such as is characteristic of most modern legal systems, or the prohibition of contractual submission to slavery.

2. *Contract and the origin of marriage.*[81] Freedom of contract in sexual affairs is not primitive. Those tribes which are most backward technologically and are least differentiated economically and socially live in *de facto* lifelong patriarchal polygamy. The horror-inspired outlawry of endogamy obviously began in the narrowest circle within the household community in connection with the relative diminution of the sexual urge through common upbringing. The exchange of one's own sister for the sister of another is probably the oldest kind of sexual contract. From this then developed the barter of the woman by her kinship group in return for commodities and ultimately the normal form of marriage, namely, wife purchase,[82] which both in India and in Rome

[78] Cf. *infra* pp. 140 *et seq.*

[79] See *infra* c. IX.

[80] See *infra* c. XI.

[81] Weber's principal sources for the following presentation of the role of contract in sex relationships seem to have been J. Kohler, *Zur Urgeschichte der Ehe* (1897), 12 Z.F. VGL. RW. 186; W. WUNDT, VÖLKERPSYCHOLOGIE (1917), vol. vii; and, above all, the book by his wife, MARIANNE WEBER, EHEFRAU UND MUTTER IN DER RECHTSENTWICKLUNG (1907). The bibliography in WEBER'S WIRTSCHAFTSGESCHICHTE (1923) 42, n. 1, does not list WESTERMARCK'S HISTORY OF HUMAN MARRIAGE, 3 vols. (5th ed. 1921). The more recent literature is listed in the bibliography following Robert H. Lowie's article on *Marriage* in 10 ENCYC. SOC. SCI. 146, 154, to which should be added C. C. ZIMMERMAN, FAMILY AND CIVILIZATION (1944); ROBERT BRIFFAULT, THE MOTHERS (1927); W. GOODSELL, HISTORY OF MARRIAGE AND THE FAMILY (1934); and P. Koschaker, *Die Eheformen der Indogermanen*, 11 Z.F. AUSL. U. INTERNAT. PRIVATRECHT (1937), Sonderheft 121; sexual relationships and their regulation are also discussed by Weber in W.u.G. 200 *et seq.*

[82] The question of whether wife purchase has really been the "normal form of marriage" in primitive or archaic civilizations cannot be regarded as definitely settled. The results of the most recent research have been summarized by Koschaker

continued to exist as the specifically plebeian form of marriage together with the aristocratic forms of marriage, i.e., wife-stealing or sacramental ceremony.[83] However, both marriage by wife-stealing and by sacramental ceremony are products of the formation of certain social organizations. The former arose as a result of the formation of military organizations, which not only tore the young men from their families but also consolidated the women and their children into maternal groups. In the men's house wife-stealing was the heroic way of obtaining a wife, but the men who lived in the community might also purchase wives from outside. Combined with the custom of wife-stealing, these practices led to the formation of cartels for the exchange of women and thus apparently to the emergence of exogamy. It came to be regulated

---

(*loc. cit.* ARCHIV ORIENTÁLNY 210, 211) as follows: "Many ancient laws know a duality of marriage forms. It has long been known to have existed in Roman Law and more recently it has been found to have existed also in several other laws. One of these forms is characterized by the fact that no price is paid for the bride. This kind of marriage for which no special formalities are prescribed, is based in the last resort upon the consent of the spouses. On the other hand, however, the husband does not acquire marital power over the wife, and the children succeed to the mother to whose family they belong. . . The normal form, however, is that kind of marriage in which the husband pays a 'bride price' and acquires marital power over her. The first-named type of marriage is the exception which occurs only in certain special type-situations, as, for instance, marriage between the abductor and the woman abducted by him, or the marriage with the woman who is the sole heir of her ancestor and through whom the husband enters the wife's family; in other words, situations in which, for one reason or another, the marriage with marital power is not suited for the particular purpose. An exceptional position is occupied by mature Roman law where marriage without marital power appears as the normal type. That in earlier times the situation may have been different and that in Rome the marriage without marital power was to serve similar functions as in other laws, is possible, but impossible to prove from the fragmentary source material. . .

"[As to marriage by purchase] we find in the literature an almost hopeless confusion. I could mention scholars of several nations of whom everyone maintains that marriage by purchase may certainly have existed among other peoples, but that it is absolutely impossible as to his own nation that it should ever have been so barbaric as to purchase women like merchandise."

Cf. also the recent articles by R. Köstler, *Die Raub- u. Kaufehe bei den Germanen* (1943), 63 SAV. Z. GERM. 62; *Die Raub- u. Kaufehe bei den Hellenen* (1944), 64 SAV. Z. ROM. 200; *Die Raub- u. Kaufehe bei den Römern* (1947), 65 SAV. Z. ROM. 43.

[83] As to Hindu forms of marriage, see JOLLY, ÜBER DIE RECHTLICHE STELLUNG DER FRAUEN BEI DEN ALTEN INDERN (1876); also, by the same author, RECHT UND SITTE (1896, transl. by G. Losh, 1928) 49. As to Roman marriage forms, *see supra* n. 27. The statement by Jolly (RECHT UND SITTE 51) and Westermarck (*op. cit.* 404) notwithstanding, it cannot be regarded as proved that marriage by purchase was the specifically plebeian form of marriage; cf. *supra* n. 82; also 1 HOWARD, HISTORY OF MATRIMONIAL INSTITUTIONS (1904) cc. 4 and 6, esp. p. 264.

totemistically where animisic conceptions of a certain sort became established, especially and originally among peoples whose phratries were also hunting groups and subsequently became magical cult-communities with sacramental rites. The less developed the phratries were, or the more they became disintegrated, the more prominent became patriarchal marriage, especially among the chiefs and *bondamenden*.[84] In their case it easily resulted in polygyny with full control of the master of the household over its members, whom he could use at will for his own purposes; or, where the kinship groups remained strong, the chief could at least use a part of the product of the labor of household members for barter with the other members of the kin group. Limits to this use of the members of the household were first imposed upon the headman by the sib of his wife. A family of high status would not sell its daughters as beasts of burden or for unlimited exploitation; they would be given to outsiders only upon reassurances as to their personal status and as to a preferred status for their children vis-à-vis the children of other wives or female slaves. In consideration of such assurances, the daughter would be endowed, upon being given away, with a dowry. It was in these ways that there arose the notion of the legitimate principal wife and legitimate children, i.e., the legal characterisics of legitimate marriage. Dowry and agreement in writing concerning continuous support for the wife, her dower, the payment to be made to her upon abandonment, and the legal position of her children became the test by which full marriage was to be distinguished from all other sexual relationships. Simultaneously, however, the freedom of the sexual contract unfolded in many different forms and degrees. Service marriage (*Dienstehe*),[85] trial marriage, and temporary companionate marriage [86] can be found, and daughters of noble families in particular were anxious to avoid the subjection to the patriarchal power of the husband. Concurrently there existed all the forms of prostitution, i.e., the rendering of sexual services for a tangible return as distinguished from the continuous support specifically provided by marriage.[87] Prostitution, both heterosexual and homosexual, is as old as the possibility of obtaining a return for it. On the other hand, there has hardly ever existed any community in which this way of earning a living would not have been regarded as dishonor-

[84] The term could not be verified.

[85] Service marriage: see WESTERMARCK, *op. cit.* 491.

[86] On trial and companionate marriage in Hellenistic Egypt, see MITTEIS, REICHSRECHT 223.

[87] On prostitution see, in addition to the literature stated *supra*, n. 81, WEBER, HISTORY c. 4 § 2, and May's article q.v. in 12 ENCYC. SOC. SCI. 553, with literature cited there.

able. This discrimination was not so much created as fortified by the specifically ethical and political evaluation of formal marriage for the sake of the militarily and religiously important purpose of procreating legitimate children. Halfway between marriage and prostitution there was, especially among the nobility, the institution of concubinage, i.e., a permanent sexual relation with a maid servant, a co-wife, a hetaera, a bayadere [88] or some other kind of woman living outside of marriage or in "free" marriage of the common or the refined type. The status of the children of such a union was mostly left to the discretion of the father, limited only by the monopoly rights of the children of the principal wife. Greater restrictions were established, however, by those who wielded the monopoly of citizenship, the politico-economic privileges of citizenship being reserved to the sons of male and female citizens. This principle was observed with peculiar force by the democracies of Antiquity. In contrast to the freedom of the sexual contract of ancient Egypt, which had its cause in the absence of all political rights of the populace, the oldest Roman law disapproved as *causas turpes* of all sexual contracts except marriage and concubinage, which was recognized as a kind of marriage of lower legal status for certain special situations.[89] But the latter was finally proscribed in the Occident by the Lateran Council [90] and the Reformation. The father's right of disposition over the children was seriously limited first by sacred law, then subjected to additional limitations, and finally abolished for military, political, and ethical reasons.

Today the chances of a return to freedom of sexual contract are more remote than ever. The great mass of women would be opposed to sexual competition for the males which, as we can conclude from the Egyptian sources, strongly increases the economic opportunities of the women of superior sex appeal at the expense of the less attractive; it would also be opposed by all traditional ethical powers, especially the

[88] *Hetaera* (Greek): girl companion, ranging from the common harlot to the geisha-like woman companion of refinement and education, often contrasted with the commonly low status of the legitimately married wife. The hetaerae gave the Greek men that intellectual stimulus which they did not find in the family. Greek life would have been unthinkable without them. Contact with them was not regarded as socially disreputable (LAMER, WÖRTERBUCH DER ANTIKE [3rd ed. 1950] q.v., where one can also find a list of historically famous hetaerae, such as Aspasia, the companion of Pericles); see also H. LICHT, LIEBE UND EHE IN GRIECHENLAND (1933).

Bayadère — Hindu dancing girl.

[89] Cf. BUCKLAND 128 *et seq.*; JÖRS AND KUNKEL 282 and literature cited there and p. 417.

[90] A.D. 1215/16.

churches. Yet, while such absolute freedom seems impossible, a similar state of affairs may be produced within the framework of legitimate marriage by a system of easy or completely free divorce combined with a system whereby the position of the wife remains both free and secure with respect to property rights. Such relative freedom has obtained, in varying degrees, in late Roman, Islamic, Jewish, as well as modern American law; it also obtained, though only for a limited period, in those legislations of the eighteenth century which were influenced not only by the contract theory of the rationalist Natural Law but also by considerations of population policy.[91] The results have varied greatly. Only in Rome and in the United States has the legal freedom of divorce been actually accompanied by a high divorce rate.[92] Both economic freedom and freedom of divorce are strongly desired by the women in the United States where their position in the home as well as in society has come to be secure, just as it had once come to be in Rome. The majority of Italian women, on the other hand, who are strongly bound by tradition, have rejected freedom of divorce even in recent times, probably because they are afraid that female competition for the male would become more acute and certainly because they do not wish to jeopardize their economic security, especially in old age, just as an aging worker would be afraid of losing his daily bread. Generally both men and women seem to favor a formally rigid or even indissoluble type of marriage where loose sexual behavior is regarded as permissible for the members of one's own sex; men may also be content with such kind of marriage where, because of weakness or opportunism, they are apt to condone a certain female license. But the decisive reason for the repudiation of freedom of divorce by bourgeois public opinion is the real or imagined danger to the children's educational chances; besides, authoritarian instincts on the part of the men have also played their part, especially where women have become economically emancipated to such a degree that the men are concerned about their position in the family and their sex vanity is thus aroused. There are, furthermore, the authoritarian interests of the political and hierocratic powers, strengthened by the idea which has become powerful through the very rationalization of life in the contractual society, that is to say, the idea that the formal integrity of the family is a source of certain vaguely specified irrational values or is the supporting supra-individual bond for needful and weak individuals. In the last generation before the [first] World

[91] Under the Prussian Code of 1794.

[92] On divorce in Rome, see 1 Friedländer und Wissowa, Sittengeschichte Roms (9th ed. 1919) 283.

War all these heterogenous motives have resulted in a backward movement away from freedom of divorce and in some respects even from economic freedom within marriage.

3. *Freedom of testation,* i.e., freedom of economic and normally intra-familial disposition, has also met in modern times with restrictive tendencies.[93] But we shall not try to trace here the formal course of legal history of testamentary disposition. Evidence of complete or almost complete substantive freedom of testation can be found only twice in history, viz., in Republican Rome and in England, i.e., among two peoples who were simultaneously strongly expansive and governed by a stratum of landowning *honoratiores.* Today its principal area of application is the United States, i.e., the area of optimal economic opportunities. In Rome freedom of testation increased with the policy of military expansion which offered to disinherited sons the prospect of material well-being in the conquered territories, while it was cut down through the practice of breaking "unnatural" wills taken over from Hellenic law as the age of colonization was coming to an end.[94] In English law freedom of testation aimed at the stabilization of the fortunes of the great families, which was also served by the very opposite institutions of landed investment, primogeniture, and strict settlement.[95] In modern democratic legislations the restriction or elimination of freedom of testation by means of generous indefeasible shares, or the prevention of primogeniture in the French Code through compulsory physical partition has been and still is largely politically determined. In the case of Napoleon, the intention of destroying the old aristocracy by compulsory partition of their estates was accompanied by the desire to establish fiefs as bearers of the new aristocracy which he was trying to create; this latter institution was referred to in his famous assertion that the introduction of the *Code* would place in the hands of the government the distribution of social power.[96]

4. *Contractual constitution of slavery.* The suppression of *slavery* [97]

[93] Cf. *supra* p. 102.

[94] See JOLOWICZ, 125 *et seq.*, 248 *et seq.*; BUCKLAND 324; for further literature, see JÖRS AND KUNKEL 307, 327, 419, 421.

[95] Cf. BRENTANO, ERBRECHTSPOLITIK (1899) 198 *et seq.*; RHEINSTEIN, DECEDENTS' ESTATES 11 *et seq.* and literature cited there and at p. 412. Significantly, freedom of testation has now been limited in favor of needy dependents even in England by the Inheritance (Family Provision) Act, 1938, 1 & 2 GEO. 6 c. 45.

[96] Letters of Napoleon to his brother Joseph, King of Naples, dated 8 March and 5 June 1806, 12 CORRESPONDENCE DE NAPOLÉON Ier 167, 432; RHEINSTEIN, DECEDENTS' ESTATES 17, n. 30.

[97] On the following, see the literature cited in WEBER'S WIRTSCHAFTSGESCHICHTE

by the prohibition of even a voluntary submission to formally slavelike relations was the product of the shift of the center of gravity of world economic factors to areas where several elements happened to coincide: slave labor was unprofitable because of the high cost of living; the wage system with its threat of dismissal and unemployment had come to provide indirect coercion to work; and direct coercion was regarded as less effective than indirect pressure to obtain work of high quality and to extort labor from the dependent strata without the great risks involved in large investments in slave labor. The religious communities, especially Christianity, played a very slight role in the suppression of slavery in antiquity, less, for example, than the Stoa; in the Middle Ages and in modern times, its role was somewhat greater but by no means decisive. In antiquity, it was rather with the pacification of the foreign relations of the Empire, which left the sale of children as the only major source of slave import for the West, that capitalistic slavery came to decline. The capitalistic slavery of the Southern United States was doomed once the supply of free land was exhausted and the cessation of the importation of slaves had raised slave prices to monopolistic levels. Its elimination through the Civil War was accelerated by the purely political and social antagonism of the democratic farmers and the Northern plutocratic bourgeoisie against the Southern planter aristocracy. In Europe it was the purely economic evolution of the medieval organization of work and labor, especially the growth of the guild system, which resulted in keeping the crafts free of slave labor even though slavery never completely disappeared from southern Europe during the Middle Ages. As far as agriculture was concerned, more intensive production for export led even in modern times at first to greater servitude in the status of the agricultural laborer; but unfree labor was finally found to be unprofitable with the emergence of modern techniques of production. However, for the final and complete elimination of personal servitude, strong ideological conceptions of natural law were ultimately decisive everywhere. The patriarchal slavery of the Near East, the ancient and characteristic seat of this institution which was much less intensively spread in East Asia and India, is on the verge of extinction as a result of the suppression of the African slave trade. Once its military

---

85, n. 1: Cairnes, The Slave Power (1862); E. von Halle, Baumwollproduktion und Pflanzungswirtschaft in den nordamerikanischen Südstaaten (2 vols. 1897, 1906); H. J. Nieboer, Slavery as an Industrial System (1900); B. du Bois, The Suppression of the African Slave Trade (1904); G. Knapp, Die Landarbeiter in Knechtschaft und Freiheit (2nd ed. 1909); see also the articles in 14 Encyc. Soc. Sci. 73 and literature cited there at p. 90.

significance, which was great in ancient Egypt as well as in the late Middle Ages, was rendered obsolete by the military technique of the mercenary armies, its economic significance, which had never been very great, also began to decline rapidly. As a matter of fact, in the Orient slavery never enjoyed a role corresponding to that played by the plantation slavery on the estates of Carthage and of late Republican Rome. In the Orient most of the slaves were domestic servants just as they had been in the Hellenic and Hellenistic regions. Some, on the other hand, constituted a sort of interest-bearing capital investment in industrial workers, as had also been the case in Babylonia, Persia, or Athens. In the Near East, and still more in Central Africa, this patriarchal slavery approximated a free labor relationship more closely than the legal form would lead one to suppose. Yet, Snouck Hurgronje's observation in Mecca that a slave would not be bought in the market unless he approved of the personal qualities of the master, and that the master would resell the slave if the latter should turn out to be grossly dissatisfied with the former,[98] seems to be the exception rather than the rule and to be brought about by the great dependence of the master on the good will especially of his domestic slaves. In Central Africa, even today, a slave who is dissatisfied with his master knows how to compel the master to give him, by way of *noxae datio*,[99] to another master for whom he has a greater preference.[100] But this, too, is certainly not universally true. Yet the nature of oriental theocratic or patrimonial authority and its inclination toward the ethical elaboration of the patriarchal side of all dependence relationships have created at least in the Near East a highly conventionalized security for the slave vis-à-vis his master. Consequently, unrestrained exploitation in the manner of late Roman slavery is practically excluded. The beginnings of this trend can be found already in ancient Jewish law, and the decisive motivation for this conduct was provided by the very circumstance that the ancient institutions of levying execution upon the debtor's person and of debt slavery entailed the probability of enslavement of one's fellow citizens.

5. *Other limitations of freedom of contract.* Finally, the social and economic interests of the influential, especially "bourgeois," strata of

[98] MEKKA IN THE LATTER PART OF THE 19TH CENTURY (1888; transl. 1931), p. 14.

[99] *Noxae datio* (Latin) — the surrender of a person, animal, or inanimate thing by which the father, master, or owner frees himself from the liability created by the child's, slave's, or animal's misdeed or the "act" of his spear, ax, or other thing. It existed in Rome and was widespread in archaic laws.

[100] Cf. GIRARD, LES ACTIONS NOXALES (1888) 62, and the review of this book by Kipp in 10 SAV. Z. ROM. 398.

society also constitute the cause of such limitations on the freedom of contract as the prohibition to put feudal or other permanent encumbrances upon land for the benefit of private parties. Such transactions were excluded in the law of Republican Rome just as they were again prohibited in the Prussian Land Redemption Laws.[101] In both instances the operative factors were bourgeois class interests and the economic conceptions associated with them. Roman legislation, which during the Republic did not recognize the emphyteusis except as *ager vectigalis* on public lands, like the present *de facto* limitation in Germany of the creation of similar tenures in lands owned by the state or by state-approved colonization corporations,[102] was a product of the concern of the bourgeois landed interests for easy marketability of land and for the prevention of manorlike land settlements.

Section 5. Extension of the Effect of a Contract beyond Its Parties — "Special Law"

Just as in Roman law, so in the modern rationalized law that type of regimentation of freedom of contract which results from the combination of all the factors just mentioned is generally achieved not by prohibiting the proscribed agreements but simply by the failure of the legal order to provide the particular type-contract or, in Rome, the particular *actio*, and by so regulating the available type-contracts that their norms are incompatible with the disapproved types of agreement. On the other hand, the technical form in which the law provides the power in a legally valid way to engage in those transactions which, like the formation of a business corporation, affect the interests of third parties, consists in the official establishment of certain standard terms which must be incorpo-

[101] As to Rome, see WEBER, AGRARGESCHICHTE 114–117; in Prussia, legislation aiming at the abolition of land encumbrances standing in the way of intensive cultivation started in 1717, with an Edict of King Frederick William I. It was continued by the Prussian Code ("Allgemeines Landrecht," abbrev. ALR) of 1794 and was vigorously promoted after the defeat of the Prussian Army in 1806 during the administration of Baron vom Stein. Final regulation was initiated after the revolution of 1848 by the Regulation Law of 2 March 1850. See F. Gutmann, *Bauernbefreiung* in 2 HANDWÖRTERBUCH DER STAATSWISSENSCHAFTEN (4th ed. 1924) 378, 544; G. F. KNAPP, DIE BAUERNBEFREIUNG UND DER URSPRUNG DER LANDARBEITER IN DEN ÄLTEREN TEILEN PREUSSENS (1887); A. MEITZEN, DER BODEN UND DER PREUSSISCHE STAAT (1868); Skalweit, *Gutsherrschaft und Landarbeiter in Deutschland* (1911), 35 SCHMOLLERS, J. B. 1339; HEDEMANN II, 34, and literature cited there.

[102] That is, organizations to promote the settlement of German farmers in the predominantly Polish regions of the eastern provinces of Prussia as constituted before 1918.

rated in every such arrangement by individual parties if it is to be legally effective not only between these parties but also against outsiders. This modern technique of leaving it to the interested parties thus to create law not only for themselves but also with operative effects as regards third parties gives those interested parties the advantages of a legal institution of *special law,* provided they comply with the substantive requirements as expressed in those terms which they have to incorporate in their arrangement. This modern type of special law differs from that type of special law which was allowed to develop in the past. The modern technique is a product of the unification and rationalization of the law; it is based on the official monopoly of law creation by, and the compulsion of membership in, the modern political organization. In the past, special law arose normally as "volitive law,"[103] i.e., from tradition, or as the agreed enactment of consensual communities of corporate-estate form or of rationally organized associations. It arose, in other words, in the form of autonomously created norms.[104] The maxim that "particularistic law" (i.e., volitive law in the above sense) "breaks" (i.e., takes precedence over) the "law of the land" (i.e., the generally valid common law) was recognized almost universally, and it obtains even today in almost all legal systems outside the Occident and even in parts of Europe, for example, for the Russian peasantry.[105] But the state insisted almost everywhere, and usually with success, that the validity of these special laws, as well as the extent of their application, should be subject to its consent; and the state did this in just the same manner in which it also transformed the towns and cities into heteronomous organizations endowed by the state with powers defined by it. In neither case, however, has this state of affairs obtained originally. For the body of laws by which a given locality or a group were governed was largely the autonomously arrogated creation of mutually independent communities between which the continuously necessitated adjustment was either achieved by mutual compromise or by imposition through those political or ecclesiastical authorities which would happen at the given time to have preponderant power. With this observation we return to phenomena which have already been touched upon above.[106]

Prior to the emergence and triumph of the purposive contract and of freedom of contract in the modern sense, and prior to the emergence of

[103] "Gewillkürtes Recht."

[104] "Durch Tradition oder vereinbarte Satzung ständischer Einverständnisgemeinschaften oder vergesellschafteter Einungen; in autonom gesatzten Ordnungen."

[105] Written before the collapse of the Czarist system.

[106] Cf. *supra*, at p. 71.

the political framework of the state, every consensual community or organization which represented a special legal order and which therefore might properly be named a "law community" [107] was a group that was either constituted in its membership by such objective characteristics as birth, political, ethnic, or religious denomination, mode of life or occupation, or was a group that arose through the process of explicit fraternization. The primitive situation, as we have seen above, was that any lawsuit that would correspond to our procedure could take place only in the form of composition-proceedings between different groups (sibs) or members of different groups. Within the group, i.e., among the members of the group, patriarchal arbitration prevailed. At the very origin of all legal history there thus prevailed, if viewed from the standpoint of the steadily growing strength of the central political authority, an important dualism, i.e., a dualism of the autonomously created law between groups, and the norms determinative of disputes among group members. At the same time, however, another fact intruded into this apparently simple situation: namely, that even at the earliest stages of development known to us the individual often belonged to several groups rather than to just one. But nevertheless, the subjection to the special law was initially a strictly personal quality, a "privilege" acquired by usurpation or grant, and thus a monopoly of its possessors who, by virtue of this fact, became "comrades in law." [108] Hence, in those groups which were politically integrated by a common supreme authority, like the Persian Empire, the Roman Empire, the kingdom of the Franks, or the Islamic states, the body of laws to be applied by the judicial officers differed in accordance with the ethnic, religious, or political characteristics of the component groups, for instance, legally or politically autonomous cities or clans. Even in the Roman Empire, Roman law was at first the law for Roman citizens only, and it did not entirely apply in the relations between citizens and noncitizen subjects. The non-Moslem subjects of the Islamic states and even the adherents of the four orthodox schools of Islamic law [109] live in accordance with their own laws; but when the former resort to the Islamic judge rather than to their own authorities, he applies Islamic law, as he is not obliged to know any other, and as in the Islamic state the non-Moslems are mere "subjects." [110]

[107] Rechtsgemeinschaft.

[108] Rechtsgenossen.

[109] Cf. p. 71, *infra*, pp. 209, 239.

[110] The text is concerned with the situation existing before the collapse of the Ottoman empire in 1918.

Under any such systems it was inevitable that difficulties were to arise in conflicts between persons subject to different bodies of law, and with them the need for a certain measure of common legal principles, which increased rapidly with the growing intensity of intercourse. There either emerges, then, as it did in Rome, a "jus gentium," which coexists together with the "ius civile" of each group; or, as occurred in England, the political or hierocratic ruler will, by virtue of his imperium, impose upon his courts an "official law" which is to be the only binding one; or it may happen that a new political group, usually a local one, will fuse the substance of different legal rules into one new body of law. In the Italian city men were well aware that the citizens had "declared" that they were living under Lombard or Roman law, but in a characteristic divergence from older legal notions, it was the *civitas,* the personification of the total body of the citizens, which was said to have accepted as its *confessio iuris* either the Lombard law or, as its supplementary source, the Roman law; or it, *the civitas,* may have adopted the Roman law, and the Lombard law as its secondary system.[111] On the other hand, in the medieval Empire, every man was entitled everywhere to be judged by that tribal law by which he "professed" to live.[112] The individual carried his *professio iuris* with him wherever he went. Law was not a *lex terrae,* as the English law of the King's court became soon after the Norman Conquest, but rather the privilege of the person as a member of a particular group. Yet this principle of "personal law" was no more consistently applied at that time than its opposite principle is today. All volitionally formed associations always strove for the application of the principle of personal law on behalf of the law created by them, but the extent to which they were successful in this respect varied greatly from case to case. At any rate, the result was the coexistence of numerous "law communities," the autonomous jurisdictions of which overlapped, the compulsory, political association being only one such autonomous jurisdiction in so far as it existed at all; and when the "comrades in law" belonging

[111] Cf. C. Calisse, *History of Italian Law,* 8 Continental Legal History Series (1928) 127–132, 165, 177; K. Neumeyer, Die gemeinrechtliche Entwicklung des internationalen Privat- und Strafrechts bis Bartolus (1901) I, 159; Engelmann, *op. cit.* (1938) 97; E. Meijers, L'histoire des principes fondamentaux du droit international privé à partir du Moyen age (Recueil des cours, [1934] III, 547, 560).

[112] This statement is correct as to the Carlovingian empire but must be qualified for the later period. The "tribal" laws had lost their significance throughout the empire at the latest in the thirteenth century, if not earlier; cf. Calisse, *op. cit.* 18, 24, 57, 97, 99, 100, 165; Huebner 2–4; Neumeyer *op. cit.*, I, 94, 155; Meijers, *loc. cit.* 558; Brunner I, part ii, 382, 399.

to a special "law community" began, by virtue of their membership in such a community, to monopolize the control of certain tangible things or objects, for example, land of a certain type such as copyholds or fiefs, when, also, these "law communities" ceased to be closed shops and, under the pressure of certain interests, it became possible for new members to join them; when, furthermore, the members of these communities increased so that any one individual member was simultaneously belonging to several groups, then the special law of any "law community" became almost identified with the ownership of the particular object so that now, in the reverse sense, such ownership became the test for membership in the particular special law community.[113] This was also a step towards the situation which prevails today, namely that those relations which are subject to a special law are formally and generally accessible to any person. Nevertheless, it was only one step in the transition to the modern situation. For all special law of the older type had an enduring quality of conferring legal privileges either directly on certain persons belonging to a group or on certain objects the possession of which provided this membership. In modern society special legal regulation may also be occasioned by the existence of certain purely technical or economic conditions such as ownership of a factory or a farm, or the exercise of the profession of attorney, pharmacist, craftsman of a certain kind, etc.

Naturally every legal system has certain special norms that are bound up with technical and economic facts. But the special bodies of laws which we are discussing at this point were of a different character. The applicability of this type of special law was founded not on economic or technical qualities but on qualities derived from "corporate status" i.e., birth, mode of life, or belonging to a circle of persons of certain qualities such as "nobleman," "knight," or "guild fellow," or on certain social relationships with respect to material objects such as a copyhold or a manor. The definition of all these qualities was indeed indirectly affected by certain "corporate status" relationships, and it has therefore always been the case that the applicability of a special law was conditional upon a particular quality of the person or upon his relationship to some material object.[114] In marginal cases, the "privilege" could even adhere

[113] On the "law communities" and their development, see PLANITZ 176, and literature stated there.

[114] On this characteristic feature of medieval law see POLLOCK AND MAITLAND I, 234–240; II, 182; HOLDSWORTH II, 35–40, 211, 379, 417, 464–466, 562; HUEBNER 4, 88–92, 96, 98, 102, 189, 334–341; A. ESMEIN, COURS ÉLÉMENTAIRE D'HISTOIRE DU DROIT FRANÇAIS (1925) 20, 159, 174, 221, 262–263, 280–282, 344.

to a single individual or object and it did so in fact quite frequently. In that case, the right coincided with the law; the privileged individual could claim as his right that he be treated in accordance with the special law. But even where it was significant that one belonged to a group of special corporate status or that one stood in a special relationship to a group of objects, it was natural to regard the application of the special legal norms as the personal right of the interested parties. The idea of generally applicable norms was not, it is true, completely lacking, but it inevitably remained in an undeveloped state; all law appeared as the privilege of particular individuals or objects or of particular constellations of individuals or objects. Such a point of view had, of course, to be opposed by that in which the state appears as the all-embracing coercive institution. At times, especially during the first period of the rising "bourgeois" strata in ancient Rome and in the modern world, the opposition was so strong that the very possibility of "privileges" was repudiated. The creation of privileges by vote of the popular assembly was regarded as impossible in Rome,[115] and the revolutionary period of the eighteenth century produced a type of legislation which sought to extirpate every form of associational autonomy and legal particularism.[116] This end was never achieved completely, however, and we shall soon see how modern law has created anew a great mass of legal particularisms. But it has done so upon a basis which differs in many important respects from that of the privileges of the older corporate status groups.

The ever-increasing integration of all individuals and all fact-situations into one compulsory institution which today, at least, rests in principle on formal "legal equality" has been achieved by two great rationalizing forces, i.e., first, by the extension of the market economy and, second, by the bureaucratization of the activities of the organs of the consensual communities.[117] They replaced that particularist mode of creating law which was based upon private power or the privilege granted to monopolistically closed organizations, in which we have recognized the autonomy of associations of a primarily corporate-status nature. This replacement was effected by two arrangements: The first is the formal, universally accessible, closely limited, and legally regulated autonomy of association which may be created by anyone wishing to

[115] See MOMMSEN 318, 322; JOLOWICZ 25.

[116] Cf. BRISSAUD, HISTORY OF FRENCH PRIVATE LAW (Howell's tr. 1912) 900; BRISSAUD, HISTORY OF FRENCH PUBLIC LAW (Garner's tr. 1915) 548; HEDEMANN I, 39, 41.

[117] Cf. W.U.G., Part III, c. vi.

do so; the other consists in the grant to everyone of the power to create law of his own by means of engaging in private legal transactions of certain kinds. The decisive factors in this transformation of the technical forms of autonomous legislation were, politically, the power-needs of the rulers and officials of the state as it was growing in strength and, economically, the interests of those segments of society that were oriented towards power in the market, i.e., those individuals who are economically privileged in the formally free competitive struggle of the market by virtue of their class-position as property owners. If, by virtue of the principle of formal legal equality, everyone "without respect of person" may establish a business corporation or a trust fund, the propertied classes as such have a sort of factual "autonomy," since they alone are able to utilize or take advantage of these powers.

However, this amorphous autonomy merits the designation of "autonomy" only in a metaphorical sense; for, unless the word "autonomy" is to lack all precision, its definition presupposes the existence of a group of persons who, though they may fluctuate, are determined in a certain way and who are all, by consent or enactment, under a special law depending on them for its modification. The particular character of the group is irrelevant for the definition; it can be a club just as well as a business corporation, a municipality, an "estate," a guild, a labor union, or a circle of vassals. The phenomenon itself is always the product of the beginning of a monopoly of lawmaking by the compulsory political organization. It always entails the idea that the state either tolerates or directly guarantees the creation of law by organs other than its own. Qualitatively, too, the autonomy enjoyed by a group through consensus or by enacted norms differs from mere freedom of contract. The line between the two coincides with the limits of the concept of norm; in other words, it lies where the order whose validity depends upon the consensus or the rational agreement of the participants is no longer conceived as the objectively valid rule imposed upon a group but as the establishment of reciprocal subjective claims, such as occurs, for instance, in the agreement of two business partners concerning the division of work and profits between them and their legal position within and outside the firm. The absence of a clear dividing line between objective law and subjective right becomes apparent at this point. From the standpoint of our modes of thought, which have developed in regard to enacted law,[118] a distinction can be found, even theoretically, only in the proposition that in the sphere of private law, which alone concerns

[118] Weber writes from the point of view of the modern continental for whom, in theory, all law is contained in the codes and statutes.

us here, autonomy is exercised where the enacted rule has its normal source in a resolution, while we have a special case of regulation by virtue of freedom of contract where the rule is supplied by an agreement between concrete individuals. This distinction was not insignificant in the past, but neither was it exclusively decisive.

As long as the distinction between objective norm and subjective claim was but incompletely developed, as long, also, as law was a quality of a person determined by his membership in a certain group, one could speak of only two kinds of rules. The first were those which were valid in a group or organization because of the special status qualities of its members; the others were valid and binding because one had created them for himself by directly participating in a contract. All special law was indeed originally the law of a group in which membership was determined by status qualities. But this state of affairs changed, as we have already indicated, with the increasing differentiation and economic scarcity of those goods which were munificently appropriated [119] by the several groups. The changes were indeed so pronounced that in the end an almost opposite rule came to obtain: namely, that special law was almost exclusively that which applied in a social or economic special relationship. To this conception certain approximations can already be found in the Middle Ages. Heusler went too far when he completely denied the existence of all estate laws (Staatsrechte).[120] But feudal law was indeed the law for the relation between lord and vassal and not the law of a "vassalic state" simply because such kind of state never existed.[121] In the same sense manorial law was the law ap-

[119] "Munifistisch appropriiert."

[120] A. Heusler, Deutsche Verfassungsgeschichte (1905) 138.

[121] Vassalic state (*Vassallenstaat*): a state in which all, or at least all political, relationships would be based upon the personal bond between lord and vassal.

The relationship between lord and vassal binds both parties together to mutual faith and loyalty. The vassal is bound to render the lord the agreed or customary services, primarily of military character, while the lord is in turn bound to protect the vassal. The relationship has repeatedly appeared in combination with the grant to the vassal by the lord of a piece of land, or an office, or both (*beneficium*), the emoluments of which are to afford the vassal the economic bases for his services to the lord. This combination constitutes the characteristic feature of feudalism. Feudalism played an essential role in the political structure of the Medieval West as well as in certain phases in oriental, especially Arab, Chinese, Japanese, and Russian development. While it does not seem that there has ever existed a state in which it would have been the sole constituent of the political organization, it might properly be said, as it is maintained by von Below (Der deutsche Staat des Mittelalters (2nd ed. 1925) I, 322; Territorium und Stadt (12th ed. 1923) 162), that the Medieval German empire was a *Feudalstaat* or *Vassallenstaat* in the sense of a state in which at least the essential relationships of public office were of

plicable to the relationships of manorial service; the law merchant was the law for merchandise and mercantile transactions; and crafts law [122] is the law relating to the transactions and the establishments of craftsmen. Yet, outside of these special relationships, the vassal, the merchant, the copyholder, and the freeman were subject to the general law of the land. An individual could own freehold and copyhold lands at one and the same time; as regards the former, he was under the jurisdiction of the common law of the land, and as regards the latter, under the law of the manor. Likewise a non-merchant who had lent money in a *commenda* [123] or upon bottomry [124] was subject to commercial law in

---

the type of the relationship between lord and vassal. Cf. MITTEIS, LEHNRECHT UND STAATSEGEWALT (1933) 448.

On feudalism, see Weber, W.u.G. Part III, cc. vii and viii, also Part I, c. iii, § 12b and 12c (tr. THEORY, 373); also articles in 6 ENCYC. SOC. SCI. 203 and literature stated there at 219; v. SCHWERIN, *op. cit.* 98, 229; D. Hintze, *Wesen und Verbreitung des Feudalismus*, SITZUNGSBERICHTE D. PREUSSISCHEN AKADEMIE D. WISSENSCHAFTEN, PHIL.-HIST. KLASSE 1929, XX, repr. 1 GESAMMELTE ABHANDLUNGEN (1941) 74; MITTEIS, *op. cit.* (1933).

[122] *Gewerberecht.* In Germany, France, and other countries it has become customary to refer to the sum total of those rules of law which relate to the crafts and industries as *Gewerberecht, droit industriel, diritto industriale.* In Germany a part of these rules has been combined in a special code, the GEWERBEORDNUNG of 1869.

[123] *Commenda*: It is "a community of two merchants of whom one stays at home while the other takes merchandise with him oversea. Originally the relationship seems to have been one of mere friendliness; among a group of merchants the members would take turns in selling the goods of the others. The necessary funds were provided either by merchants or, especially in southern Europe, by non-merchants, for instance, noblemen, who owned money and were anxious to invest their surpluses in profitable trade. Money or merchandise of a stated money value was left with the traveling *socius* to constitute the capital fund as the so-called *commenda.* The merchandise would be sold overseas; the proceeds would be used for the purchase of other goods which would be sold upon return to the home port. If the home-staying partner had furnished the entire capital, he was to receive three-fourths of the profits. If, however, the capital had been furnished by both him and the traveling partner, the profits were usually split in the relation of two to one. The transaction is the earliest one in which we find a method of capitalistic accounting. The initial capital is deducted from the end capital, and the difference is treated and distributed as profits. The *commenda* is found in Babylonian and Arabic as well as in Italian and, in a slightly modified form, in Hanseatic law." (WEBER, WIRTSCHAFTSGESCHICHTE 183/184); see also W. SILBERSCHMIDT, DIE COMMENDA IN IHRER FRÜHESTEN ENTWICKLUNG (1884); HOLDSWORTH viii, 104, 195, 275.

[124] Bottomry (*foenus nauticum*) — maritime loan: the owner or master of a ship, as his agent, borrowed money, usually for a specified voyage, pledging the ship as security but without engaging the owner's personal credit. In view of the high risk incurred by the lender, the rate of interest was high, usually 30 per cent. As the economically more powerful party the lender was usually the principal for whom the voyage was managed by the shipowner. The transaction was widely used

this, but only this, regard. However, this objective mode of treatment was by no means universal. Almost all those relationships to which a special law applied had to some degree consequences implying corporate status, i.e., touching upon the total legal status of the person. This was the case with the possession of copyholds or other "unfree" lands. Many of them were regarded as mutually incompatible in one person and the tendency to break through such corporate-status restrictions was opposed time and again by the counter-tendency towards the closure of group membership. Which of the two tendencies would be stronger was entirely determined by the concrete constellation of interests in each specific instance. In Germany, as even Heusler acknowledges, borough law (*Stadtrecht*) was a corporate-status right of the citizens rather than a law of tenure of urban land or other material relationship.[125] In England, however, the municipalities became almost entirely private corporations.

In general it is correct to say that there prevailed the tendency of treating special law as law for certain objects and situations. As a result, the integration of the special laws into the common law of the land, the *lex terrae,* as substantive special rules was greatly facilitated. The actual and final integration, however, depended predominantly on political conditions. Yet in those fields where this integration was not fully realized the problem of the relationship of the various special laws and their corresponding special courts to the common law of the land and its courts was resolved in a great variety of ways. Under the common law of the land [126] seisin in copyhold land was vested in the lord rather than the copyholder. But as to land held in fee the situation was not so simple; in the *Mirror of Saxon Law,* for instance, the problem of seisin was in dispute between the author and the glossators.[127]

This particular problem has left traces in the Roman law, too. The Roman *ius civile* was the law of the Roman citizens in so far as a person who was neither a citizen nor an assimilated person by virtue of treaty could not appear as a party before a Roman court, engage in the specific transactions of the quiritarian law,[128] or be judged according to its rules.

---

both in antiquity and the Middle Ages. Cf. WEBER, WIRTSCHAFTSGESCHICHTE 182; HOLDSWORTH v, 144; viii, 261, 277.

[125] *Institutionen des deutschen Privatrechts* (1885/86).

[126] That is, of medieval Germany.

[127] MIRROR OF SAXON LAW (SACHSENSPIEGEL), treatise on the law of Lower Saxony, by Eike von Repgow, written between 1215 and 1235. Cf. *infra* p. 211. Glosses have been added since the early fourteenth century. The extensive literature on the SACHSENSPIEGEL is listed in PLANITZ 181.

[128] Quiritarian law (*ius quiritium*), the law of the *quirites,* i.e., those who were

No Roman *lex* had any validity outside the circle of the citizenry. Its inapplicability to non-citizens was politically of considerable importance because it established the sovereign power of the officials and the Senate over the entire subjugated area which was not incorporated into the law. But on the other hand, the Roman citizen was never judged exclusively by *ius civile,* and he was never exclusively subject to the courts of the *ius civile.* The *ius civile* of historical times must rather be defined as that special law which was relevant for a person exclusively in his character as a citizen, i.e., as a member of that particular status group. Simultaneously with it we find some law spheres which covered either both citizens and non-citizens, or only a part of the citizens, and the law of which presents itself as special law either of status groups or of objective demarcation. In this context belong above all those numerous and important situations which were regulated by administrative law. Down to the time of the Gracchi, title by virtue of *ius civile* did not exist in any lands other than those which had been subjected to *ius civile* by express assignation.[129] Tenures in public lands (*ager publicus*) were neither regulated by *ius civile* nor protected by actions of *ius civile,* as they were accessible to both citizens and non-citizens. When, in the period of the Gracchi, it looked as if the citizenry would subject these lands to regulation by *lex,* i.e., by enactment of *ius civile,* the allies immediately demanded that they be made citizens. These tenures were thus subject exclusively to the cognition of the magistrates, who proceeded in this respect according to rules different from those of the *ius civile.* The latter knew neither *emphyteusis* [130] nor covenants running with the land nor copyholds. But all these institutions existed under the administrative law applicable to public lands. Furthermore, that law which applied in the relation between the public treasury and private individuals contained institutions which did not occur in the *ius civile*; even where the institutions of the former were the same as those of the latter, they were referred to by different names, as, for instance, *praes* and *praedium,* rather than *fide-iussor* and *hypotheca.*[131] This objectively defined special law was thus determined by the scope of the jurisdiction

---

members of the sibs (*gentes*) of which the Roman community seems to have been composed in its oldest period; in later times the term *ius quiritium* is frequently used as a synonym of *ius civile* as contrasted to *ius honorarium* and *ius gentium.*

[129] On the following see WEBER'S AGRARGESCHICHTE and his article on *Agrargeschichte, Altertum,* in 1 HANDWÖRTERBUCH DER STAATSWISSENSCHAFTEN (3rd ed. 1909) 52; also ROSTOVTZEV.

[130] Cf. *supra* 70.

[131] *Fideiussor* — surety; *hypotheca* — mortgage. On the *praes* see literature stated by JÖRS AND KUNKEL 213, n. 4.

of the administrative official. There did not exist any determined body of particular persons membership in which would have been the test of participation; if one would like to speak of any group one could only say that its membership consisted of all those who at a given moment would happen to be concerned with some matter subject to administrative jurisdiction. Another sphere of special law was constituted by the jurisdiction of that *praetor* who was to decide disputes between citizens and aliens. He might resort to some rule of *ius civile*, but not by virtue of a "law" of the *ius civile*, a *lex*, but simply by virtue of his magisterial power. He rather applied the *ius gentium*, a law which was derived from a different source and the validity of which rested upon different foundations. Yet, this kind of law must not be visualized as having arisen with the very establishment of the office of the *praetor peregrinus*. It rather was that international law of commerce according to which the disputes of the market had been settled from time immemorial and which probably had at first been protected only sacrally by means of the oath. Nor were the substantially feudal relations between patron and client,[132] which were of great practical importance in the early period, possible objects of litigation at *ius civile*. Just as in the Germanic law of seisin, the spheres of the *ius civile* and feudal law touched upon each other in the field of possession, viz., with respect to the *praecarium*; [133] the *ius civile* took notice of the relationship also in other respects and dealt with it in criminal law. But it was not *regulated* by *ius civile*. Genuine spheres of special law within the *ius civile* were, on the other hand, formed by certain legal institutions accessible solely to merchants and certain persons engaged in industry, viz., the *actio exercitoria*,[134] the *receptum*,[135] and the special law of the *argentarii*.[136]

A concept of great importance for future legal development, viz., that of *fides*,[136a] was contained in both the general law of commerce and the law of patron and client. It included in a peculiar way not only the obligations following from relations of loyalty but also the *fides bona*, the good faith and fair dealing of the pure commercial transactions. To the *ius civile* as such it was unknown. Yet even though technically unknown, there were elements of it in practice from the very beginning; for as regards certain fraudulent acts, the Twelve Tables

[132] On the relationship between patron and client, see BUCKLAND, 89 *et seq.*, 375.

[133] Pr[a]ecarium — tenancy at will.

[134] Action against the shipowner upon obligations contracted by the master.

[135] *Receptum nautarum, cauponum et stabulariorum* — bailment by water carriers, innkeepers, and stable owners.

[136] Bankers.

[136a] On *fides* see Kunkel, *Fides als schöpferisches Element im römischen Schuldrecht* (1939) 2 FESTSCHRIFT FÜR KOSCHAKER 1.

already threatened with the status of *improbus intestabilisque*.[137] Numerous laws expressly decreed *infamia*, the general consequences of which were in private law exclusion from giving testimony, i.e., the incapacity to bear witness or to have one's actions witnessed, which in practice amounted to a commercial boycott. It led to a limitation of acquiring property by way of testate succession; it involved, furthermore, the denegation of certain actions by the *praetor*. In spite of their informal character, the principles of *fides* were by no means the products of a vague sentimentalism either in the field of the law of patron and client or in that of commercial transactions. The entire series of sharply defined contracts, on the well marked character of which the Roman law of commerce so essentially rested, was developed on the basis of the principles of *fides*. Such ancient institutions as the *fiducia*[138] as well as the *fidei-commissum* of the imperial epoch[139] depended entirely upon *fides*. The facts that *fides* were never more than a stopgap device for the *ius civile* and that it arose only at a comparatively late stage, do by no means indicate that the institution of *fides* was created because there were not actionable in the *ius civile* certain transactions which were guaranteed only by convention, viz., legacies in favor of non-citizens and of "prohibited persons."[140] The legal institution of *clientela* is certainly as old as the legal conception of the *ius civile* itself, and yet it remained outside. Thus the concept of *ius civile* was never coexistent with that of civil law. But *fides* was not a uniform principle for the regulation of all legal relations. What one owed to another according to *fides* depended on the peculiar nature of the concrete relationship, and even in this specialization the *fides* did not, in the event of infringement, always produce the same legal consequences. *Infamia* was the consequence of certain specific acts rather than of all infringements against *fides*. Of the various reactions against offensive conduct, e.g., censorial reproof, or consular refusal to list one as a candidate for office, each had its own particular preconditions, which were identical with neither cases of *infamia* nor with the principle of *fides*, and which, moreover, fluctuated;

[137] Loss of certain civil rights, including the right to make a will.

[138] Roughly corresponding to the trust without, however, implying a right on the beneficiary's part to pursue the *res* into the hands of third purchasers.

[139] A future interest created by imposing upon a testamentary devisee or legatee a personal obligation upon a certain term or condition to transfer the *res* to a third beneficiary.

[140] These were primarily those unmarried and childless persons whom Augustus, for reasons of population policy, had declared to be either totally or partially incapable of receiving property by will. — *Lex Iulia de maritandis ordinibus*, of 18 B.C., and *Lex Papia Poppaea* of A.D. 9.

they were never bound up with infringements of *fides* purely and as such. Infringements of the obligations of clientship were originally subject to the sanctions of the patron in the household court. Later these obligations were guaranteed sacrally or conventionally and finally also by *ius civile* in the case of the purely commercial and emancipated clients.

Of the original role of *fides* in commerce we have no knowledge. We do not know the means by which the *bonae fidei* contracts were guaranteed before they were recognized in the praetorian forms of action by virtue of magisterial authority like the other institutions of the *ius gentium*. Probably there were individual or general arbitration agreements under oath, which, if broken, produced *infamia* in the same way in which in later times *infamia* was the sanction for the breach of a sworn contract of compromise. But the creation of the forms of action for the institutions of the *ius gentium* did not mean that its distinction from the *ius civile* became eliminated; the *ius civile* remained the pure corporate status group law of the citizens. Occasionally the *praetor*, through the formula *si civis Romanus esset*,[141] made a civil form of action available to non-citizens. Other institutions were imperceptibly received into the *ius gentium*. It was only during the Empire that the distinction disappeared entirely, together with other privileges of citizenship.

None of the groups of persons interested in the *fides* constituted a closed organization, although Mommsen incorrectly, as we shall subsequently see, identified them with the organization of the plebs.[142] Certainly those persons whose interests were involved in *bonae fidei* contracts or *ius gentium*, i.e., affairs which had nothing at all to do with corporate status, did not form such an organization. The praetorian law as such was naturally quite far from being identical with the *ius gentium*, and the reception of the *ius gentium* was by no means brought about only by praetorian law; indeed it was to a great extent brought about by the integration of its fundamental principles into the *ius civile* through the jurists. Both during the Republic as well as during the Empire even the genuine status groups, i.e., the slaves, the freemen, the knights, and the senatorial families, lacked any associational organization which could have been the bearer of a genuine autonomy. For reasons of politics and police, the Republic had repeatedly found itself compelled to intervene sharply against private organizations. Periods of repression alternated with periods of toleration. The period of the monarchy was naturally unfavorable to private associations. The de-

141 "[let him be treated] as if he were a Roman citizen."

142 Mommsen 15; see also W.u.G., Part III, c. viii, p. 593.

mocracy had reasons to be afraid of the associations of the socially and economically powerful; the monarchy had reasons to fear the political consequences of any sort of uncontrolled organization. The Roman law of both the Republican and the Imperial periods admitted, in effect, associational autonomy only as a law of associations or corporations in the modern sense. Autonomy existed to the very degree to which associations and corporations were tolerated or privileged. Just to what extent they existed is to be examined in connection with the general discussion of another problem, namely, that of the *legal personality* of associations.[143]

Section 6. Associational Contracts — Juristic Personality

The general transformation and mediatization of the legally autonomous organizations of the age of personal laws into the state's monopoly of law creation found its expression in the change of the forms in which such organizations were legally treated as the bearers of rights. Such treatment cannot be dispensed with when the autonomous organizations have become subject to a common body of law peacefully applied through an orderly system of adjudication within a compulsory political association, when there furthermore exist, on the one hand, monopolistically appropriated goods to be used solely by the members of the group as such and by them only for some common purpose, and when also, on the other hand, legal transactions involving these objects have become economically necessary. Where, however, this development had not yet occurred, the problem was settled in a simple way: the members of one organization held all the members of another solidarily responsible for the acts of any one of its members, including its organs. Alongside

[143] On the following, see GIERKE, GENOSSENSCHAFTSRECHT, the classical work on the history of associations and juristic personality. The most significant English contribution is Maitland's Introduction to his translation of portions of Gierke's work, published as the POLITICAL THEORY OF THE MIDDLE AGES (1900) and his essays in 3 PAPERS 210 *et seq.* (repr. s.t. SELECTED ESSAYS, 1936). The leading discussion of the development of juristic persons in Rome is MITTEIS, I, 339. The most recent comprehensive presentations are given in SCHNORR V. CAROLSFELD, GESCHICHTE DER JURISTISCHEN PERSON (1933) and H. J. WOLF, ORGANSCHAFT UND JURISTISCHE PERSON (1933/34). For Rome, see DUFF, PERSONALITY IN ROMAN LAW (as to which, see DAUBE, 1943, 33 JOURNAL OF ROMAN STUDIES 86, and vol. 34, p. 125); for further literature on Roman law, see JÖRS AND KUNKEL 73 *et seq.*, 400/401; and on medieval law, PLANITZ 151. As to Gierke's theories see also LEWIS, THE GENOSSENSCHAFT-THEORY OF OTTO VON GIERKE (1935); on "theories" of juristic personality see F. HALLIS, CORPORATE PERSONALITY (1930). For a survey, see C. S. Lobingier, *The Natural History of the Private Artificial Person* (1939, 13 TULANE L. REV. 41.

the primitive blood feud we thus find the reprisal as a universal phenomenon, i.e., the reprisal in the sense of the detention of the person or goods of a member of a group for the obligations of one or all of his fellows.[144] In the Middle Ages, negotiations about reprisals and their avoidance by reciprocal grant of access to the courts and mutual legal assistance were a constant object of discussion between the cities. Composition, too, is of the same primitive origin as the blood feud. The question of what person or persons could validly conclude a composition and represent the members of a group in dealings with outsiders was determined simply by the experiences of the outsider with respect to whose orders are in fact obeyed. The original conception, even in the early Middle Ages, was that a member of the group who had not participated in the particular resolution of the village, the guild, the market community, or other collectivity, could not be bound unless the organization's transactions with the outside were based upon an agreement of the members as expressed in a general resolution. Without either one of such bases, the transaction could not have any effects.[145] One may thus agree with Heusler that the necessity of a resolution and its binding force were characteristic elements in the development of the law of organizations.[146] But, obviously, the distinction between resolution and contract remained as fluid as that between objective norms of law and subjective rights in general; normations arrrived at through resolutions were often designated as *pactus*; [147] but virtually the distinction was always present, quite particularly in the once universal idea that a resolution would not bind anyone except those persons who had participated in and associated themselves with it, and that it had consequently to be unanimous. In appearance, at least, the idea is implied that a resolution could come into effect only as a contract. Actually, however, that conception was rather influenced by the element of revelation implied in all law, according to which only *one* law could be right. Once the magical and charismatic means for the discovery of the right law had disappeared, there could and did arise the idea that the right law was the one produced by the majority and that, therefore, the minority had the duty

[144] On reprisals cf. Jessup and Deák, 13 ENCYC. SOC. SCI. 15 and literature indicated there.

[145] "Die ursprüngliche Vorstellung war dabei auch im mittelalterlichen Recht: dass alle, die nicht an einem Beschluss der Dorfgenossen, Gildebrüder, Markgenossen ['Mark*t*genossen' is an obvious typographical error] oder um welche Gesamtheit es sich sonst handelt, teilgenommen haben, dadurch gebunden werden, dass das Auftreten des Verbandes nach aussen kraft einer durch Beschluss erzielten Willenseinigung erfolge und erfolgen müsse, um spezifische Rechtswirkungen zu haben."

[146] HEUSLER, *op. cit.* (1885/86).

[147] See *supra* p. 88.

to associate itself with it. But before the minority did so, occasionally under drastic compulsion, the majority resolution was not law and no one was bound by it.[148] Such was the practical significance of that outlook.

On the other hand, no one, of course, was considered to be obliged to conclude a contract with another. Even under these modes of thought, including the conceptions of the earliest times, the distinction between enactment as the means of creating objective law and contract as the means of creating subjective rights was a familiar one, despite the great vagueness and fluidity of the transition between them. As its complement, the resolution required an organ for its execution. The mode of its selection, e.g., election from case to case or for a longer period or hereditary appropriation of the executive functions, etc., could assume many different forms. As the process of differentiation and appropriation among and within the various organizations advanced, as individuals came to be simultaneously members of several organizations, as in the internal relations among group members the relative degrees of power of officers and members came to be subject to fixed and increasingly rational rules, and as, finally, purposive contracts both of individuals and between the organization as a whole and outsiders became more frequent in consequence of a growing exchange economy, an unambiguous determination of the significance of every action of every member and every official of an organization became necessary, and the question of the position of the organization and of the legitimation of its organs in both contractual transactions and in procedure had to arise in one way or another.

The technical legal solution of this problem was found in the concept of the juristic person. From a legal standpoint the term is a tautology, since the very concept of person is necessarily a juristic one. When a child *en ventre sa mère* is regarded as a bearer of rights and obligations just as a full citizen while a slave is not, both these rules are technical means of achieving certain effects. In this sense the determination of legal personality is just as artificial as the legal definition of "thing" — i.e., it is decided exclusively in accordance with expedientially selected juristic criteria. The more numerous alternatives available for the determination of the legal position of organizations and associations were then to create a special problem.

The most rational actualization of the idea of the legal personality of organizations consists in the complete separation of the legal spheres of

[148] On the origins and development of the principle of majority decision, see Konopczyński, 10 ENCYC. SOC. SCI. 55 and literature indicated there.

the members from the separately constituted legal sphere of the organization; while certain persons designated according to rules are regarded from the legal point of view as alone authorized to assume obligations and acquire rights for the organization, the legal relations thus created do not at all affect the individual members and their property and are not regarded as their contracts, but all these relations are imputed to a separate and distinct body of assets. Similarly, what the members as such may claim from or owe to the organization under its rules, belongs to or affects their own private assets, which are legally entirely separate from those of the organization. An individual member as such can acquire neither a right nor a duty for the organization. Legally this is possible only for the officers acting in the name of the organization, and only the assembly of qualified members called together and acting in accordance with fixed rules can, but need not, have the authority to make binding decisions. The concept of juristic personality can be extended even further to contain the control over economic goods the benefit of which is to accrue to a plurality of persons who, while they are determined in accordance with rules, are not to be associationally organized. When thus established as an *endowment*,[149] a separate bearer of rights, to be determined in accordance with fixed rules, becomes recognized as legitimated to represent the interests of those individuals. Where a consociation of persons is to be endowed with juristic personality, it can thus be constructed in two possible ways. It can be organized as a *corporation*. In that case the body of members is constituted as a fixed group of persons. The composition of that body can be changed in two ways, viz., either by succession to a position of membership in accordance with the general rules of private law, or by virtue of a resolution of a designated corporate organ. The persons designated in one of these two ways are the only ones who are entitled to any rights, and the administration is juristically carried on by virtue of their mandate. The other possible form in which a consociation of persons can be established as a juristic person is that of the *endowment* and the *institution* (*Anstalt*). When used as a juristic term of art, the

[149] The endowment (*Stiftung*) has been recognized as a special form of juristic person especially in modern German law (cf. Civil Code of 1896, §§ 80–88), where it has been defined as follows: "*Stiftung* is an organization for the pursuit of certain defined purposes, which does not constitute an association of persons but is endowed with justice personality." Cf. ENNECCERUS 274; see also 3 MAITLAND PAPERS 280, 356, where he compares "Institution" or "Foundation" with "Anstalt," saying (p. 357): "I believe that the English term which most closely corresponds to the 'Anstalt' or the 'Stiftung' of German legal literature is 'a charity,' in the sense of 'charitable trust.' "

concept of institution is different from the concept of institution as used in sociology or in political science, although there does exist a certain connection. The institution (in the juristic sense) is related to the endowment. There is no organized body of members but only an organ or organs by which the institution is represented. Membership, if one can use the word at all, is frequently based upon obligation and the accession of new members is not dependent upon the will of the older one but rather upon objective criteria or upon the discretion of the organs of the institution. Furthermore, the "members" of the institution, such as, for instance, the pupils at a school, have no influence upon its management.[150]

The three forms of organization — endowment, institution, and corporation — are not separated from each other by absolutely clear-cut legal tests. The transitions between them are rather gradual and fluid. It can certainly not be a decisive test, as Gierke assumed, whether the organization is autocephalous or heterocephalous.[151] A church is an institution, although it can be autocephalous.

From the technical legal point of view, the concept of juristic personality can be dispensed with where an organization has no property concerning which contracts in the name of the organization would be necessary. Juristic personality is inappropriate for those societies which by their very nature comprehend only a narrowly limited number of partners and which are also limited in their duration, such as certain business associations. For them the absolute separation of the legal spheres of the members from that of the collectivity would be injurious to credit since the specific credit-rating, while influenced by the existence of a separate fund, is based primarily upon the fact that all the partners are to answer for the debts of the collectivity. Likewise the establishment of separate organs for the representation of the latter would not always be expedient. For such organizations and associations the form most adequate to capitalistic credit interests is the principle of "joined hands" (*Gesamthand*),[152] which has been known, at least in an incipient state, to most legal systems of the past. It involved, first, that authority to represent the collectivity be vested in either all the participants acting jointly, or in every one, or some, or one particular participant acting in the name of all; the principle of joined hands involved, second, the liability of all with both their persons and their property. The configura-

[150] This legal concept of "Anstalt" is being used particularly in modern German administrative law. Cf. W. JELLINEK, VERWALTUNGSRECHT (1928) 174.

[151] Cf. GIERKE, PRIVATRECHT I, 458.

[152] Cf. HUEBNER 139–146, 150, 235; 3 MAITLAND, PAPERS 336, 361, 377.

tion arose from the solidary responsibility of the household community. It acquired its specific character when in a community of heirs the legal separation of the collective property from the individual property of the participants made it necessary that a distinction be made between collective and individual debts.[153] This process occurred in that course of disruption of fraternal relations by commercial influences of which we have already spoken above.[154]

From the community of heirs the institution spread and became the basis of numerous deliberately constituted communities for which the in-and-out-group relations arising from the fraternal character of the household community were either basic or adopted out of considerations of legal-technical convenience.[155] The present-day law of the partnership is, as we have seen, a direct rational development of the relations of the household community for purposes of the capitalistic enterprise. The various forms of the "société en nom commandite" [156] are combinations of this principle with the law of the *commenda* and the *societas maris* [157] as they were found everywhere. The German "limited liability company" [158] is a rational invention to serve as a substitute for the

[153] At the time Weber wrote the general statement of the text, it was doubtful whether a community of heirs had ever existed in Rome. The insufficient evidence has now been strongly fortified, however, through the discovery, in 1933, of a hitherto unknown part of the Institutes of Gaius. See JÖRS AND KUNKEL 34, 240; SCHULZ, HISTORY 105/106.

[154] Cf. *supra* pp. 106 *et seq.*

[155] As to the following, see WEBER'S GESCHICHTE DER HANDELSGESELLSCHAFTEN IM MITTELALTER (1891); Schmoller, *Die geschichtliche Entwicklung der Unternehmung* in SCHMOLLER'S JAHRBUCH, vol. 14 (1890), p. 1035, vol. 15 (1891), p. 963, vol. 16 (1892), p. 731, and vol. 17 (1893), p. 359. HOLDSWORTH viii, 192. C. T. CARR, GENERAL PRINCIPLES OF THE LAW OF CORPORATIONS (1905), c. ix, repr. s.t. *Early Forms of Corporateness* in (1909) 2 SEL. ESS. ANGLO-AMER. LEGAL HIST. 160; W. MITCHELL, ESSAY ON THE EARLY HISTORY OF THE LAW MERCHANT (1904) c. v, repr. s.t. *Early Forms of Partnership* 3 SEL. ESS. 182; S. Williston, *History of the Law of Business Corporations before 1800* (1888), 2 HARV. L. REV. 105, 149, repr. 3 SEL. ESS. 195; also A. B. DU BOIS, THE ENGLISH BUSINESS COMPANY AFTER THE BUBBLE ACT, 1720–1800 (1938); S. LIVERMORE, EARLY AMERICAN LAND COMPANIES (1939); GOLDSCHMIDT; P. REHME, GESCHICHTE DES HANDELSRECHTS (1914); K. LEHMANN, DIE GESCHICHLICHE ENTWICKLUNG DES AKTIENRECHTS BIS ZUM CODE DE COMMERCE (1895).

[156] *Société en nom commandite* (French) — that form of business association in which one or more partners with unlimited personal liability combine with one or more partners of limited liability; as to modern law, see French Commercial Code, art. 23–28 (*Code de Commerce*, 1807); German Commercial Code §§ 161–177 (*Handelsgesetzbuch*).

[157] See *supra* n. 123.

[158] "Limited liability company" (*Gesellschaft mit beschränkter Haftung*,

regular joint-stock corporation (*Aktiengesellschaft*) which is legally inadequate for the purpose of smaller family-like enterprises, especially among co-heirs, and particularly inconvenient because of the many publications required by modern legislation.

The fraternity (*agermanament* in Spanish law) of merchants, shipowners, and seamen was, by the very nature of the matter, intrinsic to the joint enterprise of a sea voyage. Corresponding to the rise of the business firm from the household community, it developed in the field of shipping into an *association of joint hands* (*Gesamthandvergesellschaftung*) of the enterprisers, whereas, on the other side, in bottomry and in the rules of general average it resulted in a single community of risk among all those interested in the voyage. In all those cases, the typical element was the replacement of a fraternal by a business relationship, i.e., of a status contract by a purposive contract, saving, however, the legally technical expediential treatment of the total group as a separate and distinct legal subject and as the separate owner of joint assets. On the other hand, the formal bureaucratization of the apparatus that would have become technically necessary in the case of a corporation was avoided. In no other legal system were the rationally transformed relationships of joint hands developed so specifically as they were in that of the Occident of the Middle Ages and later. Their absence from Roman law [159] was due more to certain elements of legal technique inherent to the nature of the national *ius civile* than to economic causes. Probably, however, the relative ease with which Roman Law could dispense with any development of such a rich variety of legal forms was connected with the peculiar character of ancient capitalism, which was both a slave capitalism and a predominantly political capitalism based upon the state. Slaves were used as business instruments through whose contracts the master could acquire unrestricted rights but only limited liabilities. The treatment of the *peculium* in the fashion of a separate fund made it possible to obtain at least part of the results which today are brought about by the various forms of limited lia-

---

G.m.b.H.) — a business corporation which does not appeal for its capital to the public and which does not have shares suitable for being bought and sold at the stock market. Invented in Germany (Law of 20 March 1898, R.G. BL. 1898, 370), the G.m.b.H. has been adopted in numerous other countries. Cf. W. Hallstein, *Die Gesellschaft mit beschränkter Haftung in den Auslandsrechten* (1939), 12 ZEITSCHRIFT F. AUSL. U. INTERN. PRIVATRECHT 34; on the German G.m.b.H. see MANUAL OF GERMAN LAW (Great Britain, Foreign Office 1950) 247.

[159] We do not know details of the development of Hellenic commercial law, from which, especially its Rhodian species, certain special institutions of the commercial law of antiquity were borrowed.

bility.[160] Of course, the fact remains that this restriction, in connection with the complete exclusion of all forms of joint hand from the law of the *societas* and the requirement of all solidary claims and obligations being created by express *sponseo correalis*,[161] is one of the legal symptoms of that absence of stable capitalistic industrial enterprises with continuous credit needs which is characteristic of the Roman economic system. The significance of the essentially political basis of ancient capitalism is indicated by the fact that those very legal institutions which were lacking for private business were recognized already in the private law of the early Empire with respect to publicans (*socii vectigalium publicorum*),[162] i.e., groups of private businessmen to whom the state farmed out the levying of taxes and the exploitation of the state-owned mines and salt works. The legal and economic structure of these associations was similar to the syndicates as they are customarily established today by banks coöperating in the issuance of bonds and other securities: one or more "leading" banks undertake toward the issuer the obligation of providing the full capital in question; other banks join the syndicate with internal liability for the full amount, while still others participate with only limited subscriptions. In Rome, the *socii* of the consortial leader (*manceps*), as they are mentioned in the *interdictum de loco publico fruendo* and in other sources,[163] were members of the *consortium*, while the *afines* subscribed only with limited liability in the manner of a modern *commanditista*; [164] both internally and externally the legal situation was thus quite similar to that of the modern phenomenon.

[160] *Peculium* — a fund legally belonging to the head of a house (*paterfamilias*), but left by him for separate management to a member of the household, such as a son or slave. For debts incurred by the member of the house the *paterfamilias* was liable in the praetorian *actio de peculio*, but he was allowed to limit his liability to an amount corresponding to the value of the *peculium* (*dumtaxat de peculio*). See MICOLIER, PÉCULE ET CAPACITÉ PATRIMONIALE (1932).

[161] INSTITUTES 3.16 pr. and Papinian in DIGEST 45.2. 11.1–2. This rule applied only to the promise of a divisible performance. The obligation of several debtors to make an indivisible performance seems in classical law to have been one of joint and several liability even without having been created by one joint promise. Our information of details is incomplete, however. See KERR WYLIE, SOLIDARITY AND CORREALITY (1925); Thayer, *Correality in Roman Law* (1943) 1 SEMINAR 11.

[162] Cf. A. Arias Bonet, *Societas publicanorum* (1949), 19 ANUARIO DE HISTORIA DEL DERECHO ESPAÑOL 218.

[163] DIGEST 43. 9.1. — injunction issued by the *praetor* to protect the lessee of the public lands and his associates in his possession.

[164] The partner in a *société en nom commandite* (*supra* n. 156), who, in contrast to the "personally liable partner or partners" is not liable for the debts of the company beyond the amount of his share.

Whether the institution of *the state* itself should be treated *as a juristic person of private law*, would depend in each case upon both legal-technical and political considerations. If it is done, it means in practice primarily that the legal spheres of the organs of state authority are to be divided into a sphere of personal rights, with claims and obligations ascribed to them as individuals, and an official sphere in which property relations are regarded as separate institutional assets; it means, furthermore, that the sphere of official activity of the organs of the state is divided into a sphere of public and one of private legal relations and that in the latter sphere, which is exclusively concerned with property matters, the general principles of the law of private transactions are applicable.[165] It is a normal consequence of the juristic personality of the state that it has capacity to sue and to be sued in ordinary civil procedure, and on an equal footing with private parties, and that claims

[165] This kind of establishment of the state as a juristic person of private law, in which the state as fisc is regarded as separate from the state as sovereign, has been worked out particularly in German theory and practice. It stands in contrast to the French and the Anglo-American systems in which the state is regarded as the sovereign even where it enters upon contractual relationships with private persons or is engaged as the owner of property. In consequence of this latter approach in the French system, the legal relations of the state as contracting party or as property owner are subject to a body of rules which, at least in theory, are different from those of ordinary private law. Also, in both the French and the Anglo-American systems, the state cannot be sued in the ordinary courts in the same way as a private person. In France actions against the state must be brought in the administrative tribunals, which are separate from the ordinary courts, have the Council of State (*Conseil d'Etat*) as their own supreme court, and are not subject to control by the Court of Cassation, the supreme court in the administration of civil and criminal justice. Cf. A. UHLER, REVIEW OF ADMINISTRATIVE ACTS (1942); GOODNOW, *op. cit.*; F. BLACHLY AND M. OATMAN, ADMINISTRATIVE LEGISLATION (1934), and INTRODUCTION TO COMPARATIVE GOVERNMENT (1938); R. D. WATKINS, THE STATE AS PARTY LITIGANT (1927).

On the historical development of the theory and practice of the state as fisc see OTTO MAYER, DEUTSCHES VERWALTUNGSRECHT (1896), I, 47; FLEINER, VERWALTUNGSRECHT (2nd ed. 1912) 34; HATSCHEK, DIE RECHTLICHE STELLUNG DES FISCUS IM BÜRGERLICHEN GESETZBUCHE (1899) 24; see also S. BOLLA, DIE ENTWICKLUNG DES FISKUS ZUM PRIVATRECHTSSUBJEKT (1938); G. JELLINEK 383; KELSEN, ALLGEMEINE STAATSLEHRE (1925) 240, and THEORY 193.

The basic investigations into the history of the juristic construction of the state in general are the following works of OTTO V. GIERKE: POLITICAL THEORIES OF THE MIDDLE AGES (Maitland's tr. 1900), esp. c. viii; NATURAL LAW AND THE THEORY OF SOCIETY (Barber's tr. 1934); also THE DEVELOPMENT OF POLITICAL THEORY (Freyd's tr. 1939), *passim*. (The former two books are parts of GIERKE'S DEUTSCHES GENOSSENSCHAFTSRECHT (1881 *et seq.*); the latter is a translation of his JOHANNES ALTHUSIUS UND DIE ENTWICKLUNG DER NATURRECHTLICHEN STAATSTHEORIEN [1880].)

may be freely prosecuted against it. From a strictly legal point of view, it is true that the juristic personality of the state has nothing to do with this latter question. The *populus Romanus* had, without any doubt, the capacity to acquire private rights, for instance by way of testate succession, but it could not be sued. The two problems are also different from a practical point of view. There seems to be no doubt that all compulsory institutional, and thus political, state structures have a juristic personality in the sense of being capable of acquiring rights, even where they avoid being subject to the ordinary process of law. Likewise the juristic personality of the state and its amenability to the process of law may be recognized while different principles may obtain for government and private contracts. But the latter phenomenon has usually been associated, as for instance in Rome, with the exclusion of the ordinary courts and the decision by administrative officials of disputes arising out of government contracts. The capacity to sue and to be sued has been recognized not only for juristic persons but also for numerous groupings of joint hands. Nonetheless, the problem of juristic personality has usually appeared in legal history in close association with the problem of the capacity of organizations, especially public ones, to sue and be sued. All the problems just discussed were bound to arise wherever the political authority could not deal with private persons as a master deals with his subjects but where it was compelled to obtain their services by free contracts. The problem had to be particularly acute where the political authority had to resort to transactions with capitalists whose credit or whose entrepreneurial organization it needed, and where, in consequence of the free movement of capital among several competing organizations, it could not coerce these services liturgically.[166] The problems were finally bound to arise where the state had to deal with free craftsmen and workers, against whom it either could not, or did not wish to, apply liturgical coercion. The security of private interests was generally increased wherever the juristic personality of the state and the jurisdiction of the ordinary courts came to be recognized. But the denial of either one did not necessarily entail an impairment of this security, as the observance of the state's contractual obligations may be adequately guaranteed by other means. The fact that the

[166] Liturgy: the financing of a political body "by means of burdens which are associated with privileges." Cf. WEBER, THEORY 312, HISTORY 95, 136, 203, 336, and literature stated there. Liturgies were of special importance in the city states of antiquity, where certain groups of the population were charged with the burden of providing and maintaining naval vessels or to provide for the public performances of the theater (so-called *choregies*).

King of England could always be sued in court did not protect the Florentine bankers against the repudiation of his enormous debt in the fourteenth century.[167] The lack of any means of procedural coercion against the Roman state treasury did not in general endanger its creditors, and when such a danger nonetheless arose during the Second Punic War, the creditors were able to obtain pledges for their loans which no one attempted to disturb. The French state has remained exempt from the compulsory jurisdiction of the courts even after the Revolution but without impairment of its credit.[168] To some extent the exemption of

[167] This statement needs qualification. In the first place, there was never a time in English medieval law when a writ could lie against the king. This followed from the fundamental theory, fully stated by Bracton, that the king could not very well issue a writ against himself or be summoned as defendant in his own court. In the second place, however, it came to be recognized in the thirteenth century that the king, being subject to the law as well as being the fountain of justice and equity, should not (or rather, ought not to) refuse to redress wrongs or satisfy claims against him. Such redress or satisfaction was sought through petitions addressed to the king or his council: but a petition, if given effect to, was substantially a remedy of grace and not one of right. Nevertheless, during the fourteenth century, petitions began to be distinguished between demands for some bonuses or some new remedy on the one hand, and claims embodying a definite legal right, enforceable by writ against anyone but the king. When this distinction was drawn, the "petition of right" grew into an effective remedy against the Crown, though perhaps not completely so before the fifteenth century. In the fourteenth century, the position was rather vague: although the petition of right had as yet not become, at any rate technically, a complete legal remedy, the king seems in practice almost always to have repaid his debts in one way or another. Such is the only conclusion that can be drawn from an examination of the fourteenth-century cases. See EHRLICH, PROCEEDINGS AGAINST THE CROWN, Oxford Studies in Social and Legal History VI, 120; POLLOCK AND MAITLAND 515; HOLDSWORTH IX, 11. As regards foreign merchants, their position was in this respect the same as that of the king's subjects. Indeed, it may actually have been better because of the close and friendly business relationship between the foreign merchants and the king. It is true that later some doubts arose whether aliens could, or could not, sue at common law; this, however, did not affect their right in the fourteenth century to address themselves to the king, to the council, or to the chancery either to recover a debt from the Crown or, indeed, for the redress of any other wrong. See HOLDSWORTH *loc. cit.*, 94–95; POLLOCK AND MAITLAND 464–467; Brodhurst, *The Merchants of the Staple*, SELECT ESSAYS IN ANGLO-AMERICAN LEGAL HISTORY 16 *et seq.* The repudiation of the king's debt to the Florentine bankers took place in January 1345. Edward III owed the leading Florentine houses, the Bardi and the Peruzzi, 1,500,000 gold florins (£500,000) so that they were now reduced to bankruptcy — "a catastrophe which plunged all Florence in distress." See SCHANZ, ENGLISCHE HANDELSPOLITIK (1881) I, 113, and authorities there cited; RAMSAY, A HISTORY OF THE REVENUES OF THE KINGS OF ENGLAND (1925) II, 189.

[168] See *supra* n. 165. In this connection it must be kept in mind, however, that the guaranties of legal security and redress obtainable against the state in the ad-

the public treasury from ordinary legal process has been connected with that principle of setting apart the state from other organizations which developed in connection with the modern concept of sovereignty. This was certainly the case in France, and in Prussia too. Frederick William I, conscious of his sovereignty, tried by all sorts of chicanery to discourage his "obstinate nobles" from invoking the Imperial Chamber Court (*Reichskammergericht*).[169] The availability of the ordinary process of law was, on the other hand, beyond doubt wherever, and as long as the corporate-status structure of the political organization resulted in the treatment of all administrative grievances as disputes between the holders of privileges or vested rights and therefore as the subject matter of ordinary litigation, in which the prince appeared not as sovereign but as the possessor of a limited prerogative or as one bearer of privileges among others in the political organization. This was the situation in England [170] and in the Holy-Roman-German Empire.

The denegation of actions against the state could, however, also be the result of essentially technical legal factors. Thus in Rome the censor was the authority for deciding all claims of individuals against the state or vice versa which, according to our modes of thought, would be claims of private law. But the censor was also the authority for disputes between private persons in so far as they turned on questions of law arising from relations touching state property.[171] All tenures in the *ager publicus* and all disputes between the capitalist owners of interests in the public lands and the state contractors (publicans), or between them and the subjects, were thus withdrawn from the high jurisdiction of the juries and referred to simple administrative cognition. This was in effect a positive rather than a negative privilege of the tremendously powerful "state capitalists." The lack of jury trial and the

---

ministrative tribunals are in no way less effective than those obtainable against private persons in the civil courts. The former are as truly courts as the latter, and the Council of State is looking upon its functions as judicial ones no less than the Court of Cassation. Cf. Ogg and Zink, Modern Foreign Governments (1949) 583.

[169] While no such incident could be verified for the reign of King Frederick William I (1713–1740), Margrave Johann is reported to have stated, in a "recess" concluded with the estates in 1552, that "in contravention to existing usage, some have been so impudent against our judgments as to appeal to the Imperial Chamber Court and thus to tie our hands with the result that quite often one family completely squeezes out the other with such chicaneries." Hence, anyone who should henceforth dare to make such an appeal should be fined 200 fl. and lose his cause. (Stölzel, Brandenburg-Preussens Rechtsverwaltung (1888) I, 214.) On the Imperial Chamber Court, see *infra* c. IX, n. 66.

[170] Cf. *supra* n. 167.

[171] See 2 Mommsen 461 *et seq.*; also Wenger 56.

dual quality of the magistrate as judge and party representative persisted and was transferred in effect to the fisc of the imperial administration when, since Claudius, following a brief fluctuation under Tiberius, the fisc increasingly acquired the character of state property and ceased to be looked upon as the personal property of the Emperor.[172] The distinction, it is true, was not complete and residues remained both terminologically (although such old terms of administrative law as *manceps*, or *praes*[173] came gradually to be replaced by the terms of private law) and in the maxim that the fisc was capable of suing and being sued. Fluctuations between the patrimonial and the institutional conceptions of the imperial property, i.e., of the conceptions of it as belonging to the emperor personally or to the state as an institution, together with considerations of administrative technique and the economic interests of the dynasty also influenced the various transformations of and differentiations between the several kinds of imperial assets which in theory were all regarded as having a regular standing in court. Actually the distinction between the Emperor as a private person and as a magistrate (ruler) was carried out only under the first emperors. Finally all the property of the emperor was regarded as property of the crown and hence it became customary for the emperor, when he acceded to the throne, to transfer his private fortune to his children. The treatment of acquisitions by way of confiscation and of the numerous legacies which were left to the emperor as a means of reinforcing the validity of testaments, was not clearly elaborated from the standpoint of either private or constitutional law.

Within the structure of Medieval estate corporatism, which we shall discuss later,[174] it was out of the question that the prince as a ruler would be differentiated from the prince as a private individual or that those of his assets which served political ends would be differentiated from those which were to serve his private ends. As we have seen, this lack of differentiation resulted in the acknowledgment of the possibility of suing the British king[175] or the German emperor. Quite the opposite effect occurred, however, when the claims to sovereignty led to the

[172] *Fiscus Caesaris* was, in the Principate, the public treasury in so far as it was managed by the emperor; as such it was distinguished from the emperor's private assets (*res privata*) and the special crown domains (*patrimonium Caesaris*); cf. 2 MOMMSEN 998; MITTEIS 347, VASSALLI, CONCETTO E NATURA DEL FISCO (1908); ROSTOVTZEV, 55, 172, 179, 186, 314, 326, 343, 357. On the fisc in the modern German system, see *supra* n. 165.

[173] See *supra*, n. 131.

[174] W.U.G., Part III, cc. vii and viii.

[175] See *supra*, n. 167.

withdrawal of the state from the jurisdiction of its own organs, although in this connection, too, legal technicalities were used for rather effective resistance to the political aspirations of the princes. The Roman concept of the fisc, which was received in Germany, was used there to serve as the instrument of legal technique which made it possible to sue the state.[176] Consequently, and as a result of the traditional corporate estate concept of the state, it also had to serve as a first basis for a genuine administrative justice far beyond the scope of private law disputes. The concept of the fisc should have produced the concept of the state as an institution already in antiquity. However, this conceptual step was never taken by the classical jurists because it would have been alien to the existing categories of ancient private law. Not even the "Auflage," as it is understood in modern law, was developed so that it could have served as a substitute.[177]

Likewise the concept of *endowment* thus remained entirely alien to Roman law. The only way available was that of establishing a corporative fund, the actual use of which is demonstrated by inscriptions. The true concept of endowment both in its substantive and technical aspects was almost everywhere developed under religious influences. The great mass of endowments have been dedicated from times immemorial to the cult of the dead or to works of religiously meritorious charity. The main interest in the definition of the legal status of such endowments was thus found among those priests to whom the supervision of the endowments' activities was entrusted. Hence a "law of endowments" arose only where the priesthood was sufficiently independent of the lay authority to develop a special body of sacred law. In Egypt, for this reason, endowments have existed from times immemorial.[178] Purely secular endowments, and particularly family endowments, however, were practi-

[176] See *supra*, n. 165.

[177] *Auflage* (Germ.) — Institution of German law practically amounting to a trust without a beneficiary; it can be used to charge the beneficiary of a testamentary disposition with a burden to be discharged for a charitable purpose; cf. German Civil Code, § 1940.

[178] In accordance with the great concern for the care of the soul after death, it was a widespread practice to insure by contract the performance of sacrifices after death. "If for this purpose [a person] made over part of his alienable estate to a priest, the law allowed him to attach to the grant a condition of forfeiture valid in perpetuity. Thus as soon as the priest or his successor in office ceased to offer up the stipulated sacrifices he was to be deprived by the public authorities of the property which should then be given to another." To this description of the Egyptian transaction, E. Seidl (*Law, Egyptian*, 9 ENCYC. SOC. SCI. 209, 210) adds: "Whether there can be seen in such and similar trusts of property beginnings of the incorporated foundation is, however, still doubtful."

cally unknown everywhere, not only because of technical legal reasons but, without doubt, also for political reasons, unless they used the form of feoffment or similar forms and thus created a dependence of the privileged families on the prince. In the *polis* they were thus completely absent. A change occurred for the first time in Byzantine law, where sacral norms were used as a technical means, after late Roman law had already made the first limited steps in this direction by means of the *fidei commissum*.[179] For reasons which we shall discuss later,[180] in Byzantium the creation of perpetual rents took the form of monastic foundations in which the management and rights to revenue were reserved for the family of the founder. The next phase in the development of this type of endowment was the *Wakf* of Islamic law, which has played there a role of immense importance economically as well as in other respects.[181] In the West, the saint was at first treated, from the legal-technical viewpoint, as the owner of the endowment fund.[182] The concept of the secular endowment of the Middle Ages began to develop once the canon law had prepared it for ecclesiastical purposes.[183]

The concept of the *institution* (*Anstalt*) was not fully developed in the purely legal sense until the period of modern theory. In substance it, too, is of ecclesiastical origin, derived from late Roman ecclesiastical law. The concept of institution was bound to arise there in some manner as soon as both the charismatic conception of the bearer of religious authority and the purely voluntary organization of the congregation had finally yielded to the official bureaucracy of the bishops and the latter had begun to seek for a legal-technical legitimation for the exercise of the ecclesiastical rights of property.

No concept of ecclesiastical institution at all had existed in antiquity. Ever since the secularization of the cult by the *polis*, the temple assets were legally regarded as its, the polis', property. Ancient legal technique aided the Christian church by means of its corporative concept; the

[179] See *infra* n. 220.

[180] W.U.G. 743.

[181] Wak'f (waq'f, wakuf) — charitable trust, endowment, of Mohammedan law.

[182] 2 GIERKE, GENOSSENSCHAFTSRECHT 526, 962.

[183] On the following, see POLLOCK AND MAITLAND I, 480; R. SOHM, KIRCHENRECHT (1892) 75; U. STUTZ, DIE EIGENKIRCHE (1895); GESCHICHTE DES KIRCHLICHEN BENEFIZIALWESENS (1895); art. *Eigenkirche* in REALENZYKLOPÄDIE FÜR PROTEST. THEOLOGIE, and art. *Kirchenrecht* in 3 HOLTZENDORFF-KOHLER, ENZYKLOPÄDIE DER RECHTSWISSENSCHAFT (1914) 301; WERMINGHOFF, VERFASSUNGSGESCHICHTE DER DEUTSCHEN KIRCHE IM MITTELALTER (1913); also Torres, M., *El órigen del sistema de iglesias proprias* (1928), 5 ANUARIO DE HISTORIA DEL DERECHO ESPAÑOL 83; also LESNE, HISTOIRE DE LA PROPRIETÉ ECCLESIASTIQUE EN FRANCE (1910/28/36).

early Middle Ages, in so far as church funds were not regarded as the property of the private owner of the church, resorted to the idea of the saint's being the owner and the church's officers his agents. After the declaration of war on the private ownership of churches in the Investiture Conflict,[184] canon law elaborated a peculiar ecclesiastical corporation law, which, in consequence of the authoritarian and institutional elements of Church structure, had to differ from the corporation law of both voluntary associations and corporate status organizations.[185] But this very ecclesiastical corporation law, in turn, markedly influenced the development of the secular corporation concept of the Middle Ages. It was the essentially technical needs of administration in the modern institutionalized state which led to the establishment as separate juristic persons of innumerable public enterprises such as schools, poorhouses, state banks, insurance funds, savings banks, etc.; having neither members nor membership rights but only heteronomous and heterocephalous organs they could not be construed as corporations and thus there was developed for them the legal concept of the institution.[186]

The rational concept of the *corporation* in the more developed form of Roman law was a product of the Imperial period, quite particularly of the law of municipal corporations.[187] Municipalities distinct from the state appeared in large numbers only after the Latin War, when hitherto sovereign cities were received into the community of Roman citizens, without impairment, however, of autonomy. In a definitive way these relationships were regulated by laws of the first emperors. In consequence of their mediatization the municipalities were deprived of their status as political institutions; *civitates privatorum loco habentur*[188] was said already in the second century and Mitteis properly points out that the adjective *commune* began at that time to replace *publicum* with reference to municipal property.[189] Of their litigations, some were treated as administrative, e.g., the *controversia de territorio*,[190] and others as private, especially those arising out of contracts, for which ordinary civil procedure was apparently available. The typical form of the municipal officialdom spread over the Empire; indeed, the

[184] Cf. v. Schwerin, Grundzüge der deutschen Rechtsgeschichte (2nd ed. 1941), §§ 30, 54, and literature stated there.

[185] See 2 Gierke, Genossenschaftsrecht 958.

[186] See *supra* n. 149.

[187] See *supra* n. 143; also Jörs and Kunkel 74 and literature stated there and at p. 400.

[188] "Cities are deemed to be private persons."

[189] Mitteis I, 348, n. 2.

[190] Controversies concerning (city) territory.

exact titles of municipal magistrates appear in the private corporations of the Imperial period. This is probably the origin of the bureaucratization of the concept of the corporation according to the pattern of the once political institution of the municipality, for which the absolute separation of the municipal property from that of the individuals was as self-evident as the maxim: *quod universitati debetur singulis non debetur.*[191] At the same time, the establishment of voluntary associations in the Julian monarchy was conditional upon a license, undoubtedly for political reasons. Whether at that time the license conferred, as it did in the later period, full, or only partial, juristic personality, is doubtful. It is probable, although not certain, that the expression *corpus collegii habere* referred to full legal capacity. The term typically used in later theory was *universitas.*[192] If it is correct, as Mitteis plausibly asserts, that the internal relations of private corporations were subject only to administrative cognition,[193] it would well fit in with that bureaucratization of the corporations which runs through the entire law of the Imperial period, and it would at the same time constitute one of those secularizing adaptations of the previously prevailing situation which are characteristic of this entire development. In the Republican period the situation was obviously different. While it is not certain it is also not improbable that the Twelve Tables, following the laws of Solon, recognized the autonomy of existing corporations. A common purse was, as shown by later prohibitive laws, a matter of course. On the other hand, there was no legal technical possibility of a civil action. It is not even certain that it was available in the Edict before the Imperial period. There was no form of action for disputes between members concerning membership rights. The reason obviously lay in the fact that the private corporations were at that time subject in part to sacral law and in part to the administrative law of the priestly or magisterial cognition; this fact, in turn, was related with the status structure of the ancient *polis*, which

[191] "That which is owed to the collective is not owed to its members." — Ulpian in D. 3.4.7.1.

[192] According to Mitteis (*loc. cit. supra* n. 143), juristic personality could not be acquired by private organizations in any way other than by grant through imperial charter. This notion is generally rejected in the recent literature, where it is maintained that it was entirely left to the discretion of the organization itself whether or not it wished to have rights and obligations of its own and distinct from those of its members. "The notion of an express grant of juristic personality was totally alien to Roman law." The term *corpus habere* is said to mean no more than "to form a club." Kunkel in Jörs and Kunkel, 75, see also now Brassloff in 1 Studi Riccobono 317.

[193] Mitteis 347, n. 21.

tolerated slaves and *metics* in the *collegium* but not in the political body of the citizenry.

Like the Hellenic phratries,[194] the voluntary organizations of the earlier period, and most other permanent associations of all legal systems as far back as the totemic clans, the oldest known Roman voluntary associations were fraternities (*sodalitates*)[195] and, as such, cult-communities. One brother could no more summon another brother into court than he could summon anyone else to whom he was bound by ties of loyalty. Traces of this state of affairs are retained even in the law of the Pandects, where criminal actions are prohibited between such brethren. In private law, these fraternal relations were significant primarily in their negative consequences, i.e., as situations excluding actionability.[196] For the same reasons, the guilds and trade associations, the existence of which in early Republican Rome is definitely established, were constituted as *collegia cultorum.*[197] Like the Chinese and medieval organizations of the kind, they were fraternities under the protection of their special patron god, who was then acknowledged as legitimate in Rome by the recognition of the *collegium* by the state; thus it was, for instance, with Mercury and the *collegium mercatorum*, which tradition marks as having been very old.[198] The obligation of mutual aid in emergencies and the cult meals, which are as characteristic of them as of the Germanic guilds or all other organizations based on fraternity, were later transformed into nationally organized assistance and burial funds. Quite a few of these *collegia* are known to have been organized during the Empire as funds of this kind.[199] They had nothing to do with the law of the citizens. As long as the sacral organization was more than a mere form, its property

[194] About the Hellenic "phratries" and similar voluntary organizations see B. LEIST, 103–175, and Weber. W.U.G., Part II, c. VIII, § 3 (p. 556); BONNER AND SMITH 118 n. 3; p. 160; and R. BONNER, ASPECTS OF ATHENIAN DEMOCRACY (1933) 91, 134, 157. These last two works were not yet accessible to Weber. The extensive literature on totemism and totemistic clans is stated in 14 ENCYC. SOC. SCI. 660. Weber seems to have relied primarily on W. WUNDT'S ELEMENTE DER VÖLKERPSYCHOLOGIE (1912, tr. by Schaub, 1916), c. II.

[195] See Mommsen, *Zur Lehre von den römischen Korporationen* (1904), 25 SAV. Z. ROM. 45; also his DE COLLEGIIS ET SODALITIBUS ROMANORUM (1843); UGO COLI, COLLEGIA E SODALITATES (1913); KARLOWA II, 59.

[196] See MITTEIS 391; KARLOWA II, 62.

[197] For a survey of the numerous kinds of guilds, cult societies, funeral societies, social clubs, etc., in Rome, see KORNEMANN, 4 PAULY-WISSOWA 381. See also MITTEIS I, 390, whose attempted distinction between organizations of public and of purely private character is being questioned by Kunkel (JÖRS AND KUNKEL 75, n. 4).

[198] On the *collegium mercatorum* (later called *mercuriales*) see MITTEIS 392. The legendary date of foundation is 495 B.C.

[199] Cf. MITTEIS 393.

was probably protected sacrally; disputes among members were settled by arbitration and conflicts with outsiders ostensibly by cognition of the magistrate. The magistrate's right of interference was obvious as to those occupational organizations which were important for state liturgies (*munera*).[200] This fact explains the easy transition to the bureaucratization of the Imperial period. It is also probable that the relationships of those agricultural organizations the persistence of which may only be surmised from our sources remained outside of the regular jury procedure. The *ager compascuus* was a rudimentary commons, and the *arbitria,* which are mentioned by the agricultural writers,[201] were the residue of a state-regulated but nonetheless autonomous arbitration of disputes among neighbors. Once the *municipium* [202] had arisen as a type that was to be increasingly influential for the entire law of corporations, the law applicable to those corporations which were still permitted grew increasingly uniform during the Imperial period. The remnants of the rights of sodality membership, as far as one could find them at all, disappeared; they remained possible only outside the area of Roman imperial law, e.g., in the craftsmen's *phylae* of Hellenistic small towns.[203] The latter are not mentioned, it is true, in the Imperial Law. This omission does not prove, however, that there had not existed certain forms of organizations which it did not pretend to regulate. To draw such a conclusion would be as unjustified as it would be to conclude from the absence in the ancient *ius civile* of any regulation of *emphyteusis* or other tenures that they actually did not exist in lands other than those which made up the *ager optimo iure privatus* and which were thus the only ones to be listed in the census rolls.

Medieval continental law stood under the threefold influence of the Germanic forms of sodality, the Canon Law, and Roman Law as received in legal practice. The Germanic forms of sodality were rediscovered by Gierke and are described in all their richness and development in his magnificent work [204] but we shall not deal with their details here. In the present context a few remarks must suffice to explain those formal principles of treatment with which we are exclusively concerned here. We find there a continuous series of structures ranging from the simple relationships of joint hands to the strictly political community,

[200] See *supra* n. 165.

[201] *Ager compascuus* and *arbitria* — see WEBER, AGRARGESCHICHTE 56, 120.

[202] *Supra* p. 169.

[203] MITTEIS 393; also E. Szanto, *Die griechischen Phylen*, (1906) AUSGEWÄHLTE ABHANDLUNGEN 216.

[204] *Supra* n. 143.

or from the household to the municipality. From the point of view of legal technology they all have in common the capacities to sue and to be sued and to own property; the relationships between the entity and the individuals were worked out, however, in the most manifold ways conceivable. The individual might be denied any share in the common fund or he might be regarded as the private owner of a share as his free property, transferable, perhaps, by some form of commercial paper, but representing a share in the total fund rather than in any one of its particular assets; or, on the very contrary, every member might be regarded as owner of a share in every particular asset. To an ever varying extent the rights of the individuals might be limited and determined as to their content by the community or, on the contrary, disposition by the community might be limited by the rights of the individuals. In varying ways, too, the community could externally be represented and internally managed by one of its officers or a particular member as such or, perhaps to a certain extent at least, by all members. Contributions might have to be made by the members in kind or through personal services. Membership might be open or closed so that it could be acquired only through a resolution of the members. The administration approximated, in varying degrees, those forms which were found in the political organizations, often to such an extent that the coercive powers within the organization or toward outsiders were distinguishable from the coercive power of the political organization only by the nature of the coercive means or by its heteronomy as to the political organization. On the other hand, the collectivity was also treated as the bearer of personal rights and obligations. Like any private person it could have the right to a name, rights of status (*Standesrechte*), or the monopoly of the exclusive use of certain inventions; it could be held liable for certain unlawful acts, especially certain acts and omissions of its agents. The latter situation was so far from being exceptional that there were entire epochs, especially in England, when collective personalities were regarded as the bearers of certain duties and in the event of failure of performance were regarded as the debtor of the fine imposed by the king.[205] The collectivities could assume almost every one of the forms which we shall encounter in the course of our examination of political organizations: [206] e.g., direct administration or representative management in the name of the participants, resting on either equality or inequality; with office holders selected by rotation or election; or management could be a lord's right, possibly limited by norms or tradition but

[205] See J. HATSCHEK, ENGLISCHE VERFASSUNGSGESCHICHTE (1913) 87/88.
[206] *Infra* c. XIII.

otherwise autocratic, pertaining either to a single individual or to a firmly delimited group of persons, and acquired through periodic election or some other type of appointment or through inheritance or through other acquisition as a transferable right, title to which could be connected with that to some piece of property. The position of the organs of the collectivity could tend toward constituting a prerogative composed of clearly defined rights, i.e., a bundle of concrete but strictly limited privileges to exercise certain particular authoritative powers as subjective rights; or it could be more like a governmental power limited by objective norms but free within its scope in the choice of means, and in that case the organization could approximate either the type of the association or that of the institution. As to its powers, management could be strictly bound to the particular ends of the organization or it could enjoy a greater or lesser freedom of choice. The latter factor was also important for the degree of autonomy enjoyed by the organization as such; it could be lacking entirely, and the acquisition of rights and obligations could be regulated automatically according to fixed rules, as, e.g., in the case of certain liturgical organizations in England; [207] or the organization could possess broad powers of autonomous enactment, limited by elastic norms of a conventional, statutory, or otherwise heteronomous character.

Which of these numerous alternatives was realized in any particular instance was, and under a system of freedom of association still is, determined by the concrete ends and, quite particularly, by the economic means of the particular organization. The organization may be a predominantly economic community. In that event the structure is essentially determined by economic factors, especially the extent and the role of the capital and its inner structure, on the one hand, and the basis of credit and risk, on the other.

In an organization aiming at capitalistic profit, such as a business corporation, a mining or a shipowners' company, or a company for financing state needs or colonial enterprise, capital is of predominant significance for the efficiency of the whole, and the prospect of a share in the profits for the interests of the members. Such an organization thus requires that, at least as a general rule, membership be closed and that the purposes be fixed in a relatively stable way; also, that the membership rights be formally inviolable and transferable upon death and, at least usually, *inter vivos*; that the management be carried on bureaucratically, with some influence, however, of an assembly of the members,

[207] See *supra*, n. 205.

in which they participate either themselves or through proxies, which is *de iure* organized democratically, but plutocratically *de facto*, and which adopts its resolutions, after discussion, by a vote proportionate to capital shares. The special aim of such organizations, furthermore, does not require personal liability of the members externally, since it is irrelevant for the credit standing of the enterprise. It can also be dispensed with internally, except, however, in the mining company, in consequence of the peculiar structure of mining capital.[208]

All this is different in the case of an organization aiming at self-sufficiency without the use of money; the more comprehensive its purposes are, the more it requires the preponderant authority of the collectivity, the absence of fixed membership rights, and an approximation to communist economy upon either a directly democratic or a patriarchal basis, such as is found in the household community, the *Gemeinderschaft*, or a system of strict communal tillage (*Feldgemeinschaft*). As membership in the organization becomes increasingly closed and internally connected with fixed appropriation, as is the case in the village and commons community,[209] the membership rights will come more to the foreground, while those benefits of the individually appropriated assets which have continued to be administered communally are transferred to the management, which may be determined either by rotation, by inheritance, or by the authority of the lord of the manor. Finally, in voluntary organizations established for the communal supplementation of individual production or consumption, as, for instance, in the modern coöperatives, membership rights, although firmly appropriated and, like membership duties, firmly delimited, are, at least ordinarily, not freely alienable; although personal liability tends to become more significant for the credit standing of the organization, it is usually limited, unless the risk can be clearly determined, in which case it may be unlimited; administration is formally bureaucratic but in practice is conducted quite frequently by honoratiores.[210] Individual membership

[208] See WEBER, HISTORY 178.

[209] *Dorf- und Markgemeinschaft* (Mark*t*gemeinschaft is clearly a typographical error). *Markgemeinschaft* or, more frequently, *Markgenossenschaft* is the community of those who are entitled to share in the use of the commons, especially the common pasture and woodland. On the various forms of agrarian communities, see WEBER, HISTORY 3; cf. POLLOCK AND MAITLAND I, 560.

[210] *Wo es sich endlich um gewillkürte Vergesellschaftungen zur gemeinwirtschaftlichen Ergänzung individueller Produktions- oder Konsumtionswirtschaften handelt, wie bei den sog. Genossenschaften des modernen Rechts, da pflegt die Mitgliedschaft Folge zu sein, da Mitgliederrechte zwar fest appropriiert und ebenso wie die Mitgliedspflichten fest begrenzt, aber regelmässig nicht frei veräusserlich*

rights in the collective fund increasingly lose their structurally determinative significance the more the organization acquires the character of an establishment for the promotion of the interests of an indeterminate plurality of persons, especially artificial ones, while the contribution of capital becomes less significant relative to periodical contributions or payments by the interested parties for the services rendered by the collectivity. Such a situation has arisen in the case of the purely economically oriented insurance mutuals, but even more so, in the case of institutions serving ends of social security or charity.[211] Where, finally, the organization appears as an economic unit meant to serve primarily noneconomic ends, the guaranteed property rights of the members become insignificant and economic considerations lose their importance in the determination of the structure of the organization.

Generally it appears, however, that the development of the legal structure of organizations has by no means been predominantly determined by economic factors. This fact is proved primarily by the sharp contrast between medieval and also modern English developments, on the one hand, and the continental, especially the German, development, on the other. In English law the sodality, as defined by Gierke, did not exist after the Norman invasion, and no concept of corporation of the continental type was developed until modern times.[212] Apart from rudimentary beginnings, there was no group autonomy in the sense and scope

---

sind, die persönliche Haftung pflegt dann an Bedeutung für die Kreditwürdigkeit des Verbandes wesentlich stärker hervorzutreten, aber entweder begrenzt oder, wo das Risiko übersehbar bleibt, unbegrenzt zu sein, die Verwaltung formell bürokratisch, faktisch nicht selten honoratiorenmässig.

As it stands, this sentence does not hang together; apparently some mistake occurred in the transcription of Weber's manuscript. The translation constitutes an attempt to reconstruct Weber's original meaning, which cannot be ascertained with certainty, however.

The different needs as to liability are neatly accommodated by the German Law on Co-operatives (*Genossenschaftsgesetz*) of May 1, 1889 (RGBl. 55), under which a coöperative may be established either with limited or unlimited liability of the members, and in the latter case either with or without a direct right of action of the creditors against the individual members.

[211] What is meant are such state institutions as public insurance funds and, quite particularly, the institutions of the German system of social security (public funds for sickness, old age, unemployment, and industrial accident insurance).

[212] Maitland, "Introduction" to GIERKE, POLITICAL THEORY OF THE MIDDLE AGES (1900).

Basic for the history of juristic personality in England are MAITLAND'S STUDIES, referred to *supra* n. 143, and POLLOCK AND MAITLAND, Bk. II, ch. 2, §§ 12, 13; for additional recent literature, see the note on p. 239 of the 1936 ed. of MAITLAND'S SELECTED ESSAYS (ed. by Hazeltine, Lapsley, and Winfield).

in which it was taken for granted in medieval Germany, and there was no normatively and generally regulated juristic personality of associations. Sodalities of the kind of Gierke's theory, have, as shown by Maitland, and later by Hatschek,[213] found almost no place in English legal life, except in that form which Gierke designated as authoritarian associations (*Herrschaftsverbände*); [214] significantly, however, these latter can be, and in England have been, subsumed under juristic categories different from those formulated by Gierke. This absence in England of the allegedly Germanic form of the law of organizations (*Verbandsrecht*) occurs not only in spite of the non-reception of Roman law but was caused, at least in part, by this very fact. The absence of the Roman corporation concept facilitated the development of a situation in England in which, through the canon law, at first only ecclesiastical institutions possessed effective corporate rights, while later on all English organizations tended to be ascribed a similar character. The theory of the corporation sole, i.e., the *dignitas* represented by the succession of officers,[215] gave in English legal doctrine the possibility of treating state and communal administration as juristic persons in the same way in which ecclesiastical authorities were treated in canon law. Until the seventeenth century the king was regarded as a *corporation sole*,[216] and if even today it is neither the state nor the exchequer (*Fiskus*) but the crown which is regarded as the bearer of all the rights and obligations of the political organizations,[217] it is a consequence of the canon law influence as well as of the earlier absence of the German corporation concept as influenced by Roman law, which absence, in turn, was brought about by the political structure of the estate corporative state (*Ständestaat*). In modern times the English corporation, once it had come to exist at all, essentially retained its character as an institution rather than an association; it never, at any rate, became a sodality of the German type. These facts make us suspect that on the Continent Roman law was less responsible for the decline of the medieval law of sodalities than has frequently been believed. The medieval organizations were, it is true, quite alien to the law of Justinian. But the romanist jurists, by whom it was interpreted, were quite ready to accommodate the existing needs. Their theories had thus to use conceptual tools of frequently questionable character, but even so it can hardly be said that they

[213] MAITLAND, *loc. cit.* supra; also HATSCHEK, *op. cit.* (1913); HATSCHEK vol. I.
[214] GIERKE, GENOSSENSCHAFTSRECHT II, 43–46, 557.
[215] On the "corporation sole" see 3 MAITLAND, PAPERS (1911) 210.
[216] See BLACKSTONE I, 469; HOLDSWORTH IV, 202 *et seq.*
[217] HATSCHEK I, 75.

undermined the existence of the medieval organizations. That the concept of the corporation came to take the place of the vague German forms of thought was not entirely due to their efforts, although they contributed a good deal. The real reasons for the developments both in England on the one side and on the Continent, specifically Germany, on the other, were primarily political ones. This statement applies to the Middle Ages as well as to the early modern period. The essential difference was this: In England royal power was strong and centralized and, under the Plantagenets and their successors, disposed of highly developed technical means of administration. In Germany, on the other hand, no political center was in existence. Another factor was constituted by the continued effectiveness of certain feudal notions in the English law of real property.

The structure of the corporation is not the only case in which in England autocratic and institutional aspects have found expression. Alongside the corporation of the English type we find, as another substitute for the continental corporation, the technique of treating certain persons or bearers of office as trustees, i.e., persons to whom certain rights are entrusted for the benefit of either some certain beneficiary or beneficiaries or of the public at large. Since the end of the seventeenth century not only the king but also certain municipal and parish officers have every now and then been regarded as trustees. Indeed, wherever we are [218] presently using the concept of "special purpose fund" (*Zweckvermögen*),[219] English law resorts to trusteeship as the most adequate technical device. The characteristic element in this institutional approach is that the trustee not only may but must do what is in his jurisdiction; it is, thus, a substitute for the concept of public office (*Amtsbegriff*). The origin of the trust in this sense lay, just as in similar cases that of the Roman *fidei commissum*, primarily in the need to circumvent certain prohibitory laws, especially the laws of mortmain and certain other limitations imposed by the legal system.[220] A second cause was the ab-

[218] Sc. in Germany.

[219] On "Zweckvermögen" see MAITLAND, PAPERS III, 359, repr. in SELECTED ESSAYS 179, and German literature cited in the latter at p. 180, n. 2.

[220] For the validity of a testamentary disposition it was essential in Rome that the testator should appoint one or more persons as heir (*heres*) or heirs, i.e., persons to whom the estate would pass in its entirety and who would become personally liable for the debts of the testator. Provided there was a valid appointment of an heir or heirs, the testator could also make special provision for legatees. He could either provide that a specific asset of the estate should pass directly to the legatee (*legatum per vindicationem*) or that the legatee should be entitled to claim from the heir or heirs the delivery of a specific object or the payment of a sum of money or some

sence in the earlier Middle Ages of any concept of corporation. When English law did finally develop such a concept, the trust was continued to be applied to those institutions which could not be construed as corporations; but a similar trend has continued persistently to play an important role in the entire English law of corporations.

It was the last mentioned situation which accounts for the fact that the structure of the village community (*Markgenossenschaft*) was much more authoritarian in English than in German law and that the landlord was usually regarded as the owner of the commons, while the peasants were looked upon as mere grantees of *iura in re aliena*.[221] In view of this consistently held theory their right of access to the king's courts was of little use. The final result was the recognition of the fee simple as the fundamental form of English real property in a far more extreme form than that in which the *ager optimo jure privatus* of Roman law[222] ever prevailed in practice. Undivided communities of heirs[223] and all the other forms which were derived from it in German law were excluded already through the feudal principle of primogeniture. The principle of tracing all land titles ultimately to a royal grant necessarily resulted in the view that the dispositive powers of all organizations were but special titles of certain persons and their legal successors which could be acquired only by way of privilege. Maitland's studies[224] have shown that, as a result of the purely automatic distribution of rights and duties to each individual in accordance with his share, which was

---

other act of performance (*legatum per damnationem*). In both cases it was necessary for the testator to comply with certain rigidly fixed formalities (presence of five witnesses and of a *libripens* — see *supra*, nn. 26, 36, and use of certain formulary phrases) and the validity of the legacy was hedged in by a variety of highly formalistic rules. In the later republican period it thus became usual by formless precatory words (*verbis precativis*) to request the heir or some other person to make a payment to a third person or to give him some specific object. Such a request, which would frequently be stated in a formless letter (*codicillum*), could only be charged upon the conscience (*fidei commissum*) of the person concerned, but would be unenforceable legally.

For certain special kinds of *fidei commissa* Augustus provided enforcement, although not in the regular procedure of the *praetor* but in the administrative *cognitio* of the consuls. Under his successors this way of enforcement was broadened until finally in the law of Justinian *legatum* and *fidei commissum* were fused into one institution of regular law. Cf. BUCKLAND; SOHM, INSTITUTIONES (ed. 1949) 634.

221 *Iura in re aliena* — rights in another person's land (or chattel).

222 *Infra* pp. 221, 316.

223 *Ganerbschaften*; the word "Ga*u*erbschaften" of the German text is a typographical error.

224 POLLOCK AND MAITLAND, Bk. II, c. III, § 7, esp. p. 620.

derived from the old hide system and transferred to all similar organization, English practice had little need to deal as an independent legal subject with the totality of the individuals participating in a community. The situation was intensified in certain respects by that feudal division of public authority which is peculiar to a society of estates.[225] It was brought about first by the laws of mortmain which prohibited, in the interests of the king and the nobility, all alienation of land to the "dead hand" including the municipalities.[226] Exemptions from this prohibition could be obtained only through special privilege, and in fact, the city privileges of the fifteenth century which, beginning with the privilege of Kingston of 1439, granted corporation rights with positive content to the cities in question, were striven for by the cities as the very means of escape from these prohibitions. But the law of corporations thus remained a law of privileges and subject to the general influences of a legal development peculiar to a society of estates. From the king and Parliament downward all authority was regarded as a complex of specific privileges and prerogatives. Whoever claimed to exercise a right acquired otherwise than through private contract had to derive it legally from a valid grant and could thus have it only within certain definitely established limits. Positive proof of grant could be dispensed with only in the case of immemorial custom. Even after the emergence of the concept of the corporation there persisted into modern times the doctrine, in all its rigor, according to which every organization, if it were to transcend in its legal actions the range of the privileges explicitly granted to it, would be acting *ultra vires*, hence be guilty of an abuse of privilege and thus subject to dissolution as it was actually exercised on a large scale by the Tudors and Stuarts.[227]

The results were that neither a public nor a private corporation could be established in any way other than that of special grant; that no such grant would be given except for a limited purpose and upon grounds of public utility; and that all corporations were political, or politically authorized, limited purpose corporations, which were to remain under constant control and supervision. In the last analysis, the origin of this legal situation can be traced to the liturgical character of the Norman administration. The king assured himself of the contributions needed for the government and the administration of justice by forming compulsory organizations with collective duties similar to those of the

[225] Cf. W.u.G., Part III, §§ 7 and 8.

[226] On the laws of mortmain, see Hazeltine in 11 Encyc. Soc. Sci. 40 and Rheinstein, Decedents' Estates 399.

[227] On the history of *ultra vires*, see Holdsworth IX, 59.

Chinese, the Hellenistic, the late Roman, the Russian, or other legal systems. A *communaltie* existed exclusively as an organization with liturgical duties toward the royal administration, and it had its rights only by virtue of royal grant or indulgence. Otherwise all such communities legally remained *bodies non corporate*, even into modern times.

In consequence of the rigorous patrimonial central administration this integration of all associations in the state was at its maximum at the beginning of English legal history and had to undergo a gradual weakening from then on. In continental legal history, on the other hand, it was the bureaucratic princely state of modern times which at last broke the bonds of the traditional corporative autonomy; subjected to its own supervision the municipalities, guilds, village communities,[228] churches, clubs, and other associations of all kinds; issued patents; regulated and controlled them; canceled all rights which were not officially granted in the patents; and thus for the first time introduced into actual practice the theory of the *legists*,[229] who had maintained that no organizational structure could have juristic personality or any rights of its own except by virtue of a grant by the *princeps*.[230]

Within those territories where it had lasting effects the French Revolution destroyed not only every formation of corporations but also every type of voluntary association which could not be expressly licensed for narrowly defined special ends, as well as all associational autonomy in general. This destruction was motivated primarily by those political reasons which are characteristic of every radical democracy, but some part was also played by doctrinaire conceptions of natural law as well as considerations of bourgeois-economic orientation which in their doctrinairism also tended towards ruthlessness. The Code excludes the very concept of juristic person by simply saying nothing about it. The trend was reversed, however, by the economic needs of capitalism and, for the noncapitalistic classes, the needs of the market economy on the one hand, the agitational needs of the political parties on the other, and, finally, the growing substantive differentiation of the cultural demands

[228] *Markgenossenschaften*; "Mark*t*genossenschaften" of the German text seems to be a typographical error.

[229] Legists — the late medieval scholars of temporal (Roman) law as distinguished from the scholars of the ecclesiastical law, the canonists.

[230] On the development of the corporation in the periods of mercantilism and early liberalism, see LEHMANN, *op. cit. supra* n. 155; W. R. SCOTT, CONSTITUTION AND FINANCE OF ENGLISH, SCOTTISH, AND IRISH JOINT-STOCK COMPANIES TO 1720 (1910–1912); J. COHN, DIE AKTIENGESELLSCHAFT (1921); J. S. DAVIS, ESSAYS IN THE EARLIER HISTORY OF AMERICAN CORPORATIONS (1917).

in connection with the personal differentiation of cultural interests among individuals.[231]

Such a sharp break with the past was never experienced in the English corporation law. English legal theory began in the sixteenth century to elaborate, at first for the cities, the concept of "organ" and of "acting as an organ" as legally distinct from the private sphere, and in doing so it used the concept of the *body politic,* i.e., the Roman concept of corpus.[232] It brought the guilds into the domain of corporation types, conferred upon the municipalities the possibility of procedural and contractual autonomy, provided they had a seal, and gave the licensed corporations a limited autonomy by allowing them to have their own bylaws on the basis of the majority principle rather than unanimity. In the seventeenth century it came to deny the delictual capacity of corporations but, until the eighteenth century, corporations were treated in matters of property as trustees for the individual members, whose claims against the corporation were enforceable only in equity.[233] It was not until the end of the eighteenth century that English law permitted, and even then only reluctantly, the termination of a stockholder's liability for the debts of the corporation after he had transferred his shares, and even then the law still excepted the case of the company's insolvency. Blackstone at last was the first to make the real distinction between corporate and private assets, referring to Roman law in doing so.

The gradually increasing influence of the needs of capitalistic enterprisers played an important role in this development. The great Companies of the mercantilist Tudor and Stuart periods were legally still state institutions, as was also the Bank of England.[234] The medieval requirements of the use of the seal for every instrument to be issued by the corporation, the treatment of the shares of stock as real property whenever some part of the corporate assets consisted of land, and the limitation of corporate purposes to public tasks or tasks of public utility

[231] On the juristic person (*personne morale*) in modern French law, see MAITLAND, PAPERS III, 312, repr. in SEL. ESS. 230, and literature listed there at p. 237. On juristic persons in present laws generally, see Kunkel, *Juristische Personen* (1933), 4 RECHTSVERGLEICHENDES HANDWÖRTERBUCH 560.

[232] Cf. BLACKSTONE I, 123. "Persons also are divided by the law into either natural persons, or artificial. Natural persons are such as the God of nature formed us; artificial are such as created and devised by human laws for the purposes of society and government, which are called corporations or *bodies politic.*" Cf. also Bk. I, c. XVIII, where Blackstone says of corporations, on p. 468: "The honour of originally inventing these political constitutions entirely belongs to the Romans."

[233] See *supra* n. 232.

[234] On the history of the Bank of England, see ANDRÉADÈS, HISTORY OF THE BANK OF ENGLAND (tr. by Meredith, 1909).

were completely impracticable for business corporations and had thus to be dropped in the course of the eighteenth century. But it was only in the nineteenth century that limited liability was generally introduced for business corporations and that a system of general normative regulation was established for all joint-stock companies, together with certain special norms for friendly and benevolent societies, learned societies, insurance companies, savings banks, and, finally, labor unions. In all these cases the norms are by and large similar to the corresponding norms of the Continent.[235] The old forms, however, were not entirely discarded. Even today the appointment of trustees is still required for the appearance in court for a whole range of recognized voluntary associations, for instance a friendly society,[236] while for an unincorporated voluntary association (club) a unanimously granted power of attorney is necessary for every legal transaction.[237] The doctrine of *ultra vires* is still alive, and an individual charter is still required for every corporation which cannot be fitted in with any one of the statutory patterns. In practice, however, the situation is not much different from that which has existed in Germany ever since the Civil Code took effect.

Not only this brief comparative sketch but every glance at the great legal systems shows that none of the great variations in legal development can be explained by the all too frequently invoked slogan of the individualistic character of the Roman law as contrasted with the social character of Germanic law.[238]

[235] On modern law of business corporations, see the world-wide critical survey by W. Hallstein, Die Aktienrechte der Gegenwart (1931).

[236] The trustees whom a "friendly society" is required to have by the Friendly Societies Act, 1896, s. 25 (1), and who are the persons to sue or be sued, *ibid.* s. 94 (1), are, in fact, regular officers of the society.

[237] The authorization may be made generally by the rules of the club; cf. 3 Encyc. Laws of Engl. (3rd ed.) 221.

[238] In nineteenth-century Germany the division of labor between the historians of Roman and German law developed into an emotionally affected controversy of political significance. To the Germanists the Roman law, by which the legal system of Germany had been deeply affected since its reception in the fifteenth century, appeared as the expression of a rigid, cold-hearted, and egoistic individualism, while Germanic law, of which English law was regarded as just one branch among others, was extolled as the embodiment of a warm-hearted spirit of folk community. Among the principal representatives of this attitude was as great a scholar as Gierke, to whom the richness of forms of the German *Genossenschaft* (sodality) appeared as one of the most beautiful expressions of the peculiar spirit of Germanic neighborliness, comradeship, and creativeness. In presenting the total body of medieval German private law in his Deutsches Privatrecht, he hoped to help re-Germanize the law of the country at the time when the new German Civil Code was just to take effect. The draft of this Code, Gierke had passionately attacked because of its

The great wealth of forms of German medieval sodalities was conditioned by quite particular, predominantly political, factors, and it was and still is unique. Russian and Oriental law, including Hindu Law, have recognized liturgical collective liability and the corresponding collective rights of the compulsory organizations, especially of village communities, but also of craftsmen.[239] They also have, although not everywhere, the solidary liability of the family community and quite frequently of familylike work fraternities like the Russian *artél*.[240] But they never found a place for such a richly differentiated law of sodalities as that of the medieval Occident or for the rational concept of the corporation as it was produced in the confluence of Roman and medieval law. The Islamic law of endowments was, as we have seen, prefigured by the ancient Oriental, particularly Egyptian, and above all Byzantine,[241] legal developments, but it contained no germs of a theory of corporations. Finally, Chinese law [242] shows in a typical way the concomitance of the authority of patrimonial princes and the maintenance of the family and kinship groups in their significance of guarantors of the individual's social status. A conception of the state as independent of the private person of the Emperor did not exist any more than a law of private corporations or voluntary associations, not to speak of the politically motivated police prohibitions against all organizations

---

alleged Romanism. The alleged contrast between the warm-hearted, "social" German and the cold and egoistic Roman law became a stock argument of those political groups which tried to stem the tide of modern capitalism and to preserve other, more patriarchalic patterns of social structure, or to create a "new," romantically conceived community of socialist or racist pattern or of the kind vaguely felt by the enthusiasts of the German Youth movement. The National-Socialist party, in which all these streams converged, increased the odiousness of the Roman law by labeling it as being in some unspecified way a product of the Jewish mind. The substitution of a new, truly German law for Roman law was thus established as a basic postulate in Article 19 of the Party Platform (see HITLER, MEIN KAMPF, New York: Reynal and Hitchcock, 1940, pp. 686, 690). Under the National-Socialist government, the newly established Academy of German Law initiated efforts to draft a new German Folk Code (*Deutsches Volksgesetzbuch*). The few parts which could be prepared before energies were diverted into other channels by the war indicate that the new law, if it could have been completed, might have constituted a well-drafted code likely to serve well the needs of modern life. It is difficult to see, however, in what respects it could have been of any peculiarly "German" character.

[239] These ideas of Weber's are developed in his GENERAL ECONOMIC HISTORY. About the Russian *Mir*, cf. pp. 17–21; about Oriental laws, cf. p. 57; and about Hindu villages, cf. pp. 22–23; literature is stated on pp. 371/372. About compulsory organizations of craftsmen, see p. 136 and literature stated on p. 375.

[240] Cf. *loc cit. supra* n. 239, at 58.

[241] *Supra* p. 168.

[242] See *infra* p. 236.

which would be neither familial, fiscal nor specially licensed. Municipalities were recognized in official law only as organizations for carrying the family liability for taxes and charges. On the basis of the kinship group membership, they still exercise the strongest conceivable authority over their members, organize common institutions of all sorts of economic activity, and manifest a degree of cohesion towards outsiders with which the officials of the imperial authority had to reckon as with the strongest local authority. These phenomena, which are no more recognized in the legal concepts of official Chinese law than they were anywhere else, have often enough impeded its effectiveness. For no clearly defined content could be acquired by an autonomy which expressed itself externally in blood feuds of kinship groups and towns but was never recognized by the official law. The situation of the private organizations other than the kinship groups and families, especially of the highly developed mutual loan and burial societies and the occupational organizations corresponds in part to the situation of the Roman imperial period and in part to that of Russian law of the nineteenth century. Despite that, the concept of juristic personality in the sense of the law of Antiquity is completely absent and the liturgical function has disappeared, if it ever existed at all, which is by no means certain. The capitalistic property communities (*Vermögensgemeinschaften*) have come to be emancipated from formal dependence on the household community just as they did in Medieval southern Europe, but in spite of the *de facto* use of such institutions as the firm name, they never reached the point of becoming definite legal types as they did in Europe in the thirteenth century. Collective liability, corresponding to the general state of the law of obligations, took as its origin the delictual liability of the kinship groups, which still persists in fragmentary form. But contractual liability, which is still a purely personal liability, has not assumed the form of solidarity but is limited to the duty of group members to bring forward an absconding fellow member; in all other respects co-debtors are liable only *pro rata* rather than solidarily. Only fiscal law recognized the solidary liability of the family and its property, while collective property did not legally exist for private associations any more than it did in Roman antiquity. Like the ancient companies of publicans, the modern Chinese business associations are legally treated as consortia or as *sociétés en commandite* with personally liable directors.[243] Just as in antiquity and in the Orient, this underdeveloped state of the Chinese law of private associations and business organizations was caused by the

[243] Cf. *supra* n. 156.

continuing significance of the kinship group, within which all economic association is taking place, also by the obstruction of autonomous corporations by political patrimonialism, and finally by the general reluctance to invest capital in anything other than fiscal enterprises.

The different course of medieval Occidental development was caused primarily by the fact that here patrimonialism was of a corporate status rather than a patriarchal character, which, in turn, was caused essentially by political and, particularly, military and fiscal reasons.[244] In addition there was the development and maintenance of the form of administration of justice associated with the folk community. Wherever it was lacking as, for example, in India [245] ever since the rise to predominance of the Brahmins, the actual variety of corporate and sodality forms of associations was never accompanied by a correspondingly rich legal development. The long and persistent absence of rational and strong central authorities, as it constantly recurred after temporary intervals, did indeed produce an autonomy of mercantile, occupational, and agricultural communities, which is explicitly recognized by the law.[246] But no legal development of the German type arose therefrom. The practical consequence of the folk community type of the administration of justice was that pressure came to be exercised upon the lord, both the political and the landlord, to render judgment or pronounce customals not in person or through friends but through members of the popular assembly or at least under their decisive influence, lest they be regarded as not really binding. No such determination could be made without the participation of the groups affected by the particular body of law. Copyholders, serfs, and retainers (*Dienstmannen*) had to be called in whenever the rights and obligations arising from their economic and personal dependence relations were involved; and vassals or townsmen, whenever rights and obligations concerning their political and contractual dependence were in issue.[247] This situation derived originally from the military character of the public court community, but with the decay of the central authority it was taken over by all organizations with granted or usurped administrations of justice. It is clear that this system constituted the strongest possible guaranty of both autonomous lawmaking and corporate or sodalian organization. The origin of this guaranty and of that *de facto* autonomy of the groups of legally affected

[244] Cf. W.U.G., Part III, esp. cc. I, VII, and VIII.

[245] For literature on Hindu law, see p. 234.

[246] Cf. WEBER, GESAMMELTE AUFSÄTZE ZUR RELIGIONSSOZIOLOGIE, II, 34 (Essays 399).

[247] See GIERKE, GENOSSENSCHAFTSRECHT II, 300 *et seq.*, 457 *et seq.*, 114, 93.

parties in the formation of their own laws, which was necessary to make possible the development of the occidental law of corporations and sodalities as well as of the specifically capitalistc forms of association, was conditioned by essentially political and technical administrative considerations. Quite generally the lord was preoccupied with military activities and he hardly had at his disposal a rational administrative apparatus which would have been dependent on him and which he could have used to supervise his subordinates; thus he had to depend on their good will and on their coöperation in meeting his claims and thus had to meet the traditional or usurped counterclaims of his dependents against him. The typification and appropriation of the rights of these dependent strata as sodality rights had their source in this situation. The guaranty of the associational norms was increased through a custom which stemmed from the form of lawfinding by the popular assembly, namely, that of periodically ascertaining the prevailing law of the consociation by oral testimony and recording it in customals, combined with the tendency of the dependents at propitious moments to ask the lord for the confirmation of this law as their privilege.[248] Such occurrences within authoritarian economic and political organizations naturally increased the probability of maintaining corporate autonomy also for the free and voluntary associations. No such situation could prevail in England, because the royal courts of the strong patrimonial power suppressed the old administration of justice by the popular assemblies of the counties, municipalities, etc. Hence the development of a law of sodalities was inhibited; customals and privileges of autonomy were rare, and those few which existed lacked the peculiar character of their continental counterparts. In Germany, too, sodalian autonomy, and with it, the law of the sodalities, declined rapidly as soon as the political and seignorial authorities had become able to create the administrative apparatus that allowed them to dispense with the folk type of administration of justice.[249]

It was, of course, no accident that this development coincided with the intrusion of Romanist traits into the system of government, but Roman law as such did not play the decisive role. In England the rise of a law of sodalities was prevented by devices of Germanist legal technique. Besides, those associations which could not be fitted into the categories of the corporation sole or the trust or the patented forms of organization were regarded as purely contractual relations of their members, with the statutes being accorded validity only in the sense of a contractual

[248] Cf. Amira 27; Planitz 188, with further literature.

[249] See Gierke, Genossenschaftsrecht II, 456.

offer to be accepted by joining membership. Such a view closely corresponds to a construction of the Romanist type. The political structure of the lawmaking organization and the peculiar characteristics of the professional bearers of the legal structure, whom we shall discuss later,[250] were the decisive factors.

Section 7. Freedom and Coercion

The development of legally regulated relationships toward contractual association and of the law itself toward freedom of contract, especially toward a system of free disposition within the framework of regulated legal type transactions, is usually regarded as signifying a decrease of constraint and an increase of individual freedom. It is clear from what we have been saying, in how relative a sense this opinion is formally correct. The possibility of entering with others into contractual relations the content of which is entirely determined by individual agreement, and likewise the possibility of making use in accordance with one's desires of an increasingly large number of type forms rendered available by the law for purposes of consociation in the widest sense of the word, has, as compared with the past, been immensely extended in modern law, at least in the spheres of exchange of goods and of personal work and services. However, the extent to which this trend has brought about an actual increase of the individual's freedom to shape the conditions of his own life or the extent to which, on the contrary, life has become more stereotyped in spite, or, perhaps, just because of this trend, cannot be determined simply by studying the development of formal legal institutions. The great variety of permitted contractual schemata and the formal empowerment to set the content of contracts in accordance with one's desires and independently of all official form patterns, in and of itself by no means makes sure that these formal possibilities will in fact be available to all and everyone. Such availability is prevented above all by the differences in the distribution of property as guaranteed by law. The formal right of a worker to enter into any contract whatsoever with any employer whatsoever does not in practice represent for the employment seeker even the slightest freedom in the determination of his own conditions of work, and it does not guarantee him any influence on this process. It rather means, at least primarily, that the more powerful party in the market, i.e., normally the employer, has the possibility to set the terms, to offer the job "take it or leave it," and, given the normally more pressing economic need of the worker, to impose his terms

[250] *Infra*, c. VII.

upon him. The result of contractual freedom, then, is in the first place the opening of the opportunity to use, by the clever utilization of property ownership in the market, these resources without legal restraints as a means for the achievement of power over others. The parties interested in power in the market thus are also interested in such a legal order. Their interest is served particularly by the establishment of "legal empowerment rules." [251] This kind of rules does no more than create the framework for valid agreements which, under conditions of formal freedom, are officially available to all. Actually, however, they are accessible only to the owners of property and thus in effect support their very autonomy and power positions.

It is necessary to emphasize strongly this aspect of the state of affairs in order not to fall into the widely current error that that type of decentralization of the lawmaking process [252] which is embodied in this modern form of the schematically delimited autonomy of the parties' legal transactions is identical with a decrease of the degree of *coercion* exercised within a legal community as compared with other communities, for instance, one organized along "socialist" lines. The increasing significance of freedom of contract and, particularly, of enabling laws which leave everything to "free" agreement, implies a relative reduction of that kind of coercion which results from the threat of mandatory and prohibitory norms. Formally it represents, of course, a decrease of coercion. But it is also obvious how advantageous this state of affairs is to those who are economically in the position to make use of the empowerments. The exact extent to which the total amount of "freedom" within a given legal community is actually increased depends entirely upon the concrete economic order and especially upon the property distribution. In no case can it be simply deduced from the content of the law. Enabling laws of the sort discussed here would certainly play a slight role in a "socialist" community; likewise, the positions from which coercion is exercised, the type of coercion, and those against whom it is directed, will also be different from what they are in an order of private economy. In the latter, coercion is exercised to a considerable extent by the private owners of the means of production and acquisition, to whom the law guarantees their property and whose power can thus manifest itself in the competitive struggle of the market. In this type of coercion the statement "coactus voluit" [253] applies with peculiar force just be-

[251] *Supra* p. 99.

[252] A felicitous phrase of Andeas Voigt's [Weber's note]. Voigt: German professor of economics, b. 1860; the citation could not be verified.

[253] "Coactus voluit" (it is his wish, although coerced) — Romanist phrase to

cause of the careful avoidance of the use of authoritarian forms. In the labor market, it is left to the "free" discretion of the parties to accept the conditions imposed by those who are economically stronger by virtue of the legal guaranty of their property. In a socialist community, direct mandatory and prohibitory decrees of a central economic control authority, in whichever way it may be conceived, would play a much greater role than such ordinations are playing today. In the event of disobedience, observance will be produced by means of some sort of "coercion" but not through struggle in the market. Which system would possess more real coercion and which one more real personal freedom cannot be decided, however, by the mere analysis of the actually existing or conceivable formal legal system. So far sociology can only perceive the qualitative differences among the various types of coercion and their incidence among the participants in the legal community.

A (democratically) socialist order (in the sense current in present-day ideologies) [254] rejects coercion not only in the form in which it is exercised in the market through the possession of private property but also direct coercion to be exercised on the basis of purely personal claims to authority. It would recognize only the validity of agreed abstract laws, regardless of whether they are called by this name. Formally, the market community does not recognize formal coercion on the basis of personal authority. It produces in its stead a special kind of coercive situation which, as a general principle, applies without any discrimination to workers, enterprisers, producers and consumers, viz., in the impersonal form of the inevitability of adaptation to the purely economic "laws" of the market. The sanctions consist in the loss or decrease of economic power and, under certain conditions, in the very loss of one's economic existence. The private enterprise system transforms into objects of "labor market transactions" even those personal and authoritarian-hierarchical relations which actually exist in the capitalistic enterprise. While the authoritarian relationships are thus drained of all normal sentimental content, authoritarian constraint not only continues but, at least under certain circumstances, even increases. The larger a structure whose existence depends in some specific way on "discipline,"

---

describe the situation of an individual who has engaged in a legal transaction under the influence of coercion, in contrast to the situation in which a person is used as the mere physical tool of another, for instance, where the latter forcibly grabs the former's hand and moves it so as to go through the physical motions of writing a signature. Cf. *supra*, p. 37.

[254] Weber here refers to the programs of the Social-Democratic parties, particularly of that which was in his time operating in Germany.

for instance a capitalistic industrial plant, the more relentlessly can authoritarian constraint be exercised in it, at least under certain conditions. It finds its counterpart in the shrinkage of the circle of those in whose hands the power to use this type of constraint is concentrated and who also hold the power to have that former power guaranteed to them by the legal order. A legal order which contains ever so few mandatory and prohibitory norms and ever so many "freedoms" and "empowerments" can nonetheless in its practical effects facilitate a quantitative and qualitative increase not only of coercion in general but quite specifically of authoritarian coercion.

Supplement to Chapter VI. The Market [255]

Up to this point we have discussed various types of communal structures.[256] They are highly diversified: they may be more amorphous or more organized, more continuous or more intermittent, more open or more closed. But, as a general rule, only part of the communal action within their framework has been rationalized. In contrast to all of them stands, as the archetype of all rational social action, the consociation through exchange in the *market*.

A market may be said to exist wherever there is competition, even if only unilateral, for opportunities of exchange among a plurality of potential parties. Their physical assemblage in one place, as in the local market square, the fair (the "long distance market"), or the exchange (the merchants' market), only constitutes the most consistent kind of market formation. It is, however, only this physical assemblage which allows the full emergence of the market's most distinctive feature, viz., dickering. Since the discussion of the market phenomena constitutes essentially the content of economics, it will not be presented here. From a sociological point of view, the market represents a coexistence and sequence of rational consociations, each of which is specifically ephemeral in so far as it ceases to exist with the act of exchanging the goods, unless a norm has been promulgated which imposes upon the transferors of the exchangeable goods the guaranty of their lawful acquisition as warranty of title or of quiet enjoyment. The completed barter constitutes a consociation only with the immediate partner. The preparatory dickering, however, is always a communal action since both

[255] W.u.G., Part II. Consociations and Associations — Chapter V (unfinished).

[256] The types of social structure discussed "up to this point" of Part II of Wirtschaft und Gesellschaft are: the house and neighborhood communities, ethnical communities (race, nation), and political communities.

the potential partners are guided in their offers by the potential action of an indeterminately large group of real or imaginary competitors rather than by their own actions alone. The more this is true, the more does the market constitute communal action. Furthermore, any act of exchange involving the use of money (sale) is a communal action simply because the money used derives its value from its relation to the potential action of others. Its acceptability rests exclusively on the expectation that it will continue to be desirable and can be further used as a means of payment. The creation of community through the use of money is the exact counterpart to any consociation through rationally agreed or imposed norms.

Money creates community by virtue of material interest relations between actual and potential participants in the market and its payments. At the fully developed stage, the so-called money economy, the resulting situation looks as if it had been created by a set of norms established for the very purpose of bringing it into being. The explanation lies in this: Within the market community every act of exchange, especially monetary exchange, is not directed, in isolation, by the action of the individual partner to the particular transaction, but the more rationally it is considered, the more it is directed by the actions of all parties potentially interested in the exchange. The market community as such is the most impersonal relationship of practical life into which humans can enter with one another. This is not due to that potentiality of struggle among the interested parties which is inherent in the market relationship. Any human relationship, even the most intimate, and even though it be marked by the most unqualified personal devotion, is in some sense relative and may involve a struggle with the partner, for instance, over the salvation of his soul. The reason for the impersonality of the market is its matter-of-factness, its orientation to the commodity and only to that. Where the market is allowed to follow its own autonomous tendencies, its participants do not look toward the persons of each other but only toward the commodity; there are no obligations of brotherliness or reverence, and none of those spontaneous human relations that grow out of intimate personal community. They all would just obstruct the free development of the bare market community, and its specific interests serve, in their turn, to weaken the sentiments on which these obstructions rest. Market behavior is influenced by rational, purposeful pursuit of interests. The partner to a transaction is expected to behave according to rational legality and, quite particularly, to respect the formal inviolability of a promise once given. These are the qualities which form the content of market ethics. In this latter respect the market inculcates, indeed, particularly rigorous conceptions. Violations of agreements, even though they may be concluded by mere signs, entirely unrecorded, and devoid of evidence, are almost unheard of in the annals of the stock exchange. Such absolute depersonalization is contrary to all the elementary forms of human relationship. Sombart has pointed out this contrast repeatedly and brilliantly.[257]

The "free" market, that is, the market which is not bound by ethical norms, with its exploitation of constellations of interests and monopoly positions and its dickering, is an abomination to every system of fraternal ethics. In sharp contrast to all other communities which always presuppose some measure of personal fraternization or even blood kinship, the market is fundamentally alien to any type of fraternal relationship.

At first, free exchange does not occur but with the world outside of the neighborhood community or the personal association. The market is a relationship which transcends the boundaries of neighborhood, kinship group, or tribe. Originally, it is indeed the only peaceful relationship of such kind. At first, fellow members of a community did not trade with one another with the intention of obtaining profit. There was, indeed, no need for such transactions in an age of self-sufficient agrarian units. One of the most characteristic forms of primitive trade, the silent trade, dramatically represents the contrast between the market community and the fraternal community. The silent trade is a form of exchange which avoids all face-to-face contact and in which the supply takes the form of a deposit of the commodity at a customary place; the counteroffer takes the same form, and dickering is effected through the increase in the number of objects being offered from both sides, until one party either withdraws dissatisfied or, satisfied, takes the goods left by the other party and departs.[258]

It is normally assumed by both partners to an exchange that each will be interested in the future continuation of the exchange relation-

[257] Die Juden und das Wirtschaftsleben (1911, Epstein tr. 1913, 1951, s.t. The Jews and Modern Capitalism); Der Bourgeois (1913); Händler und Helden (1915); Der moderne Kapitalismus, vol. III, Part I, p. 6; see also Deutscher Sozialismus (1934) (Geiser tr. s.t. A New Social Philosophy, 1937). Revulsion against the so-called "de-humanization" of relationships has constituted an important element in the German neo-romanticism of such groups and movements as the circle around the poet Stefan George, the youth movement, the Christian Socialists, etc. Through the tendency to ascribe this capitalistic spirit to the Jews and to hold them responsible for its rise and spread, these sentiments became highly influential in the growth of organized anti-Semitism and, especially, National-Socialism.

[258] On "silent trade," see *supra*, p. 107.

ship, be it with this particular partner or with some other, and that he will adhere to his promises for this reason and avoid at least striking infringements of the rules of good faith and fair dealing. It is only this assumption which guarantees the law-abidingness of the exchange partners. In so far as that interest exists, "honesty is the best policy." This proposition, however, is by no means universally applicable, and its empirical validity is irregular; naturally, it is highest in the case of rational enterprises with a stable clientele. For, on the basis of such a stable relationship which generates the possibility of mutual personal appraisal with regard to market ethics, trading may free itself most successfully from illimited dickering and return, in the interest of the parties, to a relative limitation of fluctuation in prices and exploitation of momentary interest constellations. The consequences, though they are important for price formation, are not relevant here in detail. The fixed price, without preference for any particular buyer, and strict business honesty are highly peculiar features of the regulated local neighborhood markets of the medieval Occident, in contrast to the Near and Far East. They are, moreover, a condition as well as a product of that particular stage of capitalistic economy which is known as Early Capitalism. They are absent where this stage no longer exists. Nor are they practiced by those estate and other groups which are not engaged in exchange except occasionally and passively rather than regularly and actively. The maxim of *caveat emptor* obtains, as experience shows, mostly in transactions involving feudal strata or, as every cavalry officer knows, in horse trading among comrades. The specific ethics of the market place is alien to them. Once and for all they conceive of commerce, as does any rural community of neighbors, as an activity in which the sole question is: who will cheat whom.

The freedom of the market is typically limited by sacred taboos or through estatist monopolistic consociations which render exchange with outsiders impossible. Directed against these limitations we find the continuous onslaught of the market community, whose very existence constitutes a temptation to share in the opportunities for gain. The process of appropriation in a monopolistic community may advance to the point at which it becomes closed toward outsiders, i.e., the land, or the right to participate in the market of a village community, may have become vested definitively and hereditarily. As the money economy expands and, with it, both the growing differentiation of needs capable of being satisfied by indirect barter, and the independence from land ownership, such a situation of fixed, hereditary appropriation normally creates a steadily increasing interest of individual parties in the possibility of using their vested property rights for exchange with the highest bidder, even though he be an outsider. This development is quite analogous to that which causes the co-heirs of an industrial enterprise in the long run to establish a corporation so as to be able to sell their shares more freely. In its outside relations, too, an emerging capitalistic economy, the stronger it becomes, the greater will be its efforts to obtain the means of production and labor services in the market without limitations by sacred or corporate-status bonds, and to emancipate the opportunities to sell its products from the restrictions imposed by the sales monopolies of corporate-status organizations. Capitalistic interests thus favor the continuous extension of the free market, but only up to the point at which some of them succeed, through the purchase of privileges from the political authority or simply through the power of capital, in obtaining for themselves a monopoly for the sale of their products or the acquisition of their means of production, and in thus closing the market on their own part.

The breakup of the monopolies of the corporate-status organizations is thus the typical immediate sequence to the full appropriation of all the material means of production. It occurs where those having a stake in the capitalistic system are in a position to influence, for their own advantage, those communities by which the ownership of goods and the mode of their use are regulated; or where, within a monopolistic corporate-status organization the upper hand is gained by those who are interested in the use of their vested property interests in the market. Another consequence is that the scope of those rights which are guaranteed as acquired or acquirable by the coercive apparatus of the property-regulating community becomes limited to rights in material goods and to contractual claims, including claims to contractual labor. All other appropriations, especially all estatist appropriations of opportunities of sale or purchase, are destroyed. This state of affairs, which we call free competition, lasts until it is replaced by new, this time capitalistic, monopolies which are acquired in the market through the power of property. These capitalistic monopolies differ from monopolies of corporate-status organizations [259] by their purely economic and rational character. By restricting either the scope of possible sales or the permissible terms the monopolies of corporate-status organizations excluded from their field of action the mechanism of the market with its dickering and

[259] Such as the monopoly of guild members to sell certain goods within the city, or the monopoly of the lord of a manor to grind the grain of all the peasants of the district, or the monopoly of the members of the bar to give legal advice, a monopoly which was abolished in most continental countries in the nineteenth century.

rational calculation. Those monopolies, on the other hand, which are based solely upon the power of property, rest, on the contrary, upon an entirely rationally calculated mastery of market conditions which may, however, remain formally as free as ever. The sacred, corporate-status, and merely traditional bonds, which have gradually come to be eliminated, constituted restrictions on the formation of rational market prices; the purely economically conditioned monopolies are, on the other hand, their ultimate consequence. The beneficiary of a corporate-status monopoly restricts, and maintains his power against, the market, while the rational-economic monopolist rules through the market. We shall designate those interest groups which are enabled by formal market freedom to achieve power, as market-interest groups.

A particular market may be subject to a body of norms autonomously agreed upon by the participants or imposed by any one of a great variety of different communities, especially political or religious groups. Such norms may involve limitations of market freedom, restrictions of dickering or of competition, or they may establish guaranties for the observance of market legality, especially the modes or means of payment or, in periods of interlocal insecurity, the norms may be aimed at guaranteeing the market peace. Since the market was originally a consociation of persons who are not members of the same group and who are, therefore, "enemies," the guaranty of peace, like that of restrictions of permissible modes of warfare, was ordinarily left to divine powers.[260] Very often the peace of the market was placed under the protection of a temple; later on it tended to be made into a source of revenue for the chief or prince. However, while exchange is the specifically peaceful form of acquiring economic power, it can, obviously, be associated with the use of force. The seafarer of Antiquity and the Middle Ages was pleased to take without pay whatever he could acquire by force and had recourse to peaceful dickering only where he was confronted with a power equal to his own or where he regarded it as shrewd to do so for the sake of future exchange opportunities which might be endangered otherwise. But the intensive expansion of exchange relations has always gone together with a process of relative pacification. All of the "public peace" arrangements of the Middle Ages were meant to serve the interests of exchange.[261] The appropriation of goods through free, purely economi-

[260] On market peace, cf. S. Rietschel, Markt und Stadt (1897); H. Pirenne, Villes, marchés et marchands au moyen âge (1898).

[261] On such medieval peace arrangements (*Landfrieden*), which were aimed at the elimination of feuds and private wars and which occurred either as nonagression pacts concluded, often with ecclesiastical or royal coöperation, between barons,

cally rational exchange is the conceptual opposite of appropriation of goods by coercion of any kind, but especially physical coercion, the regulated exercise of which is the very constitutive element of the political community.

---

cities, and other potentates, or were sought to be imposed on his unruly subjects by the king, see Quidde, *Histoire de la paix publique en Allemagne au moyen âge* (1929), 28 RECUEIL DES COURS DE L'ACADÉMIE DE DROIT INTERNATIONAL 449.

CHAPTER VII

THE LEGAL HONORATIORES[1] AND THE TYPES OF LEGAL THOUGHT[2]

For the development of a professional legal training and, through it, of specifically legal modes of thinking two different lines are possible. The first consists in the empirical training in the law as a craft; the apprentices learn from practitioners more or less in the course of actual legal practice. Under the second possibility law is taught in special schools, where the emphasis is placed on legal theory and "science," that is, where legal phenomena are given rational and systematic treatment.

1. A fairly pure illustration of the first type is represented by the guildlike English method of having law taught by the lawyers. During the medieval period a sharp distinction was made between advocate and attorney.[3] The need for an advocate was due to the peculiarities of procedure before the popular assemblies; the attorney emerged when procedure began to be rationalized in the royal courts with their jury trial and the increasing evidentiary importance of the record.[4] In France the

[1] Legal honoratiores — see *supra*, p. 52.

In effect the present Section is concerned with the legal profession, its various types, and their influence on the formal characteristics of the law.

A concise survey of the history of the legal profession in ancient and modern Western civilization will be found, with bibliography, in the article by Hazeltine, Radin, and Berle in 9 ENCYC. SOC. SCI. 324. To the bibliography should now be added F. SCHULZ, HISTORY, and R. POUND, THE LAWYER FROM ANTIQUITY TO MODERN TIMES (1953).

[2] W.U.G. 456–467.

[3] The most authoritative expositions on the development of the legal profession in the Middle Ages are those by H. Brunner: (1) *Die Zulässigkeit der Anwaltschaft im französischen, normannischen und englischen Rechte des Mittelalters* (1878) 1 Z.F. VGL. R. 321 *et seq.*, and the partial translation of it in 3 ILL. L. REV. 257; (2) *Wort und Form im altfranzösischen Process* in 57 SITZUNGSBERICHTE DER PHILOS.-HIST. CLASSE DER KAISERLICHEN AKADEMIE DER WISSENSCH. ZU WIEN (1868) 655; see also WEBER, HISTORY 340; ENGELMANN AND MILLAR, *op. cit.*

[4] On the development of jury trial in general see literature cited *supra* c. V, nn. 35, 36. For the connection between *attornatio* and the "records" in the royal courts, see Brunner, *Die Zuläss. der Anwlt.*, *loc. cit.* 362: both the *attornatio* and the records were allowed only in the *curia regis*, and their relationship is clearly shown in earlier English sources — *ibid.* 373; GLANVILLE, VIII, 8, § 7; Brunner, *op. cit.* 197.

verbal formalism which grew out of the strict application of the accusatorial principle in the procedure before the popular assembly, gave rise to the need of an *avant-rulier* (*avant-parlier*). The legal maxim *fautes volent exploits*[5] and the formalistic effect of the words spoken compelled the layman to seek the assistance of an *avant rulier* or "prolocutor" who, upon the party's request, would be assigned to him by the judge from among the judgment-finders,[6] and who would publicly "speak for," and in the name of, the party the words required for the progress of the case. Among other advantages there was thus conferred upon the litigant, since the formalistic words had not been pronounced by the litigant himself, the advantage that he could "amend" the verbal mistakes that might have been committed.[7] Originally, the advocate stood before the court next to the party litigating. His position was thus quite different from that of the attorney (*avoué*, *Anwalt*, *procurator*, *solicitor*), who assumed the technical tasks of preparing the case and obtaining the evidence. But the attorney could not assume these functions until procedure had undergone a considerable degree of rationalization. Originally an attorney in the modern sense was not possible at all. He could not function as the "representative" of the party until procedural representation had been made possible, as in England and France, by the development of the royal law; as a general rule, an attorney's appointment to such a representative function rested upon special privilege.[8] The advocate was not prevented by his acting for the party from participating in the actual finding of the judgments; indeed, he would not have been able to propose a judgment unless he was one of the judgment-finders. The attorney, however, became exclusively the representative of the party and nothing else. In the royal courts of England, attorneys were originally recruited, almost without exception, from among those persons who could write, i.e., the clergy, for whom this activity constituted a major source of income.[9] But the preoccupations of ecclesiastical

[5] *Fautes volent exploits* means "errors destroy the acts" (one mistake nullifies the whole procedure); concerning this maxim and the old French procedure in general, see Brunner, *Wort und Form im altfranzösischen Process*, *loc. cit.*, esp. at p. 670.

[6] Cf. *supra*, pp. 90 *et seq.*

[7] See Pollock and Maitland I, 212: "A man is allowed to put forward some one else to speak for him, not in order that he may be bound by that other person's words, but in order that he may have a chance of correcting formal blunders and supplying omissions" (Leg. Henr. 46, § 3). This was the so-called "droit d'amendment" explained by Brunner, *loc. cit.* 754–780, and also in his *Zuläss. der Anw.* 322.

[8] The appointment of an attorney rested at first upon special privilege, but this was no longer so in the time of Glanville. See Brunner, Zul. d. Anwl., *loc. cit.* 363; Holdsworth II, 315, 316.

[9] By the Lateran Council, 1215, the clergy were, however, prohibited from acting

service on the one hand, and the expansion of legal training among the upper classes on the other, resulted not only in the progressive exclusion of the clergy from the legal profession, but also in the organization of the lay lawyers in the four Inns of Court, and in the pronounced movement on their part to monopolize the judicial positions as well as those other official jobs which required legal knowledge. With the coming to the fore of rational modes of procedure, the old "prolocutors" disappeared. But a new aristocracy of legal honoratiores came into being, consisting of counsels, serjeants, and barristers, i.e., of those admitted to represent, and plead for, litigants before the royal courts.[10] Indeed, this new type of lawyer took over many of the characteristics of the old "prolocutors." He was subject to a strict professional etiquette. He refused to have anything to do with the technical services required in the case, and ultimately he lost all personal contact with the party whom he would not even see face to face.[11] The handling of the case lay in the hands of "attorneys" or "solicitors," a class of business people, neither organized in guilds nor possessing the legal education provided by the guilds; they were the intermediaries between the party and the "barrister" to prepare the "brief" or status causae so that the barrister could

---

as attorneys in secular courts, except in causes concerning themselves or concerning poor persons.

[10] The earliest time for which it is certain that in the royal courts of England litigants could appear by representation, is that of Henry II. Professional legal representation seems to begin with the thirteenth rather than with the twelfth century. For Bracton tells much about the "attorney" who can fully act for and indeed also fully commit his client. The attorney's job was, however, mainly procedural; and as the legal system became more and more complex, litigants required not only to be represented procedurally but also felt the need for lawyers who would *narrate* as well as argue their case in court. These lawyers were the *narrators* (and were later called the *serjeants*) but there is still too little known about their early history. As Plucknett has remarked, "In the present state of our knowledge it therefore seems safe to say that there certainly were professional *narrators* and attorneys during the reign of Edward I, and that possibly these professions already existed under Henry III" (204, 206).

In the following account of the methods of the Common Law as well as in his general ideas about it, Weber relied to an apparently large extent upon the writings of J. Hatschek, especially the third chapter of his ENGLISCHES STAATSRECHT I, 95 *et seq.* Weber's general ideas of legal thought as expressed throughout this work seem to have been influenced strongly by Hatschek, especially his article entitled *Konventionalregeln, oder über die Grenzen der naturwissenschaftlichen Begriffsbildung im öffentlichen Recht* (1909), 3 JAHRBUCH DES ÖFFENTLICHEN RECHTS 1–67.

[11] For a short account of the course of this complicated development, covering several centuries, see PLUCKNETT 212–215, and literature there cited. The standard work is HERMAN COHEN, HISTORY OF THE ENGLISH BAR (1929).

present it before the court. The practicing barristers lived together in communal fashion in the corporate and closed guildhouses. The judges were exclusively chosen from among them and continued to share the communal life with them. "Bar" and "bench" were two functions of the corporate and later highly exclusive legal profession; in the Middle Ages its members came largely from the nobility, and admission to the guild was regulated with an ever increasing measure of autonomy. There was a four-year novitiate, connected with instruction at the guild school; the call to the bar conferred the right to plead; for the rest, training was purely practical. The profession insisted on the maintenance of the code of etiquette, especially with regard to the observance of minimum fees, all fees, however, to be paid voluntarily and not to be actionable. The lecture courses in the Inns were only introduced as the result of the competitive struggle with the universities.[12] As soon as the monopoly was achieved, the lectures began to decline, to be ultimately discontinued altogether. Thereafter, training was purely empirical and practical and led, as in the craft guilds, to pronounced specialization. This kind of legal training naturally produced a formalistic treatment of the law, bound by precedent and analogies drawn from precedent. Not only was systematic and comprehensive treatment of the whole body of the law prevented by the craftlike specialization of the lawyers, but legal practice did not aim at all at a rational system but rather at a practically useful scheme of contracts and actions, oriented towards the interests of clients in typically recurrent situations. The upshot was the emergence of what had been called in Roman law "cautelary jurisprudence,"[13] as well as of such practical devices as procedural fictions which facilitated the disposition of new situations upon the pattern of previous instances.[14] From such practices and attitudes no rational system of law could emerge nor even a rationalization of the law as such because the concepts thus formed are constructed in relation to the material, and concretely experienceable events of everyday life, are distinguished from each other by external criteria, and extended in their scope, as new needs arise, by means of the techniques just mentioned. They are not "general concepts" which would be formed by abstraction from con-

[12] The two universities, Oxford and Cambridge, taught only civil and canon law whereas the Inns of Court concentrated on "English" law as developed in the royal courts. Cf. PLUCKNETT 208–209.

[13] See *supra*, p. 72.

[14] On the fictions which were used by the several courts of the king to extend their jurisdiction, see PLUCKNETT 152–155; HOLDSWORTH I, 235. More generally, see Morris R. Cohen, *Fictions*, 6 ENCYC. SOC. SCI. 225; Fuller, *Legal Fictions* (1930–31), 25 ILL. L. REV. 363, 513, 877; MAINE, c. II.

creteness or by logical interpretation of meaning or by generalization and subsumption; nor were these concepts apt to be used in syllogistically applicable norms. In the purely empirical conduct of legal practice and legal training one always moves from the particular to the particular but never tries to move from the particular to general propositions in order to be able subsequently to deduce from them the norms for new particular cases. This reasoning is tied to the word, the word which is turned around and around, interpreted, and stretched in order to adapt it to varying needs, and, to the extent that one has to go beyond, recourse is had to "analogies" or technical fictions.[15]

Once the patterns of contracts and actions, required by the practical needs of interested parties, had been established with sufficient elasticity, the official law could preserve a highly archaic character and survive the greatest economic transformations without formal change. The archaic case analysis of the law of seisin, for example, which originally corresponded to the conditions of peasant tenure and manorial lordship of the Norman period, persisted to the very threshold of the present epoch with, what were from a theoretical point of view, often grotesque results in the American Middle West.[16] No rational legal training or theory can ever arise in such a situation. Wherever legal education has been in the hands of practitioners, especially attorneys, who have made admission to practice a guild monopoly, an economic factor, namely, their pecuniary interest, brings to bear a strong influence upon the process not only of stabilizing the official law and of adapting it to changing

[15] Cf. the recent analysis of the methods of Common Law reasoning by EDWARD H. LEVI, INTRODUCTION TO LEGAL REASONING; see also LLEWELLYN, PRÄJUDIZIENRECHT UND RECHTSPRECHUNG IN AMERIKA (1933).

[16] Weber is obviously thinking of the continuance in modern American real property law of such concepts as tenure, estate, and fee, and of such relics as the doctrine of destructibility of contingent remainders, the doctrine of worthier title, or the Rule in Shelley's Case. The concept of tenure has practically disappeared, the meaning and functions of the others have been radically transformed; cf. R. R. POWELL, LAW OF REAL PROPERTY (1950) I, c. iv. On seisin, see Maitland, *The Mystery of Seisin* (1886), 2 L.Q. REV. 481; Bordwell, *Seisin and Disseisin* (1920/21), 34 HARV. L. REV. 592; Sweet, *Seisin* (1896), 12 L.Q. REV. 239.

An Illinois case on seisin reviving most of the old features of the English law is *Fort Dearborn v. Kline* (1885), 115 Ill. 177, 3 N.E. 272.

R. POWELL, *op. cit.* 236, n. 70, characterizes Illinois decisions as "anachronistic," "re-incarnating" old English law (with the help of A. Kales's great knowledge). Powell continues (p. 237): "In general, it can be said that English law [concerning real property] is a more constantly significant factor in the thinking of the Illinois judiciary than in most of our other states. The ghosts of the past have freer exit from their closets, without much scrutiny to determine their real utility as a part of a modern scheme of life."

needs in an exclusively empirical way but also of preventing its rationalization through legislation or legal science. The lawyers' material interests are threatened by every interference with the traditional forms of procedure, and every interference menaces that situation in which the adaptation of the scheme of contracts and actions to both the formal norms and the needs of the interested parties is left exclusively to the legal practitioners. The English lawyers, for example, were largely successful in preventing both a systematic and rational type of lawmaking and a rational legal education, such as exists in the Continental universities;[17] the relationship between "bar" and "bench" is still fundamentally different in the English-speaking countries from what it is on the Continent. In particular, the interpretation of newly made laws lay, and still lies, in the hands of judges who have come from the bar. The English legislator must, therefore, take special pains with every new act to exclude all sorts of possible "constructions" by the lawyers which, as has so frequently happened, would be directly contradictory to his intentions.[18] This tendency, partly immanent, partly caused by economic considerations, and partly the result of the traditionalism of the legal profession, has had the most far-reaching practical consequences. For example, the absence of a system of registration of title, and consequently the absence of a rationally organized system of real estate credit, has been largely due to the lawyers' economic interest with regard to the fees for that title examination which must in every transaction be made because of the uncertainty of all land titles. It has also had a deep influence upon the distribution of land ownership in England and, quite particularly, upon the peculiar form of the land lease as a "joint business."[19]

[17] For evidence of efforts by the English bar to prevent codification and law reform, see, among others, the biography of Lord Birkenhead in DICTIONARY OF NATIONAL BIOGRAPHY (1922–1930) 782. For Bentham's despair at the hostility shown toward law reform and codification by the English bar, see J. DILLON, LAWS AND JURISPRUDENCE OF ENGLAND AND AMERICA (1894) 271, 316–347, 180 *et seq.* See also Sunderland, *The English Struggle for Procedural Reform* (1926), 39 HARV. L. REV. 725. The American lawyers' aversion against codification and law reform found dramatic expression in the fight of the New York bar led by J. C. Carter, against David Dudley Field's efforts to codify the law. Cf. Dillon, *op. cit.* 255; see also REPORTS OF AMERICAN BAR ASSOCIATION (1890) 217 for Carter, and 1885, 1886 for D. D. Field; on D. D. Field, cf. CENTENARY ESSAYS of the New York University School of Law, ed. by A. Reppy (1949), Llewellyn, 3 ENCYC. SOC. SCI. 243, also CLARK, CODE PLEADING (2nd ed. 1947) 17–21.

[18] For illustrations of, and literature on, "the deep rooted common law tradition of judicial hostility to legislation" see J. STONE, 198.

[19] The source of this statement could not be located. The English term "joint business" is used in the German text.

In Germany this type of legal profession with a clearly defined status or guild organization did not exist; for a long time it was not even necessary for a litigant to be represented by a lawyer. In France the situation was similar. It is true that the formalism of the procedure before the popular tribunals had necessitated the use of a prolocutor, and the regulation of their duties had become universally necessary; the earliest such regulation was promulgated in Bavaria in 1330. But the separation of the counsel from the attorney was achieved in Germany quite early, as the result essentially of the spread of Roman law.[20] The requirement of special legal training established itself relatively late and was usually caused by complaints of the estates at a time when the Roman-law oriented university education already determined the standard of the upper-class legal practitioners.[21] A powerful guild organization was prevented from arising because of the decentralization of the administration of justice. Thus the status of the lawyers was determined by governmental regulation rather than by professional autonomy.[22]

2. Modern legal education in the universities represents the purest type of the second way of legal training. Where only law-school graduates are admitted to legal practice, the universities enjoy a monopoly of legal education.[23] At the present time it is supplemented by apprenticeship in legal practice and a subsequent examination. The Hanseatic cities were the only places in Germany where the academic degree alone was sufficient for admission to the bar, but even there the requirement of apprenticeship has recently been introduced.[24]

The legal concepts produced by academic law teaching bear the character of abstract norms, which, at least in principle, are formed and

[20] Cf. Brunner, *Die Zulässigkeit der Anwaltschaft* 324.

[21] Concerning Roman-law oriented legal education, see P. Koschaker, Europa und das Römische Recht (1947) 45 *et seq.*, 55–99, and literature there cited.

[22] See Koschaker, *loc. cit.* 94 *et seq.* and literature there cited; for the social position of lawyers in Rome, France, England, Germany, and the difference between them, see pp. 164–180, 227–234. There never was a lawyers' guild organization in Germany, *ibid.* pp. 230, 247.

[23] Night schools or other law schools outside of universities and of the atmosphere of the *universitas literarum* are unknown in continental Europe and are thus not considered by Weber.

[24] Legal education, as it has became established in the nineteenth century in Germany and Austria (-Hungary) and as it still exists there, consists of two parts, viz., theoretical study of three to four years at a university, and a practical in-service training of usually another three years in various courts and administrative agencies, the office of the public prosecutor and an attorney's office. Cf. Rheinstein, *Law Faculties and Law Schools*, [1938] Wis. L. Rev. 5; cf. also E. Schweinburg, Law Training in Continental Europe (1945) 32, 80.

distinguished from one another by a rigorously formal and rational logical interpretation of meaning. Their rational, systematic character as well as their relatively small degree of concreteness of content easily result in a far-reaching emancipation of legal thinking from the everyday needs of the public. The force of the purely logical legal doctrines let loose, and a legal practice dominated by it, can considerably reduce the role played by considerations of practical needs in the formation of the law. It took some effort, for instance, to prevent the incorporation into the German Civil Code of the principle that a lease is terminated by the sale of the land.[25] That principle had been quite adequate to the distribution of social power in antiquity. However, the plan of taking it over into the new Code was entirely due to a blind desire for logical consistency.

A peculiar special type of rational, though not juristically formal, legal education is presented in its purest form in the legal teaching in seminaries for the priesthood or in law schools connected with such seminaries. Some of its peculiarities are due to the fact that the priestly approach to the law aims at a material, rather than formal, rationalization of the law. This point will be discussed at a later stage; [26] at this place we shall only deal with those results which are produced by certain general characteristics of this type of legal education. The legal teaching in such schools, which generally rests on either a sacred book or a sacred law fixed by a stable oral or literary tradition, possesses a rational character in a very special sense. Its rational character consists in its predilection for the construction of a purely theoretical casuistry oriented less to the practical needs of the groups concerned than to the needs of the uninhibited intellectualism of scholars.[27] Where the "dialectical" method is applied it may also create abstract concepts and thus approximate rational, systematic legal doctrine. But like all priestly wisdom, this type of legal education is bound by tradition. Its casuistry, inasmuch as it serves at all practical rather than intellectual needs, is formalistic in the special sense that it must maintain, through re-interpretation, the practical applicability of the traditional, unchangeable norms to changing needs. But it is not formalistic in the sense that it would create a rational system of law. As a rule it also carries with it elements which

[25] See now Secs. 571, 581, 2 of the Civil Code; as to the rule of Roman law, under which a lease is a purely personal contract between lessor and lessee and where, consequently, the lessee has no right to remain on the land as against the purchaser from the lessor, see SOHM, INSTITUTIONEN 434; but see also BUCKLAND 499.

[26] *Infra*, c. VIII.

[27] Cf. WEBER, ESSAYS 351; W.U.G., c. IV, p. 253.

represent only idealistic religious or ethical demands on human beings or on the legal order, but which involve no logical systematization of an actually obtaining legal order.

The situation is similar in the case of law schools which, while not, or not entirely, under immediate priestly control, are yet bound to a sacred law.

In their purely external form, all "sacred" laws tend to approximate a type which is shown most purely in Hindu law.[28] The commandments of such a sacred law are either, as in the "book religions," fixed by a scriptural revelation regarded as an inspired record, or they must be transmitted "authentically," i.e., by a closed chain of witnesses. In the "book religions," the authentic interpretation of the sacred norm, as well as its supplementation, must also be guaranteed in this way. The tradition must have passed by word of mouth directly from one reliable holy man to the next. This is one of the most important reasons why Hindu law, in common with Islamic law,[29] has rejected the purely scriptural tradition. Reliance on the written word would mean that one believed more strongly in parchment and ink than in the prophets and the teacher, i.e., those persons who are charismatically qualified.[30] The fact that the Koran itself was a written work, whose chapters (*Suras*) were believed to be promulgated by Mohammed, after consultation with Allah, in carefully written form, was explained in Islamic teaching by the dogma of the physical creation by Allah himself of the individual copies of the Koran. For the hadiths [31] orality was a condition of valid-

[28] On Hindu law see S. Vesey Fitzgerald, *Hindu Law*, 9 ENCYC. SOC. SCI. 261, and literature stated there; see furthermore *infra*, c. VIII, n. 31. For an account of early "legal" education in India, see MAINE, EARLY LAW 13.

[29] In his ESSAYS ON SOCIOLOGY OF RELIGION Weber has not included one on Islam; he has considered it, however, in his chapter on Sociology of Religion in W.U.G. (c. IV). As the principal sources on Islamic law he seems to have used GOLDZIHER'S VORLESUNGEN ÜBER DEN ISLAM (1910, 2nd ed. 1925), the pertinent chapter in KOHLER AND WENGER, 82 *et seq*., and the further literature listed there on p. 152, especially the several articles of Josef Kohler's in his ZEITSCHRIFT FÜR VERGLEICHENDE RECHTSWISSENSCHAFT. For additional literature on Islamic law see the following works by J. Schacht: his articles in the ENCYCLOPAEDIA OF ISLAM (1927); his edition of G. BERGSTRAESSER'S GRUNDZÜGE DES ISLAMISCHEN RECHTS (1935); *Islamic Law*, 8 ENCYC. SOC. SCI. 344, with bibliography at p. 349; and ORIGIN OF MOHAMMEDAN LAW (1951). Books and articles on Mohammedan law in the English language are listed in Stern's bibliography (1950) 43 LAW LIBRARY J. 16; cf. also G. v. GRÜNEBAUM, MEDIEVAL ISLAM (1946).

[30] On charisma, see *infra*, p. 236.

[31] *Hadiths* — traditions concerning the exemplary deeds of the Prophet and his companions, and those sayings of the former which have not been incorporated in the Koran. They make up the *sunna,* which is regarded as authoritative by the

ity. It has only been at a later stage that a scriptural text will come to be preferred, viz., when the unity of traditional interpretation is endangered by purely oral transmission. At this stage new revelations are then rejected, typically with the argument that the charismatic age has long since come to an end. In such situations great emphasis is laid upon the proposition which is basic to the "institutional" character of a religious community and which has well been formulated recently by Freiherr von Hertling,[32] namely, that it is not the holy writ which guarantees the truth of the tradition and of ecclesiastical doctrine but rather the holiness of the church and its tradition, to which God has given the truth in trust and which thus guarantees the genuineness of the holy writ. This position is consistent and practical: the opposite principle, as it was held by the early Protestants, exposes the sacred writ to philological and historical criticism.

The Vedas are the sacred books of Hinduism. They contain little "law," even less than the Koran or the Torah. The Vedas were considered as *srufi* ("revelations"), while all derived sacred sources were viewed as *smeti* ("recollection" or tradition). The most important categories of secondary literature, the prose Dharma-Sutras and the versified Dharma-Sastras [33] (the last ranking entirely as *smeti,* while the former occupy a middle position), are, on the contrary, compendia of dogmatics, ethics, and legal teaching standing alongside the tradition of the exemplary lives and teachings of holy men. The Islamic hadiths correspond exactly to this latter source; they are traditions concerning the exemplary deeds

---

Sunnite branch of Mohammedanism, but rejected by the Shiites. When the *hadiths* were assembled in collections, only those were accepted as authoritative which could be traced through the "golden chain" of men regarded as completely reliable. On the role played in the formation and development of Islamic law by the "invention" of appropriate "traditions," see J. SCHACHT, ORIGINS OF MOHAMMEDAN LAW (1951).

[32] Georg Freiherr v. Hertling, 1843–1919, Catholic philosopher and German statesman.

[33] Dharma-Sutras "are the oldest manifestation of definite schools of law, or rather they embody (in the form of mnemonic aphorisms) the law teaching given in particular Vedic schools. With one exception, which professes to emanate from a god, each of them bears the name of some great sage of the [Vedic] period."—VESEY-FITZGERALD, *op. cit.* n. 28. They probably date from the period between 600 and 300 B.C.

The statement that according to prevailing Hindu theory all law is contained in the Dharma-Sutras is tenable only when the term is used in so broad a sense as to include the *arthasastras* and those law books of the institute-type which are known under the names of *Manu* and *Yajñavalkya.* The latter occupy a prominent position in the works of those later commentators which have become important for the development of modern Hindu law.

of the prophet and his companions, and those sayings of the former which have not been incorporated into the Koran. The difference is that in Islam the prophetic age is regarded as having ended with the prophet.

For the Hindu Dharma books one can find a counterpart neither in Islam, which is a book religion with only one holy writ, nor in Judaism or Christianity. The Dharma books, and especially one of the latest, viz, that of Manu, were important for a long time in the courts as "books of authority," i.e., private works of legal scholars, until they were displaced in legal practice by the systematic compilations and commentaries of the schools. This displacement was so complete that by the time of the British conquest legal practice was dominated by one such tertiary source, the Mihaksana, dating from the eleventh century. A similar fate befell the Islamic Sunna through those systematic compendia and commentaries which achieved canonical status. The same is also true, though to a somewhat lesser extent, of the Torah in relationship to the rabbinical works of Antiquity (the Talmud) and the Middle Ages. Rabbinical lawmaking in Antiquity, and, to a certain extent, even up to the present, and Islamic lawmaking in a great measure even today, have rested in the hands of the theologian jurists responding to concrete questions. This feature was unknown both to Hinduism and to the Christian Churches, at least after the extinction of charismatic prophecy and the Didaskalia, which were, however, of an ethical rather than a legal character.[34]

The reasons why Christianity and Hinduism did not have this type of lawmaking were quite different. In Hindu law, the house priest of the king is a member of his court, and he atones by fasting for erroneous judgments. All important cases have to come before the king's court. The unity of the secular and the religious administration of justice is thus guaranteed, and there is, therefore, no place for any licensed class of responding legal honoratiores. The Occidental Christian Church, on the other hand, had created for itself organs of rational lawmaking in the Councils, the bureaucracies of the dioceses, and the Holy See, and, quite particularly, in the papal powers of jurisdiction and infallible exposition of doctrine. No other of the great religions has ever possessed such institutions. Thus in Occidental Christianity, the legal opinions and decrees of the ecclesiastical authorities, together with the Conciliar

[34] Didaskalia (Greek: Teaching, Doctrine) — the unfolding of the teaching of Jesus in the pneumatic-charismatic manner of the earliest Christian communities, i.e., before its fixation in authoritative writings, such as the *Didache of the Apostles* and the channelization of Christian life in organized congregations. Cf. SOHM, KIRCHENRECHT 38, 41.

Canons and the papal decretals, have played the role which is played in Islam by the fetwa of the mufti, and in Judaism by the opinions of the rabbis.[35] Hindu legal erudition was to a great extent purely scholastic, theoretical, and systematizing; it was the work of philosophers and theorists and strikingly possessed those features of a socially bound, theoretical, and systematizing legal thinking which has little contact with legal practice. In all these respects it differs from Canon law. All typically "holy" laws, and thus quite particularly that of India, are products of the schools. The treatises always present an abundance of casuistry about completely obsolete institutions. Examples are provided by Manu's treatment of the four castes, or the presentation of all the obsolete parts of the Sharia [36] in the works of the Islamic schools.[37] But because of an overriding dogmatic objective and the rational nature of priestly thinking, the systematic structure of such law books frequently tends to be more rational than that of similar creations unconnected with priesthood. The Hindu law books, for example, are more systematic than the *Mirror of Saxon Law*. But the systematization is not a legal one but one concerned with the position of social classes and the practical problems of life. Since the law is to serve holy ends, these law books are therefore compendia not of law alone but also of ritual, ethics, and, occasionally, of social convention and etiquette. The consequence is a casuistic treatment of the legal data that lacks definiteness and concreteness, thus remaining juridically informal and but moderately rational in its systematization. For in all these cases, the driving force is neither the practicing lawyer's businesslike concern with concrete data and needs, nor the logical ambitions of the jurisprudential doctrinaire only interested in the demands of dogmatic logic, but is rather a set of those substantive ends and aims which are foreign to the law as such.

3. The effects of legal training are bound to be different again where it is in the hands of honoratiores whose relations with legal practice are professional but not, like those of English lawyers, specifically guildlike or income-oriented. The existence of such a special class of honoratiores is, generally speaking, possible only where legal practice is not sacredly dominated and legal practice has not yet become too involved with the needs of urban commerce. The medieval empirical jurists of the Northern European continent fall into this class. It is, of course, true that where commercial activity is intense the function of the legal

[35] *Fetwa* — opinion of the theologian-legal scholar, the mufti. Cf. also c. VIII, n. 57.

[36] *Sharia* — the totality of Allah's rules for the conduct of man.

[37] On the Islamic schools, see *supra*, p. 142. Cf. also *infra*, p. 239.

honoratiores is merely shifted from the consultants to the cautelary jurists; [38] and even this shift occurs under special conditions only. After the decline of the Roman Empire, the *notaries* were the only remaining group in Italy by whom the traditions of a developed commercial law could be perpetuated and transformed.[39] They were, for a long time, the specific and dominant class of legal honoratiores. In the rapidly growing cities they formed themselves into guilds and constituted an important segment of the *popolo grasso,* which was a politically important class of honoratiores.[40] Indeed, mercantile relations operated here from the very beginning through notarial documents. The procedural codes of the cities, such as Venice, preferred the rationality of documentary evidence to the irrational means of evidence of the ancient procedure of the popular courts. We have already spoken of the notaries' influence upon the development of commercial paper, but the notaries were one of the most decisive pioneers in the development of the law in general, and until the emergence of the class of legally trained judges in Italy they were probably the most decisive stratum. Like their forerunners in the ancient Hellenic East, they took a decisive part in the interlocal assimilation of the law and, above all, in the reception of Roman law, which, both in Italy and Greece, was first brought about in the documentary practice. Their own traditions, their long-lasting connection with the imperial courts, the necessity of quickly having on hand a rational law to meet the needs of the rapidly growing requirements of trade, and the social power of the great universities caused the Italian notaries to receive Roman law as the very law of commerce, especially since, in contrast to England, no corporate or fee interests were standing in the way. Thus the Italian notaries were not only the oldest but also one of

[38] Cautelary jurists — see *supra*, p. 72.

[39] In contrast to the *notary public* of the American type, whose primary function is that of authenticating signatures and thus creating official evidence of genuineness, the continental notary is also a specialist in legal drafting, especially of real estate conveyances, but also of important commercial documents. He is thus not only a lawyer but a lawyer of special training and competence. See Deák, *Notaries Public*, 11 ENCYC. SOC. SCI. 399, and literature cited there; also CALASSO, STORIA E SISTEMA DELLE FONTI DEL DIRITTO COMUNE (1938) I, 212, and (1934) III ARCHIVIO GIURIDICO 64. Savigny has fixed the collegium of the notaries in Bologna to the middle of the thirteenth century; cf. GESCHICHTE DES RÖMISCHEN RECHTS IM MITTELALTER 540; see also GOLDSCHMIDT 151–153.

[40] On the *popolo grasso*, see W.U.G. 587; "The State created a new nobility. It was in the period of the mediaeval communes that this class made its appearance, arising out of the 'borghesia grassa' or rich bourgeoisie, who had obtained a position of importance through commerce or participation in the government of the city, especially in time of war." — CALISSE, *op. cit.* 160.

the most important of the classes of legal honoratiores who were interested and directly participated in the creation of the usus modernus of Roman law. Unlike the English lawyers, they did not act as the bearers of a national body of law. Again, they could not compete with the universities through a guild system of legal education of their own simply because, unlike the English lawyers, they did not enjoy that nation-wide organization which was made possible in England by the concentration of the administration of justice in the royal courts. But thanks to the universities, Roman Law in Italy continued as a world force, influencing the formal structure of law and legal education even after its original political sponsor and interested protector, the Emperor,. had become politically unimportant. The *podestàs* [41] of the Italian cities were often chosen from among the honoratiores who had been trained in the universities; the Signorie [42] based themselves completely on the political doctrines which were obtained from them. In the cities of the French and Eastern Spanish coasts the notaries' position was quite the same.[43] Essentially different, however, was the status of the honoratiores in Germany and Northern France. They were, at least at first, involved less in urban legal relations than as aldermen (*Schöffen*) or officials in the legal affairs and the administration of justice of rural manors.[44] Their most influential types, such as for example, Eike von Repgow or Beaumanoir,[45] created a systematization of the law which was based

[41] The *podestà* were the magistrates of the free Italian cities; nearly always chosen from foreign honoratiores, that they might keep aloof from and yet dominate the turbulent movements within the city. In their hands was the judicial power, the police, and, partly, the administration. The foreign *podestà* brought with them a whole staff of foreign employees, among them also notaries, e.g., in Florence, 1287, the Podestà Petrus Stefani came with his staff of seven *iudices*, eighteen notaries, and twenty *beroarii*; in 1316 in Parma the Podestà brought with him two *iudices*, two knights, two notaries, and twenty soldiers, etc. Cf. ENGELMANN 59; also WEBER, W.U.G. 548; CALISSE, *op. cit.* 143, 169, 180.

[42] *Signoria* (Ital.) — (aristocratic) city council.

[43] Cf. Stouff (1887) 11 NOUVELLE REVUE HISTORIQUE 269; GOLDSCHMIDT, 200 and literature there cited; also p. 230 (n. 159); p. 153 (n. 32). On the notaries in France compare the dissertation of A. COPPIN, LES ORIGINES DU NOTARIAT FRANÇAIS (1884, Académie de Douai).

[44] See: for France, KOSCHAKER EUROPA U. DAS RÖM. RECHT 221 and literature there cited; for Germany, BRUNNER I, 209, II, 296 *et seq.*; see also the recent article of G. Schubart-Kikentscher, *Römisches Recht im Brünner Schöffenbuch* (1947), 65 SAV. Z. GERM. 86; see in general Engelmann and Millar 98 *et seq.*, 114 *et seq.*, 114 *et seq.*, 199, 519.

[45] EIKE VON REPGOW (c. 1180–c. 1250) is the author of SACHSENSPIEGEL (MIRROR OF SAXON LAW, 1224–1230); cf. v. Künssberg, 13 ENCYC. SOC. SCI. 308; E. WOLF, GROSSE RECHTSDENKER (1939) 1; PHILIPPE DE BEAUMANOIR (c. 1246–1296) is the

on the concrete problems of everyday practice and their essentially empirical concepts, slightly refined by abstraction. The "law books" which they compiled aimed at the restatement of the existing tradition; although they contained some occasional argumentation, they had little specifically juridical *ratio.* Indeed, the most important of these works, the *Mirror of Saxon Law,* contained a good many constructions of legal institutions which were not parts of the existing law at all but rather constituted fanciful attempts, inspired by the author's desire for completeness or his predilection for sacred numbers, to fill in gaps or complement other inadequacies.[46] Formally, their systematic records were private works just like those of the Hindu, Roman, and Islamic jurists. Like these, they have influenced legal practice considerably as convenient compendia and some of them even came to be recognized by the courts as authoritative source books. Their creators were representatives of a system of administration of justice by honoratiores but, unlike the English lawyers and the Italian notaries, they did not constitute a strong organized guild which, by corporate and economic interests, through a monopoly of the bench and a central position at the seat of the central courts, could have given them a measure of power which neither King nor Parliament could have easily brushed aside. Hence they could not, like the English lawyers, become the bearers of a corporate legal education and were thus unable to produce a fixed empirical tradition and a legal development that could have provided an enduring resistance against the subsequent encroachment of the jurists trained by rational university education. Formally, the law of the empirical law books of the Middle Ages was fairly well organized; systematically and casuistically, however, it was less rational, and oriented more towards concrete techniques of distinction than towards the abstract interpretation of meaning or legal logic.

The particular influence of the ancient Roman jurists[47] rested on the fact that the Roman system of administration of justice by honoratiores made only sparing use of special officials and thus minimized their interference in the concrete conduct of a lawsuit. But this specific fact

---

author of COUTUMES DE BEAUVAISIS (1283), the most influential of the medieval law treatises of France; cf. Meynial, 2 ENCYC. SOC. SCI. 486.

[46] See the introduction to the SACHSENSPIEGEL by Homeyer in his 3rd ed. (1861) 20, 105; E. Molitor, *Der Gedankengang des Sachsenspiegels* (1947), 65 SAV. Z. GERM. 15, and the most recent literature there cited.

[47] On the Roman jurists see JOLOWICZ, 88, 380; H. J. WOLFF, ROMAN LAW (1951) 91; and, particularly, F. SCHULZ, HISTORY, and W. KUNKEL, HERKUNFT UND SOZIALE STELLUNG DER RÖMISCHEN JURISTEN (1952).

which distinguished Rome from, for instance, the Hellenic democracy also excluded the "Khadi justice" [48] of the kind of the Attic people's courts. The official presidency over the course of the lawsuit was preserved together with the separation of power between the magistrate and the judgment finders. The combination of these factors created the specifically Roman practice of trial instruction (*Prozessinstruction*) through a strictly formal order of the magistrate to the citizen judge (the *judex*), giving him directions with regard to those issues of law and fact according to which he should grant or deny the plaintiff's claim.[49]

The magistrate, especially the *aedlis* and *praetor,* began to record the schemata of these trial instructions in his "edict" [50] at the beginning of his year of office. It was, however, only relatively late that, in contrast with the Nordic "*Lag saga*" [51] he was regarded as being bound by the content of these "edicts." Naturally, in composing his edict the magistrate was advised by legal practitioners, and the edicts were thus continuously adapted to newly emerging needs. In the main, however, each magistrate simply took over the edict of his predecessor in office. Hence, the great majority of the recognized causes of action had naturally to be defined not in terms of concrete facts, but by the legal concepts of everyday language. The use of a juridically inappropriate formula by the party having to choose the appropriate action thus resulted in the loss of the case. This contrasts with our principle of fact pleading, under which a presentation of facts will support an action if the facts justify the claim from some legal point of view. Obviously under the "principle" of "fact pleading" no such sharp legal definition of concepts is required as was the case under Roman law where the practitioner was forced to define the legal terms of common usage with juristic rigor and to elaborate sharp distinctions between them.[52] Even where the instructing magistrate confined his trial instruction to purely factual matters,

[48] *Khadi* — judge of the Mohammedan *sharia* court (see *supra*, n. 36), *khadi* justice (*Kadijustiz*) — used by Weber as a term of art to describe the administration of justice which is oriented not at fixed rules of a formally rational law but at the ethical, religious, political, or otherwise expediential postulates of a substantively rational law. See *infra*, chapter X; also THEORY 390 (where the word *khadi* is left out); W.U.G. 717; see also *infra*, pp. 317, 351; for additional references to Weber's use of Khadi justice see ESSAYS 216.

[49] *Supra* p. 94; also Millar, *Procedure, Legal*, 12 ENCYC. SOC. SCI. 439, 440.

[50] On the edict, see JOLOWICZ 95, 362; H. J. WOLFF, *op. cit.* 81.

[51] See *supra*, pp. 78, 87.

[52] The contrast corresponds to that between Common Law pleading and Code pleading, as it is known in American law. Cf. CLARK, *op. cit.* 5; Millar, *Procedure, Legal*, 12 ENCYC. SOC. SCI. 439, 446/447.

as he did in the *actiones in factum conceptae*,[53] the interpretation assumed a strictly formal character, as a result of the then accepted methods of legal thinking. In this state of affairs, the practical development of legal technique was at first largely left to "cautelary jurisprudence," i.e., to the activities of legal counselors who not only drafted the form of contracts for the parties but were also expert advisers to the magistrate in his "consilium," a consultation that was typical for all Roman officials in the preparation of their edicts and formulae. Finally, they were legal advisers of the citizen judge when he had to decide the questions put to him by the magistrate and to interpret his trial instructions.

According to historical tradition, the consultative activities of the jurisconsults seem first to have been carried out by the *pontifices*, of whom one was chosen annually for this purpose. Under this priestly influence the administration of justice, in spite of the codification of the Twelve Tables, might easily have assumed a sacrally bound and irrational character, similar to that produced in Mohammedan law by the consultative activity of the mufti. It is true that religious influences seem to have played only a secondary role in the substantive content of early Roman law, but in its purely formal aspects, which are also its most important aspects from a general historical point of view, the influence of sacred law was obviously considerable, as Demelius has made plausibe for at least certain important instances.[54] For example, such important legal techniques as procedural fictions seem to have arisen under the influence of the principle of sacred law that *simulata pro veris accipiuntur*.[55] We may recall the role played in the cult of the dead of many peoples by the simulated transaction [56] and also the role which the simulated transaction had to play in situations in which certain ritual obligations were formally fixed in an absolute fashion. It was the repugnance to an essentially bourgeois society of such simu-

[53] The *formula* used is one *in factum concepta*, when there is no reference to a civil law concept but the judge is simply told to condemn, if he finds certain *facts* described in the *intentio* to be true or, if not true, to absolve. Cf. JOLOWICZ 212–213; WENGER 162, 164.

[54] Gustav Demelius, Professor in Bonn. (SCHIEDSEID UND BEWEISEID IM RÖMISCHEN CIVILPROZESS [1887]); see review in 8 SAV. Z. ROM. 269, by O. Gradenwitz. On the problem of the extent to which sacred law was of influence in the development of (secular) Roman law, see *infra*, pp. 225, 233.

[55] *Simulata pro veris accipiuntur* ("the simulated transaction is regarded as the real [true] one"; SERVIUS AD AENEAM II, 116). This meant that instead of animals only their forms, modeled in bread or wax, had to be sacrificed. For other examples see JHERING I, 326.

[56] The cult of the dead and the evolution from preanimistic naturalism to symbolism is discussed by Weber in W.U.G. 229–232.

lated performances, which were also economically highly burdensome, which led to their replacement by a mere *pro forma* performance.[57] The substantive secularization of Roman life, combined with the political impotence of the priesthood, turned the latter into an instrument for the purely formalistic and legalistic treatment of religious matters. Furthermore, the early development of the technique of cautelary jurisprudence in temporal matters resulted in an obvious furtherance of the use of this technique in the sphere of the cult. But we may assume with confidence that the earliest techniques of cautelary jurisprudencce were at first largely concerned with sacred law.

One of the most important characteristics of early Roman law was its highly analytical nature; this at least is still valid among von Jhering's views, of which so many have become obsolete. A lawsuit would be reduced to the basic issues involved and legal transactions were cut down to the most elementary logical constituents: one lawsuit for just one issue; one legal transaction for just one object; one promise for just one performance.[58] The breaking up of the complex situations of life into specifically determined elements has been the main achievement of the early *ius civile*, the methodological effects of which have also been the most far-reaching. On the other hand, there has resulted from it a certain neglect of the constructive synthetic capacity in the perception of concrete legal institutions, as it arises in the case of a legal imagination unconfined by logical analysis. This analytical tendency, however, corresponds closely to the treatment of ritual obligations in the Roman national religion. We may recall that the peculiarity of the genuine Roman *religio*, namely, the conceptual, abstract, and thoroughly analytical distinction of the jurisdictions of the sacred *numina*,[59] resulted in a large measure in a rational juridical treatment of religious problems. According to tradition, the pontifices had already invented fixed schemata of admissible actions. This pontifical legal technique seems to have remained a professionally monopolized secret knowledge. The emancipation from sacral lawfinding came only in the third century. When the Censor Appius Claudius was trying to establish himself as a tyrant, one of his freedmen is said to have published the pontifical

[57] For example, the ritual of burying with the dead all their personal belongings was economically highly burdensome; the ritual was therefore replaced by the burial of [worthless] paper money. The deceased is satisfied with symbols instead of realities. "The first use of paper-money was to pay not the living, but the dead." — WEBER, W.U.G. 230.

[58] JHERING III, 27 *et seq.*

[59] *Numina* — deities.

formulary of actions.[60] The first plebeian Pontifex Maximus, Tiberius Coruncanius, is reported to have been the first to render *responsa* in public.[61] It was only from that stage that the edicts of the officials could develop to their later significance and that lay honoratiores came to fill the gap as legal consultants and attorneys. The opinion of counsel was communicated orally to private parties and in writing to the official who had requested it. Until the period of the Empire the opinion did not include any statement of reasons, resembling in this respect the oracle of the charismatic lag saga or the *fetwa* of the mufti. The expansion of professional juristic activity in step with increasing demand brought about a formal legal education as early as during the Republic, when students (*auditores*) were admitted to the consultations of the legal practitioners.

Another cause of the assumption by early Roman law of a highly formal and rational character, both regarding the substantive rules and their procedural treatment, was the growing involvement of the law in urban business activities as carried on through contracts.[62] In this respect, medieval German law presents a rather different picture, for its main concern related to such matters as social rank, property in land, or family law and inheritance.

But in spite of its formalism, Roman legal life, until well into the time of the Caesars, lacked not only a synthetic-constructive but also a rational-systematic character, and it did so much more than has at times been assumed. It was the Byzantine bureaucracy which finally systematized the existing law; but as far as the formal rigor of juridical thought was concerned, it stood far behind the achievements of the jurisconsults of the Republic and the Principate. It is strikingly significant that the systematically most useful among all the literary products of the jurisconsults, namely the Institutes of Gaius, which was an introductory compendium to the study of law, was the work of an unknown person who was certainly not an authority in his own lifetime and who stood outside the circle of the legal honoratiores; one may say that Gaius' relation to them was analogous to the relation of the modern cram book to the learned treatises of the scholars. But the difference was that the literary products of the practicing Roman jurists of that time, to whose circle Gaius did not belong, did not possess the quality of a rational

[60] C. 300 B.C.; cf. F. SCHULZ, HISTORY 9.

[61] Ti. Coruncanius was consul in 280 B.C. and is reported to have been the first to render *responsa* in public by Pomponius, in D. 1, 2, 2, 35: *Primus publice profiteri coepit*; cf. SCHULZ 10.

[62] These urban business activities are discussed by Weber in W.u.G. 514.

system, such as university teaching tends to produce; they were mainly moderately rationally organized collections of individual opinions.[63]

The jurisconsults remained a very specific class of honoratiores. To the property-owning strata of Rome they were the universal "fathers confessor"[64] in all economic matters. It is uncertain whether a formal license to render *responsa* was necessary in earlier times, as a passage in Cicero might lead us to suppose.[65] Certainly, it was not required at a later date. The *responsa*-rendering jurists emancipated themselves from the methods of the older cautelary jurisprudence, as well as the actual practice of draftsmanship, as their legal refinement increased. By the end of the Republic they formed themselves into schools. It is true that during the Republic the orators, such as Cicero, tended to argue emotionally and "ad hominem" rather than rationally, since the specifically political assize courts came close to assuming the character of popular justice. In this way, the orators contributed to the weakening of precise legal conceptualization; but in Rome this happened almost exclusively in political cases. Under the Empire, the administration of justice became entirely a specialized professional matter. A part of the jurisconsults were placed in an official status vis-à-vis the administration of justice by Augustus' grant of the privilege making their *responsa* binding on the judges.[66] The jurisconsults ceased to be attorneys (*causidici*); even less could they form a lawyers' guild whose interests and intellectual training would have been directed to daily practice and the needs of clients. The jurisconsults had nothing to do with the technical or business aspects of attorneyship but were concerned exclusively with the rendering of legal opinions about statements of fact which had been prepared by an attorney or a judge.[67] They were thus in the best possible position to elaborate a rigorously abstract scheme of juristic concepts. In this way the responding jurisconsults were sufficiently remote from the actual contact of legal business to allow them to reduce individual details to general principles by employing scientific tech-

[63] See BUCKLAND 22. On Gaius *ibid.* 29 and SCHULZ, HISTORY 159; JÖRS AND KUNKEL 33; De Zulueta, *Reflexions on Gaius* [1947], TULANE L. REV. 173.

[64] JHERING II, 440.

[65] CICERO, IN VERREM 4.9.20.

[66] "No juristic text suggests that Augustus made responsa binding. It is clear that a change in the position of the jurists did occur under Hadrian." BUCKLAND, TEXTBOOK 23. For recent literature on this famous controversy concerning the nature and origin of the *ius respondendi* see KOSCHAKER EUROPA U. DAS RÖM. RECHT 962; Siber, *Der Ausgangspunkt des ius respondendi* (1941), 61 SAV. Z. ROM. 397; Kunkel, *Das Wesen des ius respondendi* (1948), 66 SAV. Z. ROM. 423.

[67] On the distinction between the jurisconsults and the attorney, see JHERING II, 436; BUCKLAND 22.

niques. This remoteness was greater in Rome than it was in England, where the lawyer was always the representative of a client. It was, however, the controversies between the schools which forced these principles into even greater abstraction.[68] While, because of the binding character of their opinions, jurisconsults dominated the administration of justice, the responsa continued, however, at least for a time, to be rendered without a statement of reasons, like the Sage's oracle or the mufti's fetwa. But they began to be collected by the jurists and then to be published with comments indicating the legal reasons.[69] School discussions and disputations about legal cases among and with the auditores grew out of the latters' presence in the exercise of the consultative practice, but only by the end of the Republic did there develop a fixed course of training.[70] Just as the steadily increasing formal study of Hellenic philosophy took on a certain significance for juristic thought, so the Hellenic philosophical schools served, in many respects, as models for the external organization of the schools for lawyers. It was from this pedagogical and publishing activity of the law schools that the technique of Roman law developed from a stage when it was strongly empirical, despite the precision of its concepts, to increasing rationality of operation and scientific sublimation. But theoretical legal training remained secondary to legal practice and this fact explains how a slight degree of development of abstract legal concepts could go hand in hand with a high degree of abstraction in legal thinking, wherever the abstract legal concepts served essentially theoretical interests rather than practical requirements. The treatment of numerous, and apparently heterogeneous, fact situations under the one category of *locatio*, for instance, had no important practical consequences.[71] At least no direct, practical consequences can arise from the elaboration of the concept of "legal transaction," which is intended to serve a mere desire for intellectual organization. Thus neither this concept nor similar ones, like "claim" or "disposition," existed in Roman law of antiquity, and even

[68] On the two "schools" of Proculians and Sabinians, their significance, and alleged controversies, see BUCKLAND 27; SCHULZ, HISTORY 119; JÖRS AND KUNKEL 32, 394.

[69] On this literature, see now esp. SCHULZ, HISTORY 91, 173, 223.

[70] See KOHLER AND WENGER 172; JOLOWICZ 469; SCHULZ, HISTORY 119.

[71] The one concept of *locatio-conductio* ("lease"), as derived from the *actiones locati* and *conducti*, covered (1) the *locatio-conductio rei*, i.e., the lease of a piece of land or a chattel; (2) the *locatio-conductio operarum*, i.e., the contract for services, in which the worker was said to let his working power; and (3) the *locatio-conductio operis*, in which the opportunity to construct a building or to complete some other work, e.g., to make a suit of cloth, is let to an independent contractor.

in the time of Justinian its general systematization was not rationalized beyond a relatively modest degree. The sublimation of concepts took place almost exclusively in connection with some concrete type of contract or form of action.[72]

Two reasons are responsible for the fact that this sublimation nevertheless led to those results which we have before us now. Decisive was, first, the complete secularization of the administration of justice, including the office of jurisconsult. The binding *responsum* of the Roman jurist has a perfect parallel in the *fetwa* of the Islamic mufti. He too is an officially licensed legal consultant. But he receives his training in an Islamic school. These schools, to be sure, developed upon the pattern of the officially recognized law schools of the late Roman empire. Under the influence of the formal training through ancient philosophy, they also developed, for certain times at least, methods similar to those of antiquity. But their instruction remained predominantly theological, and the trends just mentioned were thwarted by the fixation of the sacred law through tradition and creed, by its vagueness, by the precariousness of its status in actual practice, and by those other features which are characteristic of all theocratic justice bound to a sacred writ. Legal education thus remained limited there to empirical and mechanical memorization and theoretical casuistry without contact with life.

The second reason for the difference between Roman and Islamic law lies in the kind of judicial organization and in the politically conditioned limits which were set to rationalization in the economic field. The theological element was completely absent from Roman legal development. The purely secular and increasingly bureaucratic late Roman state culled that unique collection of the Pandects from the products of the responding jurisconsults and their disciples, whose legal thinking was of the utmost precision, however imperfect their "system" may have been. Supplemented by autonomous Byzantine ideas, the Roman materials thus collected in the Pandects provided the stuff for the legal thought of the medieval universities for centuries to come. Already earlier, viz., during the Empire, the increasingly abstract character of the legal concepts had been added as a new element to the age-old indigenous analytical quality of the Roman legal concepts. To some extent this abstract character had been anticipated by the nature of the formulae of the Roman forms of action. In every one of them the state of the operative facts was expressed in the form of a legal concept. Some of these concepts were so formulated, however, that they afforded

[72] Weber here follows JHERING II. See also now SCHULZ, PRINCIPLES 43; WIEACKER, VOM RÖMISCHEN RECHT 7; EHRLICH 195, 312.

the practitioners, be they cautelary jurists, attorneys, or jurisconsults, the opportunity to subsume an extraordinarily diverse range of life situations under one single concept. The adaptation to new economic needs thus took place in large measure through the rational interpretation and extension of old concepts. It was in this way that legal-logical and constructive thinking was raised to the highest level to which it can be raised within the range of the purely analytical method. Goldschmidt [73] has properly pointed out the extraordinary elasticity of such legal concepts as *locatio-conductio, emptio-venditio*, *mandatum* (and especially *actio quod iussu depositum*), and above all, the unlimited capacity of stipulatio as the one *constitutum* for most of those obligations to pay a sum certain for which we have today the bill of exchange and other formal contracts.[74]

The specific character of Roman legal logic, as it developed from the given conditions, becomes especially clear when one compares it with the modes of operation of English cautelary jurisprudence. It, too, utilized and manipulated numerous individual concepts with the greatest boldness in order to achieve actionability in the most diverse situations. But we can easily see the difference between the way in which, on the one hand, the Roman jurists used the concept of *iussum* to achieve both the drawee's authority to pay for the drawer and the latter's warranty [75] and, on the other hand, the ways in which the English lawyers derived the actionability of numerous heterogenous contracts from the tort

[73] UNIVERSALGESCHICHTE 78, 93; in general, 71–89, 331.

[74] *Locatio-conductio* — lease; see *supra* n. 71; *em[p]tio-venditio* — sale; *mandatum* — mandate, i.e., contract for unpaid services; if the services are to be paid for, the contract is one of *locatio-conductio operarum*.

Actio quod iussu [*depositum*] — originally, action against one who has given to his son or slave authority to make a contract with another; *stipulatio* — promise asked for and given in certain formalized words; see *supra* c. V, n. 38.

Constitutum — the term is used here in an untechnical sense apparently meaning the legal basis (*causa*) of an actionable promise; technically *constitutum debiti* means the formless promise to pay an already existing debt of the promisor or a third party; it became actionable in praetorian law by the *actio de pecunia constituta*, an *actio in factum*. See JÖRS AND KUNKEL 189.

[75] Cf. GOLDSCHMIDT 78, 93. It must be remembered, however, that the *actio quod iussu* was not generally available, but only where the person by whom the contract had been made was a *filius familias*, a slave, or otherwise a dependent of the defendant. Cf. BUCKLAND 531, according to whom the *actio quod iussu* was only of small importance. Weber's statement is based upon GOLDSCHMIDT 78, n. 93, who speaks of the "astonishingly broad category of the *mandatum* or *iussus*" (as exemplified by D. 17.1.2), of which he says that it sufficed for those modern transactions of which Weber speaks in the text. For the present state of learning concerning *mandatum* and *iussus*, see JÖRS AND KUNKEL 213, 267, 411, 415.

concept of "trespass."[76] In the latter case the most diverse phenomena are thrown together in order to obtain actionability by indirection. In the Roman instance, however, new situations which seem to be diverse economically, i.e., externally, are subsumed under a legal concept which is adequate to the result. It is true, however, that the abstract character of many legal concepts, which today are regarded as being particularly "Roman" in their origin, is not to be found originally, and in some cases, did not even originate, in Antiquity. The much discussed Roman concept of *dominium*, for example, is a product of the denationalization of Roman law and its transformation into world law. Property, in national Roman law, was by no means a particularly abstractly ordered institution, and it was not even a unitary one in general.[77] It was

[76] Cf. PLUCKNETT 601, and the literature there cited.

[77] The comprehensive Roman concept of ownership, *dominium*, stands in contrast with the Germanic laws, in which there has been lacking not only a common legal term covering full ownership in both land and chattels, but also a term indicating the fullness of rights to possession, utilization, and disposition of land. The various ways in which a person may derive benefits from land have been traditionally expressed in the complex set of tenures, estates, and future interests which has been characteristic of the Common Law. Only in recent times have the terms "fee" and, more recently, "title" assumed a meaning which comes near to that of the Roman *dominium*, which indicates the sum total of all rights and benefits which may be derived from a piece of land (as well as from a chattel). All rights of an objectively or temporally limited character are either, as the lease, regarded as mere personal claims against the owner or as rights in the thing of another (*iure in re aliena*), i.e., encumbrances, such as an estate for life (*usufructus*), a right of way or other easement (*servitus*), or a mortgage (*hypotheca*). As long as a particular thing is encumbered with such a right of another, the owner's *dominium* is accordingly limited, immediately to expand, however, to its fullness of unlimited freedom of possession, enjoyment, use, and disposal, as soon as the encumbrance is lifted. This concept of *dominium* must not be understood, however, in the sense that a Roman property owner would have been completely unlimited in his freedom to use or abuse his thing. At all times was he limited, especially as landowner, by police power regulations established in the public interest. The concept of *dominium* is only a mental tool to facilitate mental operations concerning property rights. Indirectly, it also tends, of course, to facilitate land transactions and thus to increase the security of land titles.

As Weber observes, the highly abstract concept of *dominium* has been the product of a long process of juridical elaboration. Similar to the Germanic and other laws, older Roman law, too, operated with a variety of concepts indicating the various kinds of a person's legally recognized relationship to a thing, especially a piece of land. In the *ius civile*, *res mancipi* (citizen's land in the proper sense, slaves, cattle, and certain agricultural implements) were treated differently from the *res nec mancipi*. Ownership *ex iure Quiritium* was not the same as the *in bonis habere* of the praetorian law or the various tenures in the administratively managed public lands (see *supra*, p. 150). The elaboration of the comprehensive concept of *dominium* was the work of the jurists. According to the presently prevailing opinion,

Justinian who first abolished the fundamental differences and reduced them to the few forms which were observable in land law; and it was only after the old procedural and social conditions of the praetorian interdicts had died out that medieval analysis could concern itself with the conceptual content of the two Pandectian institutions of *dominium* and *possessio* as wholly abstract concepts. Nor was the position essentially different with many other institutions. In their earlier form, in particular, most of the genuine Roman legal institutions were not essentially more abstract than those of German law. The peculiar form of the Pandects arose out of the peculiar transformations of the Roman state. The sublimation of juristic thinking was in itself, as far as its direction was concerned, influenced by political conditions which operated in different ways in the Republican and the later imperial times. The important technical traits of the earlier administration of justice and the jurisconsults were, as we have seen, essentially the products of rule by the Republican honoratiores. But this very rule was not entirely favorable to a professional juristic training of the political upper-class magistrates with their short terms of office. While the Twelve Tables had always been taught in the schools, knowledge of the *leges*, however, was acquired by the Roman republican magistrate mostly by practical experience. His jurisconsults looked after the rest for him. In contrast, the necessity of systematic juristic studies was greatly increased by the imperial system of legal administration through appointed officials and its rationalization and bureaucratization, especially in the provincial service. The general effect of all bureaucratization of authority will be seen later in a wider context.[78] The systematic rationalization of the law in England, for example, was retarded because no bureaucratization occurred there. As long as the jurisconsults dominated the Roman legal administration of justice as the legal honoratiores, the striving for systematization was feeble, and no codifying and systematizing intervention by the political authority occurred. The downfall of the Roman aristocracy under the Severi was correlated with the decline of the role of the responding jurisconsults and parallels a rapidly increasing significance of the imperial rescripts in the practice of the courts. Legal education, carried on in the later period in state-approved schools, assumed the form of textbook instruction from the works of the jurists. The courts, too, used them as authoritative sources and, in case of dissent

---

this mental process was essentially completed by the classical jurists. On the development see Jörs and Kunkel 120, and the extensive literature stated there and at p. 405; also Buckland 188, and Noyes 131.

[78] W.u.G. Part III, c. VI; [Essays 196].

among these books, the Emperors, by the so-called "Law of Citations," established both a certain order of priority among them and the principle that the majority of the approved authors should prevail.[79] The collections of responsa thus came to occupy the position held in the Common Law by the collection of precedents. This situation conditioned the peculiar form of the Pandects and the conservation of that part of classical juristic literature which had been incorporated in them.

[79] Law of Citations — There were several; the earliest was issued by Constantine in A.D. 321; the best known is that of 426, issued by Valentinian III and Theodosius II (CODEX THEODOSIANUS 1.4.3.). The courts were ordered to consider the works of a certain number of jurists; where the jurists differed, the judge was to follow the opinion of the majority or, in the case of a tie, that of Papinian.

CHAPTER VIII

FORMAL AND SUBSTANTIVE RATIONALIZATION IN THE LAW [1]

(SACRED LAWS)

1. The considerations of the last chapter raise the important problem, already touched upon in various places, of the influence of the form of political authority on the formal aspects of the law. A definitive analysis of this problem requires an analysis of the various types of authority which we shall not undertake until later. However, a few general remarks may be made at this point. The older forms of popular justice had originated in conciliatory proceedings between kinship-groups. The primitive formalistic irrationality of these older forms of justice was everywhere cast off under the impact of the authority of princes or magistrates,[2] or, in certain situations, of an organized priesthood. With this impact, the substance of the law, too, was lastingly influenced, although the character of this influence varied with the various types of authority. The more rational the authority exercising the administrative machinery of the princes or hierarchs became, that is, the greater the extent to which administrative "officials" were used in the exercise of the power, the greater was the likelihood that the legal procedure would also become rational [3] both in form and substance. To the extent to which the rationality of the organization of authority increased, irrational forms of procedure were eliminated and the substantive law was systematized, i.e., the law as a whole was rationalized. This process occurred, for instance, in antiquity in the *jus honorarium* and the praetorian remedies,[4] in the capitularies of the Frankish Kings,[5] in the procedural innovations of the English Kings and Lords Chancellor,[6] or in

[1] W.u.G. 468–482.

[2] Imperium, bannus. [Weber's note.]

[3] In a variety of senses. [Weber's note.]

[4] *Ius honorarium* — The law created by the praetor in addition to, or in modification of, the *ius civile* as contained in the formal *leges* or in ancient tradition.

[5] See *supra*, p. 56.

[6] Cf. PLUCKNETT, 82 *et seq.*; 2 ASSOCIATION OF AMERICAN LAW SCHOOLS, SELECT ESSAYS IN ANGLO-AMERICAN LEGAL HISTORY (1908) 367.

the inquisitorial procedure of the Catholic Church.[7] However, these rationalizing tendencies were not part of an articulate and unambiguous policy on the part of the wielders of power; they were rather driven in this direction by the needs of their own rational administration, as, for instance, in the case of the administrative machinery of the Papacy, or by powerful interest-groups with whom they were allied and to whom rationality in substantive law and procedure constituted an advantage, as, for instance, to the bourgeois classes of Rome, of the late Middle Ages, or of modern times. Where these interests were absent the secularization of the law and the growth of a specialized, strictly formal mode of juridical thought either remained in an incipient stage or was even positively counteracted. In general terms, this may be attributed to the fact that the rationality of ecclesiastical hierarchies as well as of patrimonial sovereigns is substantive in character,[8] so that their aim is not that of achieving that highest degree of formal juridical precision which would maximize the chances for the correct prediction of legal consequences and for the rational systematization of law and procedure. The aim is rather to find a type of law which is most appropriate to the expediential and ethical goals of the authorities in question. To these carriers of legal development the self-contained and specialized "juridical" treatment of legal questions is an alien idea, and they are not at all interested in any separation of law from ethics. This is particularly true, generally speaking, of theocratically influenced legal systems, which are characterized by a combination of legal rules and ethical demands. Yet in the course of this kind of rationalization of legal thinking on the one hand and of the forms of social relationships on the other, the most diverse consequences could emerge from the non-juridical components of a legal doctrine of priestly make. One of these possible consequences was the separation of *fas*, the religious command, from *jus*, the established law for the settlement of such human conflicts which had no religious relevance.[9] In this situation, it was possible for *jus* to pass through an independent course of development into a ra-

[7] Legal procedure, civil or criminal, is said to be inquisitorial when the ascertainment of the facts is regarded primarily as the task of the judge, while in the so-called adversary procedure the true facts are expected to emerge from the allegations and proofs of the parties without the active coöperation of the judge. A shift from the predominantly adversary procedure of the Germanic laws was initiated in the later Middle Ages by the Church, whose model became influential for procedural development through Western Europe.

[8] Cf. W.u.G. Part II, c. IV, esp. § 10.

[9] On the Roman distinction between *ius* and *fas* see JOLOWICZ, *op. cit.* 86 *et seq.*; MITTEIS 22–30 and literature there listed. For a baroque use of the terms, see BLACKSTONE III, 2.

tional and formal legal system, in which emphasis might be either upon logical or upon empirical elements. This actually happened both in Rome and in the Middle Ages. We shall discuss later[10] the ways in which the relationship between the religiously fixed and the freely established components of the law were determined in these cases. As we shall see hereafter,[11] it was quite possible, as thinking became increasingly secular, for the sacred law to encounter as a rival, or to be replaced by, a "natural law" which would operate beside the positive law partly as an ideal postulate and partly as a doctrine with varying actual influence upon legislation or legal practice. It was also possible, however, that the religious prescriptions were never differentiated from secular rules and that the characteristically theocratic combination of religious and ritualistic prescriptions with legal rules remained unchanged. In this case, there arose an inextricable conglomeration of ethical and legal duties, moral exhortations and legal commandments without formalized explicitness and the result was a specifically nonformal type of law. Just which of these two possibilities actually occurred depended upon the already mentioned characteristics of the religion in question and the principles that governed its relation to the legal system and the state; in part it depended upon the power position of the priesthood vis-à-vis the state; and finally, upon the structure of the state. It was because of their special structure of authority that in almost all the Asiatic civilizations the last mentioned of these courses of development came to emerge and persist.

But although certain features in the logical structure of different legal systems may be similar, they may nevertheless be the result of diverse types of authority. Authoritarian powers, especially those resting on personal loyalty, and more particularly theocracy and patrimonial monarchy, have usually created a nonformal type of law. But a nonformal type of law may also be produced by certain types of democracy. The explanation lies in the fact that not only such power-wielders as hierarchs and despots, and particularly enlightened despots, but also democratic demagogues may refuse to be bound by formal rules, even by those they have made themselves, excepting, however, those norms which they regard as religiously sacred and hence as absolutely binding. They all are confronted by the inevitable conflict between an abstract formalism of legal certainty and their desire to realize substantive goals. Juridical formalism enables the legal system to operate like a technically rational machine. Thus it guarantees to individuals and groups within

[10] Cf. *infra*. pp. 233, 250.
[11] Cf. *infra* c. X.

the system a relative maximum of freedom, and greatly increases for them the possibility of predicting the legal consequences of their actions. Procedure becomes a specific type of pacified contest, bound to fixed and inviolable "rules of the game."

Primitive procedures for adjusting conflicts of interest between kinship groups are characterized by rigorously formalistic rules of evidence.[12] The same is true of judicial procedure in *Dinggenossenschaften*.[13] These rules were at first influenced by magical beliefs which required that the questions of evidence should be asked in the proper way and by the proper party. Even afterwards it took a long time for procedure to develop the idea that a fact, as understood today, could be "established" by a rational procedure, particularly by the examination of witnesses, which is the most important method now, not to speak at all of circumstantial evidence. The compurgators of earlier epochs did not swear that a statement of fact was true but confirmed the rightness of their side by exposing themselves to the divine wrath. We may observe that this practice was not much less realistic than that of our days when a great many people, perhaps a majority, believe their task as witnesses to be simply that of "swearing" as to which party is "in the right." In ancient law, proof was therefore not regarded as a "burden" but rather as a "right" of one or the other of the contending parties, and ancient law was liberal in allowing a party this right. The judge, however, was strictly bound by rules and the traditional methods of proof. The modern theory of as late a period as that of common law procedure [14] is different from ancient procedure only in that it would treat proof as a burden. It, too, binds the judge to the motions of, and the evidence offered by, the parties and, indeed, the same principle applies to the entire conduct of the suit: in accordance with the principle of adversary procedure the judge has to wait for the motions of the parties. Facts which are neither stipulated nor alleged and proved, and facts which remain undisclosed by the recognized methods of proof, be they rational or irrational, do not exist as far as the judge is concerned, who aims at establishing only that relative truth which is attainable within the limits set by the procedural acts of the parties.

Exactly alike in this respect were the oldest clear-cut forms of ad-

[12] See *supra* c. V.

[13] See *supra* c. V.

[14] Namely, of continental Europe, i.e., the procedure which was common on the Continent before the reforms introduced by the codification of the nineteenth and twentieth centuries. In this and the following sentences Weber speaks also, however, of the continental procedure of the present day, which, as will appear, is not basically different from Anglo-American procedure.

judication, i.e., arbitration and composition between contending kinship groups, with oracle or ordeal constituting the trial procedure. This ancient legal procedure was rigorously formal like all activities oriented towards the invocation of magical or divine powers; but, by means of the irrational supernatural character of the decisive acts of procedure, it tried to obtain the substantively "right" decision. When, however, the authority of, and the belief in, these irrational powers came to be lost and when they were replaced by rational proof and the logical derivation of decisions, the formalistic adjudication had to become a mere contest between litigants, regulated so as to aim at the relatively optimal chance of finding the truth. The promotion of the progress of the suit is the concern of the parties rather than that of the state. They are not compelled by the judge to do anything they do not wish to do at their own initiative. It is for this very reason that the judge cannot comply with the quest for the optimal realization of substantive demands of a political, ethical or affective character by means of an adjudication which could give effect to considerations of concrete expediency or equity in individual cases. Formal justice guarantees the maximum freedom for the interested parties to represent their formal legal interests. But because of the unequal distribution of economic power, which the system of formal justice legalizes, this very freedom must time and again produce consequences which are contrary to the substantive postulates of religious ethics or of political expediency. Formal justice is thus repugnant to all authoritarian powers, theocratic as well as patriarchic, because it diminishes the dependency of the individual upon the grace and power of the authorities.[15] To democracy, however, it has been repugnant because it decreases the dependency of the legal practice and therewith of the individuals upon the decisions of their fellow citizens.[16] Furthermore, the development of the trial into a peaceful contest of conflicting interests can contribute to the further concentration of economic and social power. In all these cases formal justice, due to its necessarily abstract character, infringes upon the ideals of substantive justice. It is precisely this abstract character which constitutes the decisive merit

[15] Weber has anticipated the procedural reforms of the modern totalitarian states which have shown marked tendencies to strengthen the inquisitorial at the expense of the adversary principle. Cf. M. Ploscowe, *Purging Italian Criminal Justice of Fascism* (1945), 45 COL. L. REV. 240; BERMAN, JUSTICE IN RUSSIA 207; EBERHARD SCHMIDT, EINFÜRHRUNG IN DIE GESCHICHTE DER DEUTSCHEN STRAFRECHTSPFLEGE (1947) 406; also SCHOENKE, ZIVILPROZESSRECHT (6th ed. 1949) 25; H. Schroeder, *Die Herrschaft der Parteien im Zivilprozess* (1943), 16 ANNUARIO DI DIRITTO COMPARATO 168.

[16] Apparently, Weber is thinking here of the democracy of the Athenian rather than of the modern Western type.

of formal justice to those who wield the economic power at any given time and who are therefore interested in its unhampered operation, and also to those who on ideological grounds attempt to break down authoritarian control or to restrain irrational mass emotions for the purpose of opening up individual opportunities and liberating capacities. To all these groups nonformal justice simply represents the likelihood of absolute arbitrariness and subjectivistic instability. Among those groups who favor formal justice we must include all those political and economic interest groups to whom the stability and predictability of legal procedure are of very great importance, i.e., particularly rational, economic, and political organizations intended to have a permanent character. Above all, those in possession of economic power look upon a formal rational administration of justice as a guarantee of "freedom," a value which is repudiated not only by theocratic or patriarchal-authoritarian groups but, under certain conditions, also by democratic groups. Formal justice and the "freedom" which it guarantees are indeed rejected by all groups ideologically interested in substantive justice. Such groups are better served by khadi-justice than by the formal type. The popular justice of the direct Attic democracy, for example, was decidedly a form of khadi-justice. Modern trial by jury, too, is frequently khadi-justice in actual practice although, perhaps, not according to formal law; even in this highly formalized type of a limited adjudication one can observe a tendency to be bound by formal legal rules only to the extent directly required by procedural technique. Quite generally, in all forms of popular justice decisions are reached on the basis of concrete, ethical, or political considerations or of feelings oriented toward social justice. The latter type of justice prevailed particularly in Athens, but it can be found even today. In this respect, there are similar tendencies displayed by popular democracy on the one hand and the authoritarian power of theocracy or of patriarchal monarchs on the other.

When, for example, French jurors, contrary to formal law, regularly acquit a husband who has killed his wife's paramour caught in the act, they are doing exactly what Frederick the Great did when he dispensed "royal justice" for the benefit of Arnold, the miller.[17]

[17] Famous case in which Frederick tried to intervene in a private lawsuit.

In 1779, upon suit by his landlord, a baron, Arnold, a humble miller, was ejected because of nonpayment of rent. Arnold turned to the king who ordered the court to vacate its judgment and restore Arnold to the possession of the mill. The judges refused to render a decision "which would be against the law." When they continued in their "obstinate" refusal to obey the king's angrily repeated command, he ordered the supreme court to sentence them to jail. When the supreme court judges declared that the law would not permit such a step, they, together with the judges

The distinctive characteristic of a theocratic administration of justice consists entirely in the primacy of concrete ethical considerations; its indifference or aversion to formalism is limited only in so far as the rules of the sacred law are explicitly formulated. But in so far as norms of the latter apply, the theocratic type of law results in the exact opposite, viz., a law which, in order to be adaptable to changing circumstances, develops an extremely formalistic casuistry. Secular, patrimonial-authoritarian administration of justice is much freer than theocratic justice, even where it has to conform with tradition, which usually allows quite a degree of flexibility.

Finally, the administration of justice by honoratiores presents two aspects depending on what legal interests there are involved, those of the honoratiores' own class or those of the class dominated by them. In England, for instance, all cases coming before the central courts were adjudicated in a strictly formalistic way. But the courts of justices of the peace, which dealt with the daily troubles and misdemeanors of the masses, were informal and representative of khadi-justice to an extent completely unknown on the Continent. Furthermore, the high cost of litigation and legal services amounted for those who could not afford to purchase them to a denial of justice, which was rather similar to that which existed, for other reasons, in the judicial system of the Roman Republic.[18] This denial of justice was in close conformity with the interests of the propertied, especially the capitalistic, classes. But such a dual judicial policy of formal adjudication of disputes within the upper class, combined with arbitrariness or de facto denegation of justice for the economically weak, is not always possible. If it cannot be had, capitalistic interests will fare best under a rigorously formal system of adjudication, which applies in all cases and operates under the adversary system of procedure. In any case adjudication by honoratiores inclines to be essentially empirical, and its procedure is complicated and expensive. It may thus well stand in the way of the interests of the bourgeois

---

of the lower court, were ordered to be arrested by the king and were sentenced by him to one year's imprisonment, loss of office, and payment of damages to Arnold. It was one of the first acts of government of Frederick's successor, Frederick William II, to comply with the demand of the public to rehabilitate the judges and to indemnify them out of the public treasury. See W. JELLINEK, VERWALTUNGSRECHT 85 and literature cited there; for an account in English, see the translation by I. Husik of R. STAMMLER, THE THEORY OF JUSTICE (1925) 243 *et seq.*

[18] Cf. A. MENDELSSOHN-BARTHOLDY, IMPERIUM DES RICHTERS (1908). The allusion points to the early period when Rome was dominated by the patricians, who entirely dominated the administration of justice, until their power was broken in the long struggle of the plebeians. Cf. MOMMSEN, HISTORY OF ROME (Dickson's tr. 1900) 341–369; JOLOWICZ 7–12.

classes and it may indeed be said that England achieved capitalistic supremacy among the nations not because but rather in spite of its judicial system. For these very reasons the bourgeois strata have generally tended to be intensely interested in a rational procedural system and therefore in a systematized and unambiguously formal and purposefully constructed substantive law which eliminates both obsolete traditions and arbitrariness and in which rights can have their source exclusively in general objective norms. Such a systematically codified law was thus demanded by the English Puritans,[19] the Roman Plebeians,[20] and the German bourgeoisie of the fifteenth century.[21] But in all these cases such a system was still a long way off.

In the administration of justice of the theocratic type, in adjudication by secular honoratiores, in a court system guided by private or officially patented jurisconsults, as well as in that development of law and procedure which is based upon the imperium and the contempt powers of magistrates, princes, or officials holding in their hands the direction of the lawsuit,[22] the view is always strictly adhered to that fundamentally

[19] Cf. I. SANFORD, STUDIES AND ILLUSTRATIONS OF THE GREAT REBELLION (1858); P. A. GOOCH, ENGLISH DEMOCRATIC IDEAS IN THE SEVENTEENTH CENTURY (2nd ed. 1927) 308; HOLDSWORTH 412.

[20] In their struggle against patrician domination the plebeians achieved one of their most important successes when they compelled the patricians to consent to the appointment of a commission to write down the laws and thus to make their knowledge generally accessible. The product of the commission's work was the law of the Twelve Tables, which is reported by Livy (III, 9 *et seq.*) to have been promulgated in 450/449 B.C. and which for centuries was taken as the basis of the Roman *ius civile.*

[21] In the fifteenth and sixteenth centuries the laws were collected and "reformed" in numerous German cities. On these "Stadtrechte," see GIERKE, PRIVATRECHT 63; STOBBE I, 488; II, 3; also BRUNNER, GRUNDZÜGE DER DEUTSCHEN RECHTSGESCHICHTE (5th ed. 1912) 270. On one of the most important city laws of this kind, the Frankfurter Reformation, see COING, DIE REZEPTION DES RÖMISCHEN RECHTS IN FRANKFURT AM MAIN (1939) 141.

[22] "Magistrates, princes, or officials holding in their hands the direction of the lawsuit": This clumsy circumlocution had to be chosen to translate the German term, "die die Prozesse instruierenden Magistrate, Fürsten, und Beamte." *Prozessinstruktion* is a term of art of German theory of procedure. It means the role and activity of those persons who keep a lawsuit, civil or criminal, going and direct the course which it has to follow.

In the type of procedure mentioned in the text, the *Prozessinstruktion* is vested in a public officer or potentate who presides over the trial or at least that part of it in which the issues are formulated, but does not himself render the final judgment. The principal illustration is constituted by the role of the Roman *praetor* who presided over the proceedings *in iure*, in which there were formulated, with his active participation, those issues of law or fact or both which had to be decided, *in iudicio*, by the *iudex*, whom the *praetor* would appoint.

the law has always been what it is and that no more is needed than an interpretation of its ambiguities and its application to particular cases. Nonetheless, as we have seen,[23] the emergence of rationally compacted norms is in itself possible even under rather primitive economic conditions, once the hold of magical stereotypization has been broken. The existence of irrational techniques of revelation as the sole means of innovation has often implied a high degree of flexibility in the norms; their absence, on the other hand, has resulted in a higher degree of stereotypization, because in that event the sacred tradition as such remained the sole holy element and would thus be sublimated by the priests into a system of sacred law.

Sacred law and sacred lawmaking have emerged in rather different ways in different geographical areas and in different branches of the law; their persistence has likewise varied. We shall completely disregard at this point of our analysis the special attention which sacred law pays to all problems of punishment and atonement, a concern originally caused by purely magical norms; nor shall we here consider its interest in political law, or the originally magically conditioned norms which regulated the times and places at which trials were allowed to take place, or the modes of proof. In the main, we shall deal only with "private law" as commonly understood. In this branch of law, the fundamental principles regarding the permissibility and the incidents of marriage, the law of the family, and, closely related to it, that of inheritance, have constituted a major branch of sacred law in China and India as well as in the Roman fas, the Islamic Shariah, and the medieval canon law. The ancient magical prohibitions of incest were early forms of religious regulation of marriage.[24] In addition there was the importance of appropriate sacrifices to the ancestors and other familial sacra, which caused the intrusion of sacred law into the law of the family and inheritance, and in the latter field the Church's interest in revenue and, consequently, in the validity of wills, tended to maintain its control, when, in the areas of Christianity, the pagan sacred interests had disappeared.[25] Secular law

Another variety is represented by popular assemblies, especially of the Germanic type, which would be presided over by a prince or his representative or by some other person of authority, while the decision would be made by all, or some, of the members of the assembly (see *supra* p. 90). Both the Roman *praetor* and the Germanic prince, etc., had the *Banngewalt*, i.e., the power to subpoena attendance upon penalty of outlawry or forfeiture of property.

[23] Cf. *supra*, c. V.

[24] See WESTERMARCK, HISTORY OF HUMAN MARRIAGE c. XIX; FREUD, TOTEM AND TABOO (Brill transl. 1927) c. I; Fortune, R., *Incest*, 7 ENCYC. SOC. SCI. 620 and further literature cited there.

[25] On the role of the Church in maintaining or reëstablishing the principle of

was liable to come into conflict with the religious norms relating to objects and places dedicated to religious purposes or consecrated for other reasons or magically tabooed. In the sphere of contract, sacred law intervened on purely formal grounds whenever a religious form of promise, especially an oath, had been used, a situation which occurred frequently and in the beginning, we may surmise, regularly.[26] On substantive grounds, sacred law became involved whenever important norms of a religious-ethical character, for instance, the prohibition of usury, entered the picture.[27]

The relations between temporal and sacred law in general can vary considerably, depending upon the particular principles underlying the religious ethics in question. As long as religious ethics remains at the stage of magical or ritualistic formalism, it can, under certain circumstances, become paralyzed and completely ineffective through its own inherent means of refined rationalization of magical casuistry. In the course of the history of the Roman Republic the fas met with just this fate. There was scarcely a single sacred norm for the circumvention of which one could not have invented some appropriate sacred device or form of evasion.[28] The College of Augurs' power of intervention in cases

---

freedom of testation, see POLLOCK AND MAITLAND II, 349; HOLDSWORTH III, 536, 541 *et seq.*

[26] Here Weber apparently follows JHERING 263. In contrast MITTEIS 23, n. 2, points to the "well-known" fact "that in Roman private life the promissory oath was hardly used in any situations other than those in which legal coercion was lacking." Explicitly referring to Jhering, Mitteis states that "the idea of a religious component in the secular law of Rome has at one time been badly abused" (*op. cit.* 24, n. 4). More recently such ideas have been resuscitated, however, even more radically by HAEGERSTROEM, DER RÖMISCHE OBLIGATIONSBEGRIFF (1927), and DAS MAGISTRATISCHE IUS IM ZUSUMMENHANG MIT DEM RÖM. SAKRALRECHT (1929).

[27] This latter point will be discussed in connection with the problem of the economic significance of religious ethics. (The reference is to 2 W.u.G., c. IV, § 11, p. 336.) See also WEBER'S PROTESTANT ETHIC AND THE SPIRIT OF CAPITALISM (Parson's transl. 1930) 73 *et seq.*, 201 *et seq.* and HISTORY, c. XXI 267 *et seq.*

[28] See JHERING I, 325 *et seq.* Recent research has thrown doubt on the correctness of applying the word *fas* to the sacred law of Rome. Cf. the following statement in JÖRS AND KUNKEL 19, n. 2: "In modern literature the distinction between *ius* and *fas* is commonly regarded as equivalent to that between temporal and sacred law. Such use of the terms does not, however, correspond to Roman usage. At first, *fas* meant that sphere which was left free by the Gods. It included quite particularly those aspects of life for which the temporal law could be effective. In an ethically deepened usage, which came to be frequent with the Ciceronian period, *fas* means that which is religiously *permitted* in contrast to *ius*, which means that which is *commanded*. Even in this sense, *fas* does not mean, however, a religiously moral order in contrast to *ius* as a man-made order. Such an idea did not arise before Christianity. Even less does *fas* mean the complex of rules concerning religious rites

of defective religious form and evil omina, which meant, practically speaking, a power to rescind the resolutions of the popular assemblies, was never formally abolished in Rome as it had been by Pericles and Ephialtes in the case of the equally sacredly conditioned power of the Athenian Areiopagus.[29] But under the absolute domination of the priesthood by the secular magisterial nobility, this power served political purposes exclusively, and its application, like that of the substantive fas, was rendered practically innocuous by peculiar sacred techniques. Thus, like the Hellenic law of the late period, the thoroughly secularized jus was guaranteed against intrusions from this direction, despite the extraordinarily large role played in Roman life by considerations of ritual obligation. The subordination of the priesthood to the profane power in the ancient polis, certain peculiar characteristics of the Roman Olympus and those modes of their treatment of which we have spoken, were the factors by which this line of development was determined in Rome.[30]

The situation was the reverse where a dominant priesthood was able to regulate the whole range of life ritualistically and thus to a considerable extent to control the entire legal system, as was the case in India.[31] According to prevailing *Hindu* theory, all law is contained in the Dharma-Sutras.[32] The purely secular development of law was con-

---

and similar problems. These rules belong to the *ius*, as *ius sacrum* or *ius pontificium*. The development of the meaning of *fas* is largely paralleled by that of the Greek word ὅσιον; cf. WILAMOWITZ, PLATON I. 61; LATTE, HEILIGES RECHT 55 n. 16." Cf. also *supra* n. 9.

[29] On the College of Augurs and its *interventio*, see JHERING I, 329 *et seq.* On the abolition of the Areiopagos, "by a decree which was carried, about B.C. 458 and by which, as Aristotle says, the Areiopagos was 'mutilated' and many of its hereditary rights abolished" (ARIST., POL. ii 9; CIC., DE NAT. DEOR. ii 29; DE REP. i 27), see the article in W. SMITH, DICTIONARY OF GREEK AND ROMAN ANTIQUITIES (1848) 128.

[30] Weber's treatment of the relations between religion and law corresponds to the prevailing opinion, as expressed especially by Mitteis. A much closer relationship and a more far-reaching influence of magico-religious ideas upon the development of Roman law has more recently been maintained by HÄGERSTRÖM, *op. cit. supra* n. 23; as to further literature on the problem see JÖRS AND KUNKEL 4, n. 3, 393.

[31] On Hindu law see the article by Vesey-Fitzgerald in 9 ENCYC. SOC. SCI. 257, and literature cited there; Weber seems to have used primarily Jolly's article in BÜHLER'S GRUNDRISS DER INDOARISCHEN PHILOLOGIE (1886; Engl. transl. by Ghosh, Calcutta, 1928) and the DIGEST OF HINDU LAW by West and Bühler (Bombay, 1867/69). Cf. the footnote in WEBER'S GESAMMELTE AUFSÄTZE ZUR RELIGIONSSOZIOLOGIE (2nd ed. 1923), HINDUISMUS AND BUDDHISMUS II, 2. He also seems to have been acquainted with the pertinent passages in KOHLER AND WENGER 102–130, and with the works of SIR HENRY MAINE: ANCIENT LAW; VILLAGE COMMUNITIES; EARLY HISTORY OF INSTITUTIONS; EARLY LAW AND CUSTOM.

[32] See *supra*, p. 207.

fined to the establishment of particular systems of law for the various vocational estates of the merchants, artisans, and so forth. No one doubted the right of the vocational groups and castes to establish their own laws, so that the prevailing state of affairs could be summarized in the maxim: "Special law prevails over general law." [33] Almost all of the actually obtaining secular law came from these sources. This type of law, which covered almost the entire field of matters of daily life, was, however, disregarded in priestly doctrine and in the philosophical schools. Since no one thus specialized in its study and administration, it escaped not only all rationalization, but also lacked a reliable guaranty of validity in cases of divergence from the sacred law, which later was in theory absolutely binding, even though it was widely disregarded in practice.

Lawfinding in India represented that same characteristic intermixture of magical and rational elements which corresponds to both the peculiar kind of the religion and the theocratic-patriarchal regulation of life. The formalism of procedure was on the whole rather slight. The courts were not of the type of popular justice. The rules that the King is bound by the decision of the chief justice and that lay members (viz., merchants and scribes in the older sources and guild masters and scribes in the later ones) must be among the members of the court are both expressive of rational tendencies. The great significance of private arbitration corresponded to the autonomous law creation by the consociations. However, appeals from the organized tribunals of the consociations to the public courts were permitted as a general rule. The law of evidence is today primarily rational in character; resort is primarily had to instruments in writing and to the testimony of witnesses. Ordeals were reserved for cases in which the results of the rational means of evidence were not sufficiently clear. In those situations, however, they preserved their unbroken magical significance. This was especially true of the oath, which was to be followed by a period of waiting to determine the consequences of the self-curse. Similarly the magical means of execution, especially the creditor's starving himself to death before the

[33] Weber uses here the old German maxim, "Willkür bricht Landrecht," which, as shown above, at p. 141, meant that in the later middle ages and the early centuries of the modern age the customary or specially created law of some group prevailed over the general law of the land. The parallel with this German state of affairs is admissible only when one considers that Hindu law could not strictly be called the law of any particular territory in the sense of the German *Landrecht* but rather the law of the believers, which was simply regarded as *the* law as long as it did not have to compete with any other legal system, i.e., in the period before the Mohammedan invasion.

door of the debtor,[34] existed along with the official enforcement of judgments and legalized self-help. A practically complete parallelism of sacred and secular law existed in criminal procedure. But there was also a tendency towards the fusion of both these types of law, and on the whole sacred and secular law constituted an undifferentiated body, which obscured the remnants of the ancient Aryan law. This body of law was, in turn, largely superseded by the autonomous administration of justice of the consociations, especially the castes, which possessed the most effective of all means of compulsion, viz., expulsion.

Within the territory where *Buddhism* prevailed as the religion of the state, i.e., in Ceylon, Siam, Malaya, Indo-China, and especially Cambodia and Burma, the legislative influence of the Buddhist ethics was far from slight.[35] The Buddhist ethics was responsible for the equal status of husband and wife as expressed, for instance, in the rule of cognatic inheritance or the system of community property, or in the duty of filial piety, established in the interest of the parents' fate in the beyond, and requiring, among other things, the heir's liability for the debts of the deceased. The whole law came to be permeated with ethical elements which found expression in the protection of slaves, the leniency of the penal law (except the often extremely cruel punishment for political crimes), and in the admissibility of giving bond for keeping the peace. Yet even the relatively worldly ethics of Buddhism was so preoccupied with conscience on the one hand and ritual formalism on the other that a system of sacred "law" could scarcely develop as the subject matter of a specialized learning. Nonetheless, a legal literature, Hindu in tone, did develop and made possible the proclamation in Burma in 1875 of the "Buddhist law" as the official law, meaning by Buddhist law a law of Hindu origin, modified in the direction of Buddhism.

In *China*,[36] on the other hand, the magical and animistic duties were

[34] See *supra*, p. 114.

[35] As to the law in the countries of Buddhist influence, see VESEY-FITZGERALD, *loc. cit.* n. 28 *supra*; also BURGE'S COMMENTARIES ON COLONIAL AND FOREIGN LAW (ed. 1908–1914), 6 vols. The following articles in 1 SCHLEGELBERGER, RECHTSVERGL. HANDWÖRTERBUCH (1929) deal with these countries' modern legal systems, in which the Buddhist traditions are still influential, although in various degrees: W. Trittel, *Siam* 470; H. Mundell, *Malaiische Staaten* 417; H. Solus, *Die französischen Besitzungen und Kolonien* 535, 553 (Cambodia); F. Grobbs, *Britisch Indien* 319–328; 324–325 (Burma). In Ceylon, Buddhist law was largely superseded in the eighteenth century by Roman-Dutch law. See LEE, INTRODUCTION TO ROMAN-DUTCH LAW (1925); PEREIRA, LAWS OF CEYLON (1913); J. KOHLER, RECHTSVERGLEICHENDE STUDIEN (1889) 211 *et seq.*, 251.

[36] The principal literature on China which was used by Weber is listed in the

restricted by the power-monopoly of the bureaucracy to the purely ritual sphere. Thus, as we have seen and shall see further,[37] it exercised profound influences on economic activity. The irrationalities of Chinese administration of justice were caused by patrimonial rather than theocratic factors. Legal prophecy, like prophecy in general, has been unknown in China, at least in historical times; there also was no stratum of responding jurisconsults and no specialized legal training. All this corresponded to the patriarchal character of the political association, which was opposed to any development of formal law. The "Wu" and the "Wei"[38] were the counselors in matters of magical ritual. Those of their members who had passed the examinations and had, accordingly, a literary education, were advisors to families, kinship groups, and villages in ceremonial and legal matters.

In *Islam*[39] there was, at least in theory, not a single sphere of life in which secular law could have developed independently of the claims of sacred norms. In fact, there occurred a rather far-reaching reception of Hellenic and Roman law.[40] Officially, however, the entire corpus of private law was claimed to be an interpretation of the Koran, or its elaboration through customary law. This took place when, after the fall of the Omayyad Caliphate and the establishment of rule of the Abbassides, the caesaro-papist principles of the Zarathustrian Sassanids were transplanted into Islam in the name of a return to the sacred tradition.[41] The status of sacred law in Islam is an ideal example of the

---

introductory note to his essay on the ethics of Confucianism and Taoism (1 GESAMMELTE AUFSÄTZE ZUR RELIGIONSSOZIOLOGIE (3rd ed. 1934) 276; tr. by H. Gerth, s.t. THE RELIGION OF CHINA [1951]). Chinese law is discussed by him especially on pp. 391 *et seq.* and 436 *et seq.* of the work just mentioned. Weber apparently used the chapter on Chinese Law (pp. 138 *et seq.*) in KOHLER AND WENGER and the literature listed there at p. 153. For further orientation on Chinese law see Escarra, *Chinese Law*, 9 ENCYC. SOC. SCI. 249 and literature listed there at p. 266; Betz and Lautenschlager, *China*, in 1 SCHLEGELBERGER'S RECHTSVERGL. HANDWÖRTERBUCH 328, and literature listed there at pp. 389–391; see also BUENGER, QUELLEN ZUR RECHTSGESCHICHTE DER T'ANG ZEIT (1949); C. H. PEAKE, RECENT STUDIES ON CHINESE LAW (1937). Weber's observations are limited, of course, to the law of pre-revolutionary China. See also *supra*, p. 184.

[37] W.u.G. Part III, VI (*passim*).

[38] Taoist magicians. [Weber's note.]

[39] Cf. *supra*, p. 206.

[40] The theory of a major reception of Roman or Hellenistic ideas or institutions in Islamic law has recently encountered well-stated opposition. See R. Vesey-Fitzgerald, *Alleged debt of Islamic to Roman Law* (1951) in 67 L.Q. REV. 81; cf. Schacht, *Origins of Islamic Jurisprudence* (1951) and *Foreign Elements in Ancient Islamic Law* (1950), 32 J. COMP. LEG. 9.

[41] Omayyads (661–750) — Arab dynasty following in the caliphate the immediate

way in which sacred law operates in a genuinely prophetically created "book religion." [42] The Koran itself contains quite a few rules of positive law.[43] But the bulk of the legal prescriptions are of a different origin. Formally, they usually appear as *hadith*, i.e., exemplary deeds and sayings of the prophet, the authenticity of which was attested to by a successive line of recognized transmitters extending back by oral transmission to the contemporaries of the prophet, which originally meant back to the specially qualified companions of Mohammed. Due to this unbroken chain of personal transmitters the prescriptions are, or are said to be, exclusively orally transmitted, and constitute the Sunna, which is not an interpretation of the Koran itself, but a tradition alongside the Koran. Its oldest parts derive mainly from the earliest period of Islamic history, particularly from the customary law of Medina, the compilation and editing of which as *Sunna* has been attributed to Malik-ibn-Anas. But neither the Koran nor the *Sunna* were by themselves the sources of the law used by the judges. These sources were rather the fikh, i.e., the product of the speculative labors of the law schools, which are collections of hadiths arranged either according to authors [44] or to subject matter.[45] The fikh comprises ethical as well as legal commands and has contained, ever since the law became crystallized, an increasingly large section of a completely obsolete character. The crystallization was officially achieved through the belief that the charismatic, juridical-prophetic power of legal interpretation [46] had been extinguished since the seventh or eighth century, that is, the thirteenth or fourteenth century of the Christian era, a belief similar to that of the Christian Church and to that of Judaism regarding their assumption that the prophetic age had come to an end. The prophets of the law, the mujtahids of the charismatic epoch, were still thought of as

---

associates of Mohammed (abu-Bekr, Omar, Osman, and Ali), leading in the Arab-Islamic expansion into Armenia, Iran, Afghanistan, the Indus area, North Africa, and Spain; revolutionary success of the Abbassids (750–1258) residing in Baghdad, marks the rise of the Persian element and the amalgamation of the Arab conquerors with their Oriental subjects. Cf. H. C. Becker, in 2 Cambridge Medieval History (1913) 355–364.

Sassanides (226–641) — last Persian dynasty before the Arab conquest.

Caesaro-papism — absolute rule over state and church by the temporal ruler.

[42] Book religion — a religion based on a sacred writ conceived as direct revelation.

[43] Such as, for instance, the abolition of the prohibition of marriage between a man and his adoptive daughter-in-law, the very liberty of which Mohammed availed himself. [Weber's note.]

[44] *Musnad.* [Weber's note.]

[45] *Mussunaf*, of which six constitute the traditional Canon. [Weber's note.]

[46] *Ijtihad.* [Weber's note.]

the agents of juridical revelation, although only the founders of the four law schools,[47] acknowledged as orthodox, were given complete recognition.[48] After the extinction of the ijtihad only commentators [49] remained and the law became absolutely fixed. The struggle among the four orthodox law schools was primarily a conflict about the components of the orthodox Sunna, but it was also a conflict over methods of interpretation, and even these differences were increasingly stereotyped once the law was fixed. Only the small Hanbalite School rejects all bida, i.e., all new law, all new hadith, and all rational schemes of interpretation. Thus, as well as because of its postulate of Coge intrare,[50] it has cut itself off from the other schools which, in principle, are tolerant of each other. The schools differ by the different roles ascribed to legal science in the creation of new law. The Malekite School was dominant for a long time in Africa and Arabia. Since it originated in the oldest political center of Islam, Medina, it was especially uninhibited, perhaps as might have been expected, in incorporating pre-Islamic law. But it was bound to a greater extent by tradition than the Hanefite School, which emerged from Iraq and was, accordingly, deeply affected by Byzantine influences.[51] Its role was particularly important in the Court of the Caliph, and it is still the official school in Turkey [52] and the dominant one in Egypt. The main contribution of the Hanefite jurisprudence, which was in close contact with the ideas of the palace, seems to have been the development of the empirical techniques of Islamic jurists, i.e., the use of analogy.[53] It also proclaimed the ra'y, i.e., the idea that learned doctrine was an independent source of law, together with the received interpretation of the Koran. The Shafiite school, which orig-

[47] *Madhas.* [Weber's note.]

[48] On the four orthodox schools, see *supra*, pp. 142, 209.

[49] *Mugallidin.* [Weber's note.]

[50] Postulate of *coge intrare* — claim of rightful compulsion against heretics, especially as made against the Donatists by Augustine (Epist. 185, ad Bonifacium, A.D. 417), who ascribes to the Church the right and duty to compel membership and obedience even on the part of the unwilling. As authority he refers to the parable of the great supper (Luke 14:23), in which the host bids the servant that he "compel to enter" (*coge intrare*) all those whom he will encounter. — SCHAFF, HISTORY OF THE CHRISTIAN CHURCH (1886) 144. The argument was also used, first, it seems, in 1009 by Bruno von Querfurt, in the agitation for the Crusades and the compulsory conversion to Christianity of Moslems and other infidels; cf. ERDMANN, DIE ENTSTEHUNG DES KREUZZUGSGEDANKENS (1935) 97.

[51] Doubtful; see *supra*, n. 40.

[52] Written before the separation of church and state by Kemal Atatürk; see now the Constitution of April 20, 1924, and the Civil Code of October 4, 1926, which is in the main a translation of the Swiss Civil Code of 1907.

[53] *Gijas.* [Weber's note.]

inated in Baghdad and spread into Southern Arabia, Egypt, and Indonesia, is regarded as opposed not only to both these Hanefite characteristics, that is, the role ascribed to learned opinion and borrowings from foreign law, but also to the Malekites' elastic attitude toward tradition. It is thus regarded as more traditionalistic, although it has nevertheless achieved similar results through its large-scale reception of hadith of questionable genuineness. The conflict between the Ashab-al-hadith, i.e., the conservative traditionalists, and the Ashab-al-fikh, i.e., the rationalistic jurists, has persisted through the entire history of Islamic law.

The sacred law of Islam is throughout specifically a "jurists' law." Its validity rests on ijmâ [54] which is defined in practice as the agreement of the prophets of the law, i.e., the great jurists.[55] Besides the infallible prophet, only the ijmâ are officially infallible. Koran and Sunna are merely the historical sources of the ijmâ. The judges do not consult the Koran or the Sunna, but the compilations of the ijmâ, and they are not allowed independently to interpret the sacred writings or traditions. The Islamic jurists were in a position similar to that of the Roman jurists, and especially the organization of their schools is reminiscent of that in Rome. The jurist's activities involved both legal consultation and the teaching of students. He was therefore in contact with the practical requirements of his clients as well as the practical pedagogical demands, which necessitated systematic classification. But the subordination both to the fixed interpretative methods laid down by the heads of the schools and to the authoritative commentaries excluded, ever since the close of the ijtihad period, all freedom of interpretation. In the official universities, like the Azhar at Cairo, which includes among its faculty representatives of all four orthodox schools, teaching became the routinized recitation of fixed sentences.[56] Certain essential characteristics of Islamic organization, viz., the absence of Councils as well as the accepted infallibility of doctrine, influenced the development of the sacred law in the direction of a stereotyped "jurists' law." Actually, however, the direct applicability of sacred law was limited to certain fundamental institutions within a range of substantive legal domain only slightly more inclusive than that of medieval canon law. However, the universalism which was claimed by the sacred tradition resulted in the

[54] *Ijmah-al-ammah* — tacit *consensus omnium*. [Weber's note.]

[55] *Fukaha*. [Weber's note.]

[56] This statement of Weber's is no longer correct. On recent reforms of Islamic legal education see A. Sékaly, *La réorganisation de l'Université d'El-Azhar* (1936), 10 RÉVUE DES ÉTUDES ISLAMIQUES 1.

fact that inevitable innovations had to be supported either by a fetwa,[57] which could almost always be obtained in a particular case, sometimes in good faith and sometimes through trickery, or by the disputatious casuistry of the several competing orthodox schools. As a consequence of these factors, together with the already mentioned inadequacy of the formal rationality of juridical thought, systematic lawmaking, aiming at legal uniformity or consistency, was impossible. The sacred law could not be disregarded; nor could it, despite many adaptations, be really carried out in practice. As in the Roman system, officially licensed jurists [58] can be called on for their opinions by the Khadis,[59] or parties, as the occasion arises. Their opinions are authoritative, but they also vary from person to person; like the opinions of oracles, they are given without any statement of rational reasons. Thus they actually increase the irrationality of the sacred law rather than contribute, however slightly, to its rationalization.

As a status group law, the sacred law applies only to the Muslim but not to the subject population of unbelievers. As a consequence, legal particularism continued to exist not only for the several tolerated denominations, which were privileged partly positively and partly negatively, but also as local or vocational custom. The scope of the maxim that "special law prevails over the general law of the land," although it claimed an absolute validity, was of doubtful application whenever particular laws happened to conflict with sacred norms, which, themselves, were subject to thoroughly unstable interpretations. The commercial law of Islam developed from the legal techniques of late antiquity a variety of norms, quite a few of which were directly taken over by the West.[60] In Islam itself, however, the validity of these commercial

[57] *Fetwa* — a jurist's opinion on a concrete case, similar to the *responsa* of the Roman jurists; cf. *supra*, p. 217.

[58] *Muftis*, with the *Sheikh-ül-Islam* at their head [the office of *Sheikh-ül-Islam* was abolished on April 10, 1938, in the course of Kemal Atatürk's reforms in Turkey].

[59] Khadi-judge of the religious court.

[60] This statement of Weber's, as also that in his HISTORY 258, seems to be based upon the works of Josef Kohler, especially KOHLER AND WENGER 97; *Die Islamlehre vom Rechtsmissbrauch* 29 Z.F.V.R. 432–444, and MODERNE RECHTSFRAGEN BEI ISLAMITISCHEN JURISTEN. EIN BEITRAG ZU IHRER LÖSUNG (1885). But compare the cautious statements by GOLDSCHMIDT 98, 99, 246, 250; and *Ursprünge des Mäklerrechts, insbesondere sensal* (1882), 28 Z.F. GES. HANDELSRECHT 115.

Strictly denying any influence is P. Rehme, *Geschichte des Handelsrechts* in 1 EHRENBERG HANDBUCH DES GESAMTEN HANDELSRECHTS (1913) 95. ("Was das Verhältnis des islamitischen Rechtes zu den romanischen anlangt, so ist festzustellen: bisher ist noch für keinen Punkt der Nachweis einer Einwirkung jenes auf dieses erbracht worden.") See also, pp. 98, 99, 102, 108. In addition to the authorities

norms did not derive from enactment or from stable principles of a rational legal system. Their guaranty consisted in nothing but the merchants' sense of honesty and economic influence. The sacred traditions rather threatened than promoted most of these particularistic institutions. They existed praeter legem.

This impediment to legal unification and consistency always existed as a natural consequence wherever the validity of sacred law or immutable tradition has been taken seriously, in China and India just as in the territories of Islam. Even in Islam the system of personal laws applied to the purely orthodox schools, in the same way in which it once applied as part of the folk laws in the empire of the Carlovingians.[61] It would have been quite impossible to create a lex terrae such as the Common Law had become since the Norman Conquest and, officially, since Henry II. We actually find in all the great Islamic empires of the present time a dualism of religious and secular administration of justice: the temporal official stands beside the khadi, and the secular law beside the Shariah. Similarly to the capitularies of the Carlovingians, this secular law [62] began to expand from the very beginning, i.e., since the times of the Omayyad Khalifs,[63] and to assume increasing importance in relation to the sacred law, the more the latter became stereotyped. It became binding for the secular courts whose jurisdiction came to prevail in all matters except those concerning honorific titles, marriage, inheritance, divorce, and, to some extent, settled lands and certain other aspects of land law. These courts are not concerned at all with the prohibitions of the sacred law but decide according to local custom, since every systematization of even the secular law was prevented by the continuous intervention of spiritual norms. Thus the Turkish Codex, which began to be promulgated in 1869, is not a Code in the true sense, but simply a compilation of Hanefite norms.[64] We shall see that this state of affairs has had important consequences as regards economic organization.

---

above mentioned, compare also about the *contractus mohatrae* (Arabic khatar), Cohn, *Die Kreditgeschäfte* in 3 ENDEMANN, HANDBUCH DES DEUTSCHEN HANDELS-, SEE- UND WECHSELRECHTS (1885) 846; 2 WINDSCHEID, LEHRBUCH DES PANDEKTENRECHTS (1900) 73; about negotiable instruments, cf. GRASSHOFF, DAS WECHSELRECHT DER ARABER (1899); REHME, *loc. cit.* 95; Kohler, *Islamrecht* in 17 Z.F.V.R. 207.

[61] See *supra*, pp. 71, 142.

[62] Q'anon. [Weber's note.] The word "quorum" in the German edition is an obvious typographical error.

[63] *Supra* n. 41.

[64] Weber's main sources seem to have been Kohler in KOHLER AND WENGER 130,

In *Persia,* where the Shiite form of Islam [65] is the established religion, the irrationality of the sacred law is even greater, since there it does not even possess the relatively firm bases given by the Sunna.[66] The belief in the invisible teacher [67] who, at any rate in official theory, is regarded as infallible,[68] is only a poor substitute. The members of the judiciary are "admitted" by the Shah, who, as a religiously illegitimate ruler, is compelled to pay the greatest regard to the wishes of the local honoratiores. This "admission" is not an appointment but rather a placement of the graduates of the professional theological schools. There are judicial districts, but the jurisdictions of the individual judges do not seem to be clearly fixed, as the parties may choose from among a number of competing judges. The charismatic character of these juridical prophets is thus clearly indicated. The rigorous sectarianism of the Shiites, which is accentuated by Zarathustrian influences, would have prohibited as unclean all economic intercourse with nonbelievers. But through a number of fictions this sectarianism claimed by sacred law has ultimately been almost completely renunciated. There was thus brought about an extensive withdrawal of sacred legal influences from almost all spheres of activity that are of any economic and political consequence. The same recession of sacred law took place in the political sphere when constitutionalism was justified, through fetwas,[69] by quotations from the Khoran. Nevertheless, the theocracy is even today far from being a negligible factor in economic life. Despite the increasing shrinkage of its range of influence, the theocratic element in adjudication was and still is — together with the peculiar features of oriental patrimonialism as a form of domination — of great significance

---

and literature cited there at p. 153. On modern Persian law see the article by Greenfield in 1 SCHLEGELBERGER, *op. cit.*, 427.

[65] Cf. *supra*, pp. 206/207.

[66] Cf. *supra*, p. 238.

[67] Imâm. [Weber's note.]

[68] The word imâm, which in general simply means teacher, has in the Shiite tradition assumed the special meaning of spiritual and temporal head of all Islam. The first Imâm is Ali, Mohammed's son-in-law. None but Ali's descendants can be his successors. The Omayads, who after Ali's assassination assumed the khalifate, are regarded as usurpers by the Shiites, among whom dissension also broke out, however, as to which of the several lines of Ali's descendants were to be regarded as the charismatically true. All agree that that imâm, whom they respectively regard as the last legitimate one, transcended from earth, has since been living concealed from man as the "invisible imâm," and will at the end of time reappear as *mahdi* to save the world from all evil and to establish his kingdom of peace and justice. Certain eminent sages are believed to have had personal contacts with the invisible imâm and to have received revelations from him. Cf. GOLDZIHER, *op. cit.* 213 *et seq.*

[69] Cf. *supra*, p. 241.

for economic activity. Here, as elsewhere, this fact is due less to the positive content of the norms of the sacred law than to the attitudes prevailing in judicial administration, which is aiming at "material" justice rather than at a formal regulation of conflicting interests. It arrives at its decisions in accordance with considerations of equity even in those cases concerning real property which belong to its jurisdiction. Such considerations are all the more likely where the law is uncodified. Predictability of decisions of Khadi justice is thus at a minimum. As long as religious courts had jurisdiction over land cases, capitalistic exploitation of the land was thus impossible, as, for instance, in Tunisia.[70] The whole situation is typical of the way in which theocratic judicial administration has interfered and must necessarily interfere with the operation of a rational economic system. It is only the precise extent of this interference which varies from place to place.

Jewish sacred law has certain formal similarities with Islamic sacred law, although its context was quite the reverse of that in which Islamic sacred law existed.[71] Among the Jews, too, the Torah and the interpretative and supplementary sacred tradition purported to obtain as a norm of universal validity in all areas of life; similarly, the sacred law obtained only for the coreligionists. But unlike Islam, the bearers of this legal system were not an estate of rulers but rather a pariah folk. Hence commerce with outsiders was juridically foreign commerce, and it was to be governed in part by different ethical norms. To the legal norms obtaining in their environment the Jews tried to adapt themselves to the extent permitted by that environment and to the extent that it did not run counter to their own ritualistic scruples. As early as in the period [72] of the kings, the old local oracles, the Urim and T'hummim, had already been supplanted by juridical prophets, who contested the king's competence to issue legal orders with much greater effectiveness than their counterparts in Germanic law.

In the post-Exilic age the Nabim, i.e., the soothsayers and law prophets

[70] Cf. Solus in 1 SCHLEGELBERGER, *op. cit.* 545.

[71] In his own book on Judaism of Antiquity (DAS ANTIKE JUDENTUM, vol. III of GESAMMELTE AUFSÄTZE ZUR RELIGIONSSOZIOLOGIE, tr. by H. Gerth s.t. ANCIENT JUDAISM [1952]) Weber does not deal with rabbinical law (the reference in the index is misleading). The literature on Jewish law which Weber is likely to have known is listed in KOHLER AND WENGER 151/152; for further information see Gulak, *Jewish Law*, 9 ENCYC. SOC. SCI. 219, and literature there at p. 264; also D. Daube, *The Civil Law of the Mischnah* (1944), 18 TULANE L. REV. 351.

[72] The Urim and T'hummim seem to have been objects attached to the breastplates of the High Priest (Exod. 28:30) and used by him to ascertain the will of God on questions of national importance (Num. 27:21). They disappeared in the period of the later kings (Ezra 2:63).

of the period of the kings,[73] were replaced by the pharisees who were originally a stratum of intellectuals of upper-class origin with marked Hellenistic traits; later they also included small middle-class people who engaged in scriptural interpretation as a pastime.[74] Thus there developed, at the latest in the last pre-Christian century, the scholastic treatment of ritual and legal questions and thereby the legal technique of the expositors of the Torah and the consulting jurists of the two Eastern centers of Judaism: Jerusalem and Babylon.[75] Like the Islamic and Hindu lawyers, they were the bearers of a tradition which in part rested on the interpretation of the Torah but was also in part independent of it. God had given that tradition to Moses during their forty-day encounter on Sinai. By means of this tradition the official institutions, for instance, levirate marriage,[76] were as markedly transformed as was the case in Islam or in India. Furthermore, like that of Islam and India, it was at first a strictly oral tradition. Its written fixation by the Tannaim [77] began with the increasing fragmentation of the diaspora and the development of a scholastic treatment in the schools of Hillel [78] and Shammai [79] after the beginning of the Christian era. This was undoubtedly done to guarantee unity and consistency once the judge had become bound to the responses of the consulting legal scholars and therefore to precedents. As in Rome and England, the authorities for the particular legal sayings were cited, and vocational training, examinations, and licensing finally replaced the formerly free legal prophecy. The Mishnah [80] is still the product of the activities of the respondents themselves, collected by Rabbi Judah the Patriarch.[81] The Gemara, its official commentary, is, on the other hand, the product of the activities of the teaching lawyers, the Amoraim, who had

[73] On divination and prophecy in Israel, see WEBER *loc. cit. supra* n. 55, at 112 *et seq.*, 179 *et seq.*, 281 *et seq.*

[74] On the sociological place and role of the Pharisees, Weber has expressed himself *loc. cit. supra* n. 71, at pp. 401 *et seq.*

[75] Both the Palestinian and the Babylonian Talmud were concluded in the later part of the fifth century B.C.

[76] Deut. 25:5–10: Where a man dies without a male descendant, the widow must not marry a stranger, but the surviving brother of the deceased must take her to wife, and the first son born of them succeeds to the name and property of the deceased, cf. Cohon, *Levirate Marriage* in FERM'S ENCYCL. OF RELIGION (1945) 441, and literature stated there.

[77] *Tannaim* (Aramaic)-Jewish scholars of the first two centuries A.D.

[78] *Ca.* 30 B.C.–A.D. 10.

[79] Contemporary of Hillel.

[80] Older layer of talmudic canon.

[81] *Ca.* 135–220.

succeeded the first interpreters and who translated into Aramaic and interpreted for the audience the Hebraic passages recited by the reader. In Palestine they bore the title Rabbi and a corresponding one in Babylon.[82] A "dialectical" treatment along the lines of occidental theology could be found in the Pambedita "academy" in Babylon. But this method became fundamentally suspect during the later period of orthodoxy and it is condemned today. Since then a speculative theological treatment of the Torah has been impossible. More explicitly than in India and in Islam the dogmatic-edifying and the legal elements in the tradition, the haggadah and the halachah, were separated from one another both in literature and in division of labor. In its external aspects the center of learned activity and organization shifted increasingly toward Babylon. The Exilarch[83] lived in Babylon from the time of Hadrian onward and into the eleventh century. His office, which was hereditarily transmitted in the Davidic family, was officially recognized by the Parthian and Persian, and later by the Islamic, rulers; he was provided with a pontifical retinue, his jurisdiction was acknowledged for a long time, even in criminal matters, and under the Arabs he had the power of excommunication. The bearers of the legal development were the two competing academies of Sura and Pambedita, of which the former was the more distinguished. Their presidents, the Gaonim, combined judicial activity as members of the Sanhedrin with consultative practice for the entire Diaspora and with academic teaching of law. The Gaonim were partly elected by the recognized teachers and partly designated by the Exilarch. The external academic organization resembled that of the medieval and oriental schools. The regular students resided at the school; in the month of the Kalla[84] they were joined from abroad by large numbers of more mature candidates for rabbinical office, who came to participate in the academic discussions of the Talmud. The Gaon issued his responses either spontaneously or after discussion in the Kalla or with the students.

The literary works of the Gaonim, which began roughly with the sixth century, were, in form, no more than commentaries. Theirs was thus a more modest task than that of their predecessors, the Amoraim, who creatively expounded the Mishnah, or that of the successors of the latter, the Saboraim, who commented on it in a relatively free manner, not to speak at all of the Tannaim. But, in practice, and as a

[82] *Mor.* [Weber's note.]

[83] *Roshgalath.* [Weber's note.]

[84] Convention of scholars, held twice annually at the Babylonian academies; see 2 LEVY, TALMUD WÖRTERBUCH 331.

result of their elaborate and strong organization, they succeeded in having the authority of the Babylonian Talmud triumph over that of the Palestinian. It is true that this supremacy was at first confined to the Islamic countries, but from the tenth century on, it was also accepted by the Jews of the Occident. It was only after that and following the extinction of the office of the Exilarch [85] that the West freed itself from the Eastern influence. The Frankish rabbis of the Carlovingian epoch, for instance, brought about the transition to monogamy. After the learned treatises of Maimonides [86] and Asher,[87] although they were rejected by the Orthodox as rationalistic, it was ultimately possible for the Spanish Jew Joseph Karo, in his Shulchan Aruch,[88] to create a compendium which, as compared with the Islamic canonic treatises, was very manageable and brief. In practice this work then replaced the authority of the Talmudic responses, and in Algiers, for example, as well as in Continental Europe, it came in many instances to guide practice like a veritable code.

Talmudic jurisprudence originated in a highly scholastic atmosphere and, during the very period of the emergence of the commentary on the Mishnah, it had much looser relations with legal practice than in both earlier and later periods. In consequence of these two factors, its formal appearance demonstrated with great clarity the typical characteristics of sacred law, i.e., its marked predominance of purely theoretically constructed, but lifeless, casuistry, which within the narrow limits of a purely rationalistic interpretation could not be elaborated into a genuine system. The casuistic sublimation of law was by no means slight. Moreover, living and dead law were thoroughly intermixed, and no distinction was made between legal and ethical norms.

In matters of substance innumerable receptions had occurred already in Talmudic times, from Near Eastern, especially the Babylonian, and later from the Hellenistic and Byzantine, environments. But not everything in Jewish law which corresponds to the common Near Eastern law

[85] A.D. 942, after an internal quarrel between the Exilarch David ben Zakkai and the philosopher Saadia ben Joseph al-Fayyumi, David's two successors were assassinated by Moslems. 3 GRAETZ, HISTORY OF THE JEWS (3rd ed.) 201.

[86] 1135(1139?)–1204, foremost Jewish Philosopher of the Middle Ages, lived in Spain and North Africa; see Guttmann in 10 ENCYC. SOC. SCI. 48. Maimonides' treatise on the law, *Mischnah torah* or *Yad-hachazakah*, was completed in 1180; for an English transl., see RABINOWITZ, THE CODE OF MAIMONIDES, Book 13, THE BOOK OF CIVIL LAWS (1949).

[87] Jacob ben Asher, born in Germany, died in Toledo, Spain; his legal treatise, *Turim*, was written between 1327 and 1340. Cf. 7 GRAETZ, *loc. cit.* (3rd ed.) 298.

[88] 1488–1575; see Ginzberg in 3 JEW. ENCYCL. 583; also B. COHEN, THE SHULHAN ARUK AS GUIDE FOR RELIGIOUS PRACTICE TO-DAY (1941).

is borrowed. On the other hand, it is intrinsically improbable that, as a modern theory holds, some of the most important legal institutions of capitalistic commerce, for instance, the instrument payable to bearer, were invented by the Jews in their own law and then imported by them into the Occident.[89] Instruments containing a bearer clause had been known already in Babylonian law of the Age of Hammurabi, and the only question is whether they were instruments simply allowing the debtor to discharge his debt by making payment to the holder or whether they were genuine negotiable instruments payable to bearer.[90] The former type of instrument can also be found in Hellenistic law.[91] But the legal construction is different from what it is in the occidental negotiable instrument payable to bearer (*Inhaberurkunden*), which was influenced by the Germanic conception of the paper as the "embodiment" of rights and was therefore much more effective for purposes of commercialization.[92] The Jewish origin of the modern types of securities is rendered improbable by an additional fact, viz., the fact that the occidental precursors of these securities originated in the peculiar needs of early medieval procedure, the various forms of which were purely national. Indeed the clauses which prepared the way for negotiability originally did not serve commercial ends at all but rather those of procedure, above all that of providing a means for substituting a representative for the true party in interest.[93] So far not a single importation of a

[89] The author referred to in the text seems to be Werner Sombart, who, in his THE JEWS AND MODERN CAPITALISM ascribes to the Jews a decisive role in giving the capitalistic organization its peculiar features, by inventing a good many details of the commercial machinery which moves the business life of today, and by coöperating in the perfecting of others (p. 11). However, in his detailed discussion of this alleged Jewish achievement, Sombart states expressly that "it would be difficult, perhaps impossible, to show what that share was by reference to documentary evidence" (p. 63). Sombart's extensive hypotheses were readily accepted in National-Socialist literature. On the problem of the influence of Jewish law, see also Kuntze, DIE LEHRE VON DEN INHABERPAPIEREN (1857) 48, who discusses some institutions of ancient and later Jewish law but leaves it expressly open whether or not they had any influence on Western developments.

[90] Cf. KOHLER, PREISER, AND UNGNAD, HAMMURABI'S GESETZ I, 117, III, 237; SCHORR, ALTBABYLONISCHE RECHTSURKUNDEN (1913) 88.

[91] Cf. FREUNDT, WERTPAPIERE IM ANTIKEN UND MITTELALTERLICHEN RECHT (1910) and extensive critical discussion of this book by Joseph Partsch (1911) 70 Z.F. HANDELSR. 437.

[92] Cf. Brunner, *Carta and Notitia, Ein Beitrag zur Geschichte der germanischen Urkunde*, in COMMENTATIONES PHILOLOGAE IN HONOREM THEODORI MOMMSENI (1877) 570, repr. 1 ABH. 458.

[93] Weber here follows Brunner, BEITRÄGE ZUR GESCHICHTE UND DOGMATIK DER WERTPAPIERE (1877/78), Z.F. HANDELSR. XXII, 87, 518; XXIII, 225; repr. FOR-

legal institution has been clearly demonstrated as attributable to the Jews.[94]

It was not in the Occident but rather in the Orient that Jewish law played a real role as an influence in the legal systems of other peoples. Important elements of the Mosaic law were incorporated with Christianization into Armenian law as one of the components of its further development.[95] In the kingdom of the Khazars, Judaism was the official religion and thus Jewish law applied there even formally.[96] Finally, the legal history of the Russians makes it seem probable that through the Khazars certain elements of the most ancient Russian law developed under the influence of Jewish-Talmudic law.[97] There was nothing similar in the Occident. Although it is not impossible that through the mediation of the Jews certain forms of business enterprise may have been imported into the Occident, it is improbable that these forms would have been of national Jewish origin. They are much more likely to have been Syrian-Byzantine institutions or, through these, Hellenistic, or ultimately perhaps, institutions of common Oriental law deriving from Babylon. We must remember that in the importation of Eastern commercial techniques into the West the Jews were in competition with the Syrians, at least in late antiquity.[98] As far as its formal character is concerned, genuine Jewish law as such and, particularly, the Jewish law of obligations, were no appropriate context at all for the develop-

---

SCHUNGEN ZUR GESCHICHTE DES DEUTSCHEN U. FRANZÖSISCHEN RECHTS (1894); and *Das französische Inhaberpapier des Mittelalters*, in FESTSCHRIFT FÜR THÖL (1879) 7; repr. 1 ABH. 487.

[94] Cf. GOLDSCHMIDT 111.

[95] Cf. Kohler, *Das Recht der Armenier* (1887), 7 Z.F. VGL. RECHTSW. 385, 396; but without any evidence.

[96] The Khazars, one of the peoples of the North-Caucasian steppes, established an empire between the Black Sea and the Caspian. They reached the zenith of their power in the eighth and ninth centuries. Refusing to yield to pressure from Christian Byzantium and the Mohammedan khalifs, the dynasty, about A.D. 740, adopted the religion of the Jews, who had been expelled from Byzantium and found refuge with the Khazars. Jewish law did not become, however, the general law of the Khazar empire but only of those who professed the Jewish faith. With the arrival of the Viking rulers (Varangians) in Kiev in the late ninth century, the Khazar empire was steadily reduced in size and finally destroyed by Svjatoslav of Kiev (964–972). KADLEC in 4 CAMBRIDGE MEDIEVAL HISTORY 187.

[97] Weber's source seems to be S. Eisenstadt, *Über altrussische Rechtsdenkmäler* (1911), 26 Z.F. VGL. R. 157, who does not state more, however, than a brief conjecture.

[98] On the role of the Syrians in late antiquity, see Scheffer-Boychorst, *Zur Geschichte der Syrer im Abendlande*, 6 MITTEILUNGEN FÜR ÖSTERREICHISCHE GESCHICHTSFORSCHUNG 521; MOMMSEN, RÖMISCHE GESCHICHTE 467.

ment of such institutions as are required by modern capitalism. Its relatively unhampered development of the contractual type of transaction in no way changes this situation.

Naturally the influence of Jewish sacred law was all the more powerful in the internal life of the family and the synagogue. It was especially significant there in so far as it was ritual. The strictly economic norms were either, like the sabbatical year,[99] confined to the Holy Land,[100] or rendered obsolete by changes in the economic system, or, like everywhere else, were made innocuous by formalistic practices of circumvention. Even before the emancipation of the Jews the extent to, and sense in, which the sacred law was still valid varied greatly from place to place. Formally, Jewish sacred law manifested no peculiar characteristics. As a special body of law and as one which was only imperfectly systematized and rationalized and which, while elaborated casuistically, was still not logically consistent, Jewish sacred law possessed the general features of a product which had developed under the control of sacred norms and their elaboration by priests and theological lawyers. However interesting the theme may be in itself, we have in this place no reason to give it special attention.

The Canon Law of *Christendom* occupies a relatively special position with reference to all other systems of sacred law.[101] In many of its parts it was much more rational and more highly developed on the formal side than the other systems of sacred law. Furthermore, from the very beginning its relation to the secular law was one of a relatively clear dualism, with the respective jurisdictions fairly definitely marked in a manner not to be found elsewhere. This situation was, first of all, due to the fact that the ancient church had refused for centuries to have anything whatsoever to do with state and law. Its relatively rational character, however, was the product of several causes. When the Church saw itself compelled to seek relations with the secular authorities, it ar-

[99] Sabbatical year: Every seventh year the Bible (Lev. 25:1–25; Deut. 15:2) ordained that loans be canceled, serfs be freed, pledged property restored, and land left fallow, with all uncultivated growth left to the poor and the stranger. To what extent these rules were ever practiced is uncertain. They became definitely meaningless with the invention of the Prosbol, which tradition has ascribed to Hillel (see *supra*, n. 78). The debtor pretended to enter upon his obligation toward the court rather than the creditor himself. Upon the basis of spurious biblical authority a debt thus created was held not to be affected by the biblical command. Cf. GREENSTONE, 10 JEWISH ENCYCL. 219.

[100] Even there it has, through rabbinical dispensation, now become obsolete. [Weber's note.]

[101] There is no comprehensive history of the Canon Law; for a concise survey, see Hazeltine, 3 ENCYC. SOC. SCI. 179, with bibliography at 185.

ranged them with the aid of the Stoic conception of "natural law," that is, a rational body of ideas. Moreover, the rational traditions of the Roman law lived on in its own administration. At the beginning of the Middle Ages the occidental church took for its model the most formal components of Germanic law in its attempt to create its first systematic body of law, the *penitentials*.[102] Furthermore, the structure of the occidental medieval university separated the teaching of both theology and secular law from that of canon law and thus prevented the growth of such theocratic hybrid structures as developed elsewhere. The rigorously logical and professional legal technique which was developed through both ancient philosophy and jurisprudence was also bound to influence the treatment of canon law. The collecting activity of the jurists of the church had to concern itself not, as almost everywhere else, with responsa and precedents but with conciliar resolutions, official rescripts and decretals, and ultimately it even began to "create" such sources by deliberate forgery — a phenomenon that did not occur in any other church.[103] Finally, and above all, after the end of the charismatic epoch of the ancient church, the character of ecclesiastical lawmaking was influenced by the fact that the church's functionaries were holders of rationally defined bureaucratic offices. This conception, which was peculiarly characteristic of the church's organization and which, too, was a consequence of the connection with classical antiquity, was temporarily interrupted by the feudal interlude of the early Middle Ages but revived and became all-powerful with the Gregorian period.[104] Thus the occidental church traveled the path of legislation by rational

[102] Cf. J. T. McNeill and H. M. Gamer, Medieval Handbooks of Penance (1938).

[103] The most famous cases were those of the Donation of Constantine and the False (or Pseudo-Isidorean) Decretals. The first-named instrument, which was fabricated, probably, in Rome between the middle and the end of the eighth century, purported to be a grant by the Emperor Constantine, in gratitude for his conversion by Pope Silvester, to that pope and his successors forever, of spiritual supremacy over all other patriarchs as well as of temporal dominion over Rome, Italy, and the entire Western region. This *Constitutum Constantini*, which was used by the medieval papacy as one of the bases for its claims of general spiritual supremacy and of temporal power of the city of Rome, was included in the ninth century in the extensive collection of spurious decretals, which purported to be the work of Isidor of Seville, the legendary author of a seventh-century Spanish collection of decretals. The principal aim of the forger was the strengthening of the power of the bishops within the church and as against the state. Both the Donation of Constantine and the False Decretals were recognized as forgeries by the humanist scholars of the sixteenth century. Cf. 7 Encyc. Brit. 127, 524, with extensive bibliographies.

[104] Gregory VII (Hildebrand), pope from 1073 to 1085.

enactment much more pronouncedly than any other religious community. The rigorously rational hierarchical organization of the church also made it possible that it could issue general decrees by which economically burdensome and hence impractical prescriptions, for instance, the prohibition of usury, could be treated as permanently or temporarily obsolete. In numerous respects, it is true, Canon law can hardly conceal the general pattern so characteristic of all theocratic law, viz., the mixture of substantive legislative and moral ends with the formally relevant elements of normation and the consequent loss of precision. But it has nonetheless been more strongly oriented towards a strictly formal legal technique than any other body of sacred law. Unlike the Islamic and Jewish legal systems, it did not grow through the activities of responding jurists. Furthermore, in consequence of the New Testament's eschatological withdrawal from the world, the basic writ of Christianity contains only such a minimum of formally binding norms of a ritual or legal character that the way was left entirely free for purely rational enactment. The *muftis*, *Rabbis*, and *Gaonim* found parallels only in the fathers-confessor and *directeurs de l'âme* [105] of the Counter Reformation, and in certain divines of the old Protestant churches. Such casuistic ministry was then promptly productive of certain remote similarities to the Talmudic products, especially within the Catholic realm.[106] But everything was under the supervision of the central offices of the Holy See, and binding norms of social ethics were currently elaborated exclusively through their highly elastic decrees. In this way, there arose that unique relationship between sacred and secular law in which Canon law became indeed one of the guides for secular law on the road to rationality. The relatively decisive factor was the unique organization of the Catholic Church as a formal institution.[107] As to the content of the law, apart from such details as the *actio spolii* [108] and the *Summariisimum*,[109] the most significant contributions of Canon law were

[105] Spiritual advisers, especially of French royalty and nobility of the seventeenth and eighteenth centuries.

[106] The allusion is to the casuistic handbooks of confessional practice and moral theology of the seventeenth and eighteenth centuries, mostly of Jesuit or Redemptorist provenience. The most celebrated is the Homo Apostolicus of St. Alfonso dei Liguori, published 1753/5.

[107] Anstalt. [Weber's note.] See *supra*, pp. 157, 168.

[108] *Actio spolii* — originally, as stated in the False Decretals (see *supra* n. 103), the action by which a bishop ousted from his see can claim restoration without having to prove his right; later, on the basis of a canon of Innocent III, of 1215, action aiming at the speedy restoration to possession pertaining to the possessor who has been forcibly ejected as well as to any other person whose interest has been affected by the ejection. Cf. EGELMANN AND MILLAR 581.

[109] *Summariissimum*: summary proceeding of utmost speed and excluding

the recognition of informal contracts,[110] the promotion in the interest of pious endowments of freedom of testation,[111] and the canonist conception of the corporation. The churches were, indeed, the first "institutions" in the legal sense, and it was here that the legal construction of public organizations as corporations had its point of departure, as we have already seen.[112] The direct practical significance of Canon law for secular law, as far as substantive private, and especially commercial, law was concerned, varied a great deal in the course of time; in the main, however, it was relatively slight even in the Middle Ages. In Antiquity Canon law had not been able to bring about the legal abolition of free divorce even as late as Justinian,[113] and the submission of any cases to the spiritual courts had remained entirely a matter of discretion. The theoretical claim to an all-embracing substantive regulation of the entire conduct of life, which Canon law shared with all other systems of theocratic law, had in the Occident relatively harmless effects upon legal technique. The reason was that Canon law had found in the Roman law a secular competitor which had achieved an extraordinary formal perfection and which, in the course of history, had become the universal law of the world. The ancient Church had regarded the Roman Empire and its laws as definitive and eternal. And where the Canon law tried to extend its dominion it met with the vigorous and successful opposition of the economic interests of the bourgeoisie, including that of the Italian cities, with which the Papacy had to ally itself. In the municipal statutes of both Germany and Italy, and in Italian guild statutes, we find severe penalties for citizens bringing suit in an ecclesiastical court, and we can also find regulations that allow with an almost astonishing cynicism the discharge of spiritual penalties that might be incurred for "usury" by lump sum payments by the guilds.[114] Furthermore,

---

defenses not susceptible of immediate proof. The judgment to be rendered in the *summariissimum* is provisional and subject to review in the *summarium* or the *ordinarium*; cf. Engelmann and Millar. The *summariissimum* of canon law procedure influenced the development of summary procedures in the temporal courts.

[110] Ames, *History of Parol Contracts Prior to Assumpsit* (1895), 8 Harv. L. Rev. 252; repr. Ass. of Amer. Law Schools, Selected Essays on Anglo-American Legal Hist. (1909) III, 304; Pollock and Maitland II, 184.

[111] Pollock and Maitland II, 331; Holdsworth III, 534; R. Caillemer, *The Executor in England and on the Continent*, Ass. of Amer. Law Schools, Selected Essays on Anglo-American Legal History III, 746.

[112] See *supra*, p. 168.

[113] 527–565. In Justinian's Corpus Iuris divorce is treated primarily in Digest 24.2.

[114] The source of this statement of Weber's could not be located. The only references that could be found are to a statute of Brescia of 1252, mentioned in Kohler, Das Strafrecht der italienischen Statuten (1897) I, 592, and a statute of

in the rationally organized guilds of the lawyers as well as in the assemblies of the estates the same material and ideal class interests, especially of the lawyers, turned against ecclesiastical law just as they did against Roman law. Apart from a few particular institutions, the main influence of the Canon law lay in the field of procedure. In contrast with the formalistic proof of a secular procedure based upon the adversary principle, the striving of all theocratic justice for substantive rather than merely formal truth produced quite early a rational but specifically substantive technique of inquisitorial procedure.[115] A theocratic administration of justice can no more leave the discovery of the truth to the arbitrary discretion of the litigants than the expiation of a wrong. It has to operate ex officio and to create a system of evidence which appears to offer the optimal possibilities of establishing the true facts. Canon law thus developed in the Western world the procedure by inquisition, which was subsequently taken over by secular criminal justice.[116] The conflicts about substantive Canon law became later an essentially political matter. Its still existing claims no longer lie in fields which are of practical economic relevance.

After the end of the early Byzantine period, the situation of the *Oriental Churches* began to resemble that of Islam as a result of the absence of both an infallible agency for the exposition of doctrine and of conciliar legislation. The difference lay only in essentially stronger caesaro-papistic claims of the Byzantine monarchs, as compared with those which could be voiced by the Sultans of the East after the separation of the Sultanate from the Abbasside Caliphate,[117] or even as compared with those which the Turkish Sultans could make effective after the transfer of the Caliphate from Mutawakkil to Sultan Selim,[118] to

---

Trieste, of 1420, mentioned by Del Giudice in 6 PERTILE, STORIA DEL DIRITTO ITALIANO (1900) Part I, p. 82, n. 35. The former threatens with punishment anyone who invokes the ecclesiastical court against the taking of interest as declared permissible by the city. The second prohibits a debtor to invoke the ecclesiastical court before he has paid the full debt as agreed and, apparently, including interest. Cf. LASTIG, ENTWICKLUNGSWEGE UND QUELLEN DES HANDELSRECHTS (1877) §§ 14–17; 34–38; same, *Beiträge zur Geschichte des Handelsrechts* (1848) 23 Z.F. HANDELSR. 138, 142.

[115] See *supra*, p. 225.

[116] See A. ESMEIN, HISTORY OF CONTINENTAL CRIMINAL PROCEDURE (transl. by Simpson, 1913) 78.

[117] In 1258 Musta'sim, the last kaliph of Baghdad, was defeated and deposed by Hulagu, the grandson of Jenghiz Khan.

[118] After their defeat by the Mongols, the Abbassides continued a shadow sovereignty in Egypt until that country was conquered by the Turkish Sultan Selim I in 1517.

say nothing of the precarious legitimacy of the Persian Shahs vis-à-vis their Shiitic subjects.[119] Still, neither the late Byzantine nor the Russian and other caesaro-papistic rulers have ever claimed to be able to create new sacred law. There were, therefore, no organs at all for this purpose, not even law schools of the Islamic sort. As a result, therefore, Eastern Canon law, thus confined to its original sphere, remained entirely stable but also without any influence on economic life.

[119] Following the fall of the Sassanian dynasty and the Arab conquest in 637, Persia was under alien rulers until its reconstitution as a national state under the Shiite dynasty of the Safavi in 1405. According to the official doctrine established at that time, the Shah is the representative of the invisible imâm (see *supra* n. 68).

CHAPTER IX

IMPERIUM AND PATRIMONIAL MONARCHICAL POWER AS INFLUENCES ON THE FORMAL QUALITIES OF LAW: THE CODIFICATIONS [1]

1. *Imperium* — The second authoritarian power which has intervened in the formalism and irrationalism of the old folk administration of justice is the imperium [2] of the princes, magistrates, and officials. We shall not consider here that special law which a prince may create for his personal retinue, his own subordinate officials — especially his army — and of which highly significant remnants still persist today.[3] These legal creations have led in the past to very important structures of special law, e.g., the law of patron and client, master and servant, and of lord and vassal, which in antiquity as well as in the Middle Ages escaped the control of the general or common law and the jurisdiction of the regular courts, and differed from the general law in various complicated ways. Although these phenomena are of political importance, they have in themselves no formal structure of their own. In accordance with the general character of the legal system, these structures of special law were governed, as for instance in antiquity the law of patron and client, by a mixture of sacred norms on the one hand and conventional rules on the other; or they had, like the medieval laws of master and serf, or lord and vassal, a status group character; or they are regulated, like the present-day law of public and military service, by certain special norms of administrative and other public law, or are simply subjected to special substantive rules and procedural authorities.

[1] W.u.G. 482–495.

[2] Some aspects of *imperium* have already been discussed. See *supra* at p. 75 *et seq.* For Weber's discussion of Patrimonialism, Patriarchalism, and Feudalism as "forms of authority" (*Formen der Herrschaft*) see W.u.G., Part III, cc. VII and VIII (pp. 679–752).

[3] Writing before the First World War, Weber is referring here to certain institutions of monarchical Germany and Austria-Hungary, especially the regulations for the princely courts and the officers' corps of the army. Where, as in the United Kingdom, monarchy still exists, similar phenomena still obtain, although only in the same formal sense in which a man-of-war is referred to as "His (or Her) Majesty's" ship or an army regiment as the "Royal" Dragoons.

What we are concerned with are rather the effects of the imperium on the general (common) law, its modification, and the emergence of a new law of general validity alongside, in place of, or in contrast to, the common law. Quite particularly shall we be concerned with the effects of this situation upon the formal structure of the law in general. Only one general point should be made here: the degree of development of structures of special laws of this kind is a measure of the mutual power relationship of the imperium to the strata with which it must reckon as supports of its power. The English kings were successful in preventing a special feudal law from emerging as a particularistic system, as it did in Germany, so that it was rather absorbed into the unified *lex terrae*, the Common Law.[4] As a consequence the entire land law, family law and inheritance law acquired a strong feudal flavor.[5] The Roman state's law took note of the *clientela* in certain isolated norms, mostly in curse formulae, but in the main it intentionally refrained from drawing this institution, important though it was for the social status of the Roman nobility, into the regulatory sphere of private law.[6] Like the English law, the Italian statuta of the Middle Ages created a uniform *lex terrae*.[7] In Central Europe no such achievement occurred until the advent of the absolutist princely state, which, however, was careful to preserve the substantive remnants of the various special laws until they were fully absorbed by the modern institutional state.[8]

The conditions under which the prince, magistrate, or official appeared legitimated to create or influence the common law and under which he had the actual power to do so, the scope to which this power extended in different geographic areas or legal spheres, as well as the motives which underlay this intervention, will be discussed later in our treatment of the forms of domination.[9] In reality, that power assumed many forms and correspondingly produced many different results. Generally, one

[4] On this achievement of the English kings, see MAITLAND, CONSTITUTIONAL HISTORY OF ENGLAND (1931) 23, 151; PLUCKNETT 10. On the relation between feudal law and common law in Germany and in Medieval Europe in general, see MITTEIS, DER STAAT DES HOHEN MITTELALTERS (1944); further literature is stated by PLANITZ 101.

[5] Cf. PLUCKNETT 487.

[6] Cf. *supra*, p. 152. For a full discussion of the status of the *clientela* and their origin, see MITTEIS 42; MOMMSEN, RÖMISCHE FORSCHUNGEN I, 355, *et seq.*, and his STAATSRECHT III, 1, 57, 64, 76.

[7] ENGELMANN AND MILLAR 452, 492.

[8] Cf. *supra*, pp. 154 *et seq.* For a recent concise account of the history of these special laws in France and Germany, see KOSCHAKER, EUROPA UND DAS RÖMISCHE RECHT 234–245, where also the full literature on the subject is referred to.

[9] Cf. *infra* pp. 233 *et seq.*

of the earliest creations of the princely power to protect the peace (*Banngewalt*) was a national penal law.[10] Military considerations as well as general interest in "law and order" demanded regulation in this particular sphere. Next to religious lynch-law, the power of the princely office has indeed been the second main source of a separate "criminal procedure." Often priestly influences, too, were directly operative in this development, as, in Christendom, because of its interest in the extirpation of blood-vengeance and the duel. In Russia, the *knyaz* (prince), who in earlier times had presumed only to a mere arbitrator's function, was immediately after Christianization induced by the bishops to create a casuistic penal law; the very word *nakazanie* ("punishment") makes its appearance at that time.[11] Similarly in the Occident, in Islam, and certainly in India, the rational tendencies of the priesthood have played a part.

It appears plausible that the establishment of those detailed tariffs of Wergeld and fines which appear in all the old legal enactments was decisively due to the influence of the princes. Once typical conditions

[10] Cf. von Bar, History of Continental Criminal Law (1927) 73. For a similar development of the "King's Peace" in England, see Pollock and Maitland II, 462–464; also Pollock, *The King's Peace in the Middle Ages* (1900), 13 Harv. L. Rev. 177, repr. 2 Selected Essays in Anglo-American Legal History 403; Goebel, Felony and Misdemeanor (1937). For France, see Engelmann and Millar 661. For Germany, see Brunner, Rechtsgeschichte II, 47.

[11] Opinions differ as to whether the *knyaz* ("prince," from German *kuning* ["king"] through Lithuanian *kuningas*) was merely functioning as an arbitrator, so that his award could be rejected by the parties and they would be free to proceed with duel or feud, or whether he exercised more effective judicial power. Cf. L. K. Goetz, *Das russische Recht* (1910), 24 Z.f. vgl. Rw. 241, 417 *et seq.*; G. Vernadsky, Medieval Russian Law 10. The feud, with the possibility of its composition by the payment of *wergilt* (*vyra*, see *supra* c. VI, n. 29), was still common when Christianity was imposed upon the Kiev realm by Vladimir I (972[980]–1015).

The opinion that a casuistic criminal law was introduced by the prince immediately after Christianization and upon the behest of the bishops finds some support in the Russian Chronicles, which are too indefinite, however, to allow a final judgment.

Public punishment by death or corporeal castigation is still exceptional in the so-called "oldest version" of the Russkaya Pravda, which was formerly ascribed to the age of Yaroslav I (1019–1054), but upon which doubt has been thrown by recent research. See *supra*, p. 93. One who was killed, injured, or otherwise offended another is ordered not only to pay *wergilt* to the person injured or his kin, but also a money fine to the prince. This combination corresponds to that of the Germanic laws where, in the period of growing royal power, an offender had to pay "peace money" (*fredus*) to the king in addition to the *Busse* (*wergilt*) payable to the injured. In Russia this fine is called *prodasha*. The word *nakazanie* as a general term for punishment seems not to occur before the time of firmly established government.

of composition had been developed, it seems that that system which Binding has shown to have existed in German law,[12] was a universal phenomenon: in it we find two sets of *wergilt,* viz., one of considerable magnitude for acts of manslaughter and other vengeance-requiring injuries, and a much smaller one indiscriminately applicable to all other kinds of injury. It was probably under princely influence that there developed those almost grotesque tariffs covering every conceivable type of misdeed, which enabled everyone to reflect in advance whether the commission of a certain crime or the institution of a lawsuit would "pay." [13] The marked preponderance of a purely economic attitude toward crime and punishment has, as a matter of fact, been common to peasant strata in all ages. However, the formalism expressed in the fixed measurement of all amends is a result of the refusal to submit to the lord's arbitrariness. Not until the administration of justice had become thoroughly patriarchal did this rigorous formalism yield to a more elastic and ultimately completely arbitrary determination of punishment.

In the sphere of private law, which could never be as accessible to the peace power (*Banngewalt*) of the prince in the same way as criminal justice — regarded as a means of guaranteeing a formal order and security — the intervention of the sovereign occurred everywhere much later and with varying results and in varying forms. In some places a princely or magisterial law arose, which, in distinction to the common law, made explicit reference to its particular source of origin, as, for instance, the Roman *ius honorarium* of the praetorian edict, the "writ" law of the English kings, or the "equity" of the English chancellors. This law was created by the special "magisterial power" (*Gerichtsbann*) of the official charged with the administration of justice; he found complacent cooperation on the part of the legal honoratiores, who, as lawyers, such as the Roman jurisconsults or the English barristers, were eager to comply with the requests of their clients. By virtue of this power the official might be entitled, as the praetor was, to issue binding instructions to the judges or, as it was finally decided in England by James I himself in the conflict between the Lord Chancellor, Francis Bacon, and the common law courts, to issue injunctions to the parties; [14]

[12] KARL BINDING, DIE NORMEN UND IHRE ÜBERTRETUNG (1890) 415.

[13] All the *Volksrechte* (*leges barbarorum*, cf. *supra*, p. 103) contain extensive catalogues of misdeeds and the corresponding amounts of payment. The basis of computation is the *wergilt* payable for the killing of a freeman. The amends (*bot*, *Busse*) for other acts are computed as fractions of the *wergilt*. For specimens of typical catalogues of this kind, see SIMPSON AND STONE, LAW AND SOCIETY (1949) I, 97. See also POLLOCK AND MAITLAND II, 451.

[14] Cf. PLUCKNETT 183; MAITLAND, EQUITY 9.

or to see to it that, by voluntary submission or through compulsion, a case be brought into the magistrate's own court, as, for instance, in England into the Royal Courts or later into the Chancery.[15]

In this way the officials created new remedies, which in the long run came to a large extent to supersede the general law (*ius civile*, common law.) The common element in these bureaucratic innovations in substantive law is that they all had their start in the desire for a more rational procedure, which emanated from groups engaging in rational economic activity, i.e., bourgeois-strata. The very ancient *interdicta* trial[16] (*Interdiktionsprozess*) and the *actiones in factum*[17] would seem to prove that the Roman praetor had acquired his predominant position in procedure, i.e., his power of instructing the jurors, quite some time before the *lex Aebutia*.[18] But as a glance at the substantive content of the Edict shows, the formulary procedure was created by the commercial needs of the bourgeoisie as the intensity of commerce increased. The same needs resulted in the elimination of certain originally magically conditioned formalities. In England and France, the greatest attraction of the royal courts was, as it had been in Rome, the emancipation from verbal formalism. In many parts of the West, the adverse party could be compelled to testify under oath. In England, the cumbersome formalities of the summons were also dispensed with; the king would issue his summons "sub poena"; also the king's court used the jury rather than judicial combat and other irrational methods of proof which were intolerable to the bourgeoisie.

In English equity innovations of substantive law did not, to any considerable extent, occur before the seventeenth century.[19] Louis IX,[20] like Henry II and his successors, especially Edward III, created above everything else a relatively rational system of evidence and eliminated the remnants of the formalism of magical or folk justice origin.[21] The

[15] On the successful extension of the jurisdiction of the royal as against the ancient popular and feudal courts, see RADIN, ANGLO-AMERICAN LEGAL HISTORY (1936) 141; PLUCKNETT 337, and literature stated there.

[16] *Special proceedings to protect possession.*

[17] See *supra*, p. 214.

[18] Second half of second century B.C.

[19] Cf. HOLDSWORTH VI, 640.

[20] Under Louis IX (the Saint, 1226–1270), trial by ordeal was abolished and the jurisdiction of the feudal lords was subjected to the supervision of the courts of the king, the *Parlements*, whose procedure dispensed with many of the formalities of the older courts. Cf. Brunner, *Wort und Form im altfranzösischen Prozess*, 57 SITZUNGSBERICHTE DER PHIL. HIST. CLASSE DER KAISERL. AKADEMIE D. WISSENSCH. IN WIEN (1868).

[21] Of the measures taken by Henry II (1154–1189), the most important is the

"Equity" of the English Chancellor in turn eliminated from its sphere what had been the great achievement of the Royal Courts — the jury. In the dualism of "Law" and "Equity" which still obtains today in England and in the United States and frequently allows the plaintiff to choose between competing remedies, the formal distinction still consists in the fact that at Law cases are tried with, and in Equity without, a jury.

The technical instruments of magisterial law are on the whole purely empirical and formalistic in character; particularly frequent, for instance, is the use of fictions which can be found already in the Frankish capitularies.[22] This feature is, of course, to be expected in the case of a legal system which grows directly out of legal practice. In consequence, the technical character of the law remains unchanged. Indeed, its formalism has often been intensified, although, as the term "Equity" indicates, ideological postulates could also provide the stimulus to intervention. Indeed, the case is one in which the imperium had to compete with a system of law, the legitimacy of which it had to accept as inviolable and the general basis of which it could not eliminate. To greater lengths it could go only where, as in the case of verbal formalism and irrationality of proof, the imperium was accommodating urgent demands of strong pressure groups.

The power of the imperium is heightened where the existing law can be changed directly by means of princely decrees of equal validity with that of the common law, as we find it, for instance, in the case of the Frankish *capitula legibus addenda*, the ordinance and decrees of the

substitution of inquisition by jury for trial by battle in the assize of novel disseisin.

Under Edward III (1327–1377) the possibility of challenging a court record by battle was abolished (EDW. 3, STAT. 1, c. 4) as well as that of bringing in the ecclesiastical court a prosecution for defamation against members of a grand jury who had indicted a person who was subsequently acquitted (1 EDW. 3, STAT. 2, c. 11). Judicial independence as against the Crown was strengthened by the Statute of Northampton (2 EDW. 3, c. 8); the police and judicial functions of the "keepers," "commissioners," or "justices of the peace" were enlarged and consolidated by a number of statutes (see PLUCKNETT 159); the scope of compelling a defendant to submit to trial by means of outlawry was extended (25 EDW. 3, STAT. 5, c. 17); and use of the English language was allowed in pleadings (36 EDW. 3, c. 15).

[22] *Capitularia* — legislative acts of the Frankish kings; see *supra*, pp. 89, 224. On the use of fictions in them, see BRUNNER, RECHTSGESCHICHTE I, 377, 379, who, among others, reports the following illustration from a *capitulare* of Charles the Bald, of 864: Under the *Lex Salica*, service of summons had to be performed *ad domum*, i.e., in the house of the defendant. At that time many houses had been destroyed, however, by the Norman invaders. The king thus ordained that in such a case the process servers might undertake a sham-service on the spot where the house formerly had stood.

signories of the Italian cities, or the decrees of the late Roman principate, which had the same validity as *leges*. In the early Empire, it will be remembered, imperial decrees were binding only upon the emperor's officials.[23] On the whole, orders of this kind were, of course, not issued without the assent of the honoratiores (Senate, assembly of imperial officials) or even of the representatives of the moot community. The attitude also persisted for a long time, at least among the Franks, that such decrees could not create real "law," and it constituted a considerable obstacle to princely legislation.[24] Between this case and the factually omnipotent manipulation of the law by Western military dictators or the manipulation of the law by Oriental patrimonial princes we can find numerous intermediate situations. Legislation by patrimonial monarchs, too, would normally respect tradition to a considerable extent. But the more it succeeded in eliminating the administration of justice by the moot community, as it generally tended to do, the more frequently it developed its own specifically formal qualities and the better it was able to impress them upon the legal system. These qualities could be of one or the other of two quite different types, corresponding to the different political conditions of existence of the power of the patrimonial monarch.

One of the forms in which princely lawmaking took place was for the prince, whose own political power was regarded as a legitimately acquired right just as any other property right, to give up some parcel of this fullness of power by granting to some one or more of his officials or subjects, or to foreign merchants, or any other person or persons some special rights (privileges), which were then to be respected by the princely administration of justice. To the extent that this was the case, law and right, "norms" and "claims," coincided in such a way that, if thought out consistently, the entire legal order would appear as a mere bundle of assorted privileges.[25] The other form of princely lawmaking occurred in just the opposite form: the prince would not grant to anyone any claims which would be binding upon him or his judiciary. In that case, there are again two possibilities. The prince gives commands from case to case according to his entirely free discretion; to that extent there is no place for the concepts of either "law" or "right."

[23] Cf. JOLOWICZ 372–374.

[24] The legislative power of the Frankish kings was strictly limited. Laws, for example, which purported to alter the custom of the people could not be enacted without their consent. The principle was, *lex fit consensu populi ac constitutione regis* (Edict of Pistoia, 864, c. 6). Cf. BRISSAUD, HISTORY OF FRENCH PUBLIC LAW 81.

[25] On this and the following, cf. WEBER, W.u.G. Part III, c. VIII (p. 724).

Or the prince would issue "regulations" containing general directives for his officials. Such regulations mean that the officials are directed, until the receipt of further directives, to order the concerns of the subjects and to settle their conflicts in the manner indicated. In that situation the prospect of an individual to obtain a certain decision in his favor is not a "right" of his but rather a factual "reflex," a by-product of the regulation, which is not legally guaranteed to him. It is the same as in the case where a father complies with some wishes of his child without thinking, however, that he thus binds himself to any formal juristic principles or fixed procedural forms. As a matter of fact, the extreme consequence of a "patriarchal" administration of justice by the *parens patriae* is but a transposition of the intrafamilial mode of settling conflicts into the political body. The whole legal system would be dissolved into "administration" if this system were ever carried to its logical consequences.[26]

We shall designate the first of these two forms as the "estate" (ständische) type of patrimonial princely justice and the second as the "patriarchal." In the estate type of judicial administration and lawmaking, the legal order is rigorously formal but thoroughly concrete and in this sense irrational. Only an "empirical" type of legal interpretation can develop. All "administration" is negotiation, bargaining, and contracting about "privileges," the content of which must then be fixed. It thus operates like judicial procedure and is not formally distinct from the administration of justice. This was the way of the administrative proceedings of the English Parliament and of the great old Royal Councils, which were all originally administrative and judicial bodies at the same time. The most important and the only fully developed instance of estate patrimonialism is the political body of the medieval Occident.

In the purely patriarchal administration of the law, the law is, on the contrary, thoroughly informal, as far as one may speak of "law" at all under such a system of pure "regulations." Judicial administration aims at the substantive truth and thus sweeps away formal rules of evidence. Hence it would come into conflict quite frequently with the old magical procedures, but the relation between the secular and sacred procedures could assume various forms. In Africa the plaintiff might have a chance to appeal from the prince's judgment to the ordeal or to the ecstatic judgment vision of the fetish-priests or (*Orghanghas*), the agents of the old sacral trial. On the other hand, the rigorously patriarchal princely justice negates the formal guaranty of rights and the principle

[26] Compare this with Weber's discussion of "public" and "private" law *supra*, p. 41.

of strict adversary procedure in favor of the attempt to settle an interest conflict objectively "right" and equitably.

Although the patriarchal system of justice can well be rational in the sense of adherence to fixed principles, it is not so in the sense of a logical rationality of its modes of thought but rather in the sense of the pursuit of substantive principles of social justice of political, welfare-utilitarian, or ethical content. Again law and administration are identical, but not in the sense that all administration would assume the form of adjudication but rather in the reverse sense that all adjudication takes the character of administration. The prince's administrative officials are at the same time judges, and the prince himself, intervening at will into the administration of justice in the form of "cabinet justice," decides according to his free discretion in the light of considerations of equity, expediency, or politics. He treats the grant of legal remedies to a large extent as a free gift of grace or a privilege to be accorded from case to case, determines its conditions and forms, and eliminates the irrational forms and means of proof in favor of a free official search for the truth. The ideal example of this type of rational administration of justice is the "Khadi-justice" of the "Solomonian" judgment, as it was practiced by the legendary hero as well as by Sancho Panza when he happened to be governor.[27] All patrimonial princely justice has an inherent tendency to move in this direction. The "writs" of the English kings were obtained by applying to the king's boundless grace. The *actiones in factum* [28] allow us to guess how far even the Roman magistrates originally were allowed to go in the free grant or denial of actions (*denegatio actionis*).[29] English magisterial justice of the post-medieval type, too, makes its appearance as equity. The reforms of Louis IX in France were of a thoroughly patriarchal character.[30] Oriental, like Indian, justice, in so far as it is not theocratic, is essential patriarchal. Chinese administration of justice constitutes a type of patriarchal obliteration of the line between justice and administration. Decrees of the emperor, both educative and commanding in content, intervene generally or in concrete cases.[31] The find-

[27] CERVANTES, DON QUIJOTE, c. 45; cf. also the story of the Ameer of Afghanistan in MAX RADIN'S LAW AS LOGIC AND AS EXPERIENCE (1940) 65.

[28] Cf. *supra*, pp. 214, 260.

[29] The text has *temporis actiones*, an obvious error of transcription; possibly, Weber meant to refer to the *actiones temporales*, i.e., praetorian-created actions which could not be brought after the expiration of a certain, usually short, period of time; see WENGER 170.

[30] Cf. *supra* n. 20.

[31] Chinese patrimonialism is discussed by Weber in W.U.G. 707, and in his HISTORY 95, 338 *et seq*. See also his GES. AUFSÄTZE ZUR RELIGIONSSOZIOLOGIE I, 276,

ing of the judgment, to the extent that it is not magically conditioned, is oriented towards substantive rather than formal standards. When measured by formal or economic "expectations," it is thus a strongly irrational and concrete type of fireside equity. This type of intervention of the imperium into the formation of law and the administration of justice occurs on quite different "cultural levels"; it is the result not of economic but, primarily, political conditions. Thus in Africa, wherever the power of the chief has grown strong because of either its combination with the magical priesthood or the significance of war or through a trade monopoly, the old formalistic and magical procedures and the exclusive rule of tradition have often completely disappeared. In their place has arisen a procedure with public summons in the name of the prince (often through *Anschwörung* [32] of the defendant), public enforcement of the judgment and rational proof by witnesses in place of the ordeal; there have also developed practices of law enactment either exclusively by the prince alone, as among the Ashantics or, as in South Guinea, by him with the acclamation of the community.[33] But often the prince or chief or his judge decide entirely according to their own discretion and sense of equity, without any formally binding rules whatsoever. This situation can be found upon culture areas so different from each other as those of the Basuto, the Baralong, of Dahomey, the realm of Muata Cazembe, or Morocco.[34] The only restraint consists in the apprehension of losing the throne because of an excessively flagrant breach of the law, and especially a breach of those traditional norms which are regarded as

---

349 (tr. by H. Gerth s.t. THE RELIGION OF CHINA [1951]), and the article by T. Sternberg, *Der Geist des chinesischen Vermögensrechts* (1911), 26 Z.F. VGL. RW. 143.

[32] *Anschwörung* is invocation for harm, curse, execrate, to swear at; see, e.g., the article by J. Kohler and M. Schmidt, *Zur Rechtsgeschichte Afrikas* (1913), 30 Z.F. VGL. RW. 33. On the monopoly of trade in Africa by the chieftains see WEBER, HISTORY 197.

[33] For Africa see the recent literature referred to *supra* c. IV, n. 45. In general compare (1913) 30 Z.F. VGL. RW. 12 *et seq.*, 25 *et seq.*, 32, 66–68, 75, etc.

[34] *Basuto* — Bantu native of Basuto Land Protectorate; *Baralong* — Bantu group in Central Bechuanaland; *Muata Cazembe* — hereditary chief whose territory stretched from the south of Lake Mweru to north of Bangweulu, between 9° and 11° S. In the late eighteenth century the authority of the Cazembe was widely recognized; it diminished in power until, toward the end of the nineteenth century, the Cazembe sank to the rank of a petty chief. At present the territory is divided between Northern Rhodesia and Belgian Congo. Cf. Royal Geographical Soc., THE LANDS OF THE CAZEMBE (1873); M. Schmidt, *Zur Rechtsgeschichte Afrikas*, 31 Z.F. VGL. RW. (1914) 350, and 34 Z.F. VGL. RW. 441. As to Morocco, see *Quellen zur ethnologischen Rechtsforschung* (1923) 40 Z.F. VGL. RW. (Ergänzungsband) 125.

sacred and on which the rulers' own legitimacy rests. This antiformal substantive character of patriarchal administration reaches its high point when the (secular or priestly) prince places himself at the service of positive religious interests and, more particularly, when he propagates a religiosity which postulates certain ethical attitudes rather than the mere performance of rituals. All the antiformal tendencies of theocracy, which in this case are freed even from the otherwise effective restraints of ritualistic and, on that account, formal sacred norms, combine with the formlessness of a patriarchal welfare policy, which aims at the nurturing of right attitudes, and the administration of which approximates the character of pastoral care of souls. The boundaries between law and ethics are then torn down just as those between legal coercion and paternal monition, and between legislative motives, ends, and techniques. The closest approach to this "patriarchal" type is presented by the edicts of the Buddhist King Asoka.[35] As a rule, however, a combination of estate and patriarchal elements, together with the formal procedures of folk justice, prevails in the patrimonial princely system of justice. The extent to which one or the other of these factors preponderates depends — as we shall see in our discussion of "domination" [36] — essentially on political conditions and power relations. In the West, in addition to these, the (originally politically conditioned) tradition of moot justice which denied, upon principle, to the king the position of judgment finder [37] was of significance for the preponderance of estate forms in the administration of justice.

The growth to preëminence of rational-formalistic elements at the expense of the typical features of patrimonial law, as it occurred in the modern Western world, arose from the immanent needs of patrimonial monarchical administration, especially with respect to the elimination of the supremacy of estatist privileges and the estatist character of the legal and administrative system in general. In this respect the needs of those interested in increased rationality, which means in this case, in growing predominance of formal legal equality and objective formal norms, coincide with the power interests of the prince as against the holders of privilege. Both interests are served simultaneously by the substitution of "reglementation" for "privilege."

[35] 264 — c. 227 B.C.; see VINCENT SMITH, ASOKA (rev. ed. 1920); V. A. SMITH, EDICTS OF ASOKA (1909), and especially Weber's discussion in GES. AUFS. ZUR RELIGIONSSOZIOLOGIE (2nd ed. 1923) II, 253.

[36] W.u.G. Part III; *passim infra*.

[37] *Supra*, p. 90.

No such coincidence existed, however, where the demand was first, for limitations of the arbitrary patriarchal discretion by fixed rules and, second, for the recognition of definite claims of the subjects against the administration of justice or, in other words, for guaranteed "rights." As we know, these two elements are not identical. A method of settling disputes which proceeds by means of fixed administrative regulations by no means signifies the existence of guaranteed "rights"; but the latter, i.e., the existence not only of objective and fixed norms but of "law" in the strict sense is, at least in the sphere of private law, the one sure guaranty of adherence to objective norms. This guaranty was sought after by economic interest groups which the princes wished to favor and tie to themselves because they served their fiscal and political power interests. Most prominent among these were the bourgeois interests, which had to demand an unambiguous and clear legal system, that would be free of irrational administrative arbitrariness as well as of irrational disturbance by concrete privileges, that would also offer firm guaranties of the legally binding character of contracts, and that, in consequence of all these features, would function in a calculable way. The alliance of monarchical and bourgeois interests was, therefore, one of the major factors which led towards formal legal rationalization. Alliance must not be understood, however, in the sense that a direct "coöperation" of these two powers would always have been necessary. The utilitarian rationalism characteristic of every sort of bureaucratic administration tended already by itself in the direction of the private economic rationalism of the bourgeois strata. The fiscal interests of the prince also drove him to prepare the way for capitalistic interests to a far greater extent than was acutally demanded at the time by those interests themselves. On the other hand, the guaranty of rights which would be independent of the discretion of the prince and his officials was by no means a product of the tendencies genuinely immanent in bureaucracy. Moreover, it was not within the unqualified interest of the capitalist groups either. The very contrary was the case with respect to those essentially politically oriented forms of capitalism which we shall have occasion to contrast, as a special type of capitalism, with its specifically modern "bourgeois" type.[38] Even early bourgeois capitalism itself showed this interest in guaranteed rights either not at all or to a slight extent only, and sometimes it pursued even the very opposite end. The position not only of the great colonial and commercial monopolists but also of the monopo-

[38] Weber, History, c. XXX; cf. also W.u.G. 211 and 621 (Essays 162).

listic large-scale entrepreneurs of the mercantilist manufacturing period regularly rested upon a princely privilege, which often enough infringed upon the prevailing common law, i.e., in this instance, the guild law. This latter fact called forth the violent opposition of the bourgeois middle class and thus induced the capitalists to pay for their privileged business opportunities by the precariousness of their legal position vis-à-vis the prince. The politically and monopolistically oriented capitalism, and even the early mercantilistic capitalism, thus came to have an interest in the creation and maintenance of the patriarchal princely power as against the estates and against the bourgeois craftsmen, as happened in the time of the Stuarts, as has been happening today, and as is likely to happen even more often in broad areas of economic life.[39] In spite of all this, the intrusion of the imperium, especially the monarch, into the legal system, has contributed to the unification and systematization of the law and thus to "codification." The stronger and more stable the monarch's power was, the more it tended in that direction. The prince desired "order" as well as "unity" and cohesion of his realm. These aims emerged not only from technical requirements of administration but also from the personal interests of his officials: legal uniformity renders possible employment of every official throughout the entire area of the realm, in which case career chances are, of course, better than where every official is bound to the area of his origin by his ignorance of the laws of any other part of the realm. While thus the bourgeois classes seek after certainty in the administration of justice, officialdom is generally interested in the law's being clear and comprehensible.

2. *The Driving Forces behind Codification* — Although the interests of officials, bourgeois business interests, and monarchical interests in fiscal and administrative ends have been the usual factors promoting codification, they have not been the only ones. Politically dominated strata other than the bourgeoisie can be interested in the unambiguous fixation of the law, and those ruling powers to whom their demands are directed and which yield to them, voluntarily or under pressure, have not always been monarchs.

Systematic codification of the law can be the product of a conscious and universal reorientation of legal life, such as becomes necessary as a result of external political innovations, or of a compromise between

[39] Written in Germany before 1918. Weber seems to think of the support of the Conservative party by certain groups of heavy industry and high finance, which often found itself in contrast to the demands of the Center party and other groups representing the political interests of the craftsmen and other middle-class strata.

status groups or classes aiming at the internal social unification of the political body, or it may result from a combination of both these circumstances. The codification may thus be occasioned by the planful establishment of a community in a new area, as, for instance, in the case of the *leges datae* of the colonies of antiquity; [40] or by the formation of a new political community which in certain respects wishes to subject itself to a unified legal system, as, for instance, the Israelite confederation; [41] or by the conclusion of revolution through the compromise of status groups or classes, as the Twelve Tables are said to have been.[42] The systematic recording of the law may also occur in the interest of legal security following a social conflict. In such situations the parties interested in the recording of the law are naturally those which had hitherto suffered most from the lack of an unambiguously fixed and generally accessible set of norms, i.e., of norms which would allow checking up on the administration of justice. In antiquity these groups were typically the peasantry and the bourgeoisie as against a system of administration of justice carried on, or dominated by, aristocratic honoratiores or priests. In such cases, the systematic recordation of the law was apt to contain a large dose of new law and it was thus quite regularly imposed as *lex data* through prophets or prophet-like fiduciaries (*Aisymnetes*) on the basis of revelation or oracle.[43] The interests to be secured were likely to be understood quite clearly by the participants. The possible modes of settlement, too, were likely so to have been clarified by previous discussion and agitation that they were ripe for the prophet's or the aisymnete's fiat. For the rest, the interested parties were more concerned with a formal and clear settlement of the points actually

[40] JOLOWICZ 69.

[41] The codes referred to are the Book of the Covenant (Exod. 21–23) and the Decalogues in Exod. 20:1–17 and 34:10–27; Deut. 27:15–26. See WEBER'S GES. AUFS. ZUR RELIGIONSSOZIOLOGIE III, 251. There should be added the more recent Deuteronomic Code in Deut. 4:44–26:19. On the Hebrew "codification" cf. J. M. POWIS SMITH, THE ORIGIN AND HISTORY OF HEBREW LAW (1931).

[42] According to tradition the Law of the Twelve Tables is the work of a Commission of Ten (*Decemviri Legibus Scribundis*) who were appointed in 451 B.C. to satisfy the Plebeian demand for a fixation of the laws. The historicity of the tradition has been doubted. Recent researchers are inclined, however, to accept it as substantially correct. Cf. JOLOWICZ 11, and JÖRS AND KUNKEL 3, 392, both with literature; cf. also *supra* c. VIII, n. 20. For a discussion of both the Hebrew and Roman Codification, see DIAMOND 102, 134.

[43] *Aisymnete* (Gr. "adjuster") — temporary ruler, endowed with full governmental powers, elected to adjust the relationship between contesting classes within a city state, as, for instance, Solon in Athens or Charondas in Catania. Cf. *supra*, p. 8; also W.U.G. 252, 569, 571.

in issue than with a systematic law. The legal normation thus used to be expressed in the epigrammatic and proverb-like brevity which is characteristic of oracles, customals, or responsa of jurisconsults. The very fact that we find this style in the Twelve Tables should suffice to dispel the doubts as to their origin in one single act of legislation. Of the same kind is the style of the Decalogue and the Book of the Covenant. In both complexes of commands and prohibitions, the Roman and the Jewish, this style is indicative of their truly law-prophetic and aisymnetic origin. Both also equally present the characteristic feature of combining civil and religious commandments. The Twelve Tables anathematize (*sacer esto*) the son who strikes his father and the patron who does not keep faith with his client. No legal consequence were provided in either case. Obviously the commandments had become necessary because domestic discipline and piety had fallen into decay. The Jewish and Roman codifications differ, however, in so far as in the Decalogue the religious context is systematized while the Roman *lex* contained but single prescriptions; the bases of religious law were fixed and there was no new religious revelation. It is a quite different and a secondary question whether the Twelve Tables, on which the law of the City of Rome as given by the legal prophets, was said to have been recorded and which are reported to have been destroyed in the conflagration of the Gallic conquest, were any more "historical" than the two tables of the Mosaic law. But the rejection of the tradition as to the age and unity of the Roman legislation is required neither by substantive nor linguistic considerations; indeed, the latter are particularly irrelevant in view of the purely oral nature of the transmission of the tradition. The opinion that the Twelve Tables were but a collection of legal proverbs or of *responsa* of jurisconsults is contradicted by internal evidence. The norms are general ones and of a fairly abstract character; a good many of them are clearly and consciously aiming in a definite direction and a good many others clearly appear as compromises between different estate groups. It is quite improbable that a mere record of the practice of jurisconsults or the literary product of an Appius Claudius Caecus [44] or some

[44] The name is misspelled in the German text (*Arlim Partus Cotus!*) Appius Claudius Caecus was a celebrated jurisconsult of the late fourth and early third centuries B.C. To his secretary, Cnaeus Flavius, tradition ascribes the publication of the pontifical calendar and a work, which was later known as *Ius civile Flavianum* and which was regarded as having contained the pontifical formulary of civil actions. Professor Pais, Italian scholar of Roman history, maintains that the "Law of the Twelve Tables" was actually identical with this Ius Flavianum and that Appius Claudius himself was its real author (STORIA CRITICA DI ROMA [1915] 203). This thesis as well as the similar ones of Lambert (26 NOUV. REV. HIST. 149; REV.

other collector of cases could have attained such an authority in a city and in an age permeated with conflicts between rationally conceived interests. Also the analogy with other aisymnetic laws is too obvious. A "systematic" codification, to be true, is produced by that situation which is typical for aisymnetic legislation and the needs to be satisfied by it only in a purely formal sense. A "systematic" codification was constituted neither for ethics by the Decalogue nor for the regulation of business activities by the Twelve Tables or the Book of the Covenant. It was only through the work of the practicing lawyers that system and legal "ratio" were introduced, and even then but to a limited extent. Greater in this respect were the effects of the needs of legal education, but the full extent of systematization and rationalization resulted from the work of monarchical officials. They are the true systematic codifiers, since they have a special interest in a "comprehensive" system as such. For this reason monarchical codifications commonly are so much more rational with respect to systematic than even the most comprehensive aisymnetic or prophetic promulgations.

Monarchical codification has thus been one way to systematize a law. The only other one has been didactic literary activity, especially the creation of so-called "books of law," which every now and then have acquired canonical prestige and have thus come to dominate legal practice almost with statutory force.[45] In both cases, however, the systematic recordation of the law is hardly ever more than a compilation of the existing law meant to eliminate doubts and controversies. A good many collections of laws and regulations created at the behest of patrimonial monarchs and appearing externally as codes, as, for instance, the official Chinese compilation,[46] have, in spite of a certain element of "systematic" classification, little to do with real codification; they are nothing but mechanical arrangements. Other "codifications" have sought no more than to arrange the prevailing law in an orderly and systematic fashion. The Lex Salica and most of the other *leges barbarorum* were such com-

---

GÉNÉRALE DE DROIT XXVI, 385, 481, and XXVII, 15; also MÉLANGES APPLETON 503) and BAVIERA, STUDI PEROZZI 3, are generally rejected by recent writers; see *supra* n. 42.

[45] The most famous examples are the SACHSENSPIEGEL and BEAUMANOIR; see *supra*, pp. 149, 211.

[46] The Chinese compilation, which was in force in the Empire until its end, was the TA CH'ING LÜ LI of 1646, promulgated by the Manchu dynasty a few years after its seizure of power. On this and the other Chinese compilations, see WEBER, ESSAYS 416 *et seq.* Cf. *supra* n. 31; see also Escarra, *Law, Chinese*, 9 ENCYC. SOC. SCI. 249, 266 (bibliography).

pilations for the practice of the moot communities.[47] The highly influential *Assize of Jerusalem*[48] embodied the precedents on commercial usages: the *Siete Partidas* and similar "codifications" as far back as the *leges Romanae* collected those parts of the Roman law which had remained alive.[49] But even this kind of compilation necessarily implied a certain measure of systematization and, in this sense, rationalization of the legal data, and the groups that are interested in bringing about such a compilation are the same as those interested in a genuine codification, i.e., in a systematic revision of the substantive content of the existing law. The two cannot be sharply distinguished from one another. In that "legal security" which results from codification a strong political interest commonly exists even apart from all other considerations. Codification has thus always been near at hand in cases of creation of a new political entity. We thus find it at the establishment of the Mongolian Empire by Genghis Khan[50] where the collection of the Yasa constituted an incipient codification, as well as in many similar cases down to the foundation of the Napoleonic Empire. Apparently against all historical order, an epoch of codification thus occurred in the West at the very beginning of its history in the leges of the Germanic kingdoms newly created on Roman soil.[51] The need to pacify these ethnically heterogeneous political structures necessarily required the determination of the law actually existing and the upheaval of the military conquest facilitated the formal radicalism with which the task was carried out.

The interest in the precise functioning of the administrative machine through the establishment of legal security, alongside the prestige-needs

[47] For the *Lex Salica* and *Leges Barbarorum*, see *supra*, p. 103; also SEAGLE 166. The most recent reliable edition of the texts is that of the series entitled *Germanenrechte*, published by the Akademie für Deutsches Recht (1935 *et seq.*).

[48] The Assizes of Jerusalem were the code of laws for the kingdom of Jerusalem as established by the Crusaders in 1099; see K. RÖHRICHT, GESCHICHTE DES KÖNIGREICHS JERUSALEM (1898).

[49] *Siete Partidas* (Span. Law of the Seven Parts). It was compiled between 1256 and 1265 by Alfonso X, king of León and Castile. Among its sources were both the *Fuero Juzgo*, i.e., the Spanish translation of the Germanic *Lex Visigothorum* (cf. c. VI, n. 13), made in 1244, and the Roman tradition, especially as rudely compiled in the Visigothic "Code" for the Roman population, the *Lex Romana Visigothorum* or *Breviarium Alarici* of 506. Similar rudimentary compilations of the Roman law as applicable to the Roman population were made in the Ostrogothic kingdom of Theodoric, the *Edictum Theodorici* (about 500), and in the Burgundian kingdom, the *Lex Romana Burgundionum* (also known as *Papian*).

[50] Cf. H. LAMB, GENGHIZ KHAN (1927) c. VII; Krause, *Cingis Han*, HEIDELBERGER AKTEN DER VON-PORTHEIM STIFTUNG (1922); G. Vernadsky, *The Scope and Content of Chingis Khan's Yasa* (1938), 3 HARV. J. OF ASIATIC STUDIES 33.

[51] See *supra* nn. 47 and 49.

of the monarch, especially in the case of Justinian, were the motives for the compilations of the late Roman empire down to the Code of Justinian, as well as of the monarchical Roman law codifications of the Middle Ages of the kind of the Spanish *Siete Partidas*.[52] In all these cases it is unlikely that private economic interests played any direct role. On the other hand, the oldest and almost completely known code, which is in this respect the most unique of all those which have come down to us, i.e., the Code of Hammurabi,[53] allows us to infer with some reasonable degree of certainty that there existed relatively strong commercial interests and that the king wished to strengthen the legal security of commerce for his own political and fiscal purposes. The situation is typically that of a city kingdom. The surviving remnants of earlier enactments allow us to infer that the estate and class conflicts which were typical of the ancient city were at work then too, except that, due to the difference in political structure, they led to a different result. It may be said of Hammurabi's Code that, in so far as the evidence of older records is available, it did not establish any really new law but rather codified the existing law and that it was not the first of its kind.[54] As in most other monarchical codifications, the political interest in the unification of the legal system as such within the entire realm played a dominant role, in addition to the economic and religious interests which are so clearly apparent in the intensive regulation of familial obligations, especially the obligation of filial piety, which there as everywhere else were lying close to the heart of the patriarchal monarch. For the same reasons which we have already come to know, most of the other monarchical codifications, too, were aimed at overcoming the old principle under which special laws were to prevail over the general law of the land. These same motives were even more influential in bringing about

[52] See *supra* n. 49.

[53] See THE CODE OF HAMMURABI, ed. and tr. by R. E. Harper (1904); KOHLER ET AL., HAMMURABIS GESETZ; G. R. DRIVER AND JOHN C. MILES, THE BABYLONIAN LAWS (1952), 6 vols. (1904–23); for concise discussions and literature see DIAMOND 22, and W. SEAGLE, MEN OF THE LAW (1947) 13.

[54] As to codes earlier than that of Hammurabi and related legal monuments, see Koschaker, *Forschungen und Ergebnisse in den Keilschriftlichen Rechtsquellen* (1929), 49 SAV. Z. ROM. 188; P. Landsberger, *Die babylonischen Termini für Gesetz und Recht* (1935) SYMBOLA KOSCHAKER. On the Sumerian Code, which has been dated 400 years earlier than the Code of Hammurabi, see the Note. Ur-Nannu, [1954] Orientalia, fasc. 1. On a Sumerian code dated 200 years earlier than the Code of Hammurabi, see F. R. Steele, *The Code of Lipit-Ishtar*, [1948] AMERICAN JOURNAL OF ARCHAEOLOGY, No. 52; on the Accadian Code, dated 80 years before the Code of Hammurabi, see Note. Sumer [1948] 4 AMERICAN JOURNAL OF ARCHAEOLOGY IN IRAQ, No. 2.

the increasing frequency of monarchical codifications in the era of the rise of the bureaucratic state.[55] They, too, brought innovations only to a limited extent. At least in Central and Western Europe, they presupposed the validity of the Roman and Canon law as a universal law. Roman law, as subsidiary law, recognized the prior claims of the local and special laws, and for Canon law the actual situation was not much different, although it claimed for itself absolute and universal effect.

None of the monarchical codifications can match the significance for the revolution in legal thought and in the actual substantive law which was brought about by the reception of Roman law.[56] This is not the place to trace the history; all we can do is to present a few observations.

3. *The Reception of Roman Law and the Development of Modern Legal Logic* — In so far as the emperors, especially Frederick I,[57] and later the territorial princes participated in it, the reception was stimulated essentially by the sovereign position of the monarch as it appears in Justinian's codification. For the rest, the question is still unresolved and perhaps not fully resolvable whether and how far economic interests were behind the reception and to what extent they were promoted by it; it is an equally open question as to what was the cause of the preëminence of the learned, i.e., university-trained, judges who were the bearers of Romanism as well as of the patrimonial-princely procedures. It is above all unsettled whether it was essentially the interested parties (Rechtsinteressenten) who, through arbitration agreements, resorted to the legally trained administrative officials of the princes instead of the courts, thus establishing decision "ex officio" instead of decision "ex lege," and

[55] Codifications of this kind were those of Denmark (King Christian V's Danish Law, of 1683), Sweden (The Law of The Realm of Sweden, of 1736), and Bavaria (1751, 1753, 1756), the Prussian Code of 1794 (see *infra*, nn. 70–72), the preparation of which was begun in 1738, the Austrian Code of 1811 with its precursors of 1766, 1786, and 1797; also the various Ordinances successively enacted in France since 1539 and dealing with certain special topics. Cf. Continental Legal History Series, I (*General Survey*), 263.

[56] Among the vast literature on the resuscitation and reception of the Roman law in medieval and Renaissance law, the sources most suitable for a general orientation are: Vinogradoff, ROMAN LAW IN MEDIEVAL EUROPE (2nd ed. 1929); SMITH; E. JENKS, LAW AND POLITICS IN THE MIDDLE AGES (1905); WIEACKER, VOM RÖMISCHEN RECHT (1944) 195; and, above all, KOSCHAKER, EUROPA UND DAS RÖMISCHE RECHT (1947); G. v. BELOW, DIE URSACHEN DER REZEPTION DES RÖMISCHEN RECHTS (1905). Cf. also MAITLAND, ENGLISH LAW AND THE RENAISSANCE (1901) and the articles in Continental Legal History Series, vol. I (GENERAL SURVEY, 1912). For an instructive case study of the reception of Roman law in a particular city, see COING, DIE REZEPTION DES RÖMISCHEN RECHTES IN FRANKFURT A. M. (1939).

[57] Frederick I, Barbarossa, 1152–1190.

starving out the ancient courts (cf. Stölzel), or whether, as Rosenthal [58] has attempted to show in detail, the courts themselves were, as a result of the initiative of the princes, increasingly staffed with legally trained "assessors" rather than with lay *honoratiores*.

Whatever the answers may be to these questions, this much seems to be clear: since, as the sources indicate, even those groups which viewed the externals of Roman law with distrust, in general did not object to the presence on the bench of some "doctors," but only opposed their preponderance and especially the appointment of foreigners, it is obvious that the advance of the trained jurists was caused by intrinsic needs of the administration of justice, especially by the need to rationalize legal procedure, and by the fact that the jurists possessed that special capacity which results from specialized professional training, viz., the capacity to state clearly and unambiguously the legal issue involved in a complicated situation. To this extent the professional interests of the legal practitioners coincided with those of the private groups interested in the law, both bourgeois and noble. Yet, in the reception of substantive Roman law the "most modern," i.e., the bourgeois groups, were not interested at all; their needs were served much better by the institutions of the medieval law merchant and the real estate of the cities. It was only the general formal qualities of Roman law which, with the inevitable growth of the character of the practice of law as a profession, brought it to supremacy, except where there existed already, as in England, a national system of legal training protected by powerful interests. These formal qualities account also for the fact that the patrimonial monarchical justice of the West did not take the path, as it did elsewhere, of turning into a patriarchal administration of justice in accordance with standards of substantive welfare and equity. A very important factor in this respect was the formalistic training of the lawyers, on whom the princes were dependent as their officials, and which was largely responsible for the fact that in the West the administration of justice acquired that juristically formal character which is peculiar to it in contrast to most other systems of patrimonial administration of justice. The respect for Roman law and Roman law training also dominated all the monarchical codifications of the early modern age, which were all the products of the rationalism of university-trained lawyers.

The reception of the Roman law created a new stratum of legal

[58] The views stated are expressed in A. Stölzel, *Die Entwicklung der gelehrten Rechtsprechung* (1910), in E. Rosenthal's extensive review of this book in 31 SAV. Z. GERM. 522, esp. 538; and in Rosenthal's own GESCHICHTE DES GERICHTSWESENS UND DER VERWALTUNGSORGANISATION IN BAYERN (1889/1906).

honoratiores, the legal scholars who, on the basis of an education in legal literature, had graduated from a university with a doctor's diploma. Indeed, this new stratum was the very basis of the strength of the Roman law. Its significance for the formal qualities of the law was far-reaching. Already during the Roman Empire, Roman law had begun to be the object of a purely literary activity, which represented something quite different from the production of "law books" by the medieval legal honoratiores of Germany or France or of elementary treatises by English lawyers, however important those books may have been in their own ways. Under the influence of the philosophical training, superficial though it may have been, of the ancient lawyers, the significance of the purely logical elements in legal thinking began to increase. Indeed, it came to be especially important for the actual legal practice as there was no sacred law with any binding force and as the mind was unencumbered by any theological or substantive ethical concerns which might have pushed it in the direction of a purely speculative casuistry. As a matter of fact, incipient tendencies toward the view that what the lawyer cannot "think" or "construe" cannot be admitted as having legal reality could be already found among the Roman jurists. In this context also belong those numerous purely logical propositions as: *quod universitati debetur singulis non debetur* [59] or *quod ab initio vitiosum est, non potest tractu temporis convalescere.*[60] Only, these maxims were but unsystematic occasional productions of abstract legal logic, added to support some concretely motivated individual decisions and totally disregarded in others, even by the same jurist. The essentially inductive, empirical character of legal thought was barely affected, or not at all. The situation was quite different, however, in the reception of the Roman law. First of all, it strengthened that tendency of the legal institutions themselves to become more and more abstract, which had begun already with the transformation of the Roman ius civile into the law of the Empire. As Ehrlich has properly emphasized,[61] in order for them to be received at all, the Roman legal institutions had to be cleansed of all remnants of national contextual association and to be elevated into the sphere of the logically abstract; and Roman law itself had to be absolutized as the very embodiment of right reason. The six centuries of Civil Law jurisprudence have produced exactly this result. At the same

[59] "That which is owed to the collective is not owed to its members." Ulpian, DIG. 3.4.7.1. Cf. Ch. VII, n. 186.

[60] "What is void from the beginning, cannot be cured by the passage of time." DIG. 50.17.29.

[61] EHRLICH 253, 297, 348, 479.

time, the modes of legal thought were turned more and more in the direction of formal logic. The occasional brilliant aperçus of the Roman jurists of the kind just noted were torn out of the context of the concrete cases of the Pandects and were raised to the level of ultimate legal principles from which deductive arguments were to be derived. Now there was created what the Roman jurists had so obviously lacked, viz., the purely systematic categories, such as "legal transaction" or "declaration of intention,"[62] for which ancient jurisprudence did not even have names. Above all, the proposition that what the jurist cannot conceive has no legal existence now acquired practical significance. Among the ancient jurists, as a result of the historically conditioned analytical nature of Roman legal thought, properly "constructive" ability, even though it was not entirely absent, was only of small significance. Now when this law was transposed into entirely strange fact situations, unknown in antiquity, the task of "construing" the situation in a logically impeccable way became almost the exclusive task. In this way that conception of law which still prevails today and which sees in law a logically consistent and gapless complex of "norms" waiting to be "applied" became the decisive conception for legal thought.[63] Practical needs, like

[62] These concepts are of fundamental importance in the present law of Germany and those related to it, especially Switzerland and Austria. A "legal transaction" (*Rechtsgeschäft*) is every transaction of a person which is intended to produce legal consequences, such as an offer, or its acceptance, the contract itself, a will, or the abandonment of the title to a chattel; it is to be distinguished from natural events creating legal consequences, such as, for instance, the avulsion of a piece of land by a torrent, and also from *Rechtshandlungen*, i.e., human activities which create legal consequences without, or even against, the will of the actors, as, for instance, the negligent causation by one person of bodily injury to another. It is one of the peculiar features of the German Civil Code that it treats in one place those legal problems which are common to all legal transactions of any kind, be it a contract, a conveyance, a marriage, a will, or the issuance of a negotiable instrument. There are thus treated in the Third Part of the First Book of the Code (Secs. 104–185): capacity, declaration of intention, contract, condition and time term, authority, and ratification.

"Declaration of intention" (*Willenserklärung*) is that particular kind of legal transaction which requires that a person make manifest his intention. An offer or an acceptance are declarations of intention; a contract, however, is a "legal transaction" consisting of the declarations of intention of offeror and offeree. The rules applicable to declarations of intention of any kind are all treated together in Secs. 116–144, which thus deal with such problems as fraud, mistake, coercion, formalities, interpretation, or invalidity. For further explanation see SCHUSTER, PRINCIPLES OF GERMAN CIVIL LAW (1907) 78; (Brit.) Foreign Office, MANUAL OF GERMAN LAW (1950) 42.

[63] In the terminology of its critics, both American and German, the method here sketched is that of "conceptual jurisprudence." As to Germany, it is described in

those of the bourgeoisie, for a "calculable" law, which were decisive in the tendency towards a formal law as such, did not play any considerable role in this particular process. As experience shows, this need may be gratified quite as well, and often better, by an amorphous empirical case law. The consequences of the purely logical construction often bear very irrational or even unforeseen relations to the expectations of the commercial interests. It is this very fact which has given rise to the frequently made charge that the purely logical law is "remote from life" (*lebensfremd*). This logical systematization of the law has been the consequence of the intrinsic intellectual needs of the legal theorists and their disciples, the doctors, i.e., of a typical aristocracy of legal literati. In troublesome cases, opinions rendered by law school faculties were the ultimate authority on the Continent.[64] The university judge and notary, together with the university-trained advocate, were the typical legal honoratiores.

Roman law triumphed wherever there did not exist a legal profession with a nation-wide organization. With the exception of England, northern France, and Scandinavia, it conquered all of Europe from Spain to Scotland and Russia. In Italy, at least at the beginning, the notaries were the chief agents of the movement, while in the North its main agents were the learned judges, with the monarchs standing behind them almost everywhere. No Western legal system, not even that of England, has kept itself entirely free of these influences. Their traces show up in the systematic structure of English law, in many of its institutions, and in the very definitions of the sources of the Common Law: judicial precedent and "legal principle," no matter what the difference of inner structure.[65] The true home of the Roman law remained, of course, in Italy,

---

detail, analyzed, and criticized by the various authors of the essays collected in 20th Century Legal Philosophy Series: Vol. II, The Jurisprudence of Interests (1948).

[64] On this function of law school faculties as appellate courts, see Engelmann; Stintzing, Geschichte der deuschen Rechtswissenschaft (1880) I, 65; Stölzel, *op. cit.* I, 187; Rheinstein, *Law Faculties and Law Schools* [1938] Wis. L. Rev. 5, 7.

[65] For a discussion of the Roman law influences on the Common Law, see Maitland, English Law and the Renaissance (1901); Scrutton, The Influence of Roman Law on the Law of England (1885).

[66] The *Reichskammergericht* (Imperial Chamber Court) was established in 1495, as a common supreme court for all parts of the Holy Empire, in the course of the — in the long run — futile attempts to rejuvenate its moribund central government. It was to render its decisions according to "The Empire's Common Law," which meant, the Roman law. Cf. Engelmann and Millar 520; R. Smend, Das Reichskammergericht (1911). See also *supra* c. VI, n. 169.

especially under the influence of the Genoese and other learned courts (*rotae*), whose elegant and constructive decisions were collected and printed in Germany in the sixteenth century and thus helped to bring Germany under the influence of the Reichskammergericht[66] and the learned courts of the territories.

4. *Types of Patrimonial Codification* — It was not until the era of fully developed "enlightened despotism" that, beginning with the eighteenth century, conscious efforts were made to transcend the specifically formal legal logic of the Civil Law and its academic legal honoratiores, which indeed constituted a unique phenomenon in the world. The decisive role was played, first of all, by the general rationalism developed by bureaucracy at its height together with its naive belief of "knowing better." Political authority with its patriarchal core assumed the form of the welfare state and proceeded without regard for the concrete desires of the groups interested in the law and the formalism of the trained legal mind. It would indeed have liked nothing better than to suppress completely this kind of thought. The ideal was to deprive the law of its specialist character and to formulate it in a way that would not only instruct the officials but, above all, would enlighten the subjects about their rights and duties exhaustively and without outside aid. This desire for an administration of justice which would strive for substantive justice unaffected by juristic hairsplitting and formalism is, as we have seen,[67] characteristic of every monarchical patriarchalism. But it has not always been able to proceed in this direction without encountering obstacles. The Justinian codifiers could not consider "laymen" as the students and interpreters of their work when they systematized the sublimated law of the jurists. They simply could not eliminate the need for specialized legal training in the face of the achievements of the classical jurists and their authority as it was officially acknowledged by the Citation Law.[68] They could do no more than put forward their work as the sole authoritative collection of citations to serve the educational needs of the students and they had thus to provide for such instruction a textbook presented in the form of a law, i.e., the *Institutes*.[69]

[67] See *supra*, p. 272.

[68] See *supra*, p. 223.

[69] Upon the promulgation of the completed work, the use of any juristic writings outside of the Code and especially of those which had been collected in the DIGEST, was forbidden. Prohibited also, under penalty of deportation and confiscation of property, was the writing of new commentaries. The Corpus Iuris was to be the exclusive source of the law. Whatever doubts would arise in its application were to be submitted to the Emperor for his own authoritative interpretation. The *Institutes* were to be the only treatise to be used in legal education.

Patriarchalism could act more freely in that classical monument of the modern "welfare state," the Prussian *Allgemeine Landrecht*.[70] In marked contrast to the one-time estatist universe of "rights," in this Prussian Code the "law" is primarily a system of duties. The universality of one's "darndest debt and duty" (*verdammte Pflicht und Schuldigkeit*) is the main characteristic of the legal order, and its most notable feature is a systematic rationalism, not of a formal but of that substantive kind which always is typical of such cases. Where "reason wants to reign" all law which has for its existence no reason other than the fact that it exists, such as, especially, customary law, must disappear. All modern codifications, down to the first draft of the German Civil Code,[71] have thus been at war with it. Those legal practices which do not rest upon the explicit provisions of the legislator, just as every traditional mode of legal interpretation, are regarded by the rationalistic legislator as inferior sources of law to be tolerated only so long as the statute has not yet spoken. Codification was thus intended to be "exhaustive" and was believed able to be so. Hence, in order to prevent all creation of new law by the hated jurists, the Prussian judge was directed, in cases of doubt, to turn to a commission specially created for the purpose. The effects of these general tendencies were apparent in the formal qualities of the law so created. In view of the fixed habits of the practitioners, who had to be reckoned with even in the Prussian *Landrecht* and who were oriented towards the concepts of the Roman law, the attempt to emancipate the law from the professional lawyers by the direct enlightenment of the public through the legislator himself of necessity resulted in a highly detailed casuistry, which, due to the striving for material justice, tended to be unprecise rather than formally clear. Yet, dependency on the categories and methodology of Roman law remained inescapable, despite numerous individual divergences and the vigorous attempt, for the first time undertaken in a German legal enactment, to use a German terminology. The occurrence of numerous provisions of a merely didactic or ethically admonitory character gave rise to many doubts as to whether or not a particular provision was really meant to constitute a legally binding norm. Despite the striving for explicitness, clarity was, furthermore, obscured by the fact that the Code's system took as its point of departure not formal legal concepts

[70] Prussian General Code, of 1 June 1794. Cf. *supra* n. 55.

[71] The Draft provided in Sec. 2 that "rules of customary law are valid only in so far as they are referred to by the [statutory] law." This provision was not taken over into the Code.

but the practical relations of life and thus frequently had to take up one and the same legal institution piecemeal in different places.

The aim of eliminating the elaboration of his law by professional jurists was, indeed, achieved by the legislator to a considerable extent, although in not exactly the way intended. A real knowledge of the law by the public could scarecly be achieved by a many-volumed work with tens of thousands of sections, and if the aim was that of bringing about an emancipation from the influence of attorneys and other legal practitioners, the very nature of things prevented its realization under modern conditions. As soon as the Supreme Court (*Obertribunal*) began to publish a series of semi-official reports of its decisions, the cult of *stare decisis* developed as strongly in Prussia as anywhere outside England. On the other hand, nobody could feel stimulated to undertake a scholarly treatment of a law which created neither formally precise norms nor clearly intelligible institutions, as neither of these was intended by this utilitarian legislation.[72] As a matter of fact, patrimonial substantive rationalism has nowhere been able to provide much stimulation for formal legal thought.

The codification thus contributed to a situation in which the scholarly juristic activity was directed either even more to Roman law or, under the influence of nationalism, to the legal institutions of older German law, with the aim to present both of them, by means of the historical method, in their original "pure" form. For Roman law the result was that, under the hands of jurists trained as professional historians, it had to shed those transformations which it had undergone since the reception to become adapted to the needs of the times. The *Usus Modernus Pandectarum*,[73] the product of the reworking of the Justinian law through the Civil Law jurists, fell into oblivion and was condemned by scientific historical purists just as much as medieval Latin had been by the humanistic philologists. And just as the latter had resulted in the elimination of Latin as the universal language of the learned, so Roman law lost its suitability to the needs of modern life. Not until then was the way completely open for abstract legal logic. Learned rationalism was thus merely shifted from one domain to another rather than overcome, as so many of the historians seem to believe.

A purely logical re-systematization of the old law was, of course, not

[72] A scholarly, systematic exposition of the Code was successfully undertaken, nevertheless, by Dernburg in his PREUSSISCHES PRIVATRECHT, 3 vols. (1894). Significantly, the author was a Romanist and the treatise did not appear until shortly before the Prussian Code was replaced by the new German Civil Code of 1896.

[73] See EHRLICH 319–340.

achieved by the historical jurists in any convincing way.[74] It is well known, and it is indeed no accident, that down to Windscheid's Compendium,[75] almost all the pandectist treatises remained unfinished. The Germanist wing of the historical school of law was no more successful in producing a rigorously formal sublimation of those institutions which were not derived from Roman law. What attracted the historians in that field were indeed those irrational and antiformalistic elements which derived from the legal order of the old society of estates.

Systematization and codification without loss of practical adaptability could thus be achieved only for those special fields which bourgeois interests had autonomously adapted to their needs and which had been empirically rationalized in the practice of special courts, i.e., commercial law and the law of negotiable instruments.[76] This achievement was possible because compelling and clearly defined economic needs were operative. But when, after seven decades of supremacy of historians, and at the high point of a development of legal historiography never achieved in any other country, the creation of the German Reich dramatically demanded the unification of the private law as a national task, the German jurists were split in the two camps of Romanists and Germanists and approached the undertaking reluctantly and not fully prepared.[77]

The type of patrimonial monarchical codification is represented by other codes, too, especially the Austrian[78] and the Russian.[79] The latter, it is true, essentially constituted an estatist law of a small group of privileged strata which left untouched the special institutions of the several estates, especially the peasantry, i.e., the great majority of the subjects. It even left them their own special administration of justice to a practically very far-reaching extent. The greater conciseness of the Russian and Austrian codes, as contrasted with the Prussian, was purchased at the expense of precision and, in the Austrian code, by a greater dependency upon Roman law. It, too, did not attract scholarly thought for all the decades preceding Unger's work,[80] and even then its treatment was

[74] On the historical school, see STONE 421. Cf. also *supra*, p. 67.

[75] WINDSCHEID, LEHRBUCH DES PANDEKTENRECHTS, 3 vols., 1862–1870. Cf. ed. by Kipp, 1906; on Windscheid see the article by Jolowicz, 15 ENCYC. SOC. SCI. 429.

[76] The law of bills of exchange and promissory notes was codified as early as 1848 in a law which was adopted by all member states of the German Confederation, including Austria. The codification of the general commercial law followed in 1861.

[77] *Supra*, p. 183.

[78] General Civil Code (*Allgemeins bürgerliches Gesetzbuch*), of 1811.

[79] SVOD ZAKONOV, begun in 1809; revised ed. 1857; covering, in 40,000 articles, the entire field of law, including public law.

[80] *System des österreichischen allgemeinen Privatrechts*, 2 vols., 1856.

carried on almost entirely within the framework of the Romanistic categories.[81]

[81] On codification in general and in the United States in particular, see now H. E. Yntema, *The Jurisprudence of Codification* (1949), DAVID DUDLEY FIELD CENTENARY ESSAYS 251.

CHAPTER X

THE FORMAL QUALITIES OF REVOLUTIONARY LAW — NATURAL LAW[1]

1. *The Unique Character of the French Civil Code.* If we compare the products of the pre-revolutionary period with that child of the Revolution, the French Civil Code,[2] and its imitations all over Western and

[1] W.u.G. 496–503.

[2] The French Civil Code was proclaimed on 21 March 1804, under the title of Code Civil des Français. In 1807 this title was changed to Code Napoléon, and in 1816 the original title was restored with the fall of the Napoleonic régime. During the reign of Napoleon III the reference to Napoleon was reinstated in the title (1852–1870). While Napoleon was the main driving force and an active participant in the making of the Code, the demand for, and the beginning of, codification in France preceded the Napoleonic era. Even before the Revolution of 1789 the diversity of local laws had come to be regarded as cumbersome and their incompleteness as a source of legal uncertainty, and the Estates General had thus petitioned for a uniform national law. Also the judges of the French *parlements* had become unpopular. The Constituent Assembly of 1790 noted that a code should be proposed, but it was left to the Convention of 1793 to create a special drafting commission, headed by Cambacérès, which was to start the actual work and indeed was charged with its completion within a month. This commission actually succeeded in completing a draft of seven hundred articles within six weeks, which, however, was rejected on the ground that it was too elaborate and detailed and might restrict the freedom of the individual! Another, much shorter, draft was presented a few years later (September 1794), but was only little debated. Of the two further drafts — one in 1796 consisting of five hundred articles and another in 1799 — equally little resulted, as the Convention was engaged in waging a war with virtually the whole of Europe; yet, as Viollet has remarked (*Cambridge Modern History* VIII, 710 at 741–742), "The Convention amidst disorders at home and war abroad peacefully deliberated on questions of inheritance, alluvial lands, illegitimate children, and the whole body of civil law. . ." The Consulate, with Napoleon as First Consul, resumed the work, and much of Cambacérès' labor was embodied in the final Code.

In the Code much of the customary law of Northern France was preserved, combined with the conceptual technique of the eighteenth-century Roman law. Extensive use was made of the work of Domat (1625–1696) and, especially, Pothier (1699–1722), who had laid, in their extensive writings, the bases of a common law of France. The whole work was permeated, however, with a strong spirit of liberalism and individualism.

The Code is still in effect in France, although modified by a large number of amendments. A Commission charged with the preparation of a total revision of the Code has been at work since 1946.

Southern Europe,[3] we can see how considerable the formal differences between them are. The Code is completely free from the intrusion of, and intermixture with, nonjuristic elements and all didactic, as well as all merely ethical admonitions; casuistry, too, is completely absent. Numerous sentences of the code sound as epigrammatic and as monumental as the sentences of the Twelve Tables, and many of them have become parts of common parlance in the manner of ancient legal proverbs.[4] Certainly none of the precepts of the *Allgemeine Land-*

On the Code, see Viollet, *loc. cit.*; Lobingier, *Code civile* and *Codification* in 3 ENCYC. SOC. SCI. 604, 606, with further literature; on the current work of revision, see J. de la Morandière, *Reform of the French Civil Code* (1948), 97 U. OF PA. L. REV. 1.

[3] Through the Napoleonic conquests the CODE CIVIL was spread outside France; but permanently it was retained only in Belgium, Luxembourg, and that part of (Russian) Poland which had been constituted by Napoleon as the Grand-Duchy of Warsaw. Until the German Civil Code of 1896 took effect in 1900, the French Code remained in effect in those parts of Germany which are situated on the left bank of the Rhine, in the Grand-Duchy of Baden, and in a small sector of the Rhine Province east of the Rhine.

During the nineteenth century the CODE CIVIL, in translation and with inconsiderable modifications, became the law of the Netherlands, Italy (now replaced by a new Code of 1942), Rumania, Egypt, Quebec, Louisiana, Portugal, and Spain. The Spanish Code, with slight amendments, is still in effect in Puerto Rico, Cuba, and the Philippine Republic, and has constituted the model for most of the codes of Latin America.

New types of codification were started with the German Civil Code of 1896 and the Swiss Civil Code of 1912. The former was taken over, with slight changes, in Japan, the latter in Turkey. In the modern codes of pre-communist China, Thailand, Brazil, Mexico (federal law), and a few other Latin American countries, the models of the French, German, and Swiss codes are combined, partly also with indigenous ideas. Cf. Fisher, *The Codes*, 9 CAMBRIDGE MODERN HISTORY 148; Amos, *The Code Napoleon and the Modern World* (1928), 10 J. COMP. LEGISL. 22; A. REPPY (ed.), DAVID DUDLEY FIELD CENTENARY ESSAYS (1949).

[4] Cf., for instance:

ART. 2. La loi ne dispose que pour l'avenir; elle n'a point d'effet rétroactif (The law disposes only for the future; it has no retroactive effect).

ART. 1134. Les conventions légalement formées tiennent lieu de loi à ceux qui les ont faites (A contract properly concluded holds the place of law for those who have made it).

ART. 1382. Tout fait quelconque de l'homme, qui a causé à autrui un dommage, oblige celui par la faute duquel il est arrivé, à le réparer (Every act of man which causes harm to another binds the one through whose fault it has occurred to make reparation).

ART. 2279, para. 1. En fait de meubles, la possession vaut titre ("As to chattels, possession amounts to title" — meaning: a bona fide purchaser from the possessor acquires a good title).

So great a French writer as Stendhal is said to have had such a high opinion of

recht [5] or any other German code has achieved such fame. As a product of rational legislation, the Code Civil has become the third of the world's great systems of law, alongside Anglo-Saxon law, a product of juristic practice, and the Roman common law, a product of theoretical-literary juristic doctrine. It has also become the foundation of the vast majority of eastern and central European codifications. The attainment of this position can be explained by its formal qualities; for the code possesses, or at least gives the impression of possessing, an extraordinary measure of lucidity as well as a precise intelligibility in its provisions. This tangible clarity of many of its precepts the Code owes to the orientation of a large number of its legal institutions to the law of the *coutumes*.[6] To this clarity and simplicity much has been sacrificed in formal juristic qualities and in the depth and thoroughness of substantive consideration.[7] However, both as a result of the abstract total structure of the legal system and the axiomatic nature of many provisions, legal thinking has not been stimulated to a truly constructive elaboration of legal institutions in their pragmatic interrelations. It has rather found itself impelled to accept as mere rules those frequent formulations of the Code which are just rules rather than articulations of broader principles, and to adapt them to the needs of practice from case to case. Quite probably, peculiar formal qualities of modern French jurisprudence are perhaps to some extent to be ascribed to these somewhat contradictory characteristics of the Code. But these characteristics are expressions of a particular kind of rationalism, namely the sovereign conviction that here for the first time was being created a purely rational law, in accordance with Bentham's ideals, free from all historical "prejudices" and deriving its substantive content exclusively from sublimated common sense in association with the particular raison d'état of the great nation that owes its power to genius rather than to legitimacy. In certain cases the Code

---

the Code's literary style that he made it a habit to read a chapter of it before sitting down to write. Cf. SEAGLE 286.

[5] Cf. *supra*, pp. 274, 280.

[6] *Coutumes* — customary law of Northern France. Apart from the law of property and contract, which was primarily derived from Roman law, almost everything else in the code was based on customary law. Thus it was the customary law as systematized by Pothier to which, as has been said, three-quarters of the code can be traced back: see EHRLICH 415–416.

[7] An instance of this kind is provided by the two articles of the code (arts. 1382 and 1383) which purport to formulate the general principles of almost the whole French law of delicts (torts). For an analysis see Walton, *Delictual Responsibility in the Modern Civil Law* (1933), 49 L.Q. REV. 70. Compare with the two laconic articles of the French Code the 951 sections of the RESTATEMENT OF THE LAW OF TORTS by the American Law Institute (4 vols. 1939).

sacrifices juristic sublimation to vivid form. This attitude towards legal logic stems directly from the personal intervention of Napoleon, while the epigrammatically dramatized character of some of its provisions corresponds to the type of formulation of the "rights of man and citizen" in the American and French constitutions. Certain axioms concerning the substantive content of legal norms are not presented in the form of matter-of-fact rules, but as postulate-like maxims, with the claim that a legal system is legitimate only when it does not contradict those postulates. With this particular method of forming abstract legal propositions we shall now deal briefly.

2. *Natural Law as the Normative Standard of Positive Law.* Conceptions of the "rightness of the law" are sociologically relevant within a rational positive legal order only in so far as the particular answer to the problem gives rise to practical consequences for the behavior of law makers, legal practitioners, and social groups interested in the law. In other words, they become sociologically relevant only when practical legal life is materially affected by the conviction of the particular "legitimacy" of certain legal maxims, and of the directly binding force of certain principles which are not to be disrupted by any concessions to positive law imposed by mere power. Such a situation has repeatedly existed in the course of history, but quite particularly at the beginning of modern times and during the Revolutionary period, and in America it still exists. The substantive content of such maxims is usually designated as "Natural Law."[8]

We encountered the *lex naturae* earlier[9] as an essentially Stoic creation which was taken over by *Christianity* for the purpose of constructing a bridge between its own ethics and the norms of the world.[10] It was the law legitimated by God's will for all men of this world of sin and violence, and thus stood in contrast to those of God's commands which were revealed directly to the faithful and are evident only to the elect. But here we must look at the lex naturae from another angle. Natural law

[8] For concise surveys of, and bibliographies on, the various forms of Natural Law concepts and their role and significance, see G. Gurvitch, *Natural Law*, 11 ENCYC. SOC. SCI. 284; STONE 215; I. W. JONES, HISTORICAL INTRODUCTION TO THE THEORY OF LAW (1947); see also C. G. HAINES, REVIVAL OF NATURAL LAW CONCEPTS IN AMERICA (1930) and ROMMEN, NATURAL LAW (1947).

[9] No such passage can be found.

[10] See E. TROELTSCH, THE SOCIAL TEACHINGS OF THE CHRISTIAN CHURCHES (2 vols., tr. by O. Wyon, London, 1931) and Weber's remarks on Troeltsch's paper on *The Stoic-Christian Natural Law* in VERHANDLUNGEN DES DEUTSCHEN SOZIOLOGENTAGS (1910) I, 196, 210, repr. in GES. AUFS. ZUR SOZIOLOGIE UND SOZIALPOLITIK (1924) 462.

is the sum total of all those norms which are valid independently of, and superior to, any positive law and which owe their dignity not to arbitrary enactment but, on the contrary, provide the very legitimation for the binding force of positive law. Natural law has thus been the collective term for those norms which owe their legitimacy not to their origin from a legitimate lawgiver, but to their immanent and teleological qualities. It is the specific and only consistent type of legitimacy of a legal order which can remain, once religious revelation and the authoritarian sacredness of a tradition and its bearers have lost their force. Natural law has thus been the specific form of legitimacy of a revolutionarily created order. The invocation of natural law has repeatedly been the method by which classes in revolt against the existing order have legitimated their aspirations, in so far as they did not, or could not, base their claims upon positive religious norms or revelation. Not every natural law, however, has been "revolutionary" in its intentions in the sense that it would provide the justification for the realization of certain norms by violence or by passive disobedience against an existing order. Indeed, natural law has also served to legitimate authoritarian powers of the most diverse types. A "natural law of the historically real" has been quite influential in opposition to the type of natural law which is based upon or produces abstract norms. A natural law axiom of this provenience can be found, for instance, as the basis of the theory of the historical school concerning the preëminence of "customary law," a concept clearly formulated by this school for the first time.[11] It became quite explicit in the assertion that a legislator "could" not in any legally effective way restrict the sphere of validity of customary law by any enactment or exclude the derogation of the enacted law by custom. It was said to be impossible to forbid historical development to take its course. The same assumption by which enacted law is reduced to the rank of "mere" positive law is contained also in all those half historical and half naturalistic theories of Romanticism which regard the *Volksgeist* [12] as the only natural, and thus the only legitimate, source from which law and culture can emanate, and according to which all "genuine" law must have grown up "organically" and must be based directly upon the sense of justice, in contrast to "artificial," i.e., purposefully enacted, law.[13] The irrationalism of such

[11] Cf. *supra*, p. 67.

[12] Folk spirit.

[13] This attitude is represented by the Historical School, especially the Germanists, among whom Gierke has been particularly prominent (cf. *supra* c. IV, n. 9; c. IX, n. 74). An American representative was James C. Carter, the chief opponent of David Dudley Field's codification plans (see the article on him by Llewellyn in 3 ENCYC. SOC. SCI. 243).

axioms stands in sharp contrast to the natural law axioms of legal rationalism which alone were able to create norms of a formal type and to which the term "natural law" has a potiori been reserved for that reason.

3. *The Origins of Modern Natural Law.* The elaboration of natural law in modern times was in part based on the religious motivation provided by the rationalistic sects; [14] it was also partly derived from the concept of nature of the Renaissance, which everywhere strove to grasp the canon of the ends of "Nature's" will. To some extent, it is derived, too, from the idea, particularly indigenous to England, that every member of the community has certain inherent natural rights. This specifically English concept of "birthright" arose essentially under the influence of the popular conception that certain rights, which had been confirmed in Magna Charta as the special status rights of the barons, were national liberties of all Englishmen as such and that they were thus immune against any interference by the King or any other political authority.[15] But the transition to the conception that every human being as such has certain rights was mainly completed through the rationalistic enlightenment of the seventeenth and eighteenth centuries with the aid, for a time, of powerful religious, particularly Anabaptist, influences.

4. *Transformation of Formal into Substantive Natural Law.* The axioms of natural law fall into very different groups, of which we shall consider only those which bear some especially close relation to the economic order. The natural law legitimacy of positive law can be connected either with formal or with substantive conditions. The distinction is not a clear-cut one, because there simply cannot exist a completely formal natural law; the reason is that such a natural law would consist entirely of general legal concepts devoid of any content. Nonetheless, the distinction has great significance. The purest type of the

[14] The role of the "rationalist" Protestant "sects," i.e., the Puritans, Baptists, Quakers, Methodists, etc., in the rise of the spirit of modern capitalism and, in this connection, in the development of formally rational modern law, constitutes one of the central themes in Weber's thought. The problem is treated extensively in the first volume of his GES. AUFSÄTZE ZUR RELIGIONSSOZIOLOGIE (Parsons' tr. 1930), where the role of the sects is discussed on pp. 207–236 (= ESSAYS 302 *et seq.* and 450–459 [Weber's footnotes contain extensive references to literature]). In W.U.G., sociology of religion is treated in Part II, c. IV (pp. 227–356 and, as to the sects in particular, at pp. 812–817); see, furthermore, HISTORY (1950 ed.) 365.

[15] The so-called Whig conception of English history; cf. H. BUTTERFIELD, THE ENGLISHMAN AND HIS HISTORY (1944). On the real and the imaginary Magna Carta see W. S. McKechnie, *Magna Carta 1215–1915*, MAGNA CARTA COMMEMORATION ESSAYS (1917) I, 18; M. Radin, *The Myth of Magna Carta* (1947) 60 HARV. L. REV. 1060.

first category is that "natural law" concept which arose in the seventeenth and eighteenth centuries as a result of the already mentioned influences, especially in the form of the "contract theory," and more particularly the individualistic aspects of that theory. All legitimate law rests upon enactment, and all enactment, in turn, rests upon rational agreement. This agreement is either, first, real, i.e., derived from an actual original contract of free individuals, which also regulates the form in which new law is to be enacted in the future; or, second, ideal, in the sense that only that law is legitimate whose content does not contradict the conception of a reasonable order enacted by free agreement. The essential elements in such a natural law are the "freedoms," and above all, "freedom of contract." The voluntary rational contract became one of the universal formal principles of natural law construction, either as the assumed real historical basis of all rational consociations including the state, or, at least, as the regulative standard of evaluation. Like every formal natural law, this type is conceived as a system of rights legitimately acquired by purposive contract, and, as far as economic goods are concerned, it rests upon the basis of a community of economic agreement created by the full development of property. Its essential components are property and the freedom to dispose of property, i.e., property legitimately acquired by free contractual transaction made either as "primeval contract" with the whole world, or with certain other persons. Freedom of competition is implied as a constituent element. Freedom of contract has formal limits only to the extent that contracts, and associational conduct in general, must neither infringe upon the natural law by which they are legitimated nor impair inalienable freedoms. This basic principle applies to both private arrangements of individuals and the official actions of the organs of society meant to be obeyed by its members. Nobody may validly surrender himself into political or private slavery. For the rest, no enactment *can* validly limit the free disposition of the individual over his property and his working power. Thus, for example, every act of social welfare legislation prohibiting certain contents of the free labor contract, is on that account an infringement of freedom of contract. Until quite recently the Supreme Court of the United States has held that any such legislation is invalid on the purely formal ground that it is incompatible with the natural law preambles to the constitutions.[16]

"Nature" and "Reason" are the substantive criteria of what is legitimate from the standpoint of natural law. Both are regarded as the

[16] *Sic.* What is meant is obviously the due process clause of the Fourteenth Amendment of the Constitution of the United States.

same, and so are the rules that are derived from them, so that general propositions about regularities of factual occurrences and general norms of conduct are held to coincide. The knowledge gained by human "reason" is regarded as identical with the "nature of things" or, as one would say nowadays, the "logic of things." The "ought" is identical with the "is," i.e., that which exists in the universal average. Those norms, which are arrived at by the logical analysis of the concepts of the law and ethics, belong, just as the "laws of nature," to those generally binding rules which "not even God Himself could change," and with which a legal order must not come into conflict. Thus, for instance, the only kind of money which meets the requirements of the "nature of things" and the principle of the legitimacy of vested rights is that which has achieved the position of money through the free exchange of goods, in other words, metallic money.[17] Some fifteenth-century fanatics therefore argued that, according to natural law, the state should rather go to pieces than that the legitimate stability of the law be sullied by the illegitimacy of "artificially" created paper money.[18] The very "concept"

[17] See WEBER, HISTORY 236 and literature cited at p. 377; also W.U.G. Part I, c. II, §§ 6, 32–36 (THEORY 173, 280 *et seq.*).

[18] The source for this statement could not be located. It is difficult to visualize how anyone could have argued against paper money in the fifteenth century. While paper money had been used repeatedly in China at earlier times (cf. Lexis, *Papiergeld*, 6 HANDWÖRTERBUCH DER STAATSWISSENSCHAFTEN, 3rd ed. 1911, p. 997; WEBER, GES. AUFS. ZUR RELIGIONSSOZIOLOGIE 286), it was practically unknown in the West before the late seventeenth century. Both Lexis (*loc. cit.*) and W. Lotz (FINANZWISSENSCHAFT [2nd ed. 1931] 885) mention the occasional use of leather and similar emergency means of payment; however, "the systematic use for the procurement of public revenue of redeemable promises of payment circulating as currency" is said to be connected with the establishment of the Bank of England in 1694. Before that time manipulations of the currency were carried on by alteration of the coinage, as it was widely practiced by princes (cf. Palyi, *Coinage*, 3 ENCYC. SOC. SCI. 622). In France, for instance, the coinage was altered no less than seventy-one times between 1351 and 1360, resulting in serious unrest and an uprising in Paris under Etienne Marcel (cf. A. LANDRY, ESSAY ÉCONOMIQUE SUR LES MUTATIONS DES MONNAIES DANS L'ANCIENNE FRANCE [1910]).

The problem of the permissibility of such manipulation was widely discussed in the literature. The legists (see *supra*, p. 181) generally supported the princes, the canonists were more reluctant, and the Aristotelians were critical, occasionally basing their position on natural law arguments. Nicolas Oresmes (c. 1320–1382) denied that the prince had any power of his own to change the coinage but conceded that he might do so with the consent of the Estates General for urgent reasons of the common weal (E. BRIDREY, NICOLE ORESME [1906]; P. Harsin, *Oresme*, 11 ENCYC. SOC. SCI. 479; A. E. MONROE, EARLY ECONOMIC THOUGHT [1924] 79). Strong criticism was also voiced by Gabriel Biel (d. in 1495; cf. W. ROSCHER, GESCHICHTE DER NATIONALÖKONOMIK IN DEUTSCHLAND [1874] 26), CYRIAKUS

of the State is said to be abused by an infringement upon the legitimate law.

This formalism of natural law, however, was softened in several ways. First of all, in order to establish relations with the existing order, natural law had to accept legitimate grounds for the acquisition of rights which could not be derived from freedom of contract, especially acquisition through inheritance. There were numerous attempts to base the law of inheritance on natural law.[19] They were mainly of philosophical rather than positively juristic origin, and so we shall disregard them here. In the last analysis, of course, substantive motives almost always enter the picture, and highly artificial constructions are thus frequent. Many other institutions of the prevailing system, too, could not be legitimated except on practical utilitarian grounds. By "justifying" them, natural law "reason" easily slipped into utilitarian thinking, and this shift expresses itself in the change of meaning of the concept of "reasonableness." In purely formal natural law, the reasonable is that which is derivable from the eternal order of nature and logic, both being readily blended with one another. But from the very beginning, the English concept of "reasonable" contained by implication the meaning of "rational" in the sense of "practically appropriate." From this it could be concluded that what would lead in practice to absurd consequences cannot constitute the law desired by nature and reason. This signified the express introduction of substantive presuppositions into the concept of reason which had in fact always been implicit in it.[20] As a matter of fact, it was with the aid of

---

SPANGENBERG (1528–1604; cf. ROSCHER, *op. cit.* 169), and, particularly, in an anonymous pamphlet, published about 1530, on the occasion of a change in the monetary system of Saxony (W. Lotz, *Die drei Flugschriften über den Münzstreit der sächsischen Albertiner und Ernestiner* [1893], esp. at p. 10). No author could be found, however, who would have radically condemned any currency change under any circumstances. Nor could there be found any writer of the eighteenth or nineteenth century taking the position stated in Weber's text (cf. A. E. MONROE, *op. cit.*; and, by the same author, MONETARY THEORY BEFORE ADAM SMITH [1923]; ROSCHER, *op. cit.*).

[19] See, for instance, Leibniz, who derives inheritance from the immortality of the soul (NOVA METHODUS DOCENDI DISCENDIQUE JURIS, Part II, Sec. 20, 17); his argumentation is also followed by Ahrens (COURS DE DROIT NATUREL [1838], Part II, Sec. 102). Grotius finds the basis of testate succession in natural freedom and that of interstate succession in its implied agreement with the will of the decedent (DE IURE PACIS AC BELLI [1625], II, c. vii; cf. on his theory MAINE 190).

The natural law theories were attacked by Pufendorf, who declared inheritance to be an institution of positive law (DE IURE NATURAE ET GENTIUM [1672], 4.10. 2–6). This opinion was followed by Blackstone (Book II, c. xiv).

[20] What Weber has in mind is the shift from natural law thinking to utilitarianism, as expressed by Bentham, John Stuart Mill, and Spencer.

this shift in the meaning of the term that the Supreme Court of the United States was able to free itself from formal natural law so as to be able to recognize the validity of certain acts of social legislation.[21]

In principle, however, the formal natural law was transformed into a substantive natural law as soon as the legitimacy of an acquired right came to be tied up with the substantive economic rather than with the formal modes of its acquisition. Lasalle, in his System of Vested Rights,[22] still sought to solve a particular problem in natural law fashion by formal means, in his case by those derived from Hegel's theory of evolution. The inviolability of a right formally and legitimately acquired on the basis of a positive enactment is presupposed, but the natural law limitation of this type of legal positivism becomes evident in connection with the problem of the so-called retroactivity of laws and the related question of the state's duty to pay compensation where a privilege is abolished. The attempted solution, which is of no interest to us here, is of a thoroughly formal and natural law character.

The decisive turn towards substantive natural law is connected primarily with socialist theories of the exclusive legitimacy of the acquisition of wealth by one's own labor. For this view rejects not only all unearned income acquired through the channels of inheritance or by means of a guaranteed monopoly, but also the formal principle of freedom of contract and general recognition of the legitimacy of all rights acquired through the instrumentality of contracting. According to these theories, all

[21] See Knoxville Iron Co. v. Harbison (1901) 183 U.S. 13; McLean v. Arkansas (1908) 211 U.S. 539; Erie R.R. v. Williams (1914) 233 U.S. 685: — statutes prescribing the character, methods, and time for payment of wages.

Holden v. Hardy (1898) 169 U.S. 366; Bunting v. Oregon (1917) 243 U.S. 426; Muller v. Oregon (1908) 208 U.S. 412; Riley v. Massachusetts (1914) 232 U.S. 671; Miller v. Wilson (1915) 236 U.S. 373; Bosley v. McLaughlin (1915) 236 U.S. 385: — statutes fixing hours of labor.

N.Y. Central R.R. Co. v. White (1917) 243 U.S. 188: — workmen's compensation laws.

Later decisions, such as Adkins v. Children's Hospital (1923) 261 U.S. 525, in which the rule of reason was temporarily nullified, or the New Deal cases, could, of course, not be considered by Weber, whose manuscript was practically complete around 1920.

For a penetrating survey and analysis, from the continental point of view, of the attitudes of the American judiciary toward social legislation, see Ed. Lambert, Le gouvernement des juges et la lutte judiciaire contre la législation sociale aux Etats-Unis (1921).

[22] Ferdinand Lassalle, 1825–1864, German socialist, founder of the General German Workers' Association, the predecessor of the German Social Democratic party. His System der erworbenen Rechte was published in 1861. On Lassalle see the article by G. Mayer in 9 Encyc. Soc. Sci. 184.

appropriations of goods must be tested substantively by the extent to which they rest on labor as their ground of acquisition.

5. *Class Relations in Natural Law Ideology*. Naturally both the formal rationalistic natural law of freedom of contract and the substantive natural law of the exclusive legitimacy of the product of labor have definite class implications. Freedom of contract and all the propositions regarding as legitimate the property derived therefrom obviously belong to the natural law of the groups interested in market transactions, i.e., those interested in the ultimate appropriation of the means of production. Conversely, the doctrine that land is not produced by anybody's labor and that it is thus incapable of being appropriated at all, constitutes a protest against the closedness of the circle of landowners, and thus corresponds with the class situation of a proletarianized peasantry whose restricted opportunities for self-maintenance force them under the yoke of the land monopolists.[23] It is equally clear that such slogans must acquire a particularly dramatic power where the product of agricultural exploitation still depends primarily upon the natural condition of the soil and where the appropriation of the land is not, at least internally, completed; where, furthermore, agriculture is not carried on in rationally organized large-scale enterprises, and where the income of the landlord is either derived entirely from the tenants' rent or is produced through the use of peasant equipment and peasant labor. All these conditions exist in large measure in the area of the "black earth." [24] As regards its positive meaning, this natural law of the small peasantry is ambiguous. It can mean in the first place the right to a share in the land to the extent of one's own labor power (*trudovaya norma*); or, secondly, a right to the ownership of land to the extent of the traditional standard of living (*potrebityelnaya norma*). In conventional terminology the postulate thus means either the "right to work" or the "right to a minimum standard of living"; thirdly, however, the two may be combined with the demand for the right to the full product of one's labor.

As far as one can judge today, the Russian revolution of the last decade will in all probability have been the last of the world's natural law-oriented agrarian revolutions.[25] It has been bled to death by its

[23] On this and the following, see Weber's discussion of the Russian revolution of 1905 in ARCHIV F. SOZIALWISSENSCHAFT (1906), XXII, 234 and XXIII, 165; see also his article on *Russlands Übergang zur Scheindemokratie* (1917) 23 DIE HILFE 272, repr. GESAMMELTE POLITISCHE SCHRIFTEN (1921) 107.

[24] Black earth — the fertile regions of the Ukraine and South Russia.

[25] In the second of the two articles mentioned in n. 23 *supra* Weber, at p. 314, predicted the coming of a new revolution in Russia, which would be oriented to-

own intrinsic contradictions including those between its ideological postulates. Those two natural law positions are not only incompatible with one another, but they are also contradictory to the historical, realistically political and practically economical programs of the peasantry, all of which are again incongruous with the evolutionist-Marxist agrarian programs. The result has been hopeless confusion among the Revolution's own basic dogmas.

Those three "socialist" rights of the individual have also played a role in the ideologies of the industrial proletariat. The first and the second are theoretically possible under handicraft as well as under capitalistic conditions of the working class; the third, however, is possible only under handicraft conditions. Under capitalism the third right of natural law is possible either not at all or only where cost prices are strictly and universally maintained in all exchange transactions. In agriculture, it can be applied only where production is not capitalistic, since capitalism shifts the attribution of the agricultural produce of the soil from the direct place of agricultural production to the shop, where the agricultural implements, artificial fertilizers, etc., are produced; and the same holds true for industry. Quite generally, where the return is determined by the sale of the product in a freely competitive market, the content of the right of the individual to the full value of his product inevitably loses its meaning. There simply is no longer an individual "labor yield," and if the claim is to make any sense it can be only as the collective claim of all those who find themselves in a common class situation. In practice, this comes down to the demand for a "living wage," i.e., to a special variant of the "right to the standard of living as determined by traditional need." It thus resembles the medieval "just price" as demanded by ecclesiastical ethics,[26] which, in case of doubt, was determined by the test (and occasionally experimentally) of whether or not at the given price the craftsmen in question could maintain the standard of living appropriate to their social status.

The "just price" itself, which was the most important natural law element in canonist economic doctrine, fell prey to the same fate. In the canonistic discussions of the determinants of the "just price" one can observe how this labor value price corresponding to the "subsistence principle" is gradually replaced by the competitive price which becomes

---

ward communism rather than natural law and which would create a state of affairs different from anything that had ever existed before (*etwas wirklich noch nicht Dagewesenes*).

[26] On the doctrine of "just price" see W.u.G. 801; cf. also the article by Salin in 8 Encyc. Soc. Sci. 504.

the new "natural" price in the same measure as the market community progresses. In the writings of Antonin of Florence[27] the latter had already come to prevail. In the outlook of the Puritans it was, of course, completely dominant. The price which was to be rejected as "unnatural" was now one which did not rest on the competition of the free market, i.e., the price which was influenced by monopolies or other arbitrary human intervention. Throughout the whole puritanically influenced Anglo-Saxon world this principle has had a great influence up to the very present.[28] Because of the fact that the principle derived its dignity from natural law, it remained a far stronger support for the ideal of "free competition" than those purely utilitarian economic theories which were produced on the Continent in the manner of Bastiat.[29]

6. *Practical Significance and Distintegration of Natural Law.* All natural law dogmas have influenced more or less considerably both lawmaking and lawfinding. Some of them survived the economic conditions of the time of their origin and have come to constitute an independent factor in legal development. Formally, they have strengthened the tendency towards logically abstract law, especially the power of logic in legal thinking. Substantively, their influence has varied, but it has been significant everywhere. This is not the place to trace in detail these influences and the changes and compromises of the various natural law axioms. The codifications of the pre-revolutionary rationalistic modern State, as well as the revolutionary codifications, were influenced by the dogmas of natural law, and they ultimately derived the legitimacy of the law which they created from its reasonableness.[30] We have already seen how easily on the basis of such a concept the shift from the ethical and juristically formal to the utilitarian and technically substantive could, and did, take place. This transformation, for reasons which we have already discussed, was very favorable to the pre-revolutionary patriarchal powers, while the codifications of the Revolution, which took place under the influence of the bourgeoisie, stressed and strengthened the formal natural law, which guaranteed to the individual his rights vis-à-vis the political authorities.

The rise of Socialism at first meant the growing dominance of sub-

[27] St. Antonio, 1389–1459, Florentine churchman and writer on ethics and economics; see the article by B. Jarrett in 2 ENCYC. SOC. SCI. 126.

[28] Cf. *supra* n. 14.

[29] Frédéric Bastiat, 1801–1850, French economist and social philosopher; see the article by P. T. Homan in 2 ENCYC. SOC. SCI. 476.

[30] For a monographic inquiry into the influence of natural law ideologies upon one particular code, viz., that of Austria, see SWOBODA, DAS ALLGEMEINE BÜRGERLICHE GESETZBUCH IM LICHTE KANTS (1924).

stantive natural law doctrines in the minds of the masses and even more in the minds of their theorists from among the intelligentsia. These substantive natural law doctrines could not, however, achieve practical influence over the administration of justice, simply because, before they had achieved a position to do so, they were already being disintegrated by the rapidly growing positivistic and relativistic-evolutionistic skepticism of the very same intellectual strata. Under the influence of this anti-metaphysical radicalism, the eschatological expectations of the masses sought support in prophecies rather than in postulates. Hence in the domain of the revolutionary theories of law, natural law doctrine was destroyed by the evolutionary dogmatism of Marxism, while from the side of "official" learning it was annihilated partly by the Comtean evolutionary scheme and partly by the historicist theories of organic growth. A final contribution in the same direction was made by Realpolitik which, under the impact of modern power politics, had come to affect the treatment of public law.[31]

The method of the public law theorists has been, and still is to a great extent, to point to certain apparent practical-political absurdities as the consequence of the juristic theory which they happen to oppose; and then to treat the theory as effectively disposed of forever after. This method is not only directly opposed to that of formal law, but it also contains nothing of substantive natural law. In the main, continental jurisprudence, even up to the most recent times, proceeds on the basis of the largely unchallenged axiom of the logical "closedness" of the positive law.[32] It seems for the first time to have been expressly stated by Bentham as a protest against the case law rut and the irrationality of the common law.[33] It is indirectly supported by all those tendencies which reject all transcendental law, especially natural law, including, to this extent, the historical school. While it would hardly seem possible to eradicate completely from legal practice all the latent influence of unacknowledged axioms of natural law, for a variety of reasons the

[31] The mode of a completely "positivist" treatment of public law was represented in Germany particularly by Paul Laband (1838–1918) and his disciples. On Laband, see the article by E. von Hippel in 8 ENCYC. SOC. SCI. 614.

[32] See *supra*, ch. IV, pp. 61 *et seq.*

[33] Weber here states an opinion expressed by Hatschek (ENGLISCHES STAATSRECHT 153), but opposed by J. Lucas (*Zur Lehre von dem Willen des Gesetzgebers*, FESTGABE FÜR LABAND [1908]), who traced the dogma of the gaplessness of the legal order to the natural law tendencies of absolute monarchy and denied any possible influence in this respect of Bentham. The controversy was carried on in a series of articles by Hatschek (1909), 24 ARCHIV. F. ÖFFENTLICHES RECHT 442; (1910) 26 *ibid.* 458; and Lukas (1910) 26 *ibid.* 67 and 465.

axioms of natural law have been deeply discredited. The conflict between the axioms of substantive and formal natural law is insoluble. Evolutionist theories have been at work in various forms. All metajuristic axioms in general have been subject to ever continuing disintegration and relativization. In consequence of both juridical rationalism and modern intellectual skepticism in general, the axioms of natural law have lost all capacity to provide the fundamental bases of a legal system. Compared with firm beliefs in the positive religiously revealed character of a legal norm or in the inviolable sacredness of an age-old tradition, even the most convincing norms arrived at by abstraction seem to be too subtle to serve as the bases of a legal system. Consequently, legal positivism has, at least for the time being, advanced irresistibly. The disappearance of the old natural law conceptions has destroyed all possibility of providing the law with a metaphysical dignity by virtue of its immanent qualities. In the great majority of its most important provisions, it has been unmasked all too visibly, indeed, as the product or the technical means of a compromise between conflicting interests.

But this extinction of the metajuristic implications of the law is one of those ideological developments which, while they have increased skepticism towards the dignity of the particular rules of a concrete legal order, have also effectively promoted the actual obedience to the power, now viewed solely from an instrumentalist standpoint, of the authorities who claim legitimacy at the moment. Among the practitioners of the law this attitude has been particularly pronounced.[34]

7. *Legal Positivism and the Legal Profession.* The vocational responsibility of maintaining the existing legal system seems to place the practitioners of the law in general among the "conservative" forces. This is true in the twofold sense that legal practitioners are inclined to remain cool not only toward the pressure of substantive postulates put forward from "below" in the name of "social" ideals but also towards those from "above" which are put forward in the name of patriarchal power, or the welfare-interests of the sovereign. Of course, this statement should not be taken as representing the whole truth without qualifications. The role of the representative of the underprivileged, and of the advocate of

[34] On positivism in Germany see G. RADBRUCH, RECHTSPHILOSOPHIE (1950) 115. This latest book of Radbruch's (as to his earlier views, see the 20th Century Legal Philosophy Series, Vol. IV, *The Legal Philosophies of Lask, Radbruch, and Dabin* [1950]) is also typical of the revival of natural law thinking in post-World-War-II Germany; cf. in this respect also H. COING, DIE OBERSTEN GRUNDSÄTZE DES RECHTS (1947), and GRUNDZÜGE DER RECHTSPHILOSOPHIE (1950); on the transformations of Radbruch's thought, see F. v. HIPPEL, GUSTAV RADBRUCH ALS RECHTSPHILOSOPHISCHER DENKER (1951).

formal equality before the law is particularly suited to the attorney by reason of his direct relationship with his clients, as well as by reason of his character as a private person working for a living and his fluctuating social status. This is why attorneys, and lawyers in general, have played such a leading role in the movements of the popolani of the Italian communes[35] and, later, in all the bourgeois revolutions of modern times as well as in the socialist parties. It also explains why in purely democratic countries, such as in France, Italy, or the United States, the lawyers, as the professionally expert technicians of the legal crafts, as honoratiores, and as the fiduciaries of their clients, are the natural aspirants to political careers.[36]

Under certain circumstances, judges, too, have maintained strong opposition to patriarchal powers, either for ideological reasons or out of considerations of status group solidarity or, occasionally, because of economic reasons. To them, the fixed and regular determinateness of all external rights and duties is apt to appear as a worth-while value to be pursued for its own sake; this specifically "bourgeois" element in their thought has determined their attitudes in the political conflicts which were fought for the purpose of limiting authoritarian patrimonial arbitrariness and favoritism.[37]

Whether the legal profession would take the side either of the authoritarian or the anti-authoritarian powers, once the "rule-boundedness" of the social order had been achieved, depended upon whether the emphasis was more upon mere "order," or upon "liberty," in the sense of guaranty and security of the individual. The choice depended, in the terminology of Radbruch, on whether law was viewed more as "regulation" or as the source of "rights." [38] But quite apart from this antinomy, it was also the previously mentioned alternative between the formal and substantive legal ideals and the vigorous, economically conditioned revival of the latter, both in the upper and lower strata of the social hierarchy, that weakened the oppositionist tendencies of the lawyers as such. We shall discuss later just what technical devices authoritative powers have used to overcome resistance from within the judiciary.[39] Among the general

[35] Cf. W.u.G. Part III, c. VIII, Sec. 4 (p. 562); also Weber's article *Die Stadt* (1920/21), 47 ARCHIV F. SOZIALWISSENSCHAFT 704, 718.

[36] Cf. Weber in *Politik als Beruf*, GES. POLITISCHE SCHRIFTEN 396 [ESSAYS 77, 94].

[37] Cf. the conflict between Frederick II of Prussia and his judges in the Arnold case, *supra* c. VIII, n. 17.

[38] Cf. RECHTSPHILOSOPHIE (1914 ed.); the terminology is no longer used, however, in the versions of 1932 and 1950.

[39] This intended investigation was not carried out by Weber.

ideological factors which account for the change in the lawyers' attitude, the disappearance of the belief in natural law has played a major role. If the legal profession of the present day manifests at all typical ideological affinities to various power groups, its members are inclined to stand on the side of "order," which in practice means that they will take the side of the "legitimate" authoritarian political power that happens to predominate at the given moment. In this respect, they differ from the lawyers of the English and French revolutionary periods and of the period of enlightenment in general. They differ also from those who had to act within the framework of patrimonial despotism or had been sitting in [German nineteenth-century] parliamentary bodies and municipal councils down to Prussia's "circuit judges' parliament" of the 1860's.[40]

[40] *Kreisrichterparlament* — so called because a considerable number of its members were *Kreisrichter* (circuit judges), who, at the time, were predominantly Liberals and opposed to the policies of Bismarck.

CHAPTER XI

THE FORMAL QUALITIES OF MODERN LAW[1]

1. *Specialization in Modern Law.* As we have seen, the specifically modern occidental type of administration of justice has arisen on the basis of rational and systematic legislation. However, its basic formal qualities are by no means unambiguously definable. Indeed, this ambiguity is a direct result of more recent developments.

The ancient principles which were decisive for the interlocking of "right" and law have disappeared, especially the idea that one's right has a "valid" quality only by virtue of one's membership in a group of persons by whom this quality is monopolized. To the past now also belongs the tribal or status-group quality of the sum total of a person's rights and, with it, their "particularity" as it once existed on the basis of free association or of usurped or legalized privilege. Equally gone are the estatist and other special courts and procedures. Yet neither all special and personal law nor all special jurisdictions have disappeared completely. On the contrary, very recent legal developments have brought an increasing specialization within the legal system. Only the principle of demarcation of the various spheres has been characteristically changed. A typical case is that of commercial law, which is, indeed, one of the most important instances of modern specialization. Under the German Commercial Code this special law applies to certain types of contracts,[2] the most important of which is the contract for acquisition of goods with the intention of profitable resale. This definition of commercial contract is entirely in accordance with a rationalized legal system; the definition does not refer to formal qualities, but to the intended

[1] W.u.G. 503–513.

[2] These transactions, which are enumerated in Sec. 1 of the German Commercial Code of 1861/97, are the following:

(a) purchase and resale of commodities or securities such as bonds; (b) enterprise by an independent contractor to do work on materials or goods supplied by the other party; (c) underwriting of insurance; (d) banking; (e) transportation of goods or passengers, on land, at sea, and on inland waterways; (f) transactions of factors, brokers, forwarding agents, and warehousemen; (g) transactions of commercial brokers, jobbers, and agents; (h) transactions of publishers, book and art dealers; (i) transactions of printers.

functional meaning of the concrete transaction. On the other hand, commercial law also applies to certain categories of persons whose decisive characteristic consists in the fact that contracts are made by them in the course of their business.[3] What is thus really decisive for the demarcation of the sphere of this type of law is the concept of "enterprise." An enterprise is a commercial enterprise when transactions of such peculiar kind are its constitutive elements. Thus every contract which "belongs" substantively, i.e., in its intention, to a commercial enterprise is under the Commercial Code, even though, when regarded alone and by itself, it does not belong to that category of transactions which are generically defined as commercial and even though, in a particular case, such a contract may happen to be made by a nonmerchant. The application of this body of special law is thus determined either by substantive qualities of an individual transaction, especially its intended meaning, or by the objective association of a transaction with the rational organization of an enterprise. It is not determined, however, by a person's membership in an estate legally constituted by free agreement or privilege, which was in the past the operative factor for the application of a special law.

Commercial law, then, inasmuch as its application is personally delimited, is a class law rather than a status-group law. However, this contrast with the past is but a relative one. Indeed, so far as the law of commerce and the law of other purely economic "occupations" are concerned, the principle of jurisdictional delimitation has always had a purely substantive character, which, while often varying in externals, has essentially been the same throughout. But those particularities in the legal system which constituted a definite status law were more significant both quantitatively and qualitatively. Besides, even the vocational special jurisdictions, so far as their jurisdictions did not depend upon the litigants' membership in a certain corporate body, have usually depended upon mere formal criteria such as acquisition of a license or a privilege. For example, under the new German Commercial Code, a person is characterized as a merchant by the mere fact that he is listed in the register of commercial firms.[4] The personal scope of application of the commercial law is thus determined by a purely formal test, while in other respects its sphere is delimited by the economic purpose which a

[3] The German Commercial Code, in Sec. 2, has the following definition: "Any enterprise which requires an established business because of its size or because of the manner in which it is carried on, is a commercial enterprise, even though it does not fall within any of the categories stated in Sec. 1." Similarly, the French Commercial Code of 1807 states in Art. 1: "Merchants are all those who carry on commercial transactions and make this activity their habit and profession."

[4] *Handelsregister* (register of firms): cf. Commercial Code, Secs. 2, 5, 8, *et seq.*

given transaction purports to achieve. The spheres of the special laws applicable to other occupational groups are also predominantly defined along substantive or functional criteria, and it is only under certain circumstances that applicability is governed by formal tests. Many of these modern special laws are also combined with special courts and procedures of their own.[5]

Mainly two causes are responsible for the emergence of these particularistic laws. In the first place, they have been a result of the occupational differentiation and the increasing attention which commercial and industrial pressure groups have obtained for themselves. What they expect from these particularistic arrangements is that their legal affairs will be handled by specialized experts.[6] The second cause, which has played an increasingly important role in most recent times, has been the desire to eliminate the formalities of normal legal procedure for the sake of a settlement that would be both expeditious and better adapted to the concrete case.[7] In practice, this trend signifies a weakening of legal formalism out of considerations of substantive expediency and thus constitutes but one instance among a whole series of similar contemporary phenomena.

2. *The Anti-Formalistic Tendencies of Modern Legal Development.* From a theoretical point of view, the general development of law and procedure may be viewed as passing through the following stages: first, charismatic legal revelation through "law prophets"; second, empirical creation and finding of law by legal honoratiores, i.e., law creation through cautelary jurisprudence and adherence to precedent; third, imposition of law by secular or theocratic powers; fourth and finally, systematic elaboration of law and professionalized administration of justice by persons who have received their legal training in a learned and formally logical manner. From this perspective, the formal qualities of the law emerge as follows: arising in primitive legal procedure from a combination of magically conditioned formalism and irrationality con-

[5] The most important special law of this kind is the labor law with its special hierarchy of labor courts. There are, furthermore, the administrative tribunals of general administrative jurisdiction and a set of special tribunals dealing respectively with claims arising under the social security laws or the war pensions laws, with tax matters, with certain matters of agricultural administration, etc.

[6] Both the commercial and the labor courts are usually organized in panels chosen from those lines of business or industry whose affairs are dealt with by the particular division of the court. Cf. ARBEITSGERICHTSGESETZ of 23 December, 1926 (R.G. BL. I, 507), Sec. 17.

[7] In the labor courts representation by attorneys is, as a general rule, not permitted at the trial stage (ARBEITSGERICHTSGESETZ of 23 December, 1926 [R.G. BL. I, 507], Sec. 11).

ditioned by revelation, they proceed to increasingly specialized juridical and logical rationality and systematization, passing through a stage of theocratically or patrimonially conditioned substantive and informal expediency. Finally, they assume, at least from an external viewpoint, an increasingly logical sublimation and deductive rigor and develop an increasingly rational technique in procedure.

Since we are here only concerned with the most general lines of development, we shall ignore the fact that in historical reality the theoretically constructed stages of rationalization have not everywhere followed in the sequence which we have just outlined, even if we ignore the world outside the Occident. We shall not be troubled either by the multiplicity of causes of the particular type and degree of rationalization that a given law has actually assumed. As our brief sketch has already shown, we shall only recall that the great differences in the line of development have been essentially influenced, first, by the diversity of political power relationships, which, for reasons to be discussed later, have resulted in very different degrees of power of the imperium vis-à-vis the powers of the kinship groups, the folk community, and the estates; second, by the relations between the theocratic and the secular powers; and, third, by the differences in the structure of those legal honoratiores who were significant for the development of a given law and which, too, were largely dependent upon political factors.

Only the Occident has witnessed the fully developed administration of justice of the folk-community (*Dinggenossenschaft*) and the status group stereotyped form of patrimonialism; and only the Occident has witnessed the rise of the rational economic system, whose agents first allied themselves with the princely powers to overcome the estates and then turned against them in revolution; and only the West has known "Natural Law," and with it the complete elimination of the system of personal laws and of the ancient maxim that special law prevails over general law. Nowhere else, finally, has there occurred any phenomenon resembling Roman law and anything like its reception. All these events have to a very large extent been caused by concrete political factors, which have only the remotest analogies elsewhere in the world. For this reason, the stage of decisively shaping law by trained legal specialists has not been fully reached anywhere outside of the Occident. Economic conditions have, as we have seen, everywhere played an important role, but they have nowhere been decisive alone and by themselves. To the extent that they contributed to the formation of the specifically modern features of present-day occidental law, the direction in which they worked has been by and large the following: To those who had interests in the commodity market, the rationalization and systematization of the law in general and, with certain reservations to be stated later, the increasing calculability of the functioning of the legal process in particular, constituted one of the most important conditions for the existence of economic enterprise intended to function with stability and, especially, of capitalistic enterprise, which cannot do without legal security. Special forms of transactions and special procedures, like the bill of exchange and the special procedure for its speedy collection, serve this need for the purely formal certainty of the guaranty of legal enforcement.

On the other hand, the modern and, to a certain extent, the ancient Roman, legal developments have contained tendencies favorable to the dilution of legal formalism. At a first glance, the displacement of the formally bound law of evidence by the "free evaluation of proof" appears to be of a merely technical character.[8] We have seen that the primitive system of magically bound proof was exploded through the rationalism of either the theocratic or the patrimonial kind, both of which postulated procedures for the disclosure of the real truth. Thus the new system clearly appears as a product of substantive rationalization. Today, however, the scope and limits of the free evaluation of proof are determined primarily by commercial interests, i.e., by economic factors. It is clear that, through the system of free evaluation of proof, a very considerable domain which was once subject to formal juristic thought is being increasingly withdrawn therefrom.[9] But we are here more concerned with

[8] Roman-canonical procedure, as it had come to be adopted generally in the continental courts, was characterized by its system of "formal proof," which was in many respects similar to the law of evidence of Anglo-American procedure. There were rules about exclusion of certain kinds of evidence and, quite particularly, detailed rules about corroboration and about the mechanical ways in which the judge had to evaluate conflicting evidence. The testimony of two credible witnesses constituted full proof (*probatio plena*); one credible witness made half proof (*probatio semiplena*), but one doubtful witness (*testis suspectus*) made less than half proof (*probatio semiplena minor*), etc.

This entire system of formal proof was swept away by the procedural reforms of the nineteenth century and replaced by the system of free or rational proof, which did away with most of the exclusionary rules, released the judge from his arithmetical shackles, and authorized him to evaluate the evidence in the light of experience and reason. Cf. ENGELMANN-MILLAR 39.

[9] Together with the rule of stare decisis and, to some extent, the jury system, the fact that the Common Law has preserved a much more formalistic law of evidence is the principal cause why in such fields as torts, damages, interpretation and construction of legal instruments, English and American law have developed so much more numerous and detailed rules of law than the systems of the Civil Law. The comparison, for instance, of the 951 sections of the Restatement of Torts

the corresponding trends in the sphere of substantive law. One such trend lies in the intrinsic necessities of legal thought. Its growing logical sublimation has meant everywhere the substitution for a dependence on externally tangible formal characteristics of an increasingly logical interpretation of meaning in relation to the legal norms themselves as well as in relation to legal transactions. In the doctrine of the continental "common law" this interpretation claimed that it would give effect to the "real" intentions of the parties; in precisely this manner it introduced an individualizing and relatively substantive factor into legal formalism. This kind of interpretation seeks to construct the relations of the parties to one another from the point of view of the "inner" kernel of their behavior, from the point of view of their mental "attitudes" (such as good faith or malice).[10] Thus it relates legal consequences to informal elements of the situation and this treatment provides a telling parallel to that systematization of religious ethics which we have already considered previously.[11] Much of the system of commodity exchange, in primitive as well as in technically differentiated patterns of trade, is possible only on the basis of far-reaching personal confidence and trust in the loyalty of others. Moreover, as commodity exchange increases in importance, the need in legal practice to guarantee or secure such trustworthy conduct becomes proportionally greater. But in the very nature of the case, we cannot, of course, define with formal certainty the legal tests according to which the new relations of trust and confidence are to be governed. Hence, through such ethical rationalization the courts have been helpful to powerful interests. Also, outside of the sphere of commodity exchange, the rationalization of the law has substituted attitude-evaluation as the significant element for assessment of events according to external criteria. In criminal law, legal rationalization has replaced the purely mechanistic remedy of vengeance by rational "ends of punishment" of an either ethical or utilitarian character, and

---

and the 31 sections dealing with torts in the German Civil Code (Secs. 823–853) or the 5 sections of the French Code (Arts. 1382–86) is revealing in this respect, just as is the comparison of the few sections of the German Code dealing with the interpretation of wills (Secs. 2087 *et seq.*) with the elaborate treatment of the topic in American law.

As to the law of evidence itself, compare the ten volumes of Wigmore's treatise (3rd ed. 1940) with the complete absence of books on evidence in Germany or the brief treatment of a few evidentiary problems in the French treatises on private law, for instance, in JOSSERAND'S COURS DE DROIT CIVIL POSITIF FRANÇAIS (1939), where the chapter on "preuves" covers 43 pages.

[10] Cf. HEDEMANN I, 117.

[11] W.U.G., Part II, c. IV, 227–356.

has thereby introduced increasingly nonformal elements into legal practice. In the sphere of private law the concern for a party's mental attitude has quite generally entailed evaluation by the judge. "Good faith and fair dealing" or the "good" usage of trade or, in other words, ethical categories have become the test of what the parties are entitled to mean by their "intention."[12] Yet, the reference to the "good" usage of trade implies in substance the recognition of such attitudes which are held by the average party concerned with the case, i.e., a general and purely business criterion of an essentially factual nature, such as the average expectation of the parties in a given transaction. It is this standard which the law has consequently to accept.[13]

Now we have already seen that the expectations of parties will often be disappointed by the results of a strictly professional legal logic.[14] Such disappointments are inevitable indeed where the facts of life are juridically "construed" in order to make them fit the abstract propositions of law and in accordance with the maxim that nothing can exist in the realm of law unless it can be "conceived" by the jurist in conformity with those "principles" which are revealed to him by juristic science. The expectations of the parties are oriented towards the economic and utilitarian meaning of a legal proposition. However, from the point of view of legal logic, this meaning is an "irrational" one. For example, the layman will never understand why it should be impossible under the traditional definition of larceny to commit a larceny of electric power.[15]

[12] For illustrations of this judicial attitude see the case surveys given in connection with Sec. 242 of the German Civil Code (good faith and fair dealing) or Sec. 346 of the Commercial Code ("good" custom of trade) in the annotated editions of these Codes. The dangers of excessive judicial resort to legal provisions referring the judge to such indefinite standards have been pointed out by HEDEMANN, DIE FLUCHT IN DIE GENERALKLAUSELN, EINE GEFAHR FÜR RECHT UND STAAT (1933).

[13] The German Supreme Court has consistently maintained, however, that a usage is not to be considered when it is unfair, and especially when it constitutes a gross abuse of a position of economic power; see, for instance, 114 ENTSCHEIDUNGEN DES REICHSGERICHTS IN ZIVILSACHEN 97; [1922] JURISTISCHE WOCHENSCHRIFT 488; [1932] o.c. 586.

[14] The possibilities of such discrepancies have been pointed out especially in the writings of Heck and other advocates of the "jurisprudence of interests." See in this respect THE JURISPRUDENCE OF INTERESTS, vol. II of this 20th Century Legal Philosophy Series.

[15] Such was the decision of the German Supreme Court in 29 ENTSCHEIDUNGEN DES REICHSGERICHTS IN STRAFSACHEN 111 and 32 o.c. 165. In Sec. 242 of the German Criminal Code larceny is defined as the unlawful taking of a chattel. Electric power is not a chattel; hence it cannot be the subject matter of larceny. The gap in the law was filled by the enactment of a Special Law Concerning the Unlawful Taking of Electric Power, of 9 April 1900 (R.G. BL. 1900, 228). The decisions just men-

It is by no means the peculiar foolishness of modern jurisprudence which leads to such conflicts. To a large extent such conflicts rather are the inevitable consequence of the incompatibility that exists between the intrinsic necessities of logically consistent formal legal thinking and the fact that the legally relevant agreements and activities of private parties are aimed at economic results and oriented towards economically determined expectations. It is for this reason that we find the ever-recurrent protests against the professional legal method of thought as such, which are finding support even in the lawyers' own reflections on their work. But a "lawyers' law" has never been and never will be brought into conformity with lay expectation unless it totally renounce that formal character which is immanent in it. This is just as true of the English law which we glorify so much today,[16] as it has been of the ancient Roman jurists or of the methods of modern continental legal thought. Any attempt, like that of Erich Jung,[17] to replace the antiquated "law of nature"[18] by a new "natural law"[19] aiming at "dispute settlement" (Streitschlichtung) in accordance with the average expectations of average parties would thus come up against certain immanent limitations. But, nevertheless, this idea does have some validity in relation to the realities of legal history. The Roman law of the later Republic and the Empire developed a type of commercial ethics that was in fact oriented towards that which is to be expected on the average. Such a view means, of course, that only a small group of clearly corrupt or fraudulent practices would be outlawed, and the law would not go beyond what is regarded as the "ethical minimum."[20] In spite of the bona fides (which a seller had to display), the maxim of caveat emptor remained valid.

New demands for a "social law" to be based upon such emotionally colored ethical postulates as justice or human dignity, and thus directed against the very dominance of a mere business morality have arisen in modern times with the emergence of the modern class problem. They are

---

tioned have become the stock "horrible" in modern German excoriations of conceptual jurisprudence.

[16] In the years preceding the First World War the English administration of justice and, particularly, the creative role and prominent position of the English "judicial kings" (*Richterkönige*) were highly praised and advocated for adoption, particularly by A. MENDELSSOHN BARTHOLDY, IMPERIUM DES RICHTERS (1908), and F. ADICKES, GRUNDLINIEN EINER DURCHGREIFENDEN JUSTIZREFORM (1906).

[17] DAS PROBLEM DES NATÜRLICHEN RECHTS (1912).

[18] *Naturrecht*. [Weber's note.]

[19] *Natürliches Recht*. [Weber's note.]

[20] Expression of G. JELLINEK, in DIE SOZIAL-ETHISCHE BEDEUTUNG VON RECHT, UNRECHT UND STRAFE (2nd ed. 1908).

advocated not only by labor and other interested groups but also by legal ideologists.[21] By these demands legal formalism itself has been challenged. Such a concept as economic duress,[22] or the attempt to treat as immoral, and thus as invalid, a contract because of a gross disproportion between promise and consideration,[23] are derived from norms which, from the legal standpoint, are entirely amorphous and which are neither juristic nor conventional nor traditional in character but ethical and which claim as their legitimation substantive justice rather than formal legality.

Internal professional ideologies of the lawyers themselves have been operative in legal theory and practice along with those influences which have been engendered by both the social demands of democracy and the welfare ideology of monarchical bureaucracy. The status of being confined to the interpretation of statutes and contracts, like a slot machine into which one just drops the facts (plus the fee) in order to have it spew out the decision (plus opinion), appears to the modern lawyer as beneath his dignity; and the more universal the codified formal statute law has become, the more unattractive has this notion come to be. The present demand is for "judicial creativeness," at least where the statute is silent. The school of "free law" has undertaken to prove that such silence is the inevitable fate of every statute in view of the irrationality of the facts of life; that in countless instances the application of the statutes as "interpreted" is a delusion, and that the decision is, and ought to be, made in the light of concrete evaluations rather than in accordance with formal norms.[24]

[21] On Gierke as the leading legal scholar in the movement for law as an expression of "social justice," see G. BÖHMER, GRUNDLAGEN DER BÜRGERLICHEN RECHTSORDNUNG (1951) II, 155; see, especially, Gierke's lecture on THE SOCIAL TASK OF PRIVATE LAW (DIE SOZIALE AUFGABE DES PRIVATRECHTS, 1899), repr. E. WOLF, DEUTSCHES RECHTSDENKEN (1948).

[22] On the development of the doctrine of economic duress in positive German law, see J. Dawson, *Economic Duress and the Fair Exchange in French and German Law* (1937), 12 TULANE L. REV. 42.

[23] In Sec. 138 the German Civil Code provides as follows:

"A legal transaction which violates good morals is void.

"Void, in particular, is any transaction in which one party, by exploiting the emergency situation, the imprudence, or the inexperience of another causes such other person to promise or to give to him or to a third person a pecuniary benefit which so transcends the value of his own performance that under the circumstances of the case the relationship between them appears as manifestly disproportionate."

[24] The School of Free Law (*Freirecht*) constitutes the German counterpart of American and Scandinavian "realism." The basic theoretical idea of these three schools, viz., that law is not "found" by the judges but "made" by them, was anticipated in 1885 by Oskar Bülow in his GESETZ UND RICHTERAMT. The first at-

For the case where the statute fails to provide a clear rule, the well-known Article 1 of the Swiss Civil Code orders the judge to decide according to that rule which he himself would promulgate if he were the

---

tack upon the Pandectist "Konstruktionsjurisprudenz" (conceptual jurisprudence) or, in Weber's terminology, rational formalism, was made in 1848 by v. Kirchmann in his sensational pamphlet ÜBER DIE WERTLOSIGKEIT DER JURISPRUDENZ ALS WISSENSCHAFT. The attack was later joined by no less a scholar than Jhering, who until then had been one of the most prominent expounders of the traditional method, but who now came to emphasize the role of the law as a means to obtain utilitarian ends in a way which would now be called "social engineering" or, in Weber's terms, "substantive rationality" (DER ZWECK IM RECHT, 1877/83; Husik's tr. s.t. LAW AS A MEANS TO AN END, 1913) and to ridicule legal conceptualism in his SCHERZ UND ERNST IN DER JURISPRUDENZ (1855; on Jhering see STONE 299). At the turn of the century the attack was intensified and combined with the postulates that the courts should shake off the technique of conceptual jurisprudence (i.e., in Weber's terminology, the technique of rational formalism), should give up the fiction of the gaplessness of the legal order, should thus treat statutes and codes as ordaining nothing beyond the narrowest meaning of the words of the text, and should fill in the gaps thus created, i.e., in the great mass of problems, in a process of free, "kingly" creativeness. The leaders of this movement were E. Fuchs, a practicing attorney (principal works: DIE GEMEINSCHÄDLICHKEIT DER KONSTRUKTIVEN JURISPRUDENZ ["The Dangers of the Conceptual Jurisprudence to the Common Weal," 1909]; WAS WILL DIE FREIRECHTSSCHULE? ["What Are the Aims of the School of Free Law?" 1929]). Professor H. Kantorowicz (writing under the pen name of Gnaeus Flavius: DER KAMPF UM DIE RECHTSWISSENSCHAFT [1908]; AUS DER VORGESCHICHTE DER FREIRECHTSLEHRE [1925]; see also the article by him and E. Patterson, *Legal Science — a Summary of its Methodology* [1928], 28 COL. L. REV. 679, and *Some Rationalizations about Realism* [1934], 43 YALE L.J., 1240, where Kantorowicz recedes from some of his earlier theses), and the judge J. G. Gmelin (QUOUSQUE? BEITRAG ZUR SOZIOLOGISCHEN RECHTSFINDUNG [1910, Bruncken's transl. in Modern Legal Philosophy Series, IX, SCIENCE OF LEGAL METHOD (1917)]). These passionate radicals were joined by E. Ehrlich, who provided for the new movement a broad historical and sociological basis (FREIE RECHTSFINDUNG UND FREIE RECHTSWISSENSCHAFT [1903, Bruncken's transl. in Modern Legal Philosophy Series, IX, SCIENCE OF LEGAL METHOD (1917), 47]; *Die juristische Logik* [1918], 115 ARCHIV FÜR DIE CIVILISTISCHE PRAXIS, nos. 2 and 3, repr. as a book in 1925; and his GRUNDLEGUNG DER SOZIOLOGIE DES RECHTS [1913], Moll's transl. s.t. FUNDAMENTAL PRINCIPLES OF THE SOCIOLOGY OF LAW [1936]).

The movement stirred up violent discussion (see especially H. REICHEL, GESETZ UND RICHTERSPRUCH [1915]; G. BÖHMER, GRUNDLAGEN DER BÜRGERLICHEN RECHTSORDNUNG [1951], II, 158) and also found some attention in the United States. (See the translations listed above in this note.) Its exaggerations were generally repudiated, however, and actual developments came to be more effectively influenced by the ideas of the so-called school of jurisprudence of interests, whose principal writings are collected in vol. II of this 20th Century Legal Philosophy Series, entitled THE JURISPRUDENCE OF INTERESTS (1948). The method was elaborated primarily by M. Rümelin, P. Heck, and their companions at Tübingen, and by R. Müller-Erzbach, who has been working at the elaboration of social and concrete bases for that "balancing of interests" which the method requires (see especially DAS PRIVATE RECHT

legislator.[25] This provision, the practical import of which should not be overestimated, however,[26] corresponds formally with the Kantian formula. But in reality a judicial system which would practice such ideals would, in view of the inevitability of value-compromises, very often have to forget about abstract norms and, at least in cases of conflict, would have to admit concrete evaluations, i.e., not only nonformal but irrational lawfinding. Indeed, the doctrine of the inevitability of gaps in the legal order as well as the campaign to recognize as fiction the systematic coherence of the law has been given further impetus by the assertions that the judicial process never consisted, or, at any rate never should consist, in the "application" of general norms to a concrete case, just as no utterance in language should be regarded as an application of the rules of grammar.[27] In this view, the "legal propositions" are regarded as secondary and as being derived by abstraction from the concrete decisions which, as the products of judicial practice, are said to be the real embodiment of the law. Going still farther, one has pointed out the quantitative infrequency of those cases which ever come to trial and judicial decision as against the tremendous mass of rules by which human behavior is actually determined; from this observation one has come derogatively to call "mere rules of decision" those norms which appear in the judicial process, to contrast them with those norms which are factually valid in the course of everyday life and independently of their reaffirmation or declaration in legal procedure, and, ultimately, to estab-

---

DER MITGLIEDSCHAFT ALS PRÜFSTEIN EINES KAUSALEN RECHTSDENKENS [1948] and DIE RECHTSWISSENSCHAFT IM UMBAU [1950]). The Jurisprudence of Interests is close to Roscoe Pound's sociological jurisprudence. It aims at replacing the system of formally rational with one of substantively rational concepts, and it has come to establish itself firmly in German legal practice (for a concise survey and evaluation see BÖHMER, *op. cit.* 190, and, very brief, W. FRIEDMANN, LEGAL THEORY [2nd ed. 1949] 225; no complete survey is as yet available in English).

The following passages in Weber's text are concerned with the School of Free Law.

[25] "The law must be applied in all cases which come within the letter or the spirit of its provisions.

"Where no provision is applicable, the judge shall decide according to the existing customary law and, in default thereof, according to the rule which he would lay down if he had himself to act as legislator.

"Herein he must be guided by tested doctrine and tradition."

[26] Cf. I. WILLIAMS, THE SOURCES OF LAW IN THE SWISS CIVIL CODE (1923) 34; see also the discussion of this provision and the similarly worded Sec. 1 of the Civil Code of the Russian Federal Soviet Socialist Republic by V. E. Greaves, *Social-economic Purpose of Private Rights* (1934/5, 12 N.Y.U.L.Q. REV. 165, 439).

[27] Cf. H. ISAY, RECHTSNORM UND ENTSCHEIDUNG (1929).

lish the postulate that the true foundation of the law is entirely "sociological."[28]

Use has also been made of the historical fact that for long periods, including our own, private parties have to a large extent been advised by professional lawyers and judges who have had technical legal training or that, in other words, all customary law is in reality lawyers' law. This fact has been associated with the incontrovertible observation that entirely new legal principles are being established not only *praeter legem* but also *contra legem*[29] by judicial practice, for instance, that of the German Supreme Court after the entry into force of the Civil Code. From all these facts the idea was derived that case law is superior to the rational establishment of objective norms and that the expediential balancing of concrete interests is superior to the creation and recognition of "norms" in general.[30] The modern theory of legal sources has thus disintegrated both the half-mystical concept of "customary law," as it had been created by historicism, as well as the equally historicist concept of the "will of the legislator" that could be discovered through the study of the legislative history of an enactment as revealed in committee reports and similar sources. The statute rather than the legislator has been thus proclaimed to be the jurists' main concern. Thus isolated from its background, the "law" is then turned over for elaboration and application to the jurists, among whom the predominant influence is ascribed at one time to the practitioners and at others, for instance, in the reports accompanying certain of the modern codes, to the scholars.[31] In this

[28] Cf. Ehrlich, esp. chapters 5 and 6.

[29] *Praeter legem* — alongside the (statute) law; *contra legem* — in contradiction to the (statute) law.

[30] So especially Lambert, *op. cit.* (1903); Ehrlich.

[31] In the last two sentences of the text three different phenomena are brought together in a way which indicates the possibility that some connecting part has been omitted. The postulate that in statutory interpretation the judge has to look upon the text "objectively" as a self-sufficient entity and that he should not, or that he is not even allowed to, inquire into the intentions of the legislature has not been confined to Germany. It has long been the established method of statutory interpretation in England and for a considerable time it was dominant in the United States. In Germany its principal representatives were A. Wach (Handbuch des Zivilprozesses [1885]) and K. Binding (Handbuch des Strafrechts [1885]); see also J. Kohler, *Über die Interpretation von Gesetzen* (1886), 13 Grünhut's Zeitschrift 1. The Theory has had some influence on the German courts but could not prevent them in the long run from paying careful attention to parliamentary hearings and other legislative materials.

The idea that statutes ought to be interpreted narrowly so as to leave free reign to free judicial law creation in the interstices constituted one of the postulates of the School of Free Law (see *supra* n. 24).

manner the significance of the legislative determination of a legal command is, under certain circumstances, degraded to the role of a mere "symptom" of either the validity of a legal proposition or even of the mere desire of such validity which, however, until it has been accepted in legal practice, is to remain uncertain. But the preference for a case law which remains in contact with legal reality — which means with the reality of the lawyers — to statute law is in turn subverted by the argument that no precedent should be regarded as binding beyond its concrete facts. The way is thus left open to the free balancing of values in each individual case.

In opposition to all such value-irrationalism, there have also arisen attempts to reëstablish an objective standard of values. The more the impression grows that legal orders as such are no more than "technical tools," the more violently will such degradation be rejected by the lawyers. For to place on the same level such merely "technical rules" as a customs tariff and legal norms concerning marriage, parental power, or the incidents of ownership, offends the sentiment of the legal practitioners, and there emerges the nostalgic notion of a transpositive law above that merely technical positive law which is acknowledged to be subject to change. The old natural law, it is true, looks discredited by the criticisms leveled at it from the historical and positivist points of view. As a substitute there are now advanced the religiously inspired natural law of the Catholic scholars,[32] and certain efforts to deduce objective standards from the "nature" of the law itself. The latter effort has taken two forms. In the aprioristic, neo-Kantian doctrines, the "right law," as the normative system of a "society of free men," is to be both a legislative standard for rational legislation and a source for judicial decisions where the law refers the judge to apparently nonformal criteria.[33] In the empiricist, Comtean, way those "expectations" which pri-

---

The phrase that the solution of certain problems be left to "legal science and doctrine" recurs constantly in the report (*Motive*) accompanying the Draft of the German Civil Code. The draftsmen used it whenever they felt that too much detail would be detrimental to the purposes of the codification. It is difficult to see what it might have to do with the Free Law tenet stated in the following sentence of the text.

[32] Especially VICTOR CATHREIN, RECHT, NATURRECHT UND POSITIVES RECHT (2nd ed. 1909); v. HERTLING, RECHT, STAAT UND GESELLSCHAFT (4th ed. 1917); MAUSBACH, NATURRECHT UND VÖLKERRECHT (1918); more recently H. ROMMEN, DIE EWIGE WIEDERKEHR DES NATURRECHTS (1936; Hanley's transl. s.t. THE NATURAL LAW, 1948), and the survey of the latest Catholic literature by I. Zeiger in (1952) 149 STIMMEN DER ZEIT 468.

[33] On Neo-Kantianism, see FRIEDMANN, *op. cit.* 91; the principal representative is R. Stammler, whose LEHRE VON DEM RICHTIGEN RECHT (1902) has been translated

vate parties are justified to have in view of the average conception existing with regard to the obligations of others, are to serve as the ultimate standard, which is to be superior even to the statute and which is to replace such concepts as equity, etc., which are felt to be too vague.[34]

At this place we cannot undertake a detailed discussion or a full criticism of these tendencies which, as our brief sketch has shown, have produced quite contradictory answers. All these movements are international in scope, but they have been most pronounced in Germany and France.[35] They are agreed only in their rejection of the once universally accepted and until recently prevalent petitio principii of the consistency and "gaplessness" of the legal order. Moreover, they have directed themselves against very diverse opponents, for instance, in France against the school of the Code-interpreters and in Germany against the methodology of the Pandectists. Depending upon who are the leaders of a particular movement, the results favor either the prestige of "science," i.e., of the legal scholars, or that of the practitioners. As a result of the continuous growth of formal statute law and, especially, of systematic codification, the academic scholars feel themselves to be painfully threatened both in their importance and in their opportunities for unencumbered

---

by Husik s.t. THE THEORY OF JUSTICE (1925). For a trenchant criticism, see E. KAUFMANN, KRITIK DER NEUKANTISCHEN RECHTSPHILOSOPHIE (1921).

[34] The reference is to the continuation and elaboration of Jhering's ideas through the school of jurisprudence of interests; see *supra*, n. 24.

[35] On French legal theory, see vol. VII of the Modern Legal Philosophy Series: MODERN FRENCH LEGAL PHILOSOPHY (1916) containing writings by A. Fouillée, J. Charmont, L. Duguit, and R. Demogue. A comprehensive, critical history is presented by J. BONNECASE, LA PENSÉE JURIDIQUE FRANÇAISE DE 1804 À L'HEURE PRÉSENTE (1933). Cf. also in the 20th Century Legal Philosophy Series, vol. IV, THE LEGAL PHILOSOPHIES OF LASK, RADBRUCH, AND DABIN (1950) 227; and, for latest trends, B. Horváth, *Social Value and Reality in Current French Legal Thought* (1952), 1 AM. J. OF COMPAR. LAW 243.

The principal representatives of the trends mentioned by Weber are François Gény, the founder of the French counterpart to the jurisprudence of interests (MÉTHODE D'INTERPRÉTATION [1899]; cf. his article in Modern Legal Philosophy Series, vol. IX, SCIENCE OF LEGAL METHOD [1917] 498); the sociological jurists Edouard Lambert (*op. cit.*), Léon Duguit (LE DROIT SOCIAL, LE DROIT INDIVIDUEL, ET LA TRANSFORMATION DE L'ÉTAT [1910]; L'ÉTAT, LE DROIT OBJECTIF ET LA LOI POSITIVE [1901]; LES TRANSFORMATIONS GÉNÉRALES DU DROIT PRIVÉ [1912], transl. in Continental Legal History Series, vol. XI, s.t. THE PROGRESS OF CONTINENTAL LAW IN THE 19TH CENTURY [1918]; LES TRANSFORMATIONS DU DROIT PUBLIC [1913], transl. by Laski s.t. LAW IN THE MODERN STATE [1919]), and RAYMOND SALEILLES (MÉTHODE ET CODIFICATION [1903]; *Le code civil et la méthode historique* in LIVRE DU CENTENAIRE DU CODE CIVIL [1904]).

intellectual activity. The rapid growth of anti-logical as well as the anti-historical movements in Germany can be historically explained by the fear that, following codification, German legal science might have to undergo the same decline which befell French jurisprudence after the enactment of the Napoleonic Code or Prussian jurisprudence after the enactment of the Allgemeine Landrecht.[36] Up to this point these fears are thus the result of an internal constellation of intellectual interests. However, all variants of the developments which have led to the rejection of that purely logical systematization of the law as it had been developed by Pandectist learning, including even the irrational variants, are in their turn products of a self-defeating scientific rationalization of legal thought as well as of its relentless self-criticism. To the extent that they do not themselves have a rationalistic character, they are a flight into the irrational and as such a consequence of the increasing rationalization of legal technique. In that respect they are a parallel to the irrationalization of religion.[37] One must not overlook, however, that the same trends have also been inspired by the desire of the modern lawyers, through the pressure groups in which they are so effectively organized, to heighten their feeling of self-importance and to increase their sense of power. This is undoubtedly one of the reasons why in Germany such continuous reference is made to the "distinguished" position of the English judge who is said not to be bound to any rational law.[38] Yet, the differences in the attribution of honorific status on the continent and in England are rather rooted in circumstances which are connected with differences in the general structure of authority.

3. *Contemporary Anglo-American Law*. The differences between continental and common law methods of legal thought have been produced mostly by factors which are respectively connected with the internal structure and the modes of existence of the legal profession as well as by factors related to differences in political development. The economic elements, however, have been determinative only in connection with these elements. What we are concerned with here is the fact that, once everything is said and done about these differences in historical developments, modern capitalism prospers equally and manifests essentially identical economic traits under legal systems containing rules and institutions which considerably differ from each other at least from the juridical point of view. Even what is on the face of it so fundamental a concept of continental law as *dominium* still does not exist in Anglo-

[36] Cf. *supra*, p. 280.

[37] Cf. W.u.G. Part II, c. IV, pp. 227 *et seq.*

[38] Cf. *supra*, n. 16.

American law.[39] Indeed, we may say that the legal systems under which modern capitalism has been prospering differ profoundly from each other even in their ultimate principles of formal structure.

Even today, and in spite of all influences by the ever more rigorous demands for academic training, English legal thought is essentially an empirical art. Precedent still fully retains its old significance, except that it is regarded as unfair to invoke a case from too remote a past, which means older than about a century. One can also still observe the charismatic character of lawfinding, especially, although not exclusively, in the new countries, and quite particularly the United States. In practice, varying significance is given to a decided case not only, as happens everywhere, in accordance with the hierarchal position of the court by which it was decided but also in accordance with the very personal authority of an individual judge. This is true for the entire common-law sphere, as illustrated, for instance, by the prestige of Lord Mansfield. But in the American view, the judgment is the very personal creation of the concrete individual judge, to whom one is accustomed to refer by name, in contrast to the impersonal "District Court" of Continental-European officialese. The English judge, too, lays claim to such a position. All these circumstances are tied up with the fact that the degree of legal rationality is essentially lower than, and of a type different from, that of continental Europe. Up to the recent past, and at any rate up to the time of Austin, there was practically no English legal science which would have merited the name of "learning" in the continental sense. This fact alone would have sufficed to render any such codification as was desired by Bentham practically impossible. But it is also this feature which has been responsible for the "practical" adaptibility of English law and its "practical" character from the standpoint of the public.

The legal thinking of the layman is, on the one hand, literalistic. He tends to be a definition-monger when he believes he is arguing "legally." Closely connected with this trait is the tendency to draw conclusions from individual case to individual case; the abstractionism of the "pro-

[39] Apparently Weber was not conversant with recent common law use of the concept of title. In the classical form of the law of real property, it is true, the various ways in which one might be entitled to the use and disposition of a piece of land were defined by the various tenures, estates, and other rights in land which had come to be recognized in the royal courts of law and equity. There did not exist, however, any term which comprehensively covered, like the Roman term *dominium*, the fullness of all rights, privileges, powers, and immunities, which can possibly exist in a piece of land. But in modern usage the terms title, fee, or fee title, are generally used in exactly this sense, especially in the United States. Cf. *supra*, p. 22.

fessional" lawyer is far from the layman's mind. In both respects, however, the art of empirical jurisprudence is cognate to him, although he may not like it. No country, indeed, has produced more bitter complaints and satires about the legal profession than England. The formularies of the conveyancers, too, may be quite unintelligible to the layman, as again is the case in England. Yet, he can understand the basic character of the English way of legal thinking, he can identify himself with it and, above all, he can make his peace with it by retaining once and for all a solicitor as his legal father confessor for all contingencies of life, as is indeed done by practically every English businessman. He simply neither demands nor expects of the law anything which could be frustrated by "logical" legal construction.

Safety valves are also provided against legal formalism. As a matter of fact, in the sphere of private law, both common law and equity are "formalistic" to a considerable extent in their practical treatment. It would hardly be otherwise under a system of stare decisis [40] and the traditionalist spirit of the legal profession. But the institution of the civil jury imposes on rationality limits which are not merely accepted as inevitable but are actually prized because of the binding force of precedent and the fear that a precedent might thus create "bad law" in a sphere which one wishes to keep open for a concrete balancing of interests. We must forego the analysis of the way in which this division of the two spheres of stare decisis and concrete balancing of interests is actually functioning in practice. It does in any case represent a softening of rationality in the administration of justice. Alongside all this we find the still quite patriarchal, summary and highly irrational jurisdiction of the justices of the peace. They deal with the petty causes of everyday life and, as can be readily seen in Mendelssohn's description, they represent a kind of Khadi justice which is quite unknown in Germany.[41] All in all, the Common Law thus presents a picture of an administration of justice which in the most fundamental formal features of both substantive law and procedure differs from the structure of continental law as much as is possible within a secular system of justice, that is, a system that is free from theocratic and patrimonial powers. Quite definitely, English law-finding is not, like that of the Continent, "application" of "legal propositions" logically derived from statutory texts.

These differences have had some tangible consequences both economically and socially; but these consequences have all been isolated single phenomena rather than differences touching upon the total structure of

[40] On *stare decisis*, *supra*, p. 73.
[41] *Das Imperium des Richters* (1908)

the economic system. For the development of capitalism two features have been relevant and both have helped to support the capitalistic system. Legal training has primarily been in the hands of the lawyers from among whom also the judges are recruited, i.e., in the hands of a group which is active in the service of propertied, and particularly capitalistic, private interests and which has to gain its livelihood from them. Furthermore and in close connection with this, the concentration of the administration of justice at the central courts in London and its extreme costliness have amounted almost to a denial of access to the courts for those with inadequate means. At any rate, the essential similarity of the capitalistic development on the Continent and in England has not been able to eliminate the sharp contrasts between the two types of legal systems. Nor is there any visible tendency towards a transformation of the English legal system in the direction of the continental under the impetus of the capitalist economy. On the contrary, wherever the two kinds of administration of justice and of legal training have had the opportunity to compete with one another, as for instance in Canada, the Common Law way has come out on top and has overcome the continental alternative rather quickly. We may thus conclude that capitalism has not been a decisive factor in the promotion of that form of rationalization of the law which has been peculiar to the continental West ever since the rise of Romanist studies in the medieval universities.

4. *Lay Justice and Corporative Tendencies in the Modern Legal Profession.* Modern social development, aside from the already mentioned political and internal professional motives, has given rise to certain other factors by which formal legal rationalism is being weakened. Irrational Khadi justice is exercised today in criminal cases clearly and extensively in the "popular" justice of the jury.[42] It appeals to the sentiments of the layman, who feels annoyed whenever he meets with formalism in a concrete case, and it satisfies the emotional demands of those underprivileged classes which clamor for substantive justice.

Against this "popular justice" element of the jury system, attacks have been directed from two quarters. The jury has been attacked because of the strong interest orientation of the jurors as against the technical matter-of-factness of the specialist. Just as in ancient Rome the jurors' list was the object of class conflict, so today the selection of jurors is attacked, especially by the working class, as favoring class justice, upon the ground that the jurors, even though they may be "plebeians," are picked predominantly from among those who can afford

[42] Written before the abolition of the jury in Germany by the Law of 1924; see *infra*, p. 352.

the loss of time. Although such a test of selection can hardly be avoided entirely, it also depends, in part at least, on political considerations. Where, on the other hand, the jurors' bench is occupied by working-class people, it is attacked by the propertied class. Moreover, not only "classes" as such are the interested parties. In Germany, for instance, male jurors can practically never be moved to find a fellow male guilty of rape, especially where they are not absolutely convinced of the girl's chaste character.[43] But in this connection we must consider that in Germany female virtue is not held in great respect anyway.

From the standpoint of professional legal training lay justice has been criticized on the ground that the laymen's verdict is delivered as an irrational oracle without any statement of reasons and without the possibility of any substantive criticism. Thus one has come to demand that the lay judges be subjected to the control of the legal experts. In answer to this demand there was created the system of the mixed bench, which, however, experience has shown to be a system in which the laymen's influence is inferior to that of the experts. Thus their presence has practically no more significance than that of giving some compulsory publicity to the deliberation of professional judges in a way similar to that of Switzerland, where the judges must hold their deliberation in full view of the public.[44] The professional judges, in turn, are threatened, in the sphere of criminal law, by the overshadowing power of the professional psychiatrist, onto whom more and more responsibility is passed, especially in the most serious cases, and on whom rationalism is thus imposing a task which can by no means be solved by means of pure science.

Obviously all of these conflicts are caused by the course of technical and economic development only indirectly, namely in so far as it has favored intellectualism. Primarily they are rather consequences of the insoluble conflict between the formal and the substantive principles of justice, which may clash with one another even where their respective protagonists belong to one and the same social class. Moreover, it is by no means certain that those classes which are underprivileged today,

[43] This passage was written before the Revolution of 1918, which resulted in the admission of women both to professional judicial office and to membership in the lay part of the mixed bench of the criminal, labor, commercial, and administrative courts. At present the percentage of women in the German judiciary, including the Supreme Court, is probably higher than in any other Western country.

[44] Weber's judgment on the inferior role of the lay members of the mixed bench is by no means shared generally in Germany, Sweden, the U.S.S.R., or those other countries in which the system has been adopted. For an objective effort at evaluating the merit of the system of the mixed bench, see R. C. K. Ensor, Courts and Judges in France, Germany, and England (1933) 68.

especially the working class,[45] may safely expect from an informal administration of justice those results which are claimed for it by the ideology of the jurists. A bureaucratized judiciary, which is being planfully recruited in the higher ranks from among the personnel of the career service of the prosecutor's office and which is completely dependent on the politically ruling powers for advancement, cannot be set alongside the Swiss or English judiciary, and even less the (federal) judges in the United States. If one takes away from such judges their belief in the sacredness of the purely objective legal formalism and directs them simply to balance interests, the result will be very different from those legal systems to which we have just referred. However, the problem does not belong to this discussion. There remains only the task of correcting a few historical errors.

Prophets are the only ones who have taken a really consciously "creative" attitude toward existing law; only through them has new law been consciously created. For the rest, as must be stressed again and again, even those jurists who, from the objective point of view, have been the most creative ones, have always and not only in modern times, regarded themselves to be but the mouthpiece of norms already existing, though, perhaps, only latently, and to be their interpreters or appliers rather than their creators. This subjective belief is held by even the most eminent jurists. It is due to the disillusionment of the intellectuals that today this belief is being confronted with objectively different facts and that one is trying to elevate this state of facts to the status of a norm for subjective judicial behavior. As the bureaucratization of formal legislation progresses, the traditional position of the English judge is also likely to be transformed permanently and profoundly. On the other hand, it may be doubted whether, in a code country, the bestowal of the "creator's" crown upon bureaucratic judges will really turn them into law prophets. In any case, the juristic precision of judicial opinions will be seriously impaired if sociological, economic, or ethical argument were to take the place of legal concepts.

All in all the movement is one of those characteristic onslaughts against the dominance of "specialization" and rationalism, which latter has in the last analysis been its very parent. Thus the development of the formal qualities of the law appears to have produced peculiar antinomies. Rigorously formalistic and dependent on what is tangibly perceivable as far as it is required for security to do business, the law has at the same time become informal for the sake of business loyalty, in so far as re-

[45] Written before the Revolution of 1918.

quired by the logical interpretation of the intention of the parties or by the "good usage" of business intercourse, which is understood to be tending toward some "ethical minimum."

The law is drawn into antiformal directions, moreover, by all those powers which demand that it be more than a mere means of pacifying conflicts of interests. These forces include the demand for substantive justice by certain social class interests and ideologies; they also include the tendencies inherent in certain forms of political authority of either authoritarian or democratic character concerning the ends of law which are respectively appropriate to them; and also the demand of the "laity" for a system of justice which would be intelligible to them; finally, as we have seen, anti-formal tendencies are being promoted by the ideologically rooted power aspirations of the legal profession itself.

Whatever form law and legal practice may come to assume under the impact of these various influences, it will be inevitable that, as a result of technical and economic developments, the legal ignorance of the layman will increase. The use of jurors and similar lay judges will not suffice to stop the continuous growth of the technical element in the law and hence of its character as a specialists' domain. Inevitably the notion must expand that the law is a rational technical apparatus, which is continually transformable in the light of expediential considerations and devoid of all sacredness of content. This fate may be obscured by the tendency of acquiescence in the existing law, which is growing in many ways for several reasons, but it cannot really be stayed. All of the modern sociological and philosophical analyses, many of which are of a high scholarly value, can only contribute to strengthen this impression, regardless of the content of their theories concerning the nature of law and the judicial process.

CHAPTER XII

DOMINATION[1]

Section 1. Power and Domination. Transitional Forms

Even in the most general sense, i.e., without reference to any concrete content, domination is one of the most important elements of communal action. Of course, not every form of communal action reveals a structure of dominancy. But in most of the varieties of communal action domination plays a considerable role, even where it is not obvious at first sight. Thus, for example, in linguistic communities the elevation by authoritative fiat of a dialect to the status of an official language of a political entity has very often had a decisive influence on the development of a large community with a common literary language, as, for instance, Germany.[2] On the other hand, political separation has determined the final form of a corresponding linguistic differentiation, as, for instance, in the case of Holland as against Germany.[3] Furthermore, the domination exercised in the schools stereotypes the form and the predominance of the official school language most enduringly and decisively. Without exception every sphere of social action is profoundly influenced by structures of dominancy. In a great number of cases the emergence of rational consociation from amorphous communal action has been due to domination and the way in which it has been exercised. Even where this is not the case, the structure of dominancy and its unfolding is decisive in de-

[1] W.u.G. Part III (Types of Domination); c. VIII (Domination) — pp. 603–612.

[2] Among numerous German dialects and ways in which the language was used in poetry, literature, and polite parlance, acceptance as the standard was achieved by that form which was used in the late fourteenth and fifteenth centuries by the imperial chancery, first in Prague and then in Vienna, especially when a style close to it was used by Luther in his translation of the Bible.

[3] The low-German dialect spoken in the present Netherlands achieved, in the form in which it is used in the Province of South Holland, the status of a separate language when the United Provinces separated from Germany and the Dutch dialect became the language of officialdom and of the Bible translation (Statenbijbel, 1626–1635). Significantly no such status as a separate language was achieved by any one of the Swiss German dialects; as there was no central chancery in the loose Swiss Confederation, High German remained the official language in spite of the political separation from Germany, which took place a century earlier than that of the Netherlands.

termining the form of communal action and its orientation toward a "goal." Indeed, domination has played the decisive role particularly in the economically most important social structures of the past and present, viz., the manor on the one hand, and the large-scale capitalistic enterprise on the other.

Domination constitutes a special case of power, as we shall see shortly. In the case of domination as well as of other forms of power, those who wield it do not apply it exclusively, or even usually, to the pursuit of purely economic ends, such as, for example, an adequate supply of economic goods. It is true, however, that the control over economic goods, i.e., economic power, is a frequent, often purposively willed, consequence of domination as well as one of its most important instruments. Not every position of economic power, however, represents "domination" in our sense of the word, as we shall see shortly. Nor does "domination" utilize in every case economic power for its foundation and maintenance. But in the vast majority of cases, and indeed in the most important ones, this is just what happens in one way or another and often to such an extent that the mode of applying economic means for the purpose of maintaining domination, in turn, exercises a determining influence on the structure of domination. Furthermore, the great majority of all economic organizations, among them, the most important and the most modern ones, reveal a structure of dominancy. The crucial characteristics of any form of domination may, it is true, not be correlated in any clear-cut fashion with any particular form of economic organization. Yet, the structure of dominancy is in many cases both a factor of great economic importance and, at least to some extent, a result of economic conditions.

Our first aim here is that of stating merely general propositions regarding the relationship between forms of economic organization and of domination. Because of this very general character, these propositions will inevitably be abstract and, for the time being, also somewhat indefinite. For our purpose we need, first of all, a more exact definition of what we mean by "domination" and its relationship to the general term "power." Domination in the quite general sense of power, i.e., of the possibility of imposing one's will upon the behavior of other persons, can emerge in the most diverse forms. If, as has occasionally been done, one looks upon the claims which the law accords to one person against one or more others as a power to issue commands to such others or to those to whom no such claim is accorded, one may thereby conceive of the whole system of modern private law as the decentralization of domination in the hands of those to whom the legal rights are accorded. From this angle, the worker would have the power to command, i.e., "domination," over the entrepreneur to the extent of his claim for wages, and the civil servant over the king to the extent of his salary claim. Such a terminology would be rather forced and, in any case, it would not be of more than provisional value since a distinction in kind must be made between "commands" directed by the judicial authority to an adjudged debtor and "commands" directed by the claimant himself to a debtor prior to judgment. However, a position ordinarily designated as "dominating" can emerge from the social relations in a drawing room as well as in the market, from the rostrum of an auditorium as well as from the command post of a regiment, from an erotic or charitable relationship as well as from scholarly discussion or athletics. Such a broad definition would, however, render the term "domination" scientifically useless. A comprehensive classification of all forms, conditions, and concrete contents of "domination" in that widest sense is impossible here. We will only call to mind that, in addition to numerous other possible types, there are two diametrically contrasting types of domination, viz., domination by virtue of a constellation of interests (in particular: by virtue of a position of monopoly), and domination by virtue of authority, i.e., power to command and duty to obey.

The purest type of the former is monopolistic domination in the market; of the latter, patriarchal, magisterial, or princely power. In its purest form, the first is based upon influence derived exclusively from the possession of goods or marketable skills guaranteed in some way and acting upon the conduct of those dominated, who remain, however, formally free and are motivated simply by the pursuit of their own interests. The latter kind of domination rests upon alleged absolute duty to obey, regardless of personal motives or interests. The borderline between these two types of domination is fluid. Any large central bank or credit institution, for instance, exercises a "dominating" influence on the capital market by virtue of its monopolistic position. It can impose upon its potential debtors conditions for the granting of credit, thus influencing to a marked degree their economic behavior for the sake of the liquidity of its own resources. The potential debtors, if they really need the credit, must in their own interest submit to these conditions and must even guarantee this submission by supplying collateral security. The credit banks do not, however, pretend that they exercise "authority," i.e., that they claim "submission" on the part of the dominated without regard to the latters' own interests; they simply pursue their own interests and realize them best when the dominated persons, acting with formal freedom, rationally pursue their own interests as they are forced upon them by objective circumstances.

Any owner of an even incomplete monopoly finds himself in that same position if, despite existing competition, he is able by and large to "prescribe" prices to both exchange partners and competitors; in other words, if by his own conduct he can impose upon them a way of conduct according to his own interests, without, however, imposing on them the slightest "obligation" to submit to this domination. Any type of domination by virtue of constellation of interests may, however, be transformed gradually into domination by authority. This applies particularly to domination originally founded on a position of monopoly. A bank, for instance, in order to control more effectively a debtor corporation, may demand as a condition for credit that some member of its board be made a member of the board of the debtor corporation. That board, in turn, can give decisive orders to the management by virtue of the latter's obligation to obey.

Or a central bank of issue causes the credit institutions to agree on uniform terms of credit and in this way tries, by virtue of its position of power, to secure to itself a continuous control and supervision of the relationships between the credit institutions and their customers. It may then utilize this control and supervision for ends of currency management or for the purpose of influencing the business cycle or for political ends such as, for instance, the preparation of financial readiness for war. The latter kind of use will be made in particular where the central bank itself is exposed to influences from the political power. Theoretically it is conceivable that such controls can actually be established, that the ends for and the ways of its exercise become articulated in reglementations, that special agencies are created for its exercise and special appellate agencies for the resolution of questions of doubt, and that, finally, the controls are constantly made more strict. In such a case this kind of domination might become quite like the authoritative domination of a bureaucratic state agency over its subordinates, and the subordination would assume the character of a relationship of obedience to authority.

The same observation can be made with respect to the domination by the breweries over the tavern owners whom they supply with their equipment, or the domination to which book dealers would have to submit if there should some day be a German publishers' cartel with power to issue and withhold retailers' licenses, or the domination of the gasoline dealers by the Standard Oil Company, or the domination exercised through their common sales office by the German coal producers over the coal dealers. All these retailers may well be reduced to employed sales agents, little different from linemen or other private employees working outside the employer's plant but subject to the authority of a department chief. The transitions are imperceptible from the ancient debtor's factual dependency on his creditor and formal servitude for debt; or, in the Middle Ages and even in modern times, from the craftsman and the market-wise merchant over the various forms of dependency of the home industry to the completely authoritarian labor regulation of the sweatshop worker. And from there other imperceptible transitions lead to the position of the secretary, the engineer, or the worker in the office or plant, who is subject to a discipline no longer different in its nature from that of the civil service or the army, although it has been created by a contract concluded in the labor market by formally "equal" parties through the "voluntary" acceptance of the terms offered by the employer. More important than the difference between private and public employment is certainly that between the military service and the other situations. The latter are concluded and terminated voluntarily, while the former is imposed by compulsion, at least in those countries where, as in ours, the ancient system of mercenary service has been replaced by the draft. Yet, even the relationship of political allegiance can be entered into and, to some extent, be dissolved voluntarily; the same holds true of the feudal and, under certain circumstances, even of the patrimonial dependency relationships of the past. Thus even in these cases the transitions are but gradual to those relationships of authority, for instance slavery, which are completely involuntary and, for the subject, normally nonterminable. Obviously, a certain minimum interest of the subordinate in his own obeying will normally constitute one of the indispensable motives of obedience even in the completely authoritarian duty-relationship. Throughout, transitions are thus vague and changing. And yet, if we wish at all to obtain fruitful distinctions within the continuous stream of actual phenomena, we must not overlook the clear-cut antithesis between such cases as, let us say, that factual power which arises completely out of possession and by way of interest compromises in the market, and, on the other hand, the authoritarian power of a patriarch or monarch with its appeal to the duty of obedience simply as such. The manifoldness of forms of power is in no way exhausted by the examples just given. Even mere possession can be a basis of power in forms other than that of the market. Even in socially undifferentiated situations wealth, accompanied by a corresponding way of life, creates prestige, corresponding to the position in present society of one who "keeps an open house" or the lady who has her "salon." Under certain circumstances, every one of these relationships may assume authoritarian traits. Domination in the broader sense can be produced not only by the exchange relationships of the market but also by those of "society"; such phenomena may range all the way from the "drawing room lion" to the patented *arbiter elegantiarum*[4] of imperial Rome or the courts of love of the ladies of Provence.[5] Indeed, such situations of domination can be found also outside the sphere of private markets and relationships. Even without any formal power of command an "empire state" or, more correctly, those individuals who are the decisive ones within it either through authority or through the market, can exercise a far-reaching and occasionally even a despotic hegemony. A typical illustration is afforded by Prussia's position within the German Customs Union[6] or, later, in the German Reich.[7] To some, although much lesser extent, New York's position within the United States affords another illustration.[8] In the German Customs Union the Prussian officials were dominant, because their state's territory constituted the largest and thus the decisive market; in the German Reich they are paramount because they dispose of the largest net of railroads, the greatest number of university positions, etc., and can thus cripple the corresponding administrative departments of the other, formally equal, states. New York can exercise political power, because it is the seat of the great financial powers. All such forms of power are based upon groups of interests. They thus resemble those which occur in the market, and in the course of development they can easily be transformed into formally regulated relationships of authority or, more correctly, into consociations with heterocephalous power of command and coercive apparatus.[9] Indeed, because of the very absence of rules, that domination which originates in the market or other groups of interests may be felt to be much more oppressive than an authority in which the duties of obedience are set out clearly and expressly. That aspect must not affect, however, the terminology of the sociologist.

In the following discussion we shall use the term domination exclu-

[4] *Arbiter elegantiarum* — According to Tacitus (Ann. XVI 18), Gaius Petronius, who is probably identical with the satirist Petronius Arbiter, was called by Nero the "arbiter of elegance" to whose judgment he bowed in matters of taste. Petronius and his title have been popularized through Henry Sienkiewicz' novel *Quo Vadis*.

[5] On courts of love, see *supra*, p. 25.

[6] The German Customs Union (*Zollverein*) was gradually established under Prussian leadership in the 1820's and 1830's. After January 1, 1834, it comprised all German states with the exception of Austria and two smaller states, i.e., practically that part of Germany which under Bismarck's leadership emerged in 1871 as the new German Reich. In this development of German unity under Prussian hegemony, but also toward the exclusion of Austria, which became final through the Prussian-Austrian war of 1866, the *Zollverein* constituted an important step.

[7] Written before the Revolution of 1918.

[8] Written before the advent of the New Deal.

[9] On the role of the coercive apparatus, see *supra*, c. II, § 1.

sively in that narrower sense which excludes from its scope those situations in which power has its source in a formally free interplay of interested parties such as occurs especially in the market but also in other groups of interests. In other words, in our terminology *domination* shall be *identical with authoritarian power of command.*

To be more specific, *domination* will thus mean the situation in which:

The manifested will (*command*) of the *ruler* or rulers is meant to influence the conduct of one or more others (*the ruled*) and actually does influence it in such a way that their conduct to a socially relevant degree occurs as if the ruled had made the content of the command the maxim of their conduct for its very own sake. Looked upon from the other end, this situation will be called *obedience.*

The definition just stated sounds cumbersome, especially because of the use of the "as if" formula. This fact is inevitable, however. The merely external fact of the order being obeyed is not sufficient to signify domination in our sense; we cannot overlook the fact that the meaning of the command is accepted as a valid norm. On the other hand, however, the causal chain extending from the command to the actual fact of its performance can be quite varied. The psychologist can find that the command may have achieved its effect upon the ruled either through empathy or through inspiration or through persuasion by rational argument or through some combination of these three principal types of influence of one person over another.[10] In a concrete case the performance of the command may have been motivated by the ruled's own conviction of its propriety, or by his sense of duty, or by fear, or by "dull" custom, or by a desire to obtain some benefit for himself. To the sociologist those differences are generally irrelevant. To him, however, different forms of domination may appear relevant in so far as they are connected with certain basic differences in the general foundation of domination.

Many imperceptible transitions exist, as we have seen, between that narrower concept of domination as we have defined it now and those situations of setting the tone in the market, the drawing room, in a discussion, etc., which we have discussed earlier. We shall briefly revert to some of these latter cases so as to elucidate more clearly the former.

It is obvious that relationships of domination may exist reciprocally. In modern bureaucracy, among officials of different departments, each is subject to the others' powers of command in so far as the latter have jurisdiction. There are no conceptual difficulties involved, but where a customer places with a shoemaker an order for a pair of shoes, can it

[10] On empathy and inspiration as factors influencing the attitude of other persons, see *supra*, p. 23.

then be said that either one has domination over the other? The answer will depend upon the circumstances of each individual case, but almost always will it be found that in some limited respect the will of the one has influenced that of the other even against that other's reluctance and that, consequently, to that extent one has dominated over the other. No precise concept of domination could be built up, however, upon the basis of such considerations; and this statement holds true for all relationships of exchange, including those of intangibles. Or what shall we say of the village craftsman who, as is often the case in Asia, is employed at fixed terms by the village? Is he, within his vocational jurisdiction, a ruler, or is he the ruled, and, if so, by whom? One will be inclined rather not to apply the concept of domination to such relationships, except with respect to the powers which he, the craftsman, exercises over his assistants or which are exercised over him by those persons who are to control him by virtue of their official position. As soon as we do this, we narrow the concept of domination to that technical one which we have defined above. Yet, the position of a village chief, that is, a person of official authority, may be exactly like that of the village craftsman. The distinction between private business and public office, as we know it, is the result of development and it is not at all so firmly rooted elsewhere as it is with us [in Germany]. In the popular American view, a judge's job is a business just as a banker's. He, the judge, simply is a man who has been granted the monopoly to give a person a decision with the help of which the latter may enforce some performance against another or, as the case may be, may shield himself against the claims of others. By virtue of this monopoly the judge enjoys directly or indirectly a number of benefits, legitimate or illegitimate, and for their enjoyment in some cases he pays a portion of his fees to the party boss to whom he owes his job.

To all of these, the village chief, the judge, the banker, the craftsman, we shall ascribe domination, wherever, but in so far only as, they claim, and to a socially relevant degree find obedience to, commands given and received as such. No usable concept of domination can be defined in any way other than by reference to power of command; but we must never forget that here, as everywhere else in life, everything is "in transition." It should be self-evident that the sociologist is guided exclusively by the factual existence of such a power of command, in contrast to the lawyer's interest in the theoretical content of a legal norm. As far as sociology is concerned, power of command does not exist unless the authority which is claimed by somebody is actually heeded to a socially relevant degree. Yet, the sociologist will normally start from the observation that "factual" powers of command usually are a superadditum to a normative order claiming to exist "by virtue of law." It is exactly for this reason that the sociologist cannot help operating with the conceptual apparatus of the law.

Section 2. Domination and Administration—Nature and Limits of Democratic Administration

We are primarily interested in "domination" in so far as it is combined with "administration." Every domination both expresses itself and functions through administration. Every administration, on the other hand, needs domination, because it is always necessary that some powers of command be in the hands of somebody. Possibly the power of command may appear in a rather innocent garb; the ruler may be regarded as their "servant" by the ruled, and he may even look upon himself in that way. This phenomenon occurs in its purest form in the so-called *immediate democratic administration.*

This kind of administration is called democratic for two reasons which need not necessarily coincide. The first reason is that it is based upon the assumption that everybody is equally qualified to conduct the public affairs. The second: that in this kind of administration the scope of power of command is kept at a minimum. Administrative functions are rotated, or determined by drawing lots, or assigned for short periods by election. All important decisions are reserved to the common resolution of all; the administrative functionaries have only to prepare and carry out the resolutions and to conduct "current business" in accordance with the directives of the general assembly. This type of administration can be found in many private associations, in certain political organizations, such as the Swiss Landsgemeinden or certain townships in the United States, or in universities (in so far as the administration lies in the hands of the rector and the deans),[11] as well as in numerous other organizations of a similar kind. However modest the administrative function may be, some functionary must have some power of command, and his position is thus always in suspense between that of a mere servant and that of master. It is against the very development of the latter that the "democratic" limits of his position are directed. However, "equality" and "minimization" of the dominant powers of functionaries are also found

[11] At the German universities both the president (*Rektor*) and the deans are elected by the full professors for one-year terms; together with the senate they administer the affairs of the university and represent it, especially as against the ministry of education, by which the universities are supervised.

in many aristocratic groupments within, and as against the members of, the ruling layer. Illustrations are afforded by the Venetian and Spartan aristocracies as well as by the full professors of a German university. They all have been using those same "democratic" forms of rotation of office, drawing lots, or short-term election.

Normally this kind of administration occurs in organizations which fulfill the following conditions:

First: the organization must be local or otherwise limited in the number of members; *second:* the social positions of the members must not greatly differ from each other; *third:* the administrative functions must be relatively simple and stable; *fourth:* however, there must be a certain minimum development of training in objectively determining ways and means. This latter requirement exists, for instance, in the direct democratic administrations in Switzerland and the United States just as it existed in the Russian *mir* [12] within the confines of its traditional scope of business. We do not look, however, upon this kind of administration as the historical starting point of any typical course of development but rather as a marginal type case, which lends itself well as the starting point of investigation. Neither taking turns nor drawing lots nor election are "primitive" forms of picking the functionaries of an organization.

Wherever it exists, direct democratic administration is unstable. With every development of economic differentiation arises the probability that administration will fall into the hands of the wealthy. The reason is not that they would have superior personal qualities or more comprehensive knowledge, but simply that they can afford to take the time to carry on the administrative functions cheaply or without any pay and as part-time jobs. Those, however, who are forced to work for a living would have to sacrifice time, which means income, and the more intense labor grows, the more intolerable does this sacrifice become. The bearers of that superiority are thus not simply those who enjoy high incomes but rather those who have an income without personal labor or derive it from intermittent labor. Under otherwise equal conditions a modern manufacturer can thus get away from his work less easily and is correspondingly less available for administrative functions than a landowner or a medieval merchant patrician, both of whom have not had to work uninterruptedly. For the same reason the directors of the great university clinics and institutes are the least suited to be rectors; although they have plenty of administrative experience, their time is too

[12] Mir — village community of the Russian peasants, as it existed before its dissolution in the Stolypin reforms following the revolution of 1905; cf. WEBER HISTORY 17.

much occupied with their regular work.[13] Hence in the measure in which those who have to work are becoming unable to get away from it, direct democratic administration will tend to turn into rule by *honoratiores*.

We have already met the type as that of the bearer of a specific social honor connected with the mode of living.[14] Here we now encounter another indispensable requirement, viz., that capacity to take care of social administration and rule as an honorific duty which derives from economic position. Hence we shall tentatively define *honoratiores* as follows:

Persons who, *first*, are enjoying an income earned without, or with comparatively little, labor, or at least of such a kind that they can afford to assume administrative functions in addition to whatever business activities they may be carrying on; and who, *second*, by virtue of such income, have a mode of life which attributes to them the social "prestige" of a specific honor and thus renders them fit for being called to rule.

Frequently such rule by *honoratiores* has developed in the form of deliberating bodies in which the affairs to be brought before the community are discussed in advance; such bodies easily come to anticipate the resolutions of the community or to eliminate it and thus to establish, by virtue of their prestige, a monopoly of the *honoratiores*. The development of the rule by *honoratiores* in this way has existed a long time in local communities and thus particularly in the neighborhood community. Those *honoratiores* of olden times had a character quite different, however, from those who develop in the rationalized direct democracy of the present. The original qualification for *honoratiores* simply was old age. In all communities which orient their communal conduct toward tradition, i.e., toward convention, customary law or sacred law, the elders are, so to speak, the natural honoratiores not only because of their prestige of wider experience. They know the traditions; their consent, advance approval (*προβούλευμα*),[15] or ratification (*auctoritas*)[16] guarantees the properness of a resolution as against the supernatural powers just as it is the most effective decision in a case of dispute. Where all members of a community are in about the same economic position, the

[13] Meaning: the rectors and deans are frequently elected from among those full professors who are directors of research laboratories, clinics, and other large institutions, i.e., from among those who have little time left to attend to the affairs of the university.

[14] See *supra*, pp. 52, 198 *et seq*.

[15] Προβούλευμα (Greek; esp. in Athens).

[16] *Auctoritas* [sc. patrum] (lat.) — the approval of the Roman Senate as required for the validity of certain resolutions of the popular assemblies (*comitia*); on the varying phases of political significance of the requirement, see Jolowicz 30.

"elders" are simply those oldest in the house community, the clan, or the neighborhood.

However, the relative prestige of age within a community is subject to much change. Wherever the food resources are scarce, he who can no longer work is just a burden. Also where war is a chronic state of affairs, the prestige of the older men is liable to sink below that of the warriors and there often then developes a democratic bias of the younger groups against the prestige of old age.[17] The same development occurs in periods of economic or political revolution, whether violent or peaceful, and also where the practical power of religious ideas and thus the veneration of a sacred tradition is little developed or on the decline. The prestige of old age is preserved, on the other hand, wherever the objective usefulness of experience or the subjective power of tradition are estimated highly.

Where the elders are deposed, power normally accrues not to youth but to the bearers of some other kind of social prestige. In the case of economic or estatist differentiation the councils of elders (*γερουσία, senate*) [18] may retain its name, but *de facto* it will be composed of *honoratiores* in the sense discussed above, i.e., "economic" *honoratiores*, or bearers of an estatist honor privilege, whose power ultimately is also based upon their kind of wealth.

On the other hand, the battle cry that a "democratic" administration must be obtained or preserved may become a powerful tool of the poor in their fight against the *honoratiores*, but also of economically powerful groups which are not admitted to status honor. In that case democratic administration becomes a matter of struggle between political parties, especially since the *honoratiores*, by virtue of their status prestige and the dependency on them of certain groups, can create for themselves a "protective guard" from among the poor. As soon as it is thus made the object of a struggle for power, direct democratic administration loses that specific feature, i.e., that it contains but a mere trace of domination. A political party, after all, is an organization for the very purpose of fighting for domination in the specific sense, and it thus necessarily follows a trend in its own organization to assume a clearly dominational structure, however carefully it may be trying to hide this fact.

In the marginal case of "pure" democracy all comrades live in sub-

[17] Cf. "Sexagenarios de ponte." [Weber's note.] — In the Roman republic both the duty of military service and the right to vote in the popular assemblies terminated at the age of sixty. Men above sixty who tried to enter the enclosure on the Campus Martius where the voting took place (*saepta*) were driven back from the bridge leading to it; hence the proverb, "Men of sixty, off the bridge!" Cf. Varro, op. Non. 523, 21 *et seq.*

[18] *Gerousia* (Greek) — council of elders, especially in Sparta.

stantially the same way. Just as in the case discussed last, democracy becomes alienated from its purity where the group grows beyond a certain size or where the administrative function becomes too difficult to be satisfactorily taken care of by anyone whom rotation, the lot, or election may happen to designate. The conditions of administration of mass structure are radically different from those obtaining in small associations resting upon neighborly or personal relationships. As soon as mass administration is involved, the meaning of democracy changes so radically that it no longer makes sense for the sociologist to ascribe to the term the same meaning as in the case discussed so far.

The growing complexity of the administrative tasks and the sheer expansion of their scope increasingly result in the technical superiority of those who have had training and experience and will thus inevitably favor the continuity of at least some of the functionaries. There always thus exists the probability of the rise of a special, perennial structure for administrative purposes, which of necessity, means for the exercise of domination. This structure may be one of *honoratiores*, acting as equal "colleagues," or it may turn out to be "monocratic," so that all functionaries are integrated into a hierarchy culminating in one single head.

Section 3. Domination through Organization — Bases of Legitimate Authority

The ruling position over the masses of the members of that circle of which we have just spoken rests upon the so-called "law of the small number." The ruling minority can quickly reach understanding among its members; it is thus able at any time quickly to initiate that rationally organized action which is necessary to preserve its position of power. Consequently it can easily squelch any action of the masses threatening its power as long as the opponents have not created the same kind of organization for the planned direction of their own struggle for domination. Another benefit of the small number is the ease of secrecy as to the intentions and resolutions of the rulers and the state of their information; the larger the circle grows, the more difficult or improbable it becomes to guard such secrets. Wherever increasing stress is placed upon "official secrecy," we take it as a symptom of either an intention of the rulers to tighten the reins of their rule or of a feeling on their part that their rule is being threatened.

But every domination established as a continuing one must in some decisive point be *secret rule*. Generally speaking, those specific measures of domination which are established by consociation show the following characteristics:

A circle of people who are accustomed to obedience to the orders of *leaders* and who also have a personal interest in the continuance of the domination by virtue of their own participation in, and the benefits derived for them from, the domination, have divided among themselves the exercise of those functions which will serve the continuation of the domination and are holding themselves continuously ready for their exercise.

This entire structure will be called *organization.* Those leaders who do not derive from grant by others the powers of command claimed and exercised by them, we shall call *masters*; while the term *apparatus* shall mean the circle of those persons who are holding themselves at the disposal of the master or masters in the manner just defined.

The sociological character of the *structure* of any particular case of domination is determined by the kind of relationship between the master or masters and the apparatus, the kind of relationship of both to the ruled, and by its specific *organization,* i.e., its specific way of distributing the powers of command. There can also be considered, of course, a good many other elements, which may then be used to establish a great number of varying sociological classifications. For our limited purposes, we shall emphasize those basic types of domination which result when we search for the ultimate grounds of the *validity* of a domination, in other words, when we inquire into those grounds upon which there are based the claims of obedience made by the master against the "officials" and of both against the ruled.

We have encountered the problem of *legitimacy* already in our discussion of the *legal order*. Now we shall have to indicate its broader significance. For a domination, this kind of justification of its legitimacy is much more than a matter of theoretical or philosophical speculation; it rather constitutes the basis of very real differences in the empirical structure of domination. The reason for this fact lies in the generally observable need of any power, or even of any advantage of life, to justify itself.

The fates of human beings are not equal. Men differ in their states of health or wealth or social status or what not. Simple observation shows that in every such situation he who is more favored feels the never ceasing need to look upon his position as in some way "legitimate," upon his advantage as "deserved," and the other's disadvantage as being brought about by the latter's "fault." That the purely accidental causes of the difference may be ever so obvious makes no difference.

This same need makes itself felt in the relation between positively and negatively privileged groups of human beings. Every highly privileged group develops the myth of its natural, especially its blood, superiority. Under conditions of stable distribution of power and, consequently, of an estatist order, that myth is accepted by the negatively privileged layers. Such a situation exists as long as the masses continue in that natural state of theirs in which thought about the order of domination remains but little developed, which means, as long as no urgent needs render the state of affairs "problematical." But also in times in which the class situation has become unambiguously and openly visible to everyone as the factor determining every man's individual fate, that very myth of the élite about everyone having deserved his particular lot has often become one of the most passionately hated objects of attack; one ought only to think of certain struggles of late antiquity and of the Middle Ages, and quite particularly of the class struggle of our own time in which such myths and the claim of legitimate domination based upon it have constituted one of the most powerful and most effective weapons of the attackers.

Indeed, the continued exercise of every domination (in our technical sense of the word) always has the strongest need of self-justification through appealing to the principles of its legitimation. Of such ultimate principles, there are only three:

The "validity" of a power of command may be expressed, first, in a system of consciously made *rational* rules (which may be either agreed upon or imposed from above), which meet with obedience as generally binding norms whenever such obedience is claimed by him whom the rule designates. In that case every single bearer of powers of command is legitimated by that system of rational norms, and his power is legitimate in so far as it corresponds with the norms. Obedience is thus given to the norms rather than to the person.

The validity of a power of command can also rest, however, upon *personal authority.*

Such personal authority can, in turn, be founded upon the sacredness of *tradition,* i.e., of that which is customary and has always been so and prescribes obedience to some particular person.

Or, personal authority can have its source in the very opposite, viz., the surrender to the extraordinary, the belief in *charisma,* i.e., actual revelation or grace resting in such a person as a savior, a prophet, or a hero.

The "pure" types of domination correspond to these three possible types of legitimation. The forms of domination occurring in historical reality constitute combinations, mixtures, adaptations, or modifications of these "pure" types.

Rationally consociated conduct of a dominational structure finds its typical expression in *bureaucracy.*

Social conduct bound in relationships of *traditional* authority is typically represented by *patriarchalism.*

The *charismatic* structure of domination rests upon that authority of a *concrete individual* which is based neither upon rational rules nor upon tradition.

CHAPTER XIII

POLITICAL COMMUNITIES[1]

Section 1. Nature and "Legitimacy" of Political Communities

The term "political community" shall apply to a community whose communal action is aimed at subordinating to orderly domination by the participants a "territory" and the conduct of the persons within it. The domination must be exercised through readiness to resort to physical force, meaning normally force of arms. The territory must at any time be in some way determinable, but it need not be constant or definitely limited. The persons are those who are in the territory either permanently or temporarily. Also, the aim of the participants may be to acquire additional territory for themselves.

"Political" community in this sense has existed neither everywhere nor always. In the sense of a specialized community it does not exist wherever the task of armed defense against enemies has been assigned to the household community, the neighborhood association, or some association of a different kind and essentially oriented toward economic interests. Nor has political community existed everywhere and at all times in the sense that its conceptual minimum, viz., "forcible maintenance of orderly dominion over a territory and its inhabitants," be conceived necessarily as the function of one and the same community. The tasks implied in this function have often been distributed among several communities whose actions partly complement and partly overlap each other. For example, "external" violence and defense have often been in the hands partly of kinship groups, partly of neighborhood associations, and partly of warrior consociations established *ad hoc*. "Internal" domination of the "territory" and the control of intragroup relations have likewise been distributed among various powers, including religious ones; and even in so far as violence has been used it has not necessarily been monopolized by any one community. Under certain circumstances, "external" violence can even be rejected in principle, as it was, for a

[1] W.u.G. Part III (Types of Domination); c. II (Political Communities) — pp. 613–618.

while, by the community of the Pennsylvania Quakers; at any rate, organized preparation for its use may be entirely lacking. As a rule, however, readiness to apply violence is associated with domination over a territory.

As a separate structure, a political community can be said to exist only if, and in so far as, a community constitutes more than an "economic group"; or, in other words, in so far as it possesses value systems ordering matters other than the directly economic disposition of goods and services. The particular content of communal action, beyond the forcible domination of territory and inhabitants, is conceptually irrelevant. It may vary greatly according to whether we deal with a raiding community, a "welfare state," a "constitutional," or a "culture" state. Owing to the drastic nature of its means of control, the political association is particularly capable of arrogating to itself all the possible values toward which associational conduct might be oriented; there is probably nothing in the world which at one time or another has not been an object of communal action on the part of some political association.

On the other hand, a political community may restrict its communal action exclusively to the bare maintenance of its dominion over a territory, and it has in fact done so frequently enough. Even in the exercise of this function, the action of a political community is, in many cases, intermittent, no matter what its general level of development may be in other respects. Such action flares up in response to external threat or to an internal sudden impulse to violence, however motivated; it dies down, yielding factually to a state of "anarchy" during "normal" peaceful times, when coexistence and communal action on the part of the inhabitants of the territory take the form of merely factual mutual respect for the accustomed economic spheres, without the availability of any kind of coercion either for external or for internal use.

In our terminology, a separate "political" community is constituted where we find (1) a "territory"; (2) the availability of physical force for its domination; and (3) communal action which is not restricted, in the frame of a communal economic enterprise, to the satisfaction of common economic needs but regulates, more generally, the interrelations of the inhabitants of the territory.

The enemy against whom the eventually violent communal action is directed may be located outside or inside the boundaries of the territory in question. Since political violence has become the monopoly of organized associations or, today, "institutions,"[2] the objects of violent

[2] In the juristic sense as explained *supra*, p. 168.

communal action are also, and indeed primarily, to be found among those very persons who have been coerced to participate in the political communal action. For the political community, even more than other institutionally organized communities, is so constituted that it imposes obligations on the individual members which many of them fulfill only because they are aware of the probability of physical coercion backing up such obligations. The political community, furthermore, is one of those communities whose communal action includes, at least under normal circumstances, coercion through jeopardy and destruction of life and freedom of movement applying to outsiders as well as to the members themselves. The individual is expected ultimately to face death in the communal interest. This gives to the political community its particular pathos and raises its enduring emotional foundations. The community of political destiny, i.e., above all, of common political struggle of life and death, has given rise to communities of memories which often have had a deeper impact than the ties of merely cultural, linguistic, or ethnic community. It is this community of memories which, as we shall see, constitutes the ultimately decisive element of "national consciousness."[3]

The political community never has been, nor is it today, the only community in which the renunciation of life is an essential part of the communal obligations. The obligations of other groups may lead to the same extreme consequences. To name but a few: blood vengeance on the part of kinship groups; martyrdom in religious communities; the "code of honor" of estate groups; or the demands of a good many athletic associations; of communities like the *Camorra*[4] or, especially, of all communities created for the purpose of violent appropriation of the economic goods of others.

From such communities the political community differs, sociologically, in only one respect, viz., its particularly enduring and manifest existence as a well-established power over a considerable territory of land and possibly also sea expanse. Accordingly, the differentiation between the political community on the one hand and, on the other, the communities enumerated above, becomes less clearly perceptible the further we go back in history. In the minds of the participants the notion that the

[3] W.u.G. Part III, c. III, § 2, p. 627.

[4] *Camorra* — well-organized large-scale criminal gang operating in Southern Italy, especially Naples; first appearance *c.* 1820; achieved effective power over Naples municipal government in the 1890's, was defeated in the elections of 1901 through the effort of the Honest Government League, but flared up repeatedly in later times, especially about 1911.

political community is just one among others turns into the recognition of its qualitatively different character in step with the change of its activities from merely intermittent reaction to active threats into a permanent and institutionalized consociation whose coercive means are both drastic and effective but which also create the possibility of a rationally casuistic order for their application.

The modern position of political associations rests on the prestige bestowed upon them by the belief, held by their members, in a specific "consecration" or "legitimacy" of those communal actions which are ordered and regulated by them. This prestige is particularly powerful where, and in so far as, communal action comprises physical coercion, including the power to dispose over life and death. It is on this prestige that the consensus on the specific legitimacy of communal action is founded.

The belief in the specific legitimacy of political action can, and under modern conditions actually does, increase to a point where only certain political communities, viz., the "states," are considered to be capable of "legitimizing," by virtue of mandate or permission, the exercise of physical coercion by any other community. For the purpose of threatening and exercising such coercion, the fully matured political community has developed a system of casuistic rules to which that particular "legitimacy" is imputed. This system of rules constitutes the "legal order," and the political community is regarded as its sole normal creator, since that community has, in modern times, normally usurped the monopoly of the power to compel by physical coercion respect for those rules.

This preëminence of the "legal order" guaranteed by political power has arisen only in the course of a very gradual development. It was due to the fact that those other communities which once had exercised their own coercive powers lost their grip on the individual. Under the pressure of economic and structural displacements they either disintegrated or subjected themselves to the action of the political community which would then delegate to them their coercive powers, but would simultaneously also reduce them.

The rise to preëminence of the politically guaranteed legal order was also due to the simultaneous development of constantly arising new interests requiring a protection which could not be provided within the earlier autonomous communities. Consequently, a steadily widening sphere of interests, especially economic ones, could find adequate protection only in those rationally regulated guaranties which none but the political community was able to create. The process by which this "statification" of all "legal norms" took place, and is still taking place, has been discussed in our chapters on Sociology of Law.[5]

Section 2. Stages in the Formation of Political Communities

Violent communal action is obviously something absolutely primordial. Every community, from the household to the political party, has always resorted to physical violence when it had to protect the interests of its members and was capable of doing so. However, the monopolization of legitimate violence by the political-territorial association and its rational consociation into an institutional order is nothing primordial, but a product of evolution.

Where economic conditions are undifferentiated, it is hardly possible to discern a special political community. As we consider them today, the basic functions of the "state" are: the enactment of law (legislative function); the protection of personal safety and public order (police); the protection of vested rights (administration of justice); the cultivation of hygienic, educational, social-welfare, and other cultural interests (the various branches of administration); and, last but not least, the organized armed protection against outside attack (military administration). These basic functions are either totally lacking under primitive conditions, or they lack any form of rational order. They are performed, instead, by amorphous *ad hoc* communities, or they are distributed among a variety of communities such as the household, the kinship group, the neighborhood association, the market community, and other loose associations formed for some specific purpose. Furthermore, private social organizations enter domains of communal action which we are used to regard exclusively as the sphere of action of political associations. Police functions are thus performed in West Africa by private secret societies.[6] Hence one cannot even include the maintenance of internal peace as a necessary component of the general concept of the political community.

If the idea of a specific legitimacy of violence is connected with any particular type of consensual group action, it is with that of the kinship group in the fulfillment of the obligation of blood vengeance. This connection is weak, on the other hand, with regard to corporate action of a

[5] *Supra*, chs. III–XI.

[6] Cf. in this respect the role of the "military societies" as police organs among the Plains Indians, as described by K. N. LLEWELLYN AND E. A. HOEBEL, THE CHEYENNE WAY (1941), esp. c. 5.

military type, directed against an external enemy, or of a police type, directed against the disturbers of internal order. It becomes more clearly perceptible where a territorial association is attacked by an external enemy in its traditional domain, and arms are taken up in its defense by the members in their totality in the manner of a home guard. Increasing rational precautions against such eventualities may engender a political organization regarded as enjoying a particular legitimacy. Such an organization can emerge as soon as there exists a certain stability of usages as well as at least a rudimentary corporate apparatus, ready to take precautions against violent attack from without. This, however, represents a fairly advanced stage.

The fact that "legitimacy" originally had little bearing upon violence, in the sense that violence did not abide by any norm, results even clearer from those situations where the most warlike members of a group on their own initiative consociate through personal fraternization to organize booty campaigns. This has been, at all stages of economic development up to the formation of the rational state, the typical way in which aggressive wars were initiated in sedentary societies. The freely selected leader is then normally legitimated by his personal qualities (charisma) and we have discussed elsewhere the kind of structure of domination which then emerges.[7] Violence acquires legitimacy only in those cases, however — at least initially — in which it is directed against members of the fraternity who have acted treasonably or who have harmed it by disobedience or cowardice. This state is transcended gradually, as this *ad hoc* consociation develops into a permanent structure. Through the cultivation of military prowess and war as a vocation such a structure develops into a coercive apparatus able to lay effective and comprehensive claims to obedience. These claims will be directed against the inhabitants of conquered territories as well as against the militarily unfit members of the territorial community from which the warriors' fraternity has emerged. The bearer of arms acknowledges only those capable of bearing arms as political equals. All others, those untrained in arms and those incapable of bearing arms, are regarded as women and are explicitly designated as such in many primitive languages. Within these consociations of warriors freedom is identical with the right to bear arms. The men's lodge, which has been studied by Schurtz with so much sympathetic care,[8] and which, in various forms, recurs in all

[7] W.u.G., Part I, c. III, Sec. 10 (THEORY 358).

[8] HEINRICH SCHURTZ, ALTERSKLASSEN UND MÄNNERBÜNDE (1902); for further literature, see R. Lowie, *Age Societies*, 1 ENCYC. SOC. SCI. 483. Cf. also *supra*, p. 103.

parts of the world, is one of those structures resulting eventually from such a consociation of warriors, or, in Schurtz's terminology, a "men's league." In the sphere of political action — assuming a high degree of development of the profession of the warrior — it is the almost exact counterpart to the consociation of monks in the monastery in the religious sphere. Only those are members who have demonstrated prowess in the use of arms and have been taken into the warriors' brotherhood after a novitiate, while he who has not passed the test remains outside as a "woman," among the women and children, who are also joined by those no longer capable of bearing arms. The man enters a family household only when he has reached a certain age, a change in status analogous to the present-day transfer to the reserves after service as a draftee. Until that moment the man belongs to the warriors' fraternity with every fiber of his existence. The members of the fraternity live, as a communistic association, apart from wives and households. They live on war booty and on the contributions they levy on nonmembers, especially on the women by whom the agricultural work is done. The only work, in addition to the conduct of war, regarded as worthy of them is the production and upkeep of the implements of war, which they frequently reserve for themselves as their exclusive privilege.

Depending on the social regulations in question, the warriors steal or purchase girls in common, or demand as their right the prostitution of all the girls of the territory dominated. The numerous traces of so-called premarital promiscuity, which so often are taken for residues of primitive, undifferentiated, endogamous sexual intercourse, would rather seem to be connected with this political institution of the men's lodge. In other cases, as in Sparta, each member of the warrior fraternity had his wife and children living outside as maternal groups. In most cases, the two forms appear in combination with one another.[9]

In order to secure their economic position, which is based on the continuous plundering of outsiders, especially women, the consociated warriors resort under certain circumstances to the use of religiously colored means of intimidation. The spirit manifestations which they stage with masked processions very often are nothing but plundering campaigns which require for their undisrupted execution that, on the first sound of the tom-tom, the women and all outsiders flee, on pain of instant death, from the villages into the woods and thus allow the "spirits" conveniently and without danger of being unmasked to take

[9] Cf. *supra*, pp. 107, 132.

from the houses whatever may please them. The well-known procession of the Duk-Duks in Indonesia is an example in point.[10]

Obviously, the warriors do not believe at all in the legitimacy of their conduct. The crude and simple swindle is recognized by them as such and is protected by the magical prohibition against entry into the men's lodge by outsiders and by the draconic obligations of silence which are imposed upon the members. The prestige of the men's league comes to an end, as far as the women are concerned, when the secret is broken by indiscretion or, as has happened occasionally, when it is intentionally unveiled by missionaries. It goes without saying that such rituals, like all uses of religion for black police purposes, are linked to popular cults. But despite its own disposition towards magical superstition, the warrior society remains specifically earthly and oriented towards robbery and booty, and thus it functions as an agent of skepticism vis-à-vis popular piety. At all stages of evolution it treats the gods and spirits with that disrespect with which the Homeric warrior society treated Olympus.

Only when the warrior group, consociated freely beyond and above the everyday round of life, is, so to speak, fitted into a permanent organization of a territorial community, and when thereby a political organization is formed, does the latter, and with it the privileged status of the warrior group, obtain a specific legitimation for the use of violence. This process, where it takes place at all, is gradual. The larger community, among whose members are the warriors who had so far been organized as marauders or as a permanent warriors' league, may acquire the power to subject the freely consociated warriors' raids to its control. It may achieve this success through either of two processes: the warriors' organization may disintegrate owing to a long period of pacification; or a comprehensive political consociation may be imposed either autonomously or heteronomously. The major community will be interested in obtaining such control because all of its members may have to suffer from the reprisals against the warriors' raids. An illustration of successful acquisition of such control is presented by the suppression by the Swiss of the practice of their young men to hire out as soldiers to foreign powers.[11]

Such control over the booty campaigns was already exercised in early Germanic history by the political community of the districts (*Lands-*

[10] Duk-Duk — secret society of the New Britain Archipelago N.E. of New Guinea; cf. Graf von Pfeil, *Duk-Duk*, 27 J. of Anthropol. Instit. 181; E. A. Weber, The Duk-Duks (1929).

[11] Cf. E. Fischer, Schweizergeschichte (3rd ed. 1947) 150.

gemeinde).[12] If the coercive apparatus is strong enough, it will suppress private violence in any form. The effectiveness of this suppression rises with the development of the coercive apparatus into a permanent structure, and with the growing interest in solidarity against outsiders. Initially it is directed only against those forms of private violence which would injure directly the military interests of the political community itself. Thus in the thirteenth century the French monarchy suppressed the feuds of the royal vassals for the duration of a foreign war conducted by the king himself. Subsequently it engenders, more generally, a form of permanent public peace, with the compulsory submission of all disputes to the arbitration of the judge, who transforms blood vengeance into rationally ordered punishment, and feuds and expiatory actions into rationally ordered legal procedures.[13]

Whereas in early times even actions which were openly recognized as felonious were not proceeded against by the organized community except upon pressure on the part of religious or military interests,[14] now the prosecution of an ever widening sphere of injuries to persons and property is being placed under the guaranty of the political coercive apparatus. Thus the political community monopolizes the legitimate application of violence for its coercive apparatus and is gradually transformed into an institution for the protection of rights. In so doing it obtains a powerful and decisive support from all those groups which have a direct or indirect economic interest in the expansion of the market community, as well as from the religious authorities. These latter are best able to control the masses under conditions of increasing pacification. Economically, however, the groups most interested in pacification are those guided by market interests, especially the burghers of the towns, as well as all those who are interested in river, road, or bridge tolls and in the taxpaying capacity of their tenants and subjects. These interest groups expand with an expanding money economy. Even before the political authority imposed public peace in its own interest, it was they who, in the Middle Ages, attempted, in coöperation with the church, to limit feuds and to establish temporary, periodical, or permanent leagues for the maintenance of public peace (*Landfriedensbünde*). And as the expansion of the market disrupted the monopolistic organizations and led their members to the awareness of their interests in the market, it cut out from under them the basis of that community of interests on

[12] The text says "Landesgemeinde"; "Landsgemeinde" is more commonly used.

[13] Cf. L. Quidde, *Histoire de la paix publique en Allemagne au moyen âge* (1929), 28 RECUEIL DES COURS DE L'ACADÉMIE DE DROIT INTERNATIONAL 449, 483.

[14] See p. 49.

which the legitimacy of their violence had developed. The spread of pacification and the expansion of the market thus constitute a development which is accompanied, along parallel lines, by (1) that monopolization of legitimate violence by the political organization which finds its culmination in the modern concept of the *state* as the ultimate source of every kind of legitimacy of the use of physical force; and (2) that rationalization of the rules of its application which has come to culminate in the concept of the legitimate legal order.

NOTE: We are unable here to carry on the interesting, but hitherto imperfectly developed, case study of the various stages in the development of primitive political organization.[15] Even under conditions of a relatively advanced property system, a separate political organization and all its organs can be completely lacking. Such, for instance, was, according to Wellhausen,[16] the situation among the Arabs during their "ethnic" age. Beyond the kinship groups with their elders (*sheiks*), they did not recognize any extra-familial permanent authority. The free community of nomads, tenting, wandering, and herding together, which arose out of the need for security, lacked any special organs and was essentially unstable, and whatever authority it accepted in the event of a conflict with outside enemies was only of an intermittent character.

Such a situation can continue for very long periods of time and under any type of economic organization. The only regular, permanent authorities are the family heads, the elders of the kinship groups, and, besides them, the magicians and diviners. Whatever disputes arise between kinship groups are arbitrated by the elders with the aid of the magicians. This situation corresponds to the form of economic life of the Bedouins. But, like the latter, it is nothing primordial. Wherever the type of settlement creates economic needs which require permanent and continuous provision beyond that which the kinship group and household can provide, the institution of village chieftain arises. The village chieftain frequently emerges from among the magicians, especially the rainmakers, or he is an especially successful leader of booty campaigns. Where the appropriation of property has reached an advanced stage, the position of chieftain becomes easily accessible to any man distinguished by his wealth and the corresponding standard of living. But he cannot exercise

[15] For a recent survey and synthesis of such studies, see R. THURNWALD, WERDEN, WANDEL UND GESTALTUNG VON STAAT UND KULTUR (1934); for illustrations of the type of society mentioned in the following sentences, see R. F. BARTON, IFUGAO LAW (1919) and THE KALINGAS (1948).

[16] *Das arabische Reich und sein Sturz* (1902; transl. by M. G. Weir, Calcutta, 1927).

real authority except in situations of emergency and even then exclusively upon the basis of some purely personal qualities of some magical or similar kind. Otherwise, especially under conditions of continuous peace, he is no more than a popular arbitrator and his directions are followed as statements of good advice. The total absence of any such chieftain is by no means a rare occurrence in peaceful periods. The consensual action of neighbors is then regulated merely by the respect for tradition and the fear of blood vengeance and the wrath of magical powers. In any case, however, the functions of the peacetime chieftain are in substance largely economic, such as the regulation of tillage, and, occasionally, magico-therapeutic or arbitrational. But, in general, there is no fixed type which could be described once and for all. Violence is legitimate only when it is applied by the chieftain, and only in those manners and cases in which it is sanctioned by fixed tradition. For its application the chieftain has to rely upon the voluntary aid of the members of the group. The more magical *charisma* and economic eminence he possesses, the more he is in a position to obtain that aid.

CHAPTER XIV

RATIONAL AND IRRATIONAL ADMINISTRATION OF JUSTICE [1]

The decisive reason for the success of bureaucratic organization has always been its purely technical superiority over every other form. A fully developed bureaucratic administration stands in the same relationship to nonbureaucratic forms as machinery to nonmechanical modes of production. Precision, speed, consistency, availability of records, continuity, possibility of secrecy, unity, rigorous coördination, and minimization of friction and of expense for materials and personnel are achieved in a strictly bureaucratized, especially in a monocratically organized, administration conducted by trained officials to an extent incomparably greater than in any collegial form of administration or in any conducted by *honoratiores* or part-time administrators. As concerns the execution of complicated tasks, paid bureaucratic work is not only more exact but it is often cheaper in its results than the formally unpaid administration by *honoratiores*. *Honoratiores* administration is an avocational undertaking, and for that reason it is normally slower, less bound by rules, more amorphous and hence less exact, and it is less unified because it is less dependent on a superior; it is less continuous and, because of the almost inevitably more uneconomical utilization of the technical and clerical staff, it is often very expensive. This is particularly true when one takes into account not only the mere charges on the public purse, which are higher in bureaucratic than in *honoratiores* administration, but also the frequent economic losses of the ruled populace through loss of time and sloppiness. The possibility of unpaid *honoratiores* administration normally exists in a stable way only where the business can be handled on a part-time basis. Its limits are reached with the qualitative intensification

[1] W.u.G. 660–665. In these pages Weber deals with certain aspects of sociology of law in general and of the interrelations between bureaucratic administration and the formal qualities of the law in particular. They form part of Chapter VI (Bureaucracy), of Part III (Types of Domination) of WIRTSCHAFT UND GESELLSCHAFT. This chapter has been translated in full and published in ESSAYS 196 *et seq*. The inclusion of the following parts of the chapter in our book has been found advisable because of their close connection with the theme of the book. The translation is by the editor.

of the tasks with which the administration is confronted, as in contemporary England. Collegially organized work, on the other hand, produces frictions and delays, requires compromises between colliding interests and viewpoints, and hence takes place less exactly, more independently of superiors, and accordingly less unifiedly and more slowly. The progressiveness of the Prussian administrative system has been based, and will have to continue to be based, upon the ever-progressing elaboration of the bureaucratic, and particularly the monocratic, principle.

The utmost possible speed, precision, definiteness, and continuity in the execution of official business are demanded of the administration particularly in the modern capitalistic economy. The great modern capitalist enterprises are themselves normally unrivaled models of thoroughgoing bureaucratic organization. Their handling of business rests entirely on increasing precision, continuity, and especially speed of operation. This in its turn is conditioned by the nature of the modern means of communication, in which we include the news services. The extraordinary acceleration of the transmission of public announcements and of economic or political events exercises a steady and definite pressure in the direction of the maximum acceleration of the reaction of the administration to the given situation; this maximum can normally be reached only by thoroughgoing bureaucratic organization. Of course, the bureaucratic system can, and often does, produce obstacles to the appropriate handling of certain situations. These problems shall not be discussed at this point.

Above all, bureaucratization offers the optimal possibility for the realization of the principle of division of labor in administration according to purely technical considerations, allocating individual tasks to functionaries who are trained as specialists and who continuously add to their experience by constant practice. "Professional" execution in this case means primarily execution "without regard to person" in accordance with calculable rules. The consistent carrying through of bureaucratic authority produces a leveling of differences in social "honor" or status, and, consequently, unless the principle of freedom in the market is simultaneously restricted, the universal sway of economic "class position." The fact that this result of bureaucratic authority has not always appeared concurrently with bureaucratization is based on the diversity of the possible principles by which political communities have fulfilled their tasks. But for modern bureaucracy, the element of "calculability of its rules" has really been of decisive significance. The nature of modern civilization, especially its technical-economic substructure, requires this "calculability" of consequences.

Fully developed bureaucracy operates in a special sense "sine ira ac studio." [2] Its peculiar character and with it its appropriateness for capitalism is the more fully actualized the more bureaucracy "depersonalizes" itself, i.e., the more completely it succeeds in achieving that condition which is acclaimed as its peculiar virtue, viz., the exclusion of love, hatred, and every purely personal, especially irrational and incalculable, feeling from the execution of official tasks. In the place of the old-type ruler who is moved by sympathy, favor, grace, and gratitude, modern culture requires for its sustaining external apparatus the emotionally detached, and hence rigorously "professional," expert; and the more complicated and the more specialized it is, the more it needs him. All these elements are provided by the bureaucratic structure. Bureaucracy provides the administration of justice with a foundation for the realization of a conceptually systematized rational body of law on the basis of "laws," as it was achieved for the first time to a high degree of technical perfection in the late Roman Empire. In the Middle Ages the reception of this law proceeded hand in hand with the bureaucratization of the administration of justice. Adjudication by rationally trained specialists had to take the place of the older type of adjudication on the basis of tradition or irrational presuppositions.

Rational adjudication on the basis of rigorously formal legal concepts is to be contrasted with a type of adjudication which is guided primarily by sacred traditions without finding therein a clear basis for the decision of concrete cases. It thus decides cases either as charismatic justice, i.e., by the concrete "revelations" of an oracle, a prophet's doom, or an ordeal; or as khadi justice non-formalistically and in accordance with concrete ethical or other practical value-judgments; or as empirical justice, formalistically, but not by subsumption of the case under rational concepts but by the use of "analogies" and the reference to and interpretation of "precedents." The last two cases are particularly interesting for us here. In khadi justice, there are no "rational" bases of "judgment" at all, and in the pure form of empirical justice we do not find such rational bases, at least in that sense in which we are using the term. The concrete value-judgment aspect of khadi justice [3] can be intensified until it leads to a prophetic break with all tradition, while empirical justice can be sublimated and rationalized into a veritable technique. Since the non-bureaucratic forms of authority exhibit a peculiar juxtaposition of a sphere of rigorous subordination to tradition

[2] Lat. — "without bias or favor."

[3] The term has been coined by R. Schmidt. [Weber's note.]

on the one hand and a sphere of free discretion and grace of the ruler on the other, combinations and marginal manifestations of both principles are frequent. In contemporary England, for instance, we still find a broad substratum of the legal system which is in substance khadi justice to an extent which cannot be easily visualized on the Continent.[4] Our own jury system, in which the reasons of the verdict are not pronounced, frequently operates in practice in the same way.[5] One should thus be careful not to assume that "democratic" principles of adjudication are identical with rational, i.e., formalistic, adjudication. The very opposite is the truth, as we have shown in another place.[6] Even American and British justice in the great national courts still is to a large extent empirical adjudication, based on precedent. The reason for the failure of all attempts to codify English law in a rational way as well as for the rejection of Roman law lay in the successful resistance of the great, centrally organized lawyers' guilds, a monopolistic stratum of honoratiores, who have produced from their ranks the judges of the great courts. They kept legal education as a highly developed empirical technique in their own hands and combated the menace to their social and material position which threatened to arise from the ecclesiastical courts and, for a time, also from the universities in their attempts to rationalize the legal system. The struggle of the common law lawyers against Roman and ecclesiastical law and against the power position of the church was to a large extent economically caused by their interest in fees, as was demonstrated by the royal intervention in this conflict. But their power position, which successfully withstood this conflict, was a result of political centralization. In Germany, there was lacking, for predominantly political reasons, any socially powerful estate of honoratiores who, like the English lawyers, could have been the bearers of a national legal tradition, could have developed the national law as a veritable art with an orderly doctrine, and could have resisted the invasion of the technically superior training of the jurists educated in Roman law. It was not the greater suitability of substantive Roman law

[4] A. Mendelssohn-Bartholdy, IMPERIUM DES RICHTERS (1908). Mendelssohn-Bartholdy vividly contrasts the refined and technical administration of justice in the Supreme Court of Judicature with the informal ways of the justices of the peace and those other inferior courts which serve the legal needs of the masses. Cf. *supra*, pp. 230, 231.

[5] Written before the unpopular jury system was replaced in Germany, in 1924, by the system of the mixed bench, consisting of a majority of laymen and a minority of professional career judges deliberating jointly on all aspects of the case. Cf. *supra*, p. 318.

[6] Cf. *supra* c. VII.

to the needs of emerging capitalism which decided the victory here. As a matter of fact, the specific legal institutions of modern capitalism were unknown to Roman law and are of medieval origin. No, the victory of the Roman law was due to its rational form and the technical necessity of placing procedure in the hands of rationally trained specialists, i.e., the Roman law trained university graduates. The increasingly complicated nature of the cases arising out of the more and more rationalized economy was no longer satisfied with the old crude techniques of trial by ordeal or oath but required a rational technique of fact-finding such as the one in which these university men were trained. The factor of a changing economic structure operated, it is true, everywhere including England, where rational procedures of proof were introduced by the royal authority especially in the interest of the merchants. The main cause for the difference which nonetheless exists between the development of substantive law in England and Germany is not, as is already apparent, to be found here but rather in the autonomous tendencies of the two types of organization of authority. In England there was a centralized system of courts and, simultaneously, rule by honoratiores; in Germany there was no political centralization but yet there was bureaucracy. The first country of modern times to reach a high level of capitalistic development, i.e., England, thus preserved a less rational and less bureaucratic legal system. That capitalism could nevertheless make its way so well in England was largely because the court system and trial procedure amounted until well in the modern age to a denial of justice to the economically weaker groups. This fact and the cost in time and money of transfers of landed property, which was also influenced by the economic interests of the lawyers, influenced the structure of agrarian England in the direction of the accumulation and immobilization of landed property.

Roman adjudication in the time of the Republic was a peculiar mixture of rational, empirical, and even of khadi elements. The use of jurors as such as well as the original praetorian practice of granting *actiones in factum* [7] only *ad hoc* and from case to case contains clear elements of khadi justice. The cautelary jurisprudence [8] and all that grew out of it, including even a part of the *responsa* [9] of the classical jurists, was "empirical" in character. The decisive turn of jurisprudence towards rational procedures was first prepared in the technical form of the trial instruc-

[7] Cf. *supra*, p. 214.
[8] Cf. *supra*, p. 72.
[9] Cf. *supra*, p. 216.

tions[10] contained in the formulae of the praetorian edicts which were expressed in legal concepts. Today, under the principle of fact pleading, under which recitation of the facts is decisive regardless of the legal concept under which the cause of action may arise, there no longer exists such a compulsion toward conceptualization as was produced by the peculiar technique of Roman law. We thus see that formalization in Roman law was largely due to procedural factors arising only indirectly from the structure of the state. But that peculiar rationalization of Roman law as a coherent, scientifically utilizable, conceptual system, by which it is distinguished from the products of the Orient and the Hellenistic cultures, was not completed before the bureaucratization of the state.

A typical instance of nonrational and yet "rationalistic" and highly traditional empirical justice is to be found in the responses of the rabbis of the Talmud. Purely untraditional khadi justice is represented in every prophetic dictum of the pattern: "It is written — but I say unto you." The more the religious character of the khadi or of a similarly situated judge is emphasized, the freer he is in his treatment of individual cases within the sphere which is not bound by sacred tradition. The fact that the Tunisian ecclesiastical court (*Chara*) could decide in real property matters in accordance with its "free discretion," as a European would say, remained a hindrance to the development of capitalism for a generation after the French occupation. But the sociological bases of all these older types of administration of justice shall be referred to another context.[11]

Now it is perfectly clear that "objectivity" and "professionalism" are not necessarily identical with the supremacy of general abstract rules, not even in modern adjudication. The idea of a gapless system of law is, as we know, under heavy attack and there have been violent objections against the conception of the modern judge as a vending machine into which the pleadings are inserted together with the fee and which then disgorges the judgment together with its reasons mechanically derived from the Code.[12] This attack has, perhaps, been motivated by the very reason that a certain approximation to that type of adjudication might actually result from the bureaucratization of the law. Even in the sphere of adjudication there are areas in which the bureaucratic judge is instructed by the legislators to arrive at his decision by "individualizing" the case in its peculiar circumstances. But in the domain of administra-

[10] Cf. *supra*, p. 213.
[11] Cf. *supra* cc. VII–X.
[12] See *supra* c. XI.

tion proper, i.e., of governmental activity other than legislation and adjudication, the claim of freedom and of the decisiveness of the circumstances of the individual situation has been put forth, in the face of which general norms should play but a negative role as mere limits on the positive, unregulatable, and creative activity of the official. The full implications of this proposition will not be discussed here. The important point is that this "freely" creative administration is not, as in prebureaucratic forms, a sphere of *free* discretion and grace, or of *personally* motivated favor and evaluation, but that it implies the supremacy of impersonal ends, their rational consideration, and their recognition as obligatory. Indeed, in the sphere of governmental administration in particular, that very proposition which does most to glorify the creative will of the official has put forward as his ultimate and highest guide the furtherance of the specifically modern and thoroughly impersonal idea of the *raison d'état*. To be sure, with this canonization of the abstractly impersonal there are fused the sure instincts of the bureaucracy for what is necessary to maintain their power in their own state, and, therewith, also as against other states. Finally, these power interests confer on the by no means unambiguous ideal of *raison d'état* a concretely applicable content and, in doubtful cases, the very decisive element. This point cannot be elaborated here. What is decisive for us is only that, in principle, behind every act of purely bureaucratic administration there stands a system of rationally discussable "grounds," i.e., either subsumption under norms or calculation of means and ends.

Here, too, the attitude of every democratic movement, i.e., in this instance, one aiming at the minimization of "authority" must necessarily be ambiguous. The demands for "legal equality" and of guaranties against arbitrariness require formal rational objectivity in administration in contrast to personal free choice on the basis of grace, as characterized the older type of patrimonial authority. The democratic ethos, where it pervades the masses in connection with a concrete question, based as it is on the postulate of substantive justice in concrete cases for concrete individuals, inevitably comes into conflict with the formalism and the rule-bound, detached objectivity of bureaucratic administration. For this reason it must emotionally reject what is rationally demanded. The propertyless classes in particular are not served, in the way in which bourgeois are, by formal "legal equality" and "calculable" adjudication and administration. The propertyless demand that law and administration serve the equalization of economic and social opportunities vis-à-vis the propertied classes, and judges or administrators cannot perform this function unless they assume the substantively ethical and hence nonformalistic character of the Khadi. The rational course of justice and administration is interfered with not only by every form of "popular justice," which is little concerned with rational norms and reasons, but also by every type of intensive influencing of the course of administration by "public opinion," that is, in a mass democracy, that communal activity which is born of irrational "feelings" and which is normally instigated or guided by party leaders or the press. As a matter of fact, these interferences can be as disturbing as, or, under circumstances, even more disturbing than, those of the star chamber practices of an "absolute" monarch.

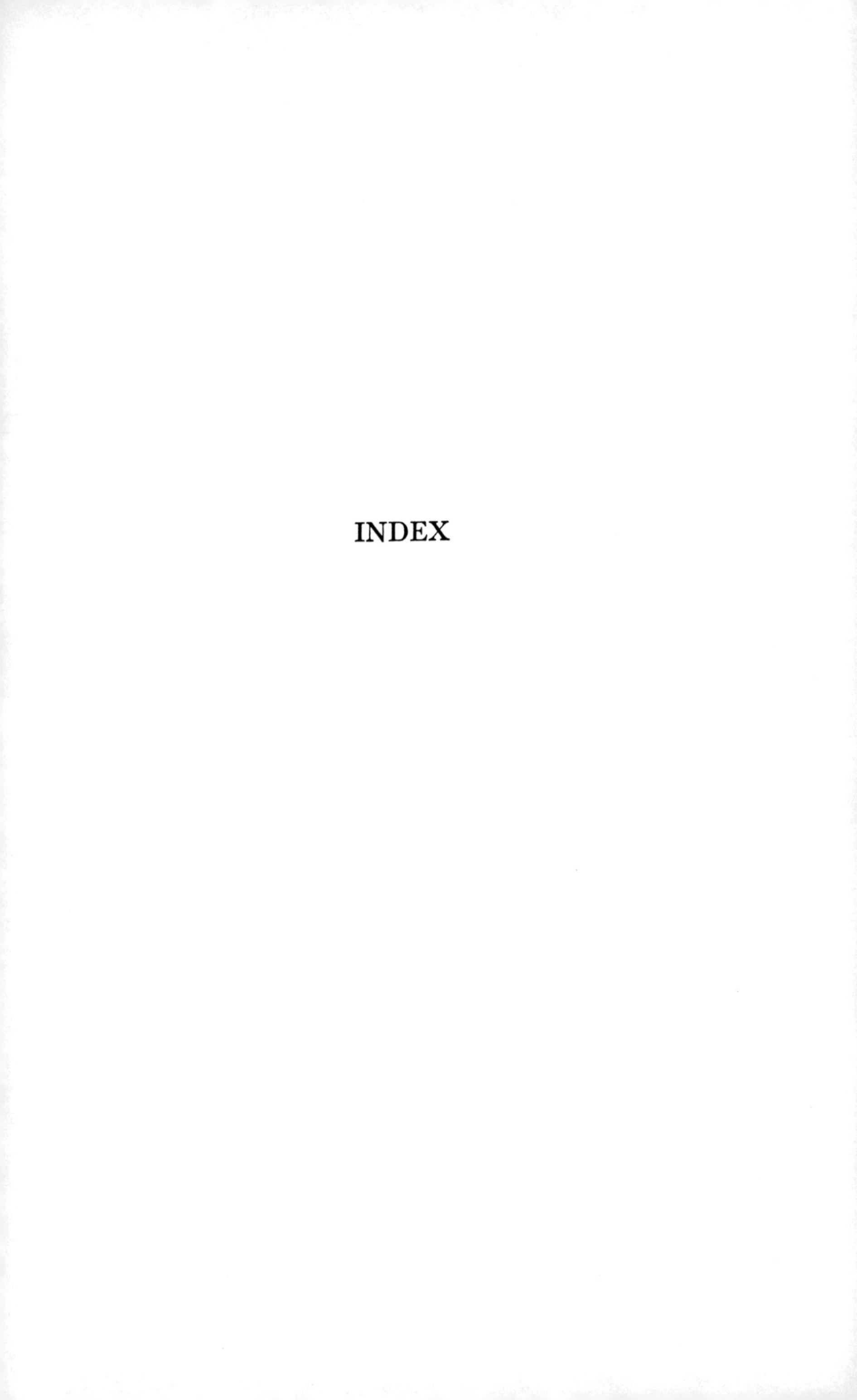
INDEX

INDEX

Abatement of debts, 54
Achilles, shield of, 91
Actio de pauperie, 51
Actio de pecunia constituta, 220
Actio in factum concepta, 214, 260, 264, 353
Actio personalis moritur cum persona, 54
Actio quod iussu, 220
Actio spolii, 252
Action of ejectment, 53
Administration, public, 44
Administrative law, 44, 48
Adoption, 130
African native law, 82, 265
Agency, 122
Ager publicus, 150
Ager vectigalis, 129
Agermanament, 160
Aisymnete, 8, 269
Anglo-American law, methods of legal thought, 315
Anstalt, *see* Institution
Arbiter elegantiarum, 327
Areiopagos, 234
Arnold, case of, 229, 299
Assignment, 123
Assize of Jerusalem, 272
Assize of novel disseisin, 78
Associations, 154
Attorney, 199
Augurs, 233
Austria, Code of 1811, 274, 282, 296
Authority, 324
Autonomy of group legislation, 146

Bann(us), 224, 232, 258
Bar, 198
Barter, 107
Bavaria, Code of 1751, 274
Beaumanoir, 211, 271
Bills of exchange, *see* Negotiable instruments
Bismarck, conflict between B. and the Prussian Diet, 32, 300
Bodenbefreiung, 130, 140
Bona fide purchaser, 54, 96
Book of the Covenant, 269
Borough laws, 231
Bottomry, 148
Brehon laws, 87
Buddhist law, 236, 266
Budget, 47
Bureaucracy, 334, 337, 349
Business associations, 159
Byzantine law, 254

Camorra, 340
Canon Law, 250
Capitularies, 89, 224, 261
Cautelary jurisprudence, 72, 201, 210
Caveat emptor, 194
Charisma, 87, 206, 336
Chinese law, 184, 236, 264
Citation Law, 223, 279
Clientela, 152, 257
Coactus voluit, 37, 189
Codification, 256
Codification, demands for, 231, 268
Codification, opposed by legal profession, 203
Coemptio, 109
Coge intrare, 239
Cognitio, 49, 150, 179
Collegia cultorum, *c. mercatorum*, 171
Commenda, 148, 159
Commercial codes, 302
Composition, 51
Compurgators, 227
Conduct, social, 1
Confarreatio, 109
Contractus literalis, 123
Contract of inheritance, 101
Convention, 5, 20
Corporation, 157, 169
Corporation sole, 177
Corpus Juris Civilis, 219, 279
Courts of love, 25, 327
Coutumes, 286
Crime and tort, 53

Crown, liability of, 164
Custom, 2
Customal, 73, 84
Customary law, 20, 66

Decalogue, 269
Demelius, G., 214
Democratic administration, 330, 352
Denmark, Code of 1683, 274
Deuteronomic Code, 269
Dharma, 114, 234
Diadikasia, 55
Didaskalia, 208
Dinggenossenschaft, *see* Thing (Germ.)
Distress, 117
Divorce, 135
Domination, 322
Domination, economic, 324
Dominium, 221
Due process clause, 290
Duel, 18
Duk-duk, 345
Duress, economic, 309

Ehrlich, E., 65, 69, 276
Eike von Repgow, 149, 211
Einlager, 118
Empathy, 328
Emphyteusis, 129, 150
Endowment, 157, 167
Equity, 260
Ethics, 7

False Decretals, 251
Fas, 225, 233
Fashion, 2
Fautes volent exploits, 199
Fee simple, 221
Fenites, 55
Fetwa, 241
Feudalism, 105, 147
Fictions, 53, 201, 214
Fidei-commissum, 152, 178, 179
Fides, 115, 151
Fisc, 162, 165, 166
Florentine bankers, loans to English crown, 164
Folk spirit, 75
Foreign attachment, 104
Formula, 214
France, codification, 284
France, legal theory in, 314
Frankish capitula, *see* Capitularies
Fraternization contract, 106
Frederick II, King of Prussia, 229, 299
Free Law, School of, 31, 309
Freedom and coercion, 31, 188
Freedom of contract, 100
Freedom of contract — limits, 125, 139
Fuero Juzgo, 272
Fundus, 54, 111

"Gapless" system of legal propositions, 62, 277, 354
Gemot, *see* Thing
Genghis Khan, 272
Genossenschaft, *see* Sodalities
Germanists — Romanists, 183, 282
Gesamthand, *see* Joined hands
Gesellschaft mit beschränkter Haftung (G.m.b.H.), 159
Gierke, O. v., 65, 158, 172, 176, 309
Government, 44

Hadiths, 206, 238
Hammurabi, Code of, 273
Hellpach, W., 23
Hereditatis petitio, 113
Hertling, G. v., 207
Heusler, A., 147
Hindu law, 186, 206, 234
Historical School, 67, 183, 282, 288
Honor code, 18
Honoratiores, 52, 198, 332
Honoratiores, administration of justice by, 230, 332, 349

Idjmâ, 67, 239
Illinois, law of real property, 202
Imâm, 243, 255
Imperium, 56, 224, 256
Imprisonment for debt, 119
Infamia, 152
In ius vocatio, 116
Inspiration, 328
Institution (Anstalt), 157, 168, 252, 339
Intercessio, 58
Interdiktionsprozess, 260
Iran, *see* Persia

Islam — Orthodox schools, 71, 142, 209, 239
Islamic law, 206, 237
Ius civile, 149
Ius cogens, 126
Ius dispositivum, 126
Ius gentium, 151
Ius honorarium, 85, 224, 260
Ius quiritium, 149
Ius respondendi, 217

Jewish law, 244
Jewish influence on capitalism and Western Law, 247
Joined hands (*Gesamthand*), 158, 160
Joint-stock company, 160
Judge-made law, 73
Judgment-finder, *see* Thing
Jurisconsults, *see* Jurists, Roman
Jurisprudence of interests, 307
Juristic personality, 151, 156
Juristic personality of state, 162
Jurists, Roman, 72, 212
Jury, 79, 93, 318, 352
Just price, 295
Justinian, Code of, 219, 279

Khadi, 213
Khazars, 249
King's peace, 258
Kleros, 54, 111

Labor law, 303
Lag saga, 78, 87, 213
Lambert, Ed., 65
Land, encumbrances upon, 130, 139
Language, differentiation of, 322
Law, criminal and private, 49
Law — definition, 5, 11
Law, public and private, 41, 263
Law, substantive law and procedure, 59
Law prophets, 86
Lawyers, 198
Legal education, 198, 204
Legal profession, 198
Leges barbarorum, 103, 259, 272
Legis actio per pignoris capionem, 117
Legists, 181, 291
Legitimate order, 3, 8, 336, 338
Lex Anastasiana, 123
Lex Poetelia, 119
Lex rogata, 85
Lex Salica, 88, 103, 261, 271
Limited liability company (G.m.b.H.), 159
Litis contestatio, 81, 104
Liturgy, 163
Locatio-conductio, 218

Magic, 49
Magna Charta, 289
Mancipatio, 108, 120
Mandatum, 220
Mansfield, Lord, 80, 316
Market, 37, 191
Market overt, 54
Marriage, early Roman, 109
Marriage, origin of, 107, 132
Men's house, 103, 343
Mendelssohn-Bartholdy, A., 317, 352
Mir (Russ.), 184, 331
Mirror of Saxon Law, 149, 211, 271
Mitteis, L., 115, 170
Money, 39
Monopoly, 324
Mortmain, 180

Napoleonic code, *see* France, codification
National-Socialism, 184, 193, 248
Natural law, 284, 308, 313
Negotiable instruments, 123, 248
Neo-Kantianism, 313
Nexum, 115, 119
Notary, 124, 210
Noxae datio, 51, 139

Oath, 81, 106, 233
Obligation, 110
Oracle, 74, 89
Oriental Church, law of, 254
Orthodox schools of Islam, *see* Islam, Orthodox Schools

Palaver, 82
Paper money, 291
Partnership, 159
Patrimonialism, 256
Peace, public, 258, 346
Peculium, 161
Peine forte et dure, 79

Penitentials, 251
Per aes et libram, transactions, 108
Perpetual rent, 130, 140
Persia, 243
Personal laws, system of, 71, 142, 242
Petition of right, 164
Phratries, 171
Podestà, 211
Political communities, 338
Pontifices, 214
Positivism, 297
Power, 322
Pr[a]ecarium, 151
Precedent, 73, 317
Private bills, 47
Privilege, 99, 267
Procedural law, origin, 104
Procedure, inquisitorial and adversary, 46, 225
Professio iuris, 143
Proof, modes of, 227, 305
Proof judgment, 80
Property, concepts in Roman and Common Law, 221
Proverbs, legal, 96
Provocatio, 93
Prussia, Code of 1794, 274, 280, 286
Public administration — personnel, 102
Puritans, 289, 296
Purposive contract, 105

Quiritarian law, 149

Rachimburgi, 87
Realist school, 310
Reception of Roman Law, 274
Receptum nautarum, cauponum et stabulariorum, 151
Rei vindicatio, 111
Rent charge, 130, 139
Responsa, 217, 241
Revolution and law, 284
Right, 15, 98
Roman law, sacred and secular elements, 233
Romanists — Germanists, *see* Germanists
Rule of law, 47
Russia, Code, 282
Russian Revolution of 1905, 294
Russkaya Pravda, 93, 95, 249, 258

Sabbatical year, 250
Sacred laws, 224
Schöffen, 86
Sects, 289, 296
Sense of justice, 75
Separation of power, 57
Shiites, 207, 243
Siete Partidas, 272
Silent trade, 107, 193
Simulata per veris accipiuntur, 214
Slavery, 137
Social-Democrats, 190
"Social Justice," law as expression of, 309
Social relationship, 2
Socialism, 190
Societas, 161
Société en nom commandite, 159, 185
Sodalitates (Roman), 171
Sodalities, 90, 154
"Special law," 127, 140, 257, 301
Specific performance, 53
Stammler, R., 27, 33, 64
Stare decisis, 75, 317
State, 338
State, juristic personality of, 162
State law, 14, 16, 30, 338
State liability, 48, 162
Status contract, 105
Statute, 47, 85
Stiftung, *see* Endowment
Stipulatio, 115, 119
Stopgap law, 126
Summariissimum, 252
Sunna (Islam), 238, 243
Sweden, Code of 1736, 274
Swiss Code, 311
"System" of legal propositions, 62, 277, 354

Ta Ch'ing Lü Li, 271
Talmud, 245
Tenure, 202
Testation, freedom of, 102, 137, 178, 232
Thesmothetes, 90
Thing, Germanic, 86, 90, 227, 266, 304
Title, 179, 221, 316

Tort and crime, 53
Trust, 178
Twelve Tables, 116, 118, 230, 269

Ultra vires, 180
Umstand, 90
United States, natural law in, 289, 293
Universitas, 169
Urim and thummim, 74, 89, 244
Urteilsschelte, 91
Usage, 2, 20, 34
Usury laws, 19, 253

Vadiatio, 119
Vassalic state, 147
Village community, 179

Wager of law, 225
Wak'f (wag'f), 168
Weistum, *see* Customal
Wergeld (*wergilt*), 110, 258

Yasa, 272

Zadruga, 17, 69
Zitelmann, H., 65
Zweckvermögen, 178